FOSSE

SAM WASSON

An Eamon Dolan Book
Houghton Mifflin Harcourt
BOSTON   NEW YORK
2013

For information about permission to reproduce selections from this book, write to Permissions, Houghton Mifflin Harcourt Publishing Company, 215 Park Avenue South, New York, New York 10003.

www.hmhbooks.com

Library of Congress Cataloging-in-Publication Data
Wasson, Sam.
Fosse / Sam Wasson.
pages cm
"An Eamon Dolan Book."
ISBN 978-0-547-55329-0 (hardback)
1. Fosse, Bob, 1927–1987. 2. Choreographers — United States — Biography. I. Title.
GV1785.F67W37 2013
792.8′2092 — dc23
[B]
2013026082

Book design by Chrissy Kurpeski
Typeset in Minion and Knockout

Printed in the United States of America
DOC 10 9 8 7 6 5 4 3 2 1

"I Wanna Be a Dancin' Man" by John H. Mercer and Harry Warren © 1951, 1952 Warner Chappell Music, Inc. 2013: Used by Permission of the Johnny Mercer Foundation, Inc.

For this book's family:
David Halpern
George Hodgman
Eamon Dolan
and Genevieve Angelson

CONTENTS

How much time do I have?

—Bob Fosse

FOSSE

THE END

GWEN VERDON, LEGALLY Mrs. Bob Fosse, was smiling big. She had perched herself in the foyer beside a tray of champagne flutes so that, with the help of a few servers, she could pass them out between air-kisses and the occasional embrace. Verdon held herself with a poise befitting her legacy as the one-time greatest musical-comedy star in the world, and though her glory days were far behind her, one could immediately recognize the naughty, adorable, masterfully flirtatious song-and-dance girl Broadway had fallen in love with. Fosse's best friend, Paddy Chayefsky, had called her the Empress.

Around eight o'clock, the flurry of famous and obscure, some of them in black tie, others dressed merely for a great time, hugged and kissed their way off the pavement and into Tavern on the Green. They passed Verdon as they headed down the mirrored hall to the Tavern's Crystal Ballroom, a fairy-tale vision of molded ceilings and twinkling chandeliers where light was low and sweet and a dark halo of cigarette smoke hovered over the ten-piece band. They played before a wide-open dance floor and dozens of tables apoof with bouquets. Each place was set with a miniature black derby, a tiny magic wand, and a little toy box that, when opened, erupted with cheers and applause.

For Fosse's haute clique of friends, lovers, and those in between, the night of October 30, 1987, was the best worst night in show-business history. In work or in love, they had all fought Fosse (in many cases, they had fought one another for Fosse), and they had always come back. No matter the pain he caused, they understood that on the other side of hurt, grace awaited them. His gift — their talent — awaited them. But now that Fosse was dead — this time permanently — many wondered how his wife, daughter, and armies of girlfriends, separated by their own claims on his love, would learn to hold his legacy.

The site of sundry Fosse movie premieres and opening-night bashes, Tavern on the Green had hosted the oddest pairings of writers, dancers, and production people, old and young, sober and drunk, but tonight, the dance floor seemed to scare them away.

People talked in separate clusters. Liza Minnelli cut a line through the procession, squeezed Verdon's hand, and made her way toward Elia Kazan. Then came Roy Scheider. Without stopping, he nodded at Verdon and eased past Jessica Lange, who was wallflowering by Fosse's psychiatrist, Dr. Clifford Sager, and Alan Heim, editor of Fosse's autobiographical tour de force *All That Jazz*. "Alan," producer Stuart Ostrow said, "you know, Bob always said you edited his life." There was Cy Coleman; Sanford Meisner; Buddy Hackett; Dianne Wiest; Herb Schlein, the Carnegie Deli maître d' who kept linen napkins set aside for Bobby and Paddy, his favorite customers for twenty years. Where was Fosse's ally and competitor Jerome Robbins? (He was free that night, though he'd RSVP'd no.) Peering into the crowd, Verdon spotted what remained of Fosse's closest friends — Herb Gardner, E. L. Doctorow, Neil Simon, Steve Tesich, Peter Maas, Pete Hamill — all writers, whom Fosse idolized for mastering the page, the one act he couldn't. They were slumped over like tired dancers and seemed lost without Paddy, Lancelot of Fosse's Round Table. "If there is an afterlife," Gardner said, "Paddy Chayefsky is at this moment saying, 'Hey, Fosse, what took you so long?'"

Before his cardiac bypass, Fosse had added a codicil to his will: "I give and bequest the sum of $25,000 to be distributed to the friends of mine listed . . . so that when my friends receive this bequest they will go out and have dinner on me."

Fosse thought the worst thing in the world (after dying) would be dying and having nobody there to celebrate his life, so he divided the twenty-five grand evenly among sixty-six people — it came out to $378.79 each — and then had them donate that money back to the party budget so that they'd feel like investors and be more likely to show up. Bob Fosse — the ace dancer, Oscar and Tony and Emmy Award–winning director and choreographer who burned to ash the pink heart of Broadway, revolutionized the movie musical *twice,* and changed how it danced — died hoping it would be standing room only at his party, and it was. Many more than his intended sixty-six shouldered in — some thought over two hundred came that night — but after a lifetime in show business, having amassed a militia of devoted associates, he had not been sure they all really *really* loved him. Had he been there, Fosse would have been studying their faces from across the room, keeping track of who told the truth and who told the best lies. Who really missed him? Who pretended to? Who was acting pretentious? Who was auditioning? He would have called Hamill and asked him later that night, waking him up, probably, at two in the morning. Fosse would fondly and faithfully deride the bereaved, but underneath he'd be worrying about the house, how many came, where they laughed, and if they looked genuinely sad.

"This is incredibly sad," said Arlene Donovan on one side of the room.

"I'm having the best time," said Alan Ladd Jr. on another.

Roy Scheider, who had played a version of Fosse in *All That Jazz,* scrutinized every detail of the party scene from behind his cigarette and said, "It was as if he was orchestrating it." He laughed.

Stanley Donen eyed Scheider. "My God," Donen thought, "I'm watching this with Fosse's ghost."

By midnight many had said their goodbyes, but you wouldn't know it to hear the band, grooving hard on their second wind. Ties were loosened. High heels dangled from fingers. Only the inner circle remained. Here was Fosse's daughter, Nicole. Here was Gwen Verdon, his wife. Here was Ann Reinking, Fosse's friend and girlfriend of many years. Along with his work, they were the living record of his fervor, adored and sinned against, difficult to negotiate, impossible to rationalize.

In a quiet room away from the clamor, Fosse's last girlfriend, Phoebe Ungerer, wept. Then she left.

Suddenly Ben Vereen flew to the dance floor. He threw his hands into the air and then onto his hips and started slithering. At first he was alone, but moments later the crowd caught on. Reinking followed with Nicole and the eternal redhead, Nicole's mother, the Empress. The bandleader upped the tempo to a funk sound with the kind of heavy percussion Fosse loved, and Fosse's three women moved closer together. Verdon, sixty-two; Reinking, thirty-eight; and Nicole, twenty-four — wife, mistress, daughter — started swaying, their arms entwined, moving together in an unmistakably sensual, sexy way. Their eyes closed and their bodies merged with the beat, pulsing together, like a hot human heart. Others joined them. First ex-girlfriends, then writers. A circle formed, closing in around the women, then opened, then closed, ceaselessly breaking apart and coming together. Grief and laughter poured out of them in waves.

SIXTY YEARS

HE WAS LOSING to the blank page. The problem was not that Bobby Fosse didn't know how to draw; it was that he didn't know what to draw to please them a second time. A year earlier, in fourth grade, he had drawn a picture they loved, a rowdy, funny Halloween parade of ghouls and goblins. His teacher was so impressed she sent his artwork to the Field Museum, one of Chicago's finest cultural institutions, and for a short time, it hung on the wall there, and his friends and family went to admire it, and him, the young genius of Ravenswood Elementary. Fosse had known then that a repeat success would be expected of him the following year, and as Halloween came around again, he felt the grownups peering over his shoulder and onto the blank page, a mean mirror as white as death. Out of ideas, he colored it with the same figures he'd used in the fourth-grade drawing, the same ghouls and goblins, and presented the finished work to his teacher, who was obviously not impressed; she did not send it to the Field Museum, his friends and family did not come, his head was not patted, and Fosse's drawing career was over.

His father, Cyril Fosse, was also a failure. He failed in show business. "By the time I was born, he was a salesman," Fosse said, "but he told me about the act." *The act:* the words lit up Cy's face. He described it to his son as the greatest show on earth. "It was probably one of the worst acts I've ever heard in my life," Fosse said. "But he was very romantic about it." Cy played the spoons, his brother did some trick stuff with the piano, and in between the four threw their arms around one another and sang barbershop quartet. For the finale, one of them would snap a bedsheet over the piano, and Richard Fosse — wearing a blindfold and thick canvas gloves — played requests to oohs and aahs. Cy told all this to little Bobby Fosse, weaving a colorful tale of bygone glories and heroic saves. He insisted that they'd made a few rounds of a third-rate vaudeville circuit before Uncle Richard got cancer. When Richard's leg was amputated, the act ended. When Richard died, Cy gave up hope of a revival.

Now the closest he got to the spotlight was singing for a local Norwegian choral group. Other than that, Cy Fosse was ordinary, no unhappier than the next guy. Round of face and gut, he was a kind enough man, a good Methodist and a proud father, but he guarded his own blandness in a way Bobby found punitive. "[Cy] would always eat a wedge of iceberg lettuce with salt [only] and wouldn't try anything else," Ann Reinking recalled. "He ate it that way until the day he died. He was so right-angled. It bothered Bob."

Cy always seemed to be on the road, supposedly hard at work for the Hershey Chocolate Company. Bob would remember him as being closer to Willy Loman than George M. Cohan, and he saw his mother, Sadie, a 235-pound former spear-carrying extra in the opera, as something like Cy's general manager. "My mother was an old-time matriarch," he said. "She left school at thirteen, but she knew every word in the dictionary. She ran the home, but she wisely allowed my father to think he did." Sadie had a heart problem. She did the best she could with the housework, but some days, or weeks, she struggled to get out of bed and make supper for the family. Her illness put an extra strain on Cy, already whipped by the Depression, but he hauled the family through on the strength of his midwestern work ethic. He bought them a home with a little front yard and a little backyard in a pleasant enough section of Chicago's middle-class North Side, where nothing was more than a few blocks away and neighbors always knew one another's business. The house at 4428 North Paulina had room enough for their five children — Cyril Jr. (called Buddy), Edward, Donald, Patsy, and Robert Louis Fosse, the youngest Fosse and by far the cutest, born June 23, 1927, sixty years before he died.

He had his mother's jalopy heart. Asthma too. Or perhaps it was his early attacks of pneumonia in both lungs — potentially fatal, especially for a small child — that branded Bobby a perennial innocent to Sadie. She cast her youngest as the defenseless good boy, and in time he found the part suited him. While the older boys wrestled one another for the football and stole cars off the street, tiny Bob went into the entertainment-of-mother business, and warm floods of attention came his way. (Lenny Bruce said, "The reason I'm in this business, I assume all performers are — it's 'Look at me, Ma!'") Sadie Fosse lived in fear that Bobby's pneumonia would come back, and she watched over his every step, admonishing him for playing too hard or running too fast, filling him with nervous caution and self-defense. "If I get pneumonia a third time," he told a friend, "I probably won't make it."

They were a bouncy bunch. Equipped with a phonograph and a radio, the Fosses could transform into a seven-person (and two-dog) repertory company at a moment's notice. Sometimes Cyril Sr. would push the furniture to the walls, steal Sadie from the kitchen, and show the boys how a man really danced with a woman. Rarely would he sing. Though Mr. Fosse had a fine tenor voice, he felt effeminate using it offstage. There was a piano too, which Sadie played, filling the room with honky-tonk as Cy, wagging fingers in the air, Suzie-Q'd around the dogs.

With so many people making so much noise, dinner could be fun, but Bobby had to fight the grownups to be heard. He would remember his father eyeing him from the head of the table. "He used to tell me, 'Always leave 'em with a joke,'" Fosse recalled. "'Don't leave the table without saying something funny.' It was heavy stuff to lay on a kid." Cy's advice sagged with his own failure. "That was one of the reasons I think he wanted me to be in show business," Fosse said. There was no doubting Bobby was born with the look. His pink cheeks called out for pinches, and his hair begged to be tousled. An aerodynamic piston, Bobby was the blond embodiment of 1927. (How this adorable rascal had sprung from Sadie's and Cyril's nineteenth-century DNA, no geneticist could possibly explain.) It might have been due to Bobby's good looks or perhaps to the fact that, as the smallest, he seemed defenseless, but whatever the reason, his father decided that Bobby would be the one to fill Cyril's dead brother's shoes. "Bob was the favorite," Ann Reinking said. "His parents decided he was the boy that was going to make it for them."

"I was a good kid," he said, "so I had to be a good kid. You're trapped by your own publicity." At too young an age, Bobby knew that not even the most capable person could outdo himself night after night, seven dinners a week, especially when his six dinner companions, all older and bigger than he was, were occupied outdoing one another. "I come from a big family," he explained. "Maybe they never paid attention to me."

He was told to escort his sister Patsy, then only ten, to dance class at the nearby Chicago Academy of Theater Arts. Patsy didn't want to go, but nine-year-old Bobby was a good boy and, according to his mother, needed the exercise. She wouldn't let him play baseball or football, and the academy was nearby, only a three-minute walk from home. And there was something in it for Bobby too — Patsy's friends. "I had a crush on one of the girlfriends," he said, "so I said, 'Gee, I'm not going to get left out of this.'"

Canopied by twin rows of sidewalk trees, those quiet blocks from the Fosse home to the academy, on the corner of Ashland and Montrose, might have made for a pleasant stroll if Patsy hadn't cried the whole way there. Bobby tried to console her but nothing he said did any good. She simply did not want to dance. If it had been 1965 instead of 1936, by which time Fosse had mastered the art of handling unwilling dancers and actors, he might have been able to soothe, or even frighten, Patsy into leaping without looking. But it was 1936, so he just walked her around the corner and across the street to a tiny upstairs studio, a converted apartment above a drugstore, where he made the acquaintance of a dozen other youngsters, mostly girls, and a spindly rake with a pencil mustache who went by the name of Frederic Weaver.

There was more than a touch of forgery about him, but Fred Weaver was the real thing, a been-everywhere, all-around veteran of the performing arts (some of those less artful than others), rumored to have led the Toronto Symphony Orchestra and studied music theory with the illegitimate son of Richard Wagner. He was (he said) a close personal friend of both Cesar Romero and Mickey Rooney's father. Who knew how old he was? Weaver had a daughter, somewhere, and a first wife he should never have married. "If you want to be in show business," he told the kids, "don't get married." He played the violin, but he'd lost his touch after the accident, he told them in his thin British accent (from central Illinois), that damaged the fingers on his left hand. That put a crimp in his piano playing too, but Mr. Weaver still played, standing up over the keys the way he'd learned to do as a pit player in silent-movie orchestras. From monocle to faded spats, his costume suggested an ersatz sophistication somewhere between Fagin and Fred Astaire, a goodhearted opportunist and an all-purpose codger who tap-danced the children in with a low bow, a straw hat in one hand and an agent's contract in the other. "I, the undersigned," it read, "offer to employ you to be my sole and exclusive personal representative and manager." Here was Weaver's way out of the Depression: turn a good kid into a good dancer, and everyone got a percentage.

His students loved him. Weaver was their mentor, their father figure, and he gave them their first taste of meaning — life lessons of the show-business world. First and foremost, he made sure they understood respect: respect for others, respect for yourself. "Mr. Weaver taught us how to act like professionals," said Charlie Grass, a classmate of Fosse's at the Chicago Academy of Theater Arts. "He told us Eddie Cantor believed in being good to the people going up the ladder of success because you're going to need them on the way down." A sign on the wall said YOUR BODY IS A TEMPLE, TREAT IT AS SUCH. And that meant no smoking, Weaver explained, lighting another cigarette as he spoke, and no hanky-panky. Respect one another's bodies. Be *professional,* Weaver had said, with *each other.*

"And remember this: There's always someone better than you. Remember that. You're not the best. There's always someone better than you, and everything's been done before."

To prove his point, Weaver told them about vaudeville, about Al Jolson and Sophie Tucker and Eddie Cantor and the Nicholas Brothers, who leapfrogged each other down flights of stairs, came up from splits with no hands, and tapped better than Fred Astaire, who could tap better than anyone. Weaver told them a great act was a performer's ticket to the top, and his signature novelty was his secret weapon. "If you do the time step," he said, "put a twist on it." Durante had his "ha-cha-cha" exit. Pat Rooney hiked his pants up and did the clog. Joe Frisco popped his derby off his head like a champagne cork as he tumbled a cigar in and out of his mouth. Groucho Marx bent his knees and zigzagged across the stage. Weaver told them about the magicians and the comics and whiz dancers and the Palace Theater in New York City and the feeling of being center stage, the volcanic high one gets after years of nights of practice when, finally, the hat falls at the right time, at just the right angle, and the cane seems to dance on its own. Once he got going, after a swig from the bottle, there was no doubting Fred Weaver's love of entertainment, of movies, opera, dance, ballet, tap . . .

Bobby Fosse fell in love with Mr. Weaver. He called him Skipper. No one else did.

The academy had a good dance floor and a ballet barre and a few small holes in the brick that could pass for windows. That was about it. Behind Weaver's desk, a cramped hallway led off to someplace the students were not allowed to investigate, but if they stayed late after class and hid behind the piano, they could hear Weaver and Marguerite Comerford, dance teacher and Weaver's sometime lover, hollering at each other from the back rooms.

Comerford knew ballet, but as a former Tiller Girl, her claims to fame were her high kicks and precision tapping, the sort of chorus choreography that would one day roll through Ziegfeld's theater and eventually influence the Rockettes. Miss Comerford was nothing special to look at — long legs and black hair — but she was terrific with the kids, and Weaver, who didn't know from ballet, knew he would have no shop without her. Trixie, he called her. At one point, they married. Together, Weaver and Comerford were a perfect instruction manual for a young hoofer, he the text and she the living illustration. "She filled me with all of these wonderful thoughts," Fosse said, "and the magic of dancing. She cared a great deal about us. So it was a woman, really, that brought me to dancing. It was a woman that brought me everywhere."

Miss Comerford, the most elegant woman Bobby had ever known, was certainly the most elegant professional to grace the academy. The rest were entertainers, circus performers, and stage acts brought in by Weaver to teach the basics of showbiz comportment. To Fosse, they were the big time. Jack Halloran, a local emcee with a speakeasy kind of mien, showed him how to address a microphone. Chris, a

Barnum and Bailey clown with a big gold tooth and a scalp as bare as an eight ball, taught the kids how to fall without getting hurt and how with pantomime they could make an audience think that a bucket of confetti was actually a bucket of water. Radio personality Gilbert Ferguson brought in scripts from his soap-opera serials and helped them practice enunciation.

None of the specialty skills gave Fosse any trouble; he could tap, clog, and tumble like a pro, but whereas his classmates seemed to double in stature when they were onstage, Fosse seemed to disappear. As much as he loved an audience, he danced away from them, rolling himself up like a crustacean, as if he were ashamed to be seen. Which he was. No one at Ravenswood Elementary knew what he did after three o'clock. He wouldn't let them. They would have called Bobby girls' names and laughed him out of recess. "They would accept the tap dancing, and the tumbling," Fosse said, "but the tights and the ballet shoes were hidden in the bottom of the drawer, and I'd sneak those in in a paper bag, you know?" Ballet stifled him. Fosse had no turnout, no extension, and he felt sissy pointing his hands and toes like a prima ballerina. "He was always told to keep his fingers together and his hands down," Grass recalled, "but up they'd go again, his palms out, his fingers spread. That was his style even then. He was doing Jolson and Eddie Cantor." Almost Jungian in resonance, these gestures of showbiz's past would one day form the syntax of Fosse's dance talk. But not yet. In Miss Comerford's class, Bobby was reprimanded for sloppy technique. That there was vaudeville: his first naughty act.

Once a year, the academy presented a recital for the parents. In Fosse's first, held at Chicago's Medinah Country Club on June 15, 1936, he played a policeman in the *Toy-Town Revue* and performed a tap solo ("Stepping It Out"). Fosse also appeared with the full com-

pany in the ballet ensemble, though he was afraid of what his fau...
would think of his son's sissy-flitting through the colored lights. Cy,
though he danced the social dances of the day, drew a hard line at
first position. And paying for it seemed a lavish indulgence. These
being Depression years, cutting some corners could make a difference to such a large family, which, in 1937, had grown one girl larger.
Marianne, Bobby's newest and fifth sibling, was added to the dinner
table next to Buddy, who had left home but then returned, bringing with him his new bride and not much income. Thus Sadie and
Cy, already stretched to the limit, stretched further: he traveling
longer hours in search of more money, she finding ways to prepare
bigger meals for more mouths. Fosse's theatrical training was not
essential.

And he had been improving too. On June 15, 1937, Fosse played the
role of Master of Ceremonies, one of his favorite parts, in "Le Petite
Café," act one of *La Folies de l'Academie,* Weaver and Comerford's
annual recital. A ten-year-old Maurice Chevalier, he tipped his hat to
the Gendarme, the Maid, and the Waiters as they crossed *le petit boulevard.* It was a good part. Keeping an eye on Fosse's progress, Weaver
ushered him from the recital to the YMCA amateur hour in 1938 and
then to a lead in a comedy sketch ("Fun in a Courthouse") for the
spring show that year. In November 1937, Fosse was the star of Myrtle
Church's fourth annual Family Nite and Armistice Celebration. *La
Folies de l'Academie of 1938,* presented by F. Weaver with dances by M.
Comerford, prominently featured Bobby Fosse's "Junior Follies." He
kept climbing. "Mr. Weaver really watched us in recitals," Grass said.
"The students he thought had talent he took to the Masons and the
Elks and then it progressed to money jobs."

Charlie Grass, one of Weaver's best ballet dancers, was part of a
trio, a pintsize version of the Ritz Brothers, and about the time Cy
Fosse fell behind on his son's dance-tuition payments, Charlie's

group lost two-thirds of its talent, which meant that Weaver, their agent, lost his commission. A double act was far easier to book than a solo, and by teaming Fosse with Grass, Weaver could get back his agent's fee plus enough to cover the tuition Cy Fosse owed him. Best of all — from Cy's point of view, at least — after Weaver was paid off, Bobby's share of the profits would go to his father. With all parties pleased, Bobby Fosse signed a contract granting Weaver 15 percent of his earnings for the next ten years, through Fosse's twenty-first birthday.

Grass and Fosse were a team, and after a round of paper-scissors-rock, they had a name, the Riff Brothers, an homage to the Nicholas Brothers, and they threw a second round of paper-scissors-rock to decide on their costumes, which would be purchased at a second-hand-clothing shop on Maxwell Street and tailored to fit them by Charlie's aunt Rita. For the first part of the act, their double, they'd dance side by side in black tails and starched collars; in the second, the singles, they'd wear white dinner jackets. For the third and final part, their competition dance, they would keep the white dinner jackets on and draw cheers one-upping each other with the kind of flash antics made famous by the Nicholas Brothers. "We'd each do tricks," Grass explained. "Squat wings, eagle wings, over-the-tops, things like that. We didn't do a lot of acrobatics. We wanted to be more like Fred Astaire. We never put our hands on the floor." The steps came compliments of Miss Comerford, but the concept — marrying Fosse's tap with Grass's ballet — was pure Weaver.

Bobby's interests expanded from his own routines to include larger matters, like overseeing life at the studio and running the academy's newsletter, "CATA Gossip," which he'd founded and which he wrote, edited, and distributed. Fosse's column, "Looking Thru the Keyhole — by the Sneak," razzed students for missing class, dished academy romances ("What blonde singer is enamoured of what blonde dancer

—and is it unrequited? [If you don't know what this means consult your Webster]"), and singled out hard workers. "Propaganda note," wrote the Sneak, "Ruthie Faltermeyer doing her stuff in Gym class at Ravenswood School. She gives the CATA good publicity." (Publicity: the concept fascinated him.) With Charlie Grass, Bobby wrote his own segue patter for academy recitals, which he was emceeing regularly.

CHAS: Well that's over.
BOB: What will we do next?
CHAS: Go on with the show.
BOB: What will we call it?
CHAS: "The Parade of Blondes."
BOB: How do you get that name?
CHAS: YOU SHOULD SEE THEM.
BOB: Oh! Yeah! Well you stay here and on with the show and I'll be back.
CHAS: Not on your life. MAYBE I'll be back.
BOB: Well, no kidding. I'll tell you what we'll do. I'll tell the folks about the show and you go out there and dig me up a nice blonde.
CHAS: O.K.
BOB: Ladies and gentlemen, this is a show from the Chicago Academy of Theater Arts on Ashland Avenue and Montrose and we hope—
CHAS: Will this do? *[Brings on Hal Felman]*
BOB: Will what do? I said a BLONDE. You sure must be colorblind.
CHAS: You don't understand. Hal's the guy with the blondes.
BOB: Oh, yeah. The blondes. Well, what does he do with them?

CHAS: He sings about them.

BOB: Well, let him sing. Introducing Mr. Hal Felman, who
        will sing you a number from *Alexander's Ragtime Band*,
        "A Pretty Girl Is Like a Melody"!

Applying himself to rehearsal every day after school and on weekends, Fosse had always showed precocious commitment to the work,
but now that he was an earner for his family, his intensity increased.
"He was starting to be a perfectionist," Grass said. "We'd practice over
and over in front of the mirror to be exactly the same, legs the same,
arms the same, perfectly extended. When someone got on the wrong
foot, we'd turn and face each other, like a mirror, and do it again and
again until we got on the same foot." Academy dancer Beth Kellough
could see the dedication on his face. "He'd furrow his little eyebrows
and concentrate," she said. "I think he wanted to be better than everybody." Bobby, dead serious now, told Grass to call him Bob. By
1940, the name Bobby Fosse had disappeared from recital programs.
He was Bob Fosse.

Astaire and Rogers held the movie slot the night he and Grass made
their first public appearance, shoulder to shoulder "with five acts
of vaudeville!" (the sign said), at Chicago's Oak Theater. Formerly
considered one of the district's grand palaces of stage entertainment,
now the Oak was just one of many theaters called, euphemistically,
presentation houses. Vaudeville was dying.

It would be a long death. Motion pictures had begun to talk, and
the more they talked, the more they grew; the more talent the movies
pillaged from the Palace stage, the more the stage talent left longed
for that lucky call from the coast. The pay was far better in Hollywood, and life under the pink canopies of Beverly Hills was less
painful than life—if you could call it that—on the road. As soon
as they could, vaudeville giants like Eddie Cantor, the Marx Broth-

ers, and Buster Keaton sold out and bought in, leaving behind them second-rate hams whose every old-hat yuk and tumble made movies seem fresher than ever. By the 1930s, most of the great vaudeville palaces, unable to command golden-age revenues, were forced to wire themselves for sound. Out went the burnished oak, the gilded arches; in slithered coal-colored cables. Some said it was a fad — they were wrong.

After *The Jazz Singer* came out, the typical vaudeville bill, as if ashamed of itself, broke into a schizophrenic split of live theater and canned film, and as the pictures got livelier and lovelier, the stage acts got worse. Then they got perfunctory. Then, unable to fall any farther, the entertainers got desperate. So they got proud. No matter what the world was telling them, the old clowns told themselves they were the *real* show business, the real talent, the neglected heart of American entertainment. Embittered, envious, and losing their grip, they stood their ground on cranky floorboards and vowed to defend their corner of the trade long after the audiences went home and the lights went out. Hence the presentation houses. With the star acts gone to Hollywood, booking agents had to bring in movies to fill the Oak Theater, which boasted almost a thousand seats, its art deco flourishes curling away the spirits of a dreamier era.

It was the only time Astaire ever opened for Fosse. As his image danced, towering twenty feet above him, Bob slipped behind the screen at the Oak Theater and followed Astaire's supersonic feet. "He wanted to dance *with* him," Grass said, "but the manager would come behind the screen and ask, 'What's all this noise back here?' So he took his tap shoes off and put on his street shoes and followed Fred Astaire."

The Riff Brothers' opening double, a light tap routine, gave way to Fosse's solo, a dance set to the heart-rendingly topical (in 1940) "Stars and Stripes Forever," in which Fosse, a soldier's cap on his head, rushed the footlights and pantomimed gunfire at the audience using his taps for bullet shots (he'd seen Astaire do it in *Top Hat*). Grass did his "Blue Danube Waltz" solo, a classy respite, then the two segued into their challenge taps. Fosse did wings; Grass beat them with knee drops and splits; Fosse destroyed those with a round of backward pullbacks, kicks, leaps, leaps from squats, and so on. To "resolve" the challenge, the Riff Brothers came together for their finale. Here Weaver demonstrated a key lesson: Sell. Dazzle them in the end, and they'll forget whatever tripe came before it. Thus, the Riff Brothers' "Bugle Call Rag." As one boy endeavored to do his trickiest, flashiest moves, the other, grinning, cheered him on, selling the performer to the audience and the audience right back, sending the room into a whistling frenzy. The whole act was eleven minutes. Bob Fosse was thirteen years old.

Weaver and Comerford bought them sundaes after the show. Being bundled up against the snow and getting loopy on ice cream with a man who seemed to be around a lot more than his father — it felt so good. "Bob spent more time at the studio than he did at home," Grass said, "and he thought of Mr. Weaver like family." Man and boy were partners now. After class, when the other boys and girls went home to dinner, Bob and the Skipper huddled by the radio listening to the fighter Joe Louis dance loops around his kill. The two shared the shorthand jive of showbiz slang — *flops* and *bombs* and *hits* — and exchanged wordless signals across the studio. Best of all, for Fosse, was the pride. The look on Mr. Weaver's face. Taking the money home.

"Weaver didn't care where he put Bobby and Charlie," classmate Dorothy Kloss said. "As long as they were working, he had what he wanted." The hotter the Riff Brothers got, the more they rehearsed, first regularly, then whenever they could grab an hour between long division and their evening shows. They were traveling more now too. "When we started performing, it was only every other weekend,"

Grass said. "Then our parents gave the okay that we could perform every weekend Friday and Saturday and even Sunday. We'd do our homework in the back of the car. Sometimes we'd hop a train to do a theater and maybe a USO." After piling into Weaver's sedan, the boys ran the act in rapid dance-speak while Weaver, behind the wheel, inserted a thought or a correction when needed. He drove them to American Legion clubs, the odd novelty show. Bob and Charlie would be thrown in with the local whistler, tenor, comic, whatever, and sometimes a semipro act to class up the evening. But not by much. "I played every two-bit beer joint in the Midwest," Fosse said, barely exaggerating — and many of those joints played him. Weaver booked the Riff Brothers into rigged competitions. But the act, Weaver assured them, was part of the act. Fosse remembered, "The booker would call you up and he'd say, 'All right, on Tuesday you win second prize at the Belmont and on Thursday I'll give you third prize at the Adelphi.'" At ten dollars a night and six bookings a week (at the Bijoux, there were five shows on Saturday alone), Bob was doing pretty well.

He went to the movies. If they were showing Fred Astaire, he'd leave the theater dancing. If it was a Saturday, they'd run four features and he would go all day, from nine in the morning till nine at night, and if it was Fred Astaire *and* a Saturday, he wouldn't get to bed until very late because he'd dance the longest possible route home — he wanted more surface area, and the more irregular the surface, the better. When the sidewalk felt too flat, he looked for fireplugs and garbage cans. He could get higher that way. Going back to the theater gave him another chance at a closer look at Astaire's shoes, and leaving gave him another chance to take it from the top and this time, seriously, do it right.

The grade-schooler took out a fresh sheet of paper and, in his best, most grown-up handwriting, penned a letter to Mr. Astaire, care of

MGM. What kind of shoes did he wear? What size were they? If Bob figured that out, maybe he would know how to be good. If he could change the size of his feet.

In 1941, having outgrown their former residence, the Fosse family moved up, slightly, to a larger house on Sheridan Road, near Lake Michigan. In the house were Edward's wife and son (Edward had left for the war in France), Don's wife and son (Don had been drafted too), and Bob's sisters, Patsy and little Marianne. While the adults were tending to the grandchildren or talking about the war, while his father drank himself to sleep in the basement or his mother put herself to bed early with cardiac pain, Bob would see to it Marianne was happily entertained. In the summers he shaved down the family's collie so that just the fur on its mane and the tip of its tail remained, and he told Marianne it had turned into a lion, and (after pouring blood-like ketchup all over his face) he wrestled it to the ground for a laugh. "He loved her so much," Ann Reinking said. "She was like his little doll." One Easter morning, Marianne awoke to a string tied to her smallest toe. She followed it out her bedroom door and found a matrix of twine cobwebbed around the house that led, finally, to an Easter basket of candy and painted eggs.

Weaver upgraded that same year. He moved the academy to 1961 West Lawrence Avenue, a bigger studio with a stage at the far end of its largest room. After school got out, Bob and Charlie would dash over to dance class, then, when class ended, they would spend the rest of the evening working on their routines. With their own set of keys, the Riff Brothers could stay as late as their bedtime, around ten. For extra money, they taught classes five days a week, writing and printing out dance notes with stencil and rubber. On weekends Bob and Charlie would take a streetcar down to the Loop, home to Chicago's theater district, to see the great acts that came to town and try to get backstage for photos and autographs.

Charlie Grass wasn't Fosse's best friend, but he was just about the only guy who knew his secret. "In those days," Grass said, "show people weren't very popular. It was considered out of place to put on makeup and a costume and perform. So we kept it quiet between ourselves." Fosse also kept quiet his crush on Beth Kellough, a cute blonde three years his junior—Kellogg, they called her, like the cereal. As Bob and Beth were about the same height, they were partnered for recitals year after year. They grew up together, changed together. "Dancing at that age," Kellough said, "you look older than you really are. Your body starts to develop early and you have on all that lipstick, rouge, and mascara." Fosse knew not to try anything. Disrespecting a dancer would be a direct violation of Weaver's number-one rule. "He treated me like family," Kellough said, "like his sister."

Miss Comerford disappeared. "All of a sudden, she was gone," Kellough said. It was tuberculosis, some thought. "It was another man," Grass recalled, "an earlier boyfriend from Iowa. He took her away." Weaver, stooped from a lifetime of hunching over a piano, stooped even lower after she left. He let his cigarettes smoke down themselves. He'd put one on his lip and forget it was there, or forget he was. Fosse—always watching him—liked the look. He slipped the cigarette into his act. With the studio lights dimmed, Bob savored his reflection in the rehearsal mirror: a Camel drooping from his mouth, turning to ash, and his eyes cutting through the snaking wisp of white. Forget the steps; the effect worked. "Ever since I was young," he said, "cigarettes were identified with work." Weaver converted to Christian Science after Comerford left, and he gave up cigarettes. So Bob smoked his while hiding on the back stairs, afraid of getting caught. He didn't want to be bad. But the mirror was right, and he loved looking good.

FORTY-FIVE YEARS

GIRLS. HALF THE STUDENTS at Amundsen Senior High School fell into that category, and half of that half fell for Bob. He had grown into an attractive young man. He was always running track or dancing, and his seemingly guileless smile (practiced but sincere) made them forget everything but that smile. "As a teenager in high school," Kellough said, "some people thought he was gay. He wasn't effeminate, but people thought any boy who was a dancer was not right. He may have gone out of his way to be a womanizer to prove to people that he wasn't." There was Marion Hauser and Miriom Wilson. There was Mary Vagos, Mary Farmakis, and Melvene Fitzpatrick. And there was only so much Bobby could tell them about what he did at night. He kept the same policy with the swim team, student government, and his teachers: he talked like a normal guy who knew nothing about show business or dance. At proms and school socials he had to be relatively well behaved when the music started. Rhythm would bring out the truth. Of course, Fosse couldn't afford to be *too* clumsy in a roomful of clapping girls enthralled with his vulnerability and charm. "He had two lives," Grass said, "a normal life, then the nightclub life." A showman in more ways than they knew, he presented beautifully.

Fosse knew right away he would be a dancer, and rather than dream big, he dreamed real. Astaire was a god and he was a mortal, and the godliest mortals danced in supper clubs — hotel ballrooms with fancily dressed couples at little tables around a dance floor — so Fosse would too. His newer models Fosse took from the middle shelf. The convenient thing about dancers Georgie Tapps and Paul Draper was they tapped to classical music, matching pirouettes and ronds de jambe to the syncopation of earthbound hoofers. It didn't get any classier, fifteen-year-old Fosse thought, than shuffling off to Bach. Years earlier, Mr. Weaver and Miss Comerford had taken him to see Draper play the Mayfair Room of Chicago's Blackstone Hotel. "I think that [Draper] was probably the most elegant performer that I had ever seen," he said, "and in subsequent performances I saw later, he maintained that elegance. For me, he created a kind of magic, and I think for everyone in the room also, a kind of enchantment that stuck in my head for a long, long time."

Elegance was only half of the equation. Filth was the other half.

"When the war came along and so many men got drafted, I became the youngest M.C. in Chicago," Fosse said. "I was sixteen years old and I played the whole burlesque wheel." But this wasn't the belle époque burlesque of parody and sexual innuendo; by the time Fosse appeared at places like the Silver Cloud and Cave of Winds, that burlesque had lost to its grimier twin. This one grew in the dank back rooms of abandoned storefronts and had no compensatory cultural merit — another way of saying it was pure entertainment, tits and laughs and that's about it. But no one watched it for the laughs. The guys who hung around the Roxy at three and four in the morning weren't there to see a couple of clowns twirling plates. At that hour, they came to see girls who couldn't cut it as actresses, didn't want to be typists, and, in some cases, had no place else to go; girls who had good enough bodies to make okay money plus kickbacks on booze; girls who could give those guys a good bad time for an hour and a half. This was not art. Art would not be out of a job when the strip joints and porn palaces moved in, but burlesque was.

"The more we talked about him wanting to be an entertainer," said a high-school girlfriend, Miriom Wilson, "the more I realized it was a lifestyle I wasn't interested in. Bob was exposed to things most of us weren't. Today's young people think nothing of promiscuity, but I knew little about nightclubs and such, places where that sort of thing went on. And so Bob kept that part of his life from me—and probably a lot of people at school—because he knew we didn't understand it."

This was not the burlesque of Gypsy Rose Lee. It was not, as today's feather dancers would have modern audiences believe, an unorthodox form of female empowerment. It was a living, and a bad one. "There wasn't much dancing," Grass said. "They just peeled it off." And it made people mean. Some came in already mean, but the real porny dives—the sort of places Fosse moved around in late at night, with no one looking out for him—made mean meaner. "These people wanted to make money," Grass said. "They didn't care if you were twelve or fifteen years old. If you looked seventeen, fine." Old toilets overflowed. Dark halls smelled of stale greasepaint and piss. In the men's room, Bob and Charlie had to walk around on their heels, and when they needed to change into their tuxedos, they had to put a piece of cardboard down first. "When we played the low-class clubs," Grass said, "we knew not to ask who was running the thing." If they had to, the club managers could mess up the girls, and the girls' boyfriends could mess up the managers, but the Mob had the final say on who came back to work. (Grass said, "You didn't bother them and they didn't bother you.") It was rough on adults, but for Fosse, a kid, it was hell aboveground, and in some cases not even aboveground.

His mother and father didn't really know, or seem to care, what it was doing to him. Neither did he, for the moment.

For the rest of his life, he would never let go of the girls, the failures, and the slimeballs. The dreck, the *true* showbiz — he understood their estrangement from the world's Astaires. In a way, he loved them. He admired their losers' tenacity. Soon, he would share it. In time, they would be Fosse's dramatis personae. The bumps and grinds would be the prepositions of his dance vocabulary, and the whining horns and beat-up drums thumping from offstage would live in his ear forever, as unforgettable as original sin, screwing him up, but screwing him up good. And something else too: there was a philosophy here. Seeing firsthand the human component in sleaze, Fosse felt the beginnings of a question he would ask his audiences, and himself, for the rest of his life: What is filth? If it makes them smile and hard, how bad could it be? Weren't the lowest common denominators what universal appeal was all about? Didn't the whole of show business, of humanity, really, come down to wanting a little peek?

Bob Fosse was the best thing ever to come out of burlesque, and he would pay for it forever.

The nights Weaver didn't send him out on his own, he appeared with Charlie Grass. Mrs. Grass, their stage mother, drove the boys from show to show, made them complete their Latin assignments in the back seat of her sedan, and advised them not to mix with the strippers. "They're not nice girls," she warned. The warnings hardly mattered. When the toilet doors in their own changing rooms wouldn't open, Bob and Charlie were detoured deeper in, to the big ladies' den, where not-nice Amazons powdered up, the boys repeating to themselves the mantras of professional conduct Mr. Weaver had been drilling into their heads for years. "Always refer to the conductor as Maestro . . ."

Strippers — twice Bobby's size in two directions, and twice as sharp—preyed on him before the show as he stood in the wings about to go on. That was the worst part, waiting for them to call his name, breathing into a moldy moth-eaten curtain and trying not to think of the twisted faces or what they would yell at him tonight. It was throw-up time.

"Oh, Bobby . . ."

"Come *on*, Bobby . . ."

When the girls found out he wasn't the eighteen-year-old he said he was, they started messing with him. Feathered gorgons appeared at the doors, all doors, backing him into dark corners. They pulled Fosse from his Latin conjugations onto their laps, crushing his face in fingers and tongues, twirling his perfect hair and the cock in his tuxedo pants. Scared and alone, he did as he was told. Even if that meant doing what no good boy should do, he did it, because if he cried out, they'd blow his cover and he'd be out of the show for good, and what would he tell his mother?

In the tense seconds before he was about to go on, they came from behind him, kneading his pants. As they jerked him off, Bobby ran the conscious part of his brain through the Cubs starting lineup and National League batting averages, while the other part of him, the part that couldn't get to Wrigley Field or Sunday school, got harder and harder and—

"Come *on*, kid."

He heard his name followed by something about "Chicago's youngest . . . ," and a drumbeat later he was pummeled with a hot beam of spotlight.

He was onstage.

"Ladies and gentlemen . . ."

The piano twanged, and without thinking, Bobby started tapping out "Tea for Two," with one sweaty hand on his top hat and the other on a coattail he held between his bulge and the audience. They laughed. Half the jokes he told he was too young to understand, so he could never be sure if they were laughing at the punch line or heck-ling him.

Then there was the war. The war he wasn't fighting in.

"Hey, where's your uniform, buddy?"

"What's the matter? You shirking?"

Even if what they were doing to him felt wrong, doing what he was told felt right.

"Oh, Bobby . . ."

His parents were so proud of him.

"Come *on*, Bobby . . ."

Something must have been seriously, shamefully wrong with him, because, despite everything he should have run from — the fondling, the sinning, the heckling, and the shirking — to him, having the strippers' attention felt a little like being a star. Years later, he would tell Janice Lynde, a girlfriend, the women were like mothers to him. "They were affectionate," Lynde said. "Maybe too affectionate." Per-haps that was the source of the confusion. Perhaps that's why night after night, he came back, like a shell-shocked veteran, even long after he left Chicago. "I can romanticize it," he said forty years later, "but it was an awful life. I was very lonely, very scared. You know, hotel rooms in strange towns, and I was all alone, thirteen or fourteen, too shy to talk to anyone, not really knowing what it was all about, and among — not the best people . . . I think it's done me a lot of harm, being exposed to things that early that I shouldn't have been exposed to . . . it left some scar that I have not quite been able to figure out." He was drawn to the girls, then hurt by them. "It was schizophrenic," Fosse said. He couldn't get away from it and he didn't want to.

"It just wasn't the same world my mother and father had told me it was," he said. "The battle going on inside me was just tremendous." On the one hand, being a dancer troubled the track star in him. On the other, being a dancer got him attention. It got him girls. And as for those girls, he knew of two kinds, separated by night and day.

One variety, at the Cuban Village, spun tassels in his face. The other variety, at Amundsen, wore skirts and demurred when kissed. And his parents, who seemed to love him, who took him to every soda counter in the neighborhood for his birthday, also condoned, by their ignorance, Bobby's scared nights alone. They abandoned him, he'd later feel, to a world no child, let alone an unaccompanied child, should be exposed to. To bolster his nerve, he would replay his mother's favorite piece of encouragement, "It will put hair on your chest!" She would be horrified if she found out about the strippers. "Bob could charm his way anywhere," Ann Reinking said, "and he probably charmed his mother into being proud of him for playing those burlesque clubs. But he later felt she encouraged him to be a bon vivant, and that she should have stopped him. He thought she was supposed to protect him and know better. He used to say, 'She shouldn't have let me.'" Fosse said, "She thought you could send a boy of that age into a roomful of naked women and it wouldn't bother him — because he was such a good boy. Obviously, she was wrong." He fucked a waitress in Springfield, who latched on to him like a suction cup and may or may not have forgotten to mention she was married. But she was, to a soldier, who returned from the war and started checking around for his wife's boyfriend. Fosse said, "I panicked at the time, still in high school and afraid my mother would find out."

The two worlds split his perceptions in two. Innocence, he discovered, lived with corruption, and there was no way to be sure what anything was, and nothing left to trust.

For decades, Fosse's hometown, like Fosse, struggled to resolve its image problem. Chicago had been considered a bad town as far back as the Great Fire of 1871. Filth sold newspapers, and over time, half-true tales of drunks and bottom-feeding hoods hardened into legends. The legends stuck. After the Valentine's Day massacre of 1929, Chicago's image problem became critical. For the city's 1933 centennial, reformers planned a full-scale makeover in the guise of a world's fair — a Century of Progress, they called it. "In 1933 the world will talk about our exposition and not our crime," Mayor Lenox Lohr announced on WGN radio. "Visitors will see our culture, our beautiful buildings and parks, our giant industries, and will carry away a different conception of Chicago." They didn't. They saw Sally Rand.

The fan dance she claimed she had invented upstaged the rest of the fair. There was a scandal; Rand became a national phenomenon. In time, the Society for the Suppression of Vice shooed fan dancing from Boston and New York back to Chicago, the greenhouse of smut, where the feathers could touch tips and multiply. As striptease scholar Rachel Shteir wrote, the gimmick suited the Depression: "The oversized fan poked fun at wealthy women who, to protect themselves from the elements, carried enormous ostrich feather fans." Sex and satire: Fosse couldn't get enough. "He was fascinated with Sally Rand," Grass said. "He loved the manipulation of the fans, when she flipped them like a baton twirler." She was the uptown version of what inflamed him downtown.

In 1943 the academy presented *Hold Ev'rything! A Streamlined Extravaganza in Two Parts*, which featured Bob Fosse's first full credit as choreographer ("Dance Numbers by Bob Fosse"), as well as his fan dance to "That Old Black Magic," one of the year's biggest hits. It was the very first Fosse number. The idea to use pitch-black ostrich feathers, twelve to a fan, likely came to the sixteen-year-old by way of the girls of the Silver Cloud, who had gotten theirs, at least spiritually, from Sally Rand. "The number was very sophisticated," recalled Beth Kellough, one of the eight glamour girls in it. "We had long formfitting gowns that were black lace over red and they were strapless. They went down to your knees and flared out a little." Fosse's exposure to tougher varieties of fan dance suggests "That Old Black Magic" might have been a touch prurient, good-boy rock 'n' roll. But how an angel of his age and guileless Andy Hardy gleam had gotten the idea (not to mention technique) to mount, in faithful miniature, the sort of number husbands would be ashamed to tell their wives they recognized, few could imagine. Of course, Mr. Weaver didn't wonder. Neither did Charlie Grass. They knew all those nights in all those shitholes had burned red sequins into Fosse's eyes. "But I like those sequins," a grown Fosse would confess. "That's show business, and I've been a showbiz person my whole life."

Show business and showbiz. One was for the real talent, the artists, and the other for the parasites that needed flash to look real. Fosse knew which side he belonged on. He would never let himself forget. "Whenever I get close to the real object," he said, "I think, whoops, that looks Tiffany to me. I better get back to the dime store." The raunch of burlesque was only half the problem; his own taste for vaudeville shtick was the other. Gags, rim shots, and whistles; rowdy, provincial audiences howling at the acts and the acts howling back; flimsy machinery, threadbare scenery; a circusy rotation of jugglers and dogs — this was his kind of show. It was real too. High theater artfully concealed what vaudeville's industrial vulgarity always seemed to expose. But Fosse loved that about vaudeville; it seemed to be *about* show business. As much as its talent, it reveled in its transparencies. Later, the acts would be called Brechtian; then, they were crude. Crude and gone.

As his beloved vaudeville sank, Fosse witnessed the final degradation of favorite acts, and his low-rent proclivities dropped, by popular standards, even lower. A decade after they were wired for sound, America's vaude-houses emptied their giants onto the streets. The performers vanished wholesale from conversation, only to reappear days or years later on ghost-town barstools, folded over or dead. Others died alive. Joe Frisco, Fosse's favorite flash dancer, turned up on a bill with a couple of trained dogs and two hand balancers. Georgie Tapps ended up a salesman in Beverly Hills. So followed a generation of the country's wackiest individuals, all flattened to sameness. Fosse knew what it meant. He could never be an Astaire. Maybe not even a Draper.

Meanwhile, the good boy cleaned up. Based on Fosse's academic performance, admirable character, and participation in school activities, in December 1944, the Amundsen faculty named him an outstanding student of the year. The story appeared in the *Tribune,* which ran a full list of his credits: "Chairman of senior class, vice president Letterman's club, prom committee, Latin club, honor society, swimming team, president of Alpha Hi-Y [the high-school branch of the YMCA], student council." The students elected him senior-class president. Buttressed, perhaps, by his popularity, Fosse decided the time was right to stop hiding his shame and dance for the toughest crowd in Chicago: his high-school class. Consisting mostly of sketches and songs, Miss Philbrick's annual variety show rarely featured dancers, but she made an exception for Bob, whom everyone loved but no one really knew. Lying, he told his drama teacher he had played the Empire Room and the Palmer House, and having seen him practice for hours at a time, perfecting pullbacks and leaps that already seemed perfect, Miss Philbrick had no reason to doubt him.

Moments after the curtains parted, the band struck up, and Fosse flew onto the stage for a showy, tap-happy rendition of "Stars and Stripes Forever" — mastered, by now, after years of presentation houses and junky burlesques — that finished up with an explosive knee slide that took him virtually into the orchestra. Trying not to gasp for breath, he was said to have held his position at the lip of the stage — arms open, Jolson-like — waiting for the shower of applause to come his way. It did.

He was a hit.

Enjoying Fosse's sudden celebrity, a few of his friends thought it might be fun to get some of their own. Fosse agreed and came up with an act. A drag act. Assuming the role of director, he taught them

to lip-synch with exact fidelity to the Andrews Sisters' "Bei Mir Bist
Du Schön." At first the boys thought it was all pretty funny. Three of
Amundsen's finest donning full drag for the senior-class assembly!
But Fosse wasn't laughing. He rehearsed his trio late into the afternoon and well into the homework hour. Racing toward perfection,
he was not content simply to have them walk across the stage. They
had to walk across the stage in character.

Between runs, George Foutris, a wrestler in mascara and heels,
pulled Bob aside. "How do you keep doing all this?" he asked.

"All what?"

"The sports, the girls, the schoolwork. And now the dancing.
How?"

"You have to learn to compartmentalize, George."

Marion Hauser correctly believed herself to be Bob Fosse's favorite girlfriend. When they were together, she believed he believed it
when he said he loved her and not the others. At least, she believed
it for a while. Hauser threw in the towel when she heard that Marion
"Smoochie" Geweke had taken Bob home to meet her parents. But
that didn't last long either. "He had his mind made up about being a
performer," Smoochie said, "and it just wasn't the life for me. I knew
he would never settle down to a nine-to-five job and I just wasn't
the kind of person who would feel comfortable with a show-business
type."

According to Charlie Grass, Fosse's parents weren't either. "I think
they didn't believe too much in entertainment," Grass recalled. "They
were against show dancing. They went with it in the beginning, the
amateur shows, because Bob was bringing home money." Cy and
Sadie endorsed the sort of ballroom style that Bob's eldest brother,
Buddy, practiced — and practiced in ways Cy and Sadie never knew.
When no one was looking, Buddy took his baby brother to junky

dime-a-dance halls and to the Rialto on State Street, a burlesque house run by the Minskys. On one occasion, Fosse invited Charlie to join them. "No, no." Grass blushed. "I'm going to go home."

Fosse's brothers had all served in the war — Buddy in the Pacific, Edward in France, Donald in England — and now that Fosse was approaching high-school graduation, the time had come for him to act. Trying to preempt Bob's being drafted to God knows where, Buddy and Ed "wrote to the Great Lakes Training Center," Grass recalled, "and told them about Bob's experience as an entertainer, hoping they would get him entertainment work and he wouldn't have to go where the fighting was." Fosse was indeed accepted into Great Lakes, a naval training facility north of Chicago, but despite the USO shows he had played, and the official letters Weaver gave him to prove his talent, Fosse was rejected by the special services entertainment division and was set to go to boot camp as soon as he graduated. He didn't know what would happen to him after that.

But first, commencement. Disguised as an ordinary high-school student, Fosse, the president of the Class of '45, approached the podium, delivered a short welcome, and then ceded the floor to Principal Perry, the main act. His speech, entitled "Post-War Opportunities," met with a rally of patriotic cheers, none of which were Fosse's. After his rejection from special services, he had managed to negotiate a six-month reprieve into his military contract. At seventeen, Fosse was going on the road, a solo act. He wouldn't have to share credit anymore.

"You want to come with me?" he asked his Riff Brother in February of 1945. They met at the studio to talk it over. Weaver was with them, managing both his interests.

"I would love to, Bob," Charlie said, "but I can't leave school." He had half a year left.

"Well, then, can I use our routines?"

This is probably what he wants anyway, Grass thought, *a solo career.* "Sure," he said. "That's fine, Bob."

Now that he had gotten a deferral from the war, Fosse negotiated himself back into Marion Hauser's arms, to which he would return, intermittently, for the next half a year. He expected to be away more, but he quickly saw the road idea wasn't working. Too old to do the kid act, too young to pull off the big time, Fosse spent his six-month reprieve playing the Midwest's remotest shitholes, lonely and far from home. Stealing, selling, and being sold, he was getting cynical about his trade, the people in it, and the places it was taking him. "I hate show business and I love it," Fosse often said. Fortunately, unfortunately, it was in him, an affliction he would never be without.

In the summer of 1945, Weaver's enrollment dropped, the academy shut down, and Bob began his nine months of boot camp. With no sense of his future, Seaman Second-Class Fosse surely felt frightened and out of place, like Eddie Bracken with a machine gun. He wrote to Mr. Weaver for help, and Weaver, mercifully, came to his aid, not for the first time or the last. The old man arranged a meeting with the training center's base commander, "a kind of audition," Grass said, bringing with him music and headshots and an agent's prayer he could somehow save Fosse from combat. On the day of the meeting, Weaver hunched over the piano and played "Stars and Stripes Forever" while Bob, in navy blues and sailor's cap, machine-gun-tapped his way to a new assignment. "That might have saved Bob's life," Grass said.

But if Weaver hadn't rescued Fosse, the subsequent world events probably would have. In September of 1945, shortly after Fosse arrived for duty, Japan surrendered, and World War II went to the Allies. Though the fighting had ended, troops held on to their Pacific island posts, keeping watch and awaiting relocation. For their amusement, Bob Fosse was transferred to the entertainment branch's Navy Liaison Unit in New York City, where the man behind the desk directed him upstate, to a naval training station in Sampson, New York. There he met former vaudevillian Tommy Sternfeld (late of Tommy Stern and His Girls), who was preparing *Hook, Line, and Sinker,* a sailor show stitched together with help from *Joe Miller's Joke Book* ("What did one wall say to the other? I'll meet you at the corner") and the talents of whoever was available. "It was songs and sketches and they threw mops on their heads and dressed up as girls," said Sternfeld's daughter Buzz Halliday. The show rehearsed, and then Fosse and his company packed up their collapsible stage and hit the Pacific in November of 1945, flying and boating from one forgotten barracks to the next.

Months later, *Hook* came to an end and Fosse resurfaced in New York City. There he met chief petty officer Joe Papirofsky, newly appointed head of yet another in-service entertainment division. Assembling a company of twelve or thirteen performing sailors, Papirofsky held informal audition/interviews at Rockefeller Center, where he encountered an unassuming, "very thin, Irish-looking kid" — Bob Fosse. Though Fosse liked Papirofsky, it took him time to feel genuinely at ease with new people. He could be shy, and his life so far had been full of vulnerability — to older siblings, older strippers, clueless parents — making distrust his default. Cigarettes gave him a comfortable piece of business. And they looked good, which was nice too. The swirl of smoke suited Fosse's natural hunch and made him seem, to all who didn't really know him, cool, out of reach, in want of nothing — which he wasn't. But it was a useful pose.

At twenty-five, Papirofsky, with his streetwise Brooklynese and hot-blooded charm, had an older brother's appeal for Fosse and cleared his trust test far quicker than most. Lifting a wave of black hair from his eyes, Papirofsky — or Papp — could quote Shakespeare easily and in an unpretentious way that brought down Fosse's guard. They shared a devilish sense of humor. "I saw at once that he was footjoy, carefree, jaunty," Papp said. "He loved to dance. On some islands he would perform in the hot sun for five or six hours. He'd go on until he nearly collapsed from the heat." They were both devoted to the same kind of popular theater: pure entertainment. "I thought plays were effete, plays were sissy," Papp said. "What I liked was vaudeville, skits, singing, and dancing." Papp brought that sensibility to the sailor shows, which he would write and direct. They had everything. Fosse said, "One guy would sing Irish songs, somebody would sing hillbilly songs, there was a tap dancer and a guy who did impressions of James Cagney." It was vaudeville on the beach.

Touring the Pacific with Papp's show *Tough Situation* was a kind of paradise for Fosse, his first time on the road with a regular, respectable gig. Palling around with guys who didn't have to hide their dance shoes, playing to grateful soldiers on warm South Pacific evenings, he felt like a man of the world, a part of something. They played ships, aircraft carriers, officers clubs, parade fields; it felt legit. "We played a different base on a different island every day," Fosse said, "places like Hawaii, Guam, Chuuk, Okinawa, Wake, all the way through to Tokyo. The guys preferred the shows with girls in them, so we had two strikes against us there, but still we were successful. We'd do sketches with a lot of inside jokes about the navy, like if an officer and a Wave got married, what would their life be like after the war. I played a girl in that skit — I was in drag with wigs and everything." Papp would toss in a ballad or tap number to break up the yocks. But no matter how crude the acts or how casual their conceptualization, Fosse and Papp took their work, and each other, very seriously.

Papp was only six years older than Fosse, but as their ship neared Japan, the end of their tour, the two developed a mentor-apprentice relationship. As the outfit's leader, Papp had an automatic authority, and Fosse, who decried his lack of education, paid very close attention to his superior's riffs on acting, literature, politics (which didn't interest Fosse), and whether Fosse was destined for film or theater. Flagrant intellectuals cooled Fosse, but Papp never went to college, and he talked as much about how to throw a custard pie as he did about psychoanalyst Karen Horney. Papp supported him through his self-described "semi-fake-arty dance period" ("with twenty thousand sailors in the South Pacific looking at me, I'd be dancing Ravel's *Bolero*") and wowed him with tales of Gene Tierney, whom Papp claimed to know personally. That amazed Fosse. He'd never met anyone who actually knew a movie star, not to mention such a hot one ("that overbite," Fosse said, "just knocked me out").

Fosse was like an ever-expanding sponge, and whenever he felt deficient, which was often, especially in the presence of an intellectual, the sponge would absorb a little more, retaining it for later use. From his front-row seat, Fosse listened intently, recording Papp in pictures that he filed away in a personality catalog he would add to consciously and unconsciously for the rest of his life, a folder for everyone. He was always filing. When rehearsal arguments broke out among cast members and Papp intervened, Fosse filed away a major lesson about directing. "If we went too far or started to get physical," Fosse said, "he would step in, as any good officer in charge of men should do. But up till then he would not only watch but also stimulate the situation a little bit." What Papp incited offstage, the performers carried into the show. People had buttons, Fosse saw, and Papp knew how to find them and when to push them.

Papp and Bill Quillin, another sailor in the outfit, sat patiently as Fosse told sad stories of a girl he loved back home. Months earlier, on leave in Chicago, Fosse had eloped with one of his high-school girlfriends — a secret he kept from everyone except one person. "I heard about it later," Grass said, "from Mr. Weaver. The girl must have told her parents because Mrs. Fosse found out about it and had it annulled after Bob left for the navy. She could do that because they were both underage. But I don't think Bob wanted to get an annulment. He wanted a girl he could write letters to." Married or not, Fosse wrote letters anyway.

There had been so many out-of-town shows — Peoria, Springfield, Dubuque — not even Charles Grass could be sure where his seventeen-year-old Riff Brother met the older stripper who arrived, pregnant, on Sadie Fosse's doorstep, long after Fosse had left for the navy. The woman told Mrs. Fosse about the pregnancy, Grass recalled, "and Mrs. Fosse went to Mr. Weaver. She kept it quiet from the family and let Mr. Weaver handle it because he got him the job and Mr. Weaver, as the second father, should have told Fosse about the birds and the bees while he was on the road." Weaver instructed Grass never to tell Fosse, as per his mother's wishes, and Grass never did. "I want you to know," Weaver assured him, "I took care of it. It's over with." And Grass maintained Fosse never knew. "Mrs. Fosse," he said, "was protecting her son."

Fosse toured *Tough Situation* for three months, appearing almost a hundred times on the troop's long way across the Pacific. The air transportation was nauseating, the weather was scorching, and the show was inane, but despite all that, and despite Fosse's gloomy, lovesick heart, he rehearsed his numbers before every show and, when he wasn't satisfied — which was always — after. Others in his company told him to take it easy. They said the soldiers, many of whom had been stationed out there for years, wouldn't know the difference. They were too shell-shocked and show-starved to discern, let alone care, whether "Fascinatin' Rhythm" was perfect or merely good enough. But Fosse cared; more than that — he feared. To the unyielding critic in his ear, the beaches were Broadway floorboards. Guam *was* the Palace, and *Tough Situation* was a rehearsal for auditions for more shows, which were auditions for more auditions. He couldn't rest after the nineteenth run-through to treat his sunburn or sigh in relief because somebody somewhere would still be going, doing it again for the twentieth time. If he stopped now, if he allowed himself a breath, there'd be no one else to blame for failure.

Dancing alone in the forest, he'd look up into the trees. He saw Japanese eyes watching him.

By the time *Tough Situation* touched down in Tokyo at the Ernie Pyle Theater, renamed after the Americans took Japan, Fosse had become the company star. He had even managed to squeeze a few of his own solos onto the bill and convince Papp to end *Tough Situation* with a version of his Andrews Sisters drag routine, a flash finish that would have made Mr. Weaver proud. They sold out the Pyle for five nights. The venue, at two thousand seats, was by far the biggest he'd ever played, and the Andrews Sisters bit went over beautifully. It was a delicious success, much of it Fosse's, and for those five nights, he crowed. Then there were the days. America had won, but the destruction of Tokyo and the way his buddies treated Japanese civilians — the women in particular — horrified Fosse. He said, "That was the first time I was really ashamed to be an American."

FORTY-ONE YEARS

LIKE VAUDEVILLE, NEW YORK CITY had something for everyone. Discharged from service in August 1946, Fosse ran toward it. He sat front row at the Lower East Side's scrappy circus of Jewish, Italian, and Russian routines; uptown, he passed the pinball machines and two-cent scams of Forty-Second Street; he swallowed up Third Avenue lying in the shadows of the El, waiting on the edge of town like a bum looking for a fight. They were all waiting for a fight. The Germans of Yorkville hated the Irish of Yorkville, and the Irish hated the Poles. They all hated the blacks. You'd hear stories about guys getting on the 2 train instead of the 1 train and ending up in Harlem with no taxi to get them back. Things were safer below Eighty-Sixth Street, near the old ladies of the West Side. All day they sat on benches in the median along Broadway. But only along Broadway. Columbus was too far in the wrong direction. Before white flight—highways ushering the rich into the suburbs —Puerto Ricans, Dominicans, fat bankers, and politicians poured in together, climbing the crumbling walls along the Hudson, fighting for space, watching the other guys' acts, learning them, absorbing them, topping them. The whole town was a mongrel work in progress.

All that cohabitation, all that bumping around, and it was only a matter of time before the right bumps begat a new species, only a matter of time before Richard Rodgers bumped Oscar Hammerstein II, who bumped Agnes de Mille, who bumped Rouben Mamoulian, and out came *Oklahoma!*, the first great musical. "In a great musical," wrote Richard Rodgers, "the orchestrations sound the way the costumes look. That's what made *Oklahoma!* work. All the components dovetailed." The reason for dovetailing music with lyrics with dance with story seems obvious today, but by 1943, it happened only piecemeal — a little in *Show Boat*, a little more in *Pal Joey*, and even more in *Lady in the Dark* — because a musical didn't have to be good to be fun, and before *Oklahoma!*, fun was really all a show needed to be.

At long last, the musical was no longer a bauble; it was an art form. Prescient, focused, and seriously assembled, Rodgers and Hammerstein's *Oklahoma!* brought content to the routinely replagiarized flapper vaudevilles of the twenties and thirties. Most of those shows' songs, many of them lovely Porter and Gershwin numbers, were unrelated to what was going on onstage, which wasn't much to begin with (mistaken identities, rags-to-riches stories), and had even less to do with what was going on in real life. *Oklahoma!* and *Carousel* put a stop to that; they made singing about the world a very serious, very dramatic thing, and they turned choreography — once just a fancy word for dancing around — into an integral part of the story. Witness the *Oklahoma!* dream ballet, "Laurey Makes Up Her Mind." Make that *Agnes de Mille's* dream ballet; fusing character and movement, traditional ballet and colloquial ease, it could have been no one else's. The choreographer had a point of view: her own. And it was about something. As the ballet's title implies, Laurey makes up her mind *in* the dance, so the number is, like any good dramatic scene, an essential and revelatory part of the musical. "Many a somber problem play," wrote *New York Times* dance critic John Martin, "has been built on just such a question of emotional compulsions and has failed to illuminate it half so clearly after several hours of grim dialogue. Yet this is a 'dance number' in a 'musical show'!"

In those days, there was a theater with a big Broadway musical on every corner, and on every corner, there was a bevy of chorus girls looking for fun — good odds for a twenty-one-year-old sailor back from the war, and better odds for a sweet and sexy one like Bob Fosse, who could pivot between a "Geez, I dunno . . ." and a "Whaddaya doing later?" in a single motion. He was that good. "When he talked to you, you just felt, *Oh my God. He's in love with me,*" said casting director Lynne Carrow. "He had a personality that drew you in. He could just click with you and pull you into his world. The touching, the looking, the little smiles as he's talking to you. I don't want to call it flirting because I think that's just how he naturally was, but maybe that's why he was such a good flirt. Just talking to him was a sensual experience."

In his cupcake way he mastered the art of not taking no for an answer. Even the girls who saw it coming were caught off-guard. That's how good he was; he could sell without selling. The girl would be upstairs with him, not knowing how she got there, and downstairs the next day, hoping to see him again. His competition didn't get it. "I had always wondered why he was always able to get all these girls," said producer Robert Greenhut. "So I asked this one stripper I knew he slept with, 'What is it about Fosse that he's always able to . . . you know. Why is he like flypaper to you guys?' She says, 'He is the greatest lay I have ever had in my life. There is absolutely no one more sexually competent than this man.' And she said his shyness was the thing that gets you to begin with. And I said, 'Well, okay. At least now I know.'"

And more girls were always around the corner. This was New York, after all, a city of corners. This was Broadway, land of the chorus girl. The streets were ablaze with talent, and there were more than enough to go around. But the girls didn't go around; they all went back to Fosse. "I think everyone was attracted to him," said sound mixer Christopher Newman. "Man, woman, piano. It didn't matter. He was insanely attractive." The preponderance of gay men in the dance world elevated Fosse to the role of high satyr almost instantly; he was more than just cute, fun, and a whiz on two feet; he was, to the fervent girls of Broadway, at the top of a very short list. The way he looked at you, you knew you were on the top of his list too. "It was like you were in a tunnel," recalled Trudy Ship, assistant editor on *Lenny* and *Liza with a Z.* "He made incredible eye contact and asked you questions. Who were your parents? Where were you born? He oozed sexuality and he was so sweet about it too."

Fosse's bed at the YMCA on Thirty-Fourth and Ninth wasn't easy to get girls to, but it was a convenient walk to Broadway and, at thirty-five cents a day, ideal for a jobless ex-sailor with only a few hundred bucks in his wallet. Full of servicemen, the Thirty-Fourth Street Y, an imposing brick tower with a red neon sign buzzing *Sloane House,* was the largest YMCA in the city. The building had over a thousand rooms, not all of them equipped with private bathrooms, so Sloane's communal showers turned social, and Sloane House, also known as the French Embassy, became one of Manhattan's most popular gay spots. Were it not for some uncomfortable bathroom attention, Fosse might have actually gotten a kick out of the place, where guests were known by their room numbers, and their keys passed through a complicit concierge. Citing the *C* in *YMCA,* scandalized members of the management hired security guards to patrol the showers, but the joke was on them: most of the guards joined in the fun.

• • •

Fosse didn't have to hang around Sloane House for long. One of his navy buddies had introduced him to MCA agent Maurice Lapue, formerly of the adagio dance team Maurice and Cordoba, and Lapue signed Fosse right away. Days later, sporting his freshly pressed sailor suit and a discharge button on his lapel, he appeared before composer Lehman Engel to audition for a part in *Call Me Mister.*

"Sing first," Engel said.

"I better dance first."

It was only his second audition, but Fosse got the job—and a pretty good one too. As the dance lead in the national production of *Call Me Mister,* he'd tap and sing (in his thinner-than-Chet-Baker's voice), touring the country's biggest second-tier theaters, finally a full-time show-business professional. A homecoming revue with songs by Harold Rome and sketches by Arnold Auerbach, *Mister* was basically for laughs: half sketches, half song and dance, and featuring an eclectic company of unknowns, from bass-baritone William Warfield to tap dancer Marian Niles to comics Buddy Hackett and Carl Reiner. The singers sang, the dancers danced, and the comics told jokes. In those days, no single person had everything.

Buddy Hackett was a trenchant wiseguy, Damon Runyon with a Catskills twang. One of his favorite bits, "The Farting Contest," pitted two guys against each other in a kind of boxing match with farts for punches. It was a sketch he liked to follow with his Peter Lorre impression. Like the hippo he resembled, he could charge an innocent passerby if the spirit moved him, barking expletives like a stripper at a speakeasy raid, then laugh and do it again. City born and raised, Hackett introduced Fosse to another side of all-night New York, leading him to underground clubs and dancehalls, tutoring him in the unwritten history of hipster comics and the wide world of Jewish shtick. Best friends, they hung out every night; by day, they rehearsed the show.

Fosse was obsessed. "He was always there early," Carl Reiner said, "warming up and doing his steps over and over again, and he was always making up new steps, always inventing. When the rest of us were resting, there was Bobby, getting there early to invent." He was inventing himself a little too. Fosse's *Call Me Mister* bio, which cited his tour of "fashionable bistros of the middle-west," was less actual than aspirational, obliquely disclosing a deep-down, never-to-be-resolved affliction of class — as in, he thought he had none. If they liked his act, he fooled them. "Bobby had the first-act finale number," Reiner said. "It was the signature song, 'Call Me Mister,' and he had a very big dance specialty in it, a solo. I was a floorwalker in the number, he was a customer, and he was dancing around getting clothes for this soldier coming out of the army. And he was just brilliant — so flashy — and he wasn't going to let anyone get in his way. Even then he had that kind of ambition. One very funny thing I'll always remember is, at one point he had leaped offstage — stage right — and my entrance was timed to his leap-off. So one day I took a head-start run before I leaped onto the stage just as he was leaping off and as we crossed in the air — I'll never forget — he said to me, 'Carl, I'm the lead dancer and you're outjumping me!' It was fantastic! Later, he said, 'Why don't you land over there, in that third of the stage?' And I said, 'But all I can *do* is jump! You dance. My thing is I jump!' Anyway, we laughed about that, I remember."

No one was more committed. "At the end of that number," dancer Jeanna Belkin said, "Fosse, who was featured, had to do *à la seconde* turns and very quickly in a two-four tempo. When the curtain started coming down, Marian Niles and I, watching from the wings, would rush downstage at just the right time to stop him from spinning into the curtain. He was that involved in the dance. He was that passionate." This happened every night. And every night, Niles reached out to save him.

Call Me Mister opened in New Haven, after which it moved on to Philadelphia and then Boston; it played to loving audiences and solid reviews for five months — a long time. "We had a pretty crazy company," said Reiner. "People were fighting, people were falling in love."

Fosse had one eye on Niles, a peppy chorus dancer with the face of a girl and the mouth of a hooker, Debbie Reynolds after a night with Mae West. They called her Spooky. She was up for anything. "Marian was a spitfire," said dancer Harvey Evans. "She was just dynamite." "I wanted to walk behind her with a tape recorder," said dancer Margery Beddow. "Everything she said was hysterical." In addition to being a career smoker, drinker, and all-night partier, Niles had what none of Fosse's former girlfriends did: talent and experience. "Spooky was a wonderful tap dancer," said Belkin. "The show called for her to do a mixture of ballet and tap, and she could move smoothly between them. There were others who were stronger in the chorus, others with longer legs, but Spooky was the best tap dancer in the bunch." Like Fosse, she had been dancing for money since she was a kid, but unlike Fosse, Niles really had played some of the most fashionable bistros, and some of them in New York. She was a *real* pro. "Bobby liked beauty but he loved talent," said dancer Deborah Geffner. "That's what he wanted to sleep with. He wanted to get as far into it as he could." Craving solace from his sense of inadequacy and adding value to his gifts, Fosse, for the rest of his life, would surround himself with an army of talent — talent of all kinds — using all means possible, including sex, to mine their value for his own. Niles was the first of many. He may even have loved her too.

They decided to team up. As a double act, Fosse and Niles were twice as appealing to club agents, and with a lot of hard work, they could move up from night holes outside Newark all the way to the Plaza Hotel. Or so they dreamed. "No matter where the show took us," Belkin said, "whether New Haven or Boston or Los Angeles, in the afternoons and on their nights off Bobby and Spooky rehearsed their tap routines." Niles was more than a great partner; she gave Fosse a foretaste of a big future, the feeling of shared ambition easily confused with love. And she had something more tangible to offer him—a repertoire. "Limehouse Blues," the jewel of her solo act, Fosse remade into a duet, heavy on drums, part tap, part Jack Cole–Oriental. It would be a Fosse-and-Niles staple. "She was a not too educated girl," Belkin said. "Too in love to see how much she was giving him."

For the newcomer, the thin line between influence and plagiarism is difficult to see. For Fosse, who had spent more time watching than inventing, who was ashamed of his showbiz instincts—the vaudeville, the burlesque—that line was almost invisible. Fearing he had nothing of his own, he drew regularly, and reluctantly, from the offerings around him. (A year earlier, in *Ziegfeld Follies*, Astaire had also danced "Limehouse Blues" as a duet.) Fosse did not consider his chameleonism or the inventions it would spawn anything but a life jacket for a drowning man, which is how he danced. Despite his flash, when he danced with Niles, Fosse moved with an inwardness comparable to shame. She "had a lot of clarity as a dancer," one dancer said, "with wonderful changes of rhythm. Bob just seemed detached as a dancer, as though he was choreographing himself out of the number." How to open up, how to play off an audience—she gave him that too.

During *Call Me Mister*'s five-week run in Boston, the company stayed at the Bradford Hotel, a few doors from the Shubert Theater. The weekend the Ice Capades came to town, the Bradford's every square foot was filled with smoke and the chatter of show folk. It was pandemonium, a cageless zoo. Instant lifelong friends threw their arms around each other, and all of them flooded strangers' suites until the sun came up or a wife walked in. Buddy Hackett turned his room into an open bar, and girls peeled off the wallpaper. Marian Niles didn't stand a chance. "Could you imagine," Hackett said, "being twenty-one years old and you're out with a musical and there's sixteen girl dancers and sixteen girl singers plus the leads and semi-leads? What a candy store!" Late in the evening, Hackett's room was mostly empty, so there wasn't much of a need for Fosse to close the bathroom door behind him, which is how Hackett, looking up from his girl, caught Bob's reflection in the medicine-chest mirror, jauntily fucking another reflection. Before Hackett had time to wonder how Fosse could have left the door open or how it was anatomically possible to achieve such an angle, Marian Niles walked in, burst into tears, and tore out of the room. ("We all knew about Bobby," Belkin said. "But we kept our mouths shut.") Hackett ran after her.

Fosse and Niles married in Chicago. The tour brought them to town, so the time seemed right for Fosse to command center stage, a professional entertainer in full view of his high-school friends and family. On the morning of July 8, the wedding party arrived at St. Chrysostom's Church, just a few blocks from Lake Michigan. Reiner appeared with an 8-millimeter camera and pointed it at ushers Hackett and William Warfield, a beaming Sadie Fosse, and the happy couple. Backstage, Fosse pouffed his ascot, and Niles, on the opposite end of the church, slipped taps onto her wedding shoes. "She was just a very sweet girl," Reiner said. "Really very in love with Bobby." When the organ sounded, she made her entrance, shuffling down the aisle.

Frederic Weaver was not in attendance. Days earlier, he warned Charlie Grass he had no intention of standing by as one of his best pupils destroyed the career he had been working toward for a decade. "Mr. Weaver was a hundred percent against marriage if you're in show business," Grass said. "It was somebody pulling you back. And family too. Bob knew how he felt about that. He'd made it very clear to us early on that you've got to be completely dedicated to show business. You're married to show business." Hackett was certain Niles was pregnant — either again or for the first time — and that the groom, wanting to do right by her, had no choice but to make it official. "He was very, very nervous and not cool at all," Hackett recalled. "That was not a guy who wanted to get married."

There was a reception that afternoon at the Fosse family home. But Fosse and Niles couldn't stay long. That night they had a show.

Call Me Mister closed in San Francisco in October 1947 and Fosse posted his final review in the scrapbook he had been keeping since the show opened. He underlined (with the help of a ruler) in red pen every mention of his name, whether good or bad, clipped every article out, and attached it to the page with long strips of tape he laid down at perfect right angles. Even duplicates were included, as though Fosse had to prove not once but twice that it had actually happened. Beside the final review (which heralded Fosse as "awfully good") he wrote, "End of 'Call Me Mister.' Also end of Bob Fosse."

Fosse and Niles arrived in New York with an agent but no money and no job. In the uneasy months to follow, which Fosse and Niles spent glaring at the phone and imploring it to ring, Maurice Lapue reached out to nightclubs as near as Long Island and as far as the Dominican Republic. But no one was buying.

Most of what they had been rehearsing was old stuff in new clothing, ballroom-type numbers with a youthful touch. Where he could, Fosse threw in a little taste of vaudeville, but nothing too crass; he and Niles were going for the uptown crowd, the Marge and Gower Champion set. Elegant and smiling, the Champions — she had her first tutu before she turned one; he signed with MCA before he graduated high school — had mastered the look of class and good breeding that Fosse feared he couldn't even fake. But he tried. With no money for studio space, the newlyweds rehearsed their act in the tiny one-room they rented above Times Square, careful not to twirl into the furniture or leap into a wall.

When they weren't rehearsing, which was rarely, they traveled with packs of other dancers, musicians, and novelty acts, hopeful that someone with an ear to the ground would bring them news of an audition before it hit the papers or they lost the job to another agent's dancers. The jobless assembled at Hansen's drugstore and the nearby Charlie's Tavern, a convenient few paces from Roseland. Those with money for a meal could find seats at the bar or in booths under the headshots Charlie hung on the peeling paint. If the place needed a little work, Charlie could turn to the young and hungry, to Fosse and Niles and the legions of unemployed comics and jazzmen of New York who stood in that patch of turf like it was their office, waiting all day (and, if they didn't have gigs, all night) for some guy who some other guy knew to show up with a lead.

In a business of lucky breaks, where the revolving door of chance turns for jerk and genius alike, patience, not talent, would get Fosse and Niles where they wanted to be. Dancing was the easy part. Sitting by the phone took work. It took cigarettes and cheap wine and skipping meals. Talking about it made it worse, but not talking about it gave them nothing to do but think about what wasn't working, and Fosse blamed himself. Never mind what was good for their feet; they should be going through the routine again. Somewhere some team was doing just that, getting better. "Bob likened show business to boxing," said Ann Reinking. "He said, 'If you can stay in the ring it will turn your way again.'" Or: What doesn't kill you will kill you later.

Winter hit. Waiting outside the theaters for their names to be called, Fosse and Niles huddled close, massaging each other's muscles to stay loose.

She couldn't leave him. They needed money, and Fosse was the closest thing she had to a chance.

He couldn't tell his mother and father what he'd told Mr. Weaver, that he'd spent all their money. "He had a drug problem," Charlie Grass said, "and Mr. Weaver helped carry him through." The maestro put tens and twenties in an envelope and directed his best and favorite student to spend the money on doctors and drug counselors. Weaver knew the signs. He had seen the top talents in vaudeville waste their lives circling the drain, and he sensed that Fosse watched them with a kind of envy. He had the jazzman's crush on burning out. "I always thought I'd be dead by twenty-five," he said. "I wanted to be. I thought it was romantic. I thought people would mourn me: 'Oh, that young career.'"

Then one day the phone rang. Lapue had booked them into the Samovar — in Montreal. In a flash, Marian changed her name to the much tonier Mary-Ann; they got on a bus and played the club on March 23, 1948, where they were, according to a local paper, "the most promising young dancers . . . in many months." A week later, they were at the Boulevard in Elmhurst, Long Island. Niles recalled, "When we got off the floor someone said, 'Did your husband hurt himself?' I said, 'What d'you mean?' She said, 'Well, he fell.' . . . He fell and got up and never knew it. Literally fell and got up." Rest was unthinkable. "They would do their nightclub act somewhere," said dancer Eileen Casey, a friend of Niles's, "and then, that night, go back and rehearse parts of the act that weren't working."

"I get terribly involved in my work," Fosse later said, "and everything else goes." Nothing was ever good enough because it came from him, and when he wasn't fooling them, he was no good. "He thought he was the best and he thought he was terrible," Ann Reinking said.

In May, Fosse and Niles played Miami's Clover Club. Onward to the Dominican Republic, to the Hotel Jaragua, where they appeared for the first time as top-liners. Then north to the Embassy Club in Jacksonville and, finally, back to New York on September 15, 1948, for Bob Fosse's first appearance on a Manhattan stage: the Belmont Hotel's Glass Hat. Then October: one night at Chicago's Drake Hotel. November: a week in Norfolk, Virginia. Come December, they were back in New York for their first TV appearance. *Kobb's Korner* was a hillbilly jamboree as stupid as it sounds, but it was also CBS and free advertising for their upcoming tenure at the Pierre Hotel's Cotillion Room, one of the most romantically appointed nightclubs in the city.

The Cotillion. Fosse and Niles could take a deep breath. They'd made it, almost.

Well located at Sixty-First and Fifth Avenue, the Cotillion was only a few steps — and, for the lucky ones, a few bookings — away from the Plaza's Persian Room, where the Champions cut the parquet for the city's most fashionable grownups. Fosse and Niles were ready. Refined over the past year, their mélange of tap, ballroom, and East Indian styles had been universally well received. It had spunk. While most café performers built their acts on a kind of pop ballet, Fosse and Niles moved fast, with a Broadway feeling of something for everyone — at least, everyone so far.

The evening of December 7, 1948, they arrived early at the Cotillion Room to scrub the glossy patches from the dance floor; too much shine, and they'd be slipping around like the Keystone Cops. Then a run-through and a quick bite in the upstairs bedroom the Pierre gave them to change in (a double-breasted business suit for him, a tasteful dress for her), after which they stubbed out their cigarettes and flurried back downstairs to wait, as they had so many times, for their introduction music.

Standing for the first time before a savvy New York audience, Fosse and Niles were about to learn how strong their act really was. This time there would be no sketch to blame for whatever bad press befell them, no dimwitted director to complain about at Hansen's after the show. There would be only failure — and all of it Fosse's. He was the choreographer.

"Ladies and gentlemen, please welcome . . ."

To the sound of applause, two silhouettes strode into the ballroom and took their starting positions under the chandelier. The room

— lined in floor-to-ceiling windows overlooking Central Park — fell silent. Then a fork clinked. Three hundred hidden faces at one hundred tiny tables, and none of them belonged to Mr. Weaver or Miss Comerford.

This was it. There was no more rehearsal.

"You've heard of Marge and Gower Champion?" Fosse asked into the darkness. "Well, we're the runner-ups."

They laughed. Good. At least he'd nailed that: knocking oneself for entertainment.

They danced two twelve-minute shows that night, an early and a late; they were fast and clean and, by the end of their final number, beat. But how were they? The act that worked so well out of town was by then old news in New York. "If they looked good they didn't have an act that showed much originality," opined *Billboard*. "Most of their steps were the same. Only their music was different for each number. An East Indian satirical dance was overplayed, and their Eddie Leonard thing with heavy taps, tho [*sic*] flashy, meant little." Neither Fosse nor *Billboard*'s critic could have known that the act, with its flash references to the early days of American entertainment, would one day emerge as a style, accrue an ideology, and change the face of dance, film, theater, and television — for good. "With more imaginative routines," concluded *Billboard*, "they can go places."

They needed a signature, an angle.

They took dancing roles in the national company of *Make Mine Manhattan*, a musical revue starring Bert Lahr in a part Sid Caesar originated on Broadway. The show opened in Boston on January 11, 1949, moved to Philadelphia two weeks later, and then went on to Baltimore, where a local critic, delighted by Fosse and Niles's big ballet number, wrote, "What faith a wife must have in her husband to allow him to lift her so high above his head, also to swing her around through space with such abandon! Suppose hubby should be angry with wifey some night — and decide to administer a bit of punishment?"

Those were dark days for Mary-Ann Niles. Fosse's infidelities humiliated her, and in the hours after the applause died down, her suffering was splintered by loneliness, the feeling that no matter how incensed those who consoled her appeared to be, no one was terribly shocked or outraged by his behavior. It was, after all, that way for all of them. That was life on the road: a hundred hotel-room doors guarded a hundred unknowns, and everyone had something on someone. Except Niles. No one had anything on Mary-Ann. She was the party on two feet, openly adored by the entire company, Fosse included. So he said.

At the show's end, Fosse and Niles returned to New York, jobless yet again. To juice up their act, they gathered what was left of their money and Mary-Ann's fortitude and enrolled in dance class with Frances Cole at her studio in the CBS building. "There were about fifteen of us in that class," said dancer Phyllis Sherwood. "In those days, you did more ballet than you did jazz, and Bobby would like to stay in the back, almost like he was embarrassed." He probably was. Ballet was Fosse's weakness, or so he believed, and for the duration, he laid low, covering up, apologizing as he sponged. "Unless he knew everything perfect," Sherwood said, "he would stand in the back there behind Mary-Ann or he would watch, like he was sucking everything in." He watched the technique, yes, but he watched the people too, inculcating in himself their emotions, imagined histories, and idiosyncrasies. They were characters, all of them richly detailed. Everyone had a walk. Everyone had a tell.

In that very same CBS building, at Broadway and Fifty-Fourth Street, Ed Sullivan taped his shows, and the network broadcast *The Fifty-Fourth Street Revue,* a live variety program with regular spots for Fosse and Niles and fellow Lapue client Carl Reiner. They made several appearances (once with Bojangles Robinson) through May and June of 1949, Fosse rising to the post of dance director and attracting the attention of twenty-six-year-old Sid Caesar. He brought them on a show of his, *The Admiral Broadway Revue*, and made Fosse and Niles his opening act at Chicago's Empire Room, where *Variety* caught them, by then a full-blown dance-comedy double. Comedy — Fosse loved to mess around; Niles lived for a laugh — that was the angle they needed. "Little bit of comedy in 'showoff' stint garners chuckles but duo really starts selling with their East Indian hoke tap, sharp travesty on the Jack Cole imitators. Satire on the old vaude days at the Palace is close to the original with youngsters getting nifty reception for cakewalk finale." Showbiz; Fosse had let it in again. Maybe that's what Caesar saw in them. Showbiz and satire.

They toured again, briefly, through the fall of 1949, and then returned to New York, where it was back to Charlie's or Hansen's and a few weeks of waiting by the phone, which soon rang with news of *Alive and Kicking*, a harebrained revue to be choreographed by Jack Cole, the slithering id of American exotica, and off they went. (The day of their audition, Gwen Verdon, Fosse's future wife and lifelong partner, was in the audience serving as Cole's right-hand dance assistant and keeper of his style.) Fosse and Niles did not get the job; in November, they signed on instead to *Dance Me a Song*, another revue, also harebrained. But it hardly mattered. The once-popular revue format was dying or dead (the *Oklahoma!* revolution already seven years in the past) and Fosse's marriage was a corpse duet, but in *Dance Me a Song*, Fosse found himself, at long last, on Broadway. On Broadway and in love.

THIRTY-SEVEN YEARS

HER NAME WAS Joan McCracken. She was a ballet dancer. Barely five feet and broad across the shoulders, she looked more like an acrobat than a swan princess, but when a soft light beamed across her eyes, a more than melancholy romance shone, and Joan became the moon. Glancing at those big, silent eyes, one might have guessed — and guessed correctly — she was in love with Poe's "Annabel Lee." "Her eyes, in particular, often looked as if she were about to cry, or had been crying," a friend observed. And yet when Joan McCracken danced, nothing like sadness came through. Laughter did. The *New York Times* once called her "practically a musical comedy in herself."

McCracken — like Fosse, like Verdon — had learned to offset her clumsy figure and irregular technique with levity. By way of splits, straddles, back bends, and contortions, she added to ballet the plucky air of a knockabout, a clown. "There are lots of ballerinas," Agnes de Mille said of McCracken, "but comediennes who can dance are rare." De Mille thought Joan's lower extremities resembled piano legs, but she had a balletic grace that tangled with something wilder, more American. "McCracken was exactly the right kind of dancer to embody the choreographic innovations de Mille was bringing to Broadway," wrote biographer Lisa Jo Sagolla, "the melding of acting and movement in a balletic yet nonclassical vein that reflected and spoke to mid-twentieth-century American sensibilities."

She was pure personality. With a quick wink to the second balcony, McCracken could smack a guy in the groin, cross his eyes, and take his heart for payment. As one of the original members of the Actors Studio, she could dance a dance as if it were a scene in a play. She was an actress. "I can fall down and make it look real," McCracken said to de Mille during an *Oklahoma!* rehearsal one afternoon — and on opening night, the whole world saw she wasn't kidding. They went nuts. "You could have sopped the audience up with a piece of bread," de Mille said. *Playbill* changed her billing to read *The Girl Who Falls Down: Joan McCracken.*

Fosse fell for McCracken and snapped Mary-Ann from his life like training wheels. It was obvious to everyone: Mary-Ann, poor thing, didn't stand a chance. In ability, looks, class, fame, and achievement, McCracken was simply the next level, an artist and a star. A full decade older than Fosse, she had appeared onstage with Charles Laughton and John Garfield and had even danced in the movies, at MGM, no less, home to the greatest names in Hollywood. Lover and mentor, McCracken was the best parts of Mary-Ann and Mr. Weaver; her attention was as invigorating to Fosse as a headline in the *New York Times*. "He would give her a flower when she came off stage," Bob Scheerer said. "It was very loving."

To Mary-Ann, Fosse gave a new washing machine, and he went out with Joan or his new friend comedian Wally Cox (who, along with Joan, was the show's breakout star) while Niles stayed at home, drinking and wringing his clean pants dry. At least he was honest about lying — once, she could let it go. But this time was different. Joan McCracken was different. But feeling sorry for herself — that's where Mary-Ann Niles drew the line. No matter who knew or how humiliating displays became, Niles would show them all that she was okay. She would laugh out loud for them to see. Ol' Spooky (she wanted them to say), always game for a good time.

That McCracken continued to upstage her onstage was a humiliation too perverse to bear. "Strange New Look" was widely considered one of the best numbers in the show, dramatic and just a touch poetic, tailor-made for McCracken's talents. Worse, *Dance Me a Song's* choreographer, Robert Sidney, seemed to give her everything she asked for — additional music here, creative freedom there, and he featured her, yet again, in "Paper," a musical-comedy-style ballet that had McCracken, the very picture of beatnik grace, in a coquettish black velvet jacket and black tights. The number was ridiculous, but McCracken was impervious and shone all the brighter by comparison. Not Niles. Bourrées, arabesques, sissonnes; the curtain call came and went, and Mary-Ann split from the group and went back to her hotel window and her cigarettes. If she left Fosse, she'd be leaving her partner, her career, and if she left her career, she'd be back to zero, just another girl Bob Fosse loved once, without a dime to dance on. So she opened another bottle and hung his pants up to dry, jabbing them with clothespins.

Dance Me a Song opened on Broadway at the Royale Theater on January 20, 1950, and it closed thirty-five performances later. But no matter: work was steady now. A few episodes of *Toni Twin Time* (Jack Lemmon, host) begat spots on *Ford Star Revue* and *The George Burns and Gracie Allen Show*. As the Lucky Strike Extra dancers on *Your Hit Parade,* Fosse and Niles appeared weekly, live, in front of studio cameras and danced in a variety of styles to the hit songs of the moment. Confined to chart-topping tunes, Fosse was forced to produce, and produce quickly, in styles not necessarily to his taste. But limitation was adaptation. Added dance modes increased Fosse's ever-expanding choreographic vocabulary, and the fear of deadlines (and public failure) whipped him on. (Gwen Verdon: "Interviewers would say, 'What is your motive? What drives you?' He would say, 'Fear.' And everyone would laugh, but Bob was telling the truth.") Flop sweat — one of Fosse's favorite expressions — was the stick he beat against his own ass. It had to hurt; stress was his muse. "Take care of myself?" He would laugh. "You've got to be kidding."

With Joan McCracken appearing (not too far away) at Connecticut's Westport Playhouse, her day- and nighttime assignations with Fosse slid easily into the cracks between rehearsals. They carried on as McCracken's current show, *Angel in the Pawnshop*, toured New England for the rest of the year; it arrived, finally, on Broadway on January 18, 1951, only a day before Fosse and Niles returned to the Cotillion Room. With little left to call a marriage, they danced better than they ever had. "Since last caught," *Billboard* said, "the kids have improved so much there's hardly any comparison. Today they are one of the freshest acts to hit the classroom circuit in many a long month. The tow-headed, boyish Fosse is more than a hoofer, tho [*sic*] he's excellent in that department; he's now a comedian with a sly approach that builds, if not for yocks, then certainly for healthy enough laughs." The place was so full, chairs had to be pushed against the walls. "The kids' walk-off, a strawhatted old vaude exit, complete with sand-steps and deliberately corny chatter, almost stopped the show." They were held over.

Club owner Marty Proser signed Fosse, and Niles, to a production in his café theater, a midsize saloon that specialized in recycling Broadway musicals into dinner-theater revues. This particular retread, a tongue-in-cheek montage of 1920s America, which cut song to song from Texas Guinan ("Hello, suckers!") to the stock-market crash of 1929, was carved from the carcass of *Billion Dollar Baby*, a hit show on Broadway. Dancer George Marcy said, "There wasn't much choreography on [that show], so Bobby did his own dances, but they weren't much, not like they became. He gave me the Charleston. He did his knee slides, his tricks, his Fred Astaire and the commercial

Gene Kelly kind of thing." Marty Proser was in the consignment business. If it's all been done before — and it has, many times — then showbiz is the act of hocking used for new, and the guy under the top hat is Elmer Gantry, at least on his best day, when they buy it. When they don't, which is most days, he's only Willy Loman, overselling to a basement of jerks. "We're all here to woo you," Fosse said of his profession. "God, it's disgusting." In early April 1951, Proser swapped out a couple numbers and retitled the show *The Roaring Twenties* so he wouldn't have to pay any royalties.

At night after the show, Fosse would lead the peach-faced boy and girl dancers out of the theater to a bar on the other side of the block to carouse in rounds of liquor dreams until late into the morning. They wanted Broadway and Hollywood. They couldn't wait anymore. "I remember going there practically every night with Bobby," said dancer George Marcy. "He would sit there and talk about what he wanted to do and how he wanted to do it. We all loved listening to him, the girls especially. He had ideas, ideas about directing and choreographing. It was so good to be around him because whatever we were feeling about ourselves, which was generally not so good — we were so poor and young and we worked so hard — Bobby would make us feel good about show business again. 'It's a wonderful thing,' he'd say. He made me believe it." And wherever there was Fosse, there was Mary-Ann. "Jesus, she was so in love with him," Marcy said. "She'd always talk about him. Even in front of him, like his mother. She'd brag about him and then she'd get embarrassed and cut him down. She was drinking so much in those days, drinking like a fish, drinking every night."

Dean Martin and Jerry Lewis, early fans of Fosse and Niles, had gone to see them at the Pierre, where they were all officially introduced. "I want you kids to choreograph my show," Lewis said, and they did. *The Colgate Comedy Hour,* a variety program on NBC, was an hour long, roomy enough to accommodate a couple of dances, including a featured spot for Fosse and Niles. Here was a challenge: The show required Fosse to stage, for the first time, an entire ensemble. From his tiny repertoire, Fosse picked the Jack Cole–inspired "Limehouse Blues," which he (in white tux and turban) and Niles danced before a giant Shiva as half a dozen others twirled around them. To downplay his lack of experience in the production department, Fosse broke the ensemble into pairs and choreographed them as duos — easier to manage that way. Sometimes the duos merged; that was about it. But, significantly, the group number showcased Fosse's details, like wrist isolations, limp hands held up high in the air, flopping like the teeny-weeny wings of a fat bird. Martin and Lewis were pleased enough with it to invite them back to choreograph another *Colgate Comedy Hour*, at Chicago's Studebaker Theater, not far from Martin and Lewis's engagement at the Chez Paree. Late in April 1951, Fosse cast a company that included his Riff Brother, Charlie Grass, for "Steppin' Out with My Baby," a white-tie-and-tails homage to Astaire. Again, the group work was generic, but the number showed an increased awareness of background and foreground space, which Fosse used to contrast grand acrobatics with cinematic close-ups of nondancers; in this case, a man in a top hat blowing cigarette smoke into the camera.

The push to large-format choreography and the acclaim it brought Fosse he owed to Joan McCracken. "She's the one who encouraged me to be a choreographer," Fosse said. "I was very showbiz, all I thought about was nightclubs, and she kept saying, 'You're too good to spend your life in nightclubs.'" Fosse thought of choreography as a means to an end, something a dancer needed in order to dance, like a floor; it wasn't a profession. The hoofer in him considered the work of the choreographer, paradoxically, both out of his creative range and a loser's plan B. Who outside of Manhattan had ever heard of Agnes de Mille? If Fosse had asked that question, McCracken would have answered, *Just wait. They will soon.* "Joan was the biggest influence in my life," Fosse said. "She was the one who changed it and gave it direction."

That she hung around with the likes of Truman Capote and Leo Lerman, read Rilke, and smoked cigarettes with gold tips made her seem, to the no-college Fosse, a storm of heady plenitude, exotic, distinctly unshowbiz. Whereas Mary-Ann reeked of tobacco, Joan bloomed with the scent of cypress and bitter fruit, a perfume one of her fancy friends must have picked up for her in Paris or Berlin. And she spoke French. And she knew about wine. And she advised Fosse to enroll in the American Theatre Wing. The GI Bill, McCracken assured him, covered a year's worth of voice, dance, and playwriting classes; all he had to pay for was the bike to take him from one place to the next, from José Limón's dance class to Anna Sokolow's. "I was always very bad in class," Fosse said, "it was slightly humiliating . . . I had a great deal of trouble with turnout and extension. To compensate for this, I used to work on other areas, such as rhythm, style of movement, taking ordinary steps and giving them some little extra twist or turn."

He took a course with Sanford Meisner, one of New York's most celebrated acting teachers. Of course it was McCracken who made the introduction.

While Lee Strasberg sank his students in psychoanalytic mires, Meisner emphasized clear, task-oriented objectives, actions as simple as opening the door, closing the window — in his words, "living truthfully under imaginary circumstances." It was simple to understand and difficult to execute. To a performer asked to play a character in fantastic or ridiculous circumstances, like those in musical theater — or, even more ridiculous, like those in musical comedy, with its cotton-candy logic — Meisner's technique offered a way through: be you. Truth and simplicity were always there, and any performer, regardless of his gifts, could harness them.

Room 3B at the Neighborhood Playhouse was, like Meisner's

technique, a model of simplicity. In the studio, beneath a window with a courtyard view, were twenty folding chairs for Fosse and his classmates — which included Gloria Vanderbilt, Farley Granger, and James Kirkwood Jr. (future co-author of *A Chorus Line*) — ten in front, ten on a riser behind. Notebooks in hand, they faced a simple stage set: two twin beds and an empty bookcase. Meisner — Sandy, they called him — sat at a hulking gray desk midway between the students and the stage and watched them working. *Working* was what Sandy called rehearsing. "Who wants to work next?" he would ask. As soon as his volunteers began, he'd stop them. If you do something, you really do it! he'd say. He told them a story about Fanny Brice, about how she got nervous when she got onstage, so nervous, he said, her hands would actually shake. And this was at the end of her career, when she was already the biggest comic in the world — Meisner would spread his hands in the air to show how big — and still she thought she was going to die. "So you're going to be nervous," Sandy said to the class. "*Be* nervous!" The real show, he encouraged them to see, was what was happening *within*. "You don't have to play at being the character," he would say, "it's right there in your doing it."

Artistically, this was a revelation to the burgeoning choreographer. Fosse said, "I think he had some sort of motto on the wall, as I remember, saying 'Don't just say something, stand there.' And I found out in choreography frequently that less movement, more economical movement, or no movement at all makes a stronger statement than fierce activity." The concept was a salve to Fosse's feeling of worthlessness. Knowing he did not have to transform himself was itself a transformative epiphany for him, almost spiritual in its emphasis on innate value and self-respect. For perhaps the first time in his professional life, he saw he could get by without irony, stolen goods, and flash. He was enough. Along with Joan, Meisner saw what few had seen: The good *inside* Bob Fosse. The potential.

By the spring of 1951, Fosse had become Joan's creation. When he

heard of an upcoming summer-stock production of *Pal Joey*, he went
straight to her for counsel. Would taking the part (Joey, of course),
if he got it, be a good next step? Or was summer stock, no matter
the part, a step back? *Joey* was one of his favorite shows, and the part
was perfect for him; it would be a real chance, his first chance, to
sing and dance in *character*. He could use the Meisner technique.
Weren't Joey's circumstances — smalltime con artist, bound to an
older woman, stopping at nothing to push his nightclub career over
the top — nearly identical to Fosse's? McCracken thought yes. Take it,
she told him, if you get it.

He got it (despite Richard Rodgers's objections to Fosse's small
size, small voice, and light complexion). Fosse and Joan were preparing the car to go to Bucks County, the first stop on *Pal Joey*'s ten-
week tour, when Fosse got a call from Maurice Lapue. MGM wanted
to screen-test him. MGM: The studio of Astaire and Gene Kelly.
Apparently, one of Metro's scouts had seen him in scenes from Saroyan's *The Time of Your Life* — Fosse played Harry, whom Saroyan
described as a "natural-born hoofer who wants to make people laugh
but can't" — at an American Theatre Wing showcase. Fosse shot the
test, and the MGM execs must have loved what they saw because on
April 16, 1951, Fosse signed the standard seven-year contract for five
hundred dollars a week, effective as soon as his summer-stock tour
ended in September of that year. Overjoyed, McCracken and Fosse
hit the road. Niles was left behind.

The *Pal Joey* tour took Bob and Joan through Cape Cod and Maine
and the most glorious seascapes of the Northeast. It was severely romantic. Her face to the moon, Joan spoke about cherishing every
moment, and she gripped his hands tight, too tight, as if she were
holding on to more than just his fingers.

She had diabetes. That had been her secret, and now it was theirs
— to know, not to discuss. Driving from inn to inn, collecting seashells and wet twinkling things from the sand, they often stopped

and stared far out over the water, into charcoal sky, never too far from the thought of the day, years from now, when her body would break down.

As Joey Evans, Fosse didn't have Gene Kelly's self-satisfied smile, and he did not attempt Kelly's signature acrobatics. Fosse's Joey was, instead, like Fosse himself, more contained, subtler, a dagger to Kelly's broadsword. Of course, Fosse's presentation was less a matter of art than of necessity. He simply wasn't good enough to put the depths of character across. But he was bashful, good-looking, and a devil of a dancer. He moved with a sense of inwardness both inviting and exclusive, almost private, like he was alone, flexing naked in front of a mirror; it made his audiences lean forward, as if by getting closer, they could see more, or even see into him. "Bobby was great in the show," said *Pal Joey* dancer Phyllis Sherwood, "because Bobby *was* Joey." But he wasn't an actor.

That is, he played a Joey better offstage, after the curtain fell. One night, perhaps with Joan away, and perhaps not, Fosse went up to Sherwood's hotel-room door and gave it a confident knock, as if she were expecting him.

"Who is it?"

"It's Bobby."

"Bobby?"

He opened the door himself, but he didn't come toward her. Like a good boy about to do wrong, he held his hands behind his back, peeking over what could have been his hundredth cigarette of the day.

"Hiya, Phyllis. May I —"

Pal Joey was Sherwood's first show, and Bob Fosse was its star, clearly the most gifted dancer in the company, so she was thrilled by his attention.

She invited him in. Standing there, he was nothing but sweet and charming, as he had been in every rehearsal and every performance. At sixteen, Sherwood wasn't quite old enough to sense what was coming; then again, she wasn't too young to guess. But never would she have imagined that Bob Fosse would calmly unzip his pants and expose himself.

"Get out!" she screamed. "Just get *out! Now!*"

He left.

"We laughed about it afterward," Sherwood remembered. "He was such a sweet guy — no matter what he did, you couldn't stay that mad." She could be speaking for any number of women, arguably every single one. "He never had a sleaziness about him," said dancer Candy Brown. "He was always — I don't know what else to say — *dear.*" Self-denying, vulnerable, soft-spoken, adorable, truthful about his lies. For men and women alike, he was impossible to refuse. "He always sort of tucked his head into his shoulder," remembered dancer Blane Savage. "You had to be so close to him to hear him talk." *Help me, come closer:* tender was what he was *and* what he needed to be.

Pal Joey was a success, and the show transferred to Broadway's Broadhurst Theater — with Harold Lang in the part of Joey. Reluctantly, Fosse dropped to understudy, and MGM postponed his official start date, banking on the chance, however slight, that Fosse might go on for Lang one lucky night, show his star to the world, and soar up, raising his stock from contract player to extremely valuable dancer — much more valuable than the old Bob Fosse — and for the bargain price of five hundred dollars a week.

But Fosse never did go on for Lang. Instead, he did a lot of waiting backstage, fooling around — dancing, that is — with chorus girls Norma Andrews and Patty Ann Jackson to keep his mind and body limber. Here and there he went out on the nightclub circuit, now as a solo, without Mary-Ann. "When he fell out of love with her, she couldn't stand that," said her friend George Marcy. "She was so much in love with him. He was her big thing in life." She talked about him so much after they separated, some wondered if Niles really understood he wasn't coming back.

For Christmas, he shared the Roxy with a Clifton Webb movie, as in the old presentation-house days. In January 1952, weeks after *Pal Joey* opened on Broadway, he appeared on the bottom part of a bill at the top part of the Waldorf-Astoria — the famed and glamorous Empire Room — with a new solo act that showed the bottom part of his heart. Reaching for pathos, he cut out the flash and "added a lot of talking to his act," and "a tragic-comedy number of the stage-struck kid auditioning was very moving." It wasn't a love story but a showbiz story that Fosse wanted to dance, and not all of it was original, which Fosse openly and apologetically acknowledged in the act. He performed his showcase, scenes from *The Time of Your Life,* and for his finale, he selected "Slaughter on Tenth Avenue," Balanchine's famous ballet-jazz duet. Fosse turned it into a scene-stealing single and tried to shine it up with jagged lights and the rumble of a jungle timpani, but he couldn't fool them into thinking it was anything new. "Fosse's 'Time of Your Life' bit, a la Gene Kelly, seems too palpably a concoction to suggest to the audience (any producers present?) that here is another prospect for Gene Kelly roles," stated *Variety.* "Fosse's dance interpretation of 'Slaughter on 10th Ave.,' which Kelly did in the Metro musical 'Words and Music,' emphasizes that thinking. This is not to discredit Fosse's ability; it's just that he should rely on new material to stress his own individuality."

Backstage at the Broadhurst, he was visibly restless. Andrews and Jackson suggested he work out a number for them, anything he wanted, for *Talent '52,* the upcoming stage managers' benefit at the Forty-Sixth Street Theater. This was one night Lang couldn't steal; eligibility was limited to nonfeatured players and understudies. Until then, Fosse's dances, which he hardly considered serious, had been confined to smaller spaces — nightclubs, mostly, as well as a TV episode or two and some regional theaters. He had merely slapped steps together and seasoned them to taste. *Talent '52* threatened to expose him. The thought of having his dances performed before an audience of his peers and New York's most discerning professionals at one of Broadway's largest theaters filled his stomach with that sour, throw-uppy feeling he got before auditions.

Although parody, no matter how refined, felt to him less like art than theft, he understood that by giving it "style" and wearing his hat at a jaunty tilt, cocking it to the side like an adventurous adulterer, he could get away with murder. At least, that was the hope as he gave Andrews and Jackson moves from famous choreographers of the day. Fosse couldn't borrow their work outright; this crowd was too hip for that. Instead, he let them in on the joke. Using his Empire Room idea, he set the pastiche in an audition sequence, each dancer appearing before an unnamed master choreographer. Based on the dances, his audience could tell whether the auditioner was dancing for Robbins or de Mille or Robert Alton. For the crowd, it was like a guessing game; for Fosse, it was a mirror trick. Had he given them Robbins or had he given them him?

The night of April 28, 1952, director Stanley Donen, whose *Singin' in the Rain* had opened two months earlier, recognized a singular voice in the chorus of styles — Fosse's. Returning to Hollywood, to MGM, Donen learned this dancer-choreographer was soon to be officially under contract. That was good; he could use him. While casting *Jumbo*, his upcoming film of Rodgers and Hart's musical, Donen ordered up Fosse's screen test, liked what he saw, and called him into the studio.

THIRTY-FIVE YEARS

JUST OUTSIDE THE high walls of MGM's main lot, on a back alley behind the Thalberg Building, the Smith and Salsbury Mortuary waited, grim and triumphant. "You know, Helen," producer Arthur Freed liked to say to his secretary, "I have a feeling they're doing better business than Leo the Lion." Louis B. Mayer hated Smith and Salsbury. They'd been there as long as anyone could remember, and they had refused his every offer to buy them out. There had been a time, years before, when Mayer might have roared their door down, but those days were behind him. TV was coming. There would be new kings.

L. B. Mayer's 167 Culver City acres of offices, sound stages, prop shops, projection rooms, bungalows, recording studios, and rehearsal halls once teemed with six thousand workers, two dozen directors, thirty stars, and one dentist; it had never spelled efficiency, but Mayer, the grand benefactor of the great American movie musical, hadn't built his reputation by being cheap.

"If I start up another studio," he said to Esther Williams one night at Chasen's, "would you come with me?"

"Thanks, Mr. Mayer," she said. "But where are you going to find a pool like the one on Stage 30? How can I go with you if you don't have a pool?"

"I'll build one."

"No, you won't," she said. "But call me if you do."

He never did.

Now Dore Schary, the pipe-smoking crusader Mayer installed to get MGM back on its feet, had the place to himself. Gone was the man who approved a five-hundred-thousand-dollar budget for a single number (the ballet from *An American in Paris*), and in came a former screenwriter, an intellectual, angling for "important" pictures. Schary's unofficial credo — Nobler and Cheaper — didn't go over well with Metro's older artists and technicians, but few were more irritated and creatively hindered than Arthur Freed, the producer Mayer had hired in 1939 to oversee every aspect of musical production at MGM, starting with *The Wizard of Oz*. Economic mandates did not work for the Freed unit. They didn't create fast, like television people did. Musicals took time. They took talent.

Before Schary, Freed had reinvented a genre that was slipping into decadence; more than simply rich in resources and luxury, his musicals, conceived holistically, were the most carefully and thoughtfully constructed productions in Hollywood history. Prior to Freed, a great many movie musicals were diminished by unintegrated musical asides, song-and-dance episodes that interrupted — rather than enhanced — the story line (*story line* being a generous term for the hey-kids-let's-put-on-a-show! scenario). Mostly, these numbers were shot head-on in long airless takes meant to simulate the natural theatrical relationship of audience and performer. The pre–Rodgers and Hammerstein dearth of resonant material didn't help. Add to that the Fred and Ginger movies, Busby Berkeley's kaleidoscopic floorshows, the many miscellaneous backstagers that seemed to vanish on the take-up reel, and one could see that the Hollywood musical was doomed to vapor. Freed changed that; he made vapor into liquid.

Elsewhere, escapist fare might escape reason, but in the glory years of Arthur Freed, *entertainment* was not a euphemism; it was a dream made real. But by 1952, when Bob Fosse sublet Buddy Hackett's place in West Hollywood, MGM was ending its tenure as American pop culture's primary producer.

Ghosts of a golden time ambled around the sound stages as if they were living people. Judy Garland. Gene Kelly making *Brigadoon*. Donald O'Connor. The Donald O'Connor knockoffs. The guileless Bob Fosse fit somewhere in there, though exactly where, no one knew for sure. He didn't have Kelly's hardy build or expansive spirit. He didn't score high on the O'Connor scale of personality. Never mind that he was one of the best dancers on the lot. Close-ups didn't care about that. Bob Fosse was mild of voice, limited of expression, and small onscreen. What did they need him for?

Fosse endured many screen tests, innumerable changes of clothes, hairstyles, poses, and expressions, until the studio finally decided who he was. They would accent the trait Fosse's women called his most compelling: his boyishness. They gave him a toupee. "That was a trauma for me," Fosse said; at twenty-five, he was certain his thinning hair predicted a lifetime of impotence.

Orders were always changing. MGM moved Fosse from the Donald O'Connor part in Stanley Donen's *Jumbo*, which had been postponed, to the Gene Kelly part in Stanley Donen's *Give a Girl a Break*; that is, the part Kelly was *supposed* to play before the picture was downgraded — thanks to the Schary regime — to a smaller-budget film. From there, more was compromised. Screenwriters Albert Hackett and Frances Goodrich knew they had a turkey on their hands. The last-minute casting (to Fosse's awe and consternation) of Marge and Gower Champion gave them only ten days to rewrite what years could not have improved. Unceasing revisions put a strain on a cast that now included Debbie Reynolds, fresh off *Singin' in the Rain*, who quickly and accurately determined that Bob Fosse, a dancer nobody had ever heard of, was her director's primary interest; she shared this gripe with the Champions, who also felt shortchanged. "They were Mr. Show Biz, and we were no talent," Reynolds said. To be fair, Donen had to think fast. With the script in a shambles, he saw Fosse as a lifeboat on the horizon. "In my opinion," Donen said, "he was going to be as good of a song-and-dance man, for lack of a better word, as any of the others — the only other two — as Kelly and Astaire. I thought, 'This guy is going to be it.'"

While the Champions worked with Reynolds, Donen and Fosse, in isolation from the company, began what would become a lifelong friendship. Like Joe Papp and Buddy Hackett, Donen shared Fosse's hoofer ethic of hard work and good humor. At sixteen, Donen had been in the chorus of the original *Pal Joey,* a major feat, Fosse thought, as was Donen's preternaturally fast transition from tap dancing to directing major MGM musicals — with Fred Astaire! Only a few years older than Fosse but with power and experience in the movie department, Donen rose quickly from friend to mentor/friend, as Papp had in the Pacific. All of Fosse's relationships, erotic or platonic, generally began this way: a boy, eager to collaborate, seeking to learn from a master. These liaisons had a political benefit too: friending talent was never a bad idea. Especially when the friend was the director and the script was being rewritten daily.

"Fosse and Donen were wrapped up in each other," Marge Champion remembered. "They really didn't give us the time of day." When the two weren't working, they were clowning. Donen was seen creeping up behind Fosse to snatch a toupee from his balding head. Fosse was seen creeping up behind Debbie Reynolds, hoping for a kiss (he didn't get one).

The bright light might have been stunning that California afternoon as Fosse shuffled across the lot with Stanley Donen, but he wouldn't have known it; the world, like the ceiling of the Sistine Chapel, was something he'd have to crane his neck to notice. Naturally hunched, he had an almost collaborative complicity with the pavement, a rehearsal space he could engage at any time. All he had to do was look down, and he disappeared.

And then, suddenly, walking across the lot, he reappeared.

He felt a rhythm he knew.

Fosse looked up.

There. Out of a distant sound stage sailed a human stripe that looked and moved alarmingly like Fred Astaire. The bounding figure appeared to recognize Donen, and he came toward them. Yes, Fosse saw it: that heedless stride. That merry pinch he gave his tie. Fosse watched a few more paces, and he was certain. It was him.

Donen made the introduction, and Astaire flung out a hand. "Hiya, Foss!"

Fosse was too thwacked to speak. Bashful under normal circumstances, he was practically unalive now. Fosse shot his hands into his pockets and looked down, zeroing in on a nail a few inches from the world's greatest dancer's shoe. Astaire toe-tapped the nail as thoughtlessly as he would flick a cigarette, but to Fosse, that nail was no cigarette — it was Ginger Rogers. And then, without warning, Astaire flicked his foot, and — *ping!* — the nail was in the air and then careening off the sound-stage wall with the force of a rifle shot. Nonplussed by Fosse's silence, God said goodbye to Donen, tipped his hat to Fosse, and headed off to eat.

Fosse was horrified. He was nothing; Astaire danced even as he stood still. The precision of the swipe and offhanded elegance of the technique made Fosse feel like that sound-stage wall a thousand nails later. He told Donen to go to lunch without him.

When the coast was clear, Fosse approached the spot where the nail had been and practiced the swipe as best he could remember it. As much as he wanted to replicate the step, he wanted to duplicate the sound. He wanted to hear the exact right scuff of shoe on pavement, the precise ping of nail on wall. He wanted to kick at the exact same angle in the identical time signature and recover, as Astaire did, with the cool look of having not performed a miracle. "You see it on the screen," Fosse would later say of Astaire, "and it looks like he just made it up. I mean, he just *happened* to have some firecrackers in his hand, he just happened to be around a piano or a set of drums. 'Well, I'll fool around a bit.'"

As the rest of the MGM employees ate their sandwiches, Fosse kicked the nail around the lot, but he never got it flying as Astaire had. Dozens of kicks later, he was still Bob Fosse.

Give a Girl a Break wrapped in early December of 1952 and Fosse, energized by his first appearance on film, flew back to New York to be with Joan. His marriage to Niles officially ended, Fosse married Mc-Cracken on December 30 in a civil ceremony, a city clerk officiating. The diabetes McCracken had tried so hard to conceal — if people found out, she feared, they'd never let her dance — had whittled her doll-like limbs to sticks. She was a marionette, brittle, wan, seemingly too delicate to move. Still, she had been cast in *Me and Juliet*, a new Rodgers and Hammerstein musical directed by George Abbott, the Zeus of Broadway comedy. By the time rehearsals began, in March, Fosse was back in Hollywood.

Returning to MGM, Fosse discovered *Give a Girl a Break*, his star-making breakthrough, now belonged to the Champions. "After they previewed it for MGM," Marge Champion said, "Stanley was told to reshoot it closer to the original script and make it as much our movie as Bob's." Donen did as he was told, but MGM was still unhappy with the picture. It was released to bland reviews.

Though it was Gower Champion who shared dance credit with Donen, Fosse had managed to slip in enough of his own material to get Mr. Weaver and Charlie Grass, watching back home, to sit straight up in their seats. "Charlie," Bob explained to his friend later,

"I showed them a couple of Riff Brothers tricks"—wings and toe stands, hammed up for the camera. Dancing "In Our United State," Fosse pulled out the old vaudeville stops, Ray Bolgering around on his heels, Chaplining at the knees, shooting up his hands as Miss Comerford had told him not to, throwing his limbs wide then snapping them shut, like a starfish going sardine. Fosse was clearly the best dancer in the movie. His articulation—sharp, fast, and exact—is the visual equivalent of Olivier's diction. The dancer can't act, but he (almost) doesn't need to; his innate gee-shucks-ness suits the part—so much so that Charlie Grass thought that Fosse, playing Bob Dowdy, was really playing himself. "That's the teenaged Bob Fosse," he said.

The picture fizzled. "I was living in a one-room apartment in Culver City, with a Murphy bed, believing in my own stardom," Fosse said. "But then, within a year I realized those people who told me I'd be a movie star weren't telling me the truth." Stopping by one of choreographer Michael Kidd's parties, he ran into Gwen Verdon, who was about to head, with Kidd, to Broadway to start rehearsing *Can-Can*, the new Cole Porter show. They recognized each other from around the MGM lot, where Gwen had been working on *The Merry Widow* as Jack Cole's assistant and lead cancan dancer ("Dance it like a lady athlete," Cole had told her). Beginning enthusiastically with discussions of Cole and Astaire, Bob Fosse and Gwen Verdon had a lot to talk about that night. Joan McCracken, Mrs. Bob Fosse, had been one of Verdon's early role models. Her performance in Joseph Losey's production of *Galileo* had made an immediate and lasting impression on the teenage Gwen. It was the first time she understood a dancer could act (this was Brecht!), that a musical-theater comedienne could be an artist, and Verdon—who at that age had danced mostly in girlie shows around Hollywood—immediately signed up for acting classes. Fosse's proximity to McCracken and Verdon's to Cole raised their esteem for each other, inflaming the flirty lure of mutual curiosity and the snug air of a second date, which, in a way, Kidd's party was. They had met before, when Fosse and Niles auditioned for *Alive and Kicking*.

They talked into the night, agreeing that movies weren't showing them at their best. Hollywood's Production Code Administration censors, frowning at every wink, had had their shears out for Verdon since her honky-tonk twist in *The I Don't Care Girl*—a dance they cut. It set a precedent. "Then came *David and Bathsheba*," she said. "David wanted to go to war but he was supposed to go home to Bathsheba, and my dance was supposed to put him in the mood to go home to her. Well, I guess it was too much, because everybody who saw it got the same idea . . ." The same thing happened to Verdon in *The Mississippi Gambler*, in *Meet Me After the Show*, in *The Farmer Takes a Wife*, and, again, as she expected, in *The Merry Widow*.

"One more body on the cutting room floor," she would say with a laugh. "So what's new?"

It gave Verdon a lift knowing someone thought she was too hot to be onscreen, even if she herself didn't really believe it. "I never think of myself as sexy," she said. "Most of the time I'm just-kidding sex, you know."

She could get away with more onstage than on film. There were no censors on Broadway.

In Los Angeles, Fosse was far from McCracken and the grimy New York streets he trusted; his disappointment over *Give a Girl a Break* turned into loneliness, and his loneliness, compounded by his worst fears, turned into despair. The despair shattered him. He blamed Hollywood, the crimes it committed in the name of creativity. He obsessed over the injustice, wondering why he looked better onstage than onscreen, why lesser talents fared better. This time, he was not just being too hard on himself. No one could tell him that his failure lived only in his fears. In *Give a Girl a Break*, he finally had the proof he needed, and his new role, in *The Affairs of Dobie Gillis*, was just as flabby. "My parts were getting smaller," Fosse said, looking back. "I knew what that meant."

He confided in Peggy King, a young singer he'd met in his first few days at the studio when they were both supposed to be in *Jumbo*. "He was depressed," she said. "There was no doubt about that. We would comfort each other. I remember telling him I couldn't get in to see Arthur Freed. I remember saying to Bobby, 'At least *you're* making a film!' We both knew if we did something wrong, we were out of there. Bobby would say, 'I feel like they're watching me.' Well, of course they were. It was Metro-Goldwyn-Mayer! We were all treated like serfs." Fosse could break his contract and try again in New York, but movie stars weren't born on Broadway. The money and fame was here, where Astaire lived. Where Fosse waited for his next lackluster assignment. "Every day was the same," King said. "We got there at nine and started our lessons. Or, if we were lucky enough to be shooting, we'd start shooting. On Saturday we were expected to be doing benefits to ballyhoo new pictures. I was doing so many benefits I had benefits coming out my ears. Or they would give us walk-ons in pictures. Otherwise, they didn't tell us anything. There was no information, just days of waiting. Why didn't they get in touch with us? We were all worried — even the big stars were worried. They thought we were going to replace them. We thought they were going to block us. Bobby and I didn't know what in the world was going on. So we hung on to each other."

He withdrew. "He lived like a monk," recalled journalist Ken Geist, "because he wanted to save all his energy for his dances." His every free hour was spent in the Eleanor Powell bungalow, rehearsing. He missed lunch. He rarely went out. "I loved him, I would have done anything for him, but he could be remote," King said. "None of us knew where Bobby lived, and we were his friends."

He nursed his loneliness with girls. The actress Pier Angeli was so beautiful, so subtle, like Garbo with a tan, her face seemingly lifted from one of those tender, timid, sinless handmaidens of mythology. Anna, as her friends called her, was said to be kind to those in the ranks, and she spoke with a sincerity unusual to the famous — or perhaps that was her native Italian translated into English. Universally beloved, Anna drew the big time; producer Arthur Loew, Kirk Douglas, and James Dean fought for her Saturday nights. Fosse had to get in line. "Anna was moving up very, very fast," said King. "Bobby would not have had a chance." Fosse blamed his broken heart on the studio. Had he shown more promise, had MGM *seen* his promise, he knew studio executives might have intervened on his behalf, setting him and Anna up on dates so they could be photographed together canoodling in little bistros, the way the studio had done with Anna and Vic Damone.

When *The Affairs of Dobie Gillis* was completed, in early February 1953, the very same Arthur Loew screened the film for Dore Schary in a projection room underneath the Thalberg Building. A meager seventy-two minutes later, Schary had seen all he needed to of Bob Fosse. "I think it would have been better if you had been in it and he had produced it," he said to Loew. Schary's mood worsened several months later, when, in the same projection room, he beheld the muddled furor of *Arena*, MGM's first — and, he hoped, last — 3-D movie. But before he could sign its death certificate, a high-ranking executive (who had invested a half a million of MGM's dollars in 3-D glasses) suggested he might let stereoscopic cinema live five hundred thousand dollars longer. Schary gave in and made *Kiss Me Kate*, MGM's final 3-D picture. Bob Fosse was cast in March 1953.

He recoiled when he saw the sound stage. "When I saw the sets for *Kate*, I thought, 'No, they're wrong . . . that's not backstage.' Everything was beautiful, glossy. The real backstage that I knew was a jungle." There was one saving grace, however. Choreographer Hermes Pan asked *Kiss Me Kate*'s top dancers — which included Fosse, Ann

Miller, Bobby Van, and Tommy Rall — to look at a section of a Gene Kelly film, *Invitation to the Dance.* He was hoping it could help them to devise something wonderful for their movie. "I met Bobby for the first time in that projection room," said Rall. "My impression of him was he wasn't too happy I had the bigger part. There was that side of him, the tough side, sometimes even mean. He hated people who didn't know what they were talking about and he would bait them to make them say more and more about things they didn't know anything about. This would amuse Bob."

After the screening, Pan broke "From This Moment On" into sections in need of choreography, and he paired off his dancers — Ann Miller with Tommy Rall, Bobby Van with Jeanne Coyne, and Fosse with Carol Haney. Formerly Gene Kelly's assistant and before that Jack Cole's, Haney fit Fosse like a pair of old shoes. At five and a half feet with a punky Beat-girl haircut and whiplash spark, she looked like jazz sounded. "You just have a way of dancing," Pan said to Fosse and Haney. "Why don't you choreograph your own piece?"

Fosse's section was short, only forty-five seconds, but it showed, for the first time, what happened when Bob Fosse danced on film in what would become known as the Fosse style.

The score, which until their entrance is an ebullient, MGM-friendly bouquet of bells and strings, is trounced by a fat swagger of brass — a stripper's vamp, to be precise — and then a leg swings up (all the way up) from camera right. It's Carol Haney's leg. Dashing to the center of the frame, she snaps her arms in the air — a burst of red-hot ecstasy contorted by gnarled charges of pain. And then, from off camera right, Bob Fosse leaps and lands in a baseball slide. There's a scream, and Fosse and Haney, a duet now, spin forward together and freeze. The music stops. A beat later, the music starts up again, slower, smoother this time, and the pair slither in syncopation, shoulders hunched and knees bent, boy and girl Fosses. They look sad. They look broken. Then — out of nowhere — a shot of music throws them in the air. Haney bolts around a pole, and Fosse — more like Gene Kelly than Bob Fosse — flies to the very top of it and opens up like a flag. The music dies again. Trancelike, the two snap to a laid-back beat, their faces down like bum junkies, and then he leaps over her, lands on his downstage knee, and begins a bizarre (and quite funny) slide camera right. Is he supposed to be a bird? His head on his shoulder and his shoulders tucked to his sides, Fosse moves his fingers like hummingbird wings and they flutter him forward as Carol Haney, in a fetal crouch beside him, crawls — with a touch of desperation — in his direction. He jumps up, lifting her off her feet, and together they take a cheery musical-comedy turn around the stage. Until the music chills and they each hit what looks like a scare-crow pose — left arm parallel to the ground, right arm at a forty-five-degree angle — and sidestep; then Fosse performs a perfect backflip, slides out with wide-open arms, and he and Haney, left arms raised as if to say *Ta-da!*, shuffle off camera in the direction they came from. (How like Fosse — who hated his backflip, who struggled to make his imperfect version Donen-ready for *Give a Girl a Break* — to insist on inserting a backflip-from-a-standing-position here and to insist on going all the way to New York to work with Joe Price, the country's foremost acrobatic teacher, not once but three times during filming.)

The Fosse influence is unmistakable to the modern viewer. One can discern his taste for showbiz symbolism and convention in the burlesque vamp, Astaire-tilted hat, and outstretched Al Jolson arms. Face-open palms, inherited from the minstrelsy tradition Fosse had seen passed through vaudeville, hang coolly on his wrists and even flicker for a moment — razzle-dazzle. Tiny pantomimes seem closer to clowning than to choreography; single joints hiccup; appendages engage, then drop. There's also an element of acting, as if he and Haney aren't merely dancing but dancing about something. They have wants. He grins; she's desperate, crawling after him. This is not de Mille–fluid, nor Robbins-robust; it's not American ballet and it's not American colloquial. It's Fosse.

And he didn't think much of the job. He said, "I thought choreographers were all rock bottom." Astaire was a star, not Hermes Pan. As for Broadway, de Mille and Robbins transcended. They were artists. At best, Fosse was an entertainer.

Kiss Me Kate was the last straw. With a full six years remaining on his contract, Bob Fosse saw no future for himself or for the movie musical. "Bob knew what was happening," Rall said. "He saw that they weren't making musicals the way they used to and he was tired of hanging around Culver City, waiting for another disappointment." MGM didn't stop him from going. In August, the studio granted Fosse a six-month leave of absence, and he flew back to New York, to Joan.

Fosse loved Joan. In light of his habitual infidelity, it was difficult to understand that, but no more difficult than understanding why Joan would take him back every time. Though hurt, in public, she played a version of herself too bohemian to care about the strictures of total monogamy, and it's true that her previous marriage to Jack Dunphy was strewn with affairs, hers with composer Rudi Revil and his, at the very end, with Truman Capote. They all tried hard to have fun. Though McCracken hadn't made peace with Fosse's indiscretions, she was certainly determined to do her best; upon his return from Hollywood, they bought waterfront land in the Pines area of Fire Island. She wanted a baby.

In town, they lived in her tenth-floor penthouse on West Fifty-Fifth Street, between Sixth and Seventh Avenues. Her eye for décor, like her conversation, was fashionably eclectic, a collage of Victorian wickerwork and Bauhaus modern. Seashore bric-a-brac dotted the shelves and tops of things, and when the wind blew through the open windows, her shells sang a round of ocean songs. On spring nights, her terrace, with its city views and salad-size garden, was home to writers, painters, and dancers invited to rehearse their work and catch up on one another's headlines over a feast that McCracken nibbled in premeasured, diabetic-safe portions. When they asked her about *Me and Juliet,* she was careful to respond modestly, embarrassed by how much the critics loved her. Especially in front of Fosse. "She was often very upset because he was so unhappy," said McCracken's *Me and Juliet* costar Isabel Bigley. "Bob was in a terrible mood because he couldn't find work." When the attention came her way, McCracken was kind enough to redirect it to him. A nimble hostess, she helped everyone to his or her moment, culling from them all their best stories, like the conductor of a tiny talking orchestra. "There were three rehearsal rooms at MGM," Fosse would begin his story. "Astaire would be in one, Kelly in the other, and I would be in the middle stealing from both." On those buoyant nights, talk would invariably turn to movies, to *Shane* and *From Here to Eternity;* to the current Broadway season of William Inge's *Picnic,* the adultery comedy *The Seven Year Itch,* Betty Comden and Adolph Green's and Leonard Bernstein's wonderful *Wonderful Town,* and Gwen Verdon, the breakout smash of *Can-Can.* Had anyone there seen it coming?

Can-Can's producers, Cy Feuer and Ernie Martin, certainly had. They first spotted Verdon months before, at Chicago's Chez Paree, where they caught her dancing it like a lady athlete, doing the Jack Cole with Jack Cole. Others could sing or dance or act, but Verdon — a luscious lollipop person with a voice she said sounded like a 78 rpm record with a wobble in it — could do all three, sometimes all at once, and better than most could do only one. She was what they called a triple threat. McCracken had the big three as well, but she never managed to launch herself out of the soubrette department. An unfortunate combination of illness, bad timing, and (ironically) versatility held her career down. But Gwen Verdon's road was clear:

leading lady. She had opportunity and she had means. A baby-woman at the eye wall of Marilyn Monroe and Irene Dunne, she had a stage persona that was complex enough to be unique to her, but basic enough to be instantly understood. To see her sing and dance was to continually fight the urge to leap, arms outstretched, from your seat. One number, one swivel of hips, and you could feel yourself wanting to run up there and squeeze to pieces all five and a half feet of her — ivory-rocket legs, tiger thighs, surging bust, twinkle nose, and very red hair — and without any guilt. She was that sweet. After they saw her at the Chez Paree, Feuer and Martin offered Verdon a fully paid weekend in New York if she'd audition there for *Can-Can*, their new show.

With Jack Cole's permission, Gwen packed up her Siamese cat and her dog and left for the Warwick Hotel in New York. She was so scared of singing for Mr. Cole Porter that when she arrived at the theater, she asked him if she could please dance first and sing second. Mr. Porter said she could. Predictably, her dance killed. But she knew it would. It was her voice, the song, that worried her. "I was so scared," she said, "my legs wouldn't hold me." Verdon asked if she could sit for the number; permission was granted, and she sang "Pennies from Heaven." Then she read a scene from the show. ("It probably sounded like, 'Run, Spot, Run,'" she later said.) The whole thing lasted just under an hour — quite a long time for an audition — and then director Abe Burrows climbed onstage.

"Well, Claudine," he said, "I guess we'll see you soon."

She looked up at him. "What?"

"Darling, you've got the job." Claudine: the character's name.

Gwen went to the Warwick Hotel alone and ordered room service. She didn't know anyone in New York, and had always wondered what it would be like to order room service.

On Sunday she went back to Hollywood, to Jack Cole. "How'd it go, honey?" he asked, blasé.

"I got the job."

He punched her. It was not the most effective way to tell Gwen he needed her with him.

Verdon returned to New York, and rehearsals went smoothly. In Philadelphia, *Can-Can* sold well and opened nicely (Cole Porter shows did that). Gwen wasn't crazy about director Michael Kidd, but the real problem was with Lilo, the show's bombshell *française*. Jealous of Verdon, Lilo insisted on restaging their numbers so Gwen ended up offstage for the applause (most of which was for Gwen); for the curtain call, Lilo arranged to hide Gwen behind a bench in far-off Siberia. Then Gwen's numbers started to disappear. Her lines too. "I don't really blame Lilo," Verdon said years later. "She was the star and I was stealing the show. In the theater, that's like another woman in a marriage triangle."

By opening night — May 7, 1953 — the company was out of steam. Cramped in her phone-booth-size dressing room off of stage left, Gwen warmed up her kicks for the big Apache number, a comedy dance that had her, the spurned girl, going after her lover with a knife. "I don't know how Michael [Kidd] did it," said Cy Feuer, "but the whole thing was done in slow motion and a waiter passed with a big cheese and there was a knife in it — in the climax of the big dance — and she in slow motion grabbed the knife, turned around, and went to her lover and stabbed him in the stomach, and came back, turned around, put the knife back in the cheese, and she walked off." It was big, juicy material and required tremendous control, which did not come easily to Verdon. "Sometimes I'm on stage," she said, "and I'm so tired but I'll kick and my legs go way up and I follow them. It's almost like they're separate from me."

On opening night, act one went well. Then came act two and the deadly Apache number.

Mostly, when people say a number stopped a show, they don't mean the show literally stopped. But when people speak of Gwen

Verdon's showstopping Apache number in *Can-Can* and of the standing ovation she got on opening night, *in the middle of the show,* they really do mean the actors stopped acting, the stage managers stopped stage-managing, and the producers stopped worrying. In fact, the response to Gwen's Apache dance was so powerful, the ovation, lasting for seven minutes, became a theatrical happening of its own. No one knew quite how to react. A few stagehands beginning to move the next scene's set into place were waved away by a cluster of dancers who were unable to leave the stage during the ovation but who were unsure of what they were supposed to do now that the show had stopped and the applause had taken over the theater.

Gwen Verdon, meanwhile, was oblivious. Following the dance, as she had been directed to do, she returned to her phone booth to change quickly for her next number. Thanks to a recalcitrant zipper, she was too busy fighting her pants to realize the roar from inside was all for her. Michael Kidd figured as much. A couple minutes into the ovation, he dashed out of the Shubert Theater, through Shubert Alley, up to the stage door, and into Gwen's dressing room. When the door opened, she heard them chanting from the house: "We want Verdon! We want Verdon!"

"You have to go out there," Kidd said.

"But —"

He grabbed her arm. The zipper would have to stay unzipped.

With only a towel to cover her, Gwen returned to the stage and faced New York. "I could have walked into Tokyo," she said of that moment. "It was just that strange to be suddenly out there."

Shubert Alley was so mobbed with fans and press after the show that to get to the Hotel Astor for the opening-night party, Gwen had to ride with a policeman on the back of his horse.

"I remember the first time I saw her in *Can-Can,*" Fosse said. "People ask if I created Gwen, and I say, 'She was hot when I met her.' That alabaster skin, those eyes, that bantam rooster walk."

Across from the Shubert, at the Majestic, Fosse would wait for
Joan. On *Me and Juliet*'s matinee days, she led a small acting class for
chorus kids. She taught Mary Tarcai, a Stanislavskian. Sometimes,
in the half darkness of the ghost light, Fosse could be seen pacing
the distant back of the theater, filling the empty house with clouds of
smoke. Joan's students — including dancer Shirley MacLaine — wondered why he, whom they semi-recognized from TV and a couple
lame movies, didn't have anywhere else to be. They would not have
known what Fosse knew, what McCracken had told Bill Hayes, her
friend, student, and costar, during the run of *Me and Juliet*. "Joan was
pregnant," Hayes said, "and she was thrilled about it. We talked about
how she was going to leave the show and have the baby." But she
never did. Before McCracken could change the size of her costume,
she lost the baby. Hayes assumed a miscarriage. "Joan had hard numbers in that show," he said, "and she danced with everything she had."
Biographer Lisa Jo Sagolla submits that McCracken's diabetes, which
she had to keep secret from the company, made a healthy pregnancy
unlikely, even dangerous. Abortion may have been her only option.
The property the Fosses bought on Fire Island, they never developed.

There was a lull out there, one that had less to do with Fosse and
McCracken than with musical comedy, which in those days, the early
1950s, had everything to do with George Abbott, the most prolific,
successful writer and director of comedy on Broadway. Everybody's
grandfather, Mr. Abbott didn't look like a musical wizard; he looked
liked Abraham Lincoln. Tall, suave, and always correct, he was basically a producer with director's responsibilities, a good man of de-
pendable taste. Not great taste, but really, really good taste, safe and
solid, just like the musical comedy of his safe and solid era. Few comedies dared what *Oklahoma!* had dared. One would have to go back
to the year 1950, to *Guys and Dolls*, to find one with a head on its
lovely shoulders. Other than that, the vestiges of the 1920s remained.
Top Banana was all gags; *Flahooley* was a mess; and *Kismet* didn't

meet its Cole dances halfway. Abbott's shows hewed closer to plot than character, nearer to frippery than to life. Revolution was not his strong suit.

That's why he didn't warm to the wildcard in McCracken when he first directed her in *Billion Dollar Baby* in 1945. But "by the time they did *Me and Juliet*," Hal Prince recalled, "he'd forgotten he'd ever objected to her in the first place." Abbott and McCracken had grown closer since; before he went out dancing, which he did most every night after the show, Abbott liked to swing by her dressing room for a chat. In November 1953, he told Joan his new musical — based on the novel *7½ Cents,* by Richard Bissell — was to be about a pajama-factory strike, an odd topic, he admitted, for a musical comedy. "Others seemed to be even more shy of the material than I was," Abbott wrote. "They felt that a garment factory and a strike was too serious and controversial a subject for a jolly musical." Was this why Jerome Robbins, whom Abbott had used on several occasions, most recently and successfully on *Call Me Madam,* had turned him down? (No: Robbins was aiming higher. He wanted to choreograph *and* direct.)

Recognizing an opportunity for her husband, McCracken took Abbott to see *Kiss Me Kate,* then playing at Radio City Music Hall, where she hoped Fosse's forty-five-second choreography debut would double as his life-changing audition, the big break he'd look back on and say, "That's when it all really started for me." McCracken's faith in him was tremendous. "Joanie sounded off about Bob every time I went into her dressing room," Abbott said. "To me, he seemed very unassuming, not very impressive at all. But she built him up to be like the next Great White Hope." The Radio City proscenium lights dimmed, and McCracken sat back, fingers crossed under her seat. She watched her director through the entire picture.

Abbott smiled. "Have you done much choreography?" he asked Fosse, days later.

"Oh, yeah, a lot."

"Where?"

(Lying.) "Canada."

That was enough for Abbott. His genius was for hiring genius. One could say he knew talent, or maybe he just knew business, because, being young and hungry, the talent he hired worked for almost nothing. Kids were good for comedy. But one of Mr. Abbott's producers, twenty-five-year-old Hal Prince, suggested, wisely, they have some kind of insurance. "Do you think we can talk Robbins into standing in the wings?" he asked. "Just in case?"

"You talk to him."

Prince called Robbins. If Robbins wouldn't choreograph the show, would he at least look over Fosse's shoulder, in case he got in trouble? Robbins, who had seen *Kiss Me Kate* and respected Fosse's work, agreed to do it. But: "I'll only do it if I can have codirecting credit."

Prince called Abbott. "He'll only do it if he can share codirecting credit."

"Give it to him."

That was a surprise. "Doesn't it seem offensive to you?" Prince asked.

"Oh, give it to him, Hal. It'll make you feel good. Everyone will know who directed the show."

Codirected by George Abbott and Jerome Robbins, based on a book by Abbott and Richard Bissell, and with songs by newcomers Richard Adler and Jerry Ross, the musical version of *7½ Cents* was to be choreographed by Bob Fosse. Walking up Fifth Avenue after a long lunch with Abe Burrows, Abbott thought of a title for the show: *The Pajama Game.*

On the street, Fosse ran into Carl Reiner. They hadn't seen each other since *Call Me Mister,* several years earlier.

"Bobby!" Reiner threw out his arms. "How are you? You look great."

"Well," he said. "Okay. I got my first job as choreographer."

"That's wonderful!"

Fosse shrugged, looked down.

"You've got to be very proud of that."

"Yeah, well, maybe." Bob tried a laugh. "I don't know."

"What? *Why?*"

"I called my dad and I told him, I said, 'Dad, I'm going to choreograph the dances for a new show, an Abbott show.' He said, 'What's *choreograph*?' I said, 'I'm going to be making up the steps for other dancers.' Then he got upset and said, 'You mean you're gonna give away your steps?'"

THIRTY-THREE YEARS

ARLY IN 1954, Fosse locked himself in a studio and tried not to panic. He had given himself eight weeks alone to come up with what he was going to show Abbott, Robbins, and the kids of *The Pajama Game,* figuring the more time he spent perfecting the steps in private, the more humiliation he would spare himself in public. Ideas did not ever simply come to him; he had to force them out. Wrestling his tricks and gimmicks, Fosse quivered around the floor with only piano music to help him, trying to see himself in that wide blank mirror without hating every reflection or blaming the failed MGM star who put it there. That way lay total paralysis. If he could simply give himself permission to *see,* to scavenge without penalty, he would at least have something to start with, a ball of clay to mold discerningly on his way to — best case — mediocrity. "[I] let everything that can come out, come out," he said, "even though it may seem ridiculous and as though I'll never use it, I kind of spill out." The clock ticking, the money slipping, he looked for ideas, half ideas, things, anything. "I go through each number and try to get a combination — or just a general feeling of what I want. Just eight bars of movement and I can build from that, with variations." Then, once he saw, he thought. He added and subtracted until the feeling of embarrassment waned. Mostly, it didn't wane. Eight weeks of this. Visualizing the horror of facing the producers and cast with nothing or, worse, with dozens of somethings and no more studio time. What would he do then? Add a knee slide? A hat trick? How many hat tricks could he stick in before they caught on?

"I need to have a sense of insecurity," Fosse said. "The feeling that I'm in over my head makes me sweat. I get up earlier and stay later." He had to fight, to stay in the swamp of certain failure long enough to see the black hole become the light at the end of the tunnel. He said, "I finally [get] to the point where I'd say to myself: 'I'm the only person here. I'm alone. And I'm just going to stand here until something comes to me.'" He worked through the nights and napped in the days, burning through cigarettes — as many as six or seven packs a day — and something always did come to him. Fosse worked out every part of every dance all on his own.

When rehearsals began in the Winter Garden Theater in March 1954, the production was still thirty thousand dollars short of the two hundred fifty thousand dollars it needed. With the specter of Joseph McCarthy looming, the theory that the regular backers had been scared away from a comedy about strikes and unions drove producers Hal Prince and Robert Griffith from Upper East Side parlor to Upper East Side parlor, glad-handing, drinking scotch, eating potato chips, and — with their spin — selling a Romeo and Juliet story with a peppy score. To make up the (considerable) shortfall, they offered the cast of Abbott's *Me and Juliet* buy-ins at thirty-five dollars each, and, after that, they deferred their own salaries. It wasn't enough. Prince and Griffith then hired themselves as stage managers and prayed that George Abbott would move through rehearsals with his legendary speed and thrifty, no-nonsense precision.

According to Abbott, the musical comedy was all about timing. The timing and placement of the numbers, the rhythm of the jokes, the length of the beats, the order of the love plots (secondary and primary). To his mathematical mind, timing was a matter of proven formula and so of higher importance than fancy flashes in the pan like "motivation" and "character." "Abbott would give you line readings," said actress Rae Allen. "He'd say, 'Do that but do it real,' and then he'd walk away." If someone started getting arty, he'd politely invite him into the lobby, fire him, and return to rehearsal. It was never personal with Abbott; there simply wasn't the time for that. He even *moved* fast. "His legs were so long," Allen recalled, "he could climb over the orchestra pit to get onstage. He was a greyhound." Comedy was a wild beast and he was there to tame it. Prince said, "He was the most disciplined man in the theater. Don't suffer fools, learn your lines, say your lines, and don't get hysterical. He didn't like crises, he didn't like contention, and he never hesitated. The theater is a breeding ground for jealousy and insecurity, but Abbott never bothered with that. Presumably, he'd already been through it. By the time we did *Pajama Game,* he was sixty-seven years old and had pretty much seen everything." He asked the kids to call him George, but they couldn't. He was that imposing. The best they could manage was an "Excuse me, George, Mr. Abbott, sir."

In other words, Abbott knew exactly what he wanted and Bob Fosse had no idea.

Fosse's mid-1950s look, a tattered trench coat and beat-up dance clothes, declared him a hipster vagrant, alternately oddball and down-to-earth. "Bobby was deeply serious," said Allen, "but he was adorable too. There was something very 'baby' about him during *Pajama Game;* he was like a scrappy kid." "He was mostly quiet," said actor Janis Paige, "watching us with a sort of timid focus, but when he wanted to make you laugh, he really could." On those occasions he would come to work with a Mickey Mouse lunch box and a Donald Duck baseball hat, as if he were auditioning for them. Struggling dancers he'd approach apologetically, as if he were the source of their errors. Shirley MacLaine, in the chorus, explained that Fosse was the king of "Forgive me, but once more from the top." Without Robbins's clout or self-assurance, Fosse had to ask nicely. At least for the moment.

Harnessing his nightclub and TV experience, Fosse found he could mount solos and duos easier than group and full-company numbers. Here his specialty worked against him; he had to change his point of view to suit the vantage of a packed house on Broadway. A bigger canvas meant bigger, more confident movements, a strategy at odds with the little inward jerks and isolations — illustrative of his own shyness — that gave a number like "From This Moment On" its louche sizzle. Furthermore, staging those numbers flummoxed Fosse. For groups big or small, he found that simply arranging the actors onstage — not to dance but to sing — presented him with challenges utterly outside his experience.

For instance: "7½ Cents," the first group vocal number in the show.

"Just stage it," Abbott decreed.

"What do I do?"

"Just have them stand there and sing."

Which is just what Fosse did. Then he turned to Abbott for his reaction.

"We better have Jerry do this one," he said.

Robbins's coat was off by the time he reached the stage. "Okay, everybody," he said, clapping at the dancers. "Offstage. Let's do it."

Fosse was awed by what followed. As he said later, "In an hour and a half, [Robbins] had this thing staged and it was brilliant." It was a lesson Fosse would never forget. He said, "You keep the actors moving — you try to get the sense of a lyric over — you never let the gesture interfere, and, at the same time, you make an interesting picture. But it's important that the lyric of a song is heard." Likewise, "Small Talk," a patter song, didn't need full-out dance but stylized movement suited to its halfway place between dialogue and duet. "In five minutes, Jerry had it solved," Rae Allen said. He gave Janis Paige a newspaper to cover her face, which gave John Raitt a reason to fight for her attention, and "Small Talk" became a chase with the potential for movement built into the conflict. "That's where Jerry Robbins came in," said actress Sara Dillon. "To help Bobby to incorporate his numbers, his little group of dancers, into what was going on around them." Jerome Robbins: a master of staging, integration, idiom, and character.

There was, however, one problem. Abbott didn't like the big ballet that opened act two. "It was a big egg," Dillon remembered. "They had about six or eight singers sort of standing around, looking silly, and about six or eight dancers behind them."

"Why don't you do something simple," Abbott suggested to Fosse. "Something with two or three people." In other words, what you do best. "Make it a pep song, a rally song. Make it a selling-to-the-union type of song. Just two or three people."

To the guy who had spent eight weeks preparing his every dancer's every move and glance, this was not a welcome suggestion.

He had the dancers for the big number to open act two; now he needed music. Fosse went to composer Richard Adler. "What else do you have? Do you have something that would fit?"

"No."

On flashed the charm. "Come on."

"Okay, maybe."

"What's it called?"

"'Steam Heat,'" Adler said. "But I hate it."

"Let me hear it."

Adler sat down at the piano and played the song he had written one day as a sort of exercise. He had held himself hostage in the bathroom, vowing not to leave until he had turned out a composition about sinks or toilets or faucets. Or radiators. The *cling-clang-psssssst* of the radiator. Once he got that, Adler had "Steam Heat" written in about ten minutes.

"That's it," Fosse said. He grabbed the sheet music off the piano and disappeared into the studio for a few weeks. Bells, bangs, honks, blocks, buzzers — Fosse was wild about novelty sounds, the accents of clowns and vaudeville comics. "Steam Heat," with its *cling-clangs* and *boink-boinks*, was a fastball down the center of the plate. And because "Steam Heat" was a nonintegrated number and so outside the story — that is, a performance within *The Pajama Game* — Fosse could run with the vaudeville concept, unencumbered by setting and character. He could fly. The original ensemble configuration still in his mind, he began thinking of the dance in two trios — three dancers and three singers. Then he cut the singers and was left with Buzz Miller, Peter Gennaro, and the dancer he had called in from Hollywood, Carol Haney. "He threw about a million steps at us," said Miller, also a former Jack Cole dancer, "and Carol, who was Bob's link, would pick them up like a magnet. He'd show us something and Carol would go 'uh-uh' meaning she hated it, or 'ah-ha!' — it works!" Haney, Miller, and Gennaro loved what Fosse did to their bodies. Cheering as he demonstrated, calling out for more, they learned the piece in only a few hours.

He knew what he was doing. "If you want to make a reputation as a choreographer," Fosse explained, "you don't do solos; you do group dances — [for] three or more [people]. If the audience sees that solo number, they come away saying, 'Ah! Wasn't he a great dancer?' With [three or] four people they say, 'Wasn't that great choreography!'" It was like starring. In a way.

Outfitting his trio like little Chaplins in matching pipe-stem pants, white gloves, and derbies, he tiny-stepped them along the footlights in the Durante manner with pelvises out, knees bent, and arms dangling behind them. "Steam Heat" was a Fred Weaver special, a deep-tissue recall of the eccentric dancers of Fosse's youth. "The actual choreography comes out of most of the stuff I'd been doing in my own act," Fosse said, "and a strong affection for a dancer . . . called Joe Frisco." The ultimate flash dancer, Joe Frisco would execute jaw-dropping feats of flimflammery with virtuosic calm. It was the manner Fosse loved as much as the moves. To achieve that cool, that ease, Fosse had his trio practice and repractice hat tricks (also à la Frisco) for hours on end, sometimes until two or three in the morning. "The tricks," wrote Shirley MacLaine, who came later to "Steam Heat," "must be effortless so that the attitude of their execution could bleed through." Accenting steps with a slouch or soft wrist, Fosse's dancers showed a tantalizing synchronicity of hot and cool, like slow-curling steam.

The first night *The Pajama Game* previewed for a real, ticket-buying audience, April 12, 1954, at New Haven's Shubert Theater, "Steam Heat" got a standing ovation. Even so, Abbott cut it. The show had to keep moving, he explained; the number was fabulous, but it meant nothing to the story. Robbins couldn't disagree with Abbott's sober evaluation, but standing ovations were standing ovations — they justified themselves. "Bob never forgot how hard Jerry fought for the number," Ann Reinking later said. "He was really touched." Before *The Pajama Game* reached Boston, Abbott put "Steam Heat" back in the show.

By the time they returned to New York, Abbott's company had reason to feel confident — but guardedly. Uncertain were the prospects for a labor comedy without stars and created by unknowns. Plus, there was still the issue of funds. "They needed money," Sara Dillon said, "because they couldn't make their production overcall. When we got back to New York, they asked everyone to give a week's salary, even the wardrobe lady. And everyone gave — except for me and Eddie Foy."

Before the opening-night curtain went up at the St. James Theater,

Hal Prince — half producer, half stage manager — changed into dinner clothes, stuffed a flashlight into his pocket, and stationed himself
backstage. Robert Griffith did the same. Abbott lowered himself into
his usual opening-night seat in the middle of the house, where he
could best experience the audience's experience of the show — then
relaxed. George Abbott could do that. Sure that he had done his best,
on opening nights, he affably resigned himself to the democracy of
popular taste; it was in the jury's hands now. Fosse, however, kept
moving. Eating smoke, he prowled nervously around the theater,
going from the mob outside to Haney backstage, where he could
hide, momentarily. He had not dreamed of this moment his whole
life long. He was a dancer.

That night, May 13, 1954, every number played beautifully. Afterward, Richard Adler looked through the clamor to see Marlene Dietrich taking people in her arms and laughing. Carol Haney said, "I
don't think any of us touched the ground the whole evening."

Prince was standing in the wings. "What do you think?" he asked
Griffith.

"Don't count your chickens," he cautioned.

But they were hatching already, one by one. "That night, Carol and
Buzz and Peter came out after 'Steam Heat' to take a bow," Janis Paige
recalled, "and [after 'There Once Was a Man'], they applauded so
much for John [Raitt] and I that *we* had to come out and take a bow.
And we were all in a daze because deep down we thought maybe the
rumors were right and doing a show about a pajama factory was a
bad idea." Prince said, "They were screaming from the rafters. We
were stunned."

Looking back, Gwen Verdon said, "I think 'Steam Heat' was
the first number on a Broadway stage that was *pure* Fosse, the way
Fosse would do it. He could have been any of the three because they
looked like Bob, danced like Bob, and it's exactly the way Bob would
have jumped up at a party and danced." Breaking from de Mille's

hegemony over Broadway ballet, "Steam Heat" announced a new, jazzy vernacular, American based, with a sly sense of humor that was indisputably Fosse's.

For the final time on opening night, May 13, the curtain came down (ten minutes late, because of the applause). The crowd filed out, work lights came on, and Prince and Griffith, first-time producers, walked across the empty stage. Saying nothing, they just looked at each other and knew. Life would be different now.

But the reviews? There were about ten papers in those days, and there was no telling what was what until Fosse had read every last one. He faked it through the requisite party chatter, his actual self clenched as he waited for the decrees of Brooks Atkinson of the *New York Times* and Walter Kerr of the *Herald Tribune*—they might grant him a stay of execution or, more likely, hang him by his neck for all New York to see. It was not until around five in the morning that the newspapers began to appear. Brooks Atkinson: "The last new musical of the season is the best . . . Bob Fosse's ballets and improvised dance turns seem to come so spontaneously out of the story." Walter Kerr: "The bright, brassy, and jubilantly sassy show that opened at the St. James Thursday is not just the best new musical of the season. That would be fairly easy. It's a show that takes a whole barrelful of gleaming new talents, and a handful of stimulating ideas as well, and sends them tumbling in happy profusion over the footlights."

Yes, they were a hit. "By 9 A.M.," Richard Adler said, "the lines had started forming, and by 10 there was a long one down the block."

Robbins gave Fosse a pair of golden cuff links, a gift to Robbins from his father. When Robbins opened his next show, Fosse returned them, but only temporarily. For the rest of their lives, they would pass the cuff links back and forth, an opening-night gift. They were in a chest of drawers by Fosse's bed on the day he died.

·   ·   ·

Weeks later, Fosse and McCracken celebrated *The Pajama Game*'s smash opening with a return to Fire Island. After selling their previous lot, they bought two adjoining spaces deeper in, against a hillside and away from the shore, where they built a cloud-gray cottage perched high over the dunes. It had a brick fireplace and two small bedrooms. Their hideaway had no phone and no electricity, which was a relief — Fosse needed the rest. He needed to think. Success had thrown him. "I'm confused," he said in May. "I really want to dance or act myself." And yet here he was, a star choreographer.

Hollywood called. He could not ignore the offer from Columbia Pictures' president Harry Cohn to stage a new round of musicals, including, maybe, Cohn's long-delayed *Pal Joey*. Reluctant to agree but unwilling to walk away — once hungry, always hungry — Fosse turned down the package (as Jerome Robbins had), opting instead to choreograph just one picture, Columbia's *My Sister Eileen*, and see what happened.

In August of 1954, Fosse and McCracken flew to Hollywood to begin rehearsal. Taking advantage of a last-minute casting change, Fosse humbly submitted himself for the small role of Frank Lippincott, soda jerk, a boy-next-door character nearly indistinguishable from his MGM roles. He got the part. Now, as choreographer/actor, Fosse could remake *My Sister Eileen* and turn it into his own personal calling card, vindicate himself in Hollywood, and become, once and for all, the next Fred Astaire.

Fully devoted to breaking in Janet Leigh and Betty Garrett, he had little time for McCracken. She needed him now. Her health had worsened but she put up a good front. Determined to show the world, and herself, she could still dance, she worked out in a sound stage next to Fosse's. Like a man in a sex farce, he would go from Joan to Janet Leigh, who had never danced in a musical before. It was immediately obvious to Fosse how much she wanted to please him. It was only slightly less obvious to Tony Curtis, her husband. But coming home after a weekend away, Curtis found a letter confirming all. "I can't wait to see you," Fosse had written to Curtis's wife. "When you're coming, please let me know."

"Bob came to the set with a sense of how his dances ought to be filmed," said costar Tommy Rall. "It was [Richard] Quine's picture, but *The Pajama Game* had done so much for Bob's reputation, Quine let him have a hand in the filming." Fosse shot his dances in the Astaire style, head to toe and flat up-front, with as few interruptions as possible. As Astaire said, "I have always tried to run a dance straight in the movies, keeping the full figure of the dancer, or dancers, in view and retaining the flow of the movement intact." His camera was like an audience on wheels.

"How do you know what you're doing?" cowriter Blake Edwards asked the first-time director.

"I don't."

"But you do. You're doing it!"

"Nahhhh."

Credited director Richard Quine looked on, admiring Fosse's persistence and humor. Fosse needed humor; levity greased the wheels, allowing him to play his own good cop when he had to get tough. "He was determined to make memorable dances," Rall said, "determined to make them a cut above what Hollywood was doing, and he tore himself apart trying to do it. He tore us apart. We'd go over the number again and again until it was absolutely perfect."

Set in an alley behind a theater, Rall's and Fosse's "Alley Dance" took the better part of two weeks to rehearse and film. *Eileen's* bravura centerpiece, Fosse made the number into a challenge dance and laced it with his own insecurities. Pitting himself against Rall, he wagered his self-perceived deficits against one of moviedom's most accomplished ballet dancers. Could jazz beat ballet? the dance asked. Could showbiz take on real grace? To level the playing field, he added echoes from "Steam Heat," like hat tricks and nods to Chaplin and

Durante, whose signature walks gave Fosse and Rall another means of competition.

Harry Cohn was so impressed with Fosse's work on *My Sister Eileen,* he encouraged him to stay on at Columbia, sweetening his initial offer with a house and, as Fosse told it, "anything I wanted." If he committed wholesale to being a choreographer, Fosse knew he could lose sight of his long-term goal, to dance, and he turned Cohn down. Besides, the Hollywood musical — at least in its present incarnation — had run its course. On the publicity tour, the cast of *Eileen* was told not to emphasize the film's singing and dancing.

Back in New York, Joan lost her bounce; her heart had been damaged by a lifetime of smoking and further compromised by complications of diabetes. Ruminating on the loss of her baby and the disappearances of her husband only worsened the situation, and she smoked more. The problems with Fosse added immeasurably to her distress, Henry Dolger, McCracken's physician, believed. But as her husband's work drew more attention, it became increasingly hard for Joan to hide her disintegration. They were supposed to be a golden couple.

The Tonys were only eight years old in March 1955. Before the American Theatre Wing tried to make the award show into a version of the Oscars — introducing the concept of nominees, announcing them well in advance, and broadcasting on television — Broadway's biggest night was no bigger than a high-priced wedding, presented with dinner and dancing in the grand ballroom of the Plaza Hotel. Fosse, neat in a little tux, came with Joan, slight as an icicle. With fewer than twenty medallions to hand out, no nominees to list, and acceptance speeches limited so the program could be broadcast on the radio, the ceremony began with coffee and ended by dessert. Joan gamely clapped and grinned as *The Pajama Game* took home best musical, best performance by a featured actress (Carol Haney), and best choreographer for twenty-seven-year-old Bob Fosse. "He was his usual cool-cat self," recalled Rae Allen, "with just a bit more I-told-you-so glint in his eye."

McCracken's condition might have hooked Fosse and drawn him back home to her, but he had already been hooked and yanked in the opposite direction. *Damn Yankees,* Abbott and company's follow-up to *The Pajama Game,* was about to unite New York's most exciting young choreographer with Prince, Griffith, Adler, Ross, a few familiar dancers, and *Can-Can's* Gwen Verdon, princess of Broadway — pending Bob Fosse's approval of her. They looked to him now. Per the grosses and the critics, he was suddenly, officially, a Tony-nominated part of the musical mainstream and of definite value to George Abbott, Mr. Mainstream himself. But Fosse had had help on *The Pajama Game.* Without Jerome Robbins, could he do it again on *Damn Yankees*? And if he could, and if Ms. Verdon — *Jack Cole's* Gwen Verdon — triumphed, what credit would they give him?

"Look," he said to Hal Prince. "I have to audition her."

"Bobby, you know she's good."

"I know. I know," he said. "But is she good for me?"

Prince conceded; she would audition.

Days later, in a tangle of forgotten props and wooden chairs, Bob Fosse and Gwen Verdon faced each other in Walton's Warehouse, a cavernous rehearsal space in midtown Manhattan. It was night. He looked like night.

"I'm very nervous," he said.

"So am I."

She saw a crumpled, soft-talking dance tramp, and he saw the sweetest, hottest dancing comedienne of the age. One with a reputation. Underneath her smile, he had heard, Verdon could be a difficult collaborator, a high-class snob with an ironclad pedigree and an almost pathological aversion to the kind of heigh-ho Broadway jumping around she called animated wallpaper. Verdon could see through him. If he tried any of those vaudeville tricks on her, she'd nail him for it in a second.

"I'm just going to show you this number," he said. "I'll just do it."

She stepped back to the mirror and waited, watching.

It was her big number, "Whatever Lola Wants," and Fosse, she saw, had filled it with all sorts of burlesque moves, moves she recognized from her early days, before Cole, playing clubs on Hollywood Boulevard at the age of fifteen, wearing a rubber bra and a body smear of gold powder. Now, watching Bob Fosse slithering and stalking his way through the oldest stripper tricks in the book, slipping off invisible gloves and shaking his imaginary tits, she felt herself giving in. He was fantastic.

Every wink, every blink, every finger curl was quite obviously the product of weeks of careful experimentation. He told her when to breathe, when to laugh, when to smile and how much. In time, her incredulity became enthusiasm; her enthusiasm gave him confidence; and his confidence inflamed her enthusiasm. Now it was her turn to be intimidated. Where another dancer would have collapsed, Gwen asked for more, to do it again, and maybe this time, if he didn't mind, with one of those robust Jack Cole turns. Did he mind? No, he didn't mind. He didn't mind at all.

They went at it for hours.

He loved what she knew. Refined over years of formal study and practice, Verdon's repertoire pulsed with a vast knowledge of tap, ballet, Denishawn training, and a hard-won supply of Jack Cole. Born and raised in Culver City, a short pony ride from the MGM lot, Gwyneth Verdon could plug into Fosse's showbiz history, body and mind, as far back as they both could remember. She had a mind like a tuning fork. Her mother had been a dance teacher, her father a gaffer at Metro. At the age of three, she had entertained at an MGM Christmas party thrown by Marion Davies; at six, she was being billed as the "fastest little tapper in the world."

"It's a vulnerability," Fosse said later. "Even if she's knocking down brick walls, you suddenly want to take care of Gwen Verdon." Crying or smiling or both at once, she was the picture of hope trying to squeeze its way out any way it can. With a winning smile, thick hair, and a voluptuous machine for a body, Verdon became the kind of grown-up girl that turned boys into men and men into idiots. Like Fosse, she had been groped, slapped, overused, underused, injured, rejected, forgotten, and fooled. The perverts, the pigs, the egos, the artists, the phonies, the producers who said yes when they meant no, the directors who said they wanted you for the show because they wanted you for the night, and the dancers who lined up against you and then called you their friend — she knew them all. Soft on the outside, on the inside, she was a dancer. "Sure, Bob's tough," she said. "He's demanding and exact, but I get a much bigger kick out of pleasing him in rehearsal than I do an entire audience in a performance." Her genius was that she made killing herself look like fun, and Bob Fosse, who also killed himself, who was never impressed, was impressed. He said, "The thing that impresses me most about her is her enthusiasm, her desire for perfection, and *endless* energy. Whenever I have an idea, I'll kind of fumble my way up to it with an 'Ah, I think we should . . .' and she'll say, 'No, I know *exactly* what you mean!' and she's off to the races."

He gave her the part, of course, of Lola in *Damn Yankees.*

They began to rehearse, exchanging pieces of their autobiographies, which they unearthed from each other's style. Those bowlers Fosse put on his dancers? From the English music-hall tradition? He got used to them covering his bald spot. Gwen's facility with hands and fingers? She learned sign language from a girl at elementary school. Her twisted, turned-in feet? "My knees were so badly knocked," she said, "that they crossed over each other. I wore braces on my legs, and orthopedic shoes and I was never without big, angry sores on my knees because they knocked together so hard." Fosse's body could speak to that; he was pigeon-toed too. Adversity became them. Those heavy black orthopedic shoes had only made little Gwen work harder, and her poor turnout forced her to compensate — with personality.

To help Gwen's legs recover, Verdon's mother enrolled her daughter in dance classes all over Los Angeles. "That child is like wild sunset!" she said. "She *will* dance!"

In the fourth grade, Gwen started signing her homework *Ginger Verdon*.

"Why Ginger?" her teacher asked.

"Because I can't [be] Fred."

Gwen didn't have technique but at fifteen, she had a winning smile; thick, delicious hair; and a killer rack, which she didn't love. But the guys did, and Gwen, who'd dance wherever they let her, took a job at the Florentine Gardens, where she got near naked before a houseful of loud and hungry men. She was underage, but Mrs. Verdon lied for her. Unlike Mrs. Fosse had done for her son, Mrs. Verdon accompanied her daughter from stage to stage, surging with pride. "My grandmother was very supportive," said Gwen's son, Jim Henaghan Jr. "She wanted my mom to dance because my mom loved it and [she] was willing to go to great lengths to see her succeed. Bob's parents were not supportive in the way my grandmother was at all. They had different ideas about showbiz. Different ideas about manhood. They weren't mean to him; they just had a different outlook on life. I don't think they objected to the point that they stopped him, but he was on his own." For Gwen, context was almost irrelevant; she didn't care if she was twirling alongside her brother in the creeks behind their bungalow or alone in her room, hopping up and down and blowing on her trumpet. As long as she was moving.

She loved to dance, but she dreamed of love. "Her dream was to have a home and a hearth and have children that were going to be okay in the world," Ann Reinking said. James Henaghan was a journalist: witty, older, dashing. Six months after they met, the couple drove down to Orange County, and Gwen told the justice of the peace she was twenty-two.

The new Mrs. Henaghan tossed her tap shoes into a cardboard box and locked the box away. It was time, she told herself, to work at being a wife.

But Henaghan drank. He lost money. When he woke up in Kansas City with no idea how he got there and a column past due, he called Gwen in the middle of the night and she wrote the piece and filed it for him. Gwen didn't love the job, but she loved loving him, and for a while she was sure she could survive on the crumbs of tenderness he transmitted by cable. For a while. Soon, they had a son, Jim Jr. Verdon didn't want to break up the family, but in a sense, the choice was made for her. On New Year's Eve 1943, she packed up her son and her animals and left her husband.

Depressed and poor and overcome with guilt, the former Venice Beach bathing-suit model and current single mother shrank to a hundred pounds. She was twenty years old. "Jimmy," she would say to her little boy later, "you and I grew up together."

They needed money. One of Henaghan's contacts asked her to review a nightclub opening. An old lover, dance was a bittersweet memory she held at arm's length, but Gwen couldn't help but raise an eyebrow at the thought of going to see Jack Cole at Slapsie Maxie's.

Cole stories were legion. He was a terrible genius, witty, bitchy, crazy, a mean man who worked out of deep pockets of brilliance and anger — and it showed in his dancers. If they survived, Cole's people were alarmingly good. When they appeared with him — tribal and half nude — on the supper-club stage, Gwen felt a yank inside of her. It was true. Cole was stunning, even standing still; he gleamed like a piece of golden technology, and when he moved, he cut the air like a rain of knives. Erotic and exotic, Cole's style drew from all aspects of world movement. When he danced, he spared no part of himself, slicing air with the grace and precision of a ballet dancer, a beast in a gentleman's body. "He would do absolutely true, real authentic East Indian dance," Verdon said. "But to jazz music." She was possessed.

Remembering who she was, or, rather, who she'd thought she might be, Gwen went backstage to introduce herself. She had good reason to be terrified.

Cole was mostly silent with Gwen. When he did talk, it was in speeches and with a grim authority unwelcoming to conversation. Art, like interlocution, was not a group effort for Jack Cole. But somehow, Gwen Verdon, whom Cole could have flicked away like a speck of dandruff, tamed the jackal inside him. Cole himself could hardly believe it. Here she was, backstage, going on about how spectacular he was and about how she needed the money and wanted to join his group, and, miraculously, the great man listened. Maybe she caught him at a good time, or maybe — knowing a good thing when he saw one — Cole felt he had caught her. "Jack was pretty amused," Verdon remembered. "For one thing, I had on such a tight skirt that I could hardly sit down." He could see that Gwen had, like him, insane drive and a combustible streak of belligerence. Her simply having the nerve to address him proved it. But could she move?

Cole invited her to audition for a chorus-girl part in *The Blonde from Brooklyn*, the film he was dance-directing at Columbia. The day of the audition, he gave her a few ballet sequences, calling them out in an esoteric dance dialect no Culver City girl could be expected to understand.

"Well, if you say it in English," she shot back, "I'll do it."

Gwen Verdon wasn't used to pretension, and Jack Cole wasn't used to gumption. So Cole repeated himself with a translation, and Gwen did as she was told, beautifully. ("Gwen's answer to Cole," Tommy Tune suggested, "was she could outdance him. She had that against him.") The assured sensuality of her dance shocked both of them.

"She had an adeptness and knowhow that showed she had lots of experience but not much real training," Cole said. "She was good but she had no strong style." He'd have to burn that into her. If she was willing. If she would move the way he told her to, read everything he said, and follow his word like it was God's law. Then he could transform her from a dancer into a Jack Cole Dancer. But she had to work. She had to study. Joining him, Gwen would have to rehearse before rehearsals so she would be prepared to prepare.

Still smarting with the pain of a broken family, Verdon wasn't sure she had the heart or the muscle to withstand Cole's strength, vision, and unsparing intelligence, which she knew — now firsthand — were more powerful than any other choreographer's.

It was true that he could wreck her if he wanted to. But what else was there? She had a baby and no money. Dance was all she could do.

"I won't let him beat me," she said.

In 1947, Gwen sold everything she owned (except for her books and records) and filed for divorce. Just after Thanksgiving, she left Jim Jr. with her parents in Culver City and joined the chorus of Cole's *Bonanza Bound* in New York. Jim Jr. said, "My mom had to decide whether to become a shop girl and take care of her kid or pursue her career, and her need to dance. That was a tough decision for her to have to make and it bothered her a great deal, but it was her choice and we all went along with it."

Devotion was innate in Gwen Verdon. As she had once belonged to Henaghan, she now belonged to Jack Cole. "She understood she had to put up with a lot of hard personality stuff to see greatness," Jim Jr. explained. "I think that's the key to all sorts of her relationships."

And as she had once belonged to Cole, she now belonged to Bob Fosse. "It was quite apparent to everyone in the [*Damn Yankees*] rehearsals that Bob Fosse was having an affair with Gwen," observed dancer Svetlana McLee, a pal of McCracken's from *Me and Juliet*. "When Joan would come into rehearsal and sit there and watch, it was uncomfortable . . . I mean uncomfortable in capital letters." Both Mc-

Cracken and Verdon needed tending, and Fosse could have split his time down the middle, running between them as he soon would run between the rehearsal studio and the editing room, night till morning, morning till night. But he didn't. He openly became Gwen's, and he cast Joan off like a first draft. "All my women have beauty and talent," he said, "and I fall in love with that, and then I don't know what happens, because it always ends. It's my fault always."

McCracken was the one to urge him to talk to someone. Her analyst made a recommendation, and Fosse, at first opposed, finally acquiesced. Mostly he talked about work, the stifling insecurity he felt creating for the public, for people he suspected were waiting for him to fail. He craved the privacy of a writer or composer, artists with the luxury to fail behind closed doors. He talked about women, about not being a good husband, about failing his first and maybe now his second marriage. He wanted to do better, to *be* better. He talked of his dreams, swollen with anxieties he couldn't name, and began to sense a profound thematic undercurrent. "In my own case these were things like the fear of not being liked," he said. "I was always very eager to please other people." He remembered the occasion, after his brothers had gotten into trouble, when he decided he would be his parents' good boy, the child they depended on. Still, he regularly found himself cheating compulsively, hurting girls, hurting Joan, especially when he worked. "I'm a pretty good husband when I'm not working," he said, "but as soon as I start a project, it's like I don't know anything else exists." It was a sinister loop, the need to win; disappointing himself in work was a virus that only more work could treat. His doctor prescribed Seconal.

Should he leave Joan? Would that be bad? Was *he* bad? He had certainly done bad things. He told his analyst about the strippers. He talked about "a rather bizarre sexual experience" when he was thirteen, something that had been done to him that made Fosse want to prove all women could be gotten, and easily. "I think he felt a sense of betrayal with women," Ann Reinking explained, "a sense of loss and betrayal early on in his life. I don't think he felt safe. I just remember him saying that his mother shouldn't have let him do burlesque and his father was always gone. He would talk about that a lot. It didn't matter that Bob's father had to go out and make a living. To a young Bob, left alone in those places, that didn't matter."

Fosse said, "I didn't realize until I got into analysis that I really hated going away from home and was scared to death, that I was in an atmosphere, with all those naked ladies running around, way over my head."

Imagination, Joyce said, is memory. Trauma, the psychologists say, compulsively seeks expression. Like a criminal, the unconscious mind obsessively returns to the scene of the crime to gain mastery over the pain, putting itself in environments and circumstances, professional and emotional, conducive to reenactment. Trauma specialist Dr. Charles Rousell: "If an adult has experienced repetitive trauma as a child at the hands of people he trusts, he might find that the residual effects become engraved into the narrative of his life. So it is not surprising that if that person had endured trauma at the hands of trusted adults in the theater world he would devote his life to the theater. Working on shows may release some of that pain and creatively forge it into constructive action." But when that pain is intimately involved with feelings of pleasure — as in sex or entertainment — untangling good from bad can be ceaselessly dissatisfying and difficult to do. "Whatever Lola Wants," a continuation of a burlesque-haunted trajectory Fosse initiated with "That Old Black Magic" in 1943, refers back to that pain.

George Abbott, who understood Gwen's power, kept growing the part of Lola. Who else could pull off the satanic Betty Boop? (Barbara Cook? Carol Channing? Ethel Merman? Mary Martin? Doubtful.)

It took Verdon, a comedienne, to make sex safe for the American musical; it took a Cole dancer to read Fosse, and an actress to legitimize Lola's humanity. Beginning March 7, 1955, she zipped among the show's separate rehearsal spaces, each on a different floor of the warehouse where Fosse and Verdon created Lola. A service elevator wheezed from one windowless studio to the next, delivering wholesale talent to Abbott's room for scene work, to Adler and Ross's floor for voice, and to Fosse's for dance. Two weeks later, the eighty-three-person company assembled for the first run-through of *Damn Yankees*.

It ran long. Prince suggested cutting the big end-of-act-one ballet, a round of musical chairs emceed by the Yankee's mascot, a gorilla. Desperate to save the number (and seize a spotlight opportunity), Fosse suggested *he* play the gorilla. Performance wasn't the issue, Prince explained, pace was. The number had to go. But Fosse pushed back; he didn't trust Hal Prince. He didn't trust producers. He assumed they were fundamentally unsympathetic to creation, their expenses and bottom lines against his requests for more time to improve. Fosse had to fail his way to success and feel safe and unpressured while he did. "We were very different minds, Bobby and me," Prince said. "He was quintessential showbiz," and Prince was a New York college boy—to Fosse, irreconcilable differences. Prince said, "Bobby was not a happy fellow. Not ever. Not with me." But in the spirit of collaboration, the producer agreed to let the first preview audience in New Haven cast the tiebreaking vote. Would the number stay or go?

The audience backed Prince. Now what? Clumped in a small bedroom of New Haven's Taft Hotel, Abbott, Prince, and Griffith shrugged and what-ifed their way through the whys and why-nots of the performance.

"Fellas," Prince began, "I think we all know what we need to do.

The gorilla number has to go. I know we put a lot into this but you saw what —"

The telephone rang.

"Excuse me," Prince said, reaching for the phone. "Hello?"

"Hal, it's Bob Fosse." (He always used his full name, afraid they'd say, "Bob who?")

"Bobby, listen," Prince said, "we're all here and we —"

"I'm in the room next door," he said. "I heard everything you said, Hal."

"Bobby . . ."

"Why don't you tell me these things to my face?"

"I'm coming right now," Prince said, and he hung up.

Seconds later, a very embarrassed, very confused Hal Prince stepped into Fosse's room and sat down in an armchair a neutral distance away. Fosse cursed at Prince, spitting smoke in the air like an angry train. Joan McCracken, waiting on the little bed, said nothing.

"Bobby," Prince muttered. "It's terrible that you heard me, just terrible. I'm so terribly sorry you did. But please understand I'm doing what I think is best for the show here, we all are —"

"You're doing it *behind my back*."

"We were in a meeting. No one's doing anything behind your back."

"Bullshit. I heard what you said."

"Bobby, I didn't say anything I didn't mean. You know what I think of the number —"

"I *know* what was going on in there!"

Joan glanced at Hal. She was embarrassed.

"It's the *number*," Prince pleaded. "It's not you, Bobby, believe me. You're great, but the show needs work."

"You're scheming!"

Joan cut in. "Enough. Stop it."

"Joanie, please."

"He *apologized*, Bobby —"

But Fosse didn't stop. Raging, he ripped into Prince, ripped into all producers, bashing their intelligence and supposed artistic sensitivity.

Long after Prince left the room, Fosse was still glowering. If they were against his work, they were against him. Even if they didn't say it, he knew they thought it.

The gorilla number went. In came "Who's Got the Pain?," a bite-size mambo for Eddie Phillips and Gwen. "Bob and I put the number together in about two hours," she said. But speed was no consolation, not to Fosse. Being *directed* by a producer — that he could not tolerate. Prince said, "I begged him to see that what I felt about him in life had nothing to do with what he did onstage. I begged him as long as I knew him."

Onward to Boston, where a new version of *Damn Yankees* was performed almost every night. "We were tossing out score all the time," said Prince, "writing new material for Gwen to beef up her part." They gave her a new number, "A Little Brains, a Little Talent." But rather than show appreciation for an expanded Lola, Verdon turned cold, as if in allegiance to Fosse. "She was very loyal, Gwen," Prince explained, "and after all that Jack Cole, so accustomed to trusting, to not questioning, especially guys."

Gwen's part continued to expand — as Lola and as Fosse's girl — as late as May 5, 1955, the night of the *Damn Yankees* Broadway opening. Before the show, McCracken went backstage to congratulate a friend, actor Ray Walston. Her hands, he noticed, were drenched in sweat. "I put it all together later," Walston said, "but it was obviously the result of what was happening between her and Bob."

She had a heart attack, then another. Then pneumonia. Though Fosse blamed himself for her decline, it was in the hospital that he left her, or began to. "Joan was in critical condition on an oxygen tank,"

Reinking said, "and she told him that everything was all right, that he shouldn't worry, that she understood. She was trying to tell him it's okay. Forgive yourself. You did not have a hand in this. You did not bring this on." He did not agree. Something was wrong with him. He saw his psychiatrist as often as five times a week in double sessions, back to back. Why couldn't he feel the good others felt in love? Beset with terrible guilt, he could not leave Joan completely, though he practically had, appearing only at odd hours to soothe both of them, or just himself, visits that became less frequent, then finally stopped.

On her own now, Joan continued to keep her heart attacks a private matter, hoping to bounce back and dance again before word of her condition spread. But Walter Winchell discovered her secret, and everyone who might have hired her found out she was unemployable — and the dominoes fell. First she stopped dancing, then she stopped exercising. Then her blood sugar levels rose. Then her heart tightened. She put on a sporting face, but Walston saw her: She was a living corpse.

She retreated to Fire Island. Alone.

Meanwhile, Gwen Verdon appeared in eight shows a week at the Forty-Sixth Street Theater to overwhelming acclaim. More than anything else in the show, Lola — a character Walter Kerr called "everything undesirable made absolutely and forever desirable" — made *Damn Yankees* matter. Verdon's smiling face appeared on the cover of *Time*, which called her "the most incendiary star on Broadway."

A few dancers on their way to say good night heard the shouts coming from her dressing room. A brave one peeked her head around the door and saw Gwen crying and Fosse against the wall.

"Why can't you do it?" she was overheard yelling at him. Gwen had finally left her boyfriend, actor Scott Brady. "Why can't you leave her?"

In a sense, he never would. For the rest of Fosse's life, he felt Joan following him, and once, he literally followed her, as she was walking down a busy avenue with a friend, dancer Doria Avila. "Look behind you," Joan said. Avila looked, and Fosse ducked behind a parked car. At night, he called Joan at Fire Island—she had finally put a telephone in, for medical emergencies—and hung up as soon as she answered.

THIRTY-TWO YEARS

WITH VERDON COMMITTED to *Damn Yankees,* Fosse seemed to stall for time. He was both waiting for her release so they could begin work on the next show — theirs — and trying to decide if he, on his own, was a star choreographer or an up-and-coming star. Once again, the chance to play *Pal Joey,* this time in a Wallingford, Connecticut, production, decided the question for him. In June of 1955, he went off to the Oakdale Theater for a week's run of the show he was determined to make his own. But audiences did not want him. Fosse might have rejected them for it and looked elsewhere for his applause, but he was trapped. "In this business," a friend said, "you are driven by insecurity. You need more love than what you're getting in life. But you'll never, never get enough. The hole stays with you, no matter what you do, and can't be fulfilled by another human being. Bob was a walking hole." His *Pal Joey* dream only deepened that hole. "Show business is really important to my life," Fosse said, "and I'm eternally grateful for all it's given me, but there is an underlying hate that I have for it. I think it's really hurt my life and I think I could have gotten more."

But where? A deli counter? Medical school? He said it many times: "I can't do anything but show business."

It was Stanley Donen who suggested Fosse might choreograph the dances for *Funny Face,* his new Audrey Hepburn/Fred Astaire musical. The job was virtually unbeatable, and Fosse accepted. Getting the green light from MGM producer Roger Edens, he jumped into a studio, and for ten hours a day, every day for four weeks, he played out ideas in the mirror, banishing from his mind the pending particulars of his salary, which he soon discovered were not all that favorable. He read the studio's terms as a personal insult, and rather than seize the chance to work with his idol, Fosse fought Edens over the deal, as if it were not a negotiation but a score he needed to settle. Money, for Fosse, wasn't about money in the bank — he was not greedy or materialistic — it was about value, his. "At the time the money seemed important," Fosse said, "but in retrospect, it was one of the dumbest things that happened in my life." The deal fell through. He'd never work with Fred Astaire.

Late in 1956, he headed to Warner Brothers, where Donen was filming *The Pajama Game,* to ensure his dances made smooth transitions to the screen. "Bob was always there and was very involved," dancer Harvey Evans recalled. "He designed some of the shots for the 'Once-a-Year Day' number, which was shot on location in a park, and he changed some of the choreography to fit the location." A notch or two more ambitious than the "Alley Dance," the "Once-a-Year Day" number favored the proscenium-style arrangements of classic Astaire, but this time, Fosse kept changing the proscenium, cutting throughout the location from one dance space to another, and rather than confine his dancers to the absolute foreground, he placed them in all corners of the frame and at all depths. Unlike the "Alley Dance," the film version of "Once-a-Year Day" could not have taken place onstage; it was expressly for the movies, made to suit the magnitude of the exterior.

In August, Fosse took an apprentice-type position, regressing slightly in his career to co-choreograph *Bells Are Ringing* with Jerome Robbins, who was also directing. Robbins felt that splitting the workload would give him more time to focus on the bigger picture — his credit would read "Entire Production Directed by Jerome Robbins" — and he also didn't think he could handle Judy Holliday, a nondancer. "Robbins would make her nervous," Buzz Miller recalled. "It was her personality type. Robbins was fairly new in directing and he really didn't know his acting that well and naturally he was defensive." Fosse learned to adapt his ambitions to Holliday's limitations. Rather than curbing his creativity, her personality actually enhanced the effects of his choreography — for no dancer, he found, no matter how grand his or her technique, could carry a number without that inner something Holliday had in superabundance. That actors couldn't dance didn't matter. Though Fosse had every step planned in advance, their natural or mundane behavior could be transformed into caricature. He would just have to watch closely and make the right choice. Once isolated, a tic or a twitch could give a whole character an inner life. Holliday's own genius would carry the rest. "To Bob, the steps were dialogue," Ann Reinking said. "He liked dancers who knew how to speak them, or even add something of themselves. Dance per se is only one part of a great dancer." Fosse devised a simple audition for the nondancers, a box step to the tune of "Yankee Doodle Dandy." On certain words, he'd have them move their hands from their hips to their heads and back again so he could be sure they could at least move and sing at the same time.

By all accounts, *Bells Are Ringing* was only a minor achievement. Fosse's stamp on "The Midas Touch," a boob-bouncing nightclub affair, was highly evident, as was his influence on "Hello, Hello, There!" a funny fandango in a Brooklyn subway. "One terrible part of the show," Robbins wrote, "is that Bob Fosse, who did most of the dances, managed to eke out a bad secondhand version of dances I've already done, so that it looks like I have just copied myself and repeated badly what I once did well." Fosse would be the first to agree that Robbins's dances weren't the only rehashes in *Bells Are Ringing*. "Mu Cha Cha," a cute-enough duet tailored to Holliday's range, was partially recycled "Who's Got the Pain?" "You develop a certain few tricks," Fosse freely admitted, "a few steps, a gimmick or so, and then you use that for the rest of your life and you keep working off of that and you protect it as though national security depended upon it."

It was working, anyway. With *Damn Yankees* still playing to happy crowds and the sensational one-thousand-show run of *The Pajama Game* only recently ended, Abbott's boys had Broadway on a string, though you wouldn't know it by the cramped offices they kept at 630 Fifth Avenue. Mr. Abbott in one room, scribbling in the margins of scripts notes like *Keep, Terrible,* or *Fix,* could hear Hal Prince and Robert Griffith on calls in another, each of them speaking on the phone and to the other simultaneously without losing the thread of either conversation. There was no desk for partner Frederick Brisson, husband of Rosalind Russell and negotiator extraordinaire, presumably because he was always at lunch someplace, negotiating extraordinarily. Nor was there a desk for Bob Fosse — their Tony winner for best choreography two years in a row — presumably because Fosse did his work standing up.

At last, the time had come for Abbott and company to discuss their next venture. With the recent death of Jerry Ross, half of the songwriting team of Adler and Ross, they couldn't return to the well. On Doris Day's recommendation — she and Abbott had met on the set of *The Pajama Game* — Abbott and his office mates listened to some wonderful songs Bob Merrill had written for a film MGM planned to make of O'Neill's *Anna Christie*. The songs were lovely. "The score," Prince said. "That's why we did the show." They bought the rights from Metro, and Abbott wrote the book in six weeks. He called it *New Girl in Town*.

Two red flags for Fosse. The first: In keeping with the seriousness of the subject, Abbott designed the show to be more sung than danced. Hence the second red flag: Abbott intended to give the part of Anna — a former prostitute trying to hide her past and make a new life — to an actress with a strong Rodgers and Hammerstein voice; not, he said, to Gwen Verdon. But Gwen wanted the part, and very badly. "I thought, 'What an extraordinary opportunity to show that musical theater acting is acting,'" she explained. "It's not different from doing just straight *Anna Christie*. It's the same." Abbott made Verdon audition — an affront to her stardom. It irritated her. Unconvinced by what he heard, he gave Verdon three weeks to rehearse and try again. In that time, Verdon, at Fosse's suggestion, had begun to work on the part with Sanford Meisner, a small threat to Abbott's control. But he gave her the part anyway; she was the biggest star on Broadway.

To maximize Verdon's time with Meisner, Fosse sketched out movement around her, ever mindful that he had to keep *New Girl in Town* a predominantly nondancing show. For weeks, he and his dance assistant Patricia Ferrier built stylized gestures and poses to mesh with *New Girl's* darker, erotic milieu. Between those gestures, ligatures developed and evolved, and glints of actual dance appeared, almost accidentally. Out came a lyrical bump-and-grind ballet, far from family-friendly. But George Abbott was nothing if not reasonable. He decided to reserve judgment until this clump of spurts and undulations — whatever it was — congealed in context, and out of town. From mud, he knew, a garden could grow. "There's a lot of serious material on the musical stage today," Abbott told the *Herald Tribune*. "*Pal Joey* is serious material. *Carousel* is. American musicals have progressed far beyond the musical comedy stage; a musical comedy implies a kind of *Follies* atmosphere. The trend of our musicals is to try to give honest characters and an honest story and have the musical development come out of that story." But was Abbott up to grown-up fare? Late in 1956, it was a question Fosse's dancers — for they were, body and mind, completely Fosse's — asked aloud. "Right away we assumed George Abbott didn't know what to do with this show," said Harvey Evans, "because it was so dark, about a prostitute."

"They live in their own world," Abbott wrote of his dancers. "They talk to the rest of us, they sometimes marry us, but at the same time they shut us out." He marveled half admiringly at their tattered slacks and sweaters, winced at their omnisexual pairings- and re-pairings-off. They thought differently, weirdly. Living on a diet of carrot sticks and coffee, these were hard-working aliens unfamiliar with the laws of reality. "Their life," Abbott wrote, "is an unending struggle against the body" — in most cases, a struggle magnified by a dictatorial choreographer. A vicious Jack Cole or a nasty Jerome Robbins spewed invective that the dancers readily accepted, rarely thinking of revolt, for the choreographer was the genius, the father, the way to success, and they themselves were disposable. "The school of choreography before Fosse was you didn't question," said Tony Stevens. "You were a slave to the dance. It was murder. They killed you and you let them. You thanked them for it."

Fosse was intimate with the dancer's drama, with its unremitting rejections and hundred-to-one-shot ambitions, and he led them all with kindness and understanding, ever aware of their suffering, which hurt him as much as his own suffering — rather, it *was* his own. Fosse's two Tonys didn't change a thing; he was still a hoofer, still a gypsy, politically and pathologically devoted to the little guy. Even when Fosse yelled or pushed too hard, his anger was all protein, no fat: fuel for them, so they could give back to him. The growing schism between the old fogy Abbott on one side and Fosse and Gwen, the hip uncle and aunt, on the other only amplified the dancers' allegiance — maybe even love — for the eternally apologetic urchin who never thought he gave them enough. "He was so tight with us on *New Girl*," Harvey Evans said, "he would have parties just for the dancers. Gwen would be there too, telling stories about Jack Cole.

She could be tough and you didn't mess around with her," Evans continued, "but on *New Girl*, Gwen was one of us. And she loved Bobby so much, and he loved her, and they loved us. We all loved each other, like a family." A kind of family.

The "Red Light Ballet," the erotic piece Fosse developed with Pat Ferrier, described Anna's dream of whorehouse squalor in ways Abbott's book hadn't dared. Performed in front of a black backdrop on a bare black stage empty of everything but a few chairs and a simple staircase leading up into the wings, the ballet, in sharp contrast to the rest of the show — a colorful Victorian affair, heavy in naturalistic detail — shifted from objective reality to the unconscious. Evans said, "It was the first time that Fosse used chairs, and the girls — prostitutes dressed in corsets and garter belts and flesh-colored tights — actually laid back on the chairs and, you know, turned their feet in and out, and pumped their crotches in the air. Their skirts fell over their heads and they writhed. But it had a lot of comedy in it too. I played a kid they brought into the whorehouse, and Gwen flirts with me, and my foot starts shaking, then my leg starts shaking and shoots up like an erection."

The lonely boom of a double bass, like a heartbeat, drove the audience farther inward, into the mind of the dreamer, hurrying Verdon toward the climax, a backward dive off the top of the stairs into the arms of dancer John Aristides. A sexy pas de deux followed. "And then at the very end of it," Evans recalled, "Aristides takes Gwen — in a back bend over his shoulder — and carries her up the stairs, we think to the bed." Verdon was so involved in the number, she didn't seem to notice when her corset loosened, partially exposing her breast. "Gwen went as far as she could," Evans added. "She really wanted to be that prostitute."

The dancers loved the number and, in rehearsal, Abbott claimed he did too. But members of New Haven's first preview audience averted their eyes and, by some accounts, shrieked in horror. When the curtain fell that night, not a single individual applauded. ("Now, I [had] never seen that," Fosse said later.) In advance of Abbott's verdict, Fosse collared a pianist and dashed to a nearby gymnasium to perform emergency surgery on the ballet. He worked for hours that night, toning and taming.

Around one in the morning, Prince, Griffith, and George Abbott appeared at the gymnasium. Their edict: The whorehouse ballet had to go. Prince said, "I think the pornographic ballet was too vulgar and not skillful. It was just not a good dance, I thought. It wasn't prudery at all. It was just — what is this? Why are we doing this? Because prostitution was not glamorous in the world of that show. It was seedy, sexless, and really grubby. Bob's number was a Vegas, Crazy Horse in Paris number." Abbott argued for narrative consistency. The character of Anna had nothing but contempt for her bordello past, so, vulgarity aside, casting prostitution in an erotic and even funny light made no sense. The whole conceit of a dream ballet, Abbott asserted, was passé. *Oklahoma!* and its dream ballet were history, fifteen years in the past.

Fosse and Verdon fought back. "They replied that it was high art," Abbott recalled, "that they didn't care what the audience liked, and that people had thrown fruit at Stravinsky. We tried to point out that the act of throwing fruit at a project was not in the strictest logic an absolute proof of its [being] high art, but our argument was not able to pierce the emotional armor with which they had invested their creation." The dancers stood with Fosse.

Arriving at rehearsal the next morning, the company met yet another shock. The theater had been padlocked, which sent an enraging message the New Haven Police were on hand to enforce: *New Girl in Town* would not play until the "Red Light Ballet" was cut. Who called in the law? Gwen alleged an angry mother had complained to a crossing guard, but no one could be sure, and it didn't matter. The ballet's forty-thousand-dollar stairway, critical to the number's most crucial innuendo, was discovered in the alley theater burned to ashes.

Fosse had no choice but to throw together a stopgap riff on Agnes de Mille (ironically more passé than the original ballet) and *New Girl* trudged on to Boston, where audiences wanted to see a dancing Gwen Verdon, which gave Abbott reason to reverse course. Ordering Fosse to add conventional dance numbers and cutting stretches of O'Neill to make room for them, he turned *New Girl in Town*, inch by inch, into an unfunny musical comedy.

An employee without a union, Fosse had no leverage. But the star did. She demanded Hal Prince deliver George Abbott.

"He's too busy to talk right now."

"Then I'm too busy to go on."

It was the flu, she said. To replace her, the production had to split the part into four different sections for four different performers. One sang and played the book scenes, and the remaining three divided the dances among them — proof that Gwen Verdon, the most threatening of triple threats, could do what no other single person could.

When she returned to the show, a week later, Verdon dove into character work. Irritating Abbott with actorly conflict, she would avenge the loss of the "Red Light Ballet."

"Just say the lines!"

"I have no more lines to say!" (He had cut that many.)

Retaliating, Abbott kept her waiting onstage all afternoon, refusing to bring on a stand-in when he rehearsed elements around her.

"You cheap son of a bitch!" she called out. "Why don't you hire someone here to stand for me?"

New Girl's trials only brought Fosse and Verdon closer. The high-pressure rush of opening night in New York, the feeling of unjust persecution, and their sense of righteous collaboration in the name of art electrified all channels of their relationship. "Gwen and Fosse were now so, so in love," Prince said, "it was almost dangerous." Conflict fired their work, work fired their romance, and romance fired the conflict. There was something conspiratorial about it. "I'd set my hair on fire if he asked me to," Verdon said. But dancers had to wonder, as they watched him raid the dressing rooms for chorus girls, would he do the same for her?

The exact parameters of their liaison did not concern Gwen's son, Jimmy. Visiting New York, he found them mutually devoted and preparing for marriage. They were just waiting on Joan McCracken, Gwen told him. "She had had a breakdown," Charlie Grass explained, "she'd been institutionalized, and Bob and Gwen helped. For years, they paid." Fosse wouldn't seek his divorce until Joan's release, when she'd recovered and was able to start performing again. (When that day came, in April 1957, Fosse went to Winston County, Alabama, quickie-divorce mecca of the South.) In the meantime, Fosse and Verdon maintained separate residences: he on the West Side of midtown, she on Lexington and Sixty-Eighth. Most nights, after *New Girl* runs at Broadway's Forty-Sixth Street Theater, Fosse and Jim would meet Gwen away from the mob, in the alley outside her dressing room, and they'd all follow it a hundred paces to Dinty Moore's back door, enter the restaurant through the kitchen, and sit down at their table.

Fosse never tried to father Jim or force a friendship. From early on, he maintained a policy of frankness and humor, with a tentative edge.

"Bob had his demons," Henaghan recalled, "but he was funny, really funny." Walking down the street with Jim and Gwen one evening, Fosse spotted an old man clonking toward them with a wonky limp.

Fosse stopped short, then turned to Jim and Gwen. "Everybody steals my steps."

At the peak of his clash with Abbott, Fosse got the most appealing offer of his life — at least, the most appealing so far — from Feuer and Martin, producers of *Can-Can,* Broadway's best. From *Where's Charley?* to *Guys and Dolls* to *The Boy Friend* to *Silk Stockings,* in pure box office, Feuer and Martin had a better record than Rodgers and Hammerstein. The envious chalked up their stunning success to good luck, but good luck didn't account for the chutzpah it took to cut a whole number from *Guys and Dolls* less than twenty-four hours before its premiere; it didn't give Feuer his Juilliard training or inborn musical charisma (his trumpet impression was a favorite of Cole Porter's); and luck didn't give Martin his show sense, an instinct so acute that he feared his actually going to the theater to see how the money was spent would disrupt it. "It's a sounder way of appraising a show from the business end of things," he said. Feuer, the more art-minded of the two, worked in the moment; Martin, account ledgers before him, figured the future. Feuer was short, pepped up, and smoked cigars; Martin, a pipe man, was tall and cool. They lived two blocks from each other — Feuer in a townhouse on East Sixty-Third, Martin in a townhouse on East Sixty-Second — and they worked in an apartment on East Fifty-Second.

Feuer and Martin's offer to Fosse — to choreograph and star in *Stay Away, Joe,* a new musical based on Dan Cushman's novel — promised Fosse his biggest showcase yet. A gloss on *Pal Joey's* Joey Evans, the part of girl-chasing, matron-swindling Joe Champlain was heaven-sent, an overdue escape from the house of Abbott and the next big break Fosse had been waiting for. In March 1957, all parties shook hands; lyricist Norman Gimbel and composer Moose Charlap signed on; and a theater was booked. A month later, MGM called Feuer and Martin. Dore Schary invited them to make *Stay Away, Joe* into a movie — needless to say, a movie that didn't star the balding Bob Fosse. His hopes dashed, the choreographer was Abbott's once again.

New Girl in Town opened on Broadway on May 15, 1957, to, as Prince said, "the reviews it deserved." The clashes of light and dark, of director and choreographer, remained unresolved, but once again, Verdon's performance transcended the material. "It would be an affecting job on any stage," rejoiced Brooks Atkinson in the *Times*. "Amid the familiar diversion of Broadway jamboree, it is sobering and admirable."

After opening, Fosse waved in the dancers. "Little by little," Harvey Evans said, "Fosse got the ballet to where it was originally, without telling anybody. We'd go in once a week and we'd rehearse a little more." On June 23, 1957, Fosse's thirtieth birthday, the "Red Light Ballet" was restored, minus the grand staircase and plus one orchestral change. The slow, sensual drum of the double bass was thrown out for something lighter and faster, and the number brought the audience to its feet.

The scuffle over the "Red Light Ballet" showed how Fosse's style and sensibility grew in the dark, and it hastened his thirst to control, to be the author of his own work and defend his artistic urges.

Though the musical drama knew how to be funny (just look at Joan McCracken), the musical comedy had no idea how to be grown-up. It was the fifties; a binary time. Man was man; woman was woman; funny was light, not dark. In 1957, no less a personage than George S. Kaufman openly endorsed their segregation. "There were long years," he wrote nostalgically, "when the outcome of the romance depended on which lad won the big football game, or the foot race, or the automobile race, or the boat race, or the airplane race. Naturally, the fellow who won the race was given permanent possession of the ingénue." Musical comedy was about basic jubilation — singing in the rain, not dancing in the dark—which posed a problem for a show that wanted to get serious and still stay up; for that to work, someone had to jubilantly pull the rug out from under jubilation.

That someone would be Fosse, but not yet. Even if Abbott had allowed it to flourish, Fosse's *New Girl in Town* would likely have contained a healthy amount of old-fashioned fun anyway. For every "Steam Heat" or "Whatever Lola Wants," Fosse seemed to stage two rousing group numbers, like *The Pajama Game*'s "Once-a-Year Day," *Damn Yankees*' "Shoeless Joe from Hannibal, Mo.," and *New Girl*'s "Roll Yer Socks Up." "Bob's choreography in the Abbott years was big and lusty," recalled Tony Stevens, "not like the micromanaging detail work that would really come to define his style. He was always very specific, but at first it was more acrobatic, like Gene Kelly with flashes of Fosse." As late as 1962, Fosse's Abbott side still existed: "I think of dancing as sheer joy," he would say, "as exhilaration, as running, as jumping, as athletic, like a trapeze artist, you know?"

In September 1957, four months after *New Girl* opened at the Forty-Sixth Street Theater, the sheer joy of dance achieved a new and depressingly (for Fosse) high benchmark. Again, the genius was Jerry Robbins. Whereas other musicals, even the great ones, had had to slow down and switch gears to go from a song to a book scene, *West Side Story* spun every disparate ingredient into one cohesive burst of dance-song-story. Worse (for Fosse), it was culturally attuned to its here-and-now gang-life setting (which gave Robbins points for sociology too). Even worse than that, *West Side Story* was bold, ending act one with two dead bodies and act two with a third. It was like a dance opera, defining and expanding character more through movement than book scenes. De Mille had presented character through dance in one memorable *Oklahoma!* number, but this was character through dance from curtain-up—complete, the whole way through—and not in ballet but in a street-ballet vernacular that was part real, part too-wonderful-to-be-true, and (still worse) in comprehensive harmony with the show's visual life, a swirl of free-floating fire escapes and carefully color-controlled costumes. Worst of all, from Fosse's point of view, it was a terrific evening. Fosse sent those golden cuff links back to Robbins.

He thought Jerome Robbins talked to God. "When I call God," Fosse said, "he's always out to lunch."

There was no denying it: After *West Side Story*, it was clear that the American musical wasn't going to go gently. Now it was mammoth. It was defiant. It had something on its mind and needed to say it. What was Bob Fosse, the entertainer, doing at that very moment? What hoary nightclub shtick was he trying not to steal from?

What Fosse was doing was *Copper and Brass*, a thin excuse to build a musical around comedienne Nancy Walker. It was such a mess, its director and second leads had withdrawn during the show's Philadelphia tryout, and Fosse — too much the gypsy to turn down a job — did what he could, which, weeks before the show's move to New York in October 1957, wasn't much. In part, the problem resided with the original choreographer, Anna Sokolow, whose work did not play well with Fosse, her former student. "Fosse was doing the best he could trying to throw things in where she would let him," said dancer Elmarie Wendel. "The poor guy was working so hard, pacing nervously around the stage, trying one thing, trying another, all scrunched up like a coiled wire. By the end of the day his little blond hair was sticking straight up." Quite mysteriously, Sokolow had insisted on setting a ballet number on the Staten Island ferry. Half of the dancers couldn't figure out why. "The dancers started to split. One side was for Sokolow and the other side was for Fosse," Wendel said. "The Sokolow side thought Fosse had no class. The Fosse side thought Sokolow was rather rarefied. The ballet ended up awkwardly in between."

On days when there were no matinee performances of *New Girl in Town*, Verdon would join Fosse in Philadelphia to show his choreography to the dancers. "We had never seen that sort of thing before," Wendel said. "We were ballet trained and ballet is the body working all in one piece. Fosse wanted us to break up the body into little pieces. The arm goes this way and the leg goes that. Roll one shoulder, flip one finger; it went against everything we knew." Unofficially his dance captain, Gwen Verdon was the living illustration of a burgeoning style that few, including Fosse, could put into words. Fosse said, "If something *felt* wrong—or if [Verdon] wanted it on the other foot—she'd say so. Or she'd say, 'I can do this twice as fast here, if you want me to.' Those are the kinds of changes she'd contribute to the finished work." She was paper talking to pen. "He would come up with something and show it to Gwen and she would knock herself out to do it," Wendel said. "She did it for us better than he had showed it to her."

But more than knowing how to move, Verdon knew how Bob Fosse thought, which elevated her above assistant, above collaborator, into a sort of creative cohabitant, beyond anything she had ever done for Jack Cole. Looking at Fosse, she could see it wasn't her dancing he was frowning at but himself, at what he wasn't doing, what he couldn't do, or what he'd done so many times before. "It was Gwen who kept Bob secure," said dancer Fred Mann III. "She was his editor, his mother." His barre. "You could see, from time to time, he'd want to impress her," dancer Leland Palmer said. "She had that power over him. That gave Bob a certain wariness too, like Gwen was the director and Bob the dancer." If the dancers wanted direction, all they had to do was turn to Verdon and Fosse watching each other in the mirror. Looking in the couple's admiring eyes, the dancers could see that Fosse's style was not just about his steps.

Sometimes Verdon and Fosse would close their eyes or turn away from the dancers to remind themselves of the basic rhythms of the piece, the rhythms they felt. They didn't have to speak in order to communicate, but when they did, they made comments in code, in a shorthand system of grunts and images mixing technical jargon and a kind of pillow talk. But despite everyone's efforts, *Copper and Brass* closed on November 16, 1957, after thirty-six dreary performances. Verdon and Fosse headed to Hollywood for a few weeks of work on the *Damn Yankees* movie — starring Verdon, choreographed by Fosse, and codirected by Abbott and Donen — and the old *New Girl* tensions returned. "Gwen wanted Bobby on the set with her at all times," said Fosse's dance assistant Pat Ferrier, "because she was still having such a hard time with Abbott." As Verdon had looked out for Fosse on *Copper and Brass*, Fosse, during Gwen's scenes, stationed himself at the camera to protect her, a difficult job given that Abbott was against her and Donen didn't like her on camera. On the first day of shooting, Gwen told Shannon Bolin, a transfer from Broadway, that Donen refused to shoot her in close-up. "But that's why Bob was there," Bolin said. "Even when he wasn't working on the dances, he was making sure Donen did right by her." The film shows that Donen may have been right; Verdon's body conveys more heart than her face.

Perhaps feeling the urge to direct, to sample his growing power, Fosse began to clash with Donen. "At the rushes," Patricia Ferrier said, "Stanley and Bobby would scream like hell at each other all the way through." Looking back to the "Red Light Ballet" and presaging the limbos he would create in *Pippin* and *Chicago*, Fosse wanted Donen to engulf "Who's Got the Pain?" in as much blackness as possible, using only a single, bright spotlight to follow the dancers. "It'll look like the black hole of Calcutta!" Donen protested. They struck a compromise.

Replacing dancer Eddie Phillips, Fosse performed the number with Verdon. It would be their only movie duet.

"The happiest times I ever had with Gwen," Fosse would say, "were when we were working together. They stimulated all sorts of things.

I mean they were fun, we had our own little jokes about rehearsals, we had something in common, I think it even affected sex." While in California, they rented a little house in Malibu, drove the red convertible Fosse called Baby up and down the coast, and visited with Gwen's son, Jimmy. Fosse knew she wanted another child. Not now, while they were on the rise, but soon.

Up late, alone, he'd call Joan in Fire Island. She had always loved the ocean, but now she needed it; the air was cool magic to what was left of her body, and living away from the theater she couldn't have was a welcome relief. But then the phone rang. And rang. At first, she'd hear only silence on the other end. Rather than ignore him, she took the call every time, leading his silence to dialogue and sustaining their conversation into the night. "I felt she was almost flattered by his bizarre behavior," said her companion Marc Adams. Joan would talk to Fosse about his depression, the failures only he saw. "I'm half Irish," he said, "which I suppose is my *up*, cheery, drinking side. And half Norwegian, which is very dark."

At night, his dark prevailed. When Fosse thought of his worthlessness, he thought of a woman, a sweet, sexy warm woman come to take him away. "I'm fascinated," Fosse admitted, "by that thin line between a person's jumping or not jumping, shooting himself or not shooting himself . . . like flirting with a girl." A flirtation that eventually would be consummated. "The problem," he said, "is you flirt so long that one day you may have to put up or shut up. I've come close to going that little step too far, just out of drunkenness, and not knowing how many sleeping pills I've swallowed. You forget, pop a couple more, and pretty soon you're in trouble." Fosse liked to joke about death and dying, but he was completely serious.

Certain nights, the pain was unbearable. That's when, if he was out of town, he'd pick up the phone. Or call a girl down the hall. Just talking helped. "An attraction to death is present in a high percentage of survivors of childhood trauma," said Dr. Charles Rousell. "These individuals frequently do not want to die but find reassurance in the fact that if emotional pain becomes unbearable they have the power to walk out that door. As they are survivors, often they never choose to do it but are soothed by the reassurance that the powerlessness they experienced as a child is replaced by the power they have as an adult. Childhood trauma survivors may also find themselves in endless pursuit of numbing agents, seeking prescription and recreational drugs, cigarettes, and alcohol."

That was the beautiful thing about amphetamines: they felt good. The warm release of dopamine gave a sense of well-being, even exhilaration. Energy increased. The heartbeat quickened; blood moved faster. Concentration, formerly expansive, homed in on close-range stimuli, things. Important things! For Fosse, punctuation, a drumbeat, a speck of dirt, dots; the amphetamines extracted total focus, obliterated unrelated thoughts (money, Jerome Robbins) and worry. There was no worry because there was no distraction. Only the sweet feeling of *bull's-eye,* of line-'em-up-and-knock-'em-down. Simply *doing* felt good. *Yes! There are thirty-six tasks to perform and I've performed all of them! Yes times thirty-six! I'm good* [dehydrated, malnourished, exhausted]*! I'm better than good! I'm five milligrams better! I'm ten better than five* [arrhythmia, hypertension]*! I see everything. I can do everything. I am everything. I am Jesus. They're trying to kill me. I heard them. I know what they're thinking. But I won't let them. I'm ten better than five! I'm five better than ten! What does he know? What do they know? They're not me. I'm me* [cardiac arrest]*! I'm better than me! Look!*

In 1937, the American Medical Association recommended Benzedrine to treat depression. Its side effects, like irritability and insomnia, both of which affected Fosse, were often addressed with a sedative barbiturate, like Seconal. The trick was to keep the balance: one for up, one for down. But there was no cause for concern: Psy-

chiatrists said amphetamines were not addictive, and they observed
no obvious physical withdrawal symptoms in their patients. Best
of all, people saw results. Athletes ran faster; Judy Garland worked
harder. The real-life equivalent of the Vitameatavegamin Lucy Ri-
cardo touted on her hugely popular sitcom, Benzedrine dried up
runny noses, gave energy to the weak, and, by 1959, it was regarded
almost as highly as aspirin and available in inhaler form without a
prescription. An estimated 3.5 billion doses were given nationwide.

And so, neither Fosse nor his psychiatrist, Dr. Clifford Sager,
would call Fosse's Seconal habit an addiction. When Fosse's lows
dropped too low, there was always Dexedrine to pick him up. But
the therapy itself weighed him down. Fosse found himself scrutiniz-
ing everything. Sometimes he'd spend a full day rehearsing a speech,
fogged in doubt, trying to analyze his behavior and then to analyze
his analysis. Was that good? Frustrated at himself, Fosse grew angry
at Dr. Sager. He skipped sessions. Was Sager's Freudian silence going
to make him into the kind of person who could sustain a loving relationship? Or into Fred Astaire?

Sager, a pioneer in the field of couples therapy, urged his clients
to make conscious the unconscious contracts they wrote with their
partners; he was among New York's most respected psychiatrists.
"Dr. Sager loved Bob, and Bob loved Dr. Sager," Ann Reinking said.
"Bob felt he genuinely wanted to help him." But Sager's specialty —
the strains of sex and marriage — conveyed only one dimension of
Fosse's struggle. An ailment far more elusive than domestic discomfort complicated his treatment. "Bob felt betrayed by his own work,
which he loved," Reinking said. "But there isn't a medicine for that,
for the psychological problems of show people. Everybody under-
stands cancer. But that's because they've been educated. Because in
show business, we're in a kind of rarefied world, this is an orphan
issue, how to protect your brains, body, and heart from the theater."

"Why can't I stop working?" Fosse would ask. "Why didn't my mother stop me? Why can't anyone stop me?"

It would be many years before psychiatrists began to understand narcissistic personality disorder, a condition that stems not from self-love but from the narcissist's feelings of utter worthlessness, often caused by a failed attachment to his caregivers early on. In ideal circumstances, Dr. Aaron Stern wrote, "Countless nurturing parental acts are employed to establish a critical level of dependency that will compel the child to view his parents as vital to his own personal survival. This dependent tie to the parents is the foundation on which the ability to love another person is built." Love, having been contaminated for the narcissist, is replaced with its thinnest simulacrum: self-gratification. Professional success, sexual conquest, power, food, drink, adulation, fame — healthy pleasures almost everyone pursues, in some degree — are, in extreme cases, pursued to the exclusion of genuine compassion. They become addictions.

"It was a constant conflict," Reinking said, "a vicious cycle of loving and running away, and he didn't know why because he wanted it badly." There it was — he could see it — happiness in real love, locked under a glass display case. Where was the key? "I don't define Bob as a complete narcissist," she added, "but there was a compounded, maybe lethal, amount in him." In order to appear capable of loving, the narcissist must razzle-dazzle. He must act the part. He must charm, produce, win, earn, score — anything for applause. But when the real thing comes back, he flees, for love is what wounded him in the first place. Efforts at intimacy become, as Reinking described it, a to-and-fro of "come closer, but stay back." Watch me from the front row; don't join me onstage. This one's a solo, and so is the next one, and the next. And the critics say it's never enough. "[The narcissist's] insatiable hungers are so great," wrote Stern, "that the slightest frustration can create the most intense pain, which often leads to depression. The more narcissistic among us are always around the corner from our next depression."

Fosse kept a spiral notebook marked "Odd Ideas" that chronicled his private self as it evolved in and out of his sessions. Challenging terms, mainly psychosexual and aesthetic concepts, were written over and over, as if he were a kid at a blackboard trying to commit them to memory. *Necrophilism, phlegmatic, narcolepsy* — each was accompanied by its definition. He collected images, like the one of a chorus girl who sat with her legs extended to keep her tights from stretching out. He collected scraps of dialogue. A short conversation between Fosse and Hal Prince concludes with Fosse saying, "I guess work is my religion." He had an idea for a therapy ballet set to a cacophony of psychoanalytic terminology that ends with the patient dancing off, happily cured, and the analyst climbing up a ladder in the middle of the stage to fix a flickering light bulb — then hanging himself.

TWENTY-EIGHT YEARS

DAVID HOCKER, FOSSE'S (and Leonard Bernstein's and Jerome Robbins's) agent at MCA, called to tell him about *Redhead,* a murder-mystery musical by lyricist Dorothy Fields, another client, and her brother Herbert Fields. In May 1958, looking for a choreographer, producers Robert Fryer and Lawrence Carr invited Fosse, Verdon, and Verdon's agent, Jack Davies, to meet at composer Albert Hague's apartment and assess their potential. The teaming of Fosse and Verdon tipped negotiations in the couple's favor. To lure one, a producer had to lure both, which gave Fosse and Verdon the cushier end of the bargain. When the moment came, Fosse, testing his new power, carefully suggested he might also play a small part in the show. The room held its smoky breath — but no one resisted him; with Verdon's participation still up in the air, Fryer and Carr had to keep every possibility in play. Fosse could be the bait. Noting this, Fryer and Carr excused themselves to a corner of the apartment, exchanged a few quiet words, and returned to the group.

"Bob," they said. "Would you like to *direct* the show?"

Verdon spoke for him. "Yes!"

"We can do this now," Hocker said. "We're all here."

The room agreed. They were all there.

Fosse?

"Guys," he said haltingly, "I'm a little overcome . . . You think I might take a little time?"

The moment he got back to his apartment, he picked up the phone. "Yes," he said. "I'll do it."

Marian Niles had started him in nightclubs. Joan McCracken had encouraged him to think bigger. Gwen Verdon, though she would deny it the rest of her life, made him a director.

"Wonderful."

"But," Fosse said, "the book has to be rewritten a little. It's not really right for Gwen."

"Fine. Fine."

"I'd like to do it myself."

Unwilling to rewrite with this untested director, the show's latest author, Sidney Sheldon, told Verdon that she would have to bring in another writer, a real writer, if she wanted further changes to the book. She suggested David Shaw, who had written the script for her 1954 television debut ("Native Dancer," an episode of *Goodyear Playhouse*), and Shaw was brought aboard. Verdonizing *Redhead,* which essentially meant slashing subplots to make room for dances, took Shaw (and, to a certain extent, Fosse) the whole summer, during which time Fosse and Verdon cast the show.

Actor Leonard Stone was among the first to be seen for the role of George Poppett, the murderer. Having never auditioned for a Broadway musical, Stone had no idea how he was going to get through the afternoon.

As he had expected, his number fizzled. Standing on the stage, hands in his pockets, Stone looked up to get his "Thank you very much."

"Do you need more time?" Fosse asked. "Would you like to do it again?"

Stone squinted into the black, trying to get a look at the face behind the gentle voice. All he caught was the red burn of a cigarette and a swirl of smoke drifting up to the balcony.

"Take your time," he heard.

It was as if the smoke were talking.

Fosse gave his hopefuls infinite leash, auditioning everyone who trembled across the stage as he would wish to be auditioned himself. Each one, he wanted to give the part. Rooting openly for their success, encouraging them on through missed steps and slips out of key, Fosse used "No" as his last recourse, and it was less a judgment against the performers than an indictment of Fosse's own inability to make them shine.

"Mr. Stone," Gwen added now. "You're doing fine."

Stone took his time and tried his best. Still not good enough.

"Thank you very much," Fosse called out. "Would you step down here, please?"

Dazed, Stone drifted offstage and into the house.

"Have a seat," Fosse said as Stone approached him and Gwen, ten seats from the orchestra.

Fosse smiled. "You got the part."

"What? Are you joking? I can't dance!"

"That makes two of us." Fosse laughed. "She's the only one here who can dance."

Gwen rolled her eyes.

"Would you mind staying through the rest of the auditions?"

"What?" Stone scanned their faces for the punch line. "Really?"

"Just watch with us and tell us what you think. Would you mind?"

Five hundred dancers, singers, and actors later, *Redhead* was cast. "At the end of every audition," Stone said, "Fosse gave the most heartfelt thanks to every performer. Sometimes he would go up onstage and put his arm around them and thank them personally. It really seemed sincere, even with the bad ones. Those were the hardest for him. When he excused them to leave, you could see his heart break. He was determined not to let them fail." Producer Robert Fryer said, "When [Richard Kiley] auditioned for *Redhead*, he was so nervous that Gwen and Bobby sang with him to give him confidence. Out came that great voice, and Kiley got the lead."

Fosse kept his envy in check throughout. "I'd do anything to be up there," he said to Stone. "Even be down here."

"You're the director. Give yourself a part."

"I did," Fosse said. "Yours."

"Mine?"

"Don't worry. They talked me out of it." Fosse would hold out for a role in the London production.

Rehearsals began in October of 1958 with dancers in one room and actors in another at the Variety Arts Studios, 225 West Forty-Sixth Street. A gray building like any other, Variety Arts housed fifteen individual studio spaces and one switchboard operator — Edith, who answered the phone in her thick New York accent, collected the dollar-per-hour rehearsal-room fee, and stood guard over a massive blackboard schedule of rehearsals and auditions listed by show name and producer as she responded to the very standard but very nervous questions of what time and how many and in which room on which of the building's four floors. "Edith knew absolutely everything that was going on in town," dancer Dan Siretta said. "She knew who was looking for what and who was doing what to who." To divide and conquer, Fosse brought on Donald McKayle, an assistant on *Copper and Brass*, and charged him with choreographing the "Uncle Sam Rag," which Fosse intended to parody Englishmen trying to dance to a low-down American rag. For two nights, McKayle struggled to cull humor from gesture. Fosse, checking in, felt his heart sink. He'd wanted to see personalities in culture clash, but instead he saw plain mincing, silliness instead of satire. The following day, his fears worsened. The time period was most definitely off; *Redhead* was set in the 1880s, but the steps were crowded with 1920s clichés. Testing his artillery, Fosse instructed McKayle to redo the choreography. They should be dancing throughout, Fosse said, even when they were singing. For the next three weeks, the dancers groaned through McKayle's innumerable variations on the "Uncle Sam Rag," none of them in keeping with Fosse's mandates. In a last-ditch effort, Fosse presented McKayle with certain poses and postures to use, small hand gestures and limb extensions, but they never seemed to survive all the bouncing around.

With only a few days until the company set out for New Haven, Fryer, Carr, Fields, Hague, Shaw, Fosse, and Verdon gathered once more at Variety Arts to see the rag's progress, and once more they were let down. Where were the touches, the little details Fosse's own numbers had? A raised hat, a limp wrist, a cocked shoulder, a carefully chosen pantomime — each gesture put a point on a dancer's character, like a colored handkerchief in a tuxedo pocket. More than that, the isolated move's cool negation of big Broadway dance could be very funny, ironic even; it was as if the dancers were playing at dancing more than actually dancing. McKayle's choreography didn't have that. As *Redhead*'s co-author David Shaw noticed, he simply didn't have the — what was the word for it?

Style. He didn't have the style.

With no other recourse, Fosse took back the number in early December 1958 and led his team to New Haven, where, to the shock of the dancers he loved and who loved him, the company was drilled to death. "He had changed," Harvey Evans said. "It wasn't as fun as *New Girl in Town* or the movie of *Pajama Game*. He was feeling the pressure like he never had before. He was a director now. He even started looking harder." Fosse replaced his boyish sweater vests and slacks with skinny dance pants and suede desert boots. He looked like a stripe, "a slick dandy," Leonard Stone said. Fosse's all-black uniform was as lean, as precise, as the emerging style he struggled to describe to McKayle. "He was getting scary," said dancer Margery Beddow, who also had known Fosse since *The Pajama Game*. "He was a slave driver," Stone added. "He wouldn't let us mark any of the steps. '*Una más!*' he'd say. '*Una más! Una más!* Get on your toes! Get up! Up! Up!' We didn't know why he was going at us so hard. He had fixed the 'Uncle Sam Rag' and the show was starting to look pretty good." But pretty good wasn't good enough. Fosse made them rehearse on Sunday, their day off, and on a slippery floor unsafe for his new order: they were to do grand jetés around the room. Scared and angry, one of the dancers approached producer Larry Carr. "You've got to give the dancers a break," Carr then said to Fosse, "or they're going to die here." A break was not what the amphetamines had in mind. A break would not guard him from the critics; it would not hurry up perfection.

There were no excuses now, no Abbotts to blame if the show went awry. There were dozens of ready dancers looking his way, waiting for Bob Fosse to be brilliant, again, a hundred times a day. Each person had one head, two legs, two arms, two hands. Each hand had five fingers. Each finger had a position. But only one choice was brilliant. "He would spend three hours on two counts of eight," one dancer said. "He would fix the height of the leg, the height of the fingers. Are they spread? Are they together? Is your hand at shoulder level; is it at ear level? He would fix the foot. Don't point with the toe; point with the heel. You're not lifting together. Don't turn out, turn in. Keep the knee forward to the audience. You want to punch the balcony rail with your knee." Sometimes Fosse had two cigarettes going, one in his hand and the other, the one he forgot about, in his mouth.

Fosse could be incredibly hard on his dancers, extensions of his own talent. "He was so influenced by all the stories about Jack Cole, Jerry Robbins, and how they used to pick on one dancer," Harvey Evans said, "and he did that in *Redhead*. The change in him was astounding." It was an unfair, but effective, approach: he found scapegoating a single dancer ignited the entire company. "I saw Bob get really mean with people," said another dancer. "It was degrading. Sometimes it was to get what he wanted from people and sometimes it was just because he was in a mood. It was painful to watch." Shouting, swearing, insults, demands. Often it was the smallest errors, like a leg not high enough, that set Fosse off. And in public, in front of everyone, he yelled. It was humiliating. "Yes, he could be cruel," one cast member said, "but only superficially. You knew behind whatever was going on, Bob was probably doing it for the good of the show. There was a plan." That his scapegoats were often women and often beautiful encouraged the sort of gossip the truth couldn't always undo. Was Fosse hardest on the girls he slept with? Or was he hardest on the ones he wanted to sleep with? The dressing room was a greenhouse for speculation and Bob Fosse the midnight sun. His persuasive combination of charisma, looks, and reputation made him the perfect target for good and bad, a theory that proved itself. "There were rumors he had a big dick," Harvey Evans remembered. "Even then, in the fifties."

Redhead changed every night of its ten-night run in New Haven. Jokes were the problem — they weren't working. New ones had to be written in the hours after the performance so they could be tested in the next day's rehearsal before they were put into the show that night. The script was significantly revised multiple times. "It got so we used a different color binder for each script that was changed," said David Shaw. "Four times we ran out of colors and had to use numbers." New songs, continually being written, had to be rewritten, arranged, scored, copied, distributed to the orchestra, rehearsed, and then revised, costing whole days of rehearsal time and upwards of $2,500 a number, and then the songs were often discarded. Scrambling, Hague and Fields wrote two new numbers — "Look Who's in Love" and "Back in Circulation" — in a day and a half. They both made it to Washington — a relief to all — but in Philadelphia, the truth became frighteningly clear: what *Redhead* needed was a new book.

To compensate for the script, Gwen Verdon — Fosse's best defense — shot into overdrive. "Essie's Dream" was by far the most challenging dance of her life. A ballet of thirty minutes that consisted of five parts — jazz, cancan, gypsy, military march, and music hall — was held together by some of the fastest costume changes Fosse had yet devised, and, of course, Gwen Verdon appeared in every section, twirling, kicking, clowning, and, once, flying. "She had an entrance in that ballet that was the best thing I've ever seen," said dancer Margery Beddow. "She was in the wings on top of a table and she jumped off the table and onto a trampoline and *dove* out on the stage absolutely horizontal." *Thirty minutes.* One night, in the middle of the ballet, Verdon turned to Harvey Evans, who was gasping for breath — they both were — and said, "I'm having the time of my life." He would never forget it. "We don't know how Gwen did it," Evans said. "The boys would come offstage almost vomiting from working so hard, and Gwen would run back out, with no break, and keep going." To keep her weight up, she guzzled root-beer floats, hot chocolate, and milk shakes, and she drank honey from the bottle as Fosse looked on in awe. She was a machine, *his* machine. Unchecked freedom terrified Fosse, but it invigorated her. "This is the first time in my life I haven't been scared," she said. Gwen had stolen *Can-Can* and *Damn Yankees; Redhead,* Fosse gave to her. Every night, she gave it back. To him, to them.

One night in Philadelphia, during "The Pickpocket Tango," the row of metal bars — as long as the stage and just as high — that was supposed to be slowly lowered from above landed hard on Gwen's feet. She cried out and fell backward. The audience gasped.

"Pull the curtain!" yelled a dancer. "Somebody pull the curtain!"

Fosse ran down the center aisle, literally leaped over the orchestra pit, and scooped her in his arms. "Pull the goddamned curtain!" he screamed, and the curtain fell.

Verdon claimed to be well enough to go on, but Fosse refused to let her. Someone asked after her understudy, and the answer came back: she was out sick. Would this mean someone *else* would go on for Gwen? The question rippled through the chorus.

"I think it's okay," Verdon said, lying. "I don't think it's broken."

"Thank the Lord it didn't fall on your head," Fosse said.

"I wish it had. I'm a dancer."

When *Redhead* opened at the Forty-Sixth Street Theater on February 5, 1959, New York saw a full evening of Fosse for the first time. The book problems had not been resolved, but the story of Essie Whimple, an innocent girl in a ghoulish world, suited his style as no story had before, showcasing his penchants for both menace and fun. As the wag of Verdon's finger could be played for either *ohh*s or *aww*s, Fosse's isolations — his adjectives — could be tender or naughty, satirical or sincere. They showed finesse. Writing in *The New Yorker*, Kenneth Tynan observed, "The amount of physical activity in which this frail-seeming creature indulges is perfectly flabbergasting; spinning, prancing, leaping, curvetting, she is seldom out of sight and never out of breath. Yet beneath the athletic ebullience is something more rarified — an unfailing delicacy of spirit."

And *Redhead*'s milieu suited Fosse's fascinations. The daughter of a vaudeville father (who abandoned her), Essie runs from death: there's a murderer on the loose. She creates wax models for a "New and Blood Curdling Exhibit — the Strangler and the Dancing Girl," selling filth for entertainment. In other words, Essie's in showbiz — and so is *Redhead*. Her dancehall history allowed Fosse to fashion the show into a medley of variety acts, each one a parody. "Uncle Sam Rag" was a gavotte burlesque, "Two Faces in the Dark" a hypersentimental Victorian duet, and, in the end, the chase for the killer was played à la Keystone Cops. The whole of *Redhead* had an air of performance, as if the show were about putting on a show. One day, that conceit would attain ontological significance—the performances we take for real life. For now, Fosse was just browsing his strengths. "Perhaps in the future," Brooks Atkinson concluded his review, "all musical comedies should be written by choreographers."

A short time later, on April 12, 1959, Bob Fosse won his third Tony for best choreography (beating Agnes de Mille), Gwen won her fourth, and *Redhead* was named outstanding musical of the year. True to form, Fosse would not accept the show's triumph as his own, though everyone else on Broadway noted his promotion from wunderkind choreographer to major director. The discrepancy between his outward success and his inward "failings" further alienated Fosse from the exciting changes around him. "By the time I got to New York, in the early sixties," said one dancer, "everyone wanted to be in a Bob Fosse show. If you were in a Fosse show, you knew you had arrived."

Bob and Gwen lived in a penthouse apartment at 91 Central Park West, a beige fifteen-story prewar building on the corner of Sixty-Ninth Street. From their terrace, vast enough to hold a vegetable garden, a Ping-Pong table, and dog run for Gwen's pets, they could watch the park below, and on fair-weather days they could entertain their small group of friends, most of them carryovers from their Long Island summers and weekends. On those afternoons, Gwen had trees and potted plants moved out to the balustrade and set up a tent and awning for shade. With high vaulted ceilings and large mirrors, the apartment itself was fairly majestic but Gwen did her best to simplify, stationing little found objects about the floor, and antiques around the living room. They loved crafts. As Fosse and McCracken had, Fosse and Verdon spent weekend time combing junkyards, beaches, and secondhand stores in search of the perfect old lamp, which they would then rehabilitate for that handmade look ex-beatniks of the Upper West Side had begun to favor. Their Tonys were not on display.

With afternoon rehearsals and evening performances, theirs or others, Fosse and Verdon didn't have much free time. Anyway, they weren't the scene type. They preferred to spend a night off at home, if not alone, then visiting with the Jule Stynes, the Sydney Chaplins, the Neil Simons, or, when he was in New York, Buddy Hackett (for dinner at Rao's). Though he enjoyed his fame, Fosse shied away from large gatherings. They were performances, too much like work. Instead, he had the guys over for poker or joined a game at Cy Coleman's, at his apartment nearby. They talked sports. To Fosse, a lifelong fan, football and baseball were essential television. He loved the Mets, the losers. "He admired the difficulty of being an athlete," Ann Reinking said. "The training, the discipline, the talent." Gwen didn't care about sports, but she loved having him home. Going back and forth from the kitchen to the TV, her shoes off to exercise the muscles in her toes, she kept the beer and pretzels flowing, occasionally attempting and failing to interest him in an eggplant or zucchini from the terrace garden. An avowed progressive in health matters, Gwen was on the nutrition train fairly early, cooking (instead of red meat) spaghetti and clam sauce and interrupting stirs with pliés. Rather than keeping the spices close by, she put them high up in a cupboard that was most easily reachable by an arabesque.

She was also early on the brain train. An active and outspoken proponent of psychoanalysis, Verdon regularly donated time and resources to the Postgraduate Center for Mental Health, the oldest low-cost psychiatric clinic in New York City. The Gwen Verdon that longed for a complete family, that lived to serve Jack Cole and then Bob Fosse, was devoted to helping children with physical disabilities, teaching them, as little Gwen in her orthopedic boots had been taught, how to get better through exercise and movement. To raise awareness, Fosse and Verdon gave premiere benefits and hosted fundraising dinner parties on their long panoramic terrace. One Postgraduate Center affair, luau themed, "made Bob such a nervous wreck," said a friend, "buzzing around worrying about the tent and the food." These were brain people, some of them from Gwen's group therapy, some of them mental-health professionals, likely to put Fosse on the defensive. "Come and get your food!" he announced at the event, and the whole party moved outside to see the tent blow off the terrace and spin down over the park. "Well," Fosse said, "there goes our fucking dinner."

Everything was two things; their collaboration crossed with love, and they danced a paradox. "You could see they really cared about each other," Leonard Stone said, "but Bob played the husband. He did it for her." Signs of the arrangement shadowed the place. "Most of it was hers," Stone said. "The paintings, the furniture." Gypsy life trained Fosse to live out of a suitcase, a lifestyle marriage did not reform. New York was his apartment. He still stayed out late, rehearsing. He went for drinks with the cast after the show; Gwen, exhausted, went home. When Fosse girled around, he girled around, but mostly at a discreet distance from Gwen, respectful of her star status, her invaluable assistance, and her emotional support, the years she'd spent darning the holes in his ego, threading her patient needle through his every burst of panic. Verdon was his night seamstress, on the nights he came home. How many women were there? "How d'you do it?" hairdresser Vidal Sassoon asked Fosse one night at dinner. "Showers," Fosse replied. "Hot showers." Some nights it seemed silly to follow Gwen uptown. His mind on tomorrow, he'd take a room at the Edison Hotel next door to Variety Arts. "All I need," Fosse said, "is a rehearsal studio and bedroom — preferably attached. I could spend all my time going from one to the other." And he did.

For dinner parties, Fosse and Verdon appeared together. At David Shaw's house in Amagansett, they met Paddy Chayefsky, Bronx-born mensch of the proletariat, playwright lion of television's golden age, and Oscar-winning screenwriter of *Marty*. His titanic intellect triggered Fosse's clam mechanism, and Fosse retreated to the back row of his personality, a bit scared of the fiery, funny, rabbinical grizzly bear holding court across the table, like Tevye by way of Sky Masterson. Chayefsky was a thought dancer, and his brain was his stage. Bursting with ideas and controversy, and as informed as a newsstand on Monday morning, he could argue either side of any debate, social or cultural, political or religious, pastrami or corned beef. He could beat himself and still win. Paddy Chayefsky was an artist, Fosse decided, maybe an entertainer on the side, but a writer first and last, a generator of stories, not lucky or slick but a real talent. Was Fosse?

With Gwen on or off his arm, Fosse was fodder for Louella Parsons's column and high up on every producer's call sheet. Agents dropped scripts at his feet for him to read whenever he could find the time. He began talks to oversee *Viva!*, a Pancho Villa musical, and briefly considered a musical of *The Farmer's Daughter*, by *Redhead*'s producers, Fryer and Carr, before switching to *Saturday Night*, a show with songs by Stephen Sondheim. An old work predating his *West Side Story* and *Gypsy* streak, *Saturday Night* was to be Sondheim's debut as composer-lyricist — prior to this, it had been lyrics only. Set in Brooklyn in the late twenties, the small-scale show followed the romantic and get-rich-quick schemes of a group of working-class kids on the eve of the stock-market crash. Acting as producer, Jule Styne knew the project would appeal to Fosse; he delivered the material to him, and talks progressed through the summer of 1959. "Bobby wanted to both direct and star in it," said Sondheim. "Though I had only seen him in movies, I had every reason to believe he'd be fine in the part. So we started having auditions for other actors and I think we had maybe one or two audition sessions and I got a feeling in the pit of my stomach that I didn't want to go back to old work and so I stopped it. And that was that."

By September, the director was directing again, this time for NBC as part of a package put together by Fosse's agents at MCA, the biggest, most powerful agency in the world (and soon to be investigated for antitrust violations). Stocked with MCA talent *and* produced by MCA executives, *Ford Startime* was a vaudeville-style anthology series of sketches, dramatic scenes, and star-filled musical numbers. Fosse's episode, "The Wonderful World of Entertainment," he codirected with Kirk Browning. Fosse and Browning split rehearsal duty, Browning focusing on the scenes and Fosse on the numbers, which he populated with a handful of dancers from *Redhead* sure to know his style and produce results fast. He drove them on for as much as eleven hours at a stretch but never went later than 7:15, when the caravan of limousines appeared to rush his dancers back to Broadway for their half-hour calls. The pressure was worse than anything he had known in the theater. "A TV show is put together so quickly," said dancer Sharon Shore, who was in the production, "there just isn't time for dances as intricate as those in the theater." At rehearsal's end, Fosse would, on occasion, drop by *Redhead* to see that its screws were tightly turned, but only on occasion. Tampering with an old show was walking across quicksand; at any moment, he could be sucked into a bottomless hole of self-doubt and lose faith in the entire enterprise. Fosse's assistants were a tremendous help in this respect, keeping an eye on the show, catching its accidental shifts — missed beats, slack cues — and reversing them before they got serious. Every morning, Fosse would be back at NBC's studios in Brooklyn.

As its title indicates, "The Wonderful World of Entertainment" gave Fosse an excuse to showcase his facility for performance styles, from vaudeville ("Ain't We Got Fun?" was a favorite) to flapper to ballet, all under the protective cover of spoof — a strategy Fosse had been refining for years and had finally perfected in *Redhead*. But it was Fosse's growing interest in eerie sensuality and in an all-black jazz look he borrowed from "Essie's Dream" that made the special momentous.

The first filmed ensemble in Fosse's signature style, "Let Me Entertain You," featured a clump of scarecrow-looking dancers in clown makeup, each in full-body black topped off with a black porkpie hat. They slunk in coagulated discontinuity, squirming en masse like a can of horny worms. The formation that would come to be known as an amoeba came to Fosse by way of coffee-table books — a great deal of his work did. Verdon said, "He was intrigued by the surrealist painters. Not just Dalí, but Hieronymus Bosch. I don't know if you're familiar with, you know, people being born out of big eggs with eight arms and legs . . . I mean having flowers for tails and a lot more than that. And people all joined together and freaks."

Before he took *Redhead* on the road, Fosse joined *The Girls Against the Boys* in Philadelphia, a few weeks before it was to open and, most likely, close. A goofball revue starring Bert Lahr, Nancy Walker, and Dick Van Dyke, the show needed a full overhaul, and fast. Unlike his *Copper and Brass* agreement, which forced Fosse to retain Sokolow's work, Fosse's present contract granted him complete approval of all artistic elements. "Fosse told us he was going to be assigning new things every day," said dancer Buzz Halliday. "And from there, it was total lunacy. I couldn't believe how quickly the ideas came. We were working so fast, I slept at the theater literally every night. Equity never knew." To inject some semblance of continuity into the sketches and the numbers, Fosse devised a series of fourth-wall-breaking, vaudeville-inspired, "Ya ready for the next number, folks?" segues. It made for cheap ligature, but Fosse loved showing the seams; it was chintzy, but unveiling desperate artistic straits struck him as real showbiz, clumsy and honest. And real showbiz it was: During the actual run, before actual audiences, Fosse would pass messages to the stage manager, who would shout them to the actors in the split seconds before they went on. "What a rush!" Halliday said. "So much had to be improvised and so much of it was about what was actually going on and going wrong. The curtain would come down between a number and a sketch and I would get the word from the stage manager to call out to Dick [Van Dyke], 'Hey, Dick, get ready for the next sketch! These people are waiting!'" Given all that metatheatrical hoofing, maybe the audience wouldn't see the dud they were seeing. (They did. *The Girls Against the Boys* played sixteen performances and died.)

What happened to the show didn't matter. Whether the production was a hit or a miss, Fosse's name would stay off the playbill, sparing him public embarrassment. He did *The Girls Against the Boys* for the work. Work: it wasn't like living, but not doing it was a lot like being dead. "Part of the work ethic," he said, "is probably a way of saying, 'You forgot me, folks. I want to remind you I'm here.'" Why stop? So Robbins could do another *West Side Story*? Hal Prince said, "I told him, 'I care as much about the theater as you do, but there's always another musical. Life, however, is not a show. Life is life. This is the only one you've got.' Bobby could never quite believe it. I thought, *Jesus, this guy is not going to live a long life.*"

One night in April 1960, Fosse called Joan McCracken. He told her where he was — in Chicago, on the road with *Redhead* and Gwen — and asked her if she ever thought about getting back together with him. Her answer was no.

The following day, on April 2, 1960, Fosse and Verdon took out a license and wed in a secret ceremony in Oak Park, Illinois. "We married because we were going to have a child," she would explain years later. "And a child needs that protection." To be a mother again, to have a complete family; it was what she had always wanted. After *Redhead* — the incessant gruel of it, the joy of it — she would take a few years off to raise the baby. Fosse? "I finally decided that I was as grown up as I'd ever be."

He had been running away from fatherhood his whole life. Surprise pregnancy and subsequent abortion had trailed him as far back as his teenage years, his time spent on the road, blackened by burlesque rim shots and human sludge. Though Fosse kept trying for clarity, healing still largely evaded him. Five years earlier, he had begun psychotherapy with the intention of breaking, or at least examining, his ruinous relationships with women. But the longer he tried to understand why he couldn't trust intimacy, the closer he came to understanding he never would, until he saw isolation as a fact of his constitution, as much a part of him as his talent, or his hopelessness.

Now that Fosse had finally remarried, he wondered if it would be appropriate to end his therapy with Dr. Sager. It had been helpful in many ways, mostly work-related; for everything the analysis did not accomplish, Fosse naturally blamed himself. But when he realized his dependency on Seconal was more of an addiction, he turned his anger on Sager and stopped both the drug and his analyst cold turkey. Despairing, he resigned himself to accepting that the pitch-blackest part of him — the remembered child in the dark of the Silver Cloud — might never be illuminated.

The search continued for a meaningful follow-up to *Redhead*, something important, a musical comedy of real substance. He knew that by turning humanity's most profound dilemmas into sources of amusement, he might prove himself to be, maybe, deeper than a mere song-and-dance man. Reinking said, "He knew that in order to be a great artist on Broadway, he'd have to have the dark as much as the light." But how? Searching with Fosse was producer Robert Whitehead, recently appointed, with Elia Kazan, to establish a repertory theater at Lincoln Center. The combination of Whitehead and Kazan, who flooded Broadway with O'Neill, Odets, Williams, Inge, and Miller, made any project an artistic behemoth, resplendent with good taste and intelligence; without question, this new concern would be no exception. It was instantly proclaimed the most exciting development in American theater in a long time. Whitehead's call must have surprised Bob Fosse.

Whitehead liked the idea of musicalizing *The Madwoman of Chaillot* with Alfred Lunt and Lynn Fontanne. Lunt and Fontanne didn't, though, and Fosse presented his benefactor with another idea: a musical of Preston Sturges's 1944 film *Hail the Conquering Hero*, about a milquetoast ex-Marine mistakenly believed to be a war hero. The coupling of fraudulence and fame had strong personal resonance for Fosse. Played in the film by Eddie Bracken, Woodrow Lafayette Pershing Truesmith spends the bulk of the picture imploring his family and the community at large to understand that he isn't a war hero but regular old Woodrow, a loser who was discharged because of his hay fever and who never saw any action. Of course, no one believes him. Woodrow's honesty is taken for extreme modesty, further proof of his nobility, which puts the poor "hero" in the front of a Kafkaesque victory march.

Whitehead got it. The story gave Fosse satirical opportunities from nearly every angle, and its attention to phoniness, to the idea of putting on a show, metaphorically speaking, was a handy entrée to song and dance. Music and lyrics went to Morris "Moose" Charlap and Norman Gimbel; book to comedy writer Larry Gelbart, who wrote Fosse's episode of *Ford Startime*; and the lead to young TV star Tom Poston — all relatively new to their careers, the men would be easier for Fosse to command. Undoubtedly, Fosse's star shone brightest. On *Conquering Hero*, only Whitehead stood above him.

In October 1960, after Fosse's usual period of studio isolation, the company gathered for the first read-through at a rehearsal space on the top floor of the New Amsterdam Theater. Abandoned for decades, the main stage — once home to Fanny Brice and George M. Cohan — had deteriorated, lush clump by lush clump, splashing green and gold pieces of art nouveau into the rainwater that filled the orchestra pit. Upstairs in the limbo of chipped porticoes and forgotten props, Fosse apologized for the cold and dust and led the company through Gelbart's book.

Gwen was there, watching them and watching Fosse. In the days leading up to rehearsal, he had been acting strangely. The amphetamines made him jumpy and impatient, and there were, of course, his dark, dark nights, but by now those were par for the course. This Fosse was scaring her. Certain days he refused to go to work. He wouldn't leave the apartment. He stopped sleeping. He was paranoid. He hallucinated. Pacing about the room, he had screamed at a cheap Mexican statue of Jesus, imploring it to save him: "*Why don't You help me?*"

It was the amphetamines. Sitting in her seat close to the stage, Gwen watched, looking for signs of another outburst.

That day, Larry Gelbart arrived halfway through rehearsals in time to hear Tom Poston reading lines — narration for a war ballet — that Gelbart, the writer, hadn't written. Baffled, he approached Fosse the next chance he got and asked about the new stuff.

"You were off fucking around somewhere," Fosse hissed. "*Somebody* had to make the changes."

The Conquering Hero was Gelbart's first Broadway show; he didn't know how things worked exactly, but he knew rudeness when he saw it. "Well, now that I'm back," he said, "I'd like to do it myself. I see what you want."

Slowly, Fosse turned away from the table of actors. Gelbart saw his skin was white and wet. Fosse looked possessed. As he opened his mouth to speak or yell, a sick-sounding gurgle ripped from his body and he tipped backward in his chair, gasping and twisting as if having a seizure. The company froze. There were screams. Gwen raced to his aid; she scooped Fosse into her arms the way he had scooped her up a year ago, after the *Redhead* set crushed her foot, and rushed him from the room. "She saw it coming," said actor John McMartin. "Gwen could tell. I don't know how."

It was a grand-mal seizure. Later, Fosse would attribute his epilepsy to a head injury he'd sustained in a horseback-riding accident many years earlier. The explanation wasn't out of the question; he did love horses. He loved the way they moved. And it's true he took Dilantin, an anticonvulsant. "It was always controlled by something," Gwen explained. "Anyway, he had an allergy. He was on three different medications and apparently it didn't mix." In an unpublished interview, Fosse offered another explanation — barbiturate withdrawal. "I got hooked on Seconal and he [Dr. Sager, Fosse's psychiatrist] didn't realize it," he said. "He had prescribed it and he wasn't aware what was happening. When I went cold turkey after I stopped using it, I had an epileptic seizure." At the time, 1960, rumors that an individual had epilepsy and drug addiction would provoke suspicious stares and put off producers, so Verdon and Fosse kept the truth to themselves and proceeded to New Haven in November, putting out fires as best they could.

The show itself was another matter. Fosse's idea for a grand antiwar ballet laden with satire (and with narration Gelbart hadn't written) disgusted Whitehead. Musical comedy, he believed, was no place for commentary about, let alone critiques of, the American military or its policy of spinning truth. "That ballet frightened the management," dancer Dick Korthaze said. "It was heavily satirical with an underlying darkness." Girl dancers played the Japanese soldiers; boys played the Americans. Dancer Margery Beddow remembered the antiwar ballet to contain "some of the most innovative work Fosse ever did." As they danced—the Japanese soldiers with knives in their teeth, the U.S. soldiers with gold glitter in their hair—Truesmith's mother, almost offstage, bragged into the phone (in Fosse's prose) about what she thought her son was doing in the South Pacific, as perhaps Fosse's mother might have bragged about what she thought Fosse was doing in late-night dives decades before. With overt theatricality and broadly pantomimed stereotypes, the ballet gave voice to an uncomfortable irony: that wishful thinking, like propaganda, was in its own way a form of show business, a myth of virtue that the nation — personified by Truesmith's mother — told itself. Whitehead rightly glimpsed, buried in the critique, a certain hostility toward the audience members who wanted to enjoy their entertainment guilt-free. Now Fosse was telling them they, like the rest of America, were fools to be duped so easily. Nor was Whitehead pleased with Fosse's parody of a political rally, a number danced to a campaign speech written in political gibberish. "Every time a word [of Truesmith's] was emphasized," Beddow said, "we'd take up the cry and start a different kind of dance to it. Even when he sneezed, we began a Spanish heel dance as we chanted, 'Ah-choo, ah-choo, ah-choo.'"

Here was Fosse's opportunity to make a meaningful statement and become a serious director, to show that war, media, and political personas were nothing more than show, an arrangement between foolers and fooled. Televisions in every home blurred the lines between news and entertainment, content and image; the censuring of Joseph McCarthy and the recent quiz-show infractions of NBC precipitated concerns over what really *is*. Fosse would have agreed with Daniel J. Boorstin, whose book *The Image* appeared that very year and bore out the national taste for razzle-dazzle and flimflam or, as Boorstin put it, "the thicket of unreality which stands between us and the facts of life." *The Conquering Hero* shouted out its cynical assent; razzle-dazzle was its medium and its message. "I'm not bothered when people refer to the razzle-dazzle aspects of my work," Fosse said, "though I think sometimes I put so many coats of paint on a thing that nobody looks to find out *what* I've painted. I mean, I stick on bugle beads and sequins until people don't see what I'm saying."

Joining Whitehead against Fosse, Gelbart shrugged off *Hero's* quote-unquote big ideas. "Bobby was getting ideas for the first time," he said. "Ideas that had been around a long time . . . but he was very enamored of them because they were new to him." Yet in musical comedy, there was no precedent for protest in choreography or for Fosse's antiwar, anti-razzle-dazzle view of national procedure. In the early sixties, dissent was not yet the fashion.

Meanwhile, Tom Poston was falling flat. "Tom wasn't right for the part," said Patricia Ferrier. "There was a weakness about him, a kind of vanilla thing. He was a good second banana, but this required more." Fosse grew furious at his leading man. (John McMartin said, "I thought, watching him, *Is he going to have another seizure?*") As if to compensate for what wasn't happening, which was everything, Fosse — already at the brink — pushed his company even harder, right over the edge, almost losing them completely. For he had not only the power to make incredible demands but also, with the Dexedrine, the physical strength and mania to shout anyone with opposing views out of the theater. "His behavior became so erratic and energetic," Beddow said, "that nobody could keep up with him." They went to war. Fosse argued that rehearsing and rehearsing and rehearsing ad infinitum even the smallest detail, like a twitch or the tiniest back bump, improved the dance; dancers saw diminishing returns. "If you watch what happens to rats when they're given stimulants," said Dr. Robert Bilder, professor of psychiatry and psychology at UCLA, "you can see as you increase the dose, they become more and more active, but in a reduced number of categories of behavior. So at low doses they may run more on the wheel or check out the water bottle or groom themselves, but when the dose gets higher, they spend all their time just licking their forepaws, licking and licking and licking and licking, over and over and over again. They don't do anything else. So it's not that they're being more productive, it's that they're spending more of their time engaged in a reduced subset of all the possible things they could be doing." Whitehead, Gelbart, Charlap, and many of the dancers who would ordinarily jump to Fosse's aid were mowed down by his oblique and tireless intractability.

"This is a busy bee among musicals," wrote the *Hartford Courant* the night of the first preview. "Twenty-five scenes, a cast as long as your arm, a tootling score, an atmosphere of brass bands and cheering crowds, dances that prance from Guadalcanal to Election Eve, and everybody on stage all the time." Problems with the book were manifest, and Gelbart considered himself available for revisions, but his instructions to revise never came. They didn't come for Whitehead either. Or Poston. Fosse was either deaf to their pleas or off with Verdon, fixated on minutiae.

What to do? Gelbart mused at one point. He and Whitehead were at a bar, drinking for ideas. Whitehead hung his head and changed the subject, slightly. "I wonder what the Israelis are going to do with Adolf Eichmann after the trial is over."

"They ought to send him out of town with a musical."

Out of town in Washington, late in November 1960, revolution seemed inevitable. But which side would shoot first? "That's when people started to get replaced," McMartin said. "They even auditioned me to replace Tom [Poston], though at the time, I had no idea that's what they were doing. I just did a few things for them out in the hall. I was too green to know that they didn't want us knowing that they didn't know what to do."

I want to do it, Fosse told Whitehead on the evening of December 1.

They had just endured another horrific preview performance and could think of no one else to replace Poston.

Whitehead laughed. "You?"

Somewhere near midnight, both sides drifted into the darkened theater and waited — Fosse in the wings, the rest in the house. It was probably what Fosse had wanted all along: *The Conquering Hero* — conceived, directed, choreographed, written by (in part), and starring Bob Fosse. And, in a perverse way, it was probably what Whitehead and the rest had been waiting for: the moment when their maniac got so high on himself, they had no choice but to overthrow him.

Gwen sneaked into the back, and a light dropped down to the stage, revealing Fosse, hunched forward, turned inward, hat tilted over his eyes like a bandit, dancing alone, as if to a mirror in himself.

Gelbart leaned to Whitehead. "He's doing *Pal Joey.*"

They were flabbergasted. Joey Evans had nothing to do with Woodrow Truesmith. Fosse's "audition" was pure showcase, outside their crisis, unrelated to anything.

Not to Gwen. She laughed through it all. "It was a folie à deux," Whitehead observed, "absolute madness, and Gwen almost seemed to be feeding it."

The next day, Fosse rehearsed the company in the opening number, a parade. "He was more intense than usual that morning," Beddow remembered. "We killed ourselves."

Afterward, he and Verdon gathered the company onstage for an announcement.

"I've been fired," Fosse said.

Some of them knew. He had called them personally, that morning or the night before. Others gasped.

"I wanted a show with edge," he said, "a funny show that really said something, and the producers wanted something different. They wanted it softer, nicer. I don't know. Please give your all to Albert Marre and Todd Bolender" — the new director, the new choreographer — "you've all done a terrific job here and I want you to keep doing a terrific job."

A pause.

"I conceived this show. I outlined it. I casted it. I choreographed it. I drew the first sketches for the design. I directed it — and — the first thing that goes wrong, they blame me."

A pause.

"I don't know."

He took Gwen's arm.

"See y'around."

TWENTY-SEVEN YEARS

FOSSE CALLED JACK PERLMAN, his lawyer. In exchange for Fosse's services as director and choreographer, the contract Perlman negotiated granted his client approval rights on all artistic matters "not to be unreasonably withheld." Perlman reasoned that having fired Fosse, effectively denying him artistic approval, Whitehead was not entitled to the benefits of Fosse's direction or choreography. There was the leverage: Fosse could withdraw his dances from the show. But there was a catch: having deferred a fee up-front in exchange for a piece of the gross, Fosse had a financial stake in seeing *The Conquering Hero* become the best show possible. His numbers would sell tickets. The deal: Fosse agreed to let Whitehead use his choreography with the understanding that it was not to be changed.

On December 5, two days after he was fired, Fosse—who had also been barred from seeing the show—heard by way of friendly dancers that changes were being made to his work. Whitehead had violated their agreement. In the spirit of compromise, Perlman suggested that if Whitehead allowed Fosse's major ballets (including the antiwar ballet) to survive in their original form, Fosse would permit

Whitehead to change as much of the remaining choreography as he wanted. Whitehead refused. The antiwar ballet went too far.

On December 7, Fosse filed a demand for arbitration with the American Arbitration Association, seeking damages and an injunction against further use of the choreography. "I am hopeful," he said to the *New York Times*, "that the association will enforce my rights by restraining the producers from altering these ballets without my consent." On December 16, partway through *Hero's* Philadelphia tryout, Whitehead claimed the whole business stank from the start. Since he felt nothing had been "unreasonably withheld" in the first place, he had not violated the contract and could therefore do what he liked with any part of *The Conquering Hero*. On January 16, the show opened in New York. The *Times* called it a dud: "An indication of the troubles it has known is the fact that the program lists neither stage director nor choreographer." On January 19, the performance was canceled. On January 21, the day *The Conquering Hero* was set to close (after only seven performances), Fosse and Verdon arrived late at the ANTA Playhouse in New York, stood behind the last row, and watched what the producers had done to him.

Standing there, he later said, and seeing how they had butchered his ballet was one of the worst experiences of his life.

By the time the curtain fell, he was fuming. When he caught sight of a bald, bespectacled man — composer Moose Charlap, Fosse was sure — coming up the aisle, he grabbed the man by the lapel and held him against the back wall of the theater.

"How the fuck can you have done this?" Fosse locked his hands around the composer's neck. "What the fuck are you trying to do to me?"

Gwen pulled Fosse away, into the lobby, and Hal Prince, who had been there to see the show, ran up to help the victim — who wasn't Charlap — off the floor. The man was Prince's partner Robert Griffith.

"What the hell was that?" Griffith asked, brushing himself off. "What did —"

"I don't know," Prince said. "But stay here."

Prince ran after Fosse, and Griffith, disregarding Prince's instructions, followed close behind. When they reached the lobby, they stopped short: Fosse was on the floor, curled up, almost catatonic. "It was very upsetting," Prince said later. "No one knew what was happening." Gwen was beside him, stroking his head, explaining to him in a whisper, "That was Bobby . . . Bobby Griffith."

"*What?*" Fosse said.

"Bobby Griffith . . . Bobby Griffith."

Fosse spent the winter miserable and unavenged. After the show folded, Whitehead conceded that he'd changed the choreography; Fosse filed for damages, but no settlement was reached for a long time. "It made him look like he couldn't choreograph," Reinking said. "The antiwar ballet meant so much to him — it was his big statement — and they ruined it." Though his name had been removed from the playbill, he knew people knew, and people talked. They would agree Fosse had tried to make a show his own, from the ground up, and he couldn't. They would call him a failure.

Soon thereafter, on December 19, 1960, Sadie Fosse died of heart disease. "He sat by her bed a long, long, long time," Reinking said. She was sixty-five. "After my mother died," Fosse said, "it all sort of disintegrated." Cy soon remarried; the siblings dispersed and lost touch. Save for his baby sister, Marianne, Fosse had never been able to relate to any of them. Now there was less reason to try. "Most of what I know about Bob," Cy Fosse would tell Charlie Grass, "I get from the gossip columns." Fosse returned home for his father's funeral (Cy died, also of heart disease, two years later) and discovered he had been seeing another woman long before Sadie had passed. Peering into the coffin, Fosse got a sad thrill glimpsing his dad in lipstick and pancake powder, looking every inch the sissy Cy had seen in his son.

From then on, family reunions became a formality. The generic and timid content of Fosse's correspondence with his siblings — news of jobs and marriages, broad good wishes, and reports of the where-abouts of nieces and nephews — written sometimes with years-old bulletins and polite queries ("If you could find a spare minute . . .") belied any real intimacy.

He might have languished the whole spring if Gus Schirmer, who had directed him in *Pal Joey* many summer-stock seasons back, hadn't approached Fosse and asked him to reappear in his favorite part in an upcoming City Center revival. How could Fosse hesitate? The part of Melba went to Eileen Heckart, an accomplished dramatic actress without musical-comedy experience. The first time she performed her big number "Zip" — Melba's story of her interview with Gypsy Rose Lee — with the orchestra, Heckart knew she had bombed. Fosse waited for her to ask his opinion. "Well," he said, "I have to tell you, it's the worst rendition of 'Zip' I've ever heard in my life." That night he and Verdon took Heckart to Downey's, a casual alternative to Sardi's, for a quick dinner, then they all packed into a cab and went downtown.

What exactly was going on? Heckart wanted to know when they reached the empty studio.

"We are going to restage your number."

She was touched. But there was no way she could accept the offer. She wasn't about to go behind the back of Ralph Beaumont. She said, "It would break [the choreographer's] heart if I did that to him."

"It's *your* ass up there, Heckart! Who gives a shit about [his] heart, for Chrissake?"

She said no but thanked him anyway.

"You know, Heckart, *that's* why you'll never be a star!"

For the next two hours, they worked. Gwen Verdon danced beside Heckart, with Fosse in front. "Yes, it was quite magnificent," Heckart would say. "For a nonmusical person to have them be as giving as they both were to me was wonderful." Wonderful, yes, and not just for Heckart. "Zip," which Melba performs for Joey, was, like any two-person exchange, essentially a pas de deux. Fosse needed her to look good in order for him to look his best.

Beaumont could not have been pleased with Fosse's attitude, but there was little the choreographer could do. New touches that were quite obviously Fosse's were popping up all over the show. According to dancer Billie Mahoney: "[There was one number] when we wore the little white gloves and had all these specific little movements, we drilled and drilled. There were eleven dance numbers in the show and more than half of the rehearsal time was spent on that one dance. And the other choreographer resented it a bit." Fosse had given the dancers so many details, Mahoney went on stage shaking with the terrible feeling she wouldn't remember all of them. But she did — and they thanked her for it. "Every night," she said, "that applause went on and on and you think, 'Boy, it is *worth* it.'"

Pal Joey was enthusiastically received, and so was Fosse, though, ironically, less for his Joey than for the choreography no critic knew was his. "The high spot," wrote the *Wall Street Journal,* "is Eileen Heckart's rendition of that wonderfully tired song simply entitled 'Zip.' . . . It's as funny as it was the first time, which is saying a great deal." Fosse registered onstage as he had onscreen, as a malfunctioning star: all sparkle and no shine. "I saw Bob in *Pal Joey,*" said Tommy Tune, a Tony-winning choreographer, "and his dancing was spectacular, but as an actor, Bobby didn't come across. I think it was his innate shyness. There was a removed quality to him. In Broadway musicals, there's got to be a lot of 'Love me! Love me!' and Bobby didn't want to ask for that."

It must have been a strange sort of horror to be a famous Broadway director, the star of a hit show (*Pal Joey* was extended, briefly), and the husband of the biggest name in musical comedy and yet feel like Bob Fosse. Few believed his self-hatred was genuine, including Stephen Sondheim. "I remember there was an interview with him where he said something like 'I don't know whether I'm a fraud or a genius,'" Sondheim said. "He was always shit-kicking. A lot of that saying 'I'm a fraud, I'm a fraud' was in itself fraudulent. He wanted people to say, 'Oh, you're not, Bobby, you're not. You're not a fraud, you're a genius.'" Buzz Halliday believed it, though. At about this time, she found him ambling around Shubert Alley looking rumpled and faraway. He was hunched over, collar up, a parenthesis with a cigarette in its mouth.

Buzz ran to him. "How are you, Bobby? What's going on?"

"Well . . ." He took a big breath. "I'm pretty depressed."

Getting away from show business, if only physically, was a relief for Fosse, even if he got restless out in East Hampton without a studio. But with friends over for dinner, he might forget for a moment about what had to be done or had been done wrong. Present that season, along with Fosse and Verdon, were Feuer and Martin; Neil Simon, piping hot on the heels of *Come Blow Your Horn*, his first play; and the composer Cy Coleman, who was known to swim the distance to lyricist Carolyn Leigh's rented Steinway to work on songs for their upcoming show, *Little Me*, then being written by Neil Simon and produced by Feuer and Martin. They called it Sardi's on the Beach. "This year [East Hampton] seems to have reached a peak," noted the *New York Times*, "with at least thirteen specific productions for the 1961–62 season being master-minded under the sun, and an indeterminate number of others being discussed to the stimulating background boom of the surf."

One show, Feuer and Martin's *How to Succeed in Business Without Really Trying*, was practically a *Guys and Dolls* reunion. Teaming Feuer and Martin with book writer/director Abe Burrows and composer-lyricist Frank Loesser, *How to Succeed* was as close to a sure thing as any unsure thing could be. However, instead of hiring Michael Kidd (as he had on *Guys and Dolls*), Feuer chose Hugh Lambert to choreograph. Lambert had never created his own dances for Broadway, but he had arranged a few numbers for the Perry Como and Ed Sullivan shows, assisted Carol Haney on *Flower Drum Song*, and, most recently, put together an extravagant trade show that impressed Feuer immensely. All this Feuer told Fosse and Verdon that summer at the beach.

Then rehearsals began. "At the first reading," one of the show's stars, Robert Morse, recalled, "everybody was laughing. People were falling down all over themselves. Abe Burrows's secretary was crying! It was just terrific. Then we started blocking the scenes and by the third day, no one laughed. There wasn't a laugh for the next four weeks." He continued, "I don't want to say it was like a burlesque show or a revue, but it felt that way because the musical numbers and book scenes weren't flowing. It was start-and-stop, like one sketch after the next. What I remember about Hugh Lambert is, he was a gifted choreographer, but he couldn't stage the numbers."

"He got us into one big clump and couldn't get us out of it," said Donna McKechnie, then appearing in her first Broadway show. "We were in that clump for three days." At the rehearsals, held in rooms without air conditioning in the late-summer heat, Feuer, Martin, Loesser, and Burrows lined up in suits like chairmen of the board and sweated through more fabric than Hugh Lambert, although who worried more — about the number, the show, his reputation — was anybody's guess. "I'd watch them from the stage," McKechnie said. "As the day went on, they'd take their jackets off, roll their sleeves up. By the time they decided to replace Lambert, they were practically in their undershirts."

Burrows, beloved by his team, was essential to the maintenance of good feeling and had a sure genius for comedy, but when it came to staging numbers, he wisely stepped aside. For backup, Feuer called

Fosse, and Fosse said he would help on the condition that Lambert retain credit and remain at rehearsals throughout the remainder of the process. "Because Bob had been fired on *Hero*," Verdon said, "he didn't want Hugh Lambert to be fired on *How to Succeed*." Feuer agreed, and Fosse arrived, with Gwen, his assistant. (Lambert moved to the balcony.)

A congenial, no-nonsense producer unaccustomed to interference, Cy Feuer was Bob Fosse's kind of guy, and Bob Fosse was Feuer's. Hanging around outside the Shubert with Loesser and Burrows — Dead End Kids all grown up — the men shared an honest-to-God, outer-borough love of show-business ritual and brotherhood. At the end of the day, they knew that human beings, at the ends of their days, were more "Did you hear the one about . . . ?" than "What light through yonder window breaks?" They ate steak, looked at girls, and went to the theater.

As a show about office life, *How to Succeed* was inherently antagonistic to musical-comedy bombast. How could one dance funny about everyday situations without compromising their everyday-ness? Fosse's priority had always been to create entertaining dances (with the odd concession to moving the story forward, adding a layer to a character, or removing a layer of propriety), but now a certain amount of reality had to be accounted for. "The main problem," he said, "was to make everything seem like it was *possible*, even remotely. They had to seem like people in an office. That put a certain number of restrictions on me and removed a number of dance conventions as well. No dancing on the desks, for one thing."

The first song Fosse and Verdon staged, or restaged, was "Coffee Break." Fosse made it into a number about addiction and withdrawal. "I took it to its extreme," he said, "treating coffee as if it were a drug — as though people needed a coffee *fix*." Fosse's isolations — more than natural, less than fantastical — helped bridge the gap between naturalism and dance. "On 'Coffee Break,' they made us rehearse our little fingers and our eyes," McKechnie said. "It was like we were dancing with our hands and faces." Fosse might have achieved close to the same effect if he'd brought in and rehearsed a real office. No matter how small their roles, all the chorus members, even if they weren't named, were asked to write up their characters' life stories, from their daily routines to the people they disliked in the office. They had become a chorus of individuals.

Particularly confounding was "A Secretary Is Not a Toy," which had been passed around the company like an unwanted orphan. Burrows tried it with four guys in front of a scrim before he gave it to Rudy Vallee, who refused to sing the song in three-four time, as Frank Loesser had written it — and Loesser quit the show. He returned three days later, and "A Secretary Is Not a Toy," a song everyone loved, was cut.

But the melody lingered on. Unwilling to part with the number, the team met one night at Philadelphia's Warwick Hotel, *How to Succeed*'s home base, for one of those headache-making sessions that turn ordinarily pleasant places like Philadelphia and New Haven into mental hospitals for theater people. At four in the morning, with no new ideas on the table and the next day's rehearsal only a few hours away, it was decided they should give up, or at least try to sleep, and the meeting adjourned. Shuffling out into the hall, Feuer heard Fosse mumbling to himself. Maybe something about a giant soft-shoe. He asked Fosse to clarify, but he didn't get much back.

Feuer resumed the line of questioning the following day. "What did you mean by that? A 'giant soft-shoe'?"

Fosse might not have looked up. "I've got an idea. Can you get me a large rehearsal hall?"

For the sake of expedience, they would have to be covert. If Loesser found out Fosse was making additional tests, he might walk off the production for another three days, wasting more time, something that, at this late juncture, they needed every second of.

Moving fast, Feuer rented Fosse a big room in the Masonic Temple across from the Shubert, and Fosse worked alone with Gwen. Macheteing his way through ideas, Fosse felt every genius he could not be or had already been glowering at his every move, blocking his escape from the jungle. Gwen knew the jungle; her job was to lead him to it, to save him from it. That alone was a dance. "The creative person is an absolute monster who tries to destroy Bob Fosse," she said. "His face changes. He'd get ropey looking. His eyes sink into his head and it looks like a death mask. I've worked in insane asylums and the inmates don't look as weird as Bob. He's driven, jumpy, crazed and all psyched up. Raw. He's like those safe-crackers in old movies who file their fingertips down to keep them sensitive." His concentration was more than merely intense; it was motorized. "When you stage a dance," he said, "you've gotta care if the dancer's hair bow is red or green. Dexedrine makes you care. A lot of people would rather I didn't say that, but it's true." Fosse called them his care pills.

His job was to know more about the dancers' bodies than the dancers did. He would say, "Do it again," when it seemed they couldn't, and he did not have to thank them. Open gratitude was for emergencies. Swollen ankles did not dissuade him, and he refused to let them just mark the steps, though he would be begged. "I want to see it full out," he would say, "again." He would say, "The word *tired* does not exist in a dancer's vocabulary." He would say, "No," and lose his temper. He would insult them. Some resented his pitilessness; others understood the fight was Fosse's gift to them. Because as he broke you down, and he did, the look in his eye — "I see you and I'm with you" — held you up. "It was his belief in you," McKechnie said, "that kept you going." There was such a thing as flawlessness, and if he could get them to believe him, they all might touch it. "We see the perfection," Ben Vereen would say. "But our humanness is holding us back."

The perfection. It was the only medicine for agony.

Three nights later, during a preview run at Shubert, Fosse and Ver-

don, alone except for a rehearsal pianist, presented the new "Secretary" to Cy Feuer in secret. Imagining upwards of forty performers
— a majority of the company — they explained how the ensemble
would break away into clusters of four or five people, each singing
a *part* of the lyric before splitting into new clusters to sing the next
part. Feuer was amazed by what he heard. "Secretary" was indeed
a giant soft-shoe of office life; it was simple enough to be a credible workplace dance yet it went to bigger, funnier extremes than its
previous incarnations, which had done little to expand on the lyric.
There's no reason to dance if the dance only reiterates — it must
build. Reaching beyond secretaries and their bosses to include every
branch of the business mechanism, Fosse and Verdon enlarged "Secretary" into a bureaucratic conspiracy, a show of self-delusion, the
idea being that office politics, like national politics, is no more than
an act. The truth? A secretary *is* a toy.

Fosse peeked up at Feuer. "Frank's gonna kill me for fucking with
his rhythm."

Feuer didn't care. He ran into the theater, directly to Loesser's
seat in the audience. "You've gotta see this," he said to Loesser, leading him back to the Masonic Temple. "And you're gonna keep your
mouth shut till it's finished."

Frank Loesser watched and kept his mouth shut — until his jaw
dropped. Between the two of them, Fosse and Verdon had worked
out everything, every part, snapping and tapping together in poly-
phonic counterpoint, playfully changing the tempo for rhythmic fun,
as if the number itself were a toy. Loesser's waltz was a thing of the
past. "Jesus Christ," he said. "I'm going to have to rewrite the whole
thing." Which he did, that night.

After many months of delays, the American Arbitration Association finally decided for Fosse in the case against Whitehead, award-

ing him a total of six cents in damages. "The results were exactly what we asked for," said Jack Perlman, Fosse's lawyer. "We wanted only 6 cents to vindicate Mr. Fosse's rights in the choreography." (Jay Topkis, lawyer for the respondent, sent Fosse a nickel and a penny.) But if Fosse wanted to protect his future work, and that of the choreographic community at large, then founding some kind of union was in order. There had been a few attempts at organization, but the Society of Stage Directors and Choreographers had gone unrecognized by the League of New York Theaters, the reigning producers and theater owners on Broadway. The league contended that directors and choreographers were supervisory personnel, not employees, and therefore had no standing as a bargaining group—a decision that left Fosse and the SSDC out in the cold. The *Hero* victory shot an arrow through all that, but whether it would yield results for the SSDC was anybody's guess.

On October 15, 1961, the drizzly morning after *How to Succeed in Business Without Really Trying* opened at the Forty-Sixth Street Theater to raves, Fosse bounded into Variety Arts, spread the papers in a circle on the studio floor, and lay down in the middle of them, grinning at the ceiling. "Crafty, conniving, sneaky, cynical, irreverent, impertinent, sly, malicious, and lovely, just lovely" (Walter Kerr, *Herald Tribune*). "The most inventive and stylized and altogether infectious new musical in recent tradition" (John McClain, *Journal-American*). "It belongs to the blue chips among modern musicals . . . *How to Succeed* arrives bearing precious gifts of an adult viewpoint and consistency of style . . . bent on fun with a helping of malice . . . an ingenious dance celebrating the point that a stenographer is not a toy keeps a tongue in cheek" (Howard Taubman, *New York Times*). For the first time, Fosse's style coated an entire show, from the dances to the book scenes. "Nobody just walked across the stage," Tommy Tune recalled. "Everybody had a stylized walk." Winking cynicism fashioned every corner of the production, and every character in it, with a fleck of irony. Even when dancers weren't performing, they *seemed* to be performing, an aesthetic gradient — or perhaps even a statement — he had intended for *Hero* but exacted here.

Moments after Fosse arrived that afternoon at Variety Arts, dancer Barrie Chase opened the studio door to find him on the floor, surrounded by the dailies. For the past week and a half, they had been rehearsing "Seasons of Youth," an hourlong Timex revue Fosse was supposed to be choreographing for ABC. But with most of Fosse's attention on *How to Succeed,* Chase spent the better part of rehearsal working with Gwen. "She was madly, madly in love with him," Chase said. "It was just so obvious." She came in every day, for free, to line up chairs and clean up the space. When a costume ripped, Gwen produced a needle and thread and started sewing. The few times Fosse and Chase rehearsed together, she found him gruff and preoccupied. "In rehearsal, my feeling was that he was very pressured," Chase said. "I wouldn't be surprised if he didn't want to be there. He wasn't giving it his best." Most of their numbers were variations on his earlier work.

Their gloss on "Who's Got the Pain?" was danced to "I Don't Think I'll End It All Today," a cheery calypso routine about suicide. In straw hats, Fosse and Chase sang, "Away with monoxide! / Away with the one-way ride!" At one point, they hold pantomime nooses over their heads and yank themselves off their knees, grinning. With considerable help from Gwen, Fosse worked out an audition number, an omnibus dance about a dancer, played by Chase, who practically kills herself to get the job. Fosse, giving voice to the off-camera director, makes her jump higher and higher through flamenco, cancan, and ballet steps — and it's never good enough. "You didn't make me cry," he sneers at her. Out of ideas, she stoops to "a little interpretive dancing" and appears in a black sequined leotard and feathered headpiece for some old-fashioned stripper stuff — this bit the director likes —

and she proceeds to the singing phase of the audition. Midway in, the voice of Fosse interrupts the dancer. She's not what he's looking for. "He knew I felt so inadequate about opening my mouth and singing," Chase said. He used it.

When the time came to film, Fosse would run back and forth from camera to stage, giving direction to both dancers and technicians and taking notes from Gwen on his own dancing, and all without pausing for a moment's consideration. "Shaking hands with Bob was like shaking hands with a grapefruit," said producer Ervin Drake. "His hand squished with all that flop sweat." Fosse was doing more than staging, filming, and dancing in the musicals scenes; he was staging the entire production, down to the comedy sketches by the Premise Players. "I went along with everything Fosse suggested," said Drake. "Everything on that screen was a choice he made, even the camera work, which he wasn't credited for." According to Drake, Joseph Cates, the credited director, "stayed away. Joe knew when he had a hit on his hands and would get the credit." His biggest TV assignment to date, the filming absorbed Fosse completely, and in ways rehearsal had not. It seemed the dances were merely a pretext for him to try his hand at the camera. "He was very involved in that aspect of it," Chase said. "But when I asked him for help on the flamenco because it was something I knew nothing about, he said it didn't matter, that we could spoof it. He said, 'You always get away with it if you spoof it.'"

They didn't get away with it. "Seasons of Youth" aroused the unproven auteur in Fosse, and he'd fumbled out his heart's ambition, unripe and grasping. The style he had harnessed onstage in dance had not translated to the camera. When the show aired, on October 25, 1961, *Variety* suggested Fosse's audition sequence ("a total cliché," Chase said) was lifted from the 1956 remake of *A Star Is Born*. Other critics reacted similarly.

The next day, Chase was back at the Plaza, packing her suitcase. The phone rang.

"Hiya, Barrie."

"Bobby?"

"What are you doing?"

"I'm packing."

With sadness: "You're leaving?"

"Well, yes. The show's over."

"When are you leaving?"

"Tonight!" She laughed.

"Where are you going?"

"Sweden. My boyfriend lives there."

"I'm downstairs."

"What?"

"In the lobby."

Then he was in her room, and then he was coming up behind her, kissing her. Trying to kiss her.

"Bobby, come on!" She shoved him off. "What are you doing?"

Chase might not have been so surprised if Fosse had shown any interest in her during rehearsal. But he hadn't. If anything, he'd been short with her, treating Chase—who was one of Fred Astaire's former partners, no less—as the out-of-shape Hollywood talent he believed her to be.

Fosse and Verdon were home the evening of November 1 when Gwen got a call from Patton Campbell, costumer of *Redhead* and *Hero*. It was something serious, Campbell said. Could he come over and see them?

When she answered the door a half an hour later, Verdon could see the news was the most serious kind of serious.

"Gwen," Campbell began, "I didn't want you to hear about it on the radio. Joanie died."

Joanie McCracken.

Gwen turned back into the apartment and told Fosse.

He was flattened. More than a wife, more even than a friend, McCracken had been a sort of angel to him. Mary-Ann Niles was a kid, a sidekick; Joan saw how good he could be. Gwen knew it; Joan had been the one to change Fosse. "Years from now," Gwen said, "you'll read how Bob enhanced so many lives, which he did. But I'm going to tell you Bob's real tragedy: Nobody, not one of us, except Joan, was ever able to enhance his."

Soon after he got the news, Fosse sat down at the typewriter. He may have thought of himself as a sporadically above-average showman, but he knew he was hopeless as a writer. Not that he wasn't capable of a cute remark here and there, but what Neil Simon, Paddy Chayefsky, and George Abbott did took more than tricks. You couldn't tap-dance on the page. You had to say something. What did Fosse have to say?

When Joan died, he tried to find out. He wrote a story about an unnamed wanderer angry to the point of madness. "He" appears in a shitty hotel in Cleveland. Feeling betrayed, he walks to the Roxy Burlesque, looking for a laugh. "He'd show her. He'd show he[r] he could go on living." Inside the theater, a baggy-pants comic in a toy derby scratches his crotch. He's followed by a beat-up stripper, then a fat man reading aloud from dirty magazines and sweating. "He hated them all," wrote Fosse. Enraged, he bolts up and screams, "Shut up! Shut up about that stuff! God damn you, shut up!" He runs up the aisle and out of the theater, wanting to hold the one he lost, damning vanity and pride, running until he can't run anymore and then collapsing on the cemetery green, crying, grasping at nothing, calling out her name in love.

The guilt—he'd never lose it.

De Mille, Robbins, and Richard Rodgers were among the standing-room-only crowd of dancers, stage managers, and wardrobe mistresses that gathered, two days later, inside a funeral parlor on

West Seventy-Second where Joan's forty-three-year-old body rested in an open casket, a pink pillow under her head. Joan's "funeral was dreadful," wrote Leo Lerman, "with this wax creature exposed in what seemed a party dress. You could not avoid it—the room was so small, many could not get into the mediocre, awful place—the sick sweet stench of perishing flowers—an utterly ordinary-voiced, black-smocked preacher reading prayers and nothing about her." It was a long fifteen minutes before the coffin was carried out into the street and placed in the hearse.

Fosse watched from the other side of Seventy-Second, and then he walked away.

Early in 1962, he got a call from Cy Feuer. It was good news. *How to Succeed* was continuing its smash run, playing to the fortunate few, like President Kennedy and Marilyn Monroe (on different nights), who could actually get tickets. How did Bob feel about codirecting Feuer and Martin's next show, *Little Me?*

"Co-?" Bob asked. "With who?"

"Me," Cy replied.

And then, the ultimate Fosse question: "Why co-?"

"Because I can handle Sid Caesar."

Good point. Having appeared with Mary-Ann Niles on Caesar's *Your Show of Shows*, Fosse knew Caesar was a handful on TV, where he was at home, so one could only imagine the headache he would be onstage (or, more likely, backstage, drinking), where he hadn't been in nearly twenty years, appearing live, without cutaways, eight shows a week—

"Playing six different parts," Feuer explained. "Maybe seven."

"What?"

Based on the novel by Patrick Dennis, author of *Auntie Mame*, *Little Me* told the story of Belle Poitrine (translation: "beautiful

breasts"), her gold-digging rise to fame and fortune, and the men
— Noble Eggleston, Mr. Pinchley, Val du Val, Fred Poitrine, Otto
Schnitzler, Prince Cherney, and Noble Junior — she married on the
way up. It was book writer Neil Simon's idea to shift the focus from
Belle to her husbands, have one actor play all seven husbands, and
have that actor be Sid Caesar — who, on top of everything else, was
known to be loose with his lines. This was one thing on TV, but onstage, with dozens of cues to knock down, he could run the whole
show into the orchestra. Also: he couldn't sing, he couldn't dance,
and he had a temper. Once, after a performance didn't go his way,
he calmly excused himself from the venue holding two double-barreled twelve-gauge shotguns under his arm and fired a round into the
woods. He was said to punch desks, tables, and horses. And he was a
genius.

Fosse accepted the job. But only if Feuer and Martin, leading
members of the League of New York Theaters, formally recognized
the Society of Stage Directors and Choreographers, now backed by
Harold Clurman, Agnes de Mille, and Elia Kazan. Fearing an SSDC
strike, Feuer and Martin wisely accepted Fosse's terms, and Fosse,
now a hero to the SSDC, looked like even more of a producer's headache than he had before, which, in light of the *Conquering Hero* scandal, was a considerable feat. Paranoid dealings lay ahead, but in the
meantime, signing the *Little Me* contract was worth more than a few
bottles of champagne.

Little Me was a healthy challenge for Fosse. The book, however
hilarious, didn't make room for dance numbers, and the sprawling
story, shifting mercilessly across decades and from place to place and
never looking back (there were no repeated sets in the show), put a
crimp in continuity. The whole affair was resistant to cohesion, and
so was Fosse: he had his own weakness in the conceptual-unity department. "You know, I never can find an overall idea for a show," he

said to a reporter covering *Little Me.* "It comes to me piece by piece, and then, if I'm lucky, the pieces fit together and style emerges. But it happens by trial and error."

As was their custom, Fosse and Verdon spent several weeks working out the steps at Variety Arts, and every night, Edith, the receptionist, closed up, shutting down the switchboard and locking the iron gate on the stairway leading up to the studios. Just beyond Edith's desk, the Variety Recording Studio stayed open for business, cutting acetate records and LPs into the quiet hours. It was soon after Edith left one evening that Fernando Vargas, the studio's co-owner, heard a rattling on the iron gate down the hall. Shouting up the stairs, Vargas demanded the rattler identify himself. He did, but Vargas didn't recognize the name that came back. When he threatened to call the police, the intruder lost his cool and blurted out, "I'm Gwen Verdon's husband!" Vargas unlocked the gate and Bob Fosse, his head down, apologized for the confusion. He'd lost his key. Fosse laughed, but Mr. Gwen Verdon was humiliated.

"Fosse loved the front room on the top floor," dancer Dan Siretta said. He and Gwen worked in a low-ceilinged space — the biggest studio in the building — with mirrors on one side and smudged windows on the other. Throughout rehearsal, Fosse kept his dance notes close at hand. He had one composition book for every show, and he filled each one with all manner of miscellany pertaining, or potentially pertaining, to dances formed or in formation, all of it scribbled in messy cursive. Uneasy with proper dance notation, Fosse relied heavily on stick-figure images and pop-culture shorthand. His *Little Me* ideas were, more than usual, bound to ghosts of showbiz past and present. Jerry Lewis's knees slid into "Rich Kid's Rag," bits of Red Buttons into "Deep Down Inside," Chaplin into "Dimples," and Jolson into "Lafayette." The picaresque show was well suited to pastiche, and pastiche was an ideal format for satire — a good fit for Fosse. *Little Me* showed the choreographer in tune with his strengths and sensibility and practicing his own language, consciously drawing from "A Secretary Is Not a Toy" and taking jumps he liked from *Redhead*.

In "The Rich Kid's Rag," a dig at the bratty rich, Fosse wasn't merely parodying popular ragtime dance but satirizing personality, and in his own style. He kept increasing and changing the tempo (a favorite technique), pushing the kids faster and faster, as if trying to break their stiff upper lips, but not a single one balked. Fosse gave a toylike quality to their jerks and snaps, their knocked knees and turned-in toes. At first it was fun and funny, but by the number's end, one couldn't help but sense that, even at play, these automatons were more like figures in a Victorian music box than real live kids. Their snootiness — a performance like any other — practically embalmed them.

"I would pass Variety Arts every night and look up," Siretta said, "and there he was. You could see him in silhouette through the windows. There was only one man on Broadway with that silhouette. There was only one man that obsessed."

In the midst of rehearsals, Barrie Chase returned to New York. How Fosse found out, she had no idea.

"Can we meet?"

"I don't think so, Bobby."

"Why not?"

As if he didn't know. "Gwen," she said. "I adore Gwen . . . I would never —"

He called Chase almost every night she was in New York, which was about a month. In time she came to expect his calls — then look forward to them. Their conversations grew longer, more personal. "We'd talk for maybe an hour," Chase said, "and about everything. We had a great time on the phone. I found him interesting and very funny. I don't know, maybe he thought he'd break me down and I'd give in. At some point in the conversation, he'd always try, he'd always slip it in."

"Come on . . . let's meet . . . just for a little . . ."

"Bobby, I'm not going over that again."

They talked of Joan McCracken. "He said he wasn't very nice to her and regretted it," Chase said. "He was much darker on the phone than in rehearsal." They talked of Gwen Verdon. "He told me she was pregnant," Chase said. "He said he told me before he told anyone else."

He and Gwen had been trying for a long time. "It looked like we couldn't have one," Fosse said. "I went through all those embarrassing things of taking your sperm out of a tube and having it tested and then when it looked like it wasn't going to happen, she was pregnant. So it was kind of a happy moment."

Neil Simon was rewriting constantly. "You know at this point," Caesar said, "nothing's funny anymore. After four weeks of rehearsal it's just a matter of logistics. It's troop movements, deployment of forces, details." This was Simon's first musical. He had no yardstick to measure exactly how far he was from where he needed to be — where *they* needed to be, where *he* wasn't getting them. Fosse, Feuer, Caesar, lyricist Carolyn Leigh, and composer Cy Coleman: six giants sharing a single bed. One couldn't move without disrupting another. But of course one moved. It was always the same one.

"You mean I got to say it exactly this way?" an exasperated Caesar asked in the middle of a dress rehearsal. "Suppose I don't think it's funny."

And so on. "He always seemed like he wanted to bite something," Feuer noted. "Basically, Sid was a brilliant, funny, nervous wreck," said one dancer. "He'd stand in the wings coughing and sweating and you'd think, *Why in the world is he doing this show?* And then he'd walk out onstage and be brilliant, absolutely brilliant." No one knew what Caesar, drunk or sober, would do from show to show. "There was a joke," a cast member recalled, "that this was going to be the only show in history with multiple-choice cues."

Late in September, fourteen crates of costumes were shipped off to Philadelphia's Erlanger Theater. (Twenty-one of the costumes were for Caesar; he had forty-eight costume changes over the course of the show, and some had to be made in under thirty-five seconds.) In October, the company said goodbye to New York. Neil Simon was uneasy about it. "It was during the Cuban Missile Crisis," he recalled, "and it really looked like the world might end." As he rewrote for Caesar, *around* Caesar, Simon took calls from his pregnant wife, Joan, begging him to come home. She was in tears. "If we're going to die," she said, "I want all of us to die together."

It was a funny thing, *Little Me*, a Chinese-food musical spun on a lazy Susan. On the one hand, the show was nothing, and on the other, it was nothing but a good time. Here, Fosse the director shone as never before. With artifice as his guide, he spun the lazy Susan at impossible speeds, changing scenes in a flash, sending his company in circles, calling attention to the sham of human motivation. But the show refuses to believe it's a nihilistic show. A cannon blast of clichés, tropes, and devices, *Little Me* took great joy in fraudulence and exposed the director's growing exasperation with the whole kit and caboodle of musical entertainment. "I don't think there is any such thing as a *realistic* musical," he said. "As soon as people start to sing to each other, you've already gone beyond 'realism' in the musical sense . . . A friend mentioned that, 'Musicals always disturb me,' he said. 'If they're singing about how they're going to kill themselves, well, that's a serious matter. And I'm sitting in the audience and wondering how, if they feel so bad, they can sing so *well?*'" They shared a certain kind of con, musicals and Fosse, masking reality with amusement.

But what would happen if that con was exposed? The question was *Little Me*. The answer was inconclusive — for Fosse aesthetically, for

Cy Feuer commercially. "I've never been in this position before," the producer said to Neil Simon the morning after the first preview. "We have a smash hit and I'm thinking maybe we should close it."

On November 17, 1962, Feuer, Simon, and Fosse, standing in tuxedos at the back of New York's Lunt-Fontanne Theater, braced themselves for what looked like the funniest, most brilliant flop of their careers and perhaps even in the history of American musical comedy. It began well—Caesar appeared to a roar of planned-for applause. But then he coughed through his first three jokes, ruining them completely. Considering this an omen, Feuer and Simon shared a pained look before turning to Fosse. He was staring straight ahead. Simon described what happened next: "Bob very simply put his arms down at his sides, closed his eyes, and fell backward, every part of his body hitting the floor simultaneously—a perfect ten at any Olympics." On the floor, he moaned quietly.

Fifteen minutes later, when Fosse was on his feet again, something around the orchestra pit caught his attention. A drunk had left the second or third row and was stumbling to the back of the house, chatting to folks he had quite obviously never met before as he made his way up the aisle. As if Caesar weren't wildcard enough. Planting himself before Feuer, Simon, and Fosse, the man patted his brow with a handkerchief and declared, "This is the worst goddamned show I've seen since My Fair Lady," and then stormed off. Fosse fell to the floor again, this time laughing himself to tears. There were still two hours to go.

"If all the theatrical platitudes of the last half-century could be turned into playing cards," Walter Kerr wrote, "and the pack scattered wildly from portal to portal, you would arrive at something like Little Me, luckily." Flip the coin—it's a wooden nickel. "I have the feeling," wrote another critic, "that this is a pressure show, a show in which pressures are applied to blind you to its weaknesses. There is nothing wrong with that tactic if it isn't too visible a tactic. There is, indeed, a word for it, a word not used often these days but still valid — showmanship. It takes skill and showmanship in combination to razzle-dazzle you into believing you are seeing a whizzer of a show when factually you are not." But was that such a bad thing? It often seemed being a good fake was not so different from being good.

Fatherhood: the realest thing of all. Fatherhood and death.

But would he be a good father?

What about names? Have you thought about names? people asked.

"If it's a boy, Nicholas," Fosse said. "Nick. It's so unphony."

Nicole Providence Fosse was born on March 24, 1963. "I can't explain it," Fosse said, "but she's the perfect love of my life."

It was a good time to be Bob Fosse, at least in theory. In theory, he could stand in the middle of Forty-Sixth Street, between Seventh and Eighth Avenues, and gaze up at the marquees — his. He could see, to one side of the street, *How to Succeed in Business Without Really Trying,* winner of the 1962 Pulitzer Prize for drama. Looking directly across, at the Lunt-Fontanne, he could smile up at the lights that spelled *Little Me,* which in April 1963 was the source of two more Tony nominations for Fosse: best director of a musical (which he'd lose to George Abbott) and best choreography (which he'd win).

That month he won yet another honor. "I've been dancing since I was nine," he said, accepting his *Dance Magazine* award, "and that's almost twenty-seven years. In that twenty-seven years I've been plagued and harassed with a fear, a doubt that I was really not very good, that I didn't have too much to offer. This feeling was — you might think it was in my imagination, and it might have been — but I can remember reviews and criticisms that seemed to add to this feeling of self-doubt. And of course I worked hard. As a matter of fact, that feeling of being a little insecure I think made me work a little harder. And I achieved some success, so much so that the people on the outside of the dance world treated me as if I knew my business. But the people on the in, the people in the dance world, always seemed to look at me as though I were sort of a commercial curiosity that occurs every so often." (If he called himself a phony, would that make him less of a phony?) He closed the speech by telling a story — one of his standards, which he told over and over, like a creation myth — of the time he broke the news of his career to his father. "Well, he asked me what a choreographer was — that's not good — and he said, 'Do you mean you're going to give away all your steps?' He then kind of threw up his arms in exasperation. Of course later on when I began to send more money home, his arms lowered and went into a gesture resembling a shrug, you know. And I think if he were here today, he might raise his arms again and hug me or pat me on the back and say, 'Do you think I could get one of those choreography jobs they're passing out?'" That last part, about the hug and the passing out, was the *two-bits!* after *shave-and-a-haircut* — compulsory, for the crowd. His father had passed away two weeks earlier.

After Fosse and Verdon married, Verdon deliberately removed herself from Broadway to live life as Mrs. Fosse, wife of Bob, mother of baby Nicole, the Fosse triangle's tallest point. If in a few years she wanted to return to the theater — and she did — Verdon knew she would have to move quickly. Nearing forty, she was far too old to be a young dancer; soon she would be too old to be an old dancer. So Gwen decided when Nicole turned three she would come back to Broadway for one giant victory lap, a Fosse-Verdon show to top *Redhead,* but this time, one they would build for themselves, from the ground up. Until then, they would search for the ideal material, something new and challenging and personal to both, with dance potential for him and a honey of a leading role for her.

But first: temptation. City Center was dedicating its spring season to Richard Rodgers with a short May-to-June cycle of *Oklahoma!, Pal Joey,* and *The King and I.* Gus Schirmer, who had directed Fosse at City Center in 1961, would direct *Joey* once more, this time with Viveca Lindfors in the part of Vera. Fosse couldn't resist the offer to reprise Joey; it was a propulsive B_{12} boost to his fading Riff Brother dream. He could shop for his next musical as he danced.

Lindfors kept her nine-year-old son, Kristoffer Tabori, backstage. He was enchanted by Fosse. "He was so charming and sweet and available," Tabori said. "I was amazed he could do Joey — dance and sing and act — with that cigarette hanging out of the corner of his mouth. It never dropped, it never moved. It did exactly what he wanted." One day Fosse let Tabori in on the secret. "After his number, he came over, threw his arms around me, and tousled my hair. 'It's like this,' he said, and told me that you had to keep your lip extremely dry so the cigarette adhered, so you had a kind of cementing. Then he said 'Here,' and put a cigarette on my lip to show me how." It worked.

If Fosse worried about his performance or the production or side-stepping George and Ethel Martin, the show's credited choreographers, he didn't let it show. "I adored him," said actress Rita Gardner. "I remember there were so many dances in the show, we ran out of time before we could rehearse my number, 'I Could Write a Book,' so Bobby cut out his rehearsal so we could go over that number for me. He knew the show backwards and forwards, but he knew I didn't. He was there for me." And he was there for Lindfors as he had been there for Heckart in 1961. "I could see him really helping her through it," Tabori said, "really helping her in her limitations. He flirted with my mother, who was a tough woman, and even she loved him. They all did. He was always surrounded by the most beautiful chorines, killing them with kindness. It was a massacre! He was so sweet to them, so dear to them, and they towered over him! I'd look up and just see Fosse in the midst of so much leg."

With several productions of the show comfortably behind him and his own personal and professional successes at an all-time high, Fosse's 1963 Joey seemed softer, with a natural confidence new to him and suitable to the part. "Fosse had an incredible sense of relaxation," Tabori said. "His Joey wasn't about finesse or cool, like Sinatra, and he wasn't as shiny-good-looking as Gene Kelly, but still we understood how he was so attractive to people. He was a performer, completely comfortable in his skin." To some, the metaphor was clear: Joey's con is his feet. The reviews were mixed.

Gwen Verdon, the star of the family, suggested the possibility of adapting Maurine Watkins's play *Chicago*. The part of Roxie had interested her for years, since she first saw Ginger Rogers in *Roxie Hart*, the 1942 film adaptation, during the run of *Can-Can* a decade earlier. She could remember flipping between the McCarthy hearings and a broadcast of the movie, thinking Watkins's flapper murderess would be a terrific part for her: sweetly criminal, sexy, and somehow innocent. Fosse and Verdon inquired after the rights but came up with nothing: Watkins, a born-again Christian, did not want her moralistic tale of sin and corruption turned into a musical comedy.

Next idea: a musical of *Breakfast at Tiffany's*. *Redhead*'s producers, Fryer and Carr, went for it. They optioned Capote's book and tempted Fosse (and writer Hugh Wheeler) with the adaptation. Holly could be a lot like Roxie — a bitter part for a sweet-tasting girl — and, from Fosse's perspective, a way to look sex in the eye and wink at the same time. He said yes.

About that time, producers Ray Stark and David Merrick, having lost Jerome Robbins to script disputes, approached Fosse to direct their as-yet-untitled show about Fanny Brice. The combination of backstage musical, underdog story, and vaudeville comedy meant it came fully equipped for Fosse — and, he thought, for Gwen — and Fosse, after expressing interest, approached Stark and Merrick with the idea of replacing Barbra Streisand, who had already been cast, with Verdon. Wisely, they turned him down. As if in retaliation, Fosse had Jack Perlman draw up a rider to the proposed contract. He would not make the same mistake twice: if Stark and Merrick ordered changes to Fosse's work without his consent, the rider stated, all rights to his dances would automatically revert to Fosse. The burn of *Hero* still with him, he refused to budge on this point, and the negotiation continued far longer than schedules permitted. Meanwhile, time was wasting. If Fosse was going to go ahead with the Fanny Brice show, he needed to get to work immediately, and for the sake of expedience, he budged slightly on the rider dispute and agreed to work on spec, for the moment, until Stark and Merrick saw some work and presumably felt more comfortable. They tabled the rights discussion in good faith.

On that tenuous note, Fosse dove into the book. He scribbled notes, took down song ideas, and sent off suggestions to writer Isobel Lennart (who seemed amenable to his input). Midway through the overture, Fosse thought, they should have the curtain rise on a pair of electricians at work on the bare stage. Checking the lights would prompt certain sparks and flashes timed to the music. A few beats later, Fanny's dressing room would roll on and Streisand would make her entrance, moving across the stage to her dressing-room door. Less inspired was Fosse's suggestion to cut the song "People." The lyrics, he said, made no sense for Fanny Brice. She was a star and stars did not "need people." They needed the stage, the audience — no more.

His brainstorming halted when Fosse heard Stark had placed a worried call to Feuer and Martin. Stark questioning Fosse's competence was a breach of good faith — Fosse identified it immediately, and he decided to quit the show. In September 1963 he wrote a six-page letter explaining how he reached his decision, sent it to the full company, and left for Feuer and Martin's *I Picked a Daisy*. When Stark found out, he fired off a telegram threatening Fosse with legal action. But it didn't take: they never had a contract in the first place.

I Picked a Daisy became *On a Clear Day You Can See Forever,* and Fosse settled into a comfortable routine of story conferences with

Feuer and Martin, producers he knew too well to distrust. As writer and lyricist Alan Jay Lerner worked (very slowly) on revisions, Fosse turned his attention to his Gwen show, to writer Hugh Wheeler and their adaptation of *Breakfast at Tiffany's*; he auditioned and rehearsed touring productions of *How to Succeed* and *Little Me*, for which he hired dancers Kathryn Doby and Leland Palmer, the latter a Broadway newcomer with a great deal of talent but, at twenty-four, without a full sense of herself.

Soon after rehearsals began, Fosse pulled her aside.

"Leland," he said, "I want to tell you something very honestly. May I?"

"Yes . . . okay." She feared the worst. He was going to fire her.

"You're not the most beautiful woman in the usual terms of beautiful," he said softly, "but you have something very unusual and very special and I don't want you to forget that."

A few nights later, Palmer's hotel-room phone rang. It was around ten o'clock.

"Hello?"

"Leland. It's Bob Fosse."

She had been deeply touched by what he had said to her in rehearsal. Never before had anyone of Fosse's stature addressed her with such conviction and grace.

"Will you come to my room?" he asked. "I want to talk to you."

A minute later, Palmer opened the door to Fosse's room. He was in bed, under the covers. She was surprised: he hadn't seemed sick that day in rehearsal.

"The light is so bright," he said to her. "Would you put a towel over the lamp?"

She did.

"I want you. Come here."

She sat beside him on the bed.

"I would like to sleep with you."

"Bob," she said, unsure of what she would, or should, say. "I respect and admire you and I respect and admire Gwen, but I won't, not tonight, not ever . . ."

"But will you kiss me?"

She thought for a moment, then kissed him on the forehead. A stranger walking in would not have known who was the grownup and who was the kid.

Palmer got up from the bed and crossed to the door. "Would you like me to take the towel off the lamp?"

"No."

"Would you like me to turn out the light?"

"No, thank you."

"Okay." She opened the door. "Good night, Bob."

"Good night."

Palmer left with a new sensation, one that, years later, she would understand to be the beginnings of sophistication and deepening self-respect. She billowed back to her room feeling fuller and new, as if a sound foundation had been slipped under the kid in her, raising her up from innocence to peek at adulthood. Fosse hadn't changed Palmer; he had seen in her what she had not yet become. And that night, for the first time, Palmer saw it too. Getting into bed, she felt special.

Sex was a medium for Fosse. It was as much a physical act as it was an opportunity to learn about and merge with his female collaborators, a way of giving to them so they could give back more and better — that is, if they didn't break under the pressure or retreat in anger. As a means of communication, sex was an exclamation point, far better than the periods of regular life. Sex improved on respect and trust — for the dancers and for him. Sex brought him closer to the epicenter of talent, as if by dipping a hand to the geyser, he could steal back a drop for himself. And all his effort brought him applause too. Fit, built, and endlessly attentive to detail, Fosse was a terrific lover, some said the best they ever had, and in bed, he worked as hard as he did in Variety Arts, giving to get. In bed he owned the spotlight, Fred Astaire performing for an audience of one (or sometimes two) night after happy night — and they really were happy — laughing, sweating, talking *together*. Sex was better than being up late and trying to drink the amphetamines to sleep on his own, without anyone there to hold back his dread.

TWENTY-FOUR YEARS

HE HAD TIME, still waiting on Lerner's revisions, to get to know his daughter. "Nicole kept Bob in life," Ann Reinking said. "She forced him to slow down, to be home." Suddenly he was anchored to someone else's physical and emotional well-being, and rather than resenting the responsibility or buckling under his fear of bungling it, he loved it. Fatherhood was bullshit repellent; it cut the fat out of Fosse's brain; it organized him. All at once, the suicidal fantasies — the ones that weren't for show — he vowed to put aside, for her. "When Nicole came along," dancer Fred Mann III said, "it opened the heavens for Bob. She was the stars, the moon, the sun. Nicole was everything to him." She was a dazzler of the most ingenious sort, and Gwen, beaming from across their living room, watched him fall for her. "He's a fabulous father to Nicole," she said. These were glorious days, rapturous days. "There was this point of great happiness," Fosse said, "and I wanted to give Gwen something wonderful. I wanted to give her the best show she ever had."

That show would not be *Breakfast at Tiffany's*. In April of 1964, with several drafts of the musical already outlined, Truman Capote decided Verdon, at thirty-eight, was too old to play Holly Golightly, and ordered Fryer and Carr's option money returned. Still itching to collaborate, the producers bounced back with another idea: What about a Fosse musical of Isherwood's *Berlin Stories*, with Gwen as Sally Bowles? It was a compelling suggestion. Sally had qualities Bob and Gwen could work with: she was happy on the outside, sad on the inside, and, like Roxie and Holly, a party girl on the down and out. But Fosse and Verdon didn't see Nazi Germany as the right setting for a musical and passed.

So they kept looking, since *On a Clear Day* wasn't going anywhere either. What if, Fosse thought, they did an evening of musicals, two or three one-acts in a single night? With Fryer and Carr's blessing, Fosse went down to Times Square to prowl the shelves of the Drama Book Shop and returned with a copy of *Modern One-Act Plays*. *A Sunny Morning*, an old Spanish comedy of 1914, stirred his interest. So did *Passionella*, a new work by Martin Charnin and Bob Kessler, which Fryer, Carr, Verdon, and Fosse heard at Gus Schirmer's apartment before deciding against it. Moving on, Fosse thought back to the spring of 1962, when Vivian Shaw, ex-wife of writer David Shaw, told him to see Fellini's film *Nights of Cabiria*, which was then playing in repertory at the Bleecker Street Cinema. As predicted, the film enthralled Fosse, and the part of Cabiria was perfect for Gwen. A low-rent hooker desperate for love, she was in many respects a modern-day (and female) Harlequin, the sixteenth-century commedia dell'arte clown Verdon saw as her personal archetype. "Harlequin is a well rounded, sensitive person," she explained. "His love for Columbine — especially when she breaks his heart — makes a man of him. He's transformed by suffering. The twirl of blue paper in his eye represents tears. The flower on his nose is a symbol of unattainable beauty — like Columbine. He hunts for it everywhere, not realizing that it is right in front of him." He was also her husband.

Without delay, Fosse screened *Nights of Cabiria* for Fryer and Carr and Gwen in Fryer and Carr's offices at 445 Park Avenue. Everyone seemed to love the movie, but midway through, Fosse knew he had a tough sell on his hands. *Cabiria* had no happy romance, and it ended on a very sad note—a bad combination for a musical comedy. In the elevator going down, Fryer admitted he felt only so-so about *Cabiria*'s Broadway potential, and Gwen, to Fosse's surprise, agreed. But Carr—driving Gwen and Bob back home to their apartment— privately encouraged Fosse to stay with it. *Cabiria* had a big little heart, he said. That had to be good for something.

That night Fosse could not sleep.

There was so much for him in *Nights of Cabiria:* the sort of crummy feelings musical comedy never touched; Fellini's hooker underground of ugly-beautiful women Fosse recognized from the clubs he did not discuss; Giulietta Masina's masterly evocation of Chaplin, that touch of vaudeville he couldn't resist; and his own ties to Cabiria, who, despite her hard shell, was sweet inside, like him. Most didn't see it but she was there, behind the black and the cigarettes and the suicide monologues and all Fosse did to imitate a brooding and far-off artist (which, ironically, he didn't have to pretend to be). But when Fosse was at home, relaxing with his friends, his stylin' desert boots kicked up on the coffee table, he let his natural state—Cabiria gamin—take over. ("Bob would be furious if I called him a nice guy," dancer Laurent Giroux said.) As much a strategy as a defense, Fosse made "cool" work for him, like a billboard or a great review in the *New York Times.* It was part of his show.

He got out of bed.

In nine pages, Fosse outlined a one-act musical of *Nights of Cabiria* and showed it to Gwen the next morning. Still, she was unconvinced. The character and milieu were stridently unglamorous, seedy even. Hadn't they learned their lesson after *New Girl in Town*'s whorehouse ballet?

Fosse got a similar response from Fryer and Carr: depressing wasn't Broadway. Which was depressing.

But what *was* Broadway? Rodgers and Hammerstein?

Not anymore: *The Sound of Music,* their last show, had climbed its last mountain on June 15, 1963. As if in reaction, the whole of musical theater scrambled for their crown, denting it somewhat on the way to high seriousness and literary good taste. The cotton-candy days of *The Pajama Game* and *Damn Yankees* had given way to "important" subjects, dutifully making good on the musical's long-term plan to sophisticate itself, like Henry Higgins did for Eliza Doolittle. In that respect, its evolution may have been natural; the Broadway musical was not a kid anymore but a college freshman, falling in love with fancy culture and the classics, like *Camelot,* as if that made him smarter. The upside was *My Fair Lady.* The downside was that "important" subjects deserved "important" productions, and shows got bigger and more expensive. With all that money onstage, producers were apt to shift their focus away from book, music, and lyrics. Musical *comedy,* the college freshman's kid brother, was particularly vulnerable. What important books should he read for fun? Or: How could an essentially antic form match *Gypsy* and *West Side Story* for guts and impact without forfeiting the silliness essential to its very being? It was an old question with many answers (*Guys and Dolls, How to Succeed,* and so on), but now that Shaw was fair game, the lure of bourgeois soft-core pulled even harder. *Bye Bye Birdie, Do Re Mi, Fade Out — Fade In:* under pressure to mature or escape maturity, comedies either sank or went puff and floated away. The old masters, meanwhile, kept getting older. In 1962, Irving Berlin opened *Mr. President,* his final show. No one knew it then, but *How to Succeed* would be Frank Loesser's last on Broadway. The great ones were dying. Hammerstein, Cole Porter; 1960, 1964, respectively. A Camelot was ending.

And another golden age was beginning. Stephen Sondheim's *A Funny Thing Happened on the Way to the Forum* was built (with Larry Gelbart and Burt Shevelove) on sound, self-aware characterization, and airtight farce — Sondheim meets the best of George Abbott. And, in contrast to many of its forebears, the 1962 comedy was as conscientiously engineered as a Russian novel, written and rewritten well in advance of the rehearsal process with the intention of grounding its silliness on the soundest possible foundations. This was a new concept — workshopping. New shows of the Abbott era had flown into rehearsal relatively quickly, relegating (somewhat counterintuitively) hard questions about the bigger picture to trials out of town (at which point, in many cases, it was too late to do anything). The post-*Forum* handling of musical books as a kind of literature was yet another facet of the new seriousness on Broadway. Seriousness of the best kind.

So, no, a musical of *Nights of Cabiria* didn't look to Verdon, Fryer, or Carr like a Broadway comedy of the early sixties. Fosse tried to move on to another project, but automatic instinct, like gravity, brought him — and then *Cabiria* — back down to the dancehall. He thought of the dime-a-dance places of his teenage years, the sort his brother Buddy took him to. He thought of the Times Square entrance to the Tango Palace, a narrow, paint-chipped artery clogged with girls' headshots: browse the dance hostesses available in every flavor, some sixteen, some forty-two, some with Louise Brooks haircuts years out of date, some from before the war, none with talent. The smart ones knew to forget about Broadway. Any soldier or college kid could buy himself a dance for a fifty-cent ticket; two tickets, and the girl would talk to him between songs. At the end of the night, each hostess turned in her tickets for a commission — half of ticket sales plus a piece of the bar. (What the girls did after that was their business.) But the ticket was a metaphor: Who could claim never to have sold one?

This time Fryer, Carr, and Verdon got it. Setting *Cabiria* in a dancehall lent theatricality to the piece, livening up the atmosphere and blurring the prostitution angle. And of course, Fosse wanted to write it. To provide himself and Gwen with the absolute best opportunities, Fosse knew he needed to man the show's conceptual entryway and keep collaboration, and therefore dissent, to a minimum. He needed control.

But he also needed a co-writer, ideally someone he could overrule in a pinch. Fryer and Carr suggested Martin Charnin, author of *Passionella;* they had recently produced his first show, *Hot Spot,* on Broadway. Fosse knew Charnin, sort of, from *The Girls Against the Boys.* As a kid of twenty-five, Charnin had been called in for last-minute revisions, and he impressed Fosse with "Love Is," a made-to-order composition with dance possibilities galore. Young, Fosse-compatible, gifted, uncelebrated, Charnin fit the job description perfectly. What up-and-comer would turn down a shot at working with one of Broadway's biggest names?

"The first day I met Fosse, at his apartment on Central Park West," Charnin said, "we watched *Nights of Cabiria.*" The film would be the basis for the first act of a two-act musical called *Hearts and Flowers,* Fosse explained. They discussed at length how to fit the piece to Gwen's strengths. "That was his first priority," Charnin said. "The other priority was that he wanted to be the controlling force of every single aspect of the piece." For the next three weeks, they worked — either at Fryer and Carr's office, where they would order up deli and rewatch *Cabiria,* or chez Fosse, in the big room that had been converted into an office. Throughout, Fosse stayed remote. "He was mind-bogglingly private," Charnin said. "Any time I attempted to ingratiate myself to him, my collaborator, the subject was dropped entirely." With Fellini's script and Fosse's outline in hand, they sat at a dining room table, tossing lines and situations back and forth. Charnin typed. "Fosse was a terrific idea man," he explained, "but not a good writer. One would have to take his disconnected thoughts and try to structure them so that they made sense." The precision Fosse wanted from his dancers, he himself could not sustain in conversation. "He didn't always know how to make language work for him," Charnin said, "and he would get impatient."

In June, they submitted the first draft of sixty pages to Fryer and Carr. "And I never heard from Fosse again," Charnin said. "Not a phone call, not a letter, nothing. My agent, Abe Newborn, chased down Fryer and Carr, but he couldn't get them on the phone. They disappeared." It would be years before Charnin knew why.

Shopping for a composer, Fosse reached out to Burton Lane. He showed *Hearts and Flowers* to Frank Loesser, who suggested turning it into a ballet. Cy Coleman had some interest, but only if he could have Dorothy Fields on lyrics. Fields was interested, but without *Hearts and Flowers*'s second-act musical decided — or even assigned — she couldn't be sure, so Fosse put his composer search aside to shop for act-two book writers, beginning a long process that ultimately broke everyone's schedule. By the time Elaine May came on, Fosse had dropped out of *On a Clear Day You Can See Forever* — still delayed — to direct and choreograph the new Loesser show *Pleasures and Palaces*, and he disappeared into the studio.

Adapted by Sam Spewack from his comedy *Once There Was a Russian* (which opened and closed in one night; you'd think they would have known), *Pleasures and Palaces* was a titanic show typical of the bigger-and-older craze, crammed with sex and jokes and political double-dealing, nobly set in the age of Catherine the Great. Fosse had been looking over Spewack's shoulder since the idea had first crossed Spewack's desk a year earlier and had helped nurse the failed play into a musical farce. He was curious about Slavic dance, and with the Cold War toying with American minds, all things Russian were in a kind of hazardous vogue. But mostly, Fosse just needed to work.

Fosse's *Pleasures* ideas burlesqued Russian acrobatics and ballet. "One man did a great big jumping split," Gwen said, "at which
point, with sound effects, his pants would rip. Another man would
do a cartwheel and his hairpiece would come undone." A mechanical
horse, belly dancers, Cossacks, girls in mustaches: *Pleasures and Palaces* was a half-a-million-dollar extravaganza, Fosse's biggest assignment yet. But, as many had predicted, the book broke underneath
him. "I knew we had trouble," he said. "But I still thought I could
pull it off . . . I really thought I could save it — but we were all doing
different things. Spewack was doing a Shavian comedy, Loesser was
doing an opera, and I was doing a Russian version of *A Funny Thing
Happened on the Way to the Forum*." Behind closed doors, everyone
blamed the other guy: Fosse didn't like the score, Loesser didn't like
the book, and Spewack was against the production.

They left for Detroit in early March 1965. "Bobby worked morning,
noon, and night," said actress Phyllis Newman, "and Gwen was with
him. They were such a team, partners in every sense. He would be
going back and forth between Gwen, working with the dancers in the
lobby, to the principals onstage." "He would always be checking with
her," said dancer Don Emmons. "He knew the show was in trouble
and was trying everything, but mostly the wrong things, changing
tiny little things, wrists there, legs there, when the whole second act
needed rewriting." Jack Cassidy replaced Alfred Marks, the show's
star. Comden and Green came to help. Then Abe Burrows and Cy
Feuer. They couldn't save the sinking ship, but just having them there
lightened the mood. "In rehearsal, Loesser told me to throw packs of
cigarettes at Bobby when he started smoking," dancer Stan Page said.
"So I did. But Bobby would pick up the cigarettes and throw them
at Loesser, who was sitting in the house. And Loesser would throw
them back on the stage."

After the first preview, few missed the writing on the wall. Loesser,
a producer, suggested they cut their losses and pack up, but Fosse

held on, urging him to give *Pleasures* another shot, in Boston this time, before opening in New York. He admitted the "Tears of Joy" number could be funnier, though he had already changed it many times, by cutting mostly, first lyrics, then music, turning what was once a ballad into a Bronx-dancehallish human drum symphony of stomps, snaps, and claps, and he knew now he could go farther. He would put up his own money. Would Loesser agree to that? He would pay for the storage and shipment of sets and scenery. He'd reconsider his plans for Nicole's education. "Well, so the kid doesn't go to Vassar," he joked with the company.

"The cast was so distraught," Kathryn Doby said, "they wanted to raise money to get orchestrations for new versions of the numbers so new backers might see it and help out." They would go that far for Fosse. He had gone that far for them, picking them out of the thousands, not just once but again and again, show after show. Fosse had proved his allegiance, demonstrated his beneficence, bestowing work, careers, and personal self-worth on those who might have floundered out of show business without him. He, the father, had given them life; and they, the children, repaid him with devotion. They called themselves Bobby's. He called them — in the parlance of choreographers — kids. He knew their lives, and he knew their boyfriends' and girlfriends' lives; he had seen them through innumerable dramas; he had watched them, and in many cases helped them to, improve. They owed him for that too. But how to repay him wasn't always clear, especially when Fosse's charisma, kindness, and intrepid sensuality blurred personal and professional dedication — which could easily backfire.

As in any family, jealousy and sibling rivalry were key factors in the creation and realignment of factions and subfactions within the company. Competition is inherent in any dancer's life — an artist consistently on the hunt for work, striving to keep her body and improve her technique — but to Bobby's girls of nineteen or twenty-five, frightened and naïve, vying to secure their slivers of stage or their sectors of the director's attention, competition was an epidemic, a sort of high-school cliquishness on overdrive. To the dancers, at least. To Fosse, conflict could be a valuable tool, a motivator like any other. "Women are very attracted to power," he said, with characteristic candor, "and to have that power is a terrific feeling." Ask the girls: "It takes two to play that game," said one dancer. "We knew what was what."

"We were almost done with Bob's new, satirical idea for 'Tears of Joy,' almost a day away, when the notice to close the show went up," Doby said. "The cast decided we should let him finish the number, so we had an extra rehearsal and he did finish the number." But no one left. Fosse watched as "Tears of Joy" evolved into a medley of his work dating back to the recollections of the oldest member of the company. Beginning with "The Pickpocket Tango," from *Redhead,* the boys and girls of *Pleasures and Palaces* reconstructed — part on the fly, part prepared — selections from "A Secretary Is Not a Toy," the (original) whorehouse ballet from *New Girl in Town,* "The Rich Kid's Rag," and, finally, *The Conquering Hero*'s war ballet. "That's how far the cast would go for Fosse," Doby said. What they thought they had forgotten, their bodies remembered; what their bodies didn't recall, they invented in his style. To watch them review the story of his life in dance, each step the product of untold deliberation, each deliberation the fruit of untold drama, one could see Bob Fosse was more than spiritually aligned with his dancers. He was in them.

Fosse took actor John McMartin for a drink across from the theater. They'd known each other since *The Conquering Hero* and despite not spending all that much time together outside rehearsal, they had developed a friendly rhythm. McMartin had always considered his director a relatively shy guy, but he found that after a few drinks, Fosse didn't have to force himself to speak.

"What are you doing when you get back?" Fosse asked.

"Nothing."

"Would you consider doing something else with me?"

McMartin hesitated.

"What's the matter?"

"Well, I've been in two of these in a row" — *these* meaning "bombs" — "and I thought you'd think, maybe, I was bringing you bad luck."

Fosse laughed. "I thought you'd think that about me."

There was no time for post-*Pleasures* blues. After returning to New York, Fosse held a backers' audition at Delmonico's for his un-named two-one-acts musical. The reading revealed Elaine May had barely completed her half of the show, "The Larger World of Faith," and Fosse's half, "Cabiria," seemed rushed. Fosse needed more stage time — a full two acts, even — if he intended to develop the relation-ship between Cabiria and Oscar, her beau, to a sensible degree, and at the suggestion of Fryer and Carr, Fosse returned to his dining room table to face the blank page.

He needed help. In May 1965 he approached a friend of his, writer David Shaw, whose ex-wife had suggested *Nights of Cabiria* in the first place; he went to Abe Burrows; he tried Hugh Wheeler. Wheeler rewrote the first seven scenes before admitting he wasn't a good match for the material, and Fosse called off the search. Better to write the two acts on his own than waste any more time auditioning writ-ers. That summer, he and Gwen rented a cottage in East Hampton only a few steps from the beach, and Fosse wrote for five days — until he got a call from Robert Fryer. Paddy Chayefsky, Fryer said, hadn't recoiled at the idea of working on the book. Would Bob be willing to meet Paddy? Almost before he got off the phone, Fosse had his desk packed up and was heading for Manhattan.

Paddy Chayefsky!

Here was a *real* artist, an Astaire of the Olivetti. Where other writ-ers merely wrote, tiptapping away like secretaries on old machines,

Chayefsky thundered with meaning and wisdom and purpose. He had something to say — something important about authenticity and compassion — and he was saying it, and in a way that hadn't been heard before. With *Marty,* first on TV in 1953 and then adapted for film in 1955, he launched a new naturalness in American drama. His characters — regular New York working-class people — spoke plainly in a common idiom but with a poetic conviction that lifted their worn-out soles a few inches off the pavement. Marty and Clara, Agnes in *The Catered Affair,* Jerry in *Middle of the Night:* they were like the rest of us, only a little bigger. "I tried in *Middle of the Night* to write about love and happiness and fulfillment in particularly mundane terms," he said, "because I believe they are mundane things, as real as the audience or electric light bulbs, palpable to the touch, recognizable to the senses." And everything he wrote, he guarded fervently. When *Marty* went to Hollywood, Chayefsky insisted on a thorough rehearsal period well in advance of shooting; he insisted Delbert Mann, director of the TV version, go on to direct the film; he insisted on attending preparatory meetings and making whatever changes to the script he deemed necessary. This was far from normal practice in the industry that he called "grasping, vicious, and pandering," but Chayefsky had been burned before. "I swore I'd never again let a script get outta my hands, outta my control," he said. It was the right move; he won the Oscar for his adaptation of *Marty,* and *Marty* won the Oscar for best picture.

Seeking to further indemnify his work, in 1957 Chayefsky founded Carnegie Productions and became his own producer. "I decided to form my own company," he said on the set of *The Goddess.* "I always figured that if you went for a low budget you could go for art, and I've tried to write *The Goddess* as a major work of art." By that decade's end, he had begun a move away from stenographic realism and toward hulking questions of philosophy and metaphysics. His play *Gideon* grew from the Old Testament. "I thought he was a funny fellow," Chayefsky said of his creation. "Other men in the Bible needed just one miracle to accept God — the burning bush sufficed for Moses — but God kept performing miracle after miracle for Gideon and Gideon didn't buy them." Like Gideon, Chayefsky kept doubting, fighting, aspiring. About his *The Passion of Josef D.*, which Chayefsky himself directed in 1964, he said, "I meant the play to be political vaudeville, the boulevard theater of the German expressionists." It closed after fifteen performances. He had taken a part-time teaching position at City College when he got the *Cabiria* call from Fryer and Carr.

Fosse's personal and professional admiration for Chayefsky was vast, but he found Chayefsky's interest in his musical comedy bewildering. Fosse drove back to Manhattan bristling with excitement. Since their first meeting, in 1959, at David Shaw's in Amagansett, Chayefsky and Fosse had impressed each other, a kind of beginners' chemistry. "From that time on," Gwen said, "there was a sort of tentative feeling out of one another." Erudition had always been like an open flame for Bob Fosse, too fascinating to look away from, too scary to touch, and Fosse's showbiz reputation read too slick for Paddy, though he couldn't help but smile at the little guy's left-right combination of shtick and insecurity.

They got to work in Paddy's office, a converted efficiency apartment eleven floors above the honks of Seventh Avenue in the heart of midtown. The kitchenette, doubling as file archive and paper repository, abutted a small foyer space and a larger corner room where Paddy sat behind his typewriter in semilight. "It was like a cave," said Karen Hassett, a friend of Chayefsky's. "Paddy kept the room dark, his back to the window, and the blinds were always drawn." He kept a couch by his desk for long nights, and — walking in and seeing this, Fosse must have smiled — a baby grand against the wall.

At their second meeting Paddy and Fosse gave up on *Cabiria*, and Fosse returned to Long Island to finish the book on his own. At the end of July, he called Neil Simon in Rome to tell him he had managed to squeeze out a first draft of what he was calling *Sweet Charity*. But it wasn't funny enough, Fosse said. He needed help. Between shooting *After the Fox* and writing the screenplay of *Barefoot in the Park*, Simon couldn't really take on another project, but he agreed to have a look, and Fosse sent out a script marked *urgent* the next day. Indeed, input was urgent; *Sweet Charity* rehearsals were scheduled to begin in August, only a few weeks away.

In lieu of major reconstruction, Simon scribbled a few suggestions in the margins and sent the script back to Fosse. Simon's phone rang a few days later.

"I love the new lines," Fosse said. "You can't stop now."

"Bob, I just don't have the time. I can barely get *Barefoot* done."

"I'm not letting you off the hook. You owe me one."

"For what?"

"I'll think of something."

A week later, Fosse was in Rome. "I'm here," Fosse said. "I brought a tape of the score. You have listen to it. Pick me up at TWA."

Hours later, Fosse was in Neil Simon's Roman living room, pushing furniture against the wall to free up dance space. On the director's cue, Simon and his wife, Joan, seated themselves, and Fosse screeched his tape player to the first bar of silence and strode to the center of the room facing the Simons. "This number," he said through the cigarette smoke, "takes place the first time we see these sleazy dance-hall girls that Charity works with." The music began.

Fosse then went on to set the stage for "Big Spender," explaining how the fan of colored lights would catch a hip or shoulder or half an ass in a line of hungry girls twisted in skin-tight sexery waiting in the dark. A loud blast of brass came from the tape player, and Fosse described how the girls, their backs to the audience, would vamp, slowly, their hips shifting with each slow step, to the long bar rising up from downstage, and then turn all at once into the bright lights with limbs held at fractured angles and looks of abject nothingness in their eyes. Each girl would freeze in mangled vogue, hanging off the bar and one another. In that soundless moment, there was no telling what came next. They'd look so cold they could be dead, but they'd also look so mean — this one carefully spreading her talons on the bar, that one a hyena . . . Then, as if seizing, they'd throw themselves back and forth — *ba-badda ba-badda* — then stop. Now there'd be little twitches no bigger than winks and finger thrusts. The shift would be eerie, as if each girl were two girls: one writhing, and the other playing it cute. They'd switch on a dime. "When you're dancing in one of Bob's shows, you're always dancing a paradox," Ann Reinking said. "In 'Big Spender,' you really want to get that guy to come to you, so from the waist up you're glamorous, you're wonderful. But from the waist down, you're tired and your legs are busted and your feet are hurt. 'Please God let me go home and get to sleep' and 'But I have to get the money' at once."

Fosse knew all about his Spender Girls, each locked in paradox, each in her own way. He knew them because he *was* them. On more than one occasion, his friend Kathy Witt accompanied him to the dime-a-dance places off Broadway. When a girl approached their table, Witt recalled, "Bob would say that he didn't wish to dance right then, but maybe one of the 'gals' would like to come and have a drink with us, some conversation? The interviewing would begin, their stories would unfold, and the night would always end in the wee hours with Bob writing most, if not all, of the 'gals,' fifty-dollar checks as tips."

Neil and Joan Simon saw the product of that research — and they were hooked. They stayed up the rest of the night listening to Fosse go through the whole show, and four days later they were still talking about it. Simon knew the first act needed a rewrite that would ultimately change the course of the second act — in other words, he would have to start the script from scratch. He squeezed in what he could between *After the Fox* and *Barefoot in the Park*, writing on yellow pads he carried with him everywhere. Working with a score already established, Simon found the writing harder than the normal hard, but he was a comedy machine. Not that he was never unfunny, but he knew how to fail and recover, and working at top speed, he could fail faster than most. He was a pro.

Fosse returned to New York comfortably on edge. The pieces of the show were clicking into place, but with each click, the pressure rose. No matter how clever the book or brilliant Gwen's comeback, *Sweet Charity* was going to be Fosse's to destroy. He knew these days it was the director who really made the musical. Apologies to Abbott, but mere expertise and showmanship no longer sufficed. With so many moving parts and so much complex material to corral, a contemporary musical needed vision and cohesion to stick together. Without Gower Champion, *Hello, Dolly* would not have gone jumbo; without Robbins, *Fiddler on the Roof* could have fallen to kitsch. They — and others — heralded the era of the director-choreographer. "People have been toying with this idea for years," Fosse said, "but I think there's been a kind of restlessness with our theater, a kind of groping around. And one of the things that we've started groping at is style. We've thought that we've become too conventional in the way we do things and that we should become more visual. And I think the first place you turn to then is someone who you believe has a keen sense of the visual . . . I think that turning toward the director-choreographer has come out of this restlessness." Striking just the right note between light and dark, combining the satirical eye of *How to Succeed* with the blowout dancing of *Redhead* and the conceptual unity of *Little Me*, Fosse had to sync his interests and plug the whole package into Gwen.

"We went to a dance hall to observe the girls," Gwen said. "They still wear the old Lana Turner hairdos and wedgie shoes, 45-year-old gals dressing like it was 1942. Boy, are they tough. One saw me eyeing her and she said, 'What are you starin' at, sister?'" They visited half a dozen dancehalls in the porniest quarters of Times Square. By his own calculations, Fosse spent about $150 on girls at $6.50 an hour; on one occasion he observed the scene with and without Gwen for well over twenty hours before realizing he was getting more groping than dancing. His wife could be conspicuous in a roomful of dancers, so Fosse set out with company member Eddie Gasper to tour the city at night. "They saw kids doing the Jerk, the Swim, all that sixties stuff," said dancer Diana Laurenson, "and then, when the clubs closed, they'd go back to the studio to work, staying sometimes to two or three in the morning lacing all those trends together."

Arthur, the most exciting new club in New York, had opened only months earlier at Fifty-Fourth Street. Proprietress Sybil Burton, recently separated from Richard Burton, had invited her friends, many of them from Broadway, to invest in her idea — novel at the time — to transfer Mod from London to New York. It was a big hit. Everyone from Warhol to John Wayne was seen against the frosted mirrors in blue-yellow-green lights. Sometimes Paddy joined Bob. Gwen said, "[Arthur] was supposed to be a disco — rock 'n' roll. Well, it was so gentle. We went there and we saw all of these people — Mrs. Kennedy, Sybil Burton — this funky music was playing, but they were so elegant. They really thought they were swingin' it around like the kids did. Well, Bob thought that was funny." A caricature of their snooty groove would go into the Aloof section of "Rich Man's Frug," a number quite like *Little Me*'s "Rich Kid's Rag" about upper-class hipsters besotted with the latest dance craze. "That's how Bob really developed his style," said Tony Stevens. "He kept reusing and improving on what he had already done. *Charity* was the pinnacle of that. Dances he had been working on since *Pajama Game* and probably before were taken to their musical-comedy height."

Facing Gwen now at Variety Arts, seeing his steps on her body,

Fosse discovered afresh how it felt to watch Gwen Verdon, his wife, become Gwen Verdon, his dancer. "When he and Gwen were working on *Sweet Charity*," Ann Reinking said, "Bob said, 'It was like our love was rekindled.' He just couldn't believe how talented she was." Watching her dance was admiring a spinning zoetrope of all they had achieved together. Lola, *Redhead*, Nicole. Now Charity. His eyes lit and she saw he wasn't grinning at her work but at her. And yes, her work too. She saw he was proud of her, and pleasing him was more stimulating than rousing an entire audience.

They worked after work. Over a sandwich at Dinty Moore's, as waiters stacked the chairs on empty tables, they talked through steps in a fevered ping-pong of what-ifs and maybes. Then something would ignite and they would have to move. Having only half finished their food, they would stride hand in hand into the kitchen, spread out over a fresh patch of floor, and finesse those what-ifs and maybes into movement while the cooks and busboys mopped the tiles around their feet. And then it would get late, later than late, and remembering life, Bob and Gwen would return home.

In those days, *Sweet Charity* was new and every discovery was an aphrodisiac. Waking with ideas or images, they'd throw off their blankets and dance out the solution on the mattress, bouncing together, high above the darkened studios of Robbins and de Mille. Gwen was tired, but it didn't matter. She was a Bob addict and always would be.

"I don't know if this is any good," she would say.

"On you, everything looks good."

Even what didn't look good. They decided Charity would be pigeon-toed and knock-kneed, like the young Verdon in orthopedic braces. It would give her a broken look that said: resilience.

Fosse was learning to choreograph people instead of patterns. Character had always been essential to his dances, but on *Sweet Charity*, whose broken types he knew more intimately than those of any other show, conveying personality took on added importance. He gave his dancers images to help them feel. He said, "It can be as pedestrian as toothpaste coming out of a tube, or you're a snake here, or your arm isn't an arm, it's a whip." Each "Big Spender" dancer had her imaginary circumstances, her wants and backstory. Each was different. "Bob never treated us like a chorus," Kathryn Doby said. "To Bob, we were all actors." The dancers loved it. "He didn't just want to put something on top of us," one said, "he wanted to bring something out of us. That's a great feeling for a performer." He found isolating inner characteristics was like isolating body parts: the right choice, the right abstraction, and a whole life came forth. In "Rich Man's Frug," each of the girls had to extend a foot while leaning back and shooting her arms down at her sides. Fosse's image helped them see *exactly* how. "Ladies," he said, "it's like a man is holding out a fur coat for you and you have to drop your arms in." There was a shoulder roll at the top of "Big Spender" when the girls came downstage. "Ladies," he said, "it's like when your hands aren't free and you have to use your shoulder to get your bra strap up." Other directors might give their dancers images for every scene; Bob and Gwen had one for just about every step. These were the lines the dancers' bodies had to speak.

Gwen was always there, watching by his side. "She wasn't *the star*," said dancer Lee Roy Reams. "She was part of the company as much as she was part of Bob." There was no set delineation of responsibility, but certain natural tendencies emerged. Where Fosse, the director, kept watch over the bigger picture, Verdon, the dancer, homed in on the details. "Gwen would break the steps down in a way Bob couldn't always," one dancer said. "Having done Bob's shows for so long, she had an eye on how to do the steps technically." He was captain and she navigator — he knew what he wanted; she knew how to *get there*.

How to get *him* there, to Hollywood. He wanted to direct movies. Broadway belonged to New York alone, but Hollywood was for everyone. Fosse knew a well-publicized effort as choreographer on a major movie would launch him to a higher plane, and in August 1965, he entertained an offer from George Cukor, the hottest film director of the summer. In April, Cukor's *My Fair Lady* had swept the Oscars, and his proposed follow-up, *Bloomer Girl,* would be a big-budget costume musical in the same tradition, prestigious and highly visible. Shirley MacLaine, a friend of Fosse's since *The Pajama Game,* had signed on to star—a good hook for Fosse, Cukor thought. But Fosse didn't need the hook. He was interested and would be available in February, a few weeks after the opening of *Sweet Charity.*

Privately, though, Fosse worried about the offer. Accepting it meant leaving Gwen and Nicole in New York. The excitement around *Charity* and the creative efficacy of rehearsals had made home life a joy he could not bear to disrupt. What's more, Fosse worried that taking the job would offend Agnes de Mille, whose ballets for the original production of *Bloomer Girl* he felt he could not improve upon. As ever, he overidentified with the loser's position. Had Warner Brothers passed him over for the films of *Pajama Game* and *Damn Yankees,* he would have been devastated, and he refused to subject de Mille to the same disappointment. And yet, bearing all that in mind, the undying gypsy in Fosse was ready to accept whatever they offered: If *Sweet Charity* was not a success, he would have to do *Bloomer Girl* for the money.

All this Fosse confessed to Fox executive Robert Linden at a lunch meeting in New York. That Gwen Verdon attended the meeting surely surprised Linden, but it was Fosse's open emotionality and pleas to remove himself from every advantageous opportunity that shocked him. So disarming was Fosse's vulnerability, Linden actually found himself arguing *against* Fosse's choreographing *Bloomer Girl,* assuring the man he was trying to hire that money was no reason for him to take the job. A professional of his stature would easily get work elsewhere. Fosse wasn't as sure, and with Gwen's nod of approval, he stuck to his original plan. They'd wait on *Charity.*

In the fall of 1965, *Charity* moved to Philadelphia for tryouts. As the first preview drew near, rumors began that Gwen — who hadn't led a show since *Redhead*, more than six years earlier; who was approaching forty-one; and who, as Charity, was on stage singing and dancing and acting virtually the entire evening — wouldn't be able to get through the night. "It was one of the hardest shows," she said, "because you never had a chance to get offstage and sit down. So the stage became the stage *and* the dressing room. [At] the dressing table for the girls who were in the 'Big Spender' number I used to put on real makeup for the next number."

The company knew Gwen was insecure about her singing. She didn't have Merman's belt or Barbara Cook's range; she had more of a novelty voice, quivery and dear. "Gwen hated singing 'Where Am I Going?'" Lee Roy Reams said of *Charity's* soaring cri de coeur late in the second act. "One day she started crying and said, 'Bobby, please, please cut the song.'" Cy Coleman wrote, "I think the true reason was that she didn't like the idea that Barbra Streisand had already recorded it before the show opened, and people might make comparisons." It was Fosse's job to differentiate between Gwen's needs and the show's, to know when she was seriously unable to sing or just afraid to, and it was Gwen's duty to take all of it, at least publicly. Privately, Fosse knew his show was hers to commandeer.

She had power and she used it. "Gwen was out from time to time," said actor Ruth Buzzi. "We would always hear that she maybe had a cold or something was wrong with her voice, but you never really know why someone's missing a show." There were theories. "I went on a hundred times for her," said Helen Gallagher, Gwen's standby. "Because she had a little girl. And if you know anything about Gwen's life, she had a boy when she was very young, and she was a nonpresent mother. And she never forgave herself for that, and so with this baby, because she was so madly in love with Bob, she said, 'I will be her mother.' And she was." How much motherhood would *Sweet*

Charity allow? How much life would Fosse permit? Their negotiations took place in hotels out of town, where the plaited strands of work and marriage twisted untold resentments into new assertions of power. Fortunately, unfortunately, Verdon and Fosse needed each other.

They previewed well in Philadelphia.

On December 23, the morning after their first Detroit preview, an ebullient Neil Simon set out for the theater. The reviews had been good for both Simon and Fosse (perhaps slightly better for Simon), and though there was clearly more work to do, he anticipated a short celebration before they buckled down.

Fosse sneered at Simon when he appeared in the theater. "Let's give a big hand to the star of the show, Neil Simon." Missing the sarcasm completely, the dancers applauded.

Star of the show?

Was that Bert Lewis talking? A month earlier, before Simon completed the *Sweet Charity* revision — a revision that ultimately turned into a full rewrite — Bert Lewis (aka Robert Louis Fosse) was the credited author. Removing his pseudonym from the byline was a preemptive move, Fosse said, to protect himself from a possible backlash. "Directed, choreographed, *and* written by Bob Fosse?" people would say. Not even Jerome Robbins had dared. But now that Simon's work had received such a warm critical response, Fosse considered the outcome an injustice. (So did Martin Charnin. When he awoke Sunday morning, October 31, 1965, to a full-page ad in the *New York Times* for a Bob Fosse musical based on *Nights of Cabiria* that did not have Charnin's name anywhere on it, he called his lawyer. "He told me I had to wait and see what of mine — mine and Bob's — was used in the show before I could claim anything. So all I could do was wait for opening night.")

Sometime after New Year's, Fosse asked Stanley Donen to come up and see the show in Detroit. A veteran collaborator and writers'-room hero, Neil Simon had a policy of welcoming outside opinion, but after Donen saw the show, he and Fosse went off to discuss it. Without Simon. The playwright returned to the hotel to wait and wonder what was going on. How could he, the writer, be excluded from his own rewrite? Had the good review cost Simon that much?

He didn't hear from Fosse until the next morning.

"The ending," Fosse said to him at breakfast. He thought it wasn't tough enough.

Neil Simon tried to laugh. He knew Fosse often confused pain and profundity. In dress rehearsals, midway into a run of "Big Spender," Fosse had decided Irene Sharaff's costumes — elaborately sequined and tailored — were far too glamorous. He wanted degradation. Sharaff reminded him he had already approved the sketches, but Fosse didn't care about the sketches; the effect was completely off. "They fought," Lee Roy Reams said. "Bob took the Spender dresses backstage and sprayed paint on the sequins, and Gwen's fishtail dress was replaced by a black slip, simple and a touch lower down." Like Sharaff's designs, Simon's ending was too polite.

"It should be grittier, darker," Fosse persisted. "Charity should be devastated and the audience should feel her pain. Now it's just funny and kind of sweet."

But how much darker could it get? The show already ended with Charity being left at the altar and then pushed into a lake and robbed. John McMartin, playing Oscar, her heartbreaker, agreed with Simon. "People in the audience would yell at me after the show," McMartin said. "It was awkward."

Look, Neil Simon said to Fosse: "To suddenly pull the rug out from under the show and make it darker and grimmer would be awkward and really pretentious."

"Who made that rule?" Bob asked him.

"I didn't."

"I want it darker."

But writers are not dancers. They can be hired and fired like dancers, but they are co-authors of the work. There are times when directors might try to blur the distinctions — indeed, that's part of their talent; it's how they get the job done — but they have to be able to restore those distinctions if they find they've gone too far. Did Fosse ever find he'd gone too far?

"I still think I'm right," he said to Simon the next day. "But I'm not positive."

Their collaboration was a dance of exploitation and recovery, anger and apology. Fosse, who wanted to control every element of his work, didn't want to need writers. He wanted to be one.

Sweet Charity would open at the Palace Theater, and — in a brilliant feat of cross-promotion — the Palace Theater would reopen with *Sweet Charity*. Once the center of the Keith-Albee circuit, home to the likes of Chaplin and Jolson and Fanny Brice, the Palace had long since fallen from its vaudeville heyday into neglect. The last movie ever to screen where *Citizen Kane* premiered was *Harlow*, in 1965. That summer, the film and the theater went down together, and the theater stayed down until the Nederlanders began renovating it. It would be ready in time for the premiere of *Sweet Charity*, the first legit production in the Palace's storied fifty-year history.

The date was January 29, 1966. Hundreds of elegantly attired guests, including Mayor Lindsay, Ethel Merman, and Paddy Chayefsky, jammed the restored lobby, hung with portraits of the Palace's most famous acts. The curtain bells rang, and they tiptoed into the auditorium and took a final look around the Palace's insides — placenta red from seats to ceiling and paneled in baroque curls of creamy gold — before the room went completely dark, and quiet, at almost seven thirty.

A level under the stage, behind a door with her name in gold letters, Gwen calmed herself in the dressing room she had designed for maximum comfort. Here was a small Victorian chair; here was a chaise longue. A knock came on her door. It was time. Gwen said, Okay, thank you, and, leaning into her reflection, drew a little black dot under each eye. No one beyond the third row would be able to see them, but she didn't do it for them, she did it for Chaplin; it was his idea. "It opens up the eye," she said. She kept his photo by her mirror. She dreamed about him.

In the first-row balcony, Martin Charnin, Martin's agent, and their wives sat with a lawyer and a court stenographer. From the moment the curtain went up on *Sweet Charity* to the moment it fell (to joyful applause), the steno typed every sung or spoken word into her machine. By the end of the night, Charnin had a script he could compare with his own mimeographed first draft. But he didn't need to. He already knew. "There was material on that stage I had nothing to do with," Charnin said, "because they had fleshed it out from a one-act into an entire musical, but most of what Fosse and I had written was up there."

He felt sick. But what could he say? He was a kid; Fosse was a prince. "The last thing I wanted to do as I was rising in the community was to reveal myself as a sore loser," Charnin said. "It was definitely loaded against me, but that's why Fosse picked me, a young guy, because he knew a young guy needed the opportunity and he could rule them better. It was deliberate. I think everything that Fosse did was deliberate. If you look at his choreography you'll see there isn't a movement that wasn't deliberate. Every pinkie move, every pointed toe is deliberate. I don't think he behaved in a manner outside of how he choreographed. I don't believe he knew how to be a human being."

Sweet Charity is an exuberant, brilliant dance show. "If My Friends Could See Me Now" — a piñata of twitches and merry distortions — plays as if Chaplin had been broken into pieces and thrown out like confetti; "Rich Man's Frug," drawn from the dance clubs of New York, stretched bodies to Giacomettis, long in every direction, and the longer the funnier. And then there was "Big Spender," Fosse's black cartoon of female credentials and his most personal number to date. "Talented Bob Fosse," Harold Clurman wrote, "has created dizzying patterns of movement out of ugliness. The rest is a kind of brilliant and ingenious hideousness which *is* a style — a style wrought from the streets and manners we observe as we enter and leave the theater." Anguish, depravity, scarcity, showmanship, seduction — it was his story in style.

But there are book problems. (Walter Kerr: "Where, for heaven's sake, did bittersweet come from?") As with many of Fosse's shows, *Charity*'s struggle to reconcile musical comedy with musical depression reveals more about Fosse's own drama than the dramas of its characters. In that mysterious ending, Charity pulls herself out of the orchestra pit dripping with lake water, and a good fairy — making her first appearance in the show — waves her wand and promises Charity all her dreams will come true. Then the good fairy turns and walks away, revealing a sign on her back: *Watch* The Good Fairy *tonight — 8:00 on CBS*. She's a fake.

The show was pivotal for Fosse. Teeming with stylized fourth-wall-breaking touches — the silent film–like titles, zippy scene changes, and iris-in techniques to create close-up effects — Fosse's grand concept, his directorial style, was a fractured thing, in pieces. It was edited. "The proscenium is all broken up, jagged, like a child made it," Reinking said. "Gwen told me that's how she thinks. That's her mind. And that's how Bob's brain worked too." *Sweet Charity* was made of defects, built on them. Charity herself was damaged; Oscar was neurotic. The story unfolded quickly, in narrative isolations, and the stage was obscured in pools of black. They all combined to give *Sweet Charity* the feel of a "Big Spender" girl — fast, dark, empty, broken.

Late in 1966, Cy Feuer called Fosse in to help on *Walking Happy*, his musical adaptation of *Hobson's Choice*. "Bob was there from the first day of rehearsal until we opened on Broadway," said dancer Dan Siretta. "He was the overall supervisor of the show." Sitting six or seven rows from the stage, Fosse saw Feuer and choreographer Danny Daniels through Detroit and Toronto. He gave his opinion only when Feuer asked for it, and he did it privately, in the back of the house at the end of the day or in the hotel lobby that evening or at breakfast the following morning. "The only time he spoke directly to us was out of town on a number called 'Think of Something Else,'" Siretta said. "Think of Something Else," a comic song about hanging around the pub, Fosse turned into a cartoon strip, playing up his dancers' character types and extreme behaviors. "He did come up with the one idea of the clog number ['Clog and Grog']," Verdon said, "where the men did wear clogs and where they did, again, a lot of tricks with hat passing. Where it would go back along the line and come forward on the line this way."

Nights alone were murder on Fosse. "Bob would get so lonely," Siretta said. "He'd call up girls at two, three in the morning and say, 'Hey, I want you to come down here to my room.' He hated the night. It wasn't just about the sex with Bobby. He was looking for kindness, tenderness. He was looking for support. He wanted to be held and treasured. He just wanted to be told he was good." The amphetamines kept him up, freaked out. "Fosse would call me at night when we were out of town," *Walking Happy* dancer Ellen Graff recalled, "and I remember being very flattered. Of course I knew he was trying to date me, but he made me feel good talking about what he was there to do. I believe he was interested in what I had to say. We talked

about how he was trying to get the performances down from caricature. I'm not sure if he succeeded." In the dressing room, girls traded
stories, some jealously. ("Did Bobby call *you* last night?" "Did you
. . . ?") Some wished they had gotten a call; others wished they hadn't.
He was so hard to say no to — or, rather, he made it so hard to say
no. "Bobby was so much a little boy," Siretta said, "but it could get
pathetic." *Walking Happy* opened and closed.

And *Sweet Charity* was a terrific hit. The credit — most of it, at least
— went to Gwen. "You are the strangest actor I have ever watched,"
Cary Grant confessed to her one night after the show.

"Why?"

"Because when you play a scene where you're just so happy, I cry.
And when you play a scene where it's very sad, I laugh."

Fosse would have snorted at this. "Whose performance do you
think she gave anyhow?" he grumbled to a friend. "Do they think a
performance comes out of the air? She didn't make it up. A performance has to be *directed.*"

For years Fosse had kept his anger to himself. Since *Damn Yankees*, it often seemed that Gwen, the star, stole his accolades. Didn't
anyone see how his talent amplified hers? With *Sweet Charity*, Fosse's
sense of injustice increased. On this show, his effort and influence
had overwhelmed, he thought, the talent of any other single con-
tributor. From book to stage, this one was Fosse's. A longtime friend,
designer Tony Walton, said, "During much of their joint professional
career, whenever they did a show together, Gwen was very much the
critics' darling, and if there was any blame to be placed, Bob was
always the recipient even though who knew how much of her performance was his creation."

Despite Fosse's gloom, Gwen remained her husband's personal
press secretary, standing at the door of their new East Hampton
home, waving in dancers by the busload. "If Fosse did anything gen-

erous or lovely," said *Sweet Charity* dancer Marie Wallace, "I some-how thought Gwen was behind it." The all-day cast parties, the silver dishes from Tiffany that said *Christmas '66 Gwen and Bob*. "She loved being with us," Wallace said. "I don't know if Bob was that way. My sense was Gwen did it for him." Gwen was certainly the more outgoing of the two, but there was no doubt Fosse enjoyed having friends over, especially his growing crop of writer pals, which now included his East Hampton neighbor Robert Alan Aurthur, an old comrade of Chayefsky's from the golden days of TV drama. Croquet, champagne, steaks on the grill — Gwen liked to show her family home was thriving. "Those were fabulous parties," one dancer said. "But knowing what we all knew about Bob and Gwen, it felt a little strange, like, Were they putting on a show?"

"I felt sorry for Gwen," Ruth Buzzi said. "She seemed so lonely, maybe because Bobby never ever came in [to her dressing room]. He never seemed to pay any attention to her backstage and he never went out with her after the show." Sensing this, Buzzi and Nick Malekos, one of the stage managers, would visit Gwen in her dressing room whenever they could. It began casually enough, with a cracked door and a hello, but soon they found themselves staying for as much as an hour, gossiping about the show or sewing stuffed animals for Nicole's birthday. "We were in there most nights of the week," Buzzi said. "It became part of the day. I remember thinking I just want to make her laugh. Gwen seemed to need it. She needed to visit with people after the show who cared." Gwen never mentioned Fosse, and Buzzi and Malekos never brought him up.

In her dressing room after a matinee one day, Gwen placed a frightened call to Robert Alan Aurthur. She needed help, fast. "Bobby called," she said, sounding scared. "He told me he's having chest pains."

"Can he get to a doctor?"

"I don't know. I called home just now and there was no answer —"

Aurthur finally reached Fosse the next morning. Was he okay? Did he see the doctor? Was he still having chest pains?

"Chest pains? There weren't any chest pains," he lied. "But I hear Gwen gave one hell of a performance last night."

TWENTY YEARS

HAVE YOU FINISHED work yet, Daddy?"
Nicole would sit outside the room Fosse designated
as his office slipping notes under his door, plying him
with the trademark Fosse tenacity no one, not even another Fosse,
could resist. At three, she already looked like the baby-girl version
of her father, possibly cuter, with her little dimples, little nose, and
dollop of bright blond hair. It was all too much for him. He needed to
find another place to work.

Fosse had an idea for a musical version of *Big Deal on Madonna
Street,* the Italian comedy about a bunch of lowlifes trying to pull off
a big heist (a story, he would admit, with a certain personal resonance), and he had decided this time he would make good on his
private vow to write the book himself. As opposed to *The Conquering Hero* and *Sweet Charity,* this idea, he wouldn't give up; he would
be responsible for every element, top to bottom. The time had come
to insist. Fosse had the clout, the financial security, and, with Paddy
Chayefsky encouraging him, the blessing of a true artist.

To be closer to Paddy, he took an eleventh-floor office at 850 Seventh Avenue, a suite literally down the hall from Chayefsky, who may

have been the only other man in New York who worked as hard as Fosse. Paddy was always around. His marriage by now a function of habit, an agreement more than a relationship, Paddy often spent nights at 850 Seventh, which seemed convenient for everyone — him, his wife, Susan, and especially Bob Fosse, whose beginning-writer questions could be answered most any hour, day or night, by one of the best in the business. All Fosse had to do was walk ten or twelve steps down the hallway and knock. Sometimes Bob and Paddy would shut the place down or wake each other up the next morning, one leaving dinner or breakfast outside the other's door before slipping back to his own office for yet another crack at the scene. "This is the manic-depressive floor," Fosse joked. "'I'm no good. I'm no good.'"

Fosse's suite was nicely disheveled, walls plastered with posters from his shows, many of them from his former life as a performer, and adoring reviews, like a clipping from one of his *Pal Joeys*. On his desk, beside a framed picture of Nicole playing in Central Park, stood a photo of his nine-year-old self in Riff Brothers' white tie and tails, as if he were trying to remind himself — as if he could ever forget — what he truly was: just a kid with a few tricks.

Down the hall from Fosse and Chayefsky, the agent Lionel Larner kept his office door open to whoever was inclined to put up his feet and browse through the day's trades or hear a funny story or use Larner's copying machine, the only one in the building. Looking more like a country home than a place of business, the offices of Lionel Larner Limited were a natural salon for the eleventh floor; Larner, at one time the agent with the highest client-renewal rate on Broadway, was convivial, witty, fluent in all dialects of industry trade-craft. He called 850 Seventh a magical place, "the Dakota of office buildings." Former tenants included Elia Kazan and the actor Dickie Moore, who had starred as Dietrich's baby in *Blonde Venus*. Larner, Fosse, and Chayefsky stuck together. They knew one another's business. When Larner heard his dear friend and client Larry Blyden had died, Bob and Paddy sat with Larner in his office until the end of the day; 850 Seventh was like that.

Located in midtown only slightly north of the theater district, the building had considerable Broadway appeal, but its secret ingredient was its landlord, Herbert Tuttle. Tuttle loved show business. He thought of himself as a patron of the arts. Every year, he renegotiated each tenant's lease, the renter's box-office figures in hand, charging only what the gross percentages promised he or she could afford. If lessees were hot, their rents would go up or stay the same; cold, and Herb would cut them a break. "The world of show business was smaller then," Larner said. "There was money to be made, of course, but there was more money elsewhere. The people of 850 Seventh were in show business because they loved show business, and Herb Tuttle was one of those people. He looked after us. We looked after each other."

On the very same hall as Fosse and Chayefsky, Herb Gardner — cartoonist, playwright of *A Thousand Clowns,* and the building's unofficial monologist — worked in blessed agony. Erupting with the spirit of quixotic Jews, Gardner was a firework rambler, discoursing in all directions at once and always — like Fosse danced and Chayefsky reasoned — on the jolly side of madness. He'd grown up at his father's Canal Street saloon, listening to nutjobs fight about cantaloupe and politics and rhapsodize about fat old girlfriends. Now Gardner was nuts. He wrote about nuts. "A man who is not touched by the earthy lyricism of hot pastrami, the pungent fantasy of corned beef, pickles, frankfurters, the great lusty impertinence of good mustard . . . is a man of stone and without heart," he wrote in one play. He wrote about people caught up in the ageless clash between trying to act like grownups on the one hand and running naked through the Lower East Side with pretty girls on the other. In Gardner's plays, the nicest thing someone could say to someone else was "You're the craziest person I've ever met." "I'd like you to fall madly in love with me and think I'm wonderful and throw yourself at my feet," says Sally in *Thieves*, "and I'd like you to do it on the phone." That was Herb Gardner. He was the ukulele type.

Masters of the hangout, Bobby, Paddy, and Herbie became best friends. Paddy was in awe of Bobby's charm; Bobby was captivated by Paddy's warmth and intellect; and they were both enthralled by Herb's lunatic whimsy. "That was a marriage between three men," said producer David Picker. "They were there for each other in any way possible. So if Herb had a play, Paddy had a play, Bobby had a [show], they were there. It was 'What can we do?' 'How can we help?'" No matter how gruesome the *Variety* headlines or the show problems or the women problems, they would be together, laughing in their ugly elevator down to lunch.

Lunch was the same every day. Thirty steps from the lobby of 850 Seventh Avenue was the Carnegie Deli, their downstairs din- ing room. Compared to the venerable Stage Deli only a block south, the Carnegie was a cluttered, cranky hole in the wall. Both delis had begun at the starting line with an equal shot, but the Stage, originally at Broadway and Forty-Eighth, was closer to the theaters and the first to go showbiz. It caught on. Stage Deli founder Max Asnas was so quotable, Fred Allen called him the "Corned Beef Confucius." Once Walter Winchell started writing about the restaurant and Asnas got on TV and radio, there was no way any other deli could keep up. In 1943, the Stage moved uptown, into Carnegie turf. Asnas opened a sidewalk conservatory, put in a bar, and became the sort of assimi- lated fancy-shmancy deli the Carnegie types loved to kvetch about. *Theirs* was a *real* deli, the Carnegie folks would say, hoping to be asked why. Why? Well, for one thing, at the Carnegie they do the same sandwich better and for less. At the Carnegie, you have to chase down a waiter to get some service and fight the kitchen noise to hear yourself complain, and you also have to eat every bite on your plate so the owner won't be insulted if he passes by, which he will, and he'll probably sit down and complain too, if not about his business, then about the Yankees, even if they're winning. This was Chayefsky's kind of place. If you left feeling more on edge than you arrived, all the better; you'd had some life for lunch.

It was the Carnegie in Chayefsky that Fosse had no trouble getting next to. Over lunch, he came to see Paddy wasn't just the brains behind *Marty*, he *was* Marty, and wasn't Marty with girls a lot like Fosse was with Fosse? Intellect aside, these were two hard-working satirists from the same metaphysical deli, not the "Broadway" one with the conservatory and fresh-squeezed orange juice, but the one with guts and loss and laughs. The deli of truths: merciless and lacerating, at all costs and on all subjects. Not many had the chutzpah to give the famous director Bob Fosse direction, especially not the kind nobody likes to get, but Paddy did. "That's bullshit, Fosse!" he would say, and Fosse would thank him. That's who they were. They hated bullshit more than they hated their own misery; they hated it together. "Paddy could tell Bob everything," Ann Reinking said, "and in such a loving way that Bob couldn't get defensive." When he was with Paddy, phoniness died on sight. "You'd see them at their table against the wall," Karen Hassett said, "the big bear and the dancing elf, debating and laughing." They loved each other. It was just Fosse's *goyishe* sandwich order — corned beef with mayo on white — that drove Paddy crazy.

In those years, the mid- to late sixties, movie-musical intelligence — taking a cue from *The Sound of Music,* a gargantuan hit — said bigger was better. To compete with the smallness of TV, which had gained on movies only in the decade since Dore Schary tried to squash it with 3-D, Hollywood bet on the extravaganza, spending more, casting more, and stretching aspect ratios ever wider to take in more of the stunning locations no TV camera could fully capture. So it hardly seemed unreasonable that Universal Pictures, now one with MCA under Lew Wasserman, poured millions into *Thoroughly Modern Millie*, an elephantine folly held up by the highly bankable promise of Julie Andrews. It would not have surprised Paddy, himself writing Paramount's twenty-million-dollar *Paint Your Wagon*, that Wasserman, looking down from his black tower in Burbank, had his sights set on *Sweet Charity* next.

But before Universal could buy the film rights from Fryer, Carr, and Joe Harris, Charnin's arbitration suit over *Sweet Charity* authorship had to be resolved. With a movie deal hanging in the balance, suddenly, after years of delays and evasions, a settlement was reached. "Fryer and Carr had to admit to it," Charnin said; that was his victory. The producers stipulated Charnin could not discuss the terms of the settlement; that was theirs.

Wasserman set Ross Hunter, producer of *Thoroughly Modern Millie*, to oversee the production of *Sweet Charity*, and signed Shirley MacLaine to star. MacLaine, who had loved Fosse since her chorus-girl days in *The Pajama Game*, considered him a life-changing influence. Fosse was one of the first to recognize her talent, the way Joan McCracken had seen his. Now a Hollywood star, MacLaine was prepared to wield her influence and make sure Fosse got to direct the movie. She reminded Wasserman there was precedent — first-time directors could make successful films of their own musicals; think of Jerome Robbins's stage-to-film transfer of *West Side Story*. According to MacLaine, Wasserman didn't counter with the obvious *Yes, but Robbins drew on the vast experience of his codirector, Robert Wise;* he said nothing but "Okay, kid. Let's get him."

"I remember feeling tentative, to say the least," Fosse said of his first movie deal, "but not wanting to communicate it. You can't express self-doubt in Hollywood; it's fatal." Instead, he led with a touch of bullshit — what little he knew of production from MGM and the television specials on his résumé — and clung to tales of his forebears Jerry Robbins and Stanley Donen.

Fosse hated Hollywood. He had a fifteen-year-old grudge against the industry that had failed him; it represented everything that was wrong with the business he loved. "I hate show business and I love it," Fosse would say. "I love working with actors and dancers and writers and designers. I think they're the most beautiful, talented, and witty people in the world. But I hate the bullshit, the Beverly Hills homes with swimming pools. I hate Mercedes. I hate Gucci bags, I hate all of that shit."

In Los Angeles, Universal paired Fosse with Robert Surtees, three-time Oscar-winning cinematographer of *My Fair Lady* and *The Graduate*, a pro at home in styles both classical and carefully avant-garde and a man well suited to Fosse's sense of humor. Surtees liked to joke that one day he would become a producer so that he could double-cross all his friends. "Bobby was fascinated with Surtees's technical expertise," said Sonja Haney, dance assistant on the film. "He wasn't afraid to ask him anything. If there was something he didn't know the answer to, he'd say, 'That's a Robert Surtees question.'" Surtees's son Bruce, an uncredited camera operator on *Sweet Charity*, remembered Fosse as glued to his father's side. "Anyone less charming than Bob could never have gotten away with so many interruptions, so many questions," Surtees said. "Even if he didn't say it, his demeanor was 'I'm just a schmuck dancer. I don't know anything about the camera.' But of course he did. He just didn't know as much as he *wanted to,* which was everything."

The side of Fosse that needed struggle in order to create may have been relieved to learn producer Ross Hunter had soft-focus ideas in store for *Sweet Charity*. "There was quite a fight," Fosse said, "about whether Charity could say 'Up yours.' I felt that if she couldn't, then we might as well make *Mary Poppins* all the way." Encouraged by Shirley MacLaine, Wasserman allied with Fosse and took Hunter off the picture, freeing the virgin filmmaker to fly solo and indulge his whims, good or bad, happy musical or sad. Other than Wasserman himself, no one could stop *Sweet Charity* from becoming a Bob Fosse picture through and through — whatever that meant.

What *did* that mean? The slate clean, Fosse set out, quite consciously, to find a film style. "He wanted to be an artist," Bruce Surtees said. "He wasn't pretentious about it; he was exploratory." He imagined the fringe elements of Charity's milieu demanded a fringe aesthetic, something outside the purview of straight-ahead musical comedy. Fosse talked to Surtees about McCracken, about ideas she had. "If there were people," McCracken had written for *Dance Magazine* in 1946, "to take full advantage of the opportunities the camera offers and the stage does not, the back would not only be photographed, but the front, side, top, and bottom all at once. Think of how nice that would be in the case of a *pirouette*. How lovely an *arabesque* turn done three times as slow would be. How amusing fast *jeté* done four times as fast would be. How interesting to see the different mood and rhythm of one dancer expressing the conflict of two driving energies, and dancing them both at the same time. Dancing is movement and the movies could make it move even more if the stage were forgotten."

They discussed John Huston's *Moulin Rouge,* one of Fosse's favorite movie musicals. "*Moulin Rouge* was the first time I saw the shot of a leg or the quick flash of a face in a pirouette," he said. "It was very exciting." Rather than approximate, as Astaire's films did, the perspective of a Broadway audience, Huston shattered his numbers with cuts and close-ups to create the frenzied effect of the Moulin Rouge. It was a style that suited Fosse's shattered dances, so often montages themselves.

Fosse began wearing a viewfinder around his neck like a membership badge. On their own in a Universal screening room, he and Surtees ordered up print after print — for two months of study. What had impressed Fosse most about *West Side Story* was Robbins's (and codirector Robert Wise's) willingness to depart from the theatrical version and his use of real locations and highly stylized film techniques to break the show free from the Broadway stage. Process shots captivated Fosse. He made note of *West Side Story*'s extreme choices, like the expressionist use of color in the gym dance and the selective blurring of actors in the background that Wise and Robbins utilized to indicate the intensity of Tony and Maria's attraction. He watched Stanley Donen's movies *Charade, Arabesque,* and *Two for the Road,* admiring their reflection shots, mirrors, glossy objects, jump cuts, rack focuses. Fosse didn't know the names for certain elements, so he asked Surtees and then made flashcards: *establishing shot, master shot, blue screen, rear projection.* His screening-room notes spawned shot lists and crude little bird's-eye diagrams, and those diagrams became the basis for further questions and possibilities. He would consider every hand on every dancer, every dancer in every shot, every shot from every angle.

Obsessively attuned to the micro, Fosse's mind was a natural for movie gadgets, which broke down sight and sound as Dexedrine broke down his dances. Macro was more of a challenge. But that's where Paddy Chayefsky came in. Along with Verdon, Paddy was in the unofficial production outfit Fosse had assembled. Sometimes it seemed that was the closest Bob Fosse came to purebred, real love — doing good work, enjoying collaboration with those he could trust. Perhaps that's why he felt closest to Gwen in rehearsal, at Variety Arts, where he couldn't be unfaithful to her.

"How do you feel about it?" he asked Gwen when Shirley Mac-Laine was cast.

"Fine."

What else could she say? The studio wasn't going to make this movie without a movie star. "It's your property," she said. "You instigated it. See it through."

When *Charity* closed on Broadway, she agreed to join him in LA to help Shirley. To help him.

While Fosse veteran Eddie Gasper ran the ensemble through countless details of "The Rich Man's Frug," Sonja Haney rehearsed Shirley MacLaine for months of preproduction, in the fall of 1967, in advance of Verdon's arrival. "I loved rehearsing with Shirley," Haney said, "because she never made the same mistake twice and she always had ideas. Fosse wanted the dances to be done his way, but he was open to her suggestions. Shirley added a hat trick from 'Steam Heat' to 'If My Friends Could See Me Now.' That wasn't in the original choreography."

With special permission from the studio, Fosse would bring Haney to their sound stage before the studio opened on weekends and plug in a pot of coffee, and the two of them would work until five in the afternoon, without breaking, blocking out every number for the camera. "Bob would start with the top of each number," Haney said, "and I would be everybody and make notes about movement, camera, and when he wanted to zoom on which bar of music." Using Haney as both model and secretary, Fosse remembered each dancer's position and pose down to the smallest unit of personality. He would isolate quirks — big eyes, long noses — for special close-ups, tailoring every shot to each dancer's signature look, and he always referred to the dancers by their names, so as to be as clear and specific as possible. "He would say, 'Have Adele here . . . and make sure we have her hair coming down over her face when she flips over . . .'" Dance was more than choreography; it was character. These weren't anonymous Ziegfeld girls but individuals, each with her own face, problem, and unfulfilled heart. Fosse and Haney covered about one number per weekend. They rehearsed the dancers during the week.

Having finished her run of *Charity* in New York, Gwen was a distant presence during the rehearsal period, careful to hover without meddling, like a mother at the school dance. Occasionally she would go in to do some barre work in an empty studio, but most days, she was there in street clothes, slacks and a scarf and a pair of nice shoes.

"How the hell do you do 'Something Better Than This'?" an exhausted Haney asked one day.

"Oh, honey." Gwen laughed. "I know when to breathe."

Few understood how Gwen, the *real* Charity, could keep up what appeared to be such a genuinely congenial attitude. "It had to be one of the worst things for her," said John McMartin, reprising his role for the film. "Her heart had to be broken that Shirley got the part. These were *her* moves. But you'd never know with Gwen. She was stoic." "The fact that she was there at all blew me away," said Chita Rivera, playing Nickie. "But dancers do what they have to do. Gwen did it for Jack Cole and she did it for Bobby. I felt no resentment coming from her. She just did her job. That was Gwen's point of view in work and in love." One would glimpse her whispering in Fosse's ear, standing over him on the ladder Fosse climbed to see the number from above. "They literally finished each other's sentences," Suzanne Charney said. "'That dancer —' '— should get there earlier.'" Gwen turned down the title role in a Broadway play, Tennessee Williams's *The Seven Descents of Myrtle,* just to be there.

When Fosse wasn't conferring with Verdon or Surtees, he was pacing. ("If I'd known how he worked," prop man Sol Martino said, "I'd never have gotten him a chair with his name on it.") Sunk under his own intensity, with his cigarette pointed downward like a rudder, Fosse was lost to the surface world of quotidian concerns and feelings, consigned to an isolation so extreme the slightest wrong turn could lock him into depression, and fast, at the ruthless speed of amphetamines. To the dancers, it didn't look like mania; it looked like focus. It looked romantic: there in the shadows, the artist. "One of the reasons you wanted to work so hard for Bobby," Lee Roy Reams said, "was because he was so obviously working so hard for you."

Word of Fosse's inscrutability made its way into the papers. "His anxieties and indecisions have everyone on edge," one columnist wrote a tad dramatically. "I knew that he felt he was under an unbelievable amount of pressure," Haney said, "but he was always quiet. He never yelled. He was too busy concentrating, trying to make a choice." Choreographing the dances offered more than enough possibilities for failure, but the number of possibilities for filming those possibilities was infinity times infinity, like looking through one kaleidoscope into another: a quarter-inch turn, and the whole vista shifted. "He missed nothing," MacLaine said. "As a result, he saw too much. Being the repository of all he saw rendered him indecisive." Thinking was quicksand. "Everything about films is so mammoth ... so much money ... every moment costing X-number of dollars ... so many people on the sets ... that it tends to overwhelm a fellow with a middle-class background," Fosse said. "But if the pressure gets to you, your talent can't function. If you let yourself be hurried, you lose your inventiveness. You have to forget those other things, lower your head and go ahead." He was constipated, and sent out for Preparation H before filming began.

On set, Gwen was the ideal antidote, the mother his dancers turned to for reassurance. If Daddy drifted too far off, she peeled back a smile that flashed *Go, team!* in blazing red lights. But at home, blaze was not her default setting. Over dinner with her old friend Pat Ferrier Kiley (Ferrier had recently married Richard Kiley), Gwen confessed she'd feared *Sweet Charity,* her comeback, might turn out to be her farewell tour. It nearly killed her. "If only all the fuses would blow," she once said to a reporter backstage, "so I wouldn't have to do this." Actors were luckier. Most got better as they got older. Gwen, a dancer, was becoming obsolescent even in her prime. Many of Fosse's new girls were teenagers.

Though being Fosse's dramaturge and ubiquitous assistant seemed to many a sad and selfless position for Gwen to take, Gwen herself thought that, considering the alternative, it was very much a good deal for her. In addition to being the director's wife, she was now the guardian of his style — its oldest representative, its most expert practitioner. And having more of Fosse's work in her brain-body than anyone else, Verdon was an unbeatable back catalog for him, poised to be essential to Fosse even after her dancer's body gave out.

"Both Gwen and I were watching every dancer to make sure their focus was right and they were looking in the right direction," Haney said. "That freed Bob up to worry about the camera." Almost oblivious to the dance, he watched the actors through his viewfinder, pushing himself to think cinematically. "Bob wasn't really into the dancing when we were shooting," said "Frug" dancer Larry Billman. "But he was right next to us or right under us, being rolled around on a little dolly cart, trying to find the perfect angle. He would only talk to us to say things like 'Angle your face more that direction.' We were literally stick figures in his frame."

"He was so involved," Haney said. "He knew everything that was going on with everyone on the set and if he didn't like the way something was going, he'd take care of it." Filming "If My Friends Could See Me Now," Fosse sat down at the lighting console and taught himself how to cross-fade at a precise speed, on the exact beat. "Bob was so focused on technique," actor Lonnie Burr said, "he'd call us to the set and then forget we were all waiting for him to finish playing with the cameras." This happened while shooting "The Rhythm of Life" number with Sammy Davis Jr. "Hey, Bob!" Sammy yelled between sips from his bourbon and Coke. "How much longer are you gonna keep me waiting? I'm a superstar, you know!" But from a technical standpoint, no number was more challenging than "Rich Man's Frug"; it contained the most elaborate camera setups, the most dancers to synchronize, the most sight and sound elements to coordinate with hairsplitting precision. "That's when Bob and I really had a hard time keeping track," Haney said. "Once he asked me, 'At what bar and what count was the crane at its furthest point back and its highest position up?' *Oh God*, I thought."

"Big Spender" Fosse shot twice, the second time after he realized he hadn't gotten in close enough. Fosse wanted to see the dancers' faces — close-ups he couldn't get onstage — but if he pushed into their faces, he would lose the painstakingly arranged composition he had in the wide shot. How to get both at once? Splitting the difference, he decided to cut two dancers from the line and move in tighter, and he reshot "Big Spender" through April 4, 1968, when the news came that Martin Luther King Jr. had been assassinated. That day he had to be told to wrap early; if it had been up to him, he would have kept shooting. Two months later, Robert Kennedy was shot. "Seeing how upset I was," said MacLaine, "Fosse switched around the shooting schedule to include a new scene in which I had to cry." What hurt in life could help in film. That's what life was: fertilizer.

The dailies were a sensation. So many thrilling pieces and jazzy angles. Fosse's editors bounded into the cutting room drunk on possibilities. But the footage didn't cut together; all that flash overwhelmed the story. But if he removed that flash, Fosse feared he'd lose his film's style. Those zooms and whips — they were proof of his vision. They had to stay.

Meanwhile, Fosse fought Universal over *Charity's* (still) problematic ending. The studio had let him shoot two, and now the brass couldn't make up their minds over which one to use. In the unhappy ending, Oscar leaves Charity. In the happy, he stops her before she jumps in the lake. (Him: "The odds against us are a hundred to one." Her: "Those are the best odds I ever had.") On the one hand, Universal knew a musical comedy had to end on an *up* note; on the other, both *Funny Girl* and *Finian's Rainbow* went out bittersweet. Was the new musical reality realer? It was a Hollywood question true to the late 1960s: the old-fashioned happy ending looked a little too easy, but these *were* comedies (right?). "That last minute in *Finian's Rainbow*," Fosse said, "where [Astaire] says he's off to Glocca Morra — I wept so . . . It was like . . . his whole career . . . suddenly . . ."

Fosse vacillated up to the very last minute. So did Universal. Both endings tested to mixed results: the sad was stronger; the happy fit better. Universal delayed the final decision for weeks, the studio executives changing their minds through the previews. "When I saw the movie for the first time," Sonja Haney said, "I didn't know how it was going to end." This was Fosse's chance. He knew the director had more power in Hollywood than on Broadway, but as a first-time filmmaker, he didn't know how to wield it. "If a director overuses it," he said, "he can start indulging his every whim — and so can the cast. On the other hand, if you underuse that power, you lose control. The picture can be taken away from you by the actors, the cameraman, or the studio itself." Ultimately, Universal went with the sadder version.

"If it's a flop," Fosse said to Shirley MacLaine, "I'll want to put my head in the oven. If it's a hit, I'll want to keep it there."

In October 1968, with the bulk of editing behind him, Fosse took a moment to repay Gwen the only way he knew how. He choreographed two pieces for her appearance on *The Bob Hope Show*, "Cool Hand Luke" and "Tijuana Brass." Each betrayed the softness he tried so hard to conceal. "Cool Hand Luke," especially — Fosse's most warm-hearted creation, a matador's lullaby devoid of ironic comment. Accompanied by Lee Roy Reams and Buddy Vest, Gwen strutted and snapped through "Luke" with elegant machismo, receiving in wide welcoming arms Fosse's plaintive offering to her sensuality. "Every moment of creating this dance," Reams said, "was a pleasure and a joy."

Fosse had reason to feel the closest he ever came to calm. On January 29, 1969, *Variety* wrote, "[*Sweet Charity*] will become one of the memorable artistic and commercial successes of this generation." He received unmitigated raves on all fronts. "Bob Fosse," the entertainment world read, "has become a major film director." The *Hollywood Reporter* followed suit, predicting *Charity* would become Universal's all-time box-office champion—and the press ride began. *Sweet Charity*'s world premiere in Boston was preceded by lavish previews in Chicago, where Fosse returned a conquering hero, and New York. Perhaps he would do *Big Deal on Madonna Street* next, as a movie musical. Keeping track of his progress in a little red pocket diary, he thought of setting the heist in Tijuana for that cool, weary Herb Alpert sound that was so popular, the style he'd used for Gwen's dance on *The Bob Hope Show*—or maybe he'd change Mexico to Harlem and make *Big Deal* an all-black show. As the Broadway success of *Cabaret* had demonstrated, the time was certainly right for a socially conscious musical.

But on April 1, 1969, his plans vaporized. *Sweet Charity* opened —and bombed at the box office. The next day, Fosse took out his red journal and wrote, "Didn't do anything except feel sorry for myself." Over the course of the next week, the box-office numbers got worse.

An autopsy of a movie gives the bereaved a feeling of power, consoling them with the cold comfort of pseudo-theories and the remote possibility of finding an explanation in the carnage. But show business is bad science. There is never a clear explanation. There is only the yes or no of an unfeeling box office, and one impossible commandment that sometimes passes for wisdom: Don't take it personally.

Bob Fosse took it all personally. "Long," "noisy," "dim," "literal." If words were spoken against his movie, they were spoken against him. He accepted the blame, encouraged it even. "That was my fault," he said. "Entirely." Screenwriter Peter Stone would indict Universal's promotional strategy; others would lament the immaturity of MCA's movie division. But these were standard snipes, transparent to any seasoned executive. Bob Fosse was through. The entirety of his film-making career had been a one hundred percent failure.

And he had no agent, nobody to leverage him some kind of recovery work. In 1962, midway into Fosse's *Little Me* deal, MCA, Fosse's agency of fifteen successful years, had sent him — and every other client — a formal breakup letter. By acquiring Universal Pictures, MCA had broken federal antitrust laws, so the conglomerate had to choose between the agency business and the production business. As the breakup letter stated, MCA chose production, abandoning Fosse midnegotiation and forcing him to seek representation elsewhere. A squabble over unpaid commissions ensued; cases were argued and settlements reached, and Fosse walked off with broken trust in agents. Since then — six years before the film of *Sweet Charity* — Fosse's lawyer Jack Perlman had done his negotiating. With a direct line to any Broadway producer in town, Fosse had decided his reputation would work for him, and he chose not to sign with another agency. But now that *Sweet Charity* had failed, no one called. And without formal representation, Fosse had no one to call on his behalf. A five-time Tony winner, he had never had to beg before. Of course, he had important friends. He could arrange a meeting with Cy Feuer or Fryer and Carr, but they were Broadway friends, and returning to the stage, Fosse knew, would underline his defeat. He wanted to be in movies. In movies, the director was the king. Maybe even the star.

Despite his circumstances, he was being courted by David Begelman of Creative Management Associates, an agency Begelman and Freddie Fields had opened with the help of certain VIP clients (Streisand, Judy Garland, Peter Sellers) they had brought over from MCA. William Morris had come up by playing the odds, signing clients big and small on the grounds that 10 percent of a dollar was still ten cents more than nothing, but CMA, a boutique agency, kept itself exclusive to haute Hollywood. The B-list need not apply. Young and slick and charming, Fields and Begelman made the movie business look fun, exchanging the Old Testament techniques of Louis B. Mayer and Jack Warner for the honey-baby mode of the hotshot generation. You wanted to be with them. Sometimes, on a call, one would pretend to be the other, carry on negotiations for a while, and then switch midstream to his real self, confounding whoever was on the other end of the phone and maybe getting a little foothold on the deal.

Fosse signed with CMA on April 9, a week after the film of *Charity* opened.

Back in New York, he kept his head down and worked on the screenplay of *Big Deal on Madonna Street,* and he lived in terror of running into a concerned friend or associate on the street or at a party and having to watch that person try to console him with the glass-half-full showings of the usual bullshit. There was a time when he would have thought of killing himself, or at least savored the fantasy ("So young!" he imagined them saying. "Such a promising career!"), but now, at forty-two, he was too old to die a tragic prodigy, and there was Nicole. Nicole: for her, he vowed to control his death wish.

When Fosse fell victim to self-pity, Paddy and Herb Gardner got him out of his office and hurried him downstairs to the Carnegie Deli, their clubhouse, where Herb Schlein, permanently concerned Jewish mother and deli maître d', lived in eager anticipation of the Bobby/Paddy/Herb lunch-hour invasion. It was the best part of his day, every day. He saved them white linen napkins. An undiscriminating collector of *Playbills*, cast albums, and signed memorabilia, Schlein was the ultimate fan, two hundred and fifty smiling pounds of "What can I do for you great men of Broadway?" (And "How is Nicole?" And "How is your infection?") "He knows every cockamamie show," Chayefsky said. "It's his totally untarnished illusions about show business, which is the way I'd like to think of it but can't."

Schlein made no secret of hating the deli. His dream was to work on a show. Acting, writing — anything. Pulling back a chair ("Do you mind if I sit?"), he'd tell about the time Kazan told him not to become an actor. Schlein knew he had a one-in-ten-billion shot, working his three-hundred-dollar-a-week job, living with his mother in Jersey, waiting for his SAG membership to come through. Fosse adored him. He identified with him.

Herbie guarded the trio's table — in the back, to the left and against the wall — like the Secret Service guarded the Oval Office. The men had no need for menus. Bob sat facing the entrance so he could keep an eye on the door (he had been known to hide when journalists came in), and Paddy sat facing the kitchen, waiting for his fruit and coffee (or, when Herbie wasn't watching him, pastrami). Fosse completed his first draft of the *Big Deal* script in June 1969 and gave it to Paddy for notes. "You would look over," Dan Siretta said, "and see pages being passed back and forth across the [deli] table." Fosse would tell Paddy to take his best shot — and Paddy always took it. Where there was trust, they knew, bullshit had no power. "[Paddy's] a very compassionate, understanding man," Fosse said. "And I don't sense that he's going to turn on me and call me a weakling or a coward ever, even though I may relate some feelings that are rather cowardly." How many women could give him that? How many men? How many writers, directors, producers, and dancers would use Fosse to move up, as Fosse would be the first to admit he had used them? Many. But Chayefsky — who had nothing to gain from Fosse's success or failure — was simply the realest man Fosse knew.

So when Paddy told Fosse *Big Deal* didn't work, Fosse knew *Big Deal* didn't work. Armed with a revised step outline (written for him by Chayefsky) and further notes from David Shaw and Bob Aurthur, Fosse started to revamp *Big Deal* in the summer of 1969. He took his manuscript to Amagansett, where he grilled and Ping-Ponged

(openly cheating) with Neil Simon, but he couldn't stop his mind
from revisiting the failure of *Sweet Charity.* Aurthur recalled a day of
waterskiing that was "marred only by Fosse's depression." There was
a time during the filming of *Charity* when Fosse had any number of
offers. That time had passed.

It's a great agent's genius to see promise and then make opportunity where others would not even think to look, mixing ideas and
personalities like a mad chemist hoping for a reaction. David Begelman was that kind of agent. By way of his CMA associate Sam
Cohn, Begelman connected Fosse with playwright and screenwriter
Steve Tesich and his script *The Eagle of Naptown.* Both won Fosse
over. The script was about a working-class midwestern kid with
Fosse's ambition — although in this case that ambition was directed
toward competitive bicycling instead of show business — and it could
be financed, all told, for an amazing $800,000, a figure Begelman
marched over to United Artists president David Picker, hoping for a
yes. But Picker passed, a blow, Begelman said, that reopened Fosse's
Sweet Charity wound. *Naptown* was turned down because of him,
wasn't it? (Ten years later, renamed *Breaking Away,* it would win Tesich an Oscar for best screenplay.)

Fosse was in awe of Tesich, a wistful, world-weary teddy bear,
another writer to add to Fosse's merry band of clown-scholars. "It's
a strange relationship, friendship," Tesich would say of their bond.
"There is no ceremony that takes place which binds you. There are
no vows taken. No birth certificate is issued when a friendship is
born. There is nothing tangible. There is just a feeling that your life
is different and that your capacity to love and care has miraculously
been enlarged without any effort on your part." No marriage would
give Fosse that enlargement, that total acceptance. "It's like having
a tiny apartment and somebody moves in with you," Tesich added,
"but instead of it becoming cramped and crowded the space expands
and you discover rooms you never knew you had." Prematurely,

Fosse sent *Big Deal* to David Picker and waited an anxious two weeks — a bad sign — for feedback, then politely excused Picker from the movie. Fosse was so desperate to work he even sent *Big Deal* to producer Ray Stark with a bury-the-hatchet note and assured him that if Stark didn't see the script as a movie, it could easily be transferred to the stage. Nothing happened.

One night, Hal and Judy Prince invited the Simons and the Fosses for dinner — their ancient feuds were long in the past — but Fosse came alone. The unspoken consensus was that the marriage was in trouble, but no one challenged Fosse's explanation that Gwen was under the weather, and the party stayed off the subject for the evening. For Fosse's sake, Simon and Prince also stayed off the subject of their careers, which, as everyone in the Broadway-speaking world knew, had soared as high as Fosse's had fallen. That left little to discuss. The Simons said they were going to rent a place in Majorca that summer. Hard up for meaningful chitchat, the quintet regrouped for coffee in the living room and Hal Prince confessed he was about to begin rehearsal on *Company*, the new Sondheim musical, so he wouldn't be directing the film of *Cabaret*, which Emanuel Wolf —

"The movie of *Cabaret*?" Bob said.

Prince had directed the show on Broadway in 1966. Fosse would not admit to liking *Cabaret*, but judging from Fosse's later shows, and none more than *Chicago*, Prince's *Cabaret* — from theme to music to stage sense — had made an impression on him. Based on Christopher Isherwood's *Berlin Stories* and John Van Druten's play *I Am a Camera*, an earlier adaptation of Isherwood, *Cabaret* was a goodtime, bad-time Nazi vaudeville. A daring crossbreed of the twentieth century's darkest hour and its lightest form of theater, musical comedy, the show's ingenious conceit was largely an accident. After weeks of rehearsal, director Hal Prince found his intended musical — the story of Sally Bowles — seemed more like a musical *within* the vaudeville world established by the introductory "this is Berlin" songs

("*Willkommen, bienvenue,* welcome!"). "There were two musicals onstage," Prince said. "One took place in real rooms, one in limbo. And in limbo were these numbers which directly commented on the real book show happening upstage." The limbo, overseen by Joel Grey's Emcee, permitted *Cabaret* to be a musical comedy. Because he was removed from the story, the Emcee could lighten the mood with jokey up-tempo numbers without compromising the seriousness of the Nazi drama unfolding "outside," in Berlin — or, for that matter, the real-life drama unfolding outside the Broadhurst Theater. "The first day of rehearsal," composer John Kander said, "Hal brought in a double-page spread from *Life* of a black couple entering a white housing development. The white crowd around them was jeering at them. He put it up on a bulletin board in the front of the room and said, 'That's what our show is about.'" It was also about the dangers of entertainment, show business as a metaphor for mass delusion. That Emcee was a kind of Hitler, and Sally Bowles, when she crossed the Mylar curtain that separated Berlin from the cabaret, chose show business instead of life. This Fosse could relate to.

After dinner that night, Prince told Fosse what he knew of the *Cabaret* movie plans. Emanuel L. Wolf at Allied Artists owned the rights and had partnered with Marty Baum at ABC Pictures. To produce, they brought on Cy Feuer, Fosse's friend of many years. Liza Minnelli would star and Jay Presson Allen would write the script, but as of yet, no one had been signed to direct.

Fosse started calling, pushing to meet with Feuer, which, oddly, Feuer seemed reluctant to do. Finally he agreed to meet Fosse for lunch.

Feuer had pasta; Fosse had cigarettes.

I have to do it, Fosse told him.

"I have to see the other guys," Feuer said. Big box-office names like Billy Wilder and Gene Kelly. "They expect it. If I don't see them, I'll seem unreasonable.

"But," Feuer added, sounding sincere, "after I see them, I'll tell Marty that I've talked to everyone and I want Fosse."

Fosse kept looking for work.

He got a call from Sue Mengers at CMA. A dumpling-shaped yenta in love with the underdog, Mengers had survived the Holocaust and the Bronx to become the funniest, toughest young agent in Hollywood. She called Larry Turman, an open-minded producer with a nice deal at Fox, and let him know Fosse was on the market. Turman didn't need to be sold. "I always, always wanted to work with Fosse," he said. "Even after *Sweet Charity* when he was persona non grata in Hollywood." Turman had taken a chance on *The Graduate;* he had taken a chance on Noel Black, director of *Pretty Poison;* and he had taken a chance on Robert Marasco's first screenplay, a wonky thriller called *Burnt Offerings* — he sent that script on to Fosse in New York. Fosse agreed to direct the movie and flew to LA as the clock struck midnight on New Year's Eve.

Turman and Fosse worked in Turman's office eight hours a day, every day, for two weeks. "Fosse was tenacious with the story," Turman said. "He had steel in his backbone, but he actually had a soft demeanor. I used to kid him and say, 'You're a tough guy, huh?' and he would sort of giggle like a kid." *Burnt Offerings* — a nonmusical about a happy family and the haunted house that destroys them — was dark even for dark material. But the contrast to *Sweet Charity* enticed Fosse, as did the (low) proposed budget and *Burnt Offerings'* central question: How much of a beating can a family withstand? On breaks, Fosse taught Turman how to skull, raising his hat with both hands and wiggling himself underneath it — an old burlesque trick used for comic emphasis, like a rim shot. "I loved the guy," Turman said. "Everyone said he was dark, but I thought he was fun." They settled on a summer 1970 shoot date, and Fosse took a trip up the California coast to look for his haunted mansion. When Fosse returned to New York, he expected to meet with Marasco for daily script discussions, but Marasco was devoted to his new play and slow to rewrite. Dissatisfied, Fosse let things fizzle from there.

Hastening the dissolution of Fosse's interest in *Burnt Offerings,* the news came that Emanuel Wolf, *Cabaret's* top-line producer, wanted to meet with Fosse. It looked like Feuer, true to his word, had indeed fought for him.

Cabaret was Wolf's second production as president and chairman of Allied Artists, a hand-to-mouth outfit with temporary office space in New York. When he heard Wolf had bought the *Cabaret* rights (for $1.5 million, the cost split with Marty Baum at ABC), Lew Wasserman told Wolf he was committing suicide. The failure of *Sweet Charity,* he explained, was not an isolated incident but part of a pattern that continued with *Paint Your Wagon* and *Star!,* flop musicals that spelled the end of the genre. And the end of Fosse. Wolf shrugged. "I knew the best time to get a talented director," he said, "was after a failure. Frank Perry [director of *Last Summer,* Allied's first film] couldn't get arrested when I hired him, but that's how I knew he was going to give me everything, and he did."

Fosse walked into Wolf's office, his eyes on the floor, and extended his fingers for a limp handshake. He seemed angry. "We were Hollywood," Wolf said, "and after what he had been through, I knew he must have hated Hollywood." They got to talking, taking shots at Lew Wasserman, and soon Fosse warmed. "He told me Wasserman misled him on *Sweet Charity,*" Wolf said. "When he met Lew, Lew told him that he should spend as much as he needed, that he'd give Fosse everything. So Fosse thought when his time ran out he was following Lew's directions." They spoke for an hour and a half, each watching the other guy for tells. "I knew this is a guy with a major distrust of people," Wolf said. "But I also knew he would go to any length he could to seek victory. I could see this was his life, and after *Sweet Charity* he was in a life-or-death situation."

To ease his worry as he waited, Fosse choreographed a number for Gwen to do on *The Ed Sullivan Show*. Through January 1970, he worked the way he usually did: at first, in three-hour shifts, from eleven to two or twelve to three, and then, as the air date drew near, every day from ten to six, a short break for dinner, and back to work from eight o'clock on into the night. To an observer, he would have appeared in a state of perfect and complete immersion, all parts of his body communing with each flash of his brain. Only Gwen, leading a group of six male dancers, could sense that his heart wasn't in the room. He was a hamster on a wheel, rehearsing only to rehearse. "The worst tragedy can befall me while I am rehearsing," he said, "and I'll still go on rehearsing." And so "A Fine, Fine Day" became imitation Fosse, a soft assemblage of bowlers, back bumps, and snaps. There was no character observation, no satire, no invention, only a literal pantomiming of lyrics. But the indefatigable Gwen played along, smiling big.

They were in trouble. "I was living like a wife and a mother," she later said, "which was really what I wanted to be, but I was the wrong kind of wife for him. I think Bob outgrew me. Bob started writing and he was involved in all kinds of things, and I was so involved with Nicole I didn't really care if I worked or not. I guess the hardest thing was I was honest with Bob and I admired him. I got sick of not being able to admire him. He began to think, 'Oh, you're my wife.' I hated that."

Soon thereafter, Fosse heard from Emanuel Wolf: Fosse would direct *Cabaret*. Production would begin the spring of the following year on location in Germany, and the money would be tight. *Cabaret* was to be a three-million-dollar picture, full stop. Fosse would get $125,000 for directing, $50,000 for choreography, and, to encourage a certain budgetary mindfulness, 7.5 percent of the profits. Wolf would stay in New York, but Feuer would accompany the production to Germany. To watch Fosse. To watch the money. "They *all* thought I could be controlled," Fosse said, "figuring I'd be too anxious after the failure of *Sweet Charity,* too scared to give anybody trouble. And I *was* scared."

Sitting across from Sam Clark and Marty Baum in the ABC offices, Fosse was as remote as he'd been at first with Wolf. "I'm here," he mumbled to the floor. "What do you want?"

Though Wolf had spoken, the ABC executives wanted to hold their own interview. "I understand you want to do *Cabaret,*" one of the men said. "Why?"

There was a pause. "I think I can make a good movie out of it."

The meeting inched along, neither side engaged. Finally, Fosse squeezed out a goodbye and left.

Baum turned to Clark. "We're going into the toilet with this."

A meeting of the *Cabaret* production team was set for January 20. Fosse joined Kander and Ebb and Jay Allen in Feuer's office for the customary get-acquainted exchange of big ideas, held mostly for Fosse's benefit. He needed to be filled in. But Fosse didn't like being filled in. *Cabaret* was his movie; he'd fill *them* in. "I didn't find him the happiest collaborator I ever had," Allen said. "For a man who dealt with women as much as he was obliged to, let's say he had an extremely parochial view of women." Fosse summoned his opinion panel for backup. Opposing Allen's approach to the script, both Neil Simon and Bob Aurthur gave Fosse the writerly ammo he needed to convince Feuer to spring for additional revisions. But Feuer wasn't dissatisfied with Allen's work, which dissatisfied Fosse even more, and so began — a full year before the first day of shooting — the old battle of "All you care about is money" versus "You do your job and I'll do mine." Wisely, the men tabled the tension, and in February, Wolf sent Feuer and Fosse on a research trip to Germany.

Munich, Hamburg, Berlin. Fosse was the bloodhound, sniffing here and there for locations, and Feuer held the leash. Too many yanks and the dog would growl; too few and Feuer would hear Emanuel Wolf growling all the way from New York. So it was that producer and director pulled each other around Germany in search of just the right castle, forest, and cobblestone street, acting like friends throughout.

Though hiring a European camera crew would have been the most cost-effective way to film the movie, Fosse was dead set on working with Robert Surtees, his *Charity* cameraman. Here Feuer tightened the leash. The issue of expenses aside, the producer felt Surtees had gone overboard on *Charity*, complicating the film with needless tricks and arty moonshine, and he asked Fosse to please consider some equally talented European cameramen, like Geoffrey Unsworth and Sven Nykvist. Fosse promised to keep an open mind, and Feuer agreed to do the same. "I lied," Feuer admitted later. "I firmly believe that there are show-business promises that have to be made — for the sake of a fragile ego or to prop up an unsteady state of mind — but that do not have to be kept." Again, they tabled the tension and returned to New York.

The time had come for Fosse to meet his star. Liza Minnelli was working the Empire Room at the Waldorf-Astoria, and she was working very hard. Wearing a fringed red-and-orange dress, she looked like she sounded, loud (too loud, the *New York Times* thought) and a touch desperate, like Judy Garland, her mother. At twenty-three, Liza Minnelli was already a strange, spastic showbiz animal, a volcano of nerdy confidence. She wasn't beautiful and she moved a little crazy, like a drunken elfin girl kept up past her bedtime to sing for her parents' guests. "Hi, everyone!" — Liza had a big voice, one that conveyed the punishing truth about making entertainment: It was mean. It was messy. It was a C-section and she was both mother and baby. "It's a long, hard battle," the *Times* wrote of her Empire act, "but she finally comes out ahead." Every night was a massacre she didn't always survive.

Fosse met Minnelli in the Waldorf coffee shop after the show. "How do you feel about going topless?" he asked.

"I won't do it."

"What if the scene calls for it?"

"It can call another way. There's always another way around, isn't there?"

"All right," he said. "I was just wondering."

So there was the line. "I knew what he was doing and he knew what I was doing," Minnelli said. She was not the sort of actress he could power into a corner.

Later that year, Fosse and Feuer returned to Europe to tie up *Cabaret*'s remaining loose ends. In London they met and cast Michael York; in Munich, Fosse oversaw sundry screen tests and dance auditions and dove deeper into research. He read the memoir of Albert Speer, a first-person account of life in the Third Reich, and studied the German expressionist George Grosz, carrying a catalog of his artwork with him from meeting to meeting and guarding it like the answers to a final exam. If Fosse had a cinematographer, he would use Grosz's paintings to help him settle on some kind of lighting scheme, but the Surtees issue had stalled the process. Over dinner one night at Fosse and Feuer's hotel, Munich's lavish Hotel Vier Jahreszeiten, Feuer, worn down, sincerely vowed to fight Marty Baum for Surtees, reiterating his allegiance to Fosse. On that note, they said good night and made for their rooms, separated, Fosse soon discovered, by a very thin wall.

"No," Fosse heard around midnight. "I don't want him. Marty, I don't want to open that up again. I do not want Surtees on the picture." Then: "Don't worry. I can control him."

Fosse listened to the entire phone call, transcribing as much as he could onto hotel stationery before calling Gwen in a fit of rage. What did she think? What should he do? She replied, simply, that he should do whatever he wanted.

Want? Fosse was persona non grata in the movie business. He *needed* the work.

He called Chayefsky in New York. Paddy told him, reasonably, "If you quit, you don't get paid, and they'll give you a bad name. Stay and if they fire you you'll be paid and they'll call it 'creative differences.'"

The next morning Fosse was still seething. He banged on Feuer's hotel-room door, and when the door opened, Fosse raged at him. "I heard your whole fucking conversation with Baum last night. I heard it through the wall. You no-good son of a bitch."

Feuer was in his bathrobe. He could see Fosse hadn't slept. His face was brittle white. "I never promised Surtees."

"That's a fucking lie. You're a two-faced shit."

Fosse accused Feuer of undermining him from the start, of betraying their years of friendship, of trying to use him for his choreography and then throwing him out as a director. It was hopeless. Feuer could do nothing but wait for Fosse to exhaust himself. "What do you want to do about it, Bob?"

"If you want me off the picture," Fosse said, "you're going to have to fire me." Fosse held the beat, watching Feuer's face show signs of pain.

SIXTEEN YEARS

MARTY BAUM HAD to fly out from Los Angeles to smooth things over. Though Fosse and Feuer had at long last settled on cinematographer Geoffrey Unsworth, Baum couldn't get Fosse to bury the hatchet. "You were either a friend or an enemy," Feuer said. "And he moved me from friend to enemy." Openly ignoring Feuer, Fosse barred him from discussions at every opportunity, forcing crew members to pick sides or at least make shows of their allegiance whenever Fosse tested them.

They needed extras. But running a call notice in the paper wouldn't do. "For six weeks," said assistant director Wolfgang Glattes, "I went to the red-light district looking for extras. Some days I wouldn't get to the production office until one o'clock in the afternoon because I had been up until five [in the morning] the night before." Nearly impossible to satisfy, Fosse tested like mad, and not just actors and locations; every last detail had to audition. "Bob was obsessed with blood," said Glattes. "He tested three or four weeks of blood on the pavement. Just blood! 'Mixture 13C!' We did ten or fifteen tests just to get the right color and the right density. Then we'd examine it the next day in dailies. If Bob wasn't happy, we'd go back for more."

Rather than depressing the crew, Fosse's ruthless perfectionism bolstered the collaborative spirit. His team wanted to help him. With money scarce, everyone did whatever he or she could to match his efforts, many of them living together under one roof at a residential hotel in Schwabing. With the right people always on hand to help Fosse try out new ideas — and Fosse was always coming up with new ideas — the boundary between production time and play time evaporated. *Cabaret* grew around the clock. That the script was still being rewritten — this time, with Fosse's blessing, by Hugh Wheeler — only enhanced the sense of communal authorship. Fosse would hear any idea.

Michael York finally mustered the courage to address the problem of his underwritten character, but he wanted to do it without seeming high maintenance. "Bob," he said, "I just reread the script on my way over and I don't know how to play this. There's nobody there!"

"Don't worry," Fosse said. "We still have two weeks."

After Fosse finished rehearsing the dancers, he, Wheeler, Minnelli, and York locked themselves in a room in Bavaria Studios and started talking about the script, beginning at page 1. "That two weeks," York said, "was one of the most creative times I have ever spent working with a director. We were all boiling, going at all cylinders."

Trailed by her dog Ocho, named for the Puerto Rican bar where she found him, Liza Minnelli came to rehearsal fully prepared. A connoisseur of Kander and Ebb, she had sung their songs (many written exclusively for her) for the better part of her singing life. Taking her father's advice, she had studied Louise Brooks and Louise Glaum, the flapper sirens Sally Bowles would have idolized. And she had already isolated the most important aspect of her character: The main act of a trashy, rundown nightclub, Sally "needed to be special." So she spotlit herself with press-on eyelashes and green-painted fingernails. Fosse understood why: failure was the province of glitz.

Minnelli cut her bangs down to a point à la Louise Brooks. "Well?"

she asked, modeling the hairstyle for her director. "You like it?"

"What if I hadn't?" he asked.

In rehearsal, Fosse found that Minnelli, still a young actress, cried too quickly, too easily. Almost as soon as the scene began, streaks of black mascara spilled down her face. It was startling, but Minnelli's gift for instant vulnerability, which worked so well in her act, ran counter to a certain inauthenticity in Sally Bowles. Fosse wanted Minnelli to clarify the tension before the tears, to work at restraining what came to her so naturally. "If you feel like crying," he told her, "I want you to fight like an animal trying not to cry." When Fosse gave her that note, she cried. But she heard him and made the adjustment permanent, and the two never stumbled again.

The night before the first day of filming, Emanuel Wolf flew in for an enormous kickoff party. Jammed into an expensive biergarten for an all-night bacchanal of schnitzel and beer, hundreds of crew members and their spouses enjoyed a rare night out on the production's dime. The only scowl in the room was Fosse's.

"What's wrong?" Wolf asked.

"Am I paying for this party?"

"What do you mean?"

"What did this cost?"

Wolf sat down beside him. "I want you to relax. Okay, Bob? *Enjoy* the party. *Enjoy* it."

"I have seven and a half percent of this movie, Manny. Am I paying for this?"

Wolf smiled. Fosse's concern was a good omen. "I will put it in writing that the cost of this party does not go against your profit percentage, okay?"

Fosse reached for a napkin. "Here."

"I'll send you a letter in the morning."

"Fine."

That night, Fosse couldn't sleep. He called Wolf.

"I got a problem."

"What's wrong?"

"Can I come see you?"

Moments later, Fosse was seated in an armchair across from Wolf's bed. "I have a big problem directing this movie."

Wolf felt a tightening in his throat. "What's wrong?"

"I'm not Jewish."

Of all the reasons to worry, and there were many, real and imagined, Fosse's religious background seemed an odd one for him to pick, especially at one in the morning. But he had been through all the others.

"I don't understand being Jewish," Fosse explained, "and I don't have a feel for it."

Fosse questioned Wolf about Jewish life, and Wolf, who wasn't religious, tried his best to answer. "I didn't know," Wolf said, "if he was addressing the real problem here or he was using it to try to get close to me." Three hours later, they were still talking.

"Manny," Fosse said, "there's this thing with Cy . . ."

He explained everything. On a certain level, Wolf was not surprised. Early on, Wolf sensed Feuer had advocated for Fosse because, as a desperate director coming off a flop, Fosse would submit himself to Feuer more willingly than a celebrated director high on his own success would.

"Bob, from here on in, *Cabaret* is your picture," Wolf said. "Your picture and my picture. Cy and Marty Baum were brought on by me, you got me? ABC put up half the money, but I have final cut, final script, final everything, and I'm telling you, Bob, if you've got any problem, any question, you come to me, okay? Not Cy."

The next morning, filming began. Separated from his American Camels, Fosse smoked Gitanes without the filters. "His concentration was so intense," Glattes said, "we'd all have to watch his cigarettes to make sure he wasn't going to burn his mouth." Glattes had met and fallen in love with Kathryn Doby, who was playing one of the Kit Kat dancers. "Because we knew him, Kathryn and I would slip by Bob, pick the cigarette out of his mouth, and throw it to the ground before it got too short. And he would go on as if nothing happened! That's how focused he was." A great respecter of focus, Geoffrey Unsworth earned Fosse's appreciation simply by working quietly. "When he was ready to go," Glattes said, "he would wait to catch my eye and just raise his hand. I knew then to get the actors ready. Geoffrey never had to speak." Calm coming down from the top pervaded the entire set. "It was always very comfortable," York said, "very friendly."

Filming began with the cabaret numbers, danced on a tiny stage only ten by fourteen feet, compelling Fosse to work within authentic restrictions. "I tried to make the dances look like the period," he said, "not as if they were done by me, Bob Fosse, but by some guy who is down and out. I tried to keep this in mind, but it's so difficult. You think, 'Oh, I can't really have them do *that*. That's embarrassing; it's so bad, so cheap.' But you think, 'But if I *were* the kind of guy who only works with cheap cabarets and clubs, what else would I do?'" And Fosse was that kind of guy, at least in part. From the wings of half-forgotten nightclubs, an emotional analogy to fascism grazed his memory, waiting to be mastered. Fosse didn't know Hitler's audience, but he knew how they must have watched their lousy cabaret acts, with excitement, horror, and lust.

The dances Fosse saw, but how exactly to film them was not clear. It wasn't like *Sweet Charity*, whose steps he had lived with for years before filming them. On that movie, anticipating what angles he needed was easy; he could close his eyes and turn around the 3-D model in his memory. But on *Cabaret*, whose multitudes of images were only beginning to flood over him, whose details and variations on details would be impossible to foresee, Fosse opted out of storyboarding to shoot somewhat on the fly. "I basically try to get an overall shot covering the choreography," he said. "Then I go in and start playing." And so, with the crew waiting and money burning, Fosse would circle the dancers, examining each one's every angle from every conceivable vantage point. "Every time I do that," he said, "I say, 'Oh my god, it's incredible to see this leg from this angle. No one's ever seen a dance from here.'" He didn't know what he wanted until he saw it; until then, he kept looking. "I keep my options open as long as possible," he said. "It's a definite problem in collaborating with me."

The cinema was perfect for his sensibility. On film, where Fosse could cut to an extreme close-up of the littlest finger performing the smallest twitch, he could reveal what was difficult, or even impossible, to see onstage. "You see, the wonderful thing about a camera that you don't have onstage," he said, "is that you can come in on a hand, you can come in to a face or some movement that you don't get in that proscenium, that you wish you could, you know, have glasses that come in on somebody's foot on a particularly right movement." Watching a performance onstage, audience members did their own editing; they picked and chose where they wanted to look. Of course, in the theater, Fosse could guide the eye with lighting and blocking, but with a film, the audience's eyes went where he wanted them to go, constantly and permanently, a perfect performance every single night. The only things keeping him from perfection were time and money. He said, "They have to keep pulling me out to say, 'Stop already.' Production managers, assistant directors are always saying, 'How many more you got?' 'I got thousands; how much time do I have?'"

Time and Cy Feuer. Their fight over a cinematographer turned into a war over light. "Feuer wanted a kind of Barbra Streisand, Harry Stradling look," said camera operator Peter MacDonald. "He wanted everything lit, everything obvious, everything normal, like an MGM musical. But Bob wanted it to be dark, very, very dark." To MacDonald and Unsworth, Fosse said, "I want this to feel like you're in a club.

I want to feel at times like the camera's frustrated by someone in the foreground and you want to push them away. If you see me doing that show-offy stuff I did in *Sweet Charity*, stop me. This isn't going to be a movie. This is real." Smoky atmosphere, light-reducing filters, long lenses ... "You had only a few points of leeway between the shot working and everything being a total disaster," MacDonald said. There was no monitor to check the shot, and since there was no way to correct underexposure in postproduction, finding out in dailies that the shot was too dark would be a disaster. "It took real nerve," MacDonald said, for Fosse to fight Cy Feuer's open opposition to *Cabaret*'s look.

"Tell me one thing you've done for me and this film," Fosse demanded of the producer at one point, his voice loud enough for all to hear.

"I'll tell you two, Bob. I hired you and so far I haven't fired you."

At Feuer's insistence, they sent the film negative to LA for a second opinion. "Some television cameraman confirmed Cy's fears the film was unviewable," MacDonald said, and Fosse got phone calls from California. "What are you doing?" they howled. "If you use one more filter we'll consider it an act of subordination!" (He did not stop using filters; in fact, he ordered stronger filters to block even more light.) One might imagine that the *Sweet Charity* debacle would make Fosse hedge his bets a little, but the scent of failure charged Fosse up, dared him to prove his opposition wrong. "All through the shooting," Michael York said, "there were guys in suits looking at their watches." It fueled Fosse's drive. "After a run-in with Feuer," MacDonald said, "you would see Bob slumped in a corner, like a boxer against the rope, thinking, *How do I get this guy? How much more of this shit do I have to take?*"

And the costumes: they weren't dingy enough for Fosse. "I'm sure it was a miscommunication," Kathryn Doby said. "The designer,

Charlotte Flemming, spoke almost no English and Bob spoke no German." The same problem had come up with Irene Sharaff on *Sweet Charity*, but this time it would not be as easy to fix. Rifling through the German studio's costume shops, Fosse and Minnelli (whose original costumes, she said, made her look like Joe Namath) soon realized they had been led to fakes. Still trying to bury evidence of war, the Germans had actually hidden their Nazi-era paraphernalia. "I asked for some real thirties clothes," Minnelli said, "slinky, no bra. I said, 'It should look like before the war.' And the Germans all said, 'What war?'" With practically the whole country against him, Fosse would be hard-pressed to find period clothing, much less a Nazi armband, which shifted his movie a big step closer to bullshit musical, and a step closer to Cy Feuer. He called Gwen. She grabbed Nicole and got on a plane.

"Gwen came and literally went to the junk shops and we all ended up with improvised things," said Michael York. She hunted through antique shops in Paris; Gwen gave Liza Fosse's vest to wear (without a shirt) in "Mein Herr," her own green blouse for "Maybe This Time," and her kimono to wear here and there. Gwen's emergency rescue enhanced the communal, us-against-them mentality. The crew loved her. Faith — theirs in her, hers in them — was contagious.

And the dailies were sensational — or terrible, depending on one's allegiance. Ordinarily, Fosse and Feuer sat at opposite sides of the screening room, like planets in angry orbit around the same sun, each ringed by his own entourage. The one occasion Feuer decided to enter Fosse's atmosphere, he sat down directly behind him in a seat regularly reserved for Peter MacDonald. Calmly, Fosse turned around and asked Feuer to move. Feuer moved. But then he started holding screenings of his own, often before Fosse's. Word of Feuer's disgust with the film would arrive just in time for Fosse's screening; some thought it was an attempt to further discourage the director and throw him off course. But if this was his plan, it didn't work. There was too much going right to quibble about lighting. "Watching dailies," Michael York said, "you felt like a creative team. Some directors don't let the actors in to dailies, but Fosse would insist. We would sit there and he would say, 'That doesn't work because . . .' or 'Now that's better because . . .'" It was too soon to get excited, but they were, struck with that knock-wood feeling of having caught something maybe very good. Fosse was already referring to *Cabaret* as the first adult musical. He grew a goatee.

Good feeling spread. There were the Kit Kat girls, gigglingly, tipsy on wine, scotch, vodka, running out for a smoke ("By the end of the shooting day," Louise Quick said, "[they] were plastered"); there was Liza and her boyfriend, drummer Rex Kramer, playing badminton on a patch of green outside stage 3; there was Joel Grey reminiscing all the way back to Mickey Katz and Joe Frisco with Fosse, three inches of ash hanging from his smile. "Friday nights after shooting," Glattes said, "we'd have dinner in Munich and then eight o'clock or nine o'clock we'd meet at the top floor of Fosse's hotel to play poker. It was me and Kathryn and Liza and Louise Quick and Bob." Fosse was nuts about poker. "It would sometimes go on to five or six in the morning," Glattes said, "and people would do crazy things. [If you lost] you'd have to go out in the corridor of the hotel and go to Joel Grey's apartment and scream at the door or say something dirty at Michael York's apartment or pour a cold bucket of water on yourself." Fosse loved what gambling did to people. He loved to watch risk exposing raw nerves, true selves. Poker was, like drugs and sex, a steadfast bullshit destroyer, and, with girls present, flirty as hell.

There was one girl in particular. Fosse had met Ilse Schwarzwald months earlier, during preproduction at the Hotel Vier Jahreszeiten, site of the Feuer blowup. She was there as an interpreter, translating for Fosse and the German designer he was interviewing with only one ear. "Ilse was a lovely lady," said Peter MacDonald. "She was one of the most beautiful people, aesthetically and as a person." Fosse and Schwarzwald's romance extended into production and grew even stronger. "It was as if he lived in some other category of ethical accountability," Feuer observed. Fosse promoted her to production secretary.

At first, the affair was known to only a few: Fosse pals and those in Ilse's small network, like Peter MacDonald, who had worked with her before.

"Do you think Bobby's gay?" Geoffrey Unsworth asked MacDonald early on.

"If he is," MacDonald said, "he's hiding it very well."

Word got around and many observed how much Ilse looked like Gwen. By the time Gwen arrived, costumes in hand and crisis averted, the comparison had been made by virtually everyone; Fosse and Ilse were quite publicly and comfortably in love. He should have known better. Back home, in the States, there were rules for breaking the rules. After suffering through a decade of Fosse's infidelity, Gwen must have felt that grace was the only vestige of couplehood (outside the work) left of the marriage. But the care Fosse took in New York to shield his wife from his latest fling evaporated in Germany. And this relationship — as they all saw — was hardly a fling.

The last thing Gwen needed — a note from Ilse's husband telling all — she got.

"She was angry, no?" Ilse asked when Bob told her what had happened.

"No," Bob said. "She wasn't angry. She was just sarcastic."

To the amazement of the crew, Gwen stayed in Munich even after she got the letter, continuing to work here and there on clothes and makeup, smiling her trademark grin. Business as usual was its own retaliation, confirming to the gossip machine that Fosse and Verdon's commitment to each other, to the *work,* went deeper than sex and bad behavior. She could not show her suffering; if people thought she suffered, they might think he did not love her, and she would lose her title as Fosse's queen. So better to stiffen and stay strong. There was dignity in transcendence. For a time.

Ilse, meanwhile, did Fosse's spying. One day, double-crossing Feuer, she warned MacDonald to stay alert: Feuer was planning to confiscate the light filters.

Five minutes later, as MacDonald was talking to Unsworth, Feuer appeared.

"Hand them over."

"Over there." MacDonald nodded to a box on the floor.

Without speaking, Feuer went through the box and then happily strode off with it.

Unsworth looked at MacDonald. "What the fuck was that?"

"Decoys."

"Ah."

In Feuer's defense, he had received a warning of his own. According to *Cabaret*'s insurers, the production was headed into dangerous overages.

"Bob," Feuer said. "We're running out of money. We have to finish on schedule."

"What happens if we don't?"

"They'll close us down. They'll make their own movie."

Neither spoke for a moment.

Then Feuer: "We have to take two days off the schedule."

"No."

"Bob, we *have* to."

"No!"

Furious, Fosse wrote a letter to Ernie Martin, Feuer's proxy in absentia, begging to be understood. First of all, he was not accountable for overages that, he claimed, he never authorized. Second, any so-called mismanagement of time was the byproduct of Jay Allen's inadequate screenplay, which had been Feuer's to oversee, not Fosse's. Finally, rather than recrimination, Fosse deserved thanks for keeping his personal expenses down and bringing Gwen in to work for free.

Adding to his insurance headache, the "If You Could See Her Through My Eyes" gorilla costume the studio had provided was, bafflingly, made of dark blue velour. Fosse had rejected it on sight, delaying the number as long as he possibly could to buy more time to get a better costume, but now, toward the end of the shoot, with pages flying off the calendar faster than ever, he had finally run out of options — and so had Charlotte Flemming, the costume designer. "He's impossible," she complained to Gwen. But she didn't know Gwen Verdon. "If the man wants a gorilla," was Verdon's reply, "then *get* a gorilla." Gwen flew to New York, to Brooks Costume, handpicked a real gorilla costume, and flew back, holding the head on her lap from JFK to Munich.

Then it happened. "She walked in on him," a friend said. "He was with a couple German girls, and that was it for her. That was the last straw."

Fosse got her letter in Berlin, where *Cabaret* had moved for the end of location photography. It said *separation*.

The evening before *Cabaret* wrapped, Fosse threw a small dinner party to honor his allies. It was a terrific evening, sad and full of enervated good feeling, and near the meal's end the host took the floor. "Now that I bought you all dinner," he declared, "I want you to all make big speeches about me, telling me how wonderful you think I am." If there was irony in this proposition, his guests missed it. Choosing not to recognize their embarrassed faces, Fosse went around the table, pulling out answers one by one. Michael York attempted very graciously to come up with something on the spot, and a baffled Peter MacDonald tried a curve ball. Standing tall, he looked Fosse in the eye. "If you don't know what I fucking think about you now, Bob, I feel sorry for you."

With money tight and relations soured, the rumor that production hadn't sprung for a wrap party occasioned an improvised get-together at the foot of the Berlin Wall. Someone found a tiny, ugly bar. Someone else turned up with meats and cheeses from a deli around the corner. Liza got up on the table to sing. "It was glorious," Peter MacDonald said, "probably the best wrap party we'd ever been to. And then to walk out at six or seven o'clock in the morning and see the streets of Berlin being washed down and first light coming up . . . it seemed the perfect way to finish the film."

Fosse was now an exile. Tax restrictions forced him to leave Germany; emotional restrictions blocked him from New York. It was too early to face Gwen.

Ilse seemed his best next move. Leaping headfirst into romance, the two flew to Madrid for what turned out to be a weeklong reenactment of the last shot of *The Graduate.* In the Spanish light of day, Ilse, no matter how lovely, could not fill the vacuum Gwen had left. He worried about Nicole; if he wasn't there for her now, she might feel he had left her too.

Had he made a mistake? (A terrible mistake?)

He called Gwen. They decided to join Neil and Joan Simon at their rented villa in Majorca, and perhaps even reconcile.

The villa turned out to be an estate overlooking a cliffy chunk of Pollensa, a coastal region on the northern corner of the island. Fosse and Verdon had all the room they needed to stroll, together and alone, through the garden tangle around the pool, or they could take a short walk behind the villa to the ruins of a Roman aqueduct, the perfect backdrop for the last act of their two-person opera. It was so hot that summer, Neil Simon said, his typewriter keys stuck to the page.

The opera ended sooner than anyone had expected. With nothing left to discuss, Fosse and Verdon said their goodbyes to the Simons, and to each other, and left. She for Nicole, he for Ilse.

And she took him back. As planned, they returned to Berlin for reshoots and pickups, the miscellaneous pieces *Cabaret* needed in order to hang together. By then, Geoffrey Unsworth had moved on to another film, so Peter MacDonald took his place behind the camera.

"Don't think you're going to get lots of money for this," Feuer told him.

"Cy, for Fosse I'd do it for nothing."

Liza Minnelli felt the same. Though she wasn't needed on camera (Louise Quick was acting as her stand-in), Minnelli loved the production too much to go home and refused even to leave the set. "I'm in the camera department!" she squealed, clapperboard in hand. "Liza was in heaven," MacDonald said. "She said she wanted to work every day on this film for the rest of her life." Fosse too, but he couldn't put off New York any longer. His film's editor, David Bretherton, and his daughter needed him.

When Fosse returned home, he was shocked to discover Bretherton had spent the previous three weeks preparing a rough cut of the film without any input from him. This was common practice in movies, but to Fosse, who had barely communicated with his editor during production, it was like someone had broken into his house and turned over the furniture.

"Well," Fosse said, "we'd better look at this stuff."

As if he wanted to situate himself to flee in case of emergency, Fosse sat in the last row. Bretherton, adjusting to his mood, gave him space. He sat with his assistant, David Ramirez, way down in the front.

They ran the picture.

Afterward, nearly four hours later, Fosse stood up. "My God," he said, "I feel sick," and he left the room.

Then he left the building.

Bretherton turned to Ramirez. "I must have really screwed up."

The next morning, Bretherton came back to the cutting room. He wasn't sure if he'd been fired, so he waited, thinking back over the previous day's events, not knowing where else to go.

Then Fosse appeared. "I didn't mean to say that," he said. "I'm sorry. Can we run it again?"

This time Fosse had questions: Why did Bretherton use these particular takes? Why weren't the dancers on the beat?

"Because," Bretherton said, "the script says it's that kind of nightclub." As in schlocky, third-rate; he had added the missteps on purpose.

This had to change. "The most important thing to me as choreographer," Fosse explained, "is for *that* toe to hit *that* floor at *that particular* split second." Bretherton took the note and recut the number, recut *all* numbers, correcting the intentional missteps.

Fosse loved watching him work. Streaming film through the smoky air, Bretherton cut with his whole body, throwing himself onto the splicer then whipping himself back, splicing and taping to an unheard beat, reaching up for a filmstrip and driving it down to the Moviola as he drifted the excised strip into the clipping bin above him, then swooping down again with yet another, and on and on through lunch and dinner and cartons of Camels, watching and rewatching take A against take F, breaking down take C into subsections one, two, and three, and comparing the feel of ba-ta-da-*dee* to ba-ta-da-*dum*.

Then Fosse stepped out. "He paced like a panther outside the editing room door," Bretherton said, "and wouldn't come in, even when invited." What now?

For three weeks, Fosse stayed out there in the hall. Bretherton, who had no idea what was happening, pressed on as best he could, but a week later he finally had to beg Fosse to join him. "I'm fiddling with three or four pieces of film," he said, "and I need you to make a quick decision."

Fosse paused outside the door. "Can I tell you something?"

Bretherton swallowed.

"I can't sit."

"What?"

"I have the worst case of hemorrhoids anyone ever had."

That got them both laughing and Fosse came back in.

Watching his director learn to edit, Bretherton was simply amazed at what he saw. Where many worked cut to cut, one deliberate piece at a time, Fosse had an automatic feel for movement and rhythm that gave him mental flickers of whole sequences, like a chess master sees checkmate long before it comes. And having shot certain numbers from as many as five angles, Fosse had provided them with a wealth of variations on every turn. Most musicals favored cuts continuous with the number, staying inside the performance as if the world outside had vanished, but Fosse and Bretherton began to see they could cut away from the number, keeping the outside reality alive, and then jump back into the number without disrupting the flow. This technique, they found, tripled the impact, made the numbers seem more natural, as if they were really happening; it allowed them to embellish the rhythm with a turn of a head or the wink of an eye and provided them with a means of commenting, by way of juxtaposition, on the number, the outside world, or both.

They caught fire. First they would cut the number the classical way, straight through, without interruption. Then they would go back and look for creative opportunities, the sort Fosse could see coming. "Every cut you make changes another cut," Bretherton said. "Then all of a sudden this opens up a new way of doing something.

[Working with Fosse] I learned that nothing is impossible." Dancers' bones broke, but celluloid did not protest. It only performed. Here in the cutting room, Fosse could realize his dream of total and precise control of every stage element, toe tap, and facial expression. Nothing fought him. The world of machines rendered thought and action nearly identical, and Fosse could finally move at the perfect speed of amphetamines. He was free.

Elsewhere in his life, he was trapped. Moving into the Hyde Park Hotel with Ilse, across the park from his old home, where his daughter lived (without him), had backed Fosse into a familiar corner. How to keep his women — for their protection and for his — separate and content? Ordinarily, he'd have the number all worked out in advance, but this time was different. This time one of those women was Nicole. She was only eight.

Fosse was lying to her about Ilse. He asked Ilse never to answer the phone, just in case it was Nicole calling. Nicole, he told Ilse, was the most important thing in his life. Then he added, "With work," and then, smiling, "and you — maybe." But the few afternoons Fosse had with his daughter brought him more pain than relief. Where once he had auditioned for the role of good father, a lead, now he would take anything, a place in her chorus even, just to be near her.

Janice Lynde soothed him. A twenty-two-year-old Texas beauty with the wholesome look Fosse couldn't resist, Janice was understudying the role of Eve Harrington in *Applause,* her first Broadway show. They had met before he took off for Germany, backstage at the Palace after her opening night.

"You're so tall," he said.

"Well, you're so short."

She had a pillow voice. It said *I can take care of you tonight.*

Fosse told her he wanted to put her in a movie, something he was working on with Herb Gardner. Friends who knew Fosse advised Janice to be careful, that he was not on the market, that he would say lovely things and then he would hurt her; Janice assured them she could take care of herself. "I wanted a career and work," she said, "so getting involved with Bob was no problem for me. I wasn't going to be his girlfriend."

That was fine for Fosse; in fact, it was better. "Unfortunately," he confessed, "and I'll never know why, I can't be a faithful husband or lover, but I can be a helpful one."

They would stick to show business.

Out at night, she could feel him looking at her hands. "Sometimes he'd watch me," she said, "and later he'd say, 'That was interesting, the way you put your hand on the table.' Or we'd go for a drink and he'd say, 'What if you lean your body and you put one leg up over here?' I'd start laughing and he'd go, 'What's so funny?' It was *all* work. *I* was work. He was looking at me through the lens, picking shots like he was directing." It was his only consistent indication of love, the attention he paid her in the form of work.

For months, they walked the goose-bumpy line between closeness and intimacy, work and more than work, occasionally crossing over and then stepping back. Was it a ploy, his little-boy look when she turned him down, or did he actually *feel* that small? He must have known what he was doing to her, having done this kind of thing so many times before. He must have known she wanted him to keep trying, that when she held her hand out to stop him, she hoped he'd take it. "I always knew, we both knew, it could never be a just-you-just-me commitment," Lynde said. "But there were spurts of things." It would be difficult to say who was leading.

"Good night, Bobby."

"Janice . . . come on, Janice . . ."

"I'm sorry, Bobby, no. I can't." She kissed him and walked off toward her building. "Good *night*, Bobby."

"You know," he called after her, "you seem very sophisticated but really you're very middle-class."

He had made this sort of remark before. It was meant to hurt.

Inside her apartment, she cried. There was no way for her to know that Bob Fosse, who seemed to her the apex of sophistication, with his black uniform and Tony Awards, was himself uncomfortable, even afraid, of the sexual excesses he was so drawn to. "I remember him saying it was wrong that in Europe men and women could be naked together on the beach," Ann Reinking said. "I thought, for him, that was an odd thing to say." He could be middle-class too.

Covetous of virtue but obsessed with corruption, Fosse was unsure where to place Janice or even himself on the sin spectrum, wanting so much to test her "goodness" against his "badness" and discover, definitively, what color they shone in the dark. "He took me to these strip clubs," Janice said. "Some of them were still doing the old-fashioned striptease he liked, some of them were becoming more go-go kind of places. I was afraid, but he was fascinated. He said the strippers he grew up with could be very motherly to him, and a couple of them really took him under their wing sexually and taught him a lot, how to be a good lover. But he also said they teased him and hurt him before he went up onstage." The contamination of innocence had obsessed Fosse since "Whatever Lola Wants," when first he stained Gwen Verdon with his touch of vice that he then spread through *Sweet Charity* and *Cabaret.*

Fosse and Janice were both night people, both talkers. "Mostly, he worried about Nicole," she said. "He worried that he was going to give her a cynical view of men, and that it would hurt her." He seemed more and more breakable every hour they stayed awake. "When he was working, when he was passionate, the adrenaline would kick in and he'd be fine," she said, "he'd be naturally up. But at nights the darkness would take him. You know how in movies when they put dark contacts over people's whole eye? That's how Bob would look to me. Like there was no one out front."

Sex and work, Lynde found, could restore him. "A lot of the time sexuality would relieve some of that darkness. It was like medication for him. Talking about working and working helped him to feel okay too, but he had a hard time following through. The Dexedrine made him feel like he could put his ideas into action. He would say, 'I have to be totally passionate or I don't want to go to work.' That's why he envied Sidney Lumet. He said Lumet was a real craftsman, that he could do every film they offered him whether he felt he could do it or not. Some of them worked, some of them didn't, but [Lumet] would always do it. Bob wanted to be that way. He wanted to be a craftsman for whom the work was easy and who could fly from project to project without too much worry of flop or hit, bad or good."

The more they saw of each other, the more anguished she became about their relationship, whatever it was. Janice knew about Ilse; he had volunteered all that. But had he told her to protect her, or to absolve himself?

"Dance for me," he said. "I want to see you dance."

They were up late again, drinking too much.

"If you choreograph it, then I'll dance it."

"No, no, no," he said. "I want to see how you move without being told anything."

Having learned from *Sweet Charity* that no career, no matter how good it looked, was ever secure and no production was a sure thing, Fosse scoured New York for his next project — or, rather, projects. He cast as wide a net as possible, spread himself all over the map, reading film scripts, TV scripts, and new musicals with the preemptive urgency of a nervous creature busily hoarding for winter. It was both inauspiciously timed, then, and very interesting that David Begelman told Fosse he was leaving CMA's New York office for the LA bureau. It was inauspiciously timed because trusting new agents was among the few talents Fosse did not possess. It was very interesting because stepping in for Begelman was Sam Cohn.

Sam Cohn was on his way to being the best agent in New York. The funny thing about Cohn — one of the funny things — was that he didn't think-Yiddish-dress-British, like Begelman, who reportedly kept a closet full of one hundred identical (numbered) black ties. He was more like a schlepster librarian in his old khakis, oversize sweaters (often stained, often torn), white gym socks, and loafers, their gold buckles sliced off so no one would know they were from Gucci. The whole package said *I don't bullshit; I'm not one of them.* "The shibboleth," Cohn explained, in his Princeton-and-Yale accent, "the image of agents, is something that frankly bothers me." He despised Los Angeles. When he had to go, he flew there and back in the same day.

At his peak, Sam Cohn saw at least five hundred movies and seventy-five plays a year. He had three assistants (phone, schedule, filing). He had a private bathroom so when he was forced to leave his desk, he didn't have to lose time mingling with others on his way to the "people other than Sam" bathroom out there in the office. Time was a problem. Cohn was rarely on time. "Sam," his client Herb Gardner said to him, "you're doomed to live in the present." Cohn's present could last a long time. His day started late, with the papers, as many as his short attention span would allow. He read them on his way to morning therapy and on his way from therapy to ICM at 40 West Fifty-Seventh Street, where he tossed them away to free up his hands — one to pitch his jacket to an assistant, the other to take the box-office figures she handed him, which he read on his way to his office, an organized mess with a view of Central Park he never had time to enjoy. By then it was almost lunch.

Lunch was generally at the Russian Tea Room, a short walk from his office, where the management kept a booth for him: the first one on the right, just beyond the bar, visible to all who walked in. And everyone walked in, many with the intention of "accidentally" running into Sam, which slowed him down even more. But he made up for lost time in the deal, whose terms he laid out as plainly as a menu ("Take it or leave it, but you really should take it" — and they took it). Eating at the Russian Tea Room was like speed-dating. In a short time, in a small space, Cohn got everyone in, and then he got out in time to get back to his desk as the West Coast woke up. He'd sit there talking on the phone with one arm slung over his head and both eyes closed, as if inspired. He'd be there all day. On the phone.

Sam Cohn's phone was legend. It rang as often as 200 times a day. On his record-breaking busiest day, Cohn hit 353. The intercom slowed him down, so Cohn shouted for his messages.

"Who is it?"

"It's Woody!"

"Put him on!"

Cohn didn't take all the calls; with that kind of volume, he simply couldn't. Many clients joked they needed an agent to get in touch with their agent. ("I would call up pretending to be Fosse," Cohn's client Paul Mazursky said, "just to get Cohn on the phone.") Thus the widespread "running into" Sam at the Russian Tea Room. Some would attempt to bribe the maître d' to be seated beside him. Once, a client sent a dime to Cohn's booth with the note reading *Please call me*. Another wrote his own obituary and sent it to the office just to get a reaction. "I have a neurotic response to some people," Cohn admitted, "and I find it very hard to call."

Most nights Cohn stayed at the office until curtain time. He decried the weakness of people who ate dinner at six, so he ate after the show — and there was always a show (*Dirty Harry*, or an oboe concerto, or, most often, the play or movie of a client). Dinner was most often at Wally's (steak, wine), where Cohn's photo hung above the coatroom doorway. Around midnight, he would return home to 25 Central Park West, where he lived, a fifteen-minute walk from the office. There he read — his clients' work. "Unless it was extremely urgent," said his associate Arlene Donovan, "Sam would never read in the office." There wasn't time.

Also, he ate paper. Script corners, napkins, checks, matchbooks, menus. Black carbon got all over his teeth. "He was supposed to meet me [once]," Donovan said, "but he got lost because he ate the directions." He ate paper absent-mindedly, as a smoker might reach for a cigarette. It didn't matter who saw him. "He seemed totally oblivious to the fact that someone might find it strange," writer Teresa Carpenter said.

"You remember that deal we made?" Cohn once asked producer Alan Ladd Jr. an hour after their lunch.

"Of course I do."

"What was it?"

Ladd paused. "You ate the deal?"

"I'm sorry."

Screwing the other guy held no appeal for Cohn. Moreover, it was bad business in those days. "It's a very small group of people," Cohn said of his kingdom, "and we can't afford to euchre each other too badly." A certain geographical intimacy (midtown, mostly) channeled the competition into close quarters, forcing show-business professionals to embrace neighborliness and even fraternity, like immigrants in steerage. "The different disciplines exist within twelve blocks of one another," he said. "One can literally go in a direct line almost from my office to Bantam Books, to United Artists, to the Shubert Theater. And, if you wanted to, you could stop by CBS or ABC on the way and you wouldn't even have to take a cab." That didn't shake the dirt off every rat, but it did encourage respect, and on both sides of the table. The goal was not the big deal (as it would be in the 1980s) but the *right* deal, and in Cohn's case, very little dealing was necessary; Liza, Mike Nichols, Sidney Lumet — his clients sold themselves. "Sam loved talent so much," Ladd said, "he would be pushing clients he didn't even represent anymore."

"His clients," said Cohn's daughter, Marya. "They were his family." And none more so than Steve Tesich, screenwriter of *Breaking Away*. He was with Cohn at the theater or at Wally's almost every night of the week. Fosse was there too. "Sam was just overwhelmed by Fosse's talent," Donovan said. "He thought Fosse was one of the most talented people he had ever come across. He worshipped him." The feeling was mutual. Cohn's professorial manner and vehement anti-Hollywoodism earned him Fosse's respect, but it was Cohn's spectacular faith in Fosse that won him his client's devotion. "Those guys had a true guy-code friendship," assistant Susan Anderson said. Cohn introduced Fosse to the writers Peter Maas and E. L. Doctorow, and, along with Tesich and Peter Stone (all Cohn clients), they joined Fosse's buddy brigade with Paddy and Herb, Falstaffs every one, with heavy undertones of Hamlet. Fosse put them — his (mostly Jewish) intellectuals — on a pedestal. "But Bobby is an extremely intelligent man," Cohn said, "though his pose is to be non-intellectual. He claims he doesn't know some of the big words Paddy uses, but I think that's a pretense. Bob would like you to think, for some obscure reason, that he's still a gypsy, a vaudeville hoofer." Cohn hung all their photos on his office wall. There were no pictures of his children. "Family dinners?" Cohn once asked a friend. "Who wants to go to *that*?" (Then, reconsidering: "What's that like?")

For the select few, Cohn's office couch was always open. Clients Robert Altman and John Guare came by for backgammon, Tesich to talk through an idea. Most called in advance. Fosse just appeared. "At any time of day," Anderson said, "Bobby would walk in laughing." If Cohn was on a call, Fosse would let himself in, get comfortable on the couch, and try to get Sam to break up. He'd mimic the way he sat, mimic his voice. "Susaaaaaaaan, would you get me —" "Susaaaaaaaan, would you get me—" He gave Cohn a telescope to put by his window, the joke being that Sam Cohn had no use for it. What did he care about the outside? One evening, with her boss away, Susan Anderson peeked through the lens, which had been turned north, toward Fosse's apartment a few blocks away. She caught Fosse standing behind his own telescope looking back at her. Then the phone rang in Cohn's office.

"Hello?"

"This is Bob Fosse. I'm a client of Mr. Cohn's. Is he in?"

Anderson laughed. "Mr. Cohn is out right now. May I have him call you in a bit?"

In the midst of cutting *Cabaret,* Fosse told Sam about an idea he had had in Germany. Watching Liza work, hard, Fosse thought of filming the making and performance of a Liza Minnelli concert for television. It would not be a canned, airless affair in the manner of most television specials (which were usually filmed at a private studio, with a limited audience, with time for retakes) but a *cinematic* stage performance, perhaps supported by interstitial interviews with Minnelli herself, backstage and in the wings, as she prepared for and recovered from her big night. As he wrote in his proposal, Fosse imagined an entertainment about the "joy, fear, anxiety, and eventual gratification" of making entertainment, a show about putting on a show. The results would be both a concert film and a documentary look at the nerve and exertion of one of the world's most entrenched representatives of show business, a fusion of razzle-dazzle and (razzle-dazzle's sometime opposite) live truth. Fosse would direct and choreograph; Kander and Ebb would oversee the production and contribute songs; and NBC would air the one-hour special the following year, in September 1972. If *Cabaret,* scheduled to open months prior, made Minnelli a movie star (as Cohn, Chayefsky, Gardner, and Fosse suspected it might), then *Liza with a Z*—a singing, dancing, confessional close-up—could promote her to phenomenon.

Amid the highs and lows of his separation, the black-and-blues of seeing Nicole, the neither-here-nor-there of his thing with Janice, Fosse sent Ilse back home, moved into a one-bedroom apartment formerly occupied by Begelman on West Fifty-Eighth Street, and threw himself into *Cabaret* for the final stretch. "Fellas, this is much too long," Wolf said after the lights came up on a rough cut one hot day in July. "I need a picture of two hours." But Fosse was reluctant to cut anything, not because he thought he had a masterpiece, but because the longer he was in the cage with a movie, the more he convinced himself he had already failed. "There's a certain amount of self-delusion that has to go on," he said. "You *think* you did this scene very well and you *think* you got the most out of the actor and you *think* you shot it well and three months later you see you really messed it up." Thus Bob Fosse would follow movie with show, Broadway with Hollywood. "Bob would do a movie," his assistant director Wolfgang Glattes said, "get disappointed and scared, then go back to the theater." Nothing was a sure thing, but the record showed he had far more success on the stage than on the screen, making Broadway a sort of safety net under Fosse's Hollywood tightrope, insuring him against the likelihood of oncoming failure. Following *Cabaret* with *Liza with a Z,* and then *Liza with a Z* with a new Broadway musical, he would buy himself insurance across three media. But what, he asked Cohn and company, should that new musical be?

In the years since the 1966–1967 Broadway season — the last time a new Fosse work had been onstage — Broadway had begun to show signs of a nervous breakdown. The late 1960s crises of race, war, sex, and national pride put traditional ideas of entertainment out to pasture, leaving Broadway to crawl, and sometimes plummet, toward new meaning and purpose. The year of *Cabaret* was also the year of *The Homecoming, A Delicate Balance, The Killing of Sister George,* and *Little Murders;* that year, comedy — ashamed of having a good time in a bad world — commingled so successfully with horror, it seemed inappropriate to laugh out loud. And everything seemed to *mean* something. Even in the most grotesque comedies, the suggestion of allegory kept the misery relatable. The breakdown cranked up a notch the following season, as *After the Rain, Rosencrantz and Guildenstern Are Dead,* and *A Day in the Death of Joe Egg* (as well as the American premiere of *Exit the King*) added meta-theatricality to the hysterical pitch-blackness. "Now, serious theater must accomplish two things," Edward Albee said in 1966. "The serious play has got to say something about the nature of the play as an art form itself; it has got to try to advance, to change that art form. It must also try to change the spectator in some fashion; alter his point of view, his view of reality, his view of the theater." So actors ran down aisles, characters marched to the lip of the stage and harassed real-life people in the front row, and Rosencrantz and Guildenstern realized they were fictional. Putting on a "show," the Broadway play of the late sixties confronted audiences with the conceptual illusions at large in the real world.

But what did that mean for the musical, obligated to contain song and dance and too expensive to shrug off popular tastes completely? The legit Broadway revolution arrived late (with the notable exception of Hal Prince's *Cabaret*) to George Abbott country. Before Fosse was offered the film of *Sweet Charity,* he momentarily considered *Promises, Promises,* a musical made from Billy Wilder's *The Apartment,* and an adaptation of Fellini's *La Strada,* perhaps with Juliet Prowse in the Giulietta Masina part. For both projects, he would have been too late. Case in point: his film of *Sweet Charity,* which opened a year after — though it seemed a generation before — *Hair.*

Hair was a landmark musical, Fosse thought, third in a triumvirate that began for him with *Oklahoma!* and *West Side Story.* Sex, drugs, and soft rock and roll, *Hair* was a counterculture parade of kid id — either chic or radical chic, depending on where one had drinks after the show. Containing none of the formal ingenuity of

Oklahoma! or *West Side Story,* *Hair* came complete with full-frontal nudity, a racially expansive cast, and an open invitation to a be-in at the show's end. Maybe these were all tricks, but who else was doing them? (Soon, everyone.) "I took somebody to an experimental play recently," said Sondheim in 1970, "and at the end of the first act we had witnessed about six rapes, seven murders, and a good deal of homosexuality and matricide. . . . And I said to my friend, 'Why is it so dull?' He said, 'Because there's no surprise.'" Even the giants had run out of good bad ideas. While Albee, the Ernst Lubitsch of bad feelings, did to happy families what *Oh! Calcutta!* did to pants, Neil Simon, Broadway comedy's Babe Ruth, fell fast and far, tumbling from *Plaza Suite* and *Last of the Red Hot Lovers* to the alcoholism of *The Gingerbread Lady* and the literal nervous breakdown of *The Prisoner of Second Avenue.* The musical tried rock, and stagnated. To really evolve, a form needs more time, or a genius.

In the case of Stephen Sondheim, the form had a genius. In the case of *Company*—music and lyrics by Sondheim, directed by Hal Prince, set design by Boris Aronson, choreography by Michael Bennett—a coven of geniuses. Described by Sondheim as a show about "the challenge of maintaining relationships in a society becoming increasingly depersonalized," *Company* reconfigured what had been the musical's basic DNA: advancing story through songs. This show went for theme. Given that it had virtually no plot—audiences watched as Bobby talked to friends, pondered his relationships, and so forth—*Company*'s episodic structure, fractured in spiritual accord with the theme of depersonalization, tossed out another musical gene: linearity. Yes, time; broken by loose chronology and Aronson's cubist designs (where are we?), one had to wonder: Was *Company* unfolding in Bobby's brain?

Follies was—well, not in Bobby's brain, but certainly in someone's, or in *something's,* unconscious, though precisely how much was difficult to say. The point was the breakdown of the American musical

was finally happening. On April 4, 1971, at the Winter Garden Theater, its subconscious was revealed: the curtain falls on two couples
at the end of their neurotic tether and comes up again on "Loveland"
—"a metaphoric explosion!" Sondheim once said—a happy place,
we're told, "where everybody loves to live" and "where everybody
lives to love" (in other words, musical comedy is a delusion). In races
a pastiche of musical forms—vaudeville, Ziegfeld, and Gershwin—
each belonging to a neurotic impulse of love, each one its own folly
and (in a great big pop-historical masterstroke) all of them follies of
musicals gone by. "I was looking at the past with affection, respect
and delight," Sondheim said. "In no way am I pointing out how silly
the songs were because I don't think they're silly. What they are is
innocent." And so, in the dawn of 1971, Sondheim, Prince, Aronson,
and Bennett eased the musical out of its cocoon, and it flew away.

Even though *Follies* wasn't to his taste (or so he claimed), Fosse
liked it and asked Sondheim if he would be interested in reading *Big
Deal*, his *Big Deal on Madonna Street* musical, now set in Mexico, with
an eye to, maybe, contributing music and lyrics. "Out of politeness
I said I would read it," Sondheim said. "You know, playwrights have
enough trouble writing librettos, what am I going to expect from a
choreographer? So I read it and to my surprise I thought it was really
good. But there was a problem and an insurmountable one. There
are only two kinds of music in the world I don't like: Mexican and
Hawaiian. I said, 'Bobby, you're not going to believe me. You're going
to think I'm copping out. You're going to think this is my polite way
of saying your book stinks, but I think the book is really good but I
can't write it. If I have to write twelve bars of mariachi music . . .'"

Fosse moved on. With music and lyrics by Stephen Schwartz and
a book by Roger Hirson, *Pippin* was a musical inspired by tales of
Pippin, son of Charlemagne. It was slight, but Schwartz had written some lovely songs, and his *Godspell* was performing sensationally
well off Broadway.

In LA, finishing postproduction on *Cabaret,* Fosse thought of John Rubinstein, an actor who'd auditioned for the part Fosse eventually gave to Michael York. "He called me up out of the blue," Rubinstein said, "and asked me if I'd be interested in the title role of *Pippin.*" Of course he was interested: the leading part in a new Bob Fosse musical? A short time later, Fosse arrived at Rubinstein's house on Beverly Glen to go through the entire script, Rubinstein reading his part and Fosse all the others.

When they finished, Rubinstein looked up.

"What do you think?" Fosse asked.

The question needed a delicate answer. The story was thin, the characters thinner. As spirited as it was, *Pippin* felt naïve, part of another era's Broadway. One had to wonder, what — other than the fact that it was a follow-up to *Godspell* — did Fosse see in it?

"Well," Rubinstein said, "I like that song 'Corner of the Sky'..." Wanting the job, the actor was in no position to challenge Fosse's taste, but not acknowledging *Pippin*'s problems could make him look foolish, especially if this was some kind of a test. Rubinstein sighed. "I'm not crazy about it."

"Yeah," Fosse said. "Neither am I."

If Rubinstein was surprised before, he was baffled now. Why had Fosse, who could direct just about anything he wanted, picked a show he didn't like?

"I need you to come to New York," Fosse said, and he left.

With a final cut of *Cabaret* behind him, Fosse returned to New York and met with Schwartz, who at twenty-four was new to Broadway and had certainly never collaborated with such a powerful director. But his talent was apparent and his success phenomenal. "Fosse told me of his enthusiasm for *Godspell,* how buoyant he had found it," Schwartz recalled. He had been working on *Pippin* since college, he told Fosse, impressing him, and they seemed to grow more excited as the meeting progressed. When Fosse left, Schwartz called up book writer Roger Hirson to celebrate.

"Isn't this terrific? We have *Bob Fosse!*"

"Yes, that's terrific," Hirson admitted. "I just want to tell you this is our last happy day on the show."

In the months that followed, Fosse and producer Stuart Ostrow met regularly to discuss what Ostrow described as "the earnestness of the book" (Fosse told him he considered the book "a piece of shit"). They had known each other socially, from poker games, as far back as the Mary-Ann Niles years (Fosse "could bluff you with a pair of deuces," Ostrow wrote), but they remained at a friendly distance professionally. None of the Feuer stuff here. Ostrow worried about producing and Fosse worried about the show, which is just how Fosse liked it. Whenever Fosse brought up financial matters — *Pippin* was budgeted at around $750,000, a figure Fosse thought far too high — Ostrow told him not to worry. "Stu Ostrow trusted Bob and that made Bob trust him," Wolfgang Glattes said. Out of trust came a respectful exchange of suggestions. Their subject was *Pippin's* perhaps too-gleeful outlook and how to profane it. Strolling through the woods around the producer's home in Pound Ridge, they decided that lampooning the show with anachronistic dialogue and modern attitudes could bring it down to earth, though how they could do it without violating Dramatists Guild regulations, which granted authors script approval, wasn't certain.

Fosse offered the part of Catherine, Pippin's pure and decent love, to Janice Lynde. That she turned it down surprised them both; that turning it down drew them closer surprised them even more. With Fosse's professional interest in her confirmed, Janice felt her caution begin to erode. They touched more. He asked her to be with him.

"I don't want to," she said. "I know what will happen."

"You don't know."

"That's how it always starts. Someone says, 'You don't know. You can't know.' But I know."

"You think being with me will hurt you in some way?"

"Yes."

"You do?"

"Yes." They'd been here before. "I don't know."

"Look at the women I've been with. Look at the women I married. We were *partners,* Janice. Look at me and Gwen. It was *good* for us."

Janice knew that being with him meant being with death. "Bob had an absolute obsession with death," Lynde said. "He would always say he didn't want to live past sixty." Sixty seemed an arbitrary age, but it came up so often, she felt it had to be meaningful. *Sixty* sounded like a mantra, the way he would repeat it, as if it soothed him. *I'll go when I'm sixty,* he would say. *Just wait until I'm sixty.*

He'd call at night or in the afternoons when he wasn't working. They lived only a few buildings apart.

"Bob?"

"Oh God," he'd say. "It's a really blue day."

She would go to him. The nights she couldn't get to his place, she'd stay with him on the phone. "No matter where I was," she said, "he would call at three or four in the morning, which was fine with me because I would go back to sleep or I was up anyway or I would be with friends. They'd say, 'There's this crazy man on the phone who wants to speak to you,' and I'd say, 'I know that man. Give me the phone.'" He would talk about dying in musical terms. It helped, sometimes. On the phone with Janice, he described death as a dance with a snake. "One sting," he said, "and you'll be in a place you want to be where you can do what you want to do without the angst and the depression and the doubt and the insecurities."

On bad nights, the nights of no music, Janice would hear a flatness in his voice, and she'd panic. She would call a doctor and run over to his apartment. "What have you taken? Are you drinking?" She wasn't sure if the Dexedrine was helping or hurting (he said it was helping), and she called a psychiatrist to lead her through the contents of his medicine cabinet, just to be sure, or try to be. On the hardest nights, Janice insisted on staying with him. "Come on," she said, "I'm going to make you dinner at my place and you're going to have to put up with my dog you *hate*." If she got him to laugh, she thought, she could get him back. "Humor," Lynde said, "made the colors change." So she kept watching his eyes. They were small eyes. When he couldn't laugh, the smallest sparkle would show her what she needed to see — Bob, in there, a sparkle.

Before getting in bed one blue night Bob spent with her, she locked her dog in the bathroom. Then the howling began.

It lasted all night.

"I'm gonna kill that thing," Bob said to her.

"You want me to let him out?"

"No!"

"I'm gonna let him out!"

"No! No! Janice!"

She got up and opened the bathroom door. A fur ball flew through the air and landed on the bed.

"Fine," Bob said. "But he's sleeping on *that* side." There — the sparkle.

She'd play him music. He loved Satie and Billy Joel. Fosse said Joel played the piano like he had a rhythm section on the keyboard — rhythm, he needed rhythm; she saw how cleanly it separated his body from the dark part of his brain. So did sex. "His darkness would often precede his sexual impulse," she said, "like he was trying to climb out of it." And she would be there for him — that worried her. "Bob knew I had very strong caretaker instincts," she said, "and I was afraid that would take over my ambition." To love too much and love Bob Fosse would be loving alone. Janice knew not to ask for a solo.

"I want to," he volunteered. "Be with just you."

"You're going to try?"

He didn't answer that.

"Bobby? Can you?"

Fosse couldn't lie about love. He could cheat and steal, but he couldn't tell a dancer she could make it if she couldn't, and he couldn't profane the trust of someone he cared for. The loneliness he could live with; the bullshit he refused to accept. He told Janice if they were together, he could not allow her to do what he did — see other people. Of course it wasn't fair, but it was the truth. He'd been Bob Fosse long enough to know jealousy shredded him. "He never agreed to anything he couldn't do," Lynde said. "I was amazed because I'd never been with anyone so honest." Somehow, his spirit of full disclosure, even at its harshest, drew her in. This too was dazzling. To a woman preparing to leave him, it was the most seductive twist of all.

"This is who I am," he said. "I don't like it, I wish it wasn't this way, but . . ."

"But what? Don't you *love*? If you love someone, then you want to be with *just them*."

They'd been here before too.

"I go out with them," he said. "But I'd come home to you."

FIFTEEN YEARS

FOR THREE CONSECUTIVE DAYS before *Cabaret* opened at New York's Ziegfeld Theater, on February 13, 1972, Fosse adjusted the house lights and levels, honing the ambience for optimum viewing. He could not be too careful, even now. An exhibition atmosphere anything less than immaculate could undo all the efforts of the past year, his work from Jay Allen to David Bretherton, from Berlin to LA. Emanuel Wolf tried to calm him, and Vincente Minnelli's response to a preview screening — he called *Cabaret* the perfect movie — was touching praise, but Fosse knew the Ziegfeld was his last line of defense against the likes of Pauline Kael and the critics from the *New York Times*, whose reviews had the power to send audiences away, taking with them Fosse's long hoped-for chances of stardom. Directors could be stars now. In the wake of Fellini, Bergman, Antonioni, and the auteur-minded critics of the late sixties, Hollywood's new filmmakers had acquired highbrow cultural prominence and, for some, even celebrity. As never before, Fosse (and others) could become an Astaire behind the camera, where every square inch of the frame was his to master and take credit for. "Bob and I were standing in the back of the Ziegfeld the night *Caba-*

ret opened," Wolf said, "and I could see his mind working, spinning and spinning, and I said to him, 'Bob, stop cutting the picture! It's over! It's *over!*'"

Cabaret pushed the movie musical past one of those through-the-looking-glass thresholds separating before and after, one era from the next. In most cases, cultural transition is gradual, intelligible only in retrospect, like the last days of a marriage. Revolution doesn't usually rush in, like brick through the glass, the way it happened the night *Cabaret* arrived at the Ziegfeld, an avalanche of newness so disruptive — *Oklahoma!* disruptive; *West Side Story* disruptive — that even those who didn't care for musicals heard the crash coming from West Fifty-Fourth Street. "Until now there has never been a diamond-hard big American movie musical," Kael wrote. "If it doesn't make money, it will still make movie history."

Where to begin? The material, for one, was blatantly radical, more so even than Prince's radical stage version, and with the added power of the crosscut, *Cabaret* could be radical in form too, contrasting showmanship and evil, the stage and reality. Working with these big ideas, Fosse could have succumbed to facile commentary, but his moral position was too slippery to reduce *Cabaret* to irony by numbers. In Fosse's film, there is no formula to soothe the audience. Joel Grey's grinning Emcee is at once maniacal and thrilling, sleazy and entertaining, and his relationship to Nazism, though it might seem to be clearly defined — he is, we think, the fascist of the cabaret, full stop — becomes more complicated on second glance. When the Emcee is joking, is he endorsing the Nazis or mocking them? When he sings "Money, Money," is he celebrating wealth or knocking the rich? It's so fun we can't be sure. That's the whole idea. Entertainment is seduction, *Cabaret* says, the happy face on *Triumph of the Will*. And it kills.

No one knew Bob Fosse was telling his own story. A film about the bejeweling of horror, *Cabaret* coruscated with Fosse's private sequins, the flash he feared made him Fosse. From those fears emerged a nihilistic worldview of political and social double-dealing perfectly synced to the war in Vietnam, the Pentagon Papers, and the mounting sense that American virtue was little more than an act. Yet that was a byproduct. Personally removed from politics and the societal unrest around him, Fosse was largely untroubled by the not-so-distant cycle of hopelessness and devastation that reached from Altamont to Kent State, My Lai to Attica, but his own gloom happened to meet the public's halfway, and he stumbled into the present.

There was no time for him to bask in his achievement. Having prepared himself for the worst, another *Sweet Charity*, Fosse was overprepared for a comeback (one he wouldn't need): a breathless sprint of prepping, auditioning, rehearsing, filming, and finally editing *Liza with a Z* as he prepped, auditioned, and rehearsed *Pippin* in time to be ready for an out-of-town opening, in Washington, DC, later that year.

For four weeks, beginning May 1, Fosse rehearsed his ten *Liza* dancers (five boys, five girls) six days a week. To say he worked harder on this production than he'd ever worked before would imply, incorrectly, that Fosse ever gave anything less than one hundred percent, but how else to describe the rehearsal atmosphere of a one-night-only show? That's right: There would be no previews and no second night. Only a dress rehearsal, and then they were on, filming live before an invitation-only black-tie audience at the Lyceum Theater, with eight cameras stationed strategically about the premises (in the wings, aisles, balcony, upper boxes, and backstage), rolling not video but 16-millimeter film. Three cameras each held a twelve-hundred-foot magazine, enough to capture the numbers in their entirety; another three cameras held only three hundred feet of film each, which meant loading and reloading constantly, and with incredible speed; two more were handheld. And the cameras had only one shot. With the exception of one day of pickups — minor shots filmed after the main part of production ended — Fosse would film only one live performance of *Liza with a Z*, upgrading the show from canned variety act to visceral experience, rich in anxiety and truth. Fosse and his crew would be like a *National Geographic* team setting out to capture a show-business creature in the full fever of performance. Shooting film — unprecedented for a television concert special — would allow for better image quality and greater mobility in editing.

Sound would be an issue. Dancing at full tilt, with no chance to catch her breath, Liza would sound better if she prerecorded her songs — but that would compromise the show's *liveness*, "the real me," as Minnelli said, "without anybody drying me off." To have it both ways, the crew would break the audio into pieces and preselect which would be sung live and which would be looped. "Fosse wanted to bring reality to the stage," said audio designer Phil Ramone. Fosse's beloved snaps, pops, and claps could be replicated in the studio, but Minnelli's breathing would not be, he decreed; that would be live. Her *effort* was the whole point of the show. Her sweat. "Bob wanted all those breathing sounds," said Ramone. "I've never seen anyone be that detailed about anything." To someone else, it might seem like splitting hairs, but to Fosse, who had internalized precise volumes and sound textures for every degree of movement, audio was as exacting an art as any.

"I can't have anybody think this is phony," said Fosse to Ramone. "If they know bar eight is going to be prerecorded for four beats and then goes back, they're going to figure it out."

"What if I keep changing it?"

"How?"

"When she goes upstage to dance, we'll go with the prerecord. When she comes downstage to sing out to the audience, she'll go live."

"But how will you match it?"

"We'll have a cue system."

It was yet another part of the show that had to be not simply practiced but *perfected*. The cue-system technique Ramone devised for *Liza* had never been tried before. "When Liza went downstage," Ramone explained, "I would open up this mic in her bra so you could hear her panting and do three or four lines if she wasn't out of breath totally. Whenever she touched her earlobe or hit her hand on her chest, we would go live. When she went upstage, we'd go to the track. Everyone was desperately afraid of being caught with the tape not working, with our pants down, so to speak. It was quite adventurous. So in rehearsal Bob would sit right in the front row to see if he could tell if she was lip-synching or not. When it worked, he smiled so big. That was rare for him."

Hiding a battery pack as big as a pack of cigarettes under Minnelli's minimalist blouse — designed by Halston just for her — proved as difficult as hiding her cleavage from the network. "When the sponsors would come around," Minnelli said, "and they'd have to let them in, Fosse would call a break. As soon as they left, we'd get back to work." A little skin was one thing on a Broadway stage, but on TV — on NBC — there were rules, rules that only tempted Bob Fosse to break them. "He could not be stopped," said director of photography Owen Roizman. "He was the ultimate leader in that respect." If he succeeded, *Liza with a Z* would break ground; it would test the conventions of filming live for TV, audio manipulation, and the strictures of the concert special. And — if Fosse could keep the sponsors away from Liza's costume — viewers would get that sensual something extra on the side.

"Now, you've gotta imagine," Minnelli said, "there's this group of guys — Bob Fosse, Fred Ebb, Marvin Hamlisch, and John Kander — and they're all challenging each other to get better. I'm in the middle saying, 'What do I do? Where do I go? How do you want it done?'" In February, Minnelli appeared as Sally Bowles on the covers of both *Newsweek* and *Time* ("The New Miss Show Biz"), but in no sense had she reached her peak. *Liza with a Z* asked her to carry an entire evening — not intimately, before fifty people in the Empire Room, or even somewhat less intimately, on Broadway, but for NBC's audience, thousands deep and close up. She was twenty-six and more nervous than she had ever been in her life. "I always watched [Fosse's] face," Minnelli said. "What was he thinking? [A step] wasn't just a step. There's a reason. There's a reason for every movement." Minnelli impressed even the most hard-working dancers, rehearsing full out, and then, when they all thought she was done for the day, joining them at a disco after work. "Liza really, really wanted to learn," said dancer Candy Brown, wanted "to do well. I remember thinking she had a real desperation, like, 'I've *got* to take everything out of life. I've *got* to enjoy it all.'"

"One night," Roizman recalled, "around three in the morning, everybody was just beat. We all had our tongues hanging out and all the dancers were exhausted from having to do this over and over again. Fosse saw this, stopped everyone, and made a speech to everybody. He said, 'Look, I know it's three o'clock in the morning, and I know you're tired, beat, and you're worn out, but when this is cut together nobody's going to know that it was three o'clock in the morning and you were tired. So you have to take the approach that this is your first time out, this is live, this is your *best,* and you have to give it your best because that's all anybody will ever see.'"

On the evening of the performance, May 31, 1972, Fosse rehearsed the company as long as he could. To many, that seemed counterintuitive, but his thinking was clear. "When you get out there on that stage," he said to Candy Brown, "then adrenaline is going to take over. But if you're already at your max when it kicks in, you're not going to be able to push much farther. You won't go from zero to sixty." At 5:30, Liza and the dancers were excused. They were out of time.

What Minnelli needed now was a moment of her own to go to her apartment and freshen up before the show. But there was no way she could get there and back in time for curtain. So instead, she took her hair, makeup, and wardrobe people to the hotel across the street, where she would try to relax in relative seclusion. As they made their way in, however, Minnelli and her entourage sensed they were in the wrong sort of establishment. ("It was a hooker hotel!" Minnelli said.) Unfazed, she settled into an upstairs room facing the theater and dressed at the window, watching the tuxedos and their dates gather at the theater door. Though she couldn't quite make out faces, she knew somewhere among them were Chita Rivera, Paddy Chayefsky, her former director Otto Preminger, Michael Bennett, Harold Arlen, Lotte Lenya, Tony Bennett, and of course her father, Vincente Minnelli.

It began to rain. Was that a bad sign? One by one, umbrellas opened over the crowd, enclosing the Lyceum in a black tie of its own.

She had only one shot.

He had only one shot.

"Liza was very nervous, exceedingly nervous," said Christopher Newman. "She was concerned that her lip-synching wouldn't be good because there hadn't been that much rehearsal and the live singing might not be perfect because it wasn't in a studio."

A few minutes before 7:30, Minnelli left the hooker hotel for her place backstage, trying to squeeze her nerves into something like energy. The faces of Bobby, Freddy, and Johnny pulsed through her panic, warming her with love. Only moments before the curtain went up, Halston appeared with a teardrop necklace, emboldening Minnelli with a propulsive surge of good feeling. Out she marched, summoning as much poise as a girl-woman could manage when about to face, alone, a theater full of the most discerning people on Broadway and, eventually, everyone watching NBC.

Kander and Ebb's songs, with their determined air of *Just listen to me and you'll understand,* suited her, helped her shrink the room to a manageable size, first face by face, as she made eye contact, establishing personal attachments, then in clusters as she picked up steam, until, finally, at the precise moment, she threw open her arms to harvest the whole house in a single immolating swoop. "I think she's great because everybody wants to take care of her," Fred Ebb said. "You kind of want to help her, although she doesn't need help." Several songs later, Minnelli was in the wings again, catching her breath before "It Was a Good Time," her big confessional number about the end of a marriage, maybe her parents'. With only a few beats to connect to that part of her where the song lived, she crossed behind the curtain to her dear old friend lyricist Fred Ebb.

"Freddy! Freddy!"

He turned.

"Gimme the story, Freddy! Gimme the story!"

"I can't." He looked drawn. "I just took a Valium, and I have to sit down."

Ebb stumbled off, and in a whirl of smoke, Fosse appeared.

"Bobby, Bobby, Bobby, help me, tell me the story."

"Okay," he said. "All right," he said. "It's a woman. Okay? A man and a woman. They have a wonderful marriage. They have a daughter —" And then he began — she thought — to cry, but she was back onstage.

> It was a good time, it was the best time
> It was a party, just to be near you.

It was a jaunty refrain about heartbreak. To accentuate the façade, Fosse gave Minnelli a small gesture. Holding her hands at hip height, with her palms open to the audience and her fingers splayed, she evoked Jolson, but with her arms at loose angles, a broken Jolson. Like a showbiz hieroglyphic, these hands signified pep, the equivalent of "the show must go on." In this case, that show — that charade — was pretending a broken family was still intact. Later in the evening, the same gesture reappeared in Liza's sweet rendition of "Mammy," down at the lip of the stage. Specifically evoking Jolson now, Fosse was placing Minnelli in the company of one of the industry's all-time greatest performers; in having Liza sing about her mammy, Fosse summoned Judy Garland to his — their — side. This time, though, the fingers on Minnelli's Jolson-palms stretched out farther, brighter, and her arms opened wider, to reinforce the sincerity of a gesture that earlier in the show had been presented ironically. She had come full circle. Where the first number drew a mean line between show business and family, the second erased it.

After the roaring subsided and the crowd left, some to sleep and some to disco, Candy Brown took the long way out through the empty theater. She saw, sitting in the back under a line of smoke, Fosse and a woman. Save for two or three ushers, they were the only people left.

"Excuse me, Mr. Fosse," she said. "I had a really good time —"

"Oh, Candy," he said. "I'd like to introduce you to someone. This is Gwen Verdon."

They would never divorce.

Pippin auditions were in full swing. The principals, including John Rubinstein, Jill Clayburgh, Leland Palmer, and Ben Vereen as the Old Man, had been cast earlier in the year, but Fosse still needed his chorus.

Fast becoming a Broadway ritual, Fosse's open calls were highly anticipated, carefully orchestrated talent marathons that could last for days or even weeks. Hopped up on Fosse's legend and rumors, dancers gathered by the hundreds at the designated theater to trade insights, many of them accurate, about the sort of girls Bob liked. "I was told cut your leotard higher, you'll get it." "Tease your hair way up." "Stuff your cleavage." "Use eyeliner." The men? "He goes for personality." "No, he goes for sexy." "Don't be sexy. *He* has to be the sexy one." "Be funny." "Don't *try* to be funny." When the offstage space filled, they lined up around the block, stretching legs up against the theater wall, crying and talking, catching up with friends or stepping back to size up the buffet of muscle and beauty Fosse had to peruse. He knew many of them personally after nearly two decades in the elimination business, which made eliminating the ones he had to — those a fraction shy of sensational, those he had seen year after year who still weren't good enough, those who were good enough but just not what he was looking for, those whom he'd promised last time he'd help next time, and those he'd fucked or fucked over or wanted to fuck — even more terrible. As best he could, he tried not to look at anyone's face until the final round.

It always began the same: first, dance captain Kathryn Doby taught them "Tea for Two," basically a ballet combination with rhythmic bits of Fosse throughout.

"What do you see in 'Tea for Two'?" dancer Chet Walker asked him.

"I see everything."

Depending on the musical being cast, "Tea for Two" would change, slightly, but the vocabulary was always the same. "It has jumps, turns, rhythm, and syncopation," Walker explained. "It showed Bob your technique, and because certain parts of it are awkward and don't come naturally, it showed how well you listened to him." By nudging the dancers off balance, Fosse got snapshots of their natural instincts, the truth between the lines. But could they master those instincts? Could they master those instincts without forfeiting their personalities? "Sometimes, he'd put in this passé leap across the stage," dancer Jane Lanier said. "He'd look at the height of the jump, the position of the arms, the point of the foot. There was a lot to fit in." Buried in the steps were the details Fosse craved. There were walks. "A lot of people wouldn't see the walks right," Kathryn Doby said, "and Bob would know."

As many dancers as could comfortably fit onstage were called out for "Tea for Two," and Fosse observed from ten or so rows back. After several runs, he would separate the ineligible from the possible without too much uneasiness or deliberation. Dividing the dancers into smaller groups, Fosse would run the combination again to watch each one close and long enough to know — or come *close* to knowing — if the dancer had really learned the combination to the best of his or her ability. Joining them onstage to help, he took on the guise of teacher so he could interact with the dancers personally. But the willingness to teach was genuine. "He was always there to make people better," said arranger and conductor Gordon Harrell. "He could get stern sometimes, but it was never for the purpose of burying anyone. It was always for their own sake." And Fosse's: before he could pass judgment, Fosse had to get them to their best. "He would tell people in the middle of their audition to step to the side and work on it and then come back," Candy Brown said. "Most choreographers wouldn't take the time." Crouching, pacing, touching, thanking, smoking, watching, playing, pushing . . . when would he accept a dancer's limitations? "I've seen Bob audition people he believed in," said dancer Laurent Giroux. "It was like he was begging them to let him hire them." If the dancers needed him to, he would dance with them.

Then, finally, having relieved himself of the fear that he was rushing to judgment, the audition could begin. "Our eyes met during the audition," said one dancer, "and I thought, *My God. He's* rooting *for me.*"

The dancers were broken down into groups of three or four to show Fosse what they had. When he was as certain as possible, he let go of the dancers he had to, first joining them onstage to excuse them one by one with a heartfelt expression of appreciation. And Fosse always meant it. ("It was like he was cutting himself," one observer said.) "He would literally walk over and practically put his arm around their shoulder," dancer Valarie Pettiford said, "and thank them." He tried, with each dancer, to wish him or her luck in a specific and credible way that could slip a stent into a damaged vessel and maybe lift the person up, a little, forever. ("I think I've turned down more people than even girls have turned me down," he said. "It's pretty close.") This took time.

The surviving dancers, all of whom had demonstrated such high levels of skill that differentiating their gifts was near impossible, were then asked to sing. Some were cut off and thanked before they finished their songs. The remaining dancers were asked to read scenes from the script, and again, more were thanked.

At this point during the *Pippin* auditions, sitting only a couple rows from the stage, Fosse, Ostrow, Schwartz, Hirson, and casting director Michael Shurtleff were taking notes on each actor. For the sake of expedience, no discussions took place until the very end of auditions each day. Then the entire pool was brought out onstage and lined up for further examination. Here they stood, watching the dark, waiting for someone to speak. Every day their faces changed.

One day, a voice — kind but firm — came out of the dark.

"Number nine, will you step forward please. Number three, step forward."

The dancers waited.

One of them was Robie Sacco; he was eighteen and from Allentown, Pennsylvania. When asked, he said that he figured the pay would be about eight hundred dollars a week but added, "I'll settle for a dollar and a quarter an hour."

On the day Sacco was cut, Fosse saw fifteen lineups of hundreds of candidates; of those hundreds, one hundred and twenty-five were cut and seventy-five asked to sing. Singing — songs they loved, which they prepared in advance — they showed something of themselves. To ensure none of them would hear what was being said about them, Fosse had the line move as far upstage as possible; it protected both sides from too much involvement. Next, he asked an assistant for his cards; he had one for each dancer. Each card listed categories, and in each category, the dancer was rated a 1, 2, or 3 — 1 being the best — with pluses and minuses for subtle distinction. The difference between, say, a 1-minus and a 2-plus in the song category was clear to Fosse. A 1-minus might signify a singer with good intonation and musicality but no power. A 2-plus singer might have a limited range but strong energy. Asterisks were for pretty girls.

Of the seventy-five asked to sing the day Sacco was cut, three were asked to read. After the reading, Fosse got up and stood next to the two who still interested him. Here they talked. He was sniffing around, going more on gut than science, reacting maybe to qualities he couldn't define or matters of conduct that had nothing to do with talent. "I remember once," dancer Ken Urmston said, "there were at least three hundred girls auditioning for one replacement, and I was sitting with Bob, who had gotten them down to five, and we said, 'What about that girl?' And he said, 'She's the best one up there but I'm not going to hire her.' We all said, 'Why not?' and he said, 'When she went to do her song, I didn't like the way she talked to the piano player.'"

"He would cast dancers over singers," Stephen Schwartz said, "so I felt we didn't have the best singers in the world and that was frustrating to me." Jennifer Nairn-Smith, a five-foot-ten Balanchine ballerina (six foot two *en pointe*), was widely considered the most beautiful girl at the audition. She wasn't a singer, but with a figure like that and ballet chops to boot, Fosse wasn't about to let Schwartz send her away. He gave Nairn-Smith a part in the chorus alongside Kathy Doby and dancers Cheryl Clark, Pam Sousa, and *Liza* alum Candy Brown. Tall, short, busty, thin: each was distinctive. "You couldn't have gotten a more eclectic group in *Pippin*," Brown said. "It wasn't just leggy blondes. It was all types."

Ann Reinking arrived at the Imperial Theater dressed to order in black tights and high heels. Black — that was one of two things she knew about Bob Fosse. The other was that he was a terrific dancer, far better than anyone gave him credit for. *The Affairs of Dobie Gillis, Kiss Me Kate, My Sister Eileen* — especially *My Sister Eileen* — she remembered seeing them on TV as a kid in Seattle, and while she didn't know how to get those dance memories into her body so she could get her body into *Pippin,* she sensed a subtle, sexy humor in his style, a mysterious quality she understood he would respond to in others. "I was drawn to him before I met him," Reinking said. He saw she had the rhythm and classical technique to pass through "Tea for Two" without difficulty. "The moment I met him, I liked him," she said, "and I knew he liked me. I thought, *This person's going to be my friend.* There's no reason for it. I don't know why. I hadn't gotten the job yet, but I started kidding him, which was nervy. I guess I felt at home with him."

He moved them into a jazzy impression of Robbins's *Afternoon of a Faun* — romantic, but tangled inward. Reinking said, "Our feet and legs were in a turned-in fourth position, torso bent over parallel to the floor, arms in fourth position mimicking the legs." Floating separate muscles in isolated harmony, her body felt to her like the inside of a clock, all parts moving together but at different speeds, one witty, one lyrical, with an innocence she would not have associated with the slick alley dancer from *My Sister Eileen.* The addition of "soft-boiled-egg hands" turned the thermostat a small notch to the erotic. "It's as if you are holding soft-boiled eggs," he explained, "at the curves of your fingers." The image described the nymphy drift of lowered, half-open fists side to side behind their backs. There was tacit power — Fosse's phrase — in slowness. At twenty-two, Reinking had only just begun to understand why.

Fosse joined them onstage, handed out personalized instructions to each dancer, watching their bodies for the results and their faces for private reactions. "He wanted to know how we responded to praise and criticism," Reinking said, "and he wanted to know if we trusted him. Trust was important for him. Very important." She found he was kind to the dancers and gentle with her. "Okay, let's try this . . . you look good . . . why don't we turn here . . . very good . . . stay elegant . . ." Once again, he separated the dancers into groups of three. "He then gave us a pantomime with a ball," she said. "You throw it up and catch it and roll it up on your shoulder, and then from the waist down is this specific dance with tiny little back bumps. You spin a web up here [with your torso] but from the waist down you're like a machine. The magic is on top; the industry is on the bottom. It was beautiful, like commedia dell'arte."

Though Reinking had the ballet dancer's shape — strong and tall and lean — she was not distant or gauzily beautiful like so many ballerinas; she was sexy in a real and neighborhood-girl way, and she smiled easily. Nervousness lit her. Like Verdon, she spoke with a rough squeak, sounding like a kid hoarse from too much fun in the sandbox, and more than anything, she really loved to dance. She was game — Fosse could see that.

"Ann extended Bob's talent," Verdon said.

That night he called her at home and asked her out. Fosse would do that: ask a dancer to dinner before telling her she got the part or, in some cases, right after. Some got nervous and lied about having boyfriends. Others got angry. What if she told him to go fuck himself? What if she said yes?

Reinking was cool. "You and me," she said, happy to hear from him, "*that* has to be outside the show."

There was something about being told to wait — when it was done by the right girl in the right way — that Bob Fosse liked. It was the straight stuff. "Okay," he said. "That's okay."

Reinking got the part, joining *Pippin*'s players' chorus, and Fosse stepped away, slightly, so she could be certain she was there because he wanted her talent, which he did, mostly.

"The thing you love can also be the death of you," Reinking said. "Dancers are aware of that much more than the average artist."

It was his first summer in the Hamptons unmarried to Gwen. "*Separate* is not the right word," she would say. "We just don't live in the same house." She oversimplified. There was something pathetic, Fosse thought, about gathering together as a family — or whatever they were — for croquet, Ping-Pong, and dinner, as if they were putting on a little show. And if they were, who was it for? Neil and Joan Simon? Paddy, Herb, and Sam? Perhaps Gwen was doing it as much for herself as for Nicole. Nicole: Fosse did it for her, though he couldn't say if she liked having him around. But his not being there could further alienate her; then again, he couldn't be sure if forced closeness helped her feel any safer. "I want to be a good father to her," he said, "to be there when she needs me. But I'm sort of on a date with my daughter; her mother lives with her, and the difference is vast. There's a day to day interdependence between them."

Of course, Fosse had fun that summer too. "Bob was the most notorious and blatant cheater I ever saw," Neil Simon said. "The wonderful thing is, he never did anything sneaky or surreptitious." He'd simply kick a promising shot away from the croquet wire or call off a game he was losing *just* before he lost it. "Or sometimes," Simon added, "he would just pick up the wire and the wicket and just place it an inch away from wherever his ball was. And then he'd smile and say, 'What's wrong?' His philosophy was that what he was doing was right. They just forgot to write 'Cheating allowed' into the rule book." Fosse was exactly eleven days older than Simon, so age became a constant source of shtick. "I always look up to you, Bob," Simon told him, "and want to be just like you when I get to be your age." "In the first eleven days of my life," Fosse replied, "before you were born, I had more girls than you'd ever have in all your life."

• • •

Fosse asked John Rubinstein to his apartment for a drink the night before the first *Pippin* rehearsal. Expecting to see the book improved since his first meeting with Fosse almost a year earlier, Rubinstein was confused by the latest revisions and wasn't sure how to discuss them without causing offense. "When I *really* read the script, when I started working on it, I said to my wife, 'Oh God, this thing ain't gonna fly. What are we going to do with this?'"

With more than a touch of concern, he walked into Fosse's building at 58 West Fifty-Eighth Street and took the elevator to the twenty-sixth floor. A welcoming blend of bachelor and cozy, Fosse's two-bedroom apartment had all the requisite guy furniture — glass coffee table, bar, audio equipment — mellowed by crisscrossing rugs, pillows, and a welcoming disarray of books, ashtrays, and antiques. He kept a tea-service tray out on the balcony; a neon Tango Palace sign (from *Sweet Charity*) over the couch; and pictures of Nicole, both in and out of Fosse's arms, seemingly everywhere. "The place had a fun and temporary feel," one dancer said, "like he was never there and when he was he wanted to have a good time."

Fosse gave Rubinstein his drink, got one for himself, led him to the living room, and they sat there for a while, saying nothing. "We were sort of looking at each other," Rubinstein explained. "I didn't know what he wanted me to do. Were we going to read the play again? Did he want to give me some sort of character analysis? Did he want to get to know me? What?"

Finally, Fosse spoke. "Yeah, I don't know, John," he said. "I just wanted to talk to you."

"About what?"

Fosse took a sip of his drink. "What the fuck are we going to do about this show?"

The floodgates opened. They proceeded to discuss the problematic aspects of the book, item by item. They weren't trashing *Pippin* but inspecting it, turning it over like a piece of produce, examining it for possibility. "He told me that the 'War Is a Science' number was going to be a vaudeville routine, an olio, with a bunch of people with tambourines going 'Ha-cha!' and all of that. I thought that was brilliant. He told me a lot of that kind of stuff, how he was planning on doing the sex scenes. He said, 'That's not going to be a pastoral thing. It's going to be you and five knock-out babes and they're going to hurl you around and be an orgiastic sex scene.'" It became evident to Rubinstein that Fosse was using Schwartz and Hirson's creation as merely a point of departure, inspiration for what sounded like a different and much darker show. The skeleton of the story — about a group of medieval players leading Pippin on a picaresque quest for self-fulfillment — worked well enough, mostly, but the show's ending needled Fosse: Rejecting the players' suggestion to find meaning in a triumphant show of self-immolation, Pippin decides instead to settle down to a normal life with Catherine, singing, "And if I'm never tied to anything / I'll never be free." Fosse knew that wasn't right. Ending a musical comedy with a happy family was pat, old-fashioned, and, furthermore, not credible, especially in light of the Old Man's offer: stardom via suicide, the best career move of all.

The Variety Arts building had burned to the ground years earlier, on July 11, 1968. The only thing salvaged from the four stories of studios was a Hammond organ, saved under the diagonal cover of a fallen wall. The morning after the fire, a sentimental stranger was spotted brushing ash off the keys and playing a chorus of "I'll Be Seeing You" for a ring of unappreciative insurance adjusters. That was the last music to come from Variety Arts; the structure was never rebuilt. But the spirit of the place followed Fosse and his dancers to *Pippin* rehearsals at Broadway Arts, at 1755 Broadway, not too far away. The new space was conveniently located. After rehearsals, Fosse headed seven blocks down, to 1600 Broadway, where, in the busy collegiate atmosphere that was New York's Pentagon of postproduction, Bob, editor Alan Heim, and assistant editor Trudy Ship cut *Liza with a Z* in their scantily furnished high-walled tenth-floor echo chamber tight on air and low on light. Cranky chairs and a few wooden tables insisted on ascetic devotion to the work. This was the war room. "Bob would always be pushing people to push people to do something deeper, something different," Heim said. "And it was always thrilling to be in that atmosphere. I mean, for me it was. For some people it was different." They clicked together, tooth in sprocket. Heim's face, glinting behind a bushy mustache and glasses, had the New York look Fosse trusted, and he spoke calmly and clearly with the assurance of serious consideration, surely a comfort to raw nerves. That Sidney Lumet had recommended Heim sealed the deal.

Stationed at their flatbed Kem, Fosse and Heim worked a few paces from Ship, in her own room syncing and sorting their film trims, always ready with the strip or the part of the strip or the part of the part when it was needed. "I arranged a very elaborate system whereby Alan could find anything he wanted," Ship explained. "It was a great big roll broken down into little sections. I had numbered the film along the edges. He knew what take it was, what song it was, what part of the number, and what angle it was. I did it with letters and numbers with a coding machine. Let's say you had the song 'Liza with a Z.' I designated it song number one. If it was shot with the A camera I would have it say 'one-A-one' [meaning part one], and then a letter telling me if it was a close-up or what kind of shot it was."

Because Fosse shot *Liza* only once, he had fewer options than usual in editing. "We had a wide-angle way in the back of the theater over the audience onto the stage," Ship said. "We had a medium angle of the same shot. We had one in each wing, so you can get side angles. And then there was a high overhead medium to really focus on Liza, and there were close-ups of Liza from both sides and the back." Her close-up shot from below was cinematographer Owen Roizman's favorite angle. As opposed to the face-forward close-up, which simulated the audience's front-row line of sight, the side angle offered a seemingly stolen intimacy with Minnelli. Watching her from this angle, the audience sees what they aren't meant to — the sweat, the feral effort behind the razzle-dazzle. It tells them, *This is not easy.*

When the day's *Pippin* rehearsal finished, Fosse appeared at Heim's side; if Heim had already left 1600 Broadway, then Fosse appeared at Trudy Ship's side, sometimes to work through the night. Fosse loved that editors didn't need to balance a hundred production schedules to do their work perfectly. Like writers, they worked as fast as their brains did, at the speed of fired neurons. Cutting film at 1600 Broadway, Fosse attained the kind of pure, monastic immersion difficult to achieve in rehearsal or production, where outside reality insisted on breaking in. "I had no idea how late we were staying," Ship said. "We worked crazy hours and we worked weekends and I didn't keep track. I didn't care. We had so much fun, and Bob was a delight."

There was a game Fosse liked to play. Out of nowhere, he would walk up to Ship and speak the lyrics of a song.

"'When you see.'"

"*Guys and Dolls.*"

"Yeah. Good."

There was another game called Would You Trust.

"Hey, Trudy?"

"Yes?"

"Would you trust . . . Tony Perkins?"

An easy one. "Not if I was taking a shower. Would you trust Timothy Carey?"

"Not if I was a racehorse." (Carey shoots a racehorse in *The Killing.*)

Sitting next to Fosse, Ship grew accustomed to his scent, Revlon's Wild Lemon cologne. She liked it so much she went out and bought a bottle for herself. Before long, the entire suite smelled of summer lemon and cigarettes and, on the days Fred Ebb stopped by with lunch, hot pastrami too. But Fosse didn't eat much. Amphetamines kept his appetite down to sandwiches and wine — "the Fosse diet," Heim called it — which worried the Carnegie Deli's Herb Schlein so much he once turned up at 1600 Broadway with a large aluminum tray and a furrowed brow. "Is Bobby around?"

"He's somewhere," Heim said.

"Has he been eating?"

"Sandwiches."

"Well, I saw him not too long ago and thought he didn't look right. Here." Peeling back the aluminum, Schlein revealed the biggest turkey Alan Heim had ever seen. With it was apple pie. "I made it myself," he said. "Make sure Bobby eats it, okay?"

Heim was amazed and a little saddened by Fosse's tenacity. "He was never sure he'd actually done it," he said. "He would always say to me, 'Get your next job before the film comes out.'" One of the hottest filmmakers in the country, well on his way to finishing a television special that would likely take him even higher, and still Fosse was looking for more to do, in sickness and in health — though telling one from the other with him was near impossible. The amphetamines gave him constant energy, so Fosse could look bad, like a figure out of Munch, and feel just fine. No one knew.

Not even Heim. "How you feeling, Bob?" he asked one day.

"Fine. Did you read it?" Fosse was talking about *Lenny,* a script by Julian Barry based on his play about the life and death of Lenny Bruce. He had had a copy sent to Heim's apartment days earlier. "What do you think?"

"I read it after my wife went to sleep," Heim said, "then I woke her up and I said, 'You've got to read this.' This was the middle of the night. She said, 'I'll read it in the morning,' and I said, 'No, no, you've gotta read this now.'"

"You liked it."

"I think it's the greatest script I've ever read."

In every way, Lenny Bruce was a perfect fit for Fosse: self-immolating, filthy, funny, and drug addicted, a man who had a short life and a pathetic demise and whose crusade against bullshit broke entertainment taboos and drove him to his death — the passion of the showbiz Christ. A no-punches-pulled First Amendment drama, *Lenny* was an opportunity for Fosse to break his own entertainment taboos, to leave singing and dancing for the sort of hard, ruthless truths Bruce himself would have respected, and to exchange razzle-dazzle for capital-*A* Art. Here also was the possibility for autobiography in biography, a chance for Fosse to continue his ongoing effort to tell his own story, from strip clubs to self-destruction. No more Mr. Musical: this film he'd shoot in black-and-white.

At *Pippin*'s first read-through, at Broadway Arts, a ten-minute walk away from 1600 Broadway, Ben Vereen faced Fosse, trying to keep the faith. His agent had told him not to do the show, that his part, the Old Man, a sort of narrator/chorus leader, would not do for him what *Jesus Christ Superstar* had. But Vereen had loved working with Fosse on *Sweet Charity*, both in the Vegas edition and in the movie, and knowing that most Broadway directors didn't generally give white roles to black actors, Vereen wanted in. Reading through the script, however, he found the character did a lot of waiting. "Enter Fastrada!" the Old Man says. (Wait.) "Enter Louis!" (Longer wait.) Whenever Vereen looked across the table hoping for a wordless answer to his unspoken *What is this?*, he saw Fosse laughing to himself.

"Don't worry about it," he whispered to Vereen after the read-through. "Go to the library. Go look at cats like Bill 'Bojangles' Robinson and Jimmy Slyde."

He did. The most esteemed black tapper of vaudeville, Bill Robinson made a name for himself in nightclubs and on Broadway before reaching stardom beside Shirley Temple in movies like *The Little Colonel*, where he performed his virtuosic stair dance. Some traced the nickname Bojangles back to the French *beau jongleur*, meaning "juggler" or "trickster," suggesting audiences may have cast Robinson as a kind of devil—Fosse would have loved that. Jimmy Slyde, Vereen read, had a slide step so smooth, when he danced he made the stage look like it was made of cream. Like Bojangles, one of his idols, Slyde slid with the utmost upper-body control, enhancing the illusion of effortlessness as he skimmed across the stage, his derby lifted high in the air. All of it would go into the Old Man. "On the page," Vereen said, "he doesn't read as evil. He reads as [Pippin's] best friend. He was the devil on his shoulder, the cat who was gonna show you everything, but inside he was a killer. He had his band of killers [the players] with him. His whole thing was to devour this young man." The Old Man became the Leading Player, a black-magic killer with the charm of an entertainer.

Schwartz and Hirson liked the idea and agreed to revise *Pippin* with the Leading Player's malevolent purpose in mind. "The show was being discovered as we went along," Schwartz said. "But then [the Leading Player] began to take over the show so much that it began to diminish Pippin. The character became basically passive and reactive and didn't have the same kind of drive, energy, and intelligence that Roger [Hirson] and I were trying to achieve with him. Yes, he was an innocent, and yes, he was naïve about things, but a lot of specific lines he had got taken away—either given away to the Leading Player or just cut—lines that showed he had a sharp sense of humor or an awareness of what was going on." Rubinstein sensed the shift right away. He said, "I realized [Fosse] was having me sit on the stage and watch these numbers, one after another after another after another. I was just the observer."

The vaudeville concept was burning up the show. Fosse's inclusion of nasty contemporary language and references to the modern day undercut the out-of-time setting Schwartz thought they had agreed on. New digs and asides at Pippin's expense clunked hard, like a bad comic's bad jokes, curdling the show's innate tenderness and naïveté.

Frederic Weaver, managing director of the Chicago Academy of Theater Arts and Fosse's first mentor. Preaching discipline, versatility, and kindness, he elevated show business from a pastime to an ethic. Fosse thought of him as a kind of father.
Courtesy of Charles Grass

The Riff Brothers, Charles and Bob, on the *Morris B. Sachs Amateur Hour*, 1940.
Courtesy of Charles Grass

Bob Fosse — professional, but not yet ready for sex — around the time he started playing Chicago's strip circuit. "I think Bob protected his mother from the fact that she hadn't been able to protect him," Ann Reinking said. "He didn't want to risk hurting her, but he needed to tell it, to talk about it, so it kept creeping out in his work." *Photofest*

Weaver's class of 1944. Charles Grass on left; Fosse on right; Beth Kellough, a crush, to Fosse's immediate right. *Courtesy of Beth Kellough*

Fosse and Mary-Ann Niles in the national tour of *Call Me Mister*, 1946. They met shortly before this picture was taken and married shortly thereafter. *Photofest*

Joan McCracken in *Dance Me a Song,* where she met and fell in love with Fosse in January 1950. *Historic Images*

Fosse, Stanley Donen, and Debbie Reynolds rehearsing *Give a Girl a Break*. "During rehearsals," Reynolds wrote, "Bobby, who was so in love with his own well-endowed self, would come up behind me and press his 'gift' into my backside to tease me." Reynolds bought him a jockstrap. *MGM*

The "Alley Dance" from *My Sister Eileen*, danced, choreographed, and directed by Bob Fosse, waged jazzy pointillism against Broadway-big, inwardness against exuberance, Bob Fosse against Tommy Rall, for Fosse's greatest performance on film until "Snake in the Grass" in *The Little Prince*. *Columbia Pictures*

Gwen Verdon acing "Whatever Lola Wants" from *Damn Yankees*, simultaneously dancing, acting, and singing where most could only hope to alternate between them.
Photofest

Fosse as Joey Evans in *Pal Joey*, City Center, 1958, with Billie Mahoney.
Courtesy of Billie Mahoney

A precious glimpse of *Pleasures and Palaces,* which closed out of town
in 1965. *Corbis/Bettmann*

Gwen Verdon in the "Pickpocket Tango" from *Redhead,* her favorite show
and Fosse's first as director/choreographer. His thing for bad girls on a line
would rear up five years later in *Sweet Charity*'s "Big Spender," and then
again, behind bars once more, in *Chicago*'s "Cell Block Tango." *Photofest*

ABOVE: This is how it looks when Paddy Chayefsky has something to say. (With Gwen and Bob.) *Photofest*

LEFT: The first-time film director rehearses Shirley MacLaine in "If My Friends Could See Me Now" from *Sweet Charity*. (He loved those desert boots.) *Photofest*

Gwen and Bob, setting up "Big Spender" for cameras, 1968.
Getty Images/Lawrence Schiller, Polaris Communications

Michael Jackson took note: "Snake in the Grass" was hip-hop before there was hip-hop. *Paramount*

But that seemed to be Fosse's intention. "I didn't feel Bob's dominance was out of ego," Schwartz said, "but at the same time it wasn't purely artistic. It felt megalomaniacal. He was working with his gut." It seemed Fosse's *Pippin* was sending up Schwartz's, as if Fosse were the Leading Player, laughing at Pippin, or Schwartz, on his way to the flames.

In fact, Fosse was as much Pippin as he was Leading Player, as much victim as invader. "He wanted to be good," Ann Reinking said. "More than anything, he wanted people to see that that's what he truly was, even if he felt he didn't deserve it, or didn't behave that way."

Angrily annotated scripts — scribbled on hard enough to rip through the pages — shuttled back and forth from director to writer. Fosse's suggestions were x'ed by Schwartz, and then Schwartz's x's were crossed out. Fosse wanted Pippin to say, "Oh, I know this is a musical comedy, but I want my life to mean something," and Schwartz and Hirson countered with "I'm getting old. Very old. And I still haven't done anything with my life." Fosse wrote *Terrible* next to that suggestion and *Up yours, Schwartz* beside another. "There's a theory," Harvey Evans said, "that Fosse picked weaker material so the critics would say, 'Oh, it's not much of a show, but what Bob Fosse did with it!'" A second theory suggests that Fosse could produce only when behind the eight ball; another that the only way he could write was by manipulating a writer; and yet another that in order to tell his story, he had to break through the stories of others.

Fosse would intrude on Schwartz's songs. In the case of "War Is a Science" — a bit of Gilbert and Sullivan that descends into minstrelsy — he corrupted the number with an occasional "Doo-dah!" from the chorus. "*Pippin* is classic vaudeville with something wrong," Ann Reinking said. "When they say 'Ta-*da!*' at the end of the number, it could be ironic and mean war is not good or it could mean war is an incredible show. Bob knew there were some people who saw war as beautiful. He was playing to both of them." Yet another point of contention with Schwartz were Fosse's *ha-chas*, *yuk-yuks*, *yeahs*, and *skiddoos* — the verbal equivalent of Fosse's pet percussion sounds. It was an interesting idea, Schwartz thought, one that was (once again) taken too far. The Leading Player's "Nyaa" — as in Jolson's "*Nyaa, folks, you ain't heard nothin' yet!*" — is a reminder that everything is entertainment, even death. It was a continuation of a philosophy Fosse had been working on since *The Conquering Hero*. He'd work on it for the rest of his life.

Fosse stormed into rehearsal late one afternoon. "There was a cloud over his head," Candy Brown recalled. "We were all kind of backing away because we didn't know what the hell was going on." They knew he lived in doubt, even fed on it, but going from *Liza* to *Pippin*, *Pippin* to *Liza*, Fosse doubled his stress, and on little sleep, doubled his exhaustion. There was no telling what, or who, had pushed him over the edge, whether that edge was real or imagined, whether he was sober or drugged. "All we could do," Brown said, "was wait."

Finally, he looked up from the floor. "I'm sorry," he said. "I'm really sorry." He slouched forward. "I was editing *Liza* today and my editor dropped a piece of ash onto the film. I'm sorry."

There was an uncertain silence.

Then Brown said, "Well, he didn't ruin any of *my* stuff, did he?"

Fosse burst out laughing, walked over to Brown, and took her in his arms. "He smelled like lemon," she said later, "and his body was almost kind of vibrating when we hugged. I know now that it was probably some kind of drug. I could feel it literally on the inner parts that his body was all vibrating, shaking like a scared animal."

Liza with a Z aired on September 10, 1972, to terrific reviews. Combining his stage sense and choreographic skill with his cinematic technique and packaging them for television, Fosse reinvented the televised concert special and mastered it in a single effort — his first. Of all the definitions of genius, fluency in the midst of discov-

ery—grace where no artist has been graceful before—seems the
most incontestable. As with Orson Welles and Noël Coward, two of
stage and screen's most expansive and fluent discoverers, Fosse had
a chameleonic intuition for both performance and presentation. His
cross-pollination of entertainment media, beginning with *Cabaret*
and continuing with *Liza with a Z*, elevated him to the exclusive
plane of absolute conqueror, the Mozart of show business.

Translation: he had a long way to fall.

Before *Pippin* left New York for tryouts in Washington, DC, Schwartz
may have spoken a little too candidly to *Newsday*. "I sort of aired
some of the dirty laundry, which did not endear me to Bob or Stuart
Ostrow," he said. "Then Bob retaliated." "I think he's very talented,"
Fosse said to the *New York Times*. "But not as talented as *he* thinks he
is." Their relationship deteriorated from there. There were outbursts
in Washington, some of them public, and all of them useful. Though
Schwartz's "ingratitude" genuinely angered Fosse, controversy was
too fortifying to waste. As Fosse had discovered many times over,
learning whom he couldn't trust helped him reach those he did.
Whether defeating Abbott or banishing Schwartz, these battles paid
artistic and social dividends, harnessing Fosse a muse, goading him
to go deeper and darker while also drawing his company closer,
strengthening their allegiance to himself and one another.

Pippin's social climate was the perfect complement to Fosse's aesthetic ambitions for the show. "Bob wanted no chorus in *Pippin*," said
dancer Pam Sousa. "He wanted everyone to have a personal role. It
really bonded us together. It made us feel a part of something." Bringing the company together offstage, Fosse enhanced their chemistry
onstage, increasing their collaborative power to lure Pippin to his
demise. The girls would have poker nights at Kathryn Doby's. "We
called Kathryn Mother," Cheryl Clark said. "She'd put our little shoes
out for us." They would play tricks on stage manager Phil Friedman,

piling into his tiny bathroom, waiting there, and pouncing on him when he opened the door. They'd hide in the shower when he called, "Places." "We were a family on *Pippin*," Candy Brown said. "Bob made us a family." Fosse would join the dancers on break and tell them stories of his MGM days, about working not too far from Gene Kelly and Fred Astaire, and about the nail that couldn't be kicked beautifully enough.

Entertainment organisms are vulnerable at every turn, to new audiences, new critics, and new personnel, and they can completely transform at the slightest provocation, like going out of town. Anxiety, jealousy, ego — functions of any collaborative environment — are roller-coastered by the very public nature of performing, quadrupled by the God-given temperament of show people, and raised to the *n*th degree by the lifespan of a company, which, no matter how successful the production, is brief. Writer Julian Barry said, "People in plays and in movies, when they are a community, and they're in danger as a community, which is what they are, they get very, very close. Then they go out of town and the danger is even greater. They fall in love with one another and they fuck one another and they vow that this is the person for me, and my wife back in New York is second rate." Even if a show is extended, an end is always looming. Time is condensed. Emotions are high. In a vinous swirl of sugared feeling, liaisons are quickly formed and quickly broken, and the other lives resume.

"He was a star director," one dancer said, "and we were so young, most of us virgins on Broadway. Many of us would have done anything he said." Washington was a heady time for all. "Most of us got those calls in the middle of the night," Brown said. "These conversations went on for about half an hour. I guess it sounds bizarre, but at the time it was — I don't know, I loved him, so if he was in pain I would try to talk to him. There was always some kind of angst about something. Just general angst." He was the best topic of discussion, the single most powerful something they all had in common. If one slept with him, they all slept with him; if one deflected his passes, they deflected him together. "I get involved in the material and the people," he said once, with spectacular cool. They were, after all, the same thing.

The extent to which Fosse reused the same dancers, drawing them so consistently into his home life, and his nightlife, meant Fosse's productions occasioned more than the standard amount of company intimacy. Adding sex complicated matters enormously, but rarely did it hurt the work. It could hurt a dancer, maybe, but never the dance. "It made me nervous and I did whatever I could do to get away," Brown said. "He was an old man to me, you know? I was nineteen or twenty. We were at a party during *Pippin* and he kept asking me to come home with him but I kept saying — I didn't know what to say — 'I gotta go home and feed my dogs!' I kept saying it over and over. He wouldn't let up." Even when Fosse was persistent, his manner could be so childlike that almost all forgave it. "I think it's fair to say Bob came on to all of us," dancer Pam Sousa said. "But it was never to a place that affected us. Some women were flattered. That was Bob being Bob." The net result of Fosse's sexual involvement was mostly positive. That many dancers described their *Pippin* relationships as familial can be attributed to Fosse's urge — creative, like the others — to build a strong family of his own. The same urge led him to Paddy and Herb and the coterie of Cohn's writers he knew would not betray him; it was the impulse that drove him to distrust. To never know sustained intimacy in love.

Jennifer Nairn-Smith, however, was not flattered by Fosse's attentions. Before coming to Washington, she'd reluctantly accepted his invitation to dinner, fearing, as many women had before her, that she would lose the job if she didn't put out. "I was never attracted to him," she said, "but he kept hounding me and hounding me, pushing and pushing." They discussed ballet, her training with Balanchine.

Nairn-Smith was tough, a self-proclaimed ballet diva, suspicious of Fosse's style and suspicious of him. But as a ballet dancer, she was of interest to Fosse, as imposing sexually as she was artistically. Ballet was the real thing; the club Fosse could never be a part of, one of the many chasms separating him from the likes of Jerry Robbins. It wasn't just ballet technique that scared him; Fosse didn't think he could sustain a dance for more than four or five minutes, the length of a Broadway musical number. He could see *Big Deal* (if he ever did it) ending with a big robbery sequence all in dance, but a full hour of uninterrupted choreography — not to mention *classical* choreography — was Mount Everest, simply beyond the clouds.

"Jennifer, the Joffrey wants me to do a ballet for them," he admitted one night. "But I can't do it."

"Why not?"

"Because I don't know the vernacular."

"They don't want the vernacular. They want your *style*."

When he made his move, Jennifer tried to flee. When he attempted to stop her, she kicked him in the groin. He made such a flagrant example of her shortcomings in rehearsals, most could guess what had (or hadn't) gone on the nights before. Fosse would do that, zero in on a girl. "There was always one person that he picked on," Candy Brown said. "But that wasn't uncommon. I saw that behavior in other choreographers. One person they yelled at constantly. 'That was sloppy! What are you doing? Get your head in it!' It's awful, especially when you know you're the person making the mistake and Bob should be berating *you*." Nairn-Smith could take it, for a while; a certain amount of punishment was part of the game. "She would be in tears, sobbing," Rubinstein said, "and two hours later they would be going out to lunch." Nairn-Smith thought Fosse's cruelty came mixed with jealousy, sexual and artistic. A ballerina with a boyfriend, she represented a double rejection to him, even when she let him have her. That's why, some thought, he made her hold a flag in *Pippin*, like a girl in the school play. "He was a director," Nairn-Smith said, "a manipulator. He knew the button to make you feel great and he knew the button to make you feel like shit."

In Washington, Nairn-Smith's boyfriend found out about Fosse, and he threatened to kill him. According to stage manager Maxine Glorsky, there were detectives trailing Fosse. "I was working in the theater and these two guys in suits came looking for him. I said, 'He's not here. It's the lunch hour.' But they'd come back and Fosse would slip past them. It kept happening. It was like some kind of funny movie." Ostrow did not think so. He put the Kennedy Center on red alert, and Fosse shifted into defense. "Bob protected me from all the creeps," Nairn-Smith said. "And he did try to get to know me but I was ice."

Candy Brown stayed at the Howard Johnson with the rest of the chorus. One night, she was standing in the elevator of the Watergate Hotel, where Fosse and the higher-ups had rooms, and the doors opened to reveal Ann Reinking waiting to leave Fosse's floor.

"Annie!"

"Candy?"

They tried smiles to buy time. Fosse had quite openly flirted with both of them, so it was possible that Reinking was coming from whence Brown was going. If so, had they betrayed each other, or had Fosse betrayed both of them? Neither could tell.

"I'm sorry," Reinking said.

"What?"

"You and Bob. I'm sorry."

"No, no!" Brown threw a hand to keep the elevator door open. "It's not like that."

A certain amount of nighttime overlap was inevitable, even intentional. ("Jennifer and Ann came in one day wearing matching jackets," one dancer said, "and we thought, *Oh Lord, Bob!*") All that crossing in the halls nicely precipitated threesomes. So did Quaaludes. "There were lots of poppers backstage on *Pippin*," one dancer said. "A couple of stagehands were handing out PCP. Lots of stuff was going on." The drugs cut both ways, building the togetherness Fosse aimed for, and sometimes shaking it apart. "Someone dropped a lude in my Seven-Up," another dancer said. "I remember a bunch of us were walking a St. Bernard through a cemetery in DC one night and I fell asleep on a tombstone."

While the company was still in Washington, Fosse called Reinking to formally and properly ask her out. She had asked him to wait and he had waited. "I talked so much on the phone that night," she said. "He made me nervous and relaxed, if that makes any sense." Reinking had told him she wanted to keep their thing outside of the show, and now that the show was up on its feet, they were as outside as they were ever going to be.

"Don't you think it's a little unfair to ask a girl out when she's still auditioning for you?" she asked him on their first date.

"Yes," he said. "But I admired you for turning me down."

Her admiration for Fosse pulled and pushed her, toward him and away. "It was like being with someone I had known forever, someone I could embrace, and also somebody I couldn't touch because he was that good." Several dinners later, she was pulled only toward him, and harder the more she saw him. Fosse recognized the feelings, hers, his. They were as good as producer's promises. "I know enough about emotions to know that nothing is permanent," he would say. But already he loved her.

Fosse kept his idea for *Pippin*'s finale a secret as long as he could, up until a day or so before the first preview. Saving it allowed him to rethink the sequence for as long as possible, and it kept the company abuzz, leaving them to wonder, from one run-through to the next, how dark *Pippin* would get, how far it would really go into existential limbo. ("You mean you want me to get into that box and set myself on fire?" Pippin asks.) "When Bob finally told us what we were going to do, we talked about it in detail," Doby said. "After Pippin decides not to kill himself, we [the players] were supposed to get audience members to come up onto the stage for the ultimate fulfillment. It became a tribal frenzy." Here the family atmosphere would pay off. Dancer Gene Foote said, "We didn't realize that at the end of this show we were going to ask someone to set themselves on fire, and kill themselves, so we could orgasm. That was the end of the show. But we didn't know anything about any of this, we just kept doing the steps."

When Pippin rejects their offer, the players push themselves into an orgiastic death collective, writhing to the lip of the stage and stretching their hands into the crowd. "I know that there are many of you out there," the Leading Player says, "extraordinary people — exceptional people — who would gladly trade your ordinary lives for the opportunity to perform one perfect act, our grand finale."

Death.

"Bob would remind us," Candy Brown said, "that we would want to get them to think committing suicide was the best deal ever." Was there a better finale?

Not to *Pippin,* but to a career?

Was there a better finale to a life?

Yes, you, in seat K116. "Some people came up," said Ken Urmston, who appeared in a later production. "You'd ask the blue-haired ladies and they didn't know what was going on but I remember asking a ten-year-old-girl and she said, 'Oh no, I like my life.' And I remember once there was a sixteen-year-old boy who was shaking — I don't know what he thought, but he came up on stage unsettled, he was very serious — and Ben Vereen took him into the wings and said, 'Look, this is just a show.'"

Ultimately, *Pippin*'s players get no volunteers, and the fabulous finale idea is dropped. Infuriated, the Leading Player strips the stage of all its scenery and commands the orchestra to shut up. Just before exiting, he says to Pippin, "You try singing without music, sweetheart." You try to make meaning without show business.

It gets quiet.

Pippin sings. Catherine, who loves him, stands with him, holding her little boy.

Then the song ends. It's quiet again.

"Pippin," she asks. "Do you feel that you've compromised?"

"No."

Quiet.

"Do you feel like a coward?"

"No."

"Well, then, how do you feel?"

His answer would be the last moment in the show. John Rubinstein said, "The audience is expecting me to say something sentimental and wrap it up. But I don't. I just stand there and I say, 'Trapped.' That first night in Washington, the audience screamed with laughter. Then the laughter dies down and Pippin feels he can't say that to this woman. He loves her. So I say, 'But happy. Which isn't too bad for the end of a musical comedy.' And I discover it for the first time as I say it. And the audience goes, *Ahhh*. It's not a laugh. It's *yes*. Because that's how we all feel. We have all this dissatisfaction. We are trapped, just like Pippin, but we're happy. We're okay. I love my kids, I love my wife, even though she's a pain in the ass. The audience was let off the cynical hook. After that audible sigh of relief in the Kennedy Center Opera House, I would then take their little hands — Jill [Clayburgh] and the boy — and pick them up over my head and go 'Ta-da!' very softly. Then the curtain would go down."

Jaundiced, sultry, satirical, *Pippin* opened September 20 at the Kennedy Center and met with sensational reviews. The show bettered the Fosse brand. It pushed more buttons harder and refined his style in staging and dance; that is, *Pippin* amplified Fosse by *simplifying* Fosse.

He was a minimalist now. Minutiae matched his smallness of stature and self-worth; it seasoned earnest displays of aerobic grandeur with irony, inviting the audience to look beyond the surface burn to the ice beneath. Or vice versa. Fosse's temperature could be hot or cool depending on any number of tiny, closely watched variables, and when those variables took the form of pantomime, running the gamut from parody (hot) to innuendo (cool), they could be quite funny too. "I used to be more involved in patterns and complex steps," he said after the show opened. "Now I try for the simplest thing that will say what I want it to say."

His ideas clarified too. In the context of the Leading Player's final entreaty, we, the audience, understand that *Pippin*'s opening number, "Magic to Do," in which the players were directed to seduce the audience to join them for the show, was actually a pretty invitation to go out with a bang. "We did not work *with* each other," said Gene Foote, "we worked out front [to the audience]. The whole show was out front." The show *was* a front — *Pippin* was only a pretense, a piece of entertainment there to disguise a cruel reality: our lives have no meaning. All we have (if we want it) is a good finale, the gift of our own destruction, and — *ha-cha!* — we might as well make the most of it. (So how destructive is entertainment, after all?)

Fosse's style seemed to degenerate as it developed. His *Pippin* was neater, wittier, and darker than *Sweet Charity, Cabaret,* and *Liza with a Z;* it showed a deathlike anti-vigor on the one hand and a clarification of his show-business vocabulary on the other. Those open-faced palms in "Magic to Do," Walter Kerr wrote, were "Jolson's, Martha Graham's, Alla Nazimova's, the *theater's.*" The burlesque bumps and Suzie Qs of "The Manson Trio," and of course Ben Vereen as the devil in Bojangles, made a definitive statement on entertainment's power of perversion and destruction, on Fosse's own downfall, which he saw hurrying toward him, coming faster and closer the harder he worked.

"I don't hesitate to lift from every form of American show business," he said. "I love the old minstrel shows." The timeless, spaceless black that surrounded the *Pippin* stage enabled him to draw from all corners of entertainment, and not just through dance, but with classic vaudeville sound effects and lighting cues. "The follow spots for Fosse were choreographed," said Maxine Glorsky. "I mean, they were *really* choreographed to be like old vaudeville. He was evoking a piece of America's folk-art history in light." With love, he underscored the show's deceit, which did not fall far from his own. As a collage artist who was never certain of his own worth, whose influences were obvious as far back as "Steam Heat"—which showed his roots in Jack Cole—the question of originality was constant, nagging Fosse to ceaseless work and self-recrimination. Those who viewed his low opinion of himself as false modesty or as an invitation for others to contradict him with love and praise—a handy mirror for the narcissist—knew him only from the press or in passing. The view from close up was much different. He was empty; the slouching, knock-kneed, burlesque kid whose own mother hadn't protected him from the fiendish strippers in the backstage of his unconscious. "I kept telling him he was a good person," Reinking said, "but I don't know if he ever believed me." It was never enough, because *he* was never enough.

He never could take care of himself. "I understand why you love him," Reinking's mother told her daughter when she first met Fosse.

"Why?"

"Because there's a lot of boy in that man."

He had to be bad to be good. That would safeguard him from critics who were hip to *Pippin*'s every move, "stolen" or otherwise: he had to add grief and depression. The more the merrier. "We now get to New York [with *Pippin*]," Rubinstein recounted, "and Bob gets nervous about the New York critics accusing him of sentimentality.

That's when he starts putting in more lines about assholes and fucks and things like that. We started cutting some corny stuff too, all of which was fun, until Bob came to me before the premiere and said, Cut 'But happy.'"

Rubinstein had protested. "But that's the whole thing!"

"Nah, it's sentimental bullshit. It's crap. I hate it."

"Now Pippin's defeated — it changes the whole character —"

"Do it," Fosse said. "The line is 'Trapped — which isn't too bad for the end of a musical comedy. Ta-da.'"

Schwartz, who, despite everything, had come to love much of what Fosse did with the show, was equally opposed to cutting "But happy," but he told Rubinstein they didn't have a choice; he had already tried, unsuccessfully, to invoke the Dramatists Guild. Fosse had the clout to overrule him.

On opening night, Fosse sent each of his dancers a bottle of Dom Pérignon and a personal note. He hated his handwriting, which was as bumpy and twisted as his dances, so he typed. "Candy, Candy, Candy, the Amazing Candy: The face of a cherub, the smile of summer. She moves with the sensuality of a panther, talent spilling out all around her. She could turn on all the boys in the band. Always with that humor that can salvage the most tense situations, always with that demanding self-knowledge. Always huggable, always lovable, always, always — what's your name again? — oh, yeah, Candy. I . . . LOVE . . . You . . . And . . . I don't care . . . who knows it. Doo-dah. Love, Bob."

Late on October 23, 1972, after the final moments of *Pippin's* Broadway premiere at the Imperial Theater, the curtain came down, and John Rubinstein felt the audience recoil at the new ending. "Part of the problem," Schwartz said later, "was that Bob was imposing his own psychological demons on a story that in many ways couldn't support that. To have the final line be 'Trapped. Which isn't too bad for a musical comedy," I felt, well, actually it *is* too bad for a musical comedy."

Fosse certainly had imposed his demons on *Pippin,* but he had also done his research. Earlier that year, the *Wall Street Journal* ran a piece about the rise of depression in the United States. One paragraph in particular caught Fosse's attention: "For those who cannot find a cure, suicide is often the result. The suicide rate of known depressives is 36 times that of the general population." That hardly meant "Trapped" would be a sure thing with critics, but Fosse knew malaise was out there, all over America, and musical comedy, to be meaningful, had a responsibility to address it. "The statement of [*Pippin*]," he told the *New York Times,* "is that life is pretty crumby but, in the end, there stands the family — pretty ugly, stripped of costumes and magic, but holding hands."

Holding hands. It wasn't the sort of magic Fosse had in mind, or even believed in. Gwen Verdon, who believed in him, who still held out a hand to Fosse, knew he needed far more than what he had. "He never seems to enjoy achieving success or love or friendship or whatever it is children give you, all the things most people aspire to and feel make up a life," she said. "Maybe he can feel the warmth of those things momentarily, but he can't retain it. Do you know what the only thing Bob can retain is? Sorrow."

"There's something deflating in that," Kerr wrote of *Pippin*'s ending, "as though we'd all gone through a lot for very little." Despite its impact, the ending was only an ending, almost literally tacked on. A comprehensive existential statement had been merely suggested.

Style over substance.

Ticket sales were mild.

Thanksgiving came around and Fosse tried to take time off. He hung out for a couple of days. Then he flew to Germany to catch up with some old *Cabaret* friends; flew to Vegas to see Liza and Joel Grey's act at the Riviera; was the guest of honor at a party Sue Mengers threw for him in Los Angeles; and took Nicole to Disneyland. Until then, the two had had the usual father-daughter dinners and crossed paths at Gwen's on Long Island, but they hadn't spent that much time together since the split. "I never use my name to get tickets or reservations," he said, "afraid someone will say, 'Bob *who?*' But I've pulled every string I can think of to get her to Disneyland." The day he came to get Nicole at Gwen's apartment, Fosse trembled with worry about the trip and confessed all to her at the door. "Don't worry about it, pal," Nicole said. She touched her tiny hand to his. "Everything's going to be all right."

Nicole at nine years old was too young to have seen her father dance in the movies, but she was old enough to know *The Little Prince,* by Antoine de Saint-Exupéry. Stanley Donen planned to adapt it into a musical film and had offered Fosse a small dancing part as the Snake. They'd shoot in Tunisia. For the longest time, Fosse brooded on the offer, first deferring, then saying no, then reconsidering and deferring again. As much as he loved performing, he knew a dancer in his midforties would never look better than he felt, which wasn't that great. It had been a long time since Fosse danced in public, let alone on film for the whole world to see. To sweeten the deal, Donen offered Fosse complete control of the number, from preproduction to post- ("You can even wear a bowler," Donen said), but still Fosse said no. "Nicole was crazy about that book," Gwen said, "so she said, 'Oh, you've got to do it!' and Bob always said, 'The next thing I knew I was in Africa.'"

The Snake: It's how he'd imagined death. "One sting," he had told Janice Lynde, "and all your worries . . ." They disappear.

Fosse bought his Snake costume — a pair of shoes from LaRay and white gloves from Bergdorf's — and rehearsed with Louise Quick at Broadway Arts. Breaking up his slow, limb-laden slither, careful turns of wrist, and vainglorious undulations of arm with kicks, sharp fingers, and staccato back bumps, Fosse made his snake appear to be both the object of his own erotic amusement and a sexual hunter, seducing outward and inward, like a proud matador. With attention on each twitch, which he overenunciated, as if rippling his scales in a full-size mirror, the Snake's showoffy air and rhythmic irregularity foreshadowed Michael Jackson, and its freezes and stutters on and through the beat presaged the pops and locks of hip-hop, a revolution still very much underground. Dazzled, Herb Gardner thought it the most incredible number Fosse had ever danced. For that honor, "Snake in the Grass" stands neck and neck with Fosse's "Alley Dance" from *My Sister Eileen* — his two greatest performances on film — but where the latter shows a Gene Kelly–type arrangement seasoned with Fosse (the tricks of "Steam Heat" in particular), "Snake" rings with his mature style.

En route to film *The Little Prince,* he flew to Madeira, a tiny island off the coast of North Africa, for a short rest. Meeting him was Ilse. They had broken up and made up more times than they could say, but considering they had never been exclusive, how could they ever really break up? With no clear starting line, there was no need to agree on a finish, and because his romances rarely ended badly — the director in him, handling them — those on the in always stayed in, and Fosse's stable, rather than narrowing with time, actually deepened. Still, there were shifts in rank and preference. His love for Ann Reinking, his growing fondness for Janice Lynde, and the occasional hot thing with Jennifer Nairn-Smith edged Ilse farther into the outer ring, where she had once been willing to wait. But now she had grown tired of waiting. Strolling the Madeira coastline, they were literally on the rocks, cliffs black and yellow and red from the giant shield volcano beneath them.

Fosse's body plunged into vacation, and his mind looked the other way. It was hard to do his famous relaxation act if he didn't have a job lined up for his return, and two, as always and with everything, was better than one. The first job was a new musical, one he had always wanted to do with Gwen — he felt he owed her — based on the Maurine Watkins play *Chicago*. For years, Watkins had rejected every offer to adapt her work. The rumor was she had become a superstitious fanatic, reading only tarot cards and *Variety* and living someplace where not even Sheldon Abend, her agent, could reach her except through a post office box in Jacksonville, Florida. To actually get Watkins in the flesh, Abend had to hire a private detective who tracked her, ultimately, to an address not far from her post office box. But once located, Watkins (now writing Hallmark cards for a living) refused to talk to him. When she died, in 1969, her estate, including the book rights to her plays, transferred to her mother. When her mother died, the rights were transferred to Abend, who, at last, sold *Chicago* to Fosse's producer Robert Fryer, and the team-building process began. Kander and Ebb signed on for music and lyrics, and Fosse and Ebb, it was decided, would collaborate on the book. Having learned the lesson many times over, Fosse would finally be credited as writer.

That was one project.

The other was *Lenny,* the film Fosse had been wanting to make about Lenny Bruce. Before it was a play directed by Tom O'Horgan, whose productions of *Hair* and *Jesus Christ Superstar* influenced *Pippin, Lenny* had actually begun as a screenplay Columbia Pictures commissioned from writer Julian Barry. But after *Love Story* hit, Columbia concluded that grim material like the Lenny Bruce story no longer suited the national taste and dropped the project. That's when Barry and O'Horgan decided to adapt the screenplay to the stage; they cast Cliff Gorman in the leading role, and he eventually won a Tony. "It played like a screenplay onstage," Barry said, "which is how Lenny's brain worked: *Cut cut cut, bang bang bang.*" Lenny's was a jazz brain, like Fosse's.

Fosse had brought with him to Madeira tapes of Bruce's routines and a draft of Barry's play. "Look, Julian," he had said to Barry at their first meeting, "I'm sure you're really pissed I haven't contacted you earlier"—he was; before getting Fosse's call, Barry had heard he was working on the script with Gardner and Chayefsky; none of Barry's calls had been returned—"but here's the thing: you've worked on this story for years, you know everything about Lenny, you've read every interview and seen every routine, but I'm new. I have to find it all out for myself. You know what I mean?"

"Yeah. I do."

"I don't want to be in a room working on a script with someone who's going to correct me on Lenny Bruce. I have to see what works and what doesn't."

Whether it was true or not, Barry was quick to accept Fosse's explanation. He wanted this job. "I understand."

"I need time."

"Okay."

"Good," Fosse said in his soft, small voice, "so how about this: while I'm in Africa, you write some new scenes. When I get back, we'll talk."

Barry smiled. "Bob, you want me to audition. That's what you're saying."

"We're in show business," he said. "We audition our whole lives."

That was true, but so was this: Fosse wanted to write. He had wanted to write *Redhead, The Conquering Hero, Sweet Charity, Pippin,* and one could argue that to varying degrees, legal and less than legal, he actually had. But on each of those projects, he had been forced to collaborate. Sole authorship—of all elements—still lay ahead of Fosse, reminding him he could not fly on his own and that his incomplete vision, stymied by his incomplete control, would forever stand between him and claims to real art. By conferring with Chayefsky and Gardner before returning Barry's calls, Fosse prepared to step into the ring a better fighter, and perhaps he even stood a chance of pinning Barry against the ropes. Beating a writer, or trying to, was a lot like trying to write.

In February 1973 Fosse said goodbye to Ilse and left Madeira for Nefta, the Saharan village where Donen's production was based. At his hotel, the Nefta Palace, he caught up with his old assistant Pat Ferrier Kiley, whose husband, Richard Kiley, had been cast as the Pilot in *The Little Prince*. They had known each other for years, since before *Redhead*. "I want to go out and find where we're shooting," Fosse told her. "Will you help me?" Fosse's Snake number — literally a sand dance — would be filmed on location, in trees and on dunes and at the tops of cliffs, and Pat would be the extra pair of eyes he needed to see himself. Just then a coughing fit hit him — it sounded deep, from the stomach, like something was trying to break out of him — and Pat froze solid, unsure whether to watch him for signs of emergency or look away to give him privacy. Before she could act, someone reached for a chair in case he wanted to sit down, or had to, but Fosse waved it off with a sharp smile as if to say this was normal and kept coughing. When he finally recovered, Pat looked him square in the eye and said what few had the courage to say: "Bobby, you've got to cut down. You've got to take it easy."

"Listen, Pat," he replied with the air of making a prepared speech. "I drink too much, I smoke too much, I take pills too much, I work too much, I girl around too much, I *everything* too much." He winked at her. "That's just the way I am."

That wink, she thought, sealed his fate.

The next day, Fosse and Pat prowled the dunes for shots. When his eyes lit on something, the two stopped. She stood in for Fosse as he played with the camera, then they switched; Fosse hid a thin slab of plywood under the sand, took his position on the board, and Pat stepped back for the view. He taught her the dance piece by piece, using a portable cassette player for the rhythm section. "Bobby came with the Snake Dance already mapped out," Pat said, "and Stanley [Donen] was occupied in other areas, so Bobby and I would get up there and literally pick out camera angles." Donen would have final cut, but he would take Fosse's suggestions, as he had since they filmed *The Pajama Game,* all the way to the editing room.

The run of *Pippin* kept Reinking from joining Fosse on location —but nothing stopped Janice Lynde. With the Snake Dance prepped and ready to shoot, she arrived just in time—for some terrible weather. The brutal cold and desert winds would be miserable under any circumstances, but to a dancer, who needed to keep warm and limber between takes, the conditions were devastating. "They told us to bring resort wear and they ended up flying in skiwear from London because it was that freezing," Lynde said. "Me and [Donen's wife] Yvette Mimieux were on the backside of those cliffs standing there with comforters and blankets. So that whole dance, Yvette and I were keeping Bob's legs and muscles warm, rubbing him, papoosing him in blankets and things and praying that he wasn't going to be blown off that cliff. It was amazing that he could even do it." They shot the number for days.

On the morning of February 13, with only a day of the Snake Dance left to film, Fosse squeezed himself into his tight black pants, slipped on his tinted shades, and angled his derby devilishly to one side. Emerging from his trailer, he saw the entire crew standing there waiting for him. They had lined up in an aisle formation stretching from his trailer door all the way to the set. What had happened? What was going on? Then someone told him: The Oscar nominations had been announced. *Cabaret* had ten, including best actress (Liza Minnelli), best supporting actor (Joel Grey), best cinematography (Geoffrey Unsworth), best editing (David Bretherton), best picture, and best director of 1972 — you. By then, a full year after *Cabaret's* release, the film and Fosse had been honored by a slew of prominent critics and had even won a few prizes, but Fosse knew not to get excited. The Oscar was not coming his way. As everyone was aware, the year 1972 was the year of *The Godfather*. "We knew what that meant," said Emanuel Wolf. "But we were just so happy to have all those nominations."

Cabaret had opened throughout Europe to enormous praise. "When we left Africa, we came back through France," Lynde said, "and Bob was the toast of Paris." The red carpet rolled out from the plane to Fosse's suite at the George V; from dinner with Janice on the Seine to the late show at the Crazy Horse. "He was fascinated with that show," Lynde said. "They did a tribute to him by doing some of the songs from *Cabaret*. Nobody sang them, they were totally dance-production numbers, but there was one with this gigantic spider web across the entire stage. Somehow they rigged it so the dancers could climb into the veins of the web and do almost aerial choreography. They called him out in the audience to a standing ovation and bravos." It was a wondrous evening. To be honored by the Crazy Horse, that esteemed purveyor of Continental grind, was to return to the slime bars of his youth and find them cleaned up, semi-assimilated into the mainstream; even better, it meant he was — to the Parisians, at least — if not an artist, then a showman king. "Bob was so happy that night," Lynde said. "It meant so much to him that they got him."

Lynde returned to their suite one afternoon to find Fosse on the floor. On his knees. Assuming he was working on a new step, she proceeded to move around him cautiously, but as she got closer, she could see he wasn't moving. His head was down.

"What is it?" she said. "What's wrong?"

He said nothing.

"Bob, what is it?"

"Wally . . ."

Fosse had known Wally Cox since 1949, when they'd met in rehearsals for *Dance Me a Song*, their first Broadway show. A shrug-
ging, bespectacled comic and sometime writer who once described
himself as "a harmless preoccupied guy in a constant state of reduced
effect," who looked as Fosse felt — as if he knew he'd drawn a losing
hand but wasn't quite ready to lose — had collapsed at his home in
Bel-Air. A heart attack, the papers said. He was forty-eight. "They
were roommates at one time," Lynde said. "Bob was devastated. He
went into a deep depression." For the rest of their stay in Paris, Fosse
and Lynde appeared where they had been invited, and Fosse tried
his best to accept the well-wishes from his hosts and give thanks in
return, but he was only halfway there.

Days later, preparing to leave the hotel for an afternoon, Janice
reached into the wardrobe for a jacket. Fosse was standing inside.

"What are you doing?"

"It should be me."

"No, it shouldn't."

"I'm the fraud. Wally wasn't a fraud. I'm the fraud."

They flew back to New York. Janice tried to assure him his success
was not in the least fraudulent, that it could not possibly be a fluke;
it was far too consistent to be accidental or lucky. He had a record.
He had accolades. But rather than comforting him, being reminded
of his sterling reputation only intensified Fosse's despair. One day,
he told Janice, he would run out of smoke. "He said his greatest fear
was that they'd find out it was all razzle-dazzle," said Lynde, "that
they'd realize he didn't have talent, like in *The Wizard of Oz,* they'd
pull back the curtain." On the heels of *Cabaret, Liza with a Z,* and the
slow-growing popular interest in *Pippin,* he sensed justice waiting for
him around the corner. On the outer rings of culture, Fosse couldn't
fail — marginalization was his destiny — but on the inside, under the

microscope of national acclaim, Fosse knew his public unmasking was inevitable, his downfall only a question of time. Gravity was the law.

Fosse and Julian Barry met at Fosse's office at 850 Seventh Avenue to work on Barry's script for *Lenny*. As soon as he walked in, Fosse blasted him with story ideas — good, awful, funny, sexy, mean, weird — in white-hot streaks of drug-induced mania. It was as if Fosse felt that the more he said, the farther he'd get from failure. "When you sat in the room with Bob Fosse," Barry said, "his mind made you so tired, you couldn't wait to get out of there. It was so intense. He was taking Dexamyl, these little green-and-white spansules, and chain-smoking the whole time. It was the most exhausting thing I've ever done in my life." Dexamyl — or Christmas trees, as they were known, for their coloring — was a combination barbiturate-amphetamine popular on the all-night disco scene. Fosse kept his in a little black attaché case he left open for all to see. "He was in the romantic period with it," Barry said. "I knew what that meant. He thought it gave him ideas, and maybe it did, but I knew he'd crash any moment." With a Seconal-like drug to counter the effects of the Dexedrine, Dexamyl provided the two-in-one solution. Aside from being highly addictive, the drug further strained Fosse's cardiovascular system, already damaged by a lifetime of cigarettes and stress.

Barry would come to 850 Seventh with scenes he had written or revised the night before, and Fosse would spend the first part of their meetings with pages in hand, reading the scenes aloud, challenging Barry's every choice. His tone was not so much contrarian as urgent. There was only one right answer — one way to save himself from slipping into mediocrity — and Fosse had to find it. Barry had to help him. Fosse's career, his life, depended on it. Barry said, "You would say something and he would say, 'Why do you think that's a good idea?' And then you would have to spend hours explaining it and defending it. I mean, he was always probing you that way. You'd be drained. He wanted to push you and he wanted to make sure you really *did* think it was going to work. He'd fucking interrogate me about everything, three hundred and sixty degrees. Then I'd go home and rewrite the scene and bring it in the next day and he'd send me back to do it again." They worked this way for a month, like a snail on speed. "We weren't using a typewriter," Barry said, "but I was taking constant notes. I would be on the couch or in a chair and he would be moving around, talking up and down, using ninety words when he could have used two."

Fosse made amphetamines look good. With the Oscars fast approaching and the Tony nominations just announced — *Pippin*'s eleven included best musical, best choreography, and best direction of a musical (two more for Fosse) — the entertainment world began to treat Fosse almost like royalty. At first, it felt good. Girls, restaurants, fame: Who wouldn't love the ride? Never mind the pressure. Never mind that no one took his stresses seriously. He was being modest. He was the king. He was a genius. What will the genius do next? (Will *Lenny* be another masterwork? Another *Cabaret*?) Then *Liza with a Z* was nominated for an Emmy. It was a show-business record: no one had ever been nominated for best director of three different works in a single year (let alone *produced* three such notable works in a single year). But where two nominations seemed prodigious, three ran him down; the Oscar, the Tony, and now the Emmy was a marathon he could not win. Thus the panic. Thus the Dexamyl. Fosse's prescription came to him from Dr. Harold Leder, his internist of many years. Before the drug was recalled, in June of 1973, around the time Fosse and Barry collaborated, Leder comfortably prescribed Dexamyl for any number of ailments. "They were diet pills," said David Freeman, a patient. "Dr. Leder kept them in a jar on

his desk like they were M and M's." Though Leder was openly concerned about Fosse's high stress and smoking, he knew better than to
interfere with the private lives of his patients. "He was not the sort of
guy to smash his fists on the table and say, 'You have to take care of
yourself,'" his son, Dr. Drew Leder, said. Even if Dr. Leder had, Fosse
would have found Dexamyl elsewhere. He had his connections.

Fosse's office phone rang like crazy. Congratulations from friends,
interview requests, and job offers were now a regular part of his day,
and though his secretary, Vicki Stein, did the lion's share of phone-
answering, Fosse couldn't always stop himself from answering it
himself. It was a reflex — muscle memory from the time he couldn't
afford a secretary. Seeing Fosse snap up the phone like a whip, Barry
sensed the gypsy in him was still waiting for those life-and-death
crumbs from his agent. Barry remembered one particular conversation: "Hello?" Fosse said into the receiver. "Yes . . ." His eyes widened.
"Yeah, that sounds really interesting . . . Well, that's great, that would
be wonderful . . ." Smiling, he held up a one-second finger to Barry.
"Great, yeah. I have to ask you one question, though. I know how you
work so I have to ask. Will you rehearse?" He waited for the answer.
Then nodded. His smile faded. "Well, Frank," he said, "I have to tell
you the truth. I can't do it." A pause. "Okay, well, thank you. Bye."
Fosse hung up, and his smile came back. "I just fucking turned down
Frank Sinatra!"

A few days later, Fosse said, "Okay, Julian. Today, *no phones.*"
"Fine."
"We're just gonna let it ring."
"Great."
"You expecting any calls?"
"Nope."
"Good, that's good. Then no calls."
They got down to work — and the phone rang. Fosse looked up to

Barry. "You think it's a job?" Barry laughed, and Fosse dove for the phone.

One day, when Barry arrived at Fosse's apartment for work, his host had on his mischievous smile. "Help me make my bed."

Barry followed him into the bedroom and looked down. The sheets were covered in dried wax. "Bob, what the hell have you been doing here?"

"Oh, they love it," he said.

Fosse got a kick, Barry thought, out of watching him react.

"He was a master watcher," said dancer Christine Colby. "He didn't always have to sleep with somebody to get to know them intimately." Dancer Dick Korthaze said, "He had a way of — how shall I say it? — *evaluating* people in social situations that would give him more of an understanding of his dancers than he would in a rehearsal or performance situation. He wanted us to be ourselves without the restriction of the professional attitude." It helped Fosse get to know his equipment, learn when to push it and how far. "You'd be talking to Bob," Alan Heim said, "and then six months later he'd hit you with something you said six months before, not to hurt you, but in order to make you better, to make the project better. He was directing. He was putting the principles of directing to use all that time. Some people might think of that as manipulative, but I don't. I think he was just doing the job."

It was one of the reasons Fosse loved to be quiet in a crowd. From party to party, Fosse took in the human spectacular, watching people's bodies for personalities, auditioning them for a show he had yet to write, and all from behind his drink across the room, where he could study them without their knowing. During the day, he could spend an hour or an afternoon on the street doing the same. Could a single blip of movement reveal a deeper meaning? Fosse loved catching it, the secret synecdoche. One afternoon, he cut through a busy slice of Fifth Avenue to stop a young woman who clearly stood out from the herd, at least to him. There's no way he could have seen the expression on her face; it was her cadence that caught his eye; it was her movement. "The way you're bounding ahead," he said to Sherri Kandell, "it looks like you're ten feet taller than everyone around you." Amazed at his perspicuity, Kandell explained she had recently given birth to her first child, a boy, and she was so happy to be in New York on her own, temporarily free, ecstatic with abandon, and full of love for her new son back home. "I was just blown away," she said years later, "that he could pick me out of rush-hour traffic and could actually see I was having the time of my life."

He was fascinated with interrogation, now more than ever. The hours of interview material he and Barry used for *Lenny* research combined with Bruce's native (and brutal) candor inspired Fosse to try some digging of his own. "Lenny Bruce would push people's buttons," Verdon said. "Bob thought that was very important." He liked to play what he called the truth game. "Why do you love your wife?" he would ask a friend in front of that friend's wife. Or "Have you ever thought of killing yourself?" He would not tolerate cop-outs and he would not stop until he touched bottom. He could be merciless about excavating the truth, or what he decided was the truth. It could kill the room. "He could get so mean about it," said Bob Aurthur's wife, Jane. "I didn't think it was fun." He would drive a wedge into the smallest admission and — *snap!* — crack a person wide open. Was he emceeing a party or tempting a breakdown? "He'd love to set up some kind of conflict," said Arlene Donovan. "If he asked you who your favorite singer was and you said Ella Fitzgerald he would give you a look and make you feel your singer should be somebody else. It wasn't mean. It was fun." Some would call it sadism, but for Fosse, pain was research, a means to an end. "What I really want to do is find out how much I really know about people," he said, "whether I can express something about them in terms that are both dramatic and valid. That's why *Lenny.*" Taking characters (or, in this case, actual people) to the moment of total hurt before the tears — that was revealing them. Directors and writers both did that job. Choreographers too. They were revealers.

"You know, Julian," Fosse said one workday. "When you're on the set, it's just different than you thought it was going to be."

"What do you mean?"

"At that point, the director really becomes the writer."

"That's just a bunch of French bullshit, Bob."

"No, think about it. It's really true."

Barry took five pieces of blank paper from his pile on the desk and handed them to Fosse. "Here," he said. "Shoot this."

They'd be sure to take lunch down at the deli. Once, Herb Schlein had caught them casually and heartlessly walking past the Carnegie on their way to a new lunch spot, one of those places where big-titted waitresses in tiny outfits served chili and hot dogs. "Herb had this look on his face that was so hurt," Barry said. "I turned to Fosse and said, 'If he finds out where we're going, he's going to start wearing bras just to keep us in there.'" Since then they had made a point of eating downstairs, often with Chayefsky and Gardner. Both were still fighting through hard times in the theater. Paddy hadn't had a new play on Broadway in almost ten years, not since the eleven-day run of *The Passion of Josef D.* in 1964, and Herb had been away since *The Goodbye People* closed after seven performances, in 1968, which was the same year Chayefsky's *The Latent Heterosexual* opened to mild reviews in Dallas (it never reached Broadway). Both men had turned to movies to recover. Gardner was trying to scrounge up funds to write and maybe direct *The Goodbye People*; Chayefsky was writing *The Hospital* (which would ultimately win him his second Academy Award — not bad for a plan B).

"How can you do this?" Chayefsky shouted at Barry in the deli one day.

"What? Do what?"

"Lenny Bruce. His mouth, his language. It's bad for the Jews."

It would be a tough table for anyone, but for the unsuspecting writer, Chayefsky's corner could be hell. Whether people asked for it or not, Chayefsky refused to soft-pedal the truth; the aim was to improve the work, not be nicer at lunch. Fuck bullshit. "Paddy was blatant," Barry said, "glowering at me." Chayefsky's fervor made it difficult to distinguish those he respected from those he didn't — as if Barry needed more feedback! First Fosse upstairs, then Paddy downstairs! Did these guys ever stop?

Fosse looked up from his sandwich. "Oh shit."

Barry and Chayefsky looked where he was looking — to the door.

"It's that guy from the newspaper."

A journalist type had spotted Fosse and was coming their way.

"I gotta get out of here," Fosse said.

"Where you going?"

"I don't know. The bathroom."

He flew off. Since the triple nomination, the record-breaker had grown tired of interviews. And he knew the more good press he got now, the more they'd want to tear him down later, when this was all done.

He was laughing to himself as he returned to the table. "This is hysterical," he said. "You spend your whole life trying to get known and then you spend the rest of it hiding in the toilet."

Awards season officially began for Bob Fosse on March 25, 1973. At the Imperial Theater, *Pippin*'s home turf, the Tony Awards opened very much in Fosse's spirit with a Broadway medley from Fosse veterans Helen Gallagher, Paula Kelly, Donna McKechnie, and Gwen

Verdon. But this was not an omen in his favor. Neither was the welcome by Richard Barr, president of the League of New York Theaters, who proudly declared to the fifteen hundred in attendance and the millions watching on ABC that half of Times Square's thirty porno palaces had been shut down to make room for family-friendlier theatergoing. The first Tonys were then presented, to Jules Fisher for best lighting design and Tony Walton for best scenic design, both from Team *Pippin,* which engendered an early surge of confidence for the show. From there, it was a fair fight with *A Little Night Music* for best musical. The tides turned with every envelope. Fosse picked up two Tonys, for best choreographer and best director. "I confess I thought I had a shot at the choreography," he said in his second acceptance speech, the one for best director, ". . . but this one . . . I have a loser's good sportsmanship–type speech I was going to give to the winner at the ball later . . . but let me just say thank you to all the marvelous people who helped with the show and say that they could not have done it without me. Thank you." Best book and best score went to Hugh Wheeler and Sondheim, respectively, for *Night Music,* and *Pippin*'s momentum vanished. The quarrel between dazzle and genuine eloquence — on view for the crème de la crème of Broadway — would have stirred Fosse's oldest doubts. The verdict: Hal Prince and *A Little Night Music* for best musical. He hadn't fooled them after all.

The very next day, with no time to rationalize his partial triumph, he flew to the Beverly Hills Hotel, his home base for the week ahead. It was Oscar time and he was in Los Angeles — two distinct reasons to move uncomfortably from party to party. But he had backup: Paddy, Herb, and Herb's girlfriend, Marlo Thomas. They'd all flown out, checked in to the Beverly Hills Hotel in rooms a few doors down from Fosse's, and stood by, champagne on ice, ready to convince their friend of his victory if he won or rage with him if he lost (and they knew he was going to lose — to Coppola). The list of night-before-

Oscar parties was as long and dull as a tax return and offered multiple opportunities for awkward run-ins between Fosse and the executive element he despised, but producer Edgar Scherick's cocktail gathering at the Hotel Bel-Air, thick with the New York vibe of Elaine May and the cast of *The Heartbreak Kid,* was the kind of evening Fosse and the Carnegie bunch (and, as it turned out, Groucho Marx) could get behind.

Janice Lynde was Fosse's date. Weeks earlier, she had accompanied him to the Directors Guild Awards (Fosse was nominated for best director of a feature film, but Coppola won, as expected). The night of the Oscars, she met Fosse for a pre-awards party at Emanuel Wolf's pink and green suite at the Beverly Hills Hotel. All of the *Cabaret* people were there: Liza Minnelli, Joel Grey, David Bretherton, Geoffrey Unsworth, and forty others. Lynde said, "He was really, really nervous then, shifty and scared." Shoring himself up with booze and tranquilizers, Fosse got sweaty cold as Wolf took the floor for one last go-get-'em-don't-worry-have-fun speech. Both *The Godfather* and *Cabaret* were tied at ten nominations each, but their little film had started with so much less: in Munich, with a tiny budget, a dilapidated genre (the movie musical), and a director on artistic parole. And yet here they were, about to go to the Academy Awards; that in itself, Wolf reminded them, was a victory. In the limo to the ceremony, Fosse repeated a discouraging statistic about how reliably the Directors Guild Awards predicted the Oscar winners. It was always best to expect the worst.

They pulled up to the Dorothy Chandler Pavilion — sitting in downtown LA, like a beached whale doing a Lincoln Center impression — and out stepped Janice in a Greek goddess dress, cut flowingly to the navel, followed by Bob Fosse in a three-piece tuxedo, his tight vest cinching him smaller than ever.

Paddy had already delivered his wisdom, and Sam Cohn, having seen many more clients lose than win, had already telegrammed a pat on the back. Variations on the good-luck theme, most of them chips off the old bullshit Fosse had heard his whole life, passed his ears; familiar and semifamiliar faces he knew (or claimed to know) claimed to know him. Hollywood people were different. Whether it was the product of more money or more sun, their alien cheer made them, like a certain kind of musical comedy, easy to write off as phony, which of course many of them were. There, Fosse's cynicism had its advantages. Broadway's gripe against the film capital of the world — based on decades of failed migrations as far back as Dorothy Parker's — made LA the voodoo doll for Fosse's pins, and it kept him at a steely distance from the in crowd he always wanted to join. And LA was clean. He didn't trust clean. The people of Broadway had a worn-in quality. They were troupers. They sweated and they stuck together. Their many weeks of rehearsal, their eight shows a week, the restrictive parameters of midtown, the small talent pool and reteamings of favorite collaborators, and the ancient rites of old theaters and restaurants made Broadway a place of tradition and familiarity. The Dorothy Chandler Pavilion conveyed an unused quality — all sparkles and high ceilings.

Ten minutes before showtime the bell sounded; every cigarette was extinguished, and the slow flood into the auditorium began.

The stage was spare. Gaunt stairways twisted behind the podium, hiding in shadow like fire escapes with stage fright. Red, orange, and blue lights peeked out from around them, as if curious to get a look at the presenters or the black lacquered runway over the orchestra and into the center aisle. The curtain bell sounded again, and the *Cabaret* company found their section near the front of the stage, Liza with boyfriend Desi Arnaz Jr. and her father, Vincente Minnelli; Joel Grey with his wife; and Bob with Janice. Soon every seat was taken, none of them in the smoking section. A man on the God mic kindly asked for silence; silence was calmly granted; there was a countdown from five; and the house lights, instead of going down, went up for the cameras. Should Janice hold Bob's hand? Was this a good time to say something? Janice decided to say nothing; she would simply *be there* with him.

Now things would get bad for almost everyone. The pre-show charge that people and their dates felt in the lobby was the happiest most of them were going to feel all night. Rather than picking up momentum, the Academy Awards invariably cool down as they progress, leaving behind each winner four bodies, and then four more and four more, so by the end of the evening, the dead so outnumber the living that most people are happy to flee. That evening was no different.

Except *Cabaret* was winning. Joel Grey heard his name and got up. One of the show's hosts, Charlton Heston, got a flat tire and missed his entrance, so Clint Eastwood, pulled from the audience, got up. The editor David Bretherton heard his name and got up, and Geoffrey Unsworth, who took Fosse's side in the darkness, got up. It was happening, and with each win, the next win seemed more likely; the next loss more humiliating. But they didn't lose; they kept sweeping: best score, best art direction, and best sound, which made it difficult to completely discount the possibility that Fosse might win, although he wouldn't. Coppola would. "He was very still," Emanuel Wolf said. "He was somewhere else." They had lost best adapted screenplay to Coppola, but the tally showed *Cabaret* was quietly, and strangely, ahead of *The Godfather*. As the bodies piled up and the ceremony approached its end, *The Godfather* had only two wins to *Cabaret*'s seven.

George Stevens and Julie Andrews, at the podium, announced the nominees for best director.

"Bob Fosse for *Cabaret*."

His head was down. Janice was not with him. The show's directors had removed the pretty girl from the edge of the frame to make for a better, more intense close-up of Fosse. Surrounded by men, seat fillers he hadn't met before, Fosse looked much more alone.

"John Boorman," Andrews said, "for *Deliverance*."

"Jan Troell for *The Emigrants*."

"Francis Ford Coppola for *The Godfather*."

"Joseph Mankiewicz for *Sleuth*."

Then the envelope and Bob Fosse heard his name again, and he was onstage, taking a cold statue from George Stevens. "My legs were like cooked spaghetti," he recalled. "I remember thinking, 'What am I going to say? I should be bright, how am I going to look on TV? I wonder if Nicole is watching? Don't make an ass of yourself. Show enough emotion. But don't slobber.'"

"Thank you," he said at the podium. "Thank you very much. Thank you. I must say I feel a little like Clint Eastwood, that you're letting me stand up here because Coppola or Mankiewicz hasn't shown up yet."

Unsteady laughter from the house.

"But being characteristically a pessimist and cynic, this and some of the other nice things that have happened to me the last couple days may turn me into some sort of hopeful optimist and ruin my whole life."

Steady laughter.

"There's so many people to thank. You've heard a lot of the names, but it's important for me to say them, and I'm sure I'm gonna miss some of the ones and regret it tomorrow. Of course Liza, and Joel, Michael York, Marisa Berenson, Marty Baum, Manny Wolf, Kander and Ebb. A terrific guy by the name of Doug Green. A dear friend of mine by the name of Gwen Verdon. And I'd also like to mention Cy Feuer, the producer, with whom I had a lot of disputes. But on a night like this, you start having affection for everybody. Thank you."

Fosse was escorted backstage for the hailstorm of press and photographs, and then he returned to his seat, woozy, for the rest of the show. Liza Minnelli heard her name, squeezed her father's arm, and got up. Then Marlon Brando's name was read and Sacheen Littlefeather, new to show business, got up. When the best-picture envelope was opened, Cy Feuer got up. Then he heard that *The Godfather* won and he sat down.

As soon as he could, Fosse called home; that is, he called Nicole at Gwen's in East Hampton.

"Hi, Dad." She was distant.

"What did you think of the show?"

"Nice."

He asked her about her new bicycle; she answered about her new bicycle; and she handed the phone to Gwen. "You should have been here," Gwen said. "When you won it, she screamed so loud she said, 'I think I broke something in my throat.'"

Somewhere around midnight, Fosse and Janice and the Academy Award for best director returned to the quiet of the Beverly Hills Hotel, where Paddy, Herb, and Marlo were waiting up for them. They convened in Fosse's suite and opened bottles and windows and looked over the one or two swimmers flying over the pool below. The occasional clink of crystal on crystal or sound of a pretty girl's laugh curled its long way up through the palms to Fosse's balcony, where he sat, smoking, laughing, unbelieving, with his friends. It was a cool evening. Nothing lasts, but Fosse knew these stubborn wisecracking maniacs belonged to him for life. "I'll walk you one more block," he had said to Herb and Paddy after lunch one afternoon, "and then I have to go back to work." "Don't you remember," Paddy shot back. "You have no work. You're finished in this business." Fosse nodded slowly. "Yeah, that's right," he said. "I forgot." They had loved him before he won and they would love him after he won and with a fervency no critic, not even him, could ever corrupt.

The next morning, Fosse ordered room service and climbed into the shower. Out of the corner of his eye, he caught Janice standing before the mirror, looking at herself holding the Oscar as if she'd won it. "Would you do *anything* to win one?" he asked.

The next week was terrific. Glorying in the attention satiated Fosse. But then the accolades passed, and he came down. "I couldn't understand why I wasn't happy," he said. "Instead of jumping down the street and being all smiles, I'd find I was badly depressed." Once a drug, the thrill of winning was starting to feel merely good; in a way, it didn't feel like winning anymore.

Then the Emmys came around. Fosse flew back to LA and won the best director award, his third, for *Liza with a Z*. He was now the only person in history to win the Tony, the Oscar, and the Emmy — the Triple Crown — in a single year. Which made him the only person in history to follow that victory with the most terrible depression of his life.

There was no achievement that could be better than winning everything, which he had just done. Here he was, a record-breaker, again: He was here. Where was he? He was alone. Public triumph brought Fosse a magic wand with a surprise curse — against him. Whenever he decided to tap it on a project or a person, to make a dream come true, there appeared from somewhere else — poof — a rejected individual furious at Fosse for not alchemizing him. There were just too many against him now, more every day. The pressure to please everyone, to share his freshly notarized genius and personally return every phone call (and happily) and weather everyone's retaliatory anger without absorbing that blame into blame against himself led Ann Reinking to observe that success for Bob Fosse was harder than failure. "He didn't understand why people seemed to be trying to tear him down," she said. "It confused him. He'd ask, 'Why am I so miserable when everything's going right?'"

He knew he couldn't complain. Discussing this sort of high-level heartache with anyone outside of Reinking (or Paddy and Herb) would further estrange him from his friends and his "friends" and those aspirants in between, so Fosse, at the pinnacle, called off the parade. He withdrew. And withdrawing, he drew more criticism. Now, they said, he thought he was too good for them. "Bob couldn't win that one," Reinking said. "He lost a lot of friends."

"His pain was extreme," Lynde said. Was this supposed to be as good as he ever felt? Was this the dream? Because if it was — and it *was,* or at least it had been — then his whole life was behind him. Except for decline.

Decline was still ahead.

"He was afraid he would not be able to figure out what to do next," Lynde said. "Nothing would ever be as good again." It would seem he had given all he had to give. Creating a new dance vocabulary, re-inventing the television special, reinventing the movie musical, and dragging all those genres to hell, both onscreen and onstage, Fosse had raised the bar on blackness impossibly high. And now he would have to raise it higher. But how? What human truth was darker than Nazism or suicide? What was darker than pitch-black? "There's this Looney Tunes cartoon," Ann Reinking said, "called *Show Biz Bugs,* with Daffy and Bugs Bunny in competing acts. The audience loves Bugs, and Daffy keeps trying to outdo him and he can't. Daffy figures out the only way he can upstage him is to blow himself up. When he finally does, the audience goes wild. Bugs loves it and claps for an encore. Daffy, his ghost floating up, says, 'I know, I know. But I can only do it once.' That's Bob." At the end of May, he checked in to the Payne Whitney psychiatry clinic.

FOURTEEN YEARS

HE WAS NO LONGER interested in therapy, not for himself. Since getting off Seconal, Fosse had stopped trying to solve his problems; he now just accepted them. Infidelity, addiction, depression, and the zero he held inside himself were, like his baldness, permanent. Like everyone else in New York, he had his theories about why he was what he was: there was the negligent mom, the loserish dad — old masks of the Freudian commedia dell'arte — and being the smallest and youngest boy in a very full house during the Depression. They were only theories. "It was too early to be Bob Fosse," Reinking said. "His doctors didn't always know how to help him. Psychiatric medicine was not what it is now." Someone, Fosse used to say, must have scared him when he was little. That boy, Dr. Sager told him, was trying to get back at someone. He was enraged, betrayed, although by whom, Dr. Sager didn't know. That was about as far as they got. Fosse hurt someplace too far down for Sager to reach. Did that make the doctor the failure, or the patient? Fosse thought both. Checking into Payne Whitney, Weill Cornell's renowned psychiatric hospital on the East River, he could have some time away, sober up, maybe, a little.

He lasted only a few days. More than his depression, Fosse hated the lithium they prescribed to combat it; the drug flatlined him, killing his sex drive, and he was happier to be unhappy and fucking than not unhappy, dull-witted, and not fucking. "I knew it was time to check out," he said to Janice Lynde one day and Ann Reinking another, "when I started to put on shows with the other inmates." It was a great line, whether or not it was true, and coming up with a great line was reason enough to get back to work. Anyway, that was the only thing that really seemed to help — that and sex — and he wasn't getting either in his white hotel.

Two scripts needed his attention. The first was *Lenny,* half completed. Marvin Worth, one of the film's producers, had notes for Barry and Fosse. He was concerned their hero was losing "hugability" and that the threesome scene Fosse had given Lenny and his ex-wife, Honey (a scene Fosse and Barry had completely invented), could get them into a libel situation. Also, Worth said all the chronological jumpings-around in space and time, from Lenny's nightclub act to his past, present, and future, threw off the story. He wanted to see *Lenny* streamlined and cleaned up. Fosse tossed Worth's notes aside and proceeded instead to revise *Lenny* with Barry in the mornings and to work with Fred Ebb on the *Chicago* book in the afternoons. Fosse had made history with Kander and Ebb's *Cabaret* and *Liza,* and so far, *Chicago* was coming along nicely, a genuine collaboration. They were having fun. At clutch intervals, Kander would join them at Fosse's office for a little volley. "We'd be talking about the form and sharing ideas," Kander said. "It was totally open, a total joy. We were all on the same page."

That Fred Ebb feared and revered Fosse made for a smoother partnership, at least from Fosse's point of view. "I was malleable," Ebb said. "I never stood up to him. I never argued with him." Fosse set the rules. As he had with Julian Barry, Fosse would spend the afternoon talking through scenes with Ebb, and then Ebb would go home to the typewriter and write, alone. In no time, Fosse had a map of Ebb's pressure points, could hover a finger over the bruise. "He would say, 'Oh, this is all right,' but he was never very wholehearted in his praise," Ebb recalled. "The mere fact that he accepted [the scenes] was terrific as far as I was concerned." The collaboration got tense. Ebb was anxious.

At the deli one day, Ebb found a moment alone with Chayefsky and Gardner. He wanted their opinion. Having respect for both sides, they encouraged Ebb to do as they would and fight Fosse. "He's an arrogant son of a bitch," they said, "but he knows what he's doing. Don't let him bully you." Ebb nodded in agreement but lost his conviction upstairs, ultimately agreeing to give Fosse what none of Fosse's other writers had: credit. No matter the division of labor, *Chicago* was going to have a book by Fred Ebb *and* Bob Fosse.

Meanwhile, with *Pippin* sales flagging, Fosse and Ostrow hit upon a wholly novel idea: a commercial. Experts believed TV audiences were uninterested in Broadway musicals, and the expense of producing commercials confined low-budget productions like *Pippin* to the more affordable print ads. But shooting on the cheap, in a studio in Princeton, Ostrow could save on major production fees. He picked a small number, "The Manson Trio," and had it filmed quickly, with one camera, on June 7, 1973. Preoccupied with *Lenny*, Fosse left the directing to William Fucci and the dancing to Vereen, Pam Sousa, and Candy Brown, who were by now more than equipped to handle the old-time Suzie Qs and flirty finger wags without him. "This cameraman was just shooting us head-on," said Sousa. "I didn't know much about film but I kept thinking, 'This can't be that interesting.' Then Bobby showed up — we never expected him to — and he had this cameraman going all over the place." In the cutting room, Fosse laid a droll voice-over on the sixty-second spot: "Here's a free minute from *Pippin*, Broadway's musical-comedy sensation, directed by Bob Fosse. You can see the other one hundred and nineteen minutes of

Pippin live, at the Imperial Theater. Without commercial interruption." It worked. Ticket sales soared, and continued to soar, through *Pippin*'s five-year run. Henceforth, the commercial would be an essential part of Fosse's promotional outreach, and it soon became a cornerstone of Broadway musical advertising. But unlike the cut-and-paste TV spots of his contemporaries, Fosse's commercials were as much short films as sales pitches, and they would grow artistically from show to show. They too were Bob Fosse productions.

Like a seesaw, winning the Triple Crown lifted Fosse up and threw him down to hell. Up, he was the king — dancing, choreographing, and directing huge movies and musicals; down, it wouldn't last. Cut with the Dexamyl, the extremes were changing him, changing the air around him. Bolstered by a fresh, substantiated arrogance and a deeper fear of failure, the new Fosse was asking for more and settling less often. Most of his dancers, writers, and editors would agree that his higher standards produced better work — and for many, his double-barreled intensity wouldn't be a problem — but post–Triple Crown Fosse was losing his patience with others. Where once he had had to cohabitate, now he had the muscle to insist on carte blanche ad infinitum. Who would stop him? This Fosse pushed hard and regularly, lodging dynamite indiscriminately, like a prospector without a lead. Though Fosse acted with stubborn assurance, many sensed he was lost. Anger and conviction seemed his way of imposing order on the turmoil. Meticulousness became compulsion. His associates asked themselves not whom but *what* they were trying to satisfy.

Therein lay the beauty of United Artists, *Lenny*'s financiers. Founded in 1919 by D. W. Griffith, Charlie Chaplin, Douglas Fairbanks, and Mary Pickford "to protect the great motion picture public from threatening combinations and trusts that would force upon them mediocre productions and machine-made entertainment," UA was premised on privileging, as its name suggested, the rights of the artist. Taking charge of the studio in 1951, Arthur Krim and Robert Benjamin, two gifted New York lawyers with appropriate amounts of creative ambition (none), restricted their business to business matters and evolved UA from a movie studio into a partner. The company flourished. Sharing profits with free agents like the Mirisch Brothers and Hecht-Hill-Lancaster (producers of Chayefsky's *Marty*), UA drew, under Krim and Benjamin, the sort of independently minded producers who were themselves drawn to the sort of independently minded talent that movie audiences of the seventies (and sixties and fifties) were hungry for. "The thing about UA was we didn't look at dailies," said UA producer and former CEO David Picker. "We approved the budget and off they went." Freedom and trust, anathema to old-school studio executives, would crown UA with the greatest postwar record of any Hollywood backer. Its films with Altman, Ashby, Coppola, Kubrick, Scorsese, and Woody Allen (and James Bond and the Pink Panther) say all. Fosse was home.

At UA, there would be no Cy Feuer. Under Picker, a tall, young veteran of show business, Fosse would have his wishes pre-granted. "I'd do anything to make it possible for Bobby to do whatever he needed to do," Picker said. "And I knew being satisfied was not his goal. He wanted to get everything he could until there was no more to get." It was love — and they were already talking honeymoon. After *Lenny*, Fosse and Picker planned to make a film of Herb Gardner's play *The Goodbye People*.

But right now they needed a star.

"I want you to play Lenny," Fosse said to Dustin Hoffman.

"Why don't you get Cliff Gorman? He did it on Broadway and he was brilliant."

"He was my first choice but the studio wouldn't finance it. So I'm coming to you."

This kind of maneuver had not been necessary before, but Fosse had never been scared of his leading actor before. On *Sweet Charity*,

Shirley MacLaine subordinated herself to his (and Verdon's) exper-tise and had wisely kept from playing the star card, and Liza Min-nelli, on *Cabaret,* was not yet star enough to cross the line of Fosse's authority. Casting his Broadway musicals in much the same way, Fosse had been very lucky, or very clever, in the diva department. *Hero, Pleasures, Pippin:* no big stars. For marquee names, he mostly kept to Verdon, his wife. (There had also been Sid Caesar in *Little Me.* And look how that turned out.) Then came *Lenny* and Dustin Hoff-man, perhaps the biggest star in Hollywood. By putting Hoffman on the defensive, Fosse was trying to take his power back — even before he lost it. "It was not the right way to begin a collaboration," Hoffman said. "I worried if I was going to be his second choice through the whole picture." He took the part.

Before he could cast Honey, Bruce's wife, Fosse had to feel out each contender, looking for a way in. He tried Raquel Welch. He tried to get Janice Lynde comfortable with stripping. He considered his sometime girlfriend Joey Heatherton, and then he found Valerie Perrine. Her mother had been a showgirl in Earl Carroll's *Vanities* and George White's *Scandals,* and Valerie had been the lead nude dancer of the Lido de Paris Extravaganza at the Stardust Hotel in Vegas. "That was," she said, "two shows a night, three shows a Satur-day night, and you never got a night off. You went to work at seven and got home at two in the morning. You had to be dying not to go to work. I've worked when I had stomach flu. I had buckets waiting for me in the wings so I could throw up into them." What Fosse would give her, he knew she could take.

"We read two hundred and fifty actresses for Honey," David Picker said. "Then we reduced them to six and screen-tested them at the Warwick Hotel." Fosse set up in a room big enough to accommodate a small crew, and over the course of several afternoons, he narrowed the six actresses down to two: dreamy Jill Robinson and fun, sexy, Valerie Perrine. On camera, they each ran the love scenes a couple of times with Hoffman, with some ad libs around the outside. *Lenny*'s every word was scripted — there would be no improvisation on Fosse's set — but hearing what the actors came up with in auditions gave Fosse and Hoffman a sense of their natural state. It was a version of the truth game.

"I'm Leonard Albert Schneider," Hoffman said, in character.

Perrine paused. "Is that Jewish or something?"

"Yes. Do you like Jewish men?"

"They have large noses and I like that."

"Why?"

"Because they give good head."

Fosse and the crew cracked up.

Perrine got the part. Fosse asked her to dinner and over drinks at the Plaza started coming on to her.

"Does this mean" — she began to cry — "I'm not going to get the part?"

Fosse laughed. "No, no, no. You've *got* the part."

"Really?"

"You don't have to do anything."

"Oh, good . . . thank you. That's good."

In lieu of carnal knowledge, he interrogated her, but gently, so it didn't seem like an interrogation. Of course she opened up. Fosse's interest was flattering, genuinely, and his voice was small and the Plaza was grand and she told him about her family, her boyfriend, her background — she told him everything, even more than she thought she had to tell. By the end of the night, she said, "He knew more about me than he would have if I slept with him." The data he filed away, and Perrine went back to her hotel brimming with the zing of a great new job but having learned nothing about her director.

There was a time when Fosse could summer with Gwen and Nicole without leaving too much life behind, but with Ann Reinking's ascension to girlfriend of girlfriends, he respectfully rented his own summer home in Quogue, a village not too far away from Gwen's place in East Hampton. "I remember how Gwen suffered through the early Ann Reinking days," said John Rubinstein. "During those summers out on the island, it was very painful for her. She knew that it was going to be serious with Bob and Annie." In the months after Payne Whitney, Fosse turned much of his depression into anger — against Gwen, against "them," whoever "they" were. "He suddenly allowed a lot of this submerged rage to emerge," set designer Tony Walton said. "The anger Bob felt toward Gwen was violent." It was all those shows where the critics gave him second billing to her star status, status she owed mostly to him; all those years he spent extolling her boundless gifts, hiding the envy that grew in him the more love she took. In *Sweet Charity*, Gwen Verdon stole the show — his — but he let her, he needed her to, because without her blush and quiver, he could not show his heart onstage. She was the cure to a Bob Fosse production.

And his cure was Quogue. Tucked behind a wall of bayberries a short distance from the sand stood a white cypress castle built by architect Jay Sears, modern and mysterious. Fosse would rent it summer after summer. A multilevel maze of decks, balconies, indoor bridges, and see-through stairways, the house was a hide-and-seeker's paradise, redolent of unplanned-for kisses and secret games. Chunky bay windows gave the structure a Rubik's Cube quality, as if sky giants, frustrated with the puzzle, had thrown it down to Earth. The whole place seemed to be in constant motion. There were rolling greens and long decks for big parties on Sundays; there were jagged, sharp-cornered culs-de-sac too small to fit more than three people and a joint. It was fun.

When Fosse entertained, he did it big, inviting dozens to stay all day and into the night. When he was working, he'd eat anything or nothing, whatever was brought to him, but when he partied, he opted for rich foods, lobster especially, and Chinese spare ribs, with French or Italian wine and after dinner, warm Courvoisier. "I would have made a terrific waiter," he said. "Sometimes I really like making people feel good, like they had a good time. I'm a good host at a party; I knock myself out. Most people clean house when they give a party. I paint the house. I want everything right. I rehearse the whole dinner — music, napkins. It takes me days." Brahms, Chopin, or (his favorite) Satie during the meal; something folky like Carly Simon after; then maybe show music, and if the evening went late enough, harder rock. No one got drunk at these gatherings, just loose. Too much scotch could take Fosse down the rabbit hole, but the right amount of wine or rum got him where he wanted to be, high and happy. "I love big parties," he said. "I enjoy all the flirtatiousness — that slightly reckless attitude." Fosse liked seeing people without their masks debating sensitive subjects with raw nerves exposed, and food, wine, and music broke down the barriers. There was something else too. Seeing people's real selves in their relaxed state, he could better grasp their up and down levers. As a dancer and choreographer, he knew that body language was personal history. "Most nondancers don't understand this," Fred Mann III said, "but we're constantly reading each other. Just the way a person walks can tell you the difference in their training. You can see their Balanchine, their forced turn-out. That kind of a thing. We're constantly reading each other." The auditioning never stopped.

East Hampton weekends, when Fosse and Reinking had time, began after Ann's last show on Saturday night and lasted through Monday, when she had to go back to town for a show. Fosse bought a Lincoln — black, of course — to take them to Quogue and back. "Quogue was a place of peace for him," she said. "He just lived." Away from New York, Fosse smoked less and cooked more. He read. Biographies, mostly, books about Lincoln and Clarence Darrow, problem solvers who suffered from depression and greatness. He and Ann played cards. They walked to the beach and scavenged the shoreline for treasure. Like Fosse and Gwen had. Like he and Joan had. "We got all these seashells," Reinking said, "and he bought these mirrors and glued the seashells all over the mirrors, layering them, and he varnished them and it looked great." At the end of the day, Fosse would take labels that he'd peeled off their empty wine bottles and decoupage them around a wastebasket. "He loved an idea like that, where you take a common ordinary thing and make it look beautiful," Reinking said, "which is exactly what he does. I said, 'You make tinsel look like a mink coat!' Even in these crafts, he wants you to feel the grit, but he wants you to feel there's beauty there too. There's the depressed side and there's the clown side; it's the best of both worlds."

They would have to have that conversation. He would have to tell her what he was not capable of, again, and she would have to pretend to feel okay about it. *This is sophisticated,* she would tell herself. *I am sophisticated.* If he came home late one night and she asked, which she knew she shouldn't, where he'd been, he would tell her where, and with whom, and she would have to show no sign of hurt. She could not ask him to apologize. This was him and she loved him, so she had to love *this.* Otherwise she didn't love him, and she *did* love him, so she wouldn't ask. But she would know, and knowing, she would hurt. "I always felt on the precipice of a cliff," she said. "Even though Bob had other women in his life, I knew he wasn't having deep relationships with them. He would talk to me about things he really cared about, and yet I'm there and I'm not there at the same time. The double standard was very hard. I didn't want to see anyone else, but I felt somehow I should. I think he felt guilty for that too. I *did* know that he loved me but I was always looking over my shoulder, frightened that he'd find someone else. Death was going to happen, there was nothing I could do about that, but I felt if I ever really lost him I would have been devastated. I wanted security. But I didn't want to lose him."

Seeing her struggle and wanting to help, Fosse encouraged Reinking to see a therapist. "Everybody needs someone to talk to," he said. "It's fine. It's good." And she went, expecting to sit down at the controls and tweak the knobs until she made him trust her or until she became more accepting of his limitations. But he knew she couldn't; they blamed each other, and the guilt slayed him. Am I taking advantage of this power? he wondered. Then he would turn on her. He'd do it before she could turn on him. Both knew the reprisal was inevitable. After all, how could she be happy with the little he gave her, and how could he be sure she really loved him? "Do you like me because I'm me or because I'm a success?" he would ask her. "If I was a janitor, would you like me?" Being together, in Quogue or in town or on the road in between, they chastised themselves for not being different people, and they each worried, when happy, that the other was worrying alone.

With his *Lenny* cast assembled, Fosse arranged an extended table read in December 1973. "We were just reading scenes, making changes," Barry recalled. It was an out-of-town tryout for the script.

"Hey, Bob," Hoffman said one afternoon. "I want to show you something."

Fosse looked up. "What's that, Dustin?"

"I got a walk — I think I worked out a walk."

"I wish you wouldn't do this."

"What?"

"The last five performances of yours degenerated into a walk."

It was untrue, but Fosse didn't care. This was the O.K. Corral and he wanted Hoffman to see the gun on his belt. And Hoffman did. Julian Barry said Hoffman's reaction evoked "one of those cats in a cartoon, thrown against a wall, when their face variegates. One piece starts to go, then another, then another . . .''

Hoffman put on a sarcastic grin and raised a finger at Fosse. "Limited gains, Bob . . ." he said. "Limited gains, talking to me that way . . ."

The more time Hoffman spent with the script, the more he came to believe that Lenny's layers, his changes and complexities, weren't on the page. The current draft, he suspected, was a carryover from the play version of *Lenny*, which seemed more of a one-man show ("Gorman was brilliant," he said, "you went to see Gorman") than a character study. So little of Bruce's biography made it into the script, Hoffman thought they might be better off turning Lenny into a fictional character and then writing freely from there. "Why not call the movie *Benny*?" Hoffman said.

Fosse agreed they had a story problem. "We don't have a movie," he announced one Friday rehearsal. "We don't have a screenplay. It doesn't work." Hoffman half expected Fosse to shelve the project right there — it might even have been something of a relief. "If I had to guess," Hoffman said, "I would guess I didn't want to do *Lenny* and I was talked into it, probably because it was the best of what was around and I wanted to go to work." Though he was in awe of Fosse's eye, Hoffman sensed Fosse didn't have an instinct for directing actors, not like Mike Nichols and John Schlesinger. He would use generalizations, results, telling Hoffman to play young Lenny with more "innocence, innocence, pure innocence." That didn't help; attitudes are ideas about performance results. They're not playable human drives, the layers Hoffman needed Fosse to help him add to the character.

But Fosse didn't call off the movie. "I think we solved it," he said Monday morning, explaining how he and Barry decided the new draft would splice into the drama naturalistic "interviews" with the film's characters, as if they were playing a scripted version of the truth game. It was an interesting concept, but was it a superficial solution? Or would the interviews really unearth *Lenny's* missing layers? Hoffman wondered. Eager to deepen the character, he volunteered to help Fosse and Barry rewrite or at least join them at Fosse's office and be a sounding board for their ideas. They turned him down. "Okay," Hoffman said. "Then I'm going to Los Angeles to do the research I can do."

No, Fosse did not want Hoffman doing research. He didn't want him getting ideas about any element outside of his approval. "He wanted me just to show up," Hoffman said, "and do what I was told. Fosse was the kind of director who would tell you what he wanted before the first take. An actor's director will guide you to surprising them. But Bob did not want me to find my own way in. He declared that very early on." But to Hoffman, a committed researcher, getting *inside* the part was his only way to personalize the performance. To give the character immediacy, he needed to find their overlap. Where in Lenny was the electric socket Hoffman could plug his heart into? Browsing through the comedian's personal interviews and writings, he had the nonfiction facts of Bruce down cold. It gave Hoffman a wealth of raw humanity to draw from, but with Fosse telling him not to think about any of it, Hoffman, who had never seen Bruce onstage, got caught. He had to choose: Lenny or Bob.

Hoffman chose Lenny. He went to Vegas to meet with Bruce's mother, Sally Marr, and she introduced him to Lenny's friends. "They all loved him," Hoffman said. "He never hurt anybody except for himself." Not Buddy Hackett ("I took a walk with Lenny on the beach and there was a dead shark and he pulled out his dick and he fucked the shark!"). Nichols and May told him Lenny played not to the audience but to the band. They were the hippest in the room; Lenny wanted to break *them* up. Hoffman said, "I came back to New York with great scenes. I found out when Lenny got a gig in LA, he advertised by getting a huge cutout of Hitler and he put it on the side of the freeway and the sign said *See Lenny Bruce! Opening* . . . I said to Bob, 'You gotta do that!' I heard a story about the time the cops would come to see Lenny and they'd wait on the stage in case he said a dirty word. This is the kind of imagination Lenny had. He asked for a hundred-foot mic cord. So when he did the show and when he had to say a dirty word, he'd tell the audience, 'I'm not allowed to say a dirty word onstage,' and he'd go out onto the street and say, 'I'm now on the corner of Hollywood and Vine, you cocksucker kike moth-erfuckers . . .' It was great! I was so excited to talk to Bob and Julian [Barry] but I had difficulty even telling him the stories. I think it was the first time I felt *This guy doesn't even want to hear it. This guy is not a collaborator.*"

Certain rehearsals Fosse devoted to Lenny's monologues. But telling jokes to a near-empty, highly critical environment of Fosse, Barry, and David Picker, Hoffman couldn't get laughs. It tried both sides.

"I'm bombing out."

"Yes," Fosse said.

"It's hard to make these jokes work because you're not an audience and your grimness is affecting me!"

"You're not funny," Fosse said.

"I'm *rehearsing*, Bob. It's just a rehearsal!"

Make it bigger, Fosse told him, and Hoffman resisted. Lenny wasn't shtick. Anyone who found his stuff funny wouldn't need his common-sense punch lines italicized.

"Bob, can I ask you a question?"

"Okay, Dustin."

"What do you find funny about Lenny Bruce?"

"I don't think Lenny Bruce is funny."

"Then why do you want to make this movie?"

"I'm interested in the ménage à trois."

The ménage à trois Fosse and Barry had invented.

Hoffman called his agent and pleaded with him to get him out of the movie. But he'd already signed.

As a favor to Liza Minnelli, Fosse directed *Liza Live at the Winter Garden,* an encore repurposing of *Liza with a Z* with some new numbers sprinkled in. As expected, the demand for Liza had not waned: thirty-six hours after tickets went on sale, the show had sold out its three-week run.

He could not complete the last piece of *Lenny* casting until he arrived on location in Miami, after *Liza* opened late in January 1974. If they were to represent a credible cross-section of midcentury Americans, *Lenny's* nightclub audiences could not be selected en masse, like extras, but face by face, depending on place and time. There were faces for LA, faces for the Catskills, faces for New York, faces for the 1940s, the 1950s, the 1960s. For the close-ups, "Bob insisted that no extra could see more than two takes to get an authentic reaction," David Picker said. "So we had to have twenty-five hundred extras for that first week, each one right for the location, and after two takes they were out."

They filmed the nightclub scenes in a dressed-up banquet hall in the Barcelona Hotel, a tired shack a déclassé distance from the beach. Filming these scenes at the hotel, a few rooms away from where most of production had been installed for the Miami leg of *Lenny,* was cheaper than shooting on location, in real nightclubs, as Fosse had promised Hoffman they would. Proximity was good news for Fosse — they lived where they worked. The all-in feel of the shoot put Fosse's crew in the right mood — summer campers after their parents drove away — and the punchy spirit of Lenny Bruce spread easily. Everyone was a little high, a little dirty, and working for last year's Oscar-winning director promised to be enriching. They could fool around with pride.

Picker's phone rang at five thirty in the morning on the first day of shooting.

"We got a problem." It was Fosse.

"What?"

"It's Dustin."

"What happened?"

"He doesn't think he can be funny."

Picker threw on his clothes, met Fosse in his hotel room, and, together, they walked into Hoffman's room. The actor was sitting on the edge of the bed. "I can't be funny," he murmured. "I don't know what to do. I can't do this." After a calm exchange, Fosse suggested they start with one of the bland routines Lenny did en route to his big breakdown and then work up to the funny material from there. Hoffman was fine with that, and Fosse, though he did not want to set an accommodating precedent, would be too. "After that," Picker said, "Dustin got comfortable."

Now Fosse had Hoffman's audience to worry about. To keep the extras loose, Fosse was not opposed to their being served a drink or two, no matter the hour, and he had hired real waiters — people who truly knew how to put down a glass — to do the pouring. Once the drinks had been served, Hoffman would tell Fosse to roll film, and he'd start to play. "Hey," he said to a guy in the front, "what's your shlong doing on that ashtray?" It didn't have to make sense, it just had to spark a reaction, something Hoffman could then push against, into another canto of Lenny's. If Hoffman stumbled, Fosse would throw him a rope, like "When you were in the hospital, Mr. Hoffman, were you faithful to your wife?" "Deny it!" Hoffman snapped back, sliding into Lenny. Even if he liked the take, Fosse went again. He was always going again. "Mr. Hoffman, what would you do if your wife came home and found a pair of pantyhose, not her size —" "Deny it!" "Mr. Hoffman . . ." "Deny it!" "Mr. Hoffman —" "I said *denyyyyy!*

Even if they have pictures, say it's a lie! Deny! Tell her a crazy woman burst into your house naked saying she had malaria and that she cried, 'Lie on top of me and keep me physically active or I'll die!'"

Anything to get an actor's horrified expression. "You're ugly! What are you doing here? Get out!" Fosse would yell into the audience, filming their shock for later use. These sneak attacks worked for Fosse, but not for Hoffman. He needed real reactions to react to. But Fosse's extras weren't laughing. From take to take, they were getting more tired and laughing less. Then they stopped laughing altogether. Hours later, Hoffman was completely on his own, catching all the flak for the downturn in mood. "It was vicious," Hoffman said, "because you're doing pieces of the monologue thirty, forty times and they're fake laughing. It got so depressing." Hoffman was beginning to lose faith, in himself, in Fosse.

"Bob, it's not working."

"It's fine. It's the wrong crowd."

"They're not laughing."

"They're stiff. Trust me. It'll cut together fine."

"Bob —"

"Trust me."

"We need to do it again."

"Please, Dustin. We got it."

Dustin Hoffman was a perfectionist and Bob Fosse was a perfectionist. Satisfaction — with themselves, with each other — rarely came, and when it did, it was even less rarely shared. The other guy's way wasn't working: Bob Fosse, the boss, put his foot down. "Dustin felt I was restricting him because I wasn't giving him enough freedom to try things," he said, sounding like the sort of executive he hated. "We'd go off together, away from the set, and battle it out. I said I'd try to give him more freedom and he said he'd try to listen." But one's "good enough" was the other's "wait, it can be better." Fosse, Hoffman felt, wasn't directing so much as pushing. For Lenny's most manic monologue, Fosse pushed Hoffman to run each take faster than the last, take after take, until the actor, gasping, finally held up a hand. "Nobody talks like this, Bob," he said. But it wasn't the speed per se Fosse was after; he liked what the speed and exhaustion were doing to Hoffman's performance. It produced an effect. Hoffman felt like shit, but shit was good! *Good?* What? Hoffman had no idea what he was *saying* anymore. He wanted to know what this scene was *about.* Here Fosse would throw up his hands. "All Dustin wants to do is talk!" Fosse said. "Someone tell Fosse I'm not a machine!" Hoffman said. "[Fosse] wanted to be Lenny," Hoffman said. "That's what he did when he'd give you a direction — it was him doing it. And inside sometimes I'd cringe because his acting was, well, you know . . ."

By breaking Hoffman down, Fosse (maybe) stood a better chance of breaking Lenny open, and there was always more to break. The broken pieces could be broken again and those fragments ground to sand and the sand pulverized to dust. After dust, *that's* what Fosse wanted. "There are not a lot of movie directors who come from the discipline of dance," David Picker observed. "Most actors are not used to working with that kind of a director." Twenty takes later, Hoffman was running the speech faster still. But whether his performance was improving or disintegrating was anybody's guess, a topic of constant debate among the crew. They saw both sides.

Production manager Robert Greenhut suspected Fosse confused extremism for efficacy. One time in particular: Fosse wanted to shoot Lenny's final routine, his gasping drug-fuddled breakdown, from an isolating distance far across the room, practically losing Hoffman in the frame. He wanted the act, which had become an utter narcissistic bore, to *feel* boring. "We can know what this means for Lenny without having to bore the audience," Greenhut said to Fosse. "We don't have to show it for ten minutes straight." But Fosse wouldn't hear of it. If Lenny was boring, then *Lenny* would be boring. "It was ballsy," cameraman Bruce Surtees said. "It was hard and it was tough. That's

what Fosse wanted *Lenny* to be. That was the business he was in."
That's why Fosse wanted black-and-white in the first place, and not
a black-and-white with soft grays. He wanted high-contrast, *mean*
black-and-white. "I want this to be like a documentary," he said to
Surtees. "No bullshit."

On the day of the contested monologue, they would shoot long
(in duration) and wide (in angle) until they literally ran out of film.
"We would just run the whole magazine and reload," Greenhut said.
Though Fosse had no intention of breaking up the scene, he told
David Picker very clearly that his decision to shoot Lenny's collapse
with three cameras was purely defensive, for emergency use only. Of
course he wouldn't tell Hoffman that; he'd want him to feel the pressure of having to get it all in one take. If Hoffman went up on his
lines or Fosse didn't like what he saw, Hoffman — and the rest of the
crew — would have to reset and take it all from the top. The shot
film would be wasted and the clock would tick on — and *Lenny* was
already behind schedule.

They shot the final monologue twice, and the second take Fosse
loved.

Already aggravated by the incessant filming, Greenhut was on his
way to becoming Fosse's next Cy Feuer. But Greenhut's job required
him to keep the production on course. "You're worse than your father," Fosse said, referring to an incident that had taken place thirty
years prior. "Your father bought me a one-way ticket to Florida and
I had to pay my way back at the end of a job." And there was a girl.
Each had seen the other prowling around her. "There was this undercurrent of competition between us," Greenhut said. It caught him
completely off-guard.

The eruption came after local judges reversed their decision to let
the production shoot one of the film's big scenes — Lenny's climactic plea for mercy — at Miami's Dade County Courthouse. Greenhut
and Neil Machlis turned Miami upside down, checking out every

possibility (and a few desperate impossibilities) for a substitute location, ever aware of the pressures of time and money. "We looked at all sorts of courtrooms," Greenhut said, "and Bob hated every one of them. Every single one. We pulled out all the stops. The only people that wanted to help was the local mafia. He thought that I was doing it to save money, that I *did* know about other courtrooms, but come on, I wasn't telling him because I'm trying to save a few hundred grand."

Fosse refused every suggestion. "Why are you doing this?" he yelled at Machlis. "Why can't you get it? *Get* somebody who can get it." But Machlis had done all he could do. There simply was not another option. "Who would ever dream of not showing Bob Fosse a location because it was too expensive?" Machlis said. "Nothing was ever good enough. Maybe the other side of that is perfectionism. I don't know. We busted our ass on that film but in his mind, he was the victim. *We* were trying to fuck *him*."

At three in the morning, Greenhut's phone rang. "Hello?"

"It's Bob." He sounded relaxed.

"Bob, what's going on? What happened?"

"I just wanted to know what shots we're starting with tomorrow."

"You know what shots we're starting with tomorrow."

"Oh, yeah, that's right. I remember. Well, there's somebody here who wants to talk to you."

"Hi . . ."

It was the girl they had both been flirting with. She was breathing hard into the phone and giggling. So Bob had wanted Greenhut to know who got her — an eye for an eye, a fuck for a fucking over. Greenhut hung up the phone and went back to sleep.

The whole crew loved Valerie Perrine. So did Fosse. She was his favorite kind of actress: talented, gorgeous, and eagerly compliant. Before shooting, she had promised Fosse she wouldn't do any research and would rely entirely on him for her information. Sally Marr, Lenny's actual mother, and the real Honey Bruce paid occasional visits to the set, but Perrine stayed clear of them. "I had complete trust in Bobby," Perrine said. "He said I was his sponge." An acting robot, he used to say; push a button and out came the emotion. And she could do it again and again, just like he liked. "He spent more time rehearsing Valerie's striptease," Fosse's assistant Larry Mark said, "than anything else in the movie." Ironically, Perrine was too good a stripper to give the effect Fosse wanted. To un-refine her technique, they rehearsed the number for a full week, breaking down each pulse and grind, down to the sparkles on her G-string.

On Valentine's Day, the day before they were to shoot the strip, Perrine asked Larry Mark to bring Fosse to her trailer.

"Hi, Bobby."

She was wearing a long terrycloth robe and had her hair up.

"Hi, Valerie."

"You know what?" she said.

"What?"

"I have a *heart*-on for you." Parting her robe, she showed him she had shaved her pubic hair into a heart.

Fosse cried out in laughter.

Mission accomplished, Perrine sauntered past him on her way to show her Valentine's Day present to the rest of the crew.

After hours, she was just as fun, lounging by the pool, going to the movies with Julian Barry, playing tennis with Hoffman. "Dustin treated me like a big brother," Perrine said. "He always wanted to make sure I had someone to hang out with." She looked out for him too. "Dustin got this horrible flu that was going around," she said. "He had a temperature of a hundred and four with a sore throat and all that the day we were supposed to shoot the scene when he pulls the covers down off of me and you can see my breasts and he's supposed to have this big 'Oh boy!' reaction but he just couldn't quite get to it because he was so sick. So I got props to get me a rubber dildo. And when he pulled the covers down . . . *boioioioiinggg!*"

For months prior to the shoot, Perrine worried about the three-some scene. Hoping to relax her, Fosse asked Perrine to cast the other girl herself. That helped somewhat. She flipped through a book of headshots and watched auditions, ultimately picking an actress with small breasts, which she imagined would make touching her more like touching a man. Still she worried, and Fosse delayed the scene to give her more time. Plus, he had an idea: he would choreograph the entire encounter, not *like* a dance but *as* a dance. With an arm on her shoulder, Fosse explained to Perrine precisely how he would shoot it, in half-lit close-ups, like a sex ballet with fingers for feet and a body for the stage. Perrine would simply follow the steps, stroking breast on one, touching face on two. "It wasn't sexual," Hoffman said. "It was surgery." The night before, Perrine tried fantasizing about women, figuring she might force herself to feel something, but it didn't work. On the day of the shoot she woke up crying. "Bobby, I can't do it," she said. "I can't, I can't . . ." He kept telling her not to worry, she should trust him, and he had her go back to her trailer and rest just a little more before they tried a take. A rose, a joint, and a bottle of champagne were there, along with a note that said *Don't come to set until you've finished these.* She drank the champagne. "Once we started, I kept thinking about camera angles and things," she said. "I had no sexual feelings at all while we were doing it."

Harder still was Perrine's big scene in court, in which Honey was sentenced to jail for drug possession. This was Honey's absolute lowest point; Fosse needed Perrine to break down. "That's why he got to know you," Perrine said, "to know how to push you." With the cameras rolling, he crouched out of frame and told her that the boyfriend she had told him all about at the Plaza had died in a plane crash. "I knew it wasn't true," she said, "but as an actress, it helped to make it real." *Remember how much you loved him? What was he wearing the*

last time you saw him? Don't you wish you could have stopped him?
Don't you wish you could have one more day together? Don't you wish
— "The thought of him being dead was too much for me," Perrine
said. "But Bobby didn't do it in a mean way. It wasn't vicious. The
problem was I couldn't turn it off. He got too much. I didn't need that
heavy of a direction." After the take, he put his arms around her. "He
could not have been more comforting," she said. "I'm embarrassed
by that story," Fosse would confess, yet it was not the only one of its
kind. Needing another outburst from Perrine later in the shoot, he
had Surtees roll camera and told Perrine to think of her Great Dane
being hit by a truck. Though she later credited her Oscar nomination to Fosse's cruelty, the crew, whose mutinous impulse grew by the
hour, was quick to come to her defense.

Their gripe was that he'd lost the movie, if indeed he'd ever had it.
His coarse manner, they said, was a cover for what he didn't know,
and since he was shooting upwards of twenty-five takes per scene,
he obviously didn't know what he wanted. Was he guessing? "In the
beginning, we were going to shoot the movie in eight weeks or forty
days or something like that," Machlis said. "A short amount of time.
But the shoot turned into something like a hundred days. And if we
would have shot another hundred days, Bobby wouldn't have cared."
"We were burning film," Greenhut said. "The guy is overrated and he
knows it," said another. "He'll do a master shot and thirty different
angles with thirty different takes per angle. He wants it all." Kodak
literally couldn't keep up. It had assembled a high-contrast black-
and-white stock specifically for *Lenny*, but the corporation simply
couldn't make and ship the film fast enough. "There came a point late
in the shoot when we were waiting for shipments to arrive," Surtees
said. The cinematographer gave Larry Mark a coconut to commemo-
rate the day they reached a million feet of film. Hoffman said, "It was
like [Fosse] was trying to get even at God for not being the genius he
wanted to be. *I'm going to prove it! I'll show you!*"

Moving from Miami to Brooklyn, *Lenny* fell even farther behind schedule. "Fosse showed no remorse for going over budget," Surtees explained, "but it got to him. He'd been a middle-class kid. He knew what a dollar meant. But he was determined to find new ways to shoot. Even the close-ups, the most basic grammar of film, he wanted to be original. That takes money." "Because there was no money," costume designer Albert Wolsky said, "we had to work fast, we had to work alone, and we had to work late." The crew, shooting all night, working six, sometimes seven days a week, up to sixteen hours a day in the acid New York cold, was overtaken by a general misery. Those awake enough at six in the morning or six at night, whenever they were waking up now, wherever they were (Brown's, a resort in the Catskills), could catch Dustin Hoffman behind a baby grand in the hotel lobby playing an old jazz song. Too tired to utter more than titles ("Tenderly" or "Stars Fell on Alabama"), they could just sit, or sleep, while Hoffman played and the resort loudspeakers whined of an open buffet in the ballroom or a phone call for Mrs. Schwartz.

It was an atmosphere Lenny's daughter Kitty Bruce called "eggshell-y, like walking on eggshells of iron. That came from Bob. He was an intense, gentle, fierce, kind soul, which was completely my dad's vibe." Along with her mother, Honey, and Lenny's mother, Sally Marr, Kitty had come to Miami to watch the filming. Eschewing real life for the pictures in his head, Fosse rarely called upon Lenny's family for technical advice, but the rest of the crew couldn't resist. Marr in particular was too much fun. Paying no heed to the eggshells, she entertained them with outrageous tales, one in particular, a true story — forget *Lenny* for a moment — when, a few years back, some sicko broke into her apartment, raped her, and then, before leaving, helped himself to a pork chop. It was the pork chop, Marr said, that pushed her over the edge; she had really been looking forward to it. After he heard the story, Hoffman bought Marr a golden necklace — twinkling with a golden pork chop. She loved it.

Fosse wouldn't be laughing with them, not during business hours. He would unwind later, at the end of the day, back in his room with a few bottles of Pouilly-Fuissé and a couple girls. Half dressed, they would pass the wine around the bed, savoring the sexy tension, then laughing at what they all knew was about to happen. "It was always like playing with Bob," Kitty Bruce said. "Never weird or lecherous."

Every day, Fosse awoke at dusk. "His cough would wake me up," Hoffman said. "It was my alarm clock." While the others slept, Fosse stalked the set alone, contemplating the arrangement of invisible actors as the sun was going down. "He just wanted to be there," Picker said. "He just wanted to absorb it." He'd pace, alone, thinking, smoking, a cup of coffee (black, sugar) in his hand. Larry Mark would stand by, waiting to exchange the empty cup for a full one, deliver the odd message, or slip him his lunch, a Swiss cheese sandwich with mustard on white, the exact same every day. Fosse would eat it in his trailer, usually alone. "He didn't like to broaden his circle," Mark said. "If it wasn't Surtees, Alan Heim on the phone, Albert Wolsky, or [script supervisor] Nick Sgarro, he would keep to himself." After lunch, he would nap, for one hour, and return to set for more pacing and thinking before the cast and crew arrived. Mark said, "Bruce Surtees would almost always say, 'Oh, Bob, please stop *looking* at this.' Because when he was alone, it invariably meant Bob would change something." Fosse spoke very little, offering no more than "We got it" to indicate he was ready to move on. He liked it quiet. When he gave notes, he spoke with his actors privately, off in a corner, in whispers. "Can you make it smaller?" he would ask. "Even less," he would say, then "even *less*."

Once, in a hotel corridor with Julian Barry, Fosse dropped to his knees beside a door and pressed an ear to the keyhole.

"What are you doing?"

Fosse shushed him. It was Dustin's room. He was in there with Valerie.

"When you're on the road with actors," he whispered, "you can learn a lot if you do this."

Barry waited.

There were literally not enough hours in the day to shoot and then analyze the dailies, but Fosse did not respect the concept of *day*. There was only work broken by naps. Sitting in the dark, most directors will lean over to their assistants or designers to make general comments like "I prefer take one" or "I liked her look in take three, but I liked her reading in take two." Fosse, however, would lean into Trudy Ship in the middle of a take with a remark like "Her finger, left hand" or "Make a note: the way she drapes her arm," or he'd ask her to note a single word of dialogue. Hoffman wanted to join, but Fosse could not expect an actor to be the film's advocate and asked him to stay away. He needed the time to work with set and costume designers. "He was never totally specific," Albert Wolsky said. "He gave you puffs of smoke, ideas. Then you worked on those." Dailies helped him communicate those puffs and turn them into actual choices. Seeing something work or fail on the screen, Fosse could figure out what he wanted and have Wolsky get him there.

"I'm so depressed," he said to Wolsky after that year's Oscar nominations were announced.

"Why?"

He was looking away. "I'm not nominated."

"Bob, you didn't make a movie last year."

"That's why I'm depressed."

Toward the end of production, Fosse told Wolsky he'd seen a big, bearded man, maybe Coppola, wandering around the set. He'd seen him a few times. Fosse would follow the stranger around trailers, planning to jump him and demand to know what he was doing there, on his location. Had they fired Fosse? He'd make Coppola tell him everything. He'd get back at them somehow: Fosse's innate paranoia conjured the fantasy, and his pills made it so. But it wasn't so. There was no Coppola on *Lenny*, no secret meetings to take the movie away from Fosse. Only Fosse, Job without God, sinned against, but by whom he didn't know. "He fought everything so hard," Hoffman said, "like he was going to prove — I don't know to who — that he was an artist. This guy wanted so desperately to be an artist — and that was his tragedy — because he already was."

Filming ended in the spring of 1974, and full-time editing began. The task: getting about 360,000 feet of printed film to a releasable 11,000. Fosse could get impatient while he cut, so Heim, relaxed, would set him up on the flatbed editing machine with a reel of reaction shots or one of Hoffman's long monologues — something to keep him busy. With bigger screens and reels, the flatbed Kem, which could take as much as a thousand feet of film, was better for screening, while the upright Moviolas — loud green monsters Heim stood before and spliced down hard into — were nimbler and better for cutting. They spent the day floating between the machines; their collaboration rarely got heated. The heat was between Fosse and *Lenny*. "He taught me how to be hard on material," Heim said. "But he was so unrelenting, sometimes I had to rescue him from his own dislike." But there was peace in postproduction. A face, an arm, an upper lip — things he spotted in dailies — they were now his to control, full stop.

Sometimes lunch would be personally delivered by Chayefsky, Gardner, or David Picker, and often for the whole family. "There were times in the cutting room," said assistant editor Jonathan Pontell, "when Fosse was very jovial, full of stories, almost literally dancing. Then there were dark times." He made no effort to hide the attaché case Heim called "the pharmacy," leaving it open by the Moviola in full view of all who passed by. "I'm positive that Bob did this intentionally," Heim said. "He didn't want to tell me that he was having these moods, but he did want me to know that it wasn't personal." Fosse did not discuss his bottom-most fears with male associates outside of his immediate circle, not even Heim, whom he had known and respected for years. Women were another matter. Whether owing to sex or friendship, in female company, Fosse opened up almost involuntarily. "Bob would talk to me about the tremendous guilt he felt not being able to stay faithful to his girlfriends," Trudy Ship said. "He was still thinking about Gwen. He said he loved her very much but that his unfaithfulness became too much for her." He would laugh at himself for dating girls closer and closer to Nicole's age, like Kim St. Leon, the nineteen-year-old extra he picked up on the set in Miami. She had followed him back to New York, and though she got a place of her own in the city, St. Leon had some accidental run-ins with Ann Reinking, one heading toward Fosse's apartment as the other headed away.

"Who was it last night?" Ship asked him one morning.

"It's complicated," he said. "But amyl nitrite helped."

One night Fosse invited Kim and Ann to 1600 Broadway, led them to seats at the Moviola, and then settled into a deep armchair. Trudy Ship cued up the reel. He gave the word and the lights went off. A few flickers in, Fosse's audience knew why they were there — it was the threesome scene. He wanted to watch them watch it.

At home, Fosse found Kim had written a man's name and number on a pad by the phone. Though she assured Fosse he was only her scene partner in acting class, he didn't care. Kim was not to see other men. It didn't have to make sense; it just was.

"If you can't go by the rules," he said, "then I guess we can't see each other."

"Well, I guess we can't, then." And that was it.

In the cutting room, Fosse could finally win his battle with Hoffman. The performance, Fosse decreed, lacked the sour edge of the real Lenny Bruce. "It was the racial monologue," Heim said. "Dustin had backed off on it, made it softer." Though Fosse, as director, had cocreated the performance, allowing Hoffman to make the choices Fosse now found distasteful, Fosse refused to assume his share of the responsibility. Hoffman became yet another Cy Feuer; this time, though, his opponent couldn't defend himself. Ship said, "[Fosse] was frequently demeaning him. Dustin would do something, or not do something, or ad lib something, and Fosse would [see it on the screen and] say, 'That little *shit.*'" To save Fosse from his emotionality, Ship mediated from behind the Moviola, defying the code of cautious silence to save good takes, or good moments in middling takes, for the sake of the picture. One particular five-second reaction struck her as one of Hoffman's best.

"Throw it out," Fosse said.

"No, no . . ."

Bob turned around.

"Oh, please save it," she begged.

"Why?"

"Because that's the best thing he does in the scene."

Fosse turned back to the Moviola. "But I can't stand this guy."

Ship was right, of course. And what Fosse hadn't caught in the masters, he uncovered in fragments, details he could muscle into a movie mosaic. Fosse had experimented with fragmentation on *Sweet Charity* and *Cabaret,* but cutting *Lenny,* Fosse and Heim freed themselves more fully from linearity. Heim said, "We discovered that by fragmenting Hoffman's performance, even more than it had been in the script, we were able to make him seem tougher, to make the film move better." There is no time in *Lenny,* at least not in the sense of chronological time; for Fosse and Heim, time was a jazz standard, there to be riffed on. The result: a network of asynchronous pieces of picture and sound that orchestrator Ralph Burns called "Fosse time."

Just as Fosse's dance style had risen from his own perceived inadequacies, Fosse time came from what Fosse perceived as a deficiency of usable film. Cutting up and around Hoffman's performance, he and Heim learned they could excavate an aspect of Lenny's personality through a chosen tempo, the speedy feeling of being everywhere at once. Intermixing past with present and the stage with the real world, they fashioned a zippy associative style closer to cogitation than reality, as if *Lenny* were thinking itself to life. It was so much about rhythm. "Film is just like music," Fosse said, "and acting is dancing. The rhythms ... the appeal to the unconscious." Tossing the script aside, Heim and Fosse finished each other's sentences on film, like Ginger leading Fred leading Ginger.

But the script belonged to Julian Barry. Early in June 1974, Fosse wrote him asking for co-credit. Fosse's tone was patient and respectful and he made it clear to Barry that if Barry decided against co-authorship, it would in no way affect their friendship. Barry owed him nothing, but after all those story meetings, Fosse felt he deserved the credit. "I wrote back and told him no," Barry said. "I said the guy who goes home with the stomachache and brings in the pages the next morning is the writer." Fosse said he'd never bring it up again, and he never did.

He was coughing all the time now. Hacking fits would overtake him in the middle of a conversation. Then he would recover, light another cigarette, and return to work. "He was coughing and coughing and coughing," Ship said, "and the whole room was tense. *Oh my God*, I thought, *his lungs are going to come out.*" Fosse wouldn't speak about it. There was little use in discussing what seemed obvious to all. "The nerve-racking thing," Robert Greenhut said, "was he would leave the cigarette between his lips and kind of forget about it. And it would burn down so much he would only remember it because his lip would get too hot. Sometimes he would burn himself. There were lots of times where people had to actually help him get it out because he couldn't take it out with his fingers. They had to swat it out of his mouth." They could miss and end up hitting him in the face or, worse, on the mouth, which was blistered up from forgotten butts he'd let burn too long. But he never ran out of lip. After singeing one side of his mouth, he would put his next cigarette on the other, burn that one, and cover the burn with a foul-tasting ointment before lighting his next and putting it on the same spot.

He was smoking and coughing when he and Paddy and Herb met to discuss, with an air of spoof seriousness, Dino De Laurentiis's proposed remake of *King Kong*. "Although we had worked on each other's stuff for years," Gardner said, "some animal instinct had kept us from working *with* each other." But this notion was too funny to pass up. Meeting at the Russian Tea Room, a place of real business, they could pretend like they were giving *King Kong* a real shot. Watching one another's eyes for signs of laughter, they slid into one of the Russian Tea Room's red-leather booths, and Fosse, the director, ordered chicken Kiev and started delegating.

"Paddy," he said. "You will handle the dignified, philosophical part of the script; that is, the boredom. Herb, you will do your usual semicomic lyrical bullshit. You'll do the whimsy. And then I'll shine it up so maybe someone will come and see it. I'll do the flash." They decided to call their *King Kong* company Boredom, Whimsy, and Flash ("It was how we referred to each other for the next fifteen years or so," Gardner said), and they agreed the movie would open at the pool at the Beverly Hills Hotel with Kong — a coked-up Hollywood has-been — being paged over the loudspeaker. Lighting a tree-size joint, Kong rises from his lounge chair and stomps through the pool on his way to the phone. He listens carefully to his agent. "Okay, Sam," he says. "I'll do the series." If only.

They had real projects to work on. Paddy's was *Network*, a movie idea he had been considering off and on since the late sixties. Now Chayefsky and his producing partner Howard Gottfried were shopping it to the studios, fishing for interest. It would not be an easy sell. *Network* drew on ugly facts of the TV nation: the perversion of truth and integrity by razzle-dazzle, the crude selling of everything, no matter how sacred, and the American appetite for entertainment that keeps it looking benign. "We used to turn on the radio," Chayefsky said, "and hear the speech [of a presidential candidate]. Today we get ten seconds of an anchorman, fifteen seconds of the reporter on the spot, and fifteen seconds of the *high* points of that speech. *That's* the speech we get. That's not *true*." But people still buy it.

Fosse was intimately invested in every nut and bolt of Chayefsky's preoccupation with the show-business-ization of network news. It meshed with his own obsession with razzle-dazzle, which he and Fred Ebb had been putting into *Chicago*, turning the show into a wicked satire of American jurisprudence, an entertainment consisting of performing lawyers, "innocent" criminals, and "impartial" journalists writing about justice. "It's all show business, kid," says *Chicago*'s lawyer Billy Flynn. "These trials, the whole world, show business." He sings "Razzle Dazzle," which could qualify as Fosse's theme song. ("Throw 'em a fake and a finagle / They'll never know you're just a bagel.")

Fosse edited *Lenny* and worked with Fred Ebb on *Chicago*'s book, and Ebb continued to meet with John Kander, every day, to write the show's music and lyrics. They lived four blocks from each other on the Upper West Side. Around ten every morning, John Kander (who liked to go out) would walk over to the apartment of Ebb (who didn't), and the coffee would be poured and the cigarettes lit. They hung about the kitchen gossiping like the old friends they were, catching up on all they'd missed since they'd seen each other the day before. Together, Ebb, an angsty, witty, waggish New Yorker, and Kander, a sweet midwestern guy, were the dialectical heart of the

Broadway musical. They got off on each other's enthusiasm. "We were pregnant a lot in those days," Ebb said. "I would look at him and a song would come out." One would shine on something that would glint in the other, and the conversation would turn to a moment in the show or a troubling phrase in a song and they would walk their glint into the small room overlooking the park, sit before the spinet piano, and try it. It wouldn't always work, but they wrote fast and tore up fast, which gave Kander and Ebb permission to dislike just about anything they wrote. After a decade together, there was no need for argument. If one mustered the confidence to assert himself, the other would nod his head okay and the thing would die, or live, for the moment.

They improvised their way to certainty. Enough good guesses about words and music eventually brought them the answers; then, their destination in mind, they'd turn around and smooth their guesswork into the beginnings of a song. But slowly, each leaving small openings in the composition for the other guy to fill in. "I would never write a completed lyric," Ebb said, "because then I would confine him to a form, which is not fair to Johnny." And Kander never handed Ebb a completed melody. They asked each other questions. An important one was "What are these characters feeling?" Or "What are these characters thinking and not saying?" "Are you with me?" "Yes, I'm with you, keep going, keep going."

"Put in two finger snaps," Ebb said on "Razzle Dazzle."

"Where?"

"Here. In the vamp."

"Oh . . . yeah, yeah . . ."

"Bobby's gonna love that."

Suddenly one would realize he was hungry, the other would remember they hadn't had anything to eat since ten o'clock, and they'd order up from the deli downstairs. Still working when the food arrived, they'd talk with bread in their mouths, one putting a mug on the spinet to free up a hand for a pencil ("Our copy was so messy," Kander said, "our copyist, the Jewish mother of copyists, would berate us for our poor notation"), the other putting on one of those old vaudeville recordings Fosse loved so they could find themselves another glint. To underline the American vaudeville of jurisprudence, they and Fosse decided *Chicago* would be a musical vaudeville too. Ebb and Fosse's book scenes were broken up by "acts" — the show's numbers — performed out to the audience in a vaudeville style suited to each character. On most days, good days, they wrote a song.

With their help, *Chicago* would be Fosse's penitent thank-you to Gwen. After all she had given him and all he had taken, *Chicago* was his way — his only way — of giving back. Perhaps he felt guilty for being a bad husband; perhaps he felt guilty for (finally) passing her on the rise to artistic renown — whatever his reasons, he told all who asked that he did it for her. Yet there was no denying that reteaming Fosse and Verdon for the first time since their separation would fuel gossip and sell tickets, and selling tickets would go a long way to ensuring Nicole's security, which was the one responsibility they shared.

Verdon's *Chicago* contract was a valentine of power. It granted her a nice piece of the profits; a strictly limited pre-Broadway run; and star billing, with her name as large and prominent as the show's title on posters and promotional materials (all subject to her approval). She also had approval of all creative elements, including but not limited to *Chicago*'s principal cast; scenic, lighting, and costume designers; their designs; her own clothes; the show's composer and compositions; orchestrator and orchestrations; librettist and libretto; dance music and dance orchestrations; and any of her understudies — whatever Lola wants.

Three years after Verdon and Fosse's separation, the dust had settled somewhat. Verdon's budding romance with actor Jerry Lanning helped them both a great deal. New love obliged Verdon to sequester the Fosse-hurt part of her heart, and her growing respect for Ann Reinking, as dancer, girlfriend to Fosse, and ally to Nicole, helped clear the debris between them. "Gwen knew a child needed both parents and was very giving in allowing us time with Nicole," Reinking said. "But it was hard for Bob that he didn't have the day-to-day of waking up every morning with his daughter and his wife. They had both gone forward since their separation and received happiness that way; it was amicable, but it was still painful." Looking at Verdon, you could see she never stopped loving Fosse. "And she continued to love him, I think, in a way he never did her," Reinking said. "I think that's why she was so good to me. She knew what I was up against. I never talked to Gwen about this, but I think she understood. She understood Bob was Bob and if you were really in love with him there was going to be a good and a bad side." Reinking clearly respected Verdon's position as Fosse's first and Nicole's only, and Verdon understood she had to retreat if she wanted to stay close. All Fosse's women did. Except Nicole.

As the summer of 1974 wore on, Fosse flew from Kander and Ebb to the cutting room and back, getting light only through the windows in his office or, after midnight, from the white flashes on the Moviola. Actual weather — that was a rumor. Actual life he lived on the side. "If you want to make something good," he said, "like a movie, it matters more than your health. So you trade a couple of years." *Lenny* nights, *Chicago* days; *Chicago* days, *Lenny* nights. Fosse said, "I'd wake up in the morning, and pop a pill. After lunch, when I couldn't get going, I'd pop another one. There was a certain romanticism about that stuff. There was Bob drinking and smoking and turning out good work. Still popping and screwing around with the girls. 'Isn't it terrific macho behavior?' they said. I probably thought I was indestructible." Fosse had his next show but he didn't have his next movie, which, whatever its subject, would have to somehow upstage *Lenny* the way *Lenny,* in its fervor and audacity, had upstaged *Cabaret,* which had upstaged *Sweet Charity.* He put Sam Cohn on the case. Together with Stuart Ostrow, who joined on as producer, they shuffled through galleys and scanned book reviews, finally touching down on *Ending,* a novel by Hilma Wolitzer about dying. "In American writing now," the *Times* review of her book began, "the romance of death seems to be challenging the romance of love. The sexual revolution has so redefined love that many of us are no longer sure what it is, while a growing existential awareness has brought death out of the funeral parlor." The review was a rave. "Above all, *Ending* made me feel how suicidally we waste our allotted time, how we often try to 'kill it,' as if it were something else and not ourselves that was being defeated." Ostrow was drawn to *Ending*'s smallness of scope, likening it to a string-quartet reprieve from Fosse's regular symphonies, and the book was optioned right away.

Ending is the story of a man's death but it is also the story of his wife's grief and the everyday ways they try to hold on and let go. With no showbiz connection, it was an odd match for Fosse. "My characters were as far from Bob Fosse as possible," Wolitzer said. "Their lives are very ordinary, very middle class." In the novel, Jay Kaufman's death is not Nazi-related or drug-induced but the result of multiple myeloma, tumors in the marrow of his bones. Which in a way makes it worse, far more arbitrary, rivaling even Hitler in the horror department. Everyone dies.

Fosse assigned Robert Alan Aurthur to the adaptation, likely anticipating the chance to pull rank if push came to shove. Aurthur had studied medicine before turning to writing and would surely be handy to have around for the script's technical elements. His first step was to try to talk Fosse out of building the story around terminal illness. No one wanted to see that in a movie; it was dramatically uninteresting and just too depressing. Instead, Aurthur suggested, they should turn the script away from the husband and toward the wife.

Exploring her choices, Aurthur could open a tunnel under the narrative cul-de-sac of the husband's inevitable death and ask how a loved one's passing changes the living. Fosse talked Aurthur into inventing a new character, a dying patient who wants to go out big, who keeps rehearsing memorable death speeches for his final close-up but who dies unceremoniously, without a word. The character manifested one of Fosse's greatest fears — not death, but an *ordinary* death. He said, "What'll happen is I'll probably die in some hospital with no glory at all. No theatrics."

Fosse bade Aurthur good luck with *Ending* and returned, with Verdon, to Broadway Arts, where they began to step through *Chicago*. They were at work for a month before Fosse summoned Kathryn Doby and Tony Stevens, his new assistant. "Don't let me do anything I've done before," Fosse told Stevens on their first day. "Keep me away from the Charleston. I want to do a twenties musical without all that flapper stuff." Stevens soon realized exactly what Fosse meant. Far from the slaphappy antics of the Prohibition age, Fosse's *Chicago* movements seemed closer to group sculpture than dance. He was draining the color. These were not people but bodies, automatons. Their eyes were still and mean. Ann Reinking called it "the Know." "You have to have the magnificent stare that bores a hole at the other end of the theater," she said. Glazed eyes give a character an air of humanless evil. Soul is missing.

The irony *Pippin* attained through exaggeration, *Chicago* was achieving through absence. One was filtered through commedia, the other through Brecht, whose epic theater had fascinated Fosse since he saw Tony Richardson's short-lived production of *Arturo Ui* in 1963, which Richardson set in 1930s Chicago. The Know was an appropriation of a Brechtian alienation technique. "The performer portrays incidents of utmost passion," Brecht wrote, "but without his delivery becoming heated." Positing a style of performance he termed *gest*, Brecht could have been describing Fosse's *Chicago* dances. "'Gest' is not supposed to mean gesticulation: it is not a matter of explanatory or emphatic movements of the hands, but of overall attitudes." The opposite of imitative, the gest is representative. It's showbiz.

Chicago days, *Lenny* nights.

For a while, Fosse had practically cut off communication with Julian Barry. "The reason I haven't called you," he said on the phone, "is because I wanted you to have a completely fresh eye when you saw the movie. Could you come down to the screening room today?"

Before he left his home in Connecticut that day, Barry stopped at his mailbox and found a letter from his wife. She had only recently taken off for Atlanta to "discover" herself (with a redneck, in a trailer), leaving Barry, miserable and alone, to care for their kids. Her latest letter said she wasn't coming back and that the redneck was not a redneck but the man of her dreams. "I went into a complete daze," Barry said, "but I got in the car and drove to New York, didn't remember how I got there, not one bridge, not one turn." He arrived at the screening room and Fosse ran the movie, and the lights came up.

"So," Fosse said. "What did you think?"

"Bob, I gotta be honest with you."

Fosse nodded for him to continue.

"I don't remember any of it."

"What do you mean?"

"I'm sorry. I couldn't see it."

"What does that mean? What's wrong with it?"

"Nothing's wrong with it —"

"Come on, Julian. Goddamn it."

"Bob, I got a letter from Pat . . . Just before I left . . ."

Barry held out the letter. Fosse scanned it and threw it on the floor. "I don't give a fuck about that bitch," he said. "I need to know what you thought of the fucking movie."

The recutting was endless. "People would walk into the editing room, see there was a black cloud in the room, and walk out," Heim said. Fosse would shred scenes down to nothing, just to see if he needed them. Heim wouldn't stop him — he knew Bob was cutting the diamond — but he'd have to stay alert. The longer they worked, the greater the chances of Bob mistaking a flaw in the stone for a flaw in himself, or someone else. "You were a better cutter before you were a father," Fosse told Heim.

At home one night with Reinking, he had a seizure, a petit mal. "He was on his back," Reinking said, "on the bed. His eyes were rolled up and his lids were fluttering." Unsure of what to do, Reinking froze in the doorway; she had never seen a seizure before. When he stopped trembling, she rushed to the bed and held him. Helping himself up, Fosse explained what had happened, that stress was likely to blame, and he calmed them both with a slow walk to the medicine cabinet for a dose of Dilantin. "He was embarrassed," she said. "I could see him thinking it was a show of weakness. Predators would see blood and come in for the attack."

While driving back from Quogue, Fosse felt his hand cramp up, which it had been doing a lot. Reinking didn't know why it kept happening. "I just don't feel good," he would say. "I just — I don't know . . ."

She had suggested they see a doctor.

"No, no, no, it's all right," he would say.

Now, as he drove, he looked nauseated, maybe carsick.

She felt his forehead. It was a little cold.

"It's okay, really. I feel okay now."

The first week of dance rehearsals began October 26 at Broadway Arts. Fosse gave them "All That Jazz," *Chicago*'s opening number, while Gwen worked on her own in another part of the studio. "All That Jazz" belonged to Velma Kelly, the star that Roxie Hart, only a showgirl, desperately wants to be. "The number started with me,

Velma, coming up on this huge lift," Chita Rivera said. "It was practically half the size of the stage. When the elevator came up, I was in the center of the platform with my back to the audience in one of my Fosse poses and this shaft of light shot down from out of nowhere. First you saw the light, then you saw the finger, then the hand, then the arm. Then there I was. Then the vamp started. It was so slow. I turned around slowly and stopped for a second and I went all the way down the stage and placed myself, and I just look. I have the whole stage to myself. The vamp is the only friend you've got at that moment. And then I start to sing." The company joins in behind her.

Fosse showed the company images of the sort of period steps he did not want them to emulate. The Charleston, the shimmy, and the black bottom were meant only to give them a context, forms to be deconstructed. Then he pointed to a black trunk in the corner of the studio. "Go over there," he said, "and pick out anything you want and then spread out." Dancers Graciela Daniele, Kathryn Doby, Cheryl Clark, Candy Brown, Pam Sousa, and a handful of others did as they were told, opening the trunk to find all sorts of vaudeville treasures (derbies, garters, canes, boas); they picked what appealed to them and spread out to different parts of the floor. "Okay," Fosse said, pointing at one dancer, "now you do the shimmy in *slow motion.*" He pointed to another. "You do the black bottom in *slow motion.*" These weren't to be flapper steps. They were streaks of blood. "In 'All That Jazz,'" dancer Gene Foote said, "he said to us, 'I want you to confront the audience with murder in your eyes and dare them to look at you.'" It was the Know in action.

The dancers kept their straw hats and derbies in a pile, but Tony Stevens guarded Fosse's bowler in a hatbox he kept with him at all times. It looked like the other bowlers with the exception of one detail: inside the brim, *Expressly made for Bob Fosse* was embroidered in gold thread. "It was the crown," Stevens said. Whenever Fosse would get up to demonstrate a step, he would signal to Stevens for his hat. "He would just open his fingers, and I would know where to aim," he said. It seemed to Stevens that Fosse couldn't dance without it. "It got so that he wouldn't put on the bowler without lighting a cigarette first," Stevens said. "I remember thinking, *Maybe it's the bowler that's killing him, not the smoke.*"

Heim said Fosse didn't look so good, that he should go home and be confident about *Lenny*, but Fosse wasn't ready to call it a day. The latest cut still wasn't working, and the release date, November 11, 1974, was only days away. That was more than enough time to rescue the picture; more than enough time, Heim feared, for Fosse to second-guess and disassemble the whole thing. But he could not assuage Fosse's doubts. After the two screened the picture (again), Fosse went (coughing) back into the editing room and cut three whole minutes from *Lenny*. No matter that his teeth ached and there was a tightening in his chest. No matter that Ann Reinking was worried about the purplish color of his lips. Every dancer learns to live with muscle aches, and what he had here, tingling aside, was routine discomfort. A pulled muscle, maybe. Nothing compared to the pain he would suffer, probably forever, if he didn't get *Lenny* right, and fast. Stress? Who wasn't stressed? They'd go until they got it.

That night, sitting with Fosse at the Moviola, Heim caught him kneading his upper arm, repeatedly clenching and unclenching his fist. And his face was white.

Bob looked away from the Moviola.

"Are you okay?"

"Just tired. Went from rehearsal to see Annie." Reinking was in the hospital. She had fractured her vertebrae in two places and had to leave *Over Here*. "Then I went back to rehearsal."

Heim said nothing.

"Now here," Fosse added.

Finally, he had to stop. Heim helped him out of his chair, walked him to the street, and put him in a cab.

"You going home?"

"Annie."

That was Saturday.

Monday, Fosse and the cast of *Chicago* assembled at Broadway Arts for the first table read. Everyone was thrilled. They all seemed to agree they were working at the top of their game. Soaring in, Chita Rivera placed a big bouquet of red roses in the middle of the table; Tony Walton showed off a model of the sleek bare set, and Kander and Ebb played their songs, which were among their rousing, cheeky best. The tastefully sinister dances Fosse had sketched out over the first week of rehearsal captivated everyone, and to see him reunited with Gwen lent a sense of rightness to their delight. Gwen may have been the only one to worry. That morning, she sensed something different in Fosse. "I was shocked," she said. "He was puffed up. He had a funny high voice. I'd never seen him like that." This time, Fosse did not deny it. He asked stage manager Phil Friedman to make him an appointment with Dr. Leder for the lunch break.

How exactly did he feel? Friedman asked.

Like a truck was driving across his chest, Fosse said.

Friedman called Leder, as directed, and the reading progressed without difficulty. Rising from the table, Fosse thanked and dismissed the company and told Friedman he should go ahead and work on "All That Jazz" if Fosse didn't make it back from Dr. Leder's office in time to start the number himself. He was clutching his chest.

On their way to lunch, producers Joe Harris and Ira Bernstein ran into Neil Simon crossing Broadway. Simon asked how the show was going; they told him the show was going great, and they all schmoozed for a moment and then parted ways. Bernstein and Harris ate their lunch and strolled back to their offices on East Forty-Eighth Street in time to pick up a ringing phone and hear a strange piece of news. Fosse had been taken to New York Hospital, and the doctors weren't letting him out. Joe Harris got in a cab.

In the hospital, Fosse — trying to keep calm — told Harris that Dr. Leder had sent him directly to the ER for further evaluation. Harris could see why. Fosse's face was slick; his breathing labored. While Leder, engaged with his stethoscope, examined the patient's chest, Fosse slipped Harris his attaché case. "The show is over," he whispered, and he told Harris to get rid of it, then put on an innocent face for cardiologist Edwin Ettinger. The pain comes and goes, Fosse explained, it wasn't serious. He'd been living with it for months; he'd just gone to Leder for a checkup, routine stuff, and now he had to get back to rehearsal. Ettinger held up a hand. Fosse was not going back to rehearsal. He was going to have a heart attack.

Fosse explained, in the clearest terms possible: He was doing a show, a Kander and Ebb show. People were counting on him.

Ettinger cut him off. Fosse needed an EKG.

"What do you mean? I have to go back. You don't understand show business."

Ettinger didn't understand that shows were not just shows; they were domino lines of careers and paychecks, and if his domino tipped, lives would fall down around him. Maybe the producers were already trying to replace him. Were they calling Robbins? Gower Champion? Hal Prince? What if his show was a hit without him and the *New York Times* wrote Hal Prince was better at Fosse than Fosse? Or what if the producers decided to shut down the whole thing and walk away with the insurance? They had a legitimate case for abandonment (which would give them 1 to 2 percent on the value of the policy) and could board up the show right then and still rake in the money. If they did, Fosse's premiums would skyrocket, and he'd be branded a liability, beholden to producers, possibly for the rest of his life. It was essential Ettinger understood this.

At 3:30, Fosse's doctors called Broadway Arts, gave the news to Phil Friedman, and asked him to get Gwen to the hospital, fast. Friedman found Verdon alone with Chita — a relief. This had to be kept private. Friedman apologized to Chita and led Gwen out of the studio and to a chair against the wall. Knitting needles in hand — she and Chita were practicing their knitting for *Chicago*'s big trial scene — Verdon seated herself where directed, and Friedman explained everything. Calmly, she changed her clothes and left the building. "[Gwen] really went through this like an actress," Friedman said. She believed this was, in a way, what he wanted, not to die, but to come to the cliff's edge of death, kiss it, and turn back. She thought it put him in touch with his talent, like fighting the producers, who in a sense were like heart attacks, like terminal illnesses, with their cruel and incessant reminders of time running out . . . last one . . . no more . . .

"Please don't let them keep me in this place," Fosse said to Gwen when she appeared in the ER.

"He's staying."

She reached a hand out for the medical papers.

"I'm his wife."

Meanwhile, Joe Harris called Ann Reinking, at her own hospital, and told her very little. No one could know anything. Razzle-dazzle damage control.

"Alan," Verdon said to Heim, "Bob won't be in for a few days."

"What is it? What's wrong?"

Big exhale. "He's exhausted."

At 5:30 that evening, producers Fryer and Harris returned to Broadway Arts to tell the dancers, if not the exact truth, then something like it. "It's exhaustion," they said. Not to worry. Rehearsals would be off for a couple of days. Fosse would return Thursday. Really, there was no reason to worry. *You know Bob. Overworked, over-stressed, over-everything . . . Go home, we'll know more tomorrow.*

Dr. Ettinger moved Fosse to a private room and recommended

immediate surgery, a cardiac bypass. There was a 98 percent chance he'd survive.

Fosse nodded. He asked if he could have a smoke and think it over.

They would take a vein from Fosse's leg, Ettinger explained, and move it to his heart. Fosse stopped him right there. Better if they didn't touch his leg; as a dancer, he'd be happier if they cut the artery out of his chest. Ettinger made the deal.

The following day, the *Chicago* company was told there would be a delay; for how long, no one knew. Maybe four months. "Do *not* worry," the producers said. "We will look out for you." They promised to call around for work and encouraged the dancers to be in touch if they needed money. If they needed *anything*. But money was not the issue for some. Having moved across the country, having said tired and fighting goodbyes to their boyfriends and girlfriends and husbands and wives, having decided, as if they had a choice, to give up, again, their lives for the barre, the dancers had put much of everything on hold to be in *Chicago*, and now that hold was being put on hold. They were in nothing, limbo. Pam Sousa booked a couple commercials and extra work in *Three Days of the Condor*.

As the company mother, Verdon held them close. She threw parties to keep spirits up. Losing one dancer to the world might inspire another to go, and then another, and though Verdon wanted them to shore themselves up with pickup gigs, she knew if the company disintegrated, schedules would fly away, and *Chicago* would be put back even farther, maybe too far, and she'd be too old.

The doctors instructed Fosse to relax. But he couldn't relax if he relaxed, so he called the theater to check up on *Pippin*, wanting to know about every dancer. How were they? How was the show? How was *Lenny*? Heim came to the hospital with a report. There were lines, he told him, all the way around the block; it was Cinema One's best opening day in twelve years. "Fosse has learned a phenomenal amount about film technique in a short time," Pauline Kael wrote.

"*Lenny* is only his third movie . . . and it's a handsome piece of work. I don't know any other movie director who entered moviemaking so late in life and developed such technical proficiency; Fosse is a true prodigy."

But lying in intensive care, awaiting the surgery that was to increase blood flow to the heart they said would attack him if he didn't get real, Fosse continued to worry. He worried about his cock. Drugged out, he called Annie in her hospital room, terrified the operation would make him impotent. The idea obsessed him. He blamed her. He said she hadn't taken care of him. Reinking knew it was the drugs talking; his words were slow to come and he drifted from subject to subject. He wondered whether he should have the open-heart surgery at all ("I'm going to a real opening," he joked). He wondered how he would live if he couldn't fuck; how he would work if he couldn't move; how he would live if he couldn't work. He could die. He would die. Maybe not here, but somewhere. Then again, maybe here. Maybe tomorrow.

The big yank, the end without end.

There was only one thing he could do about dying now: fuck as much as he could. In anticipation of an unsuccessful "opening night," Fosse made a pass at almost every nurse who came in to see him. The one who took his blood pressure got a hand on her hips. Another had her chest examined by a toy stethoscope. The nurse assigned to massage duty arrived to find lemon oils on his bedside. Some didn't mind; others were less amenable. Outside his door, the ICU nurses held a private conference to discuss the sex-and-comedy routine they termed Fosse's defense mechanism.

He called Janice in LA.

"Bob, are you smoking?"

"Yeah. It's not a big deal."

"Are you on oxygen?"

"Yeah."

"Bob, if you don't put that out right now, I'm calling the hospital!"

"You're not my mother."

"You could blow the whole place up!"

"Sometimes you act like my mother . . ."

"I'm calling them right now. I'll tell them to turn *off* the oxygen, Bob!"

"Okay" — chuckling — "okay."

At nine o'clock the evening before the operation, he called Paddy Chayefsky and Herb Gardner into his hospital room to witness the signing of his new, revised will. They arrived moments after the lawyers and hung over Fosse's bed, staring. It was depressing. To see this life-hungry maniac lying there semiconscious weighing next to nothing and hooked into tubes and drips and beeping screens was to behold a baffling and tragic ridiculousness. To the lawyers' shock, Paddy and Herb actually started laughing. Then Fosse started laughing. "We were lifetime friends," Gardner said at Fosse's memorial, "and we knew it and reveled in the security of it and attacked each other's weakness and laughed every day at each other's expense knowing there was plenty to spend. Paddy hunched over with his evil little cackle, and Bobby with his head thrown back laughed till he cried, one of us having just led a search-and-destroy mission to a weakness in the other."

It began with Chayefsky. In his rabbinical way, he declared he wasn't going to sign any document without reading it first. Snatching the will from Fosse's hand, he crossed to a chair in the corner of the room and read every word of the entire thirty-page document.

"Hey," Chayefsky mumbled. "I'm not in here." He flipped back to the beginning, just to make sure.

"Paddy," Fosse said, with a certain amount of feeling. "You're in good shape. You can take care of yourself. I've got Nicole and Gwen to plan for."

"I'm your oldest and best friend, and I'm not in your will?"

Fosse hesitated. This was not the response he expected. "There are people who really need taking care of," he said. "This has nothing to do with my love for you."

"You left me out of your will?"

"Yes, Paddy. I did."

Chayefsky took a portentous beat and then spoke. "Fuck you!" he said. "*Live!*"

Fosse exploded laughing. The wires hooked into him started flapping like fish on a boat, and one of the lawyers had to brace the heart monitor to make sure it didn't go down with the food tray that had been kicked off the bed, which got Chayefsky laughing, which started Gardner laughing, and the harder they laughed, the more embarrassed the lawyers got, until finally Chayefsky took pity on them and signed the will. It said, in part, "I give and bequeath the sum of $25,000 to be distributed to the friends of mine listed . . . so that when my friends receive this bequest they will go out and have dinner on me. They have all at one time or another during my life been very kind to me. I thank them."

After the signing, the sedation kicked in and Fosse fell asleep, leaving Chayefsky and Gardner to small-talk with the suits. It must have been one or two o'clock in the morning when one of the lawyers, endeavoring to fill the silence, said he heard the director Joshua Logan had put a similar clause in his will.

Fosse opened one eye. "For how much?"

The lawyer told him.

"Make mine ten grand more," he said and closed his eye.

So now Chayefsky and Gardner fell down laughing, which actually got the lawyers laughing, and then the surgeon came in, and just seeing them all laughing, he started to laugh. Trying to pull himself together, the doctor put on a solemn face and approached Fosse's bedside. This was serious, he said, and he led the patient through the steps of the next day's operation — the whole number, from top to bottom. The surgeon took out a pen and pointed it at a diagram of Fosse's heart. Highlighting the damaged tissue, he showed Fosse exactly how they'd be taking a vein from his chest and putting it into his heart, which —

The surgeon dropped his pen.

"Whoops," the surgeon said.

Everyone froze. Whoops?

"Operation canceled," Fosse murmured. They all started laughing again, harder than before, laughing as if they weren't in New York Hospital but at their table at the Carnegie Deli. "Doc," Fosse said to the surgeon, a man by the name of William Gay, "Doc, I won't let you operate unless you promise one thing, okay?"

"Well, okay," Gay said. "What's that?"

Fosse cleared his throat. "You gotta promise not to kiss me during the operation."

That killed them.

A half hour before the operation, Robert Alan Aurthur called Fosse. They talked a little about Aurthur's progress on *Ending*.

"We sure picked the right subject, didn't we?" Fosse said. "I'm getting a lot of material here."

"Maybe you'd rather do a comedy."

"Don't think I haven't given it a lot of thought."

Fosse mentioned the party clause in his new will.

Aurthur told him he'd done the same.

Deadpanning, Fosse said that between him, Aurthur, and Logan, maybe everyone was doing it. But how well were they doing it? If Fosse got Stuart Ostrow to produce *his* memorial party, he could probably do it for a thousand dollars less than anyone else.

On November 15, 1974, the doctors wheeled Fosse out of the ICU and into the operating theater. They put him under, hooked him up to a massive heart-lung machine, and stopped the beat.

THIRTEEN YEARS

BY THE 1970S, America had become a showbiz nation, obsessed with image, depressed by its own fraudulence and failure. The assassinations of Martin Luther King Jr. and Robert F. Kennedy, the unceasing devastation in Vietnam, and waves upon waves of Watergate lies and cover-ups ended the long-running musical comedy of the 1950s and early 1960s, a period when the nation agreed on what was good and what was bad. They were years of stunning credulity. America bought what it sold.

By the 1970s, that changed; there seemed to be no sin greater than trust. Cynicism was the new enlightenment; nothing was what it appeared to be. Certain females — feminists — acted like men, and men acted like women, or were told to. The book *Type A Behavior and Your Heart*, published in 1974, warned against intense, competitive compulsions, saying "masculine" behaviors could lead to illness or even death. The new man had to be delicate. David Bowie was delicate. He changed his costume, and Bob Dylan changed his sound, both delighting, it seemed, in a radical new approach to identity: the performance of self. "We all have to put on to make it through the day," Fosse said a year before his death. "One time I was going to do a film, a semidocumentary, about how everyone has to put on a show, how everybody wakes up and says, 'It's showtime!'"

Nixon was no different. He too performed, only not well. Printing copies of copies, Warhol made a cult of fakes, but he was merely taking his cues from a nation that had made a religion of show business. "The 70s was the decade in which people put emphasis on the skin, on the surface, rather than on the root of things," Norman Mailer wrote. "It was the decade in which image became preeminent because nothing deeper was going on." In fact, there *was* something deeper — depression, disenchantment, the search for new meaning that Tom Wolfe saw in the Me Decade. If I'm not my image, my "self," then what am I *really?* Thus would President Jimmy Carter — a figure dull on the surface but, many hoped, substantial inside — try to heal a nation he called "sick at heart."

So America had caught up to Bob Fosse.

By the time of his open-heart surgery, Fosse was only one of many musical impresarios to use show business allegorically, to explicate the modern condition. Of course, Broadway had always been fair game for a Broadway musical, but the backstage setting of a traditional backstager like *42nd Street* served not as a device to examine entertainment as metaphor but as a convenient pretext for songs and dances. The showbiz epidemic of the 1970s reversed all that, reviving and revising the backstage concept to fit America's image crisis. Each visionary had his own slant. Alongside Fosse, there was Hal Prince's *Cabaret,* and Prince and Sondheim's *Company* and *Follies.* And there was Michael Bennett's forthcoming *A Chorus Line.* But that show wasn't rife with metaphor like the others; it was just about a chorus line. And unlike the corny backstagers of yore, it was not glamorized. *A Chorus Line* was the real chorus line, a documentary in musical form.

Fosse had any number of reasons to dislike Michael Bennett, but the most immediate — that he was improving *A Chorus Line* every day that Fosse was in the hospital not improving *Chicago* — was nothing next to the headline, the critical consensus, the growing sense that Bennett's work was omnivorous, absorbing more theatricality, more ways to dance, while Fosse's work was narrow, confined to the limitations of his style. Or so Fosse feared. That made Fosse less of a shoo-in to inherit Robbins's mantle — up for grabs since he'd left Broadway after *Fiddler on the Roof* — than the still-running *Pippin*'s success would suggest. Worse, Michael Bennett was a full sixteen years Fosse's junior, with a splendid, Sondheim-rich résumé and a show-to-Tony ratio chillingly close to Fosse's own.

In public, they socialized around their enmity as best they could. "Bob took me to Patsy's for dinner," said dancer Deborah Geffner, "and Michael Bennett was sitting there with his back to us at a huge round table full of people. And as we went past, Bob, in a gesture that was sort of like patting him on the shoulder, pushed his head almost all the way down into his plate. And Michael turned around, and Bob looked back and said, 'Hey, Michael, how are you?' And Michael said, 'Fine.' There was really no love lost between them."

"Young choreographers," Fosse would growl to Alan Heim, "I wish they'd all die." One in particular.

"It was spy versus spy with those two," Tony Stevens said. "The stories you'd hear about them working it behind the scenes." Poaching Stevens, Chita Rivera's longtime friend and collaborator, from the workshops of *A Chorus Line* to the rehearsals of *Chicago*, Fosse could enjoy the added bonus of hitting Bennett where it hurt. Bennett knew what hurt Fosse too, and (according to rumor) by titling his show *A Chorus Line* instead of *Chorus Line*, he made sure it would precede *Chicago* on any alphabetical listing. Catching on to their bosses' feud, some of the shows' dancers chose sides. Some were forced to. Donna McKechnie, who began as a Fosse dancer and became Bennett's number one muse and collaborator, found herself caught in a high-school war of cliques. "I remember when I walked into a restaurant during *Chorus Line,*" she said, "and saw dancers from *Chicago,* people I knew, just snubbing me. I couldn't believe it. It was like a bad dream."

Fosse awoke on the recovery floor after surgery. They had him on an ice mattress to keep his temperature down. He had a tube up his nose and another up his cock.

As soon as he could talk, he called Annie. She was still at St. Clare's Hospital, recovering from injuries sustained in *Over Here.* "Bob? How was it? How are you?"

"For six hours," he drawled, "I was dead."

His anger surprised her. "Bob, this is a really good operation."

"I was dead, Annie. My heart stopped."

"You were on the machine. You were fine."

"What if I spring a leak?"

He sounded terrible, but Reinking was not alarmed. She had been told to expect this sort of hopelessness; depression was common after open-heart surgery. "You just have to trust this," she said. "If you don't trust this, the stress will get you, and then you'll be right back where you started."

The recovery floor frightened him. The new nurses were less attentive, at times even distant. He tried humor, which, since the surgery, had fallen from dark to black. But they didn't respond, and the antipathy isolated Fosse further. Soon, he was telling Annie — crying to her — that he felt unsafe, that something bad was going to happen. He told her a man in a bed directly across from him was dying. (The man was young, in his thirties or forties. It took two days.)

They moved Fosse to a private room on the fifteenth floor.

He thought. "There is this profound period of realization," said nurse Nancy Bird, an associate of Fosse's, "in recovery from open-heart surgery, when patients think about what they've gone through and what they've done in their lives. It's not a happy time." He thought,

What's the point of musical comedy? Of show business? It's so much ef-
fort, so much agony, for what? How much is a good laugh really *worth?*
He said later, "It is a little difficult to, you know, think that *d-da-d-da-*
ta-dum is that important, you know, after you've been close to death.
But of course, maybe it is. I don't know. Maybe *d-da-d-da-ta-dum*
is the most important thing I have in life." But *maybe* was not good
enough.

He sank.

Paddy and Herb, sitting in chairs by the patient's bed, saw that telling Fosse a dirty joke or funny story could make the needle on his
heart monitor jump into the red. So they made a game out of it. To
win Can You Top This? you had to get the needle up higher than the
other guy (extra points for cardiac arrest), but discreetly. If the nurses
found out, the game would be shut down. So Paddy and Herb whispered their jokes, but they couldn't whisper their hysterical laughter, and soon after the game began, one of the nurses appeared to
tell them the heart monitor was not an applause-o-meter. Herb and
Paddy respectfully disagreed.

He got sentimental one night, about Gwen, about Nicole. "If I
go . . ."

Paddy frowned. "*Awwww,* who cares?"

To get Fosse off the subject, Chayefsky promised Bob that if Bob
died first, Chayefsky would deliver a tedious eulogy at his funeral.
Fosse told Chayefsky that if Chayefsky died first, Fosse would do a
tap dance at the memorial.

Word of Fosse's ordeal spread through Broadway, and to keep his
spirits up (and the stress level down), his closest friends and collaborators prescribed a little postoperative party. In came Kander and
Ebb and Stuart Ostrow and Sam Cohn and Tony Walton and a dozen
others. Actor John McMartin called in the middle of it and could
barely hear Bob over the cheering. The *Pippin* cast took up a collection and sent one of the girls to FAO Schwarz to buy him puzzles, one

of which had a harem girl that looked like Ann. Garson Kanin sent a book called *How to Get Control of Your Time and Your Life*. Valerie Perrine sent a life-size naked poster of herself. Dustin sent zinnias. Shirley MacLaine wired, "How long has it been since you've had your blah-blah blahed?" (Not that long.) Others brought in books, cigarettes, movie posters, and friends of friends. Tony Walton came with his wife, Gen. "Tony," Fosse said, "watch the heart monitor," and pulled Gen in for a kiss. Paddy and Herb sneaked in sandwiches from the deli. Wolfgang Glattes saw someone smuggle in white wine. The music was loud, the laughter was louder, and the telephone — like the phone of a hit show's producer — rang around the clock. Nurses unplugged it. He had to rest, they told him.

Rest?

Student nurse Kathy Zappola took his blood pressure, and he slid a hand up her thigh. When she came in to massage Fosse's legs, she saw he had his stash of erotic oils already waiting for her. She lathered up and got to work.

"Oh, that feels good . . ." he cooed, "but I might have an erection."

"Don't do that!"

As soon as Fosse could walk, he brought flowers to the old ladies on his floor. Some died on his watch.

At all hours, girlfriends crossed in the hallway. There were fights. While Fosse slept, Gwen appeared to negotiate the peace, ushering crying dancers from his door, giving motherly understanding as she walked them to the waiting room. Her sensitivity amazed Dr. Ettinger. It confused him. As wife, she had legal say-so in certain medical matters, and she presided over Fosse's paperwork with the full force of her authority, but exactly which one of her husband's girlfriends had spiritual and emotional jurisdiction, which ones loved him, which he loved back, and how to include them, Ettinger couldn't say. No one could. "The hospital staff didn't know who to relate to," the doctor recalled. "They didn't know who was the person to be given important information. I would make my rounds and see Gwen and Ann — as if they were *sisters*. It was unbelievable."

They didn't allow children on the recovery floor so Gwen had to disguise Nicole and sneak her in. There were so many dancers, their bodies so small, coming in and out of Fosse's room, Gwen knew she could squeeze in one more if she painted her daughter's eleven-year-old face with a thick coat of makeup and put chunky platform shoes on her feet. This Verdon did (although the shoes were three sizes too big for Nicole, so Gwen had to strap them on with heavy-duty rubber bands she stole from the hospital supply closet), capping the whole look with a wide-brimmed floppy hat before sending Nicole teetering to Fosse's room.

They were both shocked to see each other. Tangled in beeps and wires, he looked to her more like a machine than a person, and she looked to him more like a girlfriend than a girl. He asked her if she had bust pads in. It embarrassed her. She couldn't understand why his mood had darkened; he was supposed to be relieved. There was a lot Nicole didn't understand about this. Though she had asked her mother questions, most of them had not been answered to Nicole's satisfaction. Everyone changed the subject around her. Even if the biological *how* of death had been clearly and expertly explained to her with charts and graphs and box-office figures, she could not know the *why* of any of it, and so she tested what she saw, prodding the scene for answers. She prodded Fosse. As Gwen looked on, Nicole put his heart through an obstacle course, going silent to get him to notice her and telling him he looked like a machine, as if by drawing his attention, and maybe love, she could guarantee his permanence. He would be her father, and fathers didn't die. Long after she left, his mind was still sutured to her face.

Being in the hospital was starting to do weird things to his head. Fosse churned under the influence of medication and the erratic postoperative depression they warned him about, and his sense of reality took a turn for the kaleidoscopic. He had too much time to think and rethink, and his regrets lined up at the foot of his bed like Ziegfeld girls and pointed angry fingers in his face. They admonished him for working too hard, for not taking care of his body. When his room wasn't occupied by friends or lovers or the hopeful types in between, when he wasn't making quiet, shaky love to Ann Reinking or another girlfriend, it became a white-walled cage where he was made to wait —like an actor auditioning for the role of himself—for a doctor to come in and tell him he was still a person, or at least that, with the right treatment, he stood a good chance of becoming one. "It didn't bother me that Bob's girlfriends came to the hospital," Reinking said. "Bob was sick. I worried about him. That's all that mattered." Having sex with Reinking, he wept with relief that impotence hadn't set in. She had never seen him cry before.

As afternoon became night, the doctors got younger and the nurses got uglier. The get-well flowers gave the place a funereal look, and all the books and posters that had been brought in were not enough to color the anemic white of his empty room. He was losing his memory. Cue the Ziegfeld girls, the pointed fingers. Someone, they said, scared Bob Fosse out of loving. But who? When? Or was Bob Fosse's heart mechanism actually perfectly calibrated—to love Bob Fosse forever and ever? Narcissist, they said. Egomaniac. Selfish. Heartless. But if he was so in love with himself, why did he sometimes want to die? Which was it? It couldn't be both. (Could it?)

Ann Reinking was sitting beside him when the pain came back.

"I don't feel good," he said. "Get the nurse."

She took one look at his ashen face and called for help. She knew the symptoms.

"I don't feel good," he repeated.

"They're coming."

They weren't. Still recovering from her own injury, Reinking, moving as quickly as she could, skidded into the hall to call again for help. Finding no one, she limped back into Bob's room to make sure. He looked worse; his lips had turned that bluish color.

"Annie . . ."

"I'm coming right back."

She went out again, hauling herself down the empty corridors, yelling for help, but no one answered. Where was everyone? For a moment, she considered bursting into patients' rooms, just throwing the doors open, hoping to find an ally, someone — and then a nurse appeared.

"You have to help me. I think he's having another heart attack."

The old woman turned up an eyebrow. "We just gave him his shot."

"He's in pain! He needs another one!"

"I'm sorry, ma'am, I —"

Shaking, Reinking raced, limping, down the hall to Fosse's room.

"I'm just going to stand here until they come," she said to him. "I'm just going to stand here with you."

He was breathing hard. Like he was drowning, very slowly.

"I'm right here," she said.

She called out again for help, but she wouldn't scream — that would scare him. She would just hold his hand, calling out with gentle forcefulness, and wait.

He was sweating. "Annie . . ."

Two nurses arrived, took a look at Fosse, and knew right away it was real. He *was* having another heart attack.

He was someplace else, in the heart of his brain, dreaming, crying, singing Nicole a rhythmic song called "Every Time My Heart Beats," which he didn't know but sang perfectly, and nuns appeared, and as the nuns danced, Nicole listened and he explained to her what it felt like to die. And she understood. They both did. The dream's rhythm told him so.

Shirley MacLaine was holding his hand when he woke up. Gwen

had caught her up on everything, and MacLaine had expected to see him coming back to life. Instead she saw, in his eyes, something like the Know.

"I had a strange dream under the anesthetic," he said. "More like a vision or a real picture."

"What was it?"

"I was dying," he said. He described everything he could remember: the rhythm; Nicole; how the number about dying came to him, not in fragments, but all at once, complete from beginning to end.

Fosse said, "I thought to myself, Even as I'm dying, I'm working."

But he didn't die. He was discharged on December 10, 1974. Leaving the hospital, Fosse and Reinking must have made quite a pair — she in her back brace and he, like someone's grandmother, being wheeled to the curb. The New York freeze stung their bodies, but these two were dancers; pain was negotiable. Shredded by the stage, unsure of their future as show people or the real-life prospects of their love, the twenty-five-year-old ballerina and her shrunken forty-seven-year-old boyfriend ducked into a cab, huddled close, and headed home for the first time in six weeks, trapped but happy.

Fosse quit smoking. Gwen threw a Christmas party, reuniting him with the company of *Chicago*. On New Year's Eve, at Herb Gardner's party, he got drunk.

He had to get out of town. Being in New York and not working was like being in bed with Jennifer Nairn-Smith and not touching. He called Janice.

"Can you get me some Dexies?"

"No, Bob."

"Please."

"That will kill you. You'll be dead."

"Well, so what?"

"I won't. No."

"But it's the only thing. I will not work if I don't have it."

"Then maybe you need to take a break from work."

He took off for Palm Desert, and then Los Angeles, to the Beverly Hills Hotel, where he ran into Emanuel Wolf. "Bob looked terrible," Wolf said, "as limp as a rag. I wanted to pick him up and carry him to his room." Three days later, Wolf ran into Fosse again, this time at a Beverly Hills disco, where Bob was partying like crazy. Wolf could not believe he had the stamina.

"Manny! Manny!" Fosse shouted from across the room. "I want you to meet the most beautiful, wonderful woman I've ever met."

Fosse introduced him to Raquel Welch, who looked every inch the most beautiful, wonderful woman he had ever met. Wolf and Welch said their hellos and their goodbyes, and Wolf left.

Welch and Fosse were awed by each other: he by the complete package of her beauty and intelligence, she by how he used creativity to free himself from depression. He explained to Welch that when he had to contain his ideas, as he had in the hospital, it kept all that was potentially good about him from coming out. It kept him locked inside. If Fosse could share that good with the world, he might cross the bridge out of his isolation, but only if what he shared matched exactly what was in his brain — and there was so much of it to share, too much, more than he could get out. So he often felt stranded on the other side of his good ideas, kept from creative potential and convinced, again, of his failures. Explaining this to Welch helped; it was a little like crossing that bridge.

At three o'clock that morning, Emanuel Wolf's hotel phone rang.

"Manny, I've never met a woman like this."

"Bob . . . I'm sleeping."

Fosse kept him on the phone for twenty minutes, exulting in Raquel Welch's every detail. She was gorgeous, lovely, the *most* perfect, incredible . . .

"Bob, let's talk tomorrow, okay? I gotta sleep."

"Sure, sure, Manny. Sure."

Two hours later the phone rang again.

"I have to finish telling you about Raquel Welch."

"Bob —"

"You really can't believe this woman."

"I gotta go now, Bob." Wolf hung up and turned over. As he drifted off, Wolf thought: *She brought him back to life.*

TWELVE YEARS

N MARCH 1975, Fosse returned to Broadway Arts, to *Chicago*, meaner than he left it. "After the heart attack, he was getting angry and scared," Reinking said. "He was scared to go back. According to Bob, they would make more money if he died than if he lived. You have to be in a certain mood to find that funny." The insurance policy legitimized a paranoia that later proved to be half true. *Chicago*'s producers had no intention of closing the show and collecting a profit, but they did discuss contingencies with Robbins and Prince. "Hal offered in the spirit of trying to help out," producer Ira Bernstein said. "Naturally, the decision was made to wait for Bobby."

Fosse's body no longer worked as fast as his brain, and he wondered if they wondered if he was still the same Fosse, as if talent were the same thing as stamina. "He got winded; he got tired," Pam Sousa said, "and it made him angry. He couldn't be as alert and creative for eight hours." As if *Chicago* were a part of Fosse's body, its dances slowed almost to a stop, and the show's tone began to change. "That will hold," he would say, meaning slow to a freeze. *Chicago* had always been cynical; now it was sinister. Protracting the movement underscored the sense of suspense, of predatory intent, even death.

Pippin's chorus was wicked; these girls were zombies. "It got creepy," Tony Stevens said. "When we first heard 'They Both Reached for the Gun,' we thought, *What a fun number!* But when Bob staged it, no one could believe how *slow* it was. It was like swimming underwater. There was this sinking feeling. I was like, *Okay, this is the dance of a very depressed man.*" Fred Ebb begged Stevens to pick up the tempo, but he didn't. "You want me to tell Bob Fosse to go faster?" he replied. "I don't think so!"

"I'm not sure he even wanted to be there," said Cheryl Clark. He always said he undertook *Chicago* for Gwen, and through the early stages he wore his duty comfortably, but returning to rehearsal after surgery, he seemed to resent the obligation. He could be distant, almost apathetic, like he didn't care, didn't want to be there. On the waltz section of "They Both Reached for the Gun," Fosse told the dancers to "treat this section like an E. E. Cummings poem." This was bafflingly abstract, totally unlike Fosse's famously specific directives. "Bobby doesn't know how he wants to handle the jury scene," stage manager Phil Friedman told Dick Korthaze, "but he wants you to go through that trunk and see what you come up with." Picking a cloche hat, a red nose, a bad toupee, a flask, a pince-nez, and an ear horn (among other things), Korthaze created a half a dozen personalities, snapping different attitudes from jury chair to jury chair. Fosse's sole remark after seeing Korthaze's wondrous creation was "When you make the change, do it when the focus is on Gwen."

Gwen. More than ever, his resentment tangoed with his reverence. "Their love was reinitiated in the rehearsal room," Stevens said. "It was a true love affair in the sense that there were arguments, pushing and pulling, passive-aggression, misunderstandings, and total trust." One could say he was trying to get her to dance her best, but one could also say he was breaking her down. One could say he wasn't yet completely fluent in Verdon's new, older body, but one could also say he was as fluent as he needed to be in the terms of her contract, which held him to the wall. "They were having a difficult time," Kander said. "I remember once she said, 'They can pack his heart in a sawdust box for all I care.'" The show's ending was a source of consistent disagreement. If everyone runs out on Roxie, Verdon argued, then Roxie needs to have a triumphant moment, like "Rose's Turn" from *Gypsy*, to take back power and win the day. "She asked Fosse for it," Stevens said, "she begged him for it, but he wouldn't give it to her." One could say he wanted Roxie to wind up wounded, like Pippin. One could say he wanted to wound Gwen, either to keep her from walking away with the show ("She knew," Stevens said, "that it would be her show if she had that moment") or to keep her fighting, fighting as Roxie Hart fought, for *her own* moment. One could say he was directing.

"I thought Bob was like the Emcee from *Cabaret*," Stevens said. "The observer, the manipulator. He would do things to get a reaction. He'd say something to someone, give them a note, and he knew it was going to just raise their ire. He just *knew* it. He'd say, 'Watch what I'm going to do to so-and-so,' and I'd say, 'Don't tell me that. I don't want to know that.' He would do it to create competition, to bring people closer to their parts, or to make an example of someone for the company. Sometimes his dancers were a bit full of themselves — they knew they were the best, they were Fosse dancers — and he would use that to get them to go even farther, which is what he was always doing with himself." There were two ways to get results, Fosse told Reinking: one positive, one negative. Negative is when you force it out of them. Positive is when you draw it out of them. "If you ever want anything from anybody," he once said to Laurent Giroux, "the first thing you do is you put your hand on their shoulder and you give them a compliment, like 'You're really fantastic . . .' And just as they're going, 'Oh, really?,' you slip in what you want and you'll always get it."

On "Funny Honey," Roxie's phony love song to her fall-guy husband, Fosse seemed to be using the negative. "He made Gwen unattractive," Stevens said. "Some of the poses, the way she sat on the piano, Roxie was supposed to be drinking and he wanted her to get more and more drunk as it went on. Some people thought he wanted to destroy her there. Bob would say it was appropriate for the piece, but not everyone was sure. You see, you're dealing with very clever people here. Bob knew Gwen would salvage herself no matter what he gave her. Maybe that's why he was doing it, to give her something to outshine, to showcase how far her talent would go." Similarly, Fosse's original idea for "Razzle Dazzle," lawyer Billy Flynn's courtroom number, was a circus-like orgy ruder than the erotic spectaculars of *New Girl in Town* and *Pippin,* and less artful. Whatever satire Fosse intended, he lost to the gut punch of gnarled, self-humping globs of groans and limbs. He lost Verdon in it too. "That's the great Gwen Verdon up there," Chita Rivera protested to Ebb, "and look what they're doing!"

"*Chicago* was always cynical but there was supposed to be something joyous about it too," John Kander said. "There was this feeling that sex was bad. I don't know where that came from. It was ugly." It was vengeful, like a retaliation. But against whom? The producers, for banking on his early death; the dancers, for dancing freely, as if they weren't wrecked from bypass surgery; Gwen, for roping him into it; Fred Ebb, for questioning Fosse's story instincts; or the New York critics for handing Fosse — he could only imagine — the same old razzle-dazzle rap? Or was *Chicago* railing against the audience, soon to fill the Forty-Sixth Street Theater, for buying its own bullshit? Was Fosse preemptively hating them before they could hate him? "There was a feeling of tension all the time," John Kander said. "We didn't know what to do."

He began smoking again, Hav-A-Tampas and cigarillos, putting the dancers in the awkward position of wondering how and if they should ask him to stop. "I'm walking off the stage unless you put that cigarette out," Chita would say, and Fosse would oblige. When she went away, he'd light another. Once, Chayefsky bounded across the room and, in front of the entire cast, slapped the cigarette out of his mouth. "I felt pretty bad about it," Fosse said later, "and then I realized it was an act of love." Love — he could accept it only from Paddy.

After he left the relative security of the New York studio for tryouts in Philadelphia, Fosse's depression met Fosse's fear. "Going out of town was a sad time for Bob," Pam Sousa said, "because he had to let go. He really felt, leaving the studio, eighty percent [of the show] had to work. Once you're up and running, there's the added expense of changing the show and of course it's hard on the company, rehearsing at day and performing at night. In Philly he told us, 'I'm going to make this darker and meaner.'" Neon set pieces, part of the older, brighter *Chicago,* were discovered in the alleyway.

Rewriting the book, or getting Ebb to, Fosse could exorcise his desperation at little cost to the producers. But at great cost to Ebb; as Fosse's scapegoat, and a natural sufferer, he agonized through every rewrite. "Their angsts were not well matched," Stevens said, "and neither were their ideas for the show. Fred missed its pizzazz, and out of town he realized he wasn't going to get it back." Fosse snapped at him publicly, but Fred Ebb admired his director too much to deny him and was, by nature, too gentle to fight. During rehearsal, Candy Brown found Ebb in the bathroom, crying alone. "Why don't we get on a train and go back to New York?" John Kander offered one night. "This isn't worth it. No show is worth dying for." One afternoon, after a particularly dark episode, Kander, Ebb, and Chita Rivera met in the back of the theater to weigh their options. "We made a pact," she said. "We agreed that if one of us goes, we *all* go."

They were staying at the Bellevue-Stratford, a five-minute walk from the theater, and unwinding as a group at the local Variety Club, where an Equity card bought you drinks at reduced "theatrical" rates and where there was a little dance floor in the back to release tension. Fosse was drinking more than usual, putting Stevens in the tricky position of having to monitor him. On a few occasions, Stevens literally had to carry Bob to his hotel room and slip him into bed. "His suite was so clean," Stevens said. "I expected to see the place a debauched nightmare, with pills on the bathroom floor and cigarette holes in the pillows, but it was like no one was living there." One night, hanging up Fosse's jacket, Stevens discovered a closet full of black — shirts, pants, jackets — all nearly identical, one after the next. He asked Fosse where he shopped. "Gwen bought them," Fosse said. In the suite again, stumbling to bed, he said, "They don't like me, do they?"

"What do you care?"

Fosse laughed. "I'm not a bad guy, you know."

"I don't know," Stevens teased. "You might be."

"I hear Michael Bennett's a *really* nice guy."

"Oh, he is — nice, talented, good-looking . . ."

"Get the fuck out of here."

(Fosse called Stevens Mary Sunshine, and Stevens called Fosse the Prince of Darkness.)

"Is there a Hershey bar in there?" Fosse asked next, pointing to a jacket.

Stevens dug through the pockets, past a folded-up picture Nicole had drawn, found the candy, and tossed it across the room.

"My dad," Fosse said, "he used to work for Hershey."

No matter how late they stayed up or how drunk he was at bedtime, Fosse was never anything less than completely prepared for the next day's rehearsal. Turning to Stevens, who was Fosse's inside line to Michael Bennett (or so he hoped), he would ask, with increasing regularity and decreasing irony, "Is this better than *A Chorus Line*?"

"Bobby, it's totally different." "Do you think Michael Bennett could do this?" "It's apples and oranges." "But what do you *think?*"

Chicago's first preview was a disaster, a sign many took to mean the show was too nasty, but to Fosse it meant *Chicago* was not nasty enough. The anger he once turned inward, against himself, he now turned outward. Critics, dancers, writers — they were Fosse's post-operative antagonists. Seeking vengeance, he scoured preview audiences for signs of discomfort; when people walked out in the middle of the show, he would say, "We got 'em!" Their laughter meant they missed the point; Fosse did not intend *Chicago* to be a comedy.

"I'm afraid this show is my image of America right now," he said. "It's about the lack of justice in our legal procedure: how justice and law hardly function at all. It makes some interesting comments on the press, about the way they make celebrities out of killers, exploiting and glamorizing criminals. When you think of people like Charlie Manson, or see Mafia killers publishing their autobiographies, you can see that *Chicago* isn't just about the 20s. It says some things that are pertinent for today, for now." The poor reviews he regarded as vendettas against him. "I'm a target now," he said, "because of the success I've had in the past few years. People tend to want to knock a target down." They said the show didn't have heart; he said, *Heart?* In 1975? "*Chicago* was theater and politics," Verdon said, "Bob's response to Watergate."

Further marginalizing Fred Ebb, Fosse asked Gardner, Chayefsky, and Neil Simon to have a look at troublesome book scenes and contribute jokes. Herb and Paddy did their share, writing between them new material for Roxie and the "Cell Block Tango," but Simon refused to help. Ebb asked Fosse why. "Neil hated it," Fosse told him. "But don't feel bad." How could Ebb not feel bad? The funniest man on Broadway saw no hope for his musical comedy. "And by the way,"

Fosse said to Ebb a little while later, "why didn't you ever give me the rewrite on the 'Roxie' number?"

What rewrite? Fosse had never asked for a rewrite.

"We were in Philadelphia for twelve years," Kander said. "It never ended."

After each of the many previews, Tony Stevens and Kathryn Doby would work for an hour, collating Fosse's notes: notes for Gwen, notes for Chita, notes for the boy dancers, the girl dancers, the conductor, and Jerry Orbach. Stevens would take the dancing notes and Doby the directing notes, type them up, and the following morning, they would go door to door at the Bellevue-Stratford, delivering Fosse's feedback as if it were room service. But the inevitable morning knock rarely brought pleasure. It meant there were to be more changes tonight, changes different from last night, which had been different from the night before, and not always totally different, but generally *slightly* different, a matter of inches or seconds. "They were the tiniest things," Rivera said. "Bobby wants you to do *this*, Bobby wants you to do *that* . . ." Keeping notes up to the moment is part of any performer's job, but for *Chicago*'s company, finding their way was like finding the door in a house of mirrors. *Knock knock knock.*

"Come in, honey."

Chita opened the door. Stevens had painted black bags under his eyes and wrinkle lines on his face, like an old man. They'd been in Philadelphia that long.

"Just one . . . more . . . note . . ."

Most of the dancers were sharing rooms, two to a room, which cut down on Stevens's and Doby's travel time but presented the awkward problem of how a girl was supposed to handle Fosse's nighttime phone calls without offending the roommate whom he hadn't picked (assuming she had wanted to be picked). This midnight tension Fosse naturally used to his advantage. Asking to speak with one dancer and not the other, he sparked an arterial fuse of jealousy that snaked from the switchboard through the twenty-some floors of the hotel, often circling back to the first spark for the *other* girl, upping the temperature from jealousy to anger ("He called me *first*"; "He likes *me* better"), which he could direct — now that the air was hot and emotions malleable — into a threesome, either with him and them, or him, one of them, and another girl a phone call away.

The phone rang in Cheryl Clark's room around eleven. Her roommate, who had been with Fosse, picked it up.

"Hi, it's Bob. Can I talk to Cheryl?"

This was typical. No hello. No hi, how are you? She handed Cheryl the phone and withdrew to the other side of the room.

"Bob?"

"Can you come to my room and we can talk?"

Cheryl couldn't say she wasn't flattered. That afternoon, in rehearsal, he had put his hand on her leotard ("That's good, Cheryl"), and that night, at the Variety Club, they looked at each other differently. It was a look she understood, a pressure she recognized. Though relatively naïve, Clark had seen all the big girls go through this on *Pippin*. Now it was her turn.

"I'm ready for bed," Cheryl said on the phone, "but I'll see you in the morning for rehearsal." After the third night of phone calls, she went.

A full cart of liquor waited for her inside Fosse's suite. There was no need to pretend they didn't know what was about to happen. He poured Cheryl a screwdriver and they started dancing, closer, to Harry Nilsson, to Neil Diamond, and then slower. Another drink and they were touching more than moving; another drink and they weren't moving. The record ended. There was no intent in his embrace, no innuendo. He held her, not to take her, but to feel her, because feeling felt good. "He was so happy," she recalled. "I mean, like a kid. I've never seen anybody happier. He was in heaven and I felt fabulous." It rested him.

The attraction she had never known was there was suddenly there. "He was a beautifully built man," she said, "a gorgeous guy." Three hours later, around three in the morning, she fell to the bed, exhausted. "It was such a beautiful, intimate encounter, the whole evening." But Fosse — nearly fifty years old and just four months out of open-heart surgery — still had more to give and take. "We felt such serenity," Clark said. He begged her to stay.

"Bob, I've got to get some sleep."

"Are you sure?"

"We've got *rehearsal*. At ten in the morning."

"Okay," he said. "Come on."

He insisted on walking her back to her bedroom, though she begged him not to.

"We'll take the stairs," he said. "No one will see us."

"That's a lot of stairs."

"It's fine."

"No, Bob, this is crazy. You just got out of the hospital."

"I'm fine."

"You have a death wish."

"No, no, no. Let's go."

More than three flights of stairs later, she was afraid he was going to have another heart attack. "Come on," she insisted. "I'm taking you back."

Fosse shook his head no. Taking Cheryl's hand, he walked her to her door and said good night.

Weeks later, they were still in Philadelphia.

They needed a new ending. What they had was, at last, Roxie and Velma's club act, their happy ending, and celebrity's victory over justice. They might be criminals, but what a show! Consisting of two numbers, "It" and "Loopin' the Loop," the finale began with Gwen playing the saxophone and Chita the drums. They would dance triumphantly, and then face their audience to thank them for everything.

> VELMA: A lot of people have lost faith in America —
> ROXIE: And what America stands for —
> VELMA: But we're the living examples of what a wonderful
>   country it is.

It wasn't working, Tony Stevens thought, for the reasons Gwen said: Roxie needed her big moment. "She was screaming and crying and hollering in the lobby of the theater downstairs," Stevens said, "and Bob knew he was in trouble. She had had it with him." Stevens understood Gwen wasn't just out for her own solo. She knew ending *Chicago* on the cynical note that began it wasn't ending the show at all. The story needed to take the audience somewhere else; Roxie needed to change. But even that posed a problem. Roxie couldn't simply reform. It was too late in the 1970s for that sort of hokum. What *Chicago* needed was to have it both ways. If they ended the show with something sincere, even ironically sincere — whatever that meant — they would amend, slightly, the cynical pose that opened *Chicago* and allow the audience to leave the theater feeling good about feeling bad. "We had to toe a line," Stevens said, "between a happy ending and a hard one. This was a musical comedy!"

Fosse went to Kander and Ebb and asked them to ditch the two bouncy numbers for a single sophisticated one. After a bitter evening, there could be a kind of pathos in class. "Bobby was almost embarrassed when he came to us," Kander said. "He wanted to know if we'd be upset. Freddy and I didn't even look at each other. We looked at our shoes and said, 'Oh, gosh . . .' And we turned and walked out of the hotel ballroom. And the minute we hit the street we started skipping because we were so happy to be out of there." They returned to their hotel piano and wrote "Nowadays" in half an hour. To make their effort seem more effortful, they took the rest of the day off.

The next morning, while Stevens and Doby worked the dancers on the stage, Gwen, Rivera, and Fosse met downstairs, in the Forrest Theater's lounge, to hear what Kander and Ebb had taken "all day" to write.

"Nowadays" is a beautiful song — resilient, not tart; wistful, not saccharine — and it's composed of such rich romance, one could even believe, against the obvious truth, that Roxie and Velma really were as classy as they were pretending to be. What else could pass for good? Where there is no absolute, panache may be all we have — sadly, gladly, trapped but happy — and "Nowadays" is the perfect resolution, ending a show about the dangers of razzle-dazzle with a soaring display of classic showmanship: top hat, white tie, and tails.

Kander and Ebb had done it: the ending was, amazingly, ironic and sincere.

Gwen said, "I want this song, Bobby," in front of everyone. "Chita and I are very close, so this is going to be fine with her. I want that song."

Standing up to Fosse was clearly a struggle for Gwen. Though she had been a star for twenty years and his wife for fifteen, she was not accustomed to contradicting him in public, and it showed; her intensity embarrassed everyone. Kander and Ebb looked down, away from Chita. No one spoke.

Fosse asked to hear the song again, this time with Gwen singing.

She began. "She was standing at the end of the piano," Rivera remembered, "and there were tears in her voice and an unhappy feeling in the room. But she never stopped singing."

Sensing Kander's embarrassment at having to hear Gwen sing through such unhappiness — and why she was unhappy, they could not say for sure, but maybe it was because she had come so close to the big moment she wanted and Fosse, dangling it, still hadn't given it all to her — Chita spoke up. "Bobby, can we do this another time, maybe?"

"She'll do as I say."

As Gwen sang, Chita, her frustration mounting, scribbled a note on a piece of paper and slipped it to John Kander. "I was sitting at the piano," he said, "slumping, so I didn't have to see the blood that was about to spill." When he was sure Fosse couldn't see him, he opened Chita's note. *Give her the song,* it said. She just wanted peace.

Of course who sang what was Fosse's call to make. Ultimately, he had them split the number, a strategy he may have intended to provoke backstage tension that Verdon and Rivera could transfer on-stage, to Roxie and Velma. "Bobby, I know what you're doing," Gwen was overheard saying, "and I want you to stop. Chita and I won't go for any of that." Or perhaps by splitting "Nowadays," Fosse was doing his best to delegate, giving his stars equal time. "Sharing the wealth is a difficult thing to do," Ann Reinking said, "and Bob had to make them all equal and equally good. He had to be Henry Kissinger and Sigmund Freud and Bob Fosse." That evening — on the day he first heard "Nowadays" — Fosse told Reinking the song had the perfect melody, haunting, beautiful, simple, and true, and what he witnessed in the bathroom lounge reached the highest level of artistry and professionalism. "Annie," he said, "I just saw magnificent talent in front of me."

Chicago moved back to New York, to the Forty-Sixth Street Theater, for more previews. The former home of *Damn Yankees, New Girl in Town, Redhead,* and *How to Succeed in Business Without Really Trying,* the Forty-Sixth Street Theater was the closest Fosse and Verdon came to a good-luck charm, which was something they needed, now more than ever. On May 21, just over a week ahead of *Chicago*'s New York opening, *A Chorus Line* premiered at the Public Theater to once-in-a-generation sensational reviews. Bennett's "choreography and direction burn up superlatives as if they were inflammable," wrote Clive Barnes in the *Times*. "In no way could it have been better done." It was a landmark, respectful of its progenitors and brazenly innovative, opening with an audition number that Bennett realized with exacting and naturalistic attention to the most granular detail. As in life, some learn the routine faster than others, some wander, some tic nervously in a corner trying to will their bodies to move. None behave as if they're in a musical — and yet, *A Chorus Line* is half fantasy. Bennett whirls dream dances from his characters' confessionals, curling reality and hope in an infinite loop of objective and subjective time. His show is always moving, and his control of the moving parts appears seamless to the point of being innate. It's masterful.

"*A Chorus Line* is a great *concept* for a musical," Fosse told the *Times*, "but if you see it again, watch how much they sing and talk about dancing and how little they do." They do talk, and most of the time like they're in a TV movie, but behind Bennett's schmaltz is a real and intense passion for the entire theatrical enterprise, for wanting it, making it, living it, and, most meaningfully, loving it. Abundant with joy, the musical laid bare what Fosse made a career prestidigitating: a big Broadway heart.

A Chorus Line, he knew, would erase *Chicago*. "They can only buy one hit a season," Fosse told Ebb.

Chicago opened on June 3 to an ecstatic audience. "Well, we fooled 'em again," Fosse said to restaurateur Joe Allen as they partied afterward in the Rainbow Room. Gwen arrived in a sequined spaghetti-strap gown with a boa thrown around her neck, and Nicole came in an offhandedly glamorous floppy hat, a streak of blond hair bouncing down her back. Every day, it seemed, Nicole was showing more of her father's lissome appeal. Now twelve, she needed a chaperone for the boy-girl parties Gwen allowed her (with one rule: no closed doors). Leading her to the dance floor, Fosse watched his daughter with a smile of perfect happiness, as if discovering, in her, in her joy of movement, a creation he could be unequivocally proud of. The only trouble was now she wanted to be a dancer. A ballerina, she said. How was he supposed to respond to that? "I would say it's not a good life," he said. "There are so many rejects in the field. It's great when you're winning, but boy, it sure isn't when you're not. It can toughen a person in the wrong way. It's odd because the very thing that makes you good is the softness you bring to the work, the sensitivity. This business tends to make you callous because you get so many no's. You have to develop a suit of armor on the outside to be tough and protect that little thing inside of you that makes you want to be an artist." It would be hypocritical to discourage Nicole — after all, she had him for a father and Gwen Verdon for a mother — but what else could he say? He was a father. It was his life's other job to protect her.

(He had said to her, at one point, "I'd rather you swallowed flaming swords in the circus."

"But Daddy, why?"

"You get applause a lot longer." Then: "If you really want to be a dancer then you need to go to class."

She nodded. "I'll go tomorrow."

"You have to go today, every day."

"It's too late for the four o'clock class."

"What about a five o'clock class?")

In the Rainbow Room, word of Clive Barnes's review spread. *Chicago* was old news, derivative of *Pippin,* "one of those shows," Barnes wrote, "where a great deal has been done with very little." Again, the show trumped the book; attitude prevailed. Fosse's hostility was too thick a gravy for such a light dish. Where were the laughs? *Chicago*'s dud puns, yuks, and gags (all in the vaudeville spirit) had a way of making a gloomy evening gloomier. And then there was *Cabaret.* Hal Prince's *Cabaret.* "It was a steal," Prince said, "he unabashedly stole

Cabaret." Kerr saw it, Barnes saw it, Frank Rich saw it. And then there was *Follies.* Sondheim said, "What happened is [Fosse] saw *Follies,* he saw the last twenty minutes of *Follies,* and thought, *Oh boy* . . . and made a career out of it. Simple as that. I saw what his work was pre-*Follies* and after *Follies.* If anything, I wouldn't say he refined it, he just used it with great skill, like any idea, whether it's been used before or not, if it's wielded with skill is worth doing. If you look at the songs at the end of *Follies* and you look at the songs in *Chicago* and the way they're treated, it's the same thing." Certainly both shows made good on a similar device, but to separate effect. Sondheim's vaudeville is abstract, a metaphoric depiction of a nervous breakdown; Fosse's is representational, a description of corrupt America in show-business terms.

Where *Pippin* borrowed liberally from diverse traditions of world entertainment to create an all-in language for an out-of-time fable — Esperanto in dance — *Chicago* excavated vaudeville, the Hebrew of our showbiz past, to satirize the pandemic of our showbiz present, in which everything, even truth and politics, is an act. Popular American amusement has been around since the first Americans paid two pennies to look at the Liberty Bell, but vaudeville, the first industrialized road show, was the original shared performance idiom, spreading and standardizing national tastes, giving Americans their initial looney salmagundi of entertainment personality. *Chicago* turns the founding fathers of the Palace into folklore, a Brechtian-American commedia dell'arte for the post-Watergate era. Fosse replaced commedia's stock characters — Harlequin, Pierrot, Columbine — with the changeable personae of our vaudeville heritage. Texas Guinan (Velma in "All That Jazz"), Helen Morgan (Roxie in "Funny Honey"), Sophie Tucker (Mama in "When You're Good to Mama"), Ted Lewis (Billy Flynn in "All I Care About Is Love"), Eddie Cantor (Roxie in "Me and My Baby"), and Bert Williams (Amos in "Mr. Cellophane")

—they are America's stock company, parts played by *Chicago*'s corrupt and powerful.

Roxie, Velma, Billy Flynn, and the rest aren't *literally* the entertainers whose styles they co-opt, but they are literally American showmen, using a good act to cover their bad deeds, and the joke's on us: we in the audience are the schmoes who paid the pennies, loving every dumb minute of our own swindling. That was bound to offend someone, or a lot of someones, if Fosse got his wish. But *Chicago* isn't all jeremiad. "At first Fosse seems to be saying that America treats criminals like superstars," Stephen Farber wrote after the critics weighed in, but "he ends up saying something subtly different; that entertainers are like killers." Lie, cheat, kill, die. Whatever keeps you in the act.

Turned off by Fosse's vitriol and unmoved by the praise of some critics, audiences stayed away from *Chicago* for some time. Here Fosse could feel misunderstood. Where once he would have blamed himself, he now blamed them. "For a while," Tony Stevens said, "it looked like we weren't going anywhere." Then Gwen sucked down some of the confetti they threw at her in "My Own Best Friend" and blistered her vocal cords. She had to leave the show, temporarily, for surgery. And Liza Minnelli stepped in, but covertly. Fosse decreed there was to be no promotional fanfare in advance of the change, and hence no new reviews. If Liza got better press, it could kill Verdon and very likely kill *Chicago* when she returned. They would treat the substitution as they would any other understudy, like Liza Minnelli was no big deal, which actually made the switch a *bigger* deal, an inside secret everyone wanted to know.

"Liza learned the show in a *week*," said Tony Stevens. "All of a sudden," he said, "I was teaching her Roxie. Dialogue, staging, steps, everything." They stayed up until four every night the week of the show, switching from the stage (when it was vacant, in the afternoons), to the studio, to Liza's house, working in side trips to the show to see Lenora Nemetz in the part so Minnelli could have a better grasp of the bigger picture when her time came. Stevens said, "We would get in the limousine, run lines, arrive at the theater, watch the show, go back to Liza's, and rehearse. It was crazy." There weren't many changes. Fosse would cut Velma from "My Own Best Friend" to make it a solo for Minnelli, and he'd strip some of the ballet from "Me and My Baby." Fosse and Minnelli were in heaven. "What you have to understand is Bob and Gwen and Liza were show-business animals," Stevens said. "They *lived* in that rehearsal room, they *came to life* on that stage." Rehearsing the second half of "All That Jazz," Minnelli jumped on the bed, threw up her arms, and called out, "I love show business, Bobby!"

Minnelli's name would not be listed in the program or written in lights above the theater. Only a five-foot billboard placed discreetly outside the entrance noted the change: "At this performance of CHICAGO the role of ROXIE HART usually played by GWEN VERDON will be played by LIZA MINNELLI." A simple announcement was made before every performance. "When they heard Liza's name," Stevens said, "the audience just lost control of itself." In an era predating that of the obligatory standing ovation, they were on their feet for Minnelli every night she was in the show. "It was a rock show," Stevens said. "People weren't sitting in a Broadway theater anymore, but an intimate stadium." They stationed security guards on the street and security guards at the lip of the stage.

"That was terrific," Fosse said to Tony Stevens after the show one night. "But what about Gwen?"

"She'll be happy for her. She's a pro."

"Pros are happy for each other?"

Fosse tried his best to keep the critics away, but Clive Barnes threatened a *New York Times* boycott of Fryer and Cresson's future shows if he was kept from writing about the new *Chicago,* and the embargo was lifted. He wrote, "The cast seems altogether tighter and tauter, and although the far weaker second half of the show remains a problem, this Walpurgisnacht of Chicago in the nineteen-twenties, with its cynicism, irony, and biting wit, has some beautifully decadent charms." The show that had both disappointed and impressed Barnes now dazzled him. And the ticket buying began: seats were so scarce, producer Martin Richards, who had given his ticket to Julie Styne (who had given his to some high-ranking diplomat), had to stand in the back of his own show.

New York mayor Abraham Beame took the stage and presented Minnelli with a key to the city. "Never before," he declared, "has one great star stepped in for another on such short notice for so brief a period a time, with no advance publicity and, most incredibly, without any billing throughout the entire five weeks." It was the night of her final performance — so those people lining up around the Forty-Sixth Street Theater the next day couldn't have been buying tickets for Liza Minnelli. They were there for *Chicago*. For Gwen.

"Good," Fosse said. "But I could have done better for her." He might not have been talking about the show. "I could have done better."

To keep Nicole's heart unmarried to show business, Fosse deliberately led his daughter to all sorts of sports and literature (she was named, he liked to say, for Nicole in *Tender Is the Night*), but dance kept pulling her back. Ballet in particular. It was the basis for all movement, she told her father, as her mother had told her many times before. Tendues and pliés, he agreed, were pennies in the bank; they seem small, but with practice, each becomes a fortune. Talking like this, Fosse and the young Nicole, the Dalton School girl, seemed to be meeting now for the first time. He knew they had only a short window. Soon she would be gone from him, lost to her teen years, too embarrassed to dance impromptu with Reinking on the backyard deck at Quogue or to giggle openly. The day would come when she wouldn't let him

push her around in shopping carts, which she used to love, he dancing down the aisle, goofing on fake ballet to the supermarket Muzak,
she screaming out for more, *Do it again, Daddy, again.* Those laughs
were blood transfusions. "No matter how hard the work, or how depressed he would get over something, there was always an element of
humor," she said. "I could get him to laugh about things." Soon he'd
be lecturing her about drinking (with a drink in hand) and warning
her to pick her boyfriends carefully (as girls cycled in and out of his
bedroom). Soon he'd be telling her about the casting couch. But first,
seventh grade.

Exhausted, he tried not to think too much about future projects,
about *Ending*, but Aurthur's script needed his attention. They sent
pages back and forth through the fall of 1975, rewriting and interviewing doctors about medicine, hospital culture, and grief. Then,
suddenly, a shift occurred. Researching *Ending*, speaking with health-
care professionals about his own hospital experience, remembering
his symptoms and the emotions of his recent history, Fosse began to
give body to his own story, adding to *Ending* pieces of primary evidence he knew to be true.

Aurthur's adaptation was terrific, doggedly attuned to the quotidian trials of deaths, and grim. A little too grim. To lighten the mood
without compromising the principle, they took a cue from *Lenny*,
weaving into the hospital drama a series of into-the-camera interviews, all scripted, with various "doctors," "patients," and "research-
ers." Like musical numbers, the interviews commented on aspects of
the story, adding and shading and offering a kind of relief — that was
good — but Fosse and Aurthur still hadn't found their big idea. How
would they make this movie entertaining? (*Should* they?) Caught between death and Hollywood, they set *Ending* aside and turned their
attention to other matters.

With *Chicago* going strong and *Pippin* still bringing in royalties,
Fosse wrote urgently to Lennie Strauss, his accountant, suggesting

that since his earning capacity was at its highest, they should invest a part of his savings now, before the inevitable decline set in. Unsurprisingly, Fosse viewed his financial good fortune as he did his professional success — with suspicion. "The black attaché case Fosse carried with him was always overflowing with bank savings-account books," Julian Barry said, "and I remember asking him why. He told me he had put his money into a variety of savings accounts as he felt that was the best way to protect his assets. He said he didn't trust the usual route." As a boy, Fosse had personally defended his pennies, storing them safely in a shoebox he kept close at all times. Now that shoebox was diversified — perhaps too diversified. "I'd come home and he'd have yet another bankbook," Reinking said. "He had coins and dollar bills stashed all over the place. And when he felt frightened, he'd count it. Some of it was in socks, some of it was in a paper bag. 'Just in case,' he said." How much of it was there? "Bob was not a multimillionaire, but he had money," said Fosse's friend and financial adviser Kenny Laub. "When Bob came to me to ask me to manage his money, I thought it was a joke at first until he called me a second and third time. He came and told me how much he had and it wasn't an earthshattering amount."

Progress on *Ending* was briefly and pleasantly interrupted by a call from Herb Gardner offering Fosse a cameo (one scene, a few lines) in John Berry's film of *Thieves,* which Gardner adapted from his own 1974 play. Gardner cast Fosse as Mr. Day, a junkie who tries to rob strait-laced Martin Cramer, played by Charles Grodin, in an alley behind a Broadway theater. Regular members of Gardner's inner circle, Fosse and Grodin had hung out many times before, mostly at Herb's. "We had this jokingly competitive relationship," Grodin said. "At a party in LA, I asked Bob's date to dance very close with me just to see what it would do to him. When he saw it, he leaped off the sofa and cut in."

Thieves turned out to be a troubled shoot. Midway into production, Gardner replaced John Berry, and the obstacles only increased from there. A slow and stubborn collaborator, Gardner alienated people on both sides of the table, dragging *Thieves* many months behind schedule and forcing Sam Cohn into a tough spot with the studio. If Cohn could not keep his client in control, he knew, Paramount would take the picture away from him. But controlling Herb Gardner was even more difficult than controlling Bob Fosse. At least Fosse collaborated. Grodin said, "Herb said once he'd rather not do the whole thing if he had to cut two lines." With a phone to each ear, the businessman-therapist in Cohn tried to talk Paramount off his back and Gardner off the ledge, but all he managed were reprieves. *Thieves* was going to bust.

Sam called Chayefsky, Fosse, and *Thieves'* editor Craig McKay to join him and Gardner for an emergency dinner at Wally's. *Thieves* wasn't Herb Gardner's mess, it was *their* mess, and Cohn made sure they would clean it up, all of them together, with five brains and one heart. "We were Sam's children," said editor Cynthia Scheider. "He was like the king of New York and we were princes and princesses. He did not care if you were down and out. He didn't care about money. If you had talent, Sam would stick by you no matter what. He just wanted us all working. We were a family." Wally's was the family's dining room.

Fosse, McKay, and Chayefsky joined Sam and Herb at a table in the back corner, specifically selected by Cohn so they would not turn heads at the outburst he expected from Gardner, which came right on schedule.

"What do they want from me? I'm giving those schmucks every-thing I've got!"

"Herbie," Sam said. "In fairness —"

"In fairness? I'm in there every day! What do they want from me?"

"They have a budget, Herbie . . ."

Chayefsky spoke up. "Sam," he said. "Listen to him. Let him speak."

Cohn did as he was told and waited for Gardner, like one of the crazies in a Herb Gardner play, to run out of steam. He waited through several minutes of expletives, jokes, impassioned appeals — he was practically singing — romantic visions, political diatribes, calls to arms.

Then Sam spoke. "Herbie, I love you," he said, "but you're not doing enough."

"I'm doing everything I can!"

"You're not doing enough to placate the studio."

"Placate the studio? I don't want to placate the studio! Fuck *them!* Fuck *them!*"

Diners' heads turned.

"Well, you've got to do something."

Gardner's expression changed. "Well, fuck you too, Sam."

"Herbie, Jesus . . ." Paddy said.

Cohn waited for a retraction. It didn't come. "All right. If that's the way you want it, I'm outta here."

"Yeah, that's the way I want it. You're outta here."

"Okay, guys," Fosse said, "everyone calm down . . . calm down."

Days later, Herb's back went out. "Herb was in agony," said McKay. "He would drink Myers's Rum with pineapple juice and painkillers. We even tried working in his apartment. Nothing worked. He couldn't move." Their snail's pace came to a full stop, and Gardner asked Fosse to cut the picture for the interim. Baiting the hook by inviting Fosse to cut his own scene, Gardner hoped Fosse would stay on as long as Gardner was laid out on the floor of his apartment. Of course, Fosse agreed.

When he arrived in the cutting room the first day, Fosse told McKay he did not want to override Gardner's work, only add and subtract where needed. "Fosse never hesitated," McKay said. "He knew what he wanted and when he didn't; he'd say, 'Craig, you know what it should be. Do it.' But I have no idea how he saw anything with all that smoke in front of his face." Soon Fosse settled in. "He was cutting in his style," McKay said. "The way he went to certain places and how quickly he did it. He was always trying to get a lot of detail, cutting more than you would have normally, punctuating stuff with short cuts. He liked to get around a lot, image-wise. I think he got more humor out of it that way."

They were at it for three weeks, Fosse, McKay, and Fosse's veteran assistant editor Trudy Ship. "Craig," he announced one afternoon, "today I became a millionaire" (courtesy of *Pippin* and *Chicago*), and he took him out to lunch.

Another day, he was standing behind the Moviola, behind Ship, a cigarette dangling from his mouth and a copy of Kübler-Ross's block-buster *On Death and Dying* tucked under his arm. "You're carrying *that* book *and* smoking?" she asked. His reply was flat: "Uh-huh."

He'd heard about the book from Stuart Ostrow, who had bor-rowed its five stages of grief — denial, anger, bargaining, depression, and acceptance — to frame his first play, *Stages,* then still in process. Though Ostrow had left *Ending,* Fosse considered borrowing what Ostrow had borrowed for Aurthur's script, which in the spring of 1976 still needed work. The same questions remained. Chayefsky had weighed in with notes and the latest was out to Gardner, but it was Fosse's pal Pete Hamill who came back with the most inspired feed-back of all. *Ending* was relentless, Hamill explained, more like jour-nalism than a work of art. Fosse's problem wasn't dying-related but form-related. What if he, for instance, took those *Lenny*-style docu-mentary interludes and turned them into musical sequences? They could be illustrative of the Kübler-Ross phases. If Jay, the dying man, could somehow visualize these concepts, then Fosse could maybe give denial, anger, bargaining, depression, and acceptance a sort of grandeur that would make them cinematic and emotionally relat-able to all. And making Jay a dancer or choreographer would justify that kind of dreamlike maneuver. After all, one could not make a straight documentary-like film about dying, as *Ending* endeavored to be. It was impossible. There were no reports from the deceased, no primary-source accounts of life's final moments. The only way to show it was to imagine it, to dance it. To dance what it felt like to die? Did that make sense to Fosse? Yes — yes, it did — to be truthful about the unknowable, one *had* to invent. To know death, Bob Fosse had to turn to fantasy, to entertainment. Reality: That was the bullshit. But show business — singing and dancing and all that jazz — held the absolute truth.

ELEVEN YEARS

ANN REINKING WAS his date to the Tonys, held that year at Broadway's Shubert Theater, where *A Chorus Line* had moved from the Public and would remain for the next fifteen years. There's no such thing as home-court advantage for the Tonys, but nonetheless, *A Chorus Line* had it. Velocity and industry support — it had those too. "We were pretty sure they were going to win everything," Reinking said, "but you always hope." The nomination breakdown gave no hint of the outcome. *A Chorus Line* had twelve and *Chicago* had eleven. Bob Fosse had three and Michael Bennett (without book credit) had two, and their respective partners (muses? Best friends?), Gwen Verdon and Donna McKechnie, stars of each show, were up against each other. "It was hell," Tony Stevens said. "Bob was in hell."

Category by category, *Chicago* lost. "It was like you start disappearing," Reinking said. "You watch as you're slowly being erased." The Tonys were going to *A Chorus Line*, first in trickles, then in waves. "Every time they cut back to Bob," said Alan Heim, who was watching on TV, "he sunk a little deeper in his chair." Best score went to Marvin Hamlisch and Edward Kleban (cynical remark: "conventional"), best book to James Kirkwood and Nicholas Dante (cynical remark: "sentimental"), best actress to McKechnie ("You know she can't act," Gwen said. "She was just playing her own story"), Michael Bennett for choreography (cynical remark: "unimaginative"), and Michael Bennett for direction (cynical remark . . . none). By the time the envelope for best musical of the year appeared onstage, all suspense was gone — the audience actually laughed as it was opened. The Tony went to Fosse's old friend Joe Papp, producer of *A Chorus Line*. They had known each other since they were kids in the navy, doing drag shows on Pacific island shores, and Fosse barely acknowledged him on his way out. *Chicago* lost everything.

If winning defeated Bob Fosse, then losing was actually a running start. "Being depressed is not a bad thing," he would say, looking back. "It makes you think. It makes you say, what's wrong? Why am I feeling this way?"

"He put himself down," Reinking said, "then he defended himself."

Quogue: his parry-riposte to New York. There he worked on *Ending* with Bob Aurthur. Taking Hamill's notes, Fosse decided to turn the movie into a story of his own death, that is, how he imagined his death would have been if instead of checking out of New York Hospital, he'd never left. Tape recorders in hand, Fosse and Bob Aurthur interviewed everyone, friend and foe, who had been around for the *Lenny*/heart attack/*Chicago* episode. Fosse wanted to know the truth about that period, the mean truth, and started asking questions, which some took to be a pretext for persecution, as if by interrogating the witnesses under the auspices of Art, he could finally get them to open up about what they really thought of him. Aurthur and Fosse divided up the list.

Aurthur got Dustin Hoffman. "What do you think?" Aurthur asked. "Do you think Bob's queer?"

"Bob?" Dustin had never considered it. "They called him Mr. Multiples." Girls.

"Do you think he's covering up?"

"I would not say he was queer. But I wouldn't say Bob didn't have any . . . *characteristics.*" It went right into the script.

Fred Ebb got a call in California. Fosse asked, "Can I use the song title 'All That Jazz' for the movie? Because it's yours."

"Actually, it's not. I was reading one of the *Time-Life* book series, and there was a chapter entitled 'All That Jazz.' I took it from there. I didn't really invent it, Bob."

This impressed Fosse. "If there is a line that you take from some-body," he said, "you acknowledge it. I never do. The sincerest form of flattery is to steal." Clicking on the tape recorder, he asked, "When I had my heart attack during *Chicago,* when you knew that I wasn't going to be back for rehearsals for a while, and that it might have meant closing down the show, what was your reaction?"

"I was horrified, Bob. I was disappointed and sad."

"What about the rest of the people who were involved with the show? Was anybody happy?"

"No, nobody was happy."

"I thought people were happy. Gwen told me a couple of people were happy."

"Nobody was happy. It was the loss of a job if nothing else, and a concern for you, who we all clearly idolized."

"What about Hal Prince?"

"What about Hal Prince?"

"When you and Kander went to Hal Prince to have him take over the show . . . You apparently thought I was going to die."

The more Ebb denied, the harder Fosse pushed.

All through the summer of 1976, each of Fosse's comrades got a phone call. Each was told to speak fearless truths about Bob Fosse; no matter how hurtful the revelations, he wanted everyone's best shot. Herb Gardner said when Fosse openly condemned himself, it was not to repent but to be absolved, to be forgiven by someone who then says, You're wonderful, don't be so hard on yourself, I love you. Gardner said the pity play was Fosse's biggest con of all. Nicole confessed she knew all about the girls, going back to Mary-Ann Niles. She confessed she knew he'd married Niles because she was pregnant. Verdon, interviewed by Aurthur, remembered how Fosse, jealous of her talent, had hated her when they first met. Wasn't she jealous of all his girls? Not really. She knew Death was the only real affair of his life. Ann admitted that he'd changed after his operation. Chayefsky said he was punishing Ann for making him fall in love with her. It's the same story with every girl, Hoffman said. Fosse starts as their gay best friend; that's how he gets them. He loses them, Paddy said, when things get serious and he knows he's going to fail them. Then Fosse turns against them. Then, as he expected, he loses and — the slingshot draws back — Fosse is himself once again. He couldn't have anyone love him. But, Dr. Sager explained, he let himself be adored. For some reason, probably having to do with something that had happened to him as a kid in burlesque, he had to prove every woman was a whore. Those with self-respect would and should leave him. His only chance for love, Sager said, for a future, was Nicole.

As Fosse swam through these unvarnished opinions, in Quogue that summer, an idea for a ballet began to take shape. He imagined a company of boring businessmen aboard a cross-country flight from LA to New York, or vice versa. In midair, to the spoken music of a Richard Pryor or Bob Newhart monologue, an orgy breaks out aboard the plane, and as more suits are sucked in, the aircraft expands, opening up, pulling apart to clear space for the action, leaving only the movie screen and the seats to dance around. When the plane lands at the end of the ballet, the businessmen reach for their briefcases and walk off as they came on, as if nothing had happened. He wrote to Robert Joffrey in June 1976, accepting an invitation he had been putting off answering for over a year, since his release from New York Hospital, an offer to give him an original Bob Fosse ballet.

To at last measure his choreographic worth against ballet — perhaps the only true metric — was, at his age and in his condition, beginning to look like a now-or-never proposition.

But the ballet he imagined for Joffrey never got to Joffrey. It went instead to the movie Fosse was bringing to life with Bob Aurthur. Secluded in Quogue, the two Bobs took the best of their transcripts (almost a hundred, Fosse claimed), and began to discuss *All That Jazz*, their unwritten movie about a director-choreographer tired of mounting the same old irrelevant musical comedies and striving to make a piece of meaningful entertainment before he dies. What scenes from Fosse's life would make good scenes in Fosse's movie? Using actual names, an early scene at Wally's would have Bob, Herbie, Paddy, and Sam discussing *NY to LA*, Bob's next musical, which he's dreading ("the thought of one more time step . . .") but that he owes to Gwen, his estranged wife. There would be scenes from his past: strippers, an alcoholic mother, an absent father. The heart attack, the hospital. A hallucination. Coming to, Bob would tell Paddy and Herbie he has an idea: a movie of his life, strippers, mother, father, hospital, hallucination. Then a second heart attack, one he doesn't survive. He's dead. We cut to his memorial at Wally's. Bob's ghost is there, watching. He tries to get his guests' attention. They don't hear him. Why don't they hear him? Someone has to hear him. Returning to the hospital, his spirit implores the sick and dying to enjoy their lives while they can, to live while they're alive, and then in some middle-reality limbo apart from life and death, he sings a farewell number, maybe "Bye Bye Life," borrowed from "Bye Bye Love." Then his spirit expires. Hard cut: Bob's time on earth is summed up in "interviews" with characters from the film, and *All That Jazz* ends on opening night of his last show, *NY to LA*. And it's a hit. Hal Prince gets the credit.

Aurthur wrote a first draft quickly, in a week, Fosse said. But the new story idea had changed their working relationship. Returning to the city, the Bobs were unsure of each other. Fosse's idea for a limbo world between death and life worried the other Bob. It was too arty. Arty? Fosse countered. It's my brain. As in: Not yours, *mine.* "Bob Aurthur said that I was crazy, that it was far out, pretentious," Fosse said. "But I saw a big room with cobwebs, junk, old scenery and costumes, theatrical memorabilia; the scene was in the character's head and his head was a mess." They were a long way from *Ending* and Paramount had let their option lapse, so Sam Cohn, in search of new funds, sent *All That Jazz* to Dan Melnick at Columbia. Cohn admired Melnick. He knew his boss, studio president David Begelman, had a solid history with Fosse and would be open to teaming again. And he was right. Columbia picked up *All That Jazz,* and Fosse signed on as director, coproducer, cowriter, and (though he denied it) subject of his autobiography. Emotionally and artistically, the project was without question the most ambitious work of his career and, judging by his constant cough, very likely his last. "I've only got one more film in me," he said to editor Craig McKay during *Thieves,* "and this is it." McKay knew Fosse wasn't talking about retiring. "He knew he was going," the editor said, "there was no question about that."

Fosse flew to LA to meet with Melnick and begin casting. Like most executives, Melnick dressed his Beverly Hills home with impeccable works of art and a kind of standard-issue modernism that told artists he was arty and his bosses that he wasn't. Despite his house and shiny car, Melnick was New York all the way; Fosse liked that. His reputation tended toward the kinky, and his dark and wily appearance — he looked like a Jewish Cassavetes — did little to contradict it. Melnick wasn't afraid of leveling with you; he was afraid of you thinking he was afraid to. So he leveled with you all the time, compulsively, sometimes on subjects he wasn't quite prepared to level with you on, and if you asked for more, asked him to elaborate, he'd tell you, on the level, he wasn't quite prepared to, probably relieved to finally be on the level with the level. He was a truth junkie; Fosse liked that too.

It was time to talk stars. Who would play the character they now called — borrowing from Chayefsky's play *Gideon* — Joe Gideon? The studio encouraged Melnick to encourage Fosse into casting an actor *likable* enough to undercut Gideon's distasteful qualities. Jack Nicholson and Warren Beatty were obvious choices. But Beatty (after his customary period of intense deliberation) asked Fosse to let Gideon live at the end, and Nicholson, who took Fosse to a Laker game, wasn't quite the dancing type — but that didn't stop Jack from trying. When Fosse arrived at his house for a meeting, Nicholson came to the door in a pair of tap shoes. Fosse approached Dustin Hoffman, and Hoffman, an admirer of Bob Aurthur's, read the script and found it surprisingly moving, but he declined. Once with Fosse was enough. Keith Carradine?

In Hollywood, Fosse met Jessica Lange. On the verge of her film debut — the *King Kong* remake Boredom, Whimsy, and Flash had turned down — Lange was by all standards a beauty, airy like Marilyn Monroe but serene and more relatable. Few in Hollywood had any faith in her talent. "I think you're wonderful," Fosse said. It was catnip to a young actress. "He befriended me in a very unfriendly town," Lange said. "I mean, he really cared about me and how I did. He was a great friend. Nobody was ever more loyal and caring than Fosse and I knew he wanted to do something for me." In other words, they were lovers. He had her in mind for *All That Jazz*, for Angelique, the Angel of Death who presides over limbo, flirting Gideon's life away from him. That's how Fosse had always described his fascination with death — a flirtation. "This is a man who did not want to die," Reinking said. "But he did want to flirt." Putting Lange in the role, he literalized the metaphor. "When you think something's about to happen to you in a car," he said, "or on an airplane, coming close to The End, this is a flash I'll get — a woman dressed in various outfits, sometimes a nun's habit, that whole hallucinatory thing. It's like the Final Fuck."

Angelique, Fosse said, was the one character Joe Gideon couldn't bullshit. He expects her to be repulsed by the ugly, self-destructive aspects of his life, but in fact, destruction being her greatest achievement, the closer he comes to death, the more she loves him. Killing himself is wooing her. Fosse — the real Gideon — was practicing off camera. "He used to tell people how he was trying to woo me," Lange said; that is, he knew she was seeing someone else and wanted her all to himself. In New York, she came to one of Fosse's parties with Charles Grodin, her *King Kong* costar. "He assumed she was my girlfriend," Grodin said, "and made a quick move on her, which I didn't dispute. I guess he felt guilty [for trying to seduce her away] because he disappeared into another room and came back with a record from *Evita*, which hadn't come to America yet."

Still without a star, Fosse couldn't move on *All That Jazz*, and he directed his attention to putting Ann Reinking into *Chicago*. After almost two years, Verdon was finally stepping out of Roxie; and in February of 1977, Reinking took off from *A Chorus Line* — she had taken over Cassie, the lead — to step in. Technique and personality made her, like Gwen, a Fosse dancer nonpareil, but their intimacy — unmatched by any other Fosse dancer — licensed both Svengali and Trilby to push her that much harder, and more than just her body.

"Is it good?" he asked about the show one night.

"Yes," she said. "It's good."

"You think it's mediocre."

"No, I think it's *good*."

"I don't think you do."

"Yes, Bob . . ."

He refused to accept it, so she reached for a dictionary and took him through each definition of *good*. There was no mention of mediocrity. "See?" she said. "I said *good* and I meant *good*. If you think it isn't good, stop taking it out on me."

"He was hooked on his stress," Reinking said. "He knew the stress was killing him and knew he couldn't work without it. It was a drug like any other. I think that's why he created his own bad guy, to push him. But then that persona which once helped him actually started to hurt him. It hurt his heart; it hurt his mind. It hurt me that people began to see him as so dark. But he wasn't so dark. Not always."

Dancer Laurent Giroux suspected Fosse didn't want to be thought of as a nice guy. The two were at a party, standing in a corner, when Giroux decided to call him on it, to Fosse Bob Fosse.

"You know what?" he said.

"What, Larry?"

"You know, with all the *black* and the *brooding* and the *women* and all this *stuff*, you don't fool me one fucking bit."

"What do you mean?"

"I know you and I know that underneath that rough exterior, you've got a heart of gold" — Giroux pinched his thumb and forefinger together — "*that* big."

Fosse loved that. "Jesus, Larry, that's good," he said, his laugh taking over. "That's really, fucking good."

In a life apart from Paddy and Herb, Fosse indulged in goodtime friendships with guys' guys, like real estate maven Kenny Laub. Chartering a boat for an island vacation, Fosse and Laub could skim off the top where the deli boys plumbed and plumbed the depths. He might escape — to the extent that he could — the panics of work and kick back al fresco for a hot week on the sea. Laub said, "If Bob had a free evening and didn't have a broad he wanted to call, he wasn't going to call Paddy. He was going to have some fun. I was his break and Bob took breaks as hard as he worked. He was an extremist, and fun was one extreme. Kindness was another." Joining them on St. Martin might be Cy Coleman or Laub's close friend the comedian Dick Shawn. There would be dancing, eating, and time enough for nothing at all. With girls. "On those trips," Laub said, "I would *occasionally* see him reading on the beach. *Occasionally.*"

Partying with Fosse, Laub played among the beauty and beauties of show business, and Fosse, with Laub as his guide, reveled in New York's other high life: money. Laub knew money. Fosse did not. At dinner at Elaine's one night, Laub grinned across the table. "Bob," he said, "we're a bunch of chauvinist pigs."

"Showbiz and women." Fosse lit a cigarette. "Assholes and vaginas."

Meanwhile, *All That Jazz* had no star, Columbia kept ordering changes to the script, and Fosse, getting less young every day, had to do something, anything, before Michael Bennett made his next move, before the clock ran out on Fosse's knees, his back, his ventricles. He didn't have much of an idea, but he had ideas — plural — for an all-dance show with no book and no story, a Broadway musical written the way Bob Fosse wrote, in dance. "I think he wanted to prove to himself that just dancing was enough," Reinking said. "That he could make a great show without the other elements." In July 1977, a month after his fiftieth birthday, he stepped into Broadway Arts with no book, half a century of unsettled scores, and one question: How much did he know about dance?

Before it was too late, he wanted to see if he could carry a show, alone, on the strength of his own talents. He wanted to show those talents to be diverse, richer, and more expansive than his own style, having touched its bottom in *Chicago*. He wanted to escape the strictures of the musical for a paradise of free movement where no writer, designer, actor, or formal convention could stop him from checking off the ideas he had left to check off on his dream list. Refusing to be refused, he wanted to push the body farther than was healthy. He wanted to show that *A Chorus Line* had nothing to do with dance. He wanted to do a show about love, which is to say about dance, and he wanted to star. As *All That Jazz* was his life in death, *Dancin'* would be his life in dance, an autobiography of style. And it had to push him; merely too far was not far enough. For the project to interest Fosse, *Dancin'* would have to ask more of him, emotionally and artistically, than *Redhead, The Conquering Hero, Pippin,* or *Chicago* had and take him through a deeper pit to a deeper triumph.

Selecting the music was the closest he came to writing an actual book. To begin, Fosse delivered music director Gordon Harrell a list of potential songs twenty pages long. "I don't know what I want to do with these," Fosse said, handing him the document, "but I circled seven or eight I know I want to use." One of them was Benny Goodman's "Sing Sing Sing," a piece Jack Cole had used in his club act. Another was Neil Diamond's "Crunchy Granola Suite."

Language had a ceiling. With Harrell as interpreter, Fosse spoke pre-verbally, in images and rhythms, groping through the air for a melody he could bring down to earth. "I want to do a number for two boys and two girls," he might say, "and it needs to be Latin." Then Harrell would fly off to the library or to his own record collection, spread samples before Fosse, and match music to notion. Once the piece had been selected, Harrell would break the score down into danceable phrases and counts and render it on piano for Fosse to test his body against. It didn't always work out. Fosse took a Cat Stevens song to the mirrors and poked at it from all sides before turning back to Harrell with the verdict: "There's nothing here for me."

But it wasn't always that clear. Often, as if he were auditioning a dancer he didn't want to turn down, Fosse would have to exhaust his brain exhausting a song before he could permit himself to accept it had no life for him. But rather than fail the song, Fosse would fail himself. "I saw him in major black holes," Harrell said. "He was paralyzed. Nothing happened. He was staring at the floor with his head between his hands. Not saying anything, not sharing anything, not emoting. He would go over to the window and look out and sort of like leave the room for a little while. Or he'd get on the phone and call Annie. I remember one day he put the stool into the middle of the room and sat there staring at himself in the mirror for a good thirty minutes. [Sometimes] this could go on for five minutes. Sometimes for half an hour. Sometimes all day and I would just sit there, stone-cold silent. I don't get up, I don't get a cup of coffee, I don't play anything, I don't even go to the bathroom. Only he could pull himself up from this bottom. The room was full of depression. You could feel his machinery had stopped working. Nothing could happen. At those points, no person — no Annie, no Sam Cohn, no Kathy Doby — could even get near Bob. People understood that without it being discussed. There were occasions when I would arrive at ten o'clock in the morning, and he would be looking like this, like Bob was caught out there looking for a clue or a stargate."

But he could not force himself to move; he had to *be* moved. That's what they were waiting for.

"Wait!" Fosse said. "Go back. Play me that section. Do it again."

His body answered with a reflex, a snap — good. That was something.

"Okay, try that again."

To the snap, a flicker was added, to the reflex a wink.

"Okay, if she's gonna do *that*, then he's —" He pointed at the piano. "Gordon, one more time."

Taking it from the top, he worked on the mirror image. He'd keep switching invisible partners until the pieces fit together, then he'd call in Kathryn Doby and others, teach them, see it whole for the first time, and make the necessary improvements. His grandmother glasses dangling from a chain around his neck, his ash collecting on the lenses, Fosse would jimmy up the kneepads from his ankles and demonstrate what he couldn't say, in gesture to his dancers, in *badda-*

*dum*s to Harrell at the piano. "In a way, I was like a tailor," Harrell said. "'Take the coat out a little bit here. Hem that cuff there.'"

Harrell hauled in a trunk of percussion instruments to keep Fosse in the mood. Next to the piano, he kept a vertical stand of bells, a ratchet, and woodblocks in a half a dozen pitches. "Most choreographers would not be able to hear the difference between a piccolo woodblock and a bass woodblock, but Bob would know every time." When Fosse connected to the rhythm, he could achieve a musical clarity uncommon to many professionals. Harrell was floored. "He'd say, 'Put a wrist flick on the sixth count of the seven-eight of section C. I want a little *ting* right there.'" Micromanaging bodies and frames of film had been his prerogative for years, but excising the composer from the process, he could sweat the caesuras and sixteenth notes without objection.

Dancin' was a playground without a chaperone. Reinking said, "He was moving closer to absolute control."

In the old days, before Nicole could dance or think, the love they had stayed at home, in the slivered hours Fosse carved off work. But when she was old enough to have an opinion, he unlocked the studio door and treated her to his most vulnerable self. Looking to her face after a number, he got the truth no child could hide. At that age, Nicole was too young to tiptoe around his feelings and not yet old enough to know Balanchine or Robbins or what people wrote about him in the *New York Times*. She saw only good and bad. Fosse could count on that. As she grew older and prettier and stayed out later, they would cross paths in the elevator on the way home and walk their conversation into the living room. He would reach for a drink and put on a record and tell her about his day in the studio working on *Dancin'*.

"Hey," he said once. "You know what?"

She looked up — a teenage girl, admiring and faraway.

"Would you stand there, behind those glass doors, and do the ballet version of what I do?"

At night, with the lights turned down, figures on the other side of the glass doors looked out of focus, like memories.

The ballerina took her position behind the glass, and the hoofer changed the record to Jerry Jeff Walker's "Mr. Bojangles." At this point, it was just an idea his feet had: humble little taps. *Toe-toe, heel-heel.* Simple and depleted but crystal clear. Like an old-timer returning to the fundamentals. But the step did not take Fosse back to Bill Bojangles Robinson, the tap-dancing clown of vaudeville; Fosse's Bojangles was not flashy; he was delicate, almost ghostly. "Don't dance," he would tell one Bojangles, by which he meant, Don't dance well. Bojangles is too tired for the precise angles and splayed fingers of showbiz Fosse. He's a faded pair of slacks run through the washing machine too many times, the gutter soul of entertainment remembering all he was, which is all he has left. "I don't want a caricature," Fosse would say. "You've got to feel this. This is sacred. This is me." His memory—Nicole behind the glass doors—dances the same steps, but better, and with the glow of ballet to incarnate the grace he either had lost or had never had to lose. "The character of Bojangles never danced well, no matter what his age," Gordon Harrell said. "I've always thought the piece was about a phenomenon that exists in the dance world that every dancer faces—their time in the spotlight being very limited. Their bodies cannot sustain for very long the pressure and the pounding that dance requires. So, just as in the opera world, as the voice goes, the singer morphs (should he or she want to) into an extension of his career as a character opera singer." At the end of his career, Fosse's Bojangles is reduced to type: he dances in blackface, a panderer.

"It wasn't that we drifted apart," Reinking said, "it was that we got too close. It scared the hell out of him." Their old arguments, once fought at surprise intervals, took permanent seats in the front rows of conversation. They knew every word. She wouldn't live with the double standards and the jealousy. Yes, years ago she had said she could, and she'd tried to, but she couldn't. She loved him too much for that. Maybe that was her failing (they both said), wanting to change him. Maybe it meant she didn't love him enough. But she didn't think so. Grievance begot grievance until blame engulfed their whole history, shared and apart, going back to their parents and their parents' failures, until all they had left to condemn was fate, their shrinks, and DNA. That's where the truth game always ended. But not fighting seemed like not talking, which was like not loving. "You only love me because I'm Bob Fosse," Bob Fosse said to her. "You wouldn't love me if I was a butcher." That almost amused her. "Yes, I would," she said, laughing, "because you'd be the best butcher on the block." Hurt, he would try anything. "You know nobody loves me." "Bob, that's not true. You know that's not true." Then he would smile. "Yes, yes" — looking away — "I know that's not true." It was always going to be his mistake. Not just with her, with everyone. "Nobody's wrong here," Ann concluded. "Our dreams jibe but our reality doesn't."

It was a contagious theme that summer. Chayefsky had been working on a story about alternate consciousnesses and the primal origins of human impulse, improbably inspired by Boredom, Whimsy, and Flash's aborted *King Kong* jam many Wally's dinners ago. Somehow the old Jekyll/Hyde dialectic had stuck in his brain's craw. What, *really*, was "self"? What lived at the very bottom, and how do we get there? Chayefsky began with Freud, and the rest poured in behind him. Genetics, anthropology, biology, meditation, and isolation tanks chain-reacted a detailed outline for *Altered States,* a science-fiction postulate about a doctor, both Frankenstein and his monster, that devolves himself to an animal state. Dan Melnick convinced Chayefsky to make the outline a novel, sell the novel, sell *him* (that is, Columbia) the rights, then write the screenplay for the film, collecting a paycheck at every stop along the way. Chayefsky did — with troublesome side effects. Writing *Altered States,* his first (and only) novel, Chayefsky pushed through and peeled back so many skins upon skins of tender self-delusion and so pitilessly whipped his brain down to new and still newer depths on his way up to epiphany, he had a heart attack before completing the final chapter and woke up in the hospital. His doctors wouldn't let him near a typewriter, so he smuggled in a notebook and scribbled away when no one was looking, at last finishing *Altered States.* He was discharged. As he and Fosse yin-yanged across their table at the Carnegie — where both ordered the pastrami, though they weren't supposed to — so did *Altered States* and *All That Jazz;* the two works traded chromosomes, as *Chicago* and *Network* had years before. The razzle-dazzle of American media culture became the condition of modern consciousness. Showbiz wasn't just on TV and in the White House; it was in Americans' brains.

In that spirit, Chayefsky rolled a fresh page into his Olympia manual and, with the haiku economy of a master screenwriter, put down a few words about his funeral. "Our family has never taken death all that seriously, and the main point of this testament is I don't want my death taken all that seriously either," he wrote. "Do what has to be done to maintain tradition and then back to the comfort of somebody's home where I honestly wish everybody a good time."

Chicago closed on August 27, 1977, after nearly a thousand performances, and the very next day, rehearsals for the national tour began, Bob Fosse presiding. For five weeks, he overlooked no detail. After years of modification and careful realignment, his visuals hit his dancers with perfect accuracy. "In 'All That Jazz,' there's a movement where people have their palms flat downstage," explained Susan Stroman, then a dancer in the tour, "and they sort of wipe their palms back and forth, and Fosse always told us to make believe we had blood all over our hands and like we were trying to wipe it off on a wall, kind of like the way the Manson family did." After a tech run at Boston's Colonial Theater, Fosse appeared onstage wholly dissatisfied with the state of "All I Care About Is Love." Hovering above the near-naked girls — on their backs, their crotches raised — he whispered, smoothly, "I wanna smell you girls from the back row." It was shocking, unforgettable, and persistently effective. "You could see his joy and sexuality about what they were doing," said Maxine Glorsky. Touching a microphone to his lower lip, Fosse would purr and moan through the numbers, as if turning him on turned them on, which turned him on even more. "It was like applause," Glorsky said. "He gave so they gave back."

The Colonial's stage-door exit opened into an alley behind the theater. One night, walking out with dancer Carolyn Kirsch, Fosse looked up from his conversation to see some kind of commotion in the darkness up ahead. Drawn in, Fosse and Kirsch pushed through the crowd and saw it: a lifeless man propped up against the theater wall.

"Is he dead?" Fosse was urgent, in need of an answer. None came, and he kept asking it to no one in particular. "Is he dead? Is he dead?" "It scared him," Kirsch said. "He wasn't fascinated, he wasn't worried, he was scared."

It was decided that Richard Dreyfuss could probably play Joe Gideon. Released only two weeks apart, *The Goodbye Girl* and *Close Encounters of the Third Kind* lifted Dreyfuss's star and showed his mastery of the manic yet likable intensity that Gideon needed. A dancing Dreyfuss wouldn't be a problem — Fosse could cheat that — if the performance was strong enough, which it probably would be. So they met: Dreyfuss was noodgy and nervous; Fosse was remote. "As soon as we got together, you could smell disaster," Fosse said. But he didn't have a better option, and the production was running out of time. When Dreyfuss expressed his doubts to Dan Melnick, Melnick nailed him to the wall. "Sign this or I'll kill you," he half joked. Drey-fuss signed.

Finding exactly the right dancers was difficult on any show, but *Dancin'* had no parts, at least not yet. Without a book, freed from the cumbersome dictates of story and character, Fosse could hire dancers exclusively on talent and personality. There was no composer to fight for his favorite singer, no writer to point out the best actor. *Dancin'* was his, and the dancers were there to *dance*. Who blew him away? "So what do you think of that one?" he'd whisper to assistants Gail Benedict and Kathryn Doby. "Do you see anything there?" He was on a shopping spree with a blank check. "Eh," he said to Benedict, "that one looks like she has dirty fingernails." (What did that mean?) They roared in from outside — people waited in a line around the theater for two hours — and danced for Fosse all afternoon, for as many as six hours, and in all styles, from ballet to jazz to Fosse. What did he have in mind? He didn't know. Impress him. "He didn't want to see your technique," said dancer Christine Colby. "He wanted to see *you*." He wanted a full company of *yous*, principal dancers every one. No chorus, all thoroughbreds; white contracts, not pink. That too hadn't been done before. "We were afraid the show was not going to work," Benedict admitted. "We were without a book, without new music, without stars. What was that? It was just a dance concert." A talent show of the top talent in New York, a ballet company minus ballet.

He held callbacks.

Then he held callbacks again, this time to *really* see them, to audition the qualities in them he couldn't see. He had them improvise. They talked. Who were they?

"What's this show about?" they asked.

"I don't know."

"What are you doing?"

"I really don't know."

Jill Cook brought a snake to her audition. At the final callback, Fosse warned Sandahl Bergman to think twice about leaving *A Chorus Line* for him. "That show's a huge hit," he muttered, "and I have no idea what I'm doing, so I'm telling you, you have the job, but don't take it." This was, she suspected, the final combination she had to perform. She could twirl, but could she leap? Could she trust? (She said yes.) What about Ann Reinking? Despite their problems, could she trust? (She said yes.)

Dancin' rehearsals took place toward the wintry end of 1977. Sixteen dancers as diverse in look and personality as Fosse's musical selections met in a large studio above the Minskoff Theater with little or no sense of what was coming. Both a trampoline and a black hole, their ignorance precipitated as much imagination as worry and — to Fosse's advantage — competition. "We all wanted Bob's approval," Benedict said. "There were a lot of high emotions and people on edge. The air was hot." Perfect: where brains melt, bodies follow.

Benedict came to one rehearsal in a tight, formfitting body suit. "Gail," Doby said, "if you wore that the first day of rehearsal, you'd have a solo right now."

"Oh," she said, "you mean I'm still auditioning?"

Fosse's thoroughbreds were all stars, but who would be *the* star? Who would take the front spot in the big number? (What was the big number?) Who would have the most numbers? The hardest numbers? The best numbers? "Everyone was fighting for fucking everything," said dancer Wayne Cilento. "People were killing each other to try to get parts, and he knew it. He used a lot of that with a lot of the girls. He played them against each other." It fed the show. "He definitely used all that to get the best performances he could," Cilento said.

With no story to maintain, Fosse could recast and "rewrite" on a whim, making moves rational and impulsive to better his show and, as was his prerogative, to protect his favorites and punish his betray-ers. The dancers' best bet was to err on the side of increase, to dance harder and flirt more, with him and one another. The sparks between Sandahl Bergman and Blane Savage flipped Fosse's idea switches, permitting him new access to real offstage emotions. "He really liked Sandahl," said Savage. "There was a lot of giving her special atten-tion, always choreographing with her, always demonstrating with her. And all of this stuff was very sexy, so he'd be rolling around with her. And when Bob Fosse was focused on someone, it was a total focus. He looked at you like he was having a relationship with you. Other people would see that, and they'd want it." Savage reasoned that Fosse thought his open flirtation with Savage's girlfriend would provoke jealousy and that Savage would use that, perhaps against Bergman, perhaps against Fosse, in their number together on the floor. But Bergman didn't take Fosse to be flirtatious, not seriously; rather, she sensed he wanted to bring out the two dancers' passion for each other. Their heat could help him through a block. "You know," Fosse said, standing over their tangled bodies, "you guys do this every night, so why don't you just figure it out?" And he walked away.

Fosse watched all from above, on a stepladder he brought into the Minskoff. He would sit up there all day — Ahab with an ashtray — admiring, editing, calculating, "looking like a raptor, ready to dive down," Savage said. "He was the most compelling guy to watch doing nothing." But he was never doing nothing. Looking down on them, he was looking down on himself, trying to erase the defects he called limitations. "I've really tried to vary my choices to try to get rid of whatever it is that people call my style," he said. *Dancin'* was the fire; he was the phoenix. "One valve is still partially clogged," he told a visiting reporter, "and I still have angina, but I take medication daily." He would run out of the room in the middle of a coughing fit.

He was almost written off as uninsurable. The Shubert Organiza-tion's first attempts to insure Fosse were outright denied, forcing the producers into an expensive and highly provisional agreement with Lloyd's of London. Rightfully concerned, the producers asked the dancers to monitor Fosse as best they could. But the dancers didn't need to be told. *Dancin'* was their show too, but unlike *Chicago,* unlike any musical (was this a musical?), there could be no replacement if Fosse went under. So if he said he was going out for a slice, two or three dancers would get hungry for pizza. Socializing en masse became the norm. "We were always together on that show," Bergman said. "We'd dance together, then we'd hang out together." That worked for Fosse; togetherness gave him new insight into his materials.

The baroque emotional atmosphere took a turn for the rococo as Ann Reinking fell in love with Charles Ward, a singularly gifted dancer who had come to *Dancin'* by way of the American Ballet Theater, making him an object of Fosse's envy and admiration well before Ward's romance with Reinking — who may or may not have still been seeing Fosse — went public. "Everyone was talking about it," said Savage. "Bob was clearly getting off watching Charles with Annie just like he was getting off watching me with Sandahl. That's when Bob started to get a little bit competitive. He would say things to try to get her jealous; she would say things to try to get him jealous. It got a little crazy and a little complex." It was painful. It was an opportunity.

In "The Dream Barre," Fosse had Ward play a nerdy ballet student who fantasizes about the girl in his class, danced by Reinking. To the music of Bach, Ward's character translated his ballet master's dance instructions into erotic terms, performing on Reinking visual double-entendres that struck many as a burlesque of their romance and too crass to be funny. "It was obvious yuk-yuk humor," said Christine Colby. "I don't know whether he did it to subconsciously hurt them or to get more dynamic performances." That was the question Gordon Harrell asked himself as Fosse made "Ionisation," Ward's big solo, progressively more and more difficult, stretching him and the number to the point where "Ionisation" came to be known as the dance of death. "It was like he was killing Charles," rehearsal pianist Don Rebic said. "It was that hard." Drummer Allen Herman recalled they kept an oxygen tank offstage just in case. But Ward had the talent. The end result, the most virtuosic endurance test that Fosse ever choreographed, Fosse placed, respectfully, at the end of act one. The number finished as Ward threw his hands up and said, "That's all, folks!"

Ann Reinking's Trumpet Solo section of "Sing, Sing, Sing," a slinky, exuberant tribute to her long limbs and power, eerily slow and then wild, combined a range of small, insular movements with rocket-launch kicks and impossible extensions. She seemed to morph from panther to eagle, ending the number almost by climaxing out of her skin. Using the whole palette, *her* palette, Fosse painted the portrait of Reinking in full motion; Annie dancing naked, he told Christine Colby, alone before her mirror. Colby said, "I remember looking at the Trumpet Solo thinking, *That's a language, a language only the two of them know.*" Reinking said, "The Trumpet Solo was primarily choreographed when we were still going together. It's about having that strong, educated stem in the midst of improvisation. That's what jazz is all about. You're sticking to the structure; then you're free. Then you're back to the structure. Really good jazz musicianship is like that. You're constantly listening, constantly concentrating, and yet you have to perform. You are yourself and you are the music. That struggle is constant. It's about having wildness in the control." It looked like a fight.

The worst snowstorm in a decade froze Boston white and rerouted Fosse's dancers from plane to train. Power was out all over town, and the winds were so mean, taxis refused to drive. The production hired horse-drawn carriages to get people to the hotel. Stagehands met dancers at the station, taking them by the hand to form a human chain against the blizzard. Unable to see, company members were shuffled to the hotel and then down into the basement, where a strip of floor had been cleared for rehearsal. Bone-cold and lit only by candles, they worked in the shadows, aching and undeterred. *Dancin'* was the hardest show of their lives, as strenuous as any ballet, and, looking ahead to a Broadway schedule of eight shows a week, far more hazardous. Sprains, twisted ankles, tweaked knees, bruises, torn Achilles tendons, groin problems, lower back problems, muscle spasms, a crushed L4 vertebra; the comprehensive dance show invited comprehensive injury. The show that began with two swings (understudies) — one boy, one girl — brought on two more in Boston to pad the bunkers. "It was absurdly hard," said Gail Benedict, "like playing a Super Bowl every day." But there was no complaining. These dancers, largely unknown, were there to work, and work with Bob Fosse.

One couldn't be certain if drugs helped or hurt. Cocaine, aside from being the disco drug of choice, was, for a few *Dancin'* dancers, the only way to master the exhaustion and pain. "The dressers would lay out your lines in your quick change booth," one dancer said. "You pick up your tissue and there would be lines and a straw and in thirty seconds you'd be back out there." Quaaludes, marijuana, sleeping pills for hard nights — most everything was available and passed freely from room to room. A good policy was give to get; you never knew what you were going to need when. The counterargument said drugs made risky situations more dangerous, pushing dancers farther than their bodies could go, twisting ankles and swinging moods. But so what? There were more drugs for that. "We were so tired," one dancer said, "we weren't thinking. When a life raft comes, do you question it? You get on and keep going."

Early one morning, Blane Savage found himself with Fosse at the hotel's breakfast counter. Hunched over an untouched plate of hash browns and eggs, Fosse smoked, staring down at his food. "I haven't been asleep for three days," he said.

"What do you mean?"

"I haven't been asleep for three days."

"Bob, you need to sleep."

"I will eventually," he said. "I'm trying."

He had more than one reason to stay awake. A few blocks from *Dancin'*, at the Colonial, *Pippin* was playing the Shubert, and although it had been five years since it opened at the Imperial, Fosse was still trying to improve the show. "Don't spend your life at the mall," he told the *Pippin* company. "Teach each other. Give classes. Talk, learn . . ." The *Pippin* ensemble thrived on that kind of community. Helping them get there was his break from *Dancin'*.

"You look tired," *Pippin* dancer Diane Duncan told Fosse.

"I literally never sleep."

Reinking's relationship with Ward, who the dancers thought was obviously gay, puzzled most everyone. Maybe they didn't have sex, they speculated; maybe she did it just to get to Fosse, but the truth was Reinking cared for Ward, and from a purely tactical vantage point, it would have been foolish to provoke Fosse. She cared for him too. "All she wanted to do was please him," Allen Herman said. Bob was no longer her lover, but he was still Bob Fosse, her director, her friend, the best butcher on the block. "There were a few bars of the Trumpet Solo that stifled Ann," Allen Herman said, "and we were all sitting around watching him put her through the wringer until finally she broke down crying." Fosse called ten. He stepped onto the stage, put an arm around Reinking, and led her off, into the house and out into the lobby, where they sat and spoke privately, away from the drama.

But he would not be the best butcher without the blades he kept twinkling in the dark, like Jessica Lange, who appeared one day in Boston, dressed all in white, as if in snow scooped up from the street. Months earlier, he had had the idea to get her to the studio. She said, "He really knew the way he was going to get me was by dancing for me, like, so I would really appreciate his extraordinary talent."

Suspecting another man in her life, Fosse overrehearsed the entire seduction number, from the offhand hello to the lean-in and kiss. When she came in, he saw himself standing before the mirror, the lights lowered to let Manhattan through the window, then he would start, and she would fall as planned. But their meeting was delayed, and he soon realized that the other man, someone named Misha, was not just another man but Mikhail Baryshnikov. Fosse quickly dropped the studio idea, but he hadn't given up. Now Jessica Lange was in Boston, in white, in the darkened back of the theater. "All of our eyes popped out of our heads," said Christine Colby, and Reinking simply left the stage. The following day she came late to rehearsal. After a run of "The Dream Barre," which still wasn't working, she snapped at dancer René Ceballos, who returned, "It's not just *your* rehearsal, Annie. It's our rehearsal too!" and Reinking stormed off again; Charles Ward went after her. Fosse looked up from the ground. "René," he said into the hush, "she's not angry at *you*."

Labeling *Dancin'* a plotless musical ("They've forgotten there's a thing called the revue form," Fosse countered), Boston critics put the wrong frame on the show and then blamed the show, leaving some in *Dancin'*, as they returned to New York for the opening, to ask if they were part of an innovation or an aberration. "Precision and style mark the evening at its best; but too frequently they are in the service of very little," the *New York Times* noted in its review. "The hollowness shows; it becomes a gaudy and elaborate mask covering nothing: a deification of emptiness," another way of saying *Dancin'*, like *Pippin*, endeavored to peel skin from the bones of entertainment and evaluate the skeleton for meaning. *Here is everything I know,* Fosse says. *What am I worth?*

Only as much as you always were, the *New Yorker's* Arlene Croce replied, which was never much to begin with. "Fosse knows his limitations," she wrote, "and he knows how to make them look like powerful artistic choices marked by daring and style." He went big wherever possible. But by flaunting Fosse's showstoppers — powerhouse music, an all-black stage, breathtaking endurance challenges — *Dancin'* inadvertently revealed how hollow the old tricks were. One Fosse-imposed challenge — nailing his dancers' clogs to the floor — took footwork out of the picture, but "footwork has about as much to do with Fosse style as lariat-twirling," Croce wrote, "gyrating body shapes are the essence of that style." The panorama of human experience, of styles, evaded him. The showiness upended the show.

"Don't look too close, folks," he liked to say, "watch the rabbit, don't watch where it's coming from."

Soon after the New York opening of *Dancin'*, Fosse called Ann Reinking from Payne Whitney. "He was afraid he was going to kill himself," she said, "and this time he came near to believing it." She went to see him. "He told me about all the stuff they took away from him so he didn't hurt himself." It was important for him to put her at ease. She could see that soothing her calmed him. He could see she believed he was going to be okay.

"Love is total acceptance," Reinking said, "and the only way for me to totally accept him was as his friend. Gwen ultimately saw it the same way. The best way to be with him was to not be with him." They would talk on the phone. They would have lunch. Reinking was virtually starring in *Dancin'*, appearing about town in cabaret acts and getting her picture taken with other men, and he could see she was happy. They grew closer. "You can't kill love," she said. "You can mess it up but it doesn't die." Removing sex only nurtured the friendship that, years ago, had begun their romance, and though one could only borrow Fosse, he was a devoted ally, as married to Annie as he was to Paddy and Herb. "You can't live without trust," she said, "and I never stopped trusting Bob."

NINE YEARS

WITH *DANCIN'* BEHIND him, a star onboard for *All That Jazz*, and a script in working order, Fosse leaped feet first into the project, finally. Casting the film was an exercise in innuendo. "I want you to do the Gwen Verdon role," he said to Leland Palmer. They had barely communicated since *Pippin*, when Palmer played Fastrada, considered by many to be that show's Gwen Verdon role. Now he was asking her to play Mrs. Joe Gideon, practically a one-to-one copy of the real-life Gwen (Shirley MacLaine had turned him down, and casting Gwen as herself would have made it impossible for Fosse to deny he was filming his autobiography). Fosse had not seen Palmer for almost a decade, and when she stepped into his office, he took a quick look at her and furrowed his brow. "What's happened to you?" he whispered. Recovering from a difficult illness, Palmer had gone through an enormous spiritual transformation Fosse knew nothing about—until that second. "I know," he said. "You found God." But before she could answer (yes, she had), he asked, "Did you bring an orange towel?" That towel— he still remembered they put it over the lamp the night they didn't make love on the road with *Little Me* many shows ago. He had everyone's key: knowledge of an actor's most private trauma, a dancer's secret ambition, a girlfriend's biggest fear. Fosse could reach a hand into any head; he could draw from everyone's biography the very thing he needed to get what he wanted. Reinking he made audition for Katie Jagger, the Ann Reinking character (she got the part). Cliff Gorman, the original Lenny on Broadway, whom Fosse couldn't cast in *Lenny,* was cast as Dustin Hoffman à clef. He put Sidney Lumet in the Chayefsky role, and when he cut the part, he moved Lumet into Lucas Sergeant, Gideon's nemesis, who, like Hal Prince, wore his glasses up on his head. Jules Fisher, Alan Heim, Phil Friedman, and Kathryn Doby (excused from *Dancin'*) all played themselves.

To find the young actress-dancer to play Michelle, Joe Gideon's daughter, Fosse ran hundreds of girls through the audition process he reserved for child actors. "You're not going to read a hundred kids separately," Fosse explained to Larry Mark. "That's not what it's about. So what I would do was, I'd tell groups of ten to stand at one end of the stage and I'd stand at the other. Then I tell them to run like hell and jump into my arms. Only about two of a hundred kids would trust me enough to really do that." He added, "I wish I could do that with adults." Erzsebet Foldi, a twelve-year-old student at the School of American Ballet, made her way through auditions and callbacks and screen-tested with Dreyfuss until it was down to her and one other girl. To break the tie, Fosse gave them a single very little, very big task. "Will you light my cigarette?" he asked the first girl, kneeling down to her height and putting a cigarette in his mouth. Without thinking, she scratched off a match as swiftly as Tatum O'Neal in *Paper Moon.* After thanking her, Fosse brought in Foldi — Liz, they called her — and asked her to do the same thing. With the lit match in one hand, she took the cigarette out of his mouth with the other and then touched the cigarette to the flame like they were the tips of two fingers. Then she handed Fosse his cigarette. "You got the job," he said.

Relinquishing as little as possible to the casting department, Fosse and Aurthur swallowed their tensions, or tried to, for more auditions. They needed strippers, the strippers who torment young Joe Gideon backstage before he goes on. As the line of zaftig possibilities moved by, this one too young, that one too pretty, Fosse's mood darkened. The room grew tense. "Finding those strippers was churning up something in Bob," Ann Reinking noted. "He got a little angry, a little aggressive." Further unsettling his company, Fosse asked Aurthur to take a seat in front of him and read the part of Young Joe. Fosse gave no explanation, and Aurthur obliged. After the next stripper introduced herself, Fosse instructed her to approach Aurthur and "disturb" him. The request and subsequent interaction was so uncomfortable, Ann Reinking had to look away. Pretending not to notice, Fosse called for the next stripper and told her to really go for Aurthur. Aurthur, again, obliged him. "As he encouraged the strippers to be more aggressive and more aggressive," Reinking said, "something came out of Bob Fosse that didn't belong, that wasn't really directed at Bob Aurthur. He went back in time. It was like watching someone almost relive it, and with a hard edge I had never seen before. I think Bob Aurthur took it [in stride] but it was hard to tell."

Screen tests took place at Astoria Studios, a long-abandoned warehouse in Queens, across the river from the Manhattan skyline. In sound stages squeezed between factories, Fosse and Dreyfuss read actors for uncast parts, and Fosse's bad feeling got worse. He suspected Dreyfuss was talking to the actors between takes, giving them notes as Joe Gideon might have — that would be the actor's defense — but Fosse saw something else, a movie star usurping his authority. "In my test, they were fighting," Sandahl Bergman recalled. "I remember getting into the elevator with Dreyfuss and he said, 'Sandahl, I'm so sorry about this.'" To Melnick, Dreyfuss said, worried, "I can't get up there with my big Jewish ass and try to be a dancer."

To his pal Roy Scheider, Dreyfuss said, "I don't think I want to do this movie." They were having dinner at Scheider's apartment. "I don't like Fosse and he doesn't like me. I just don't feel mentally prepared to do this thing." Patience was failing both Dreyfuss and Fosse, but at this point neither could walk away that easily. Dreyfuss had a contract, Fosse a schedule, and Dan Melnick, suddenly, had a studio to run. It happened quickly. After David Begelman, Fosse's former agent, pleaded nolo contendere to embezzling studio funds and resigned, Melnick — without forfeiting his producership of *All That Jazz* — assumed the position of president and COO of Columbia Pictures. By releasing Dreyfuss, Melnick would incur further delays and additional costs, and he would likely bear the criticism of authorizing, as studio head, his own wastefulness as producer — a doubly bad proposition for any executive, but for one so new to the job, *doubly* doubly. Buying time without money, Melnick begged Dreyfuss to hold on; Sam Cohn begged Bob Aurthur, also a producer, to hold on; and they all held off from telling Fosse what everyone else knew: Richard Dreyfuss wanted out. Then Aurthur told Fosse.

"I want to play the part" was his response.

Aurthur was stupefied. "If I propose this to Melnick, he will say I'm crazy."

"You must support me in this."

Which Aurthur did — but Melnick shut him down. Fosse would not star, cowrite, coproduce, and direct a picture he was making *about himself.* It was outrageous, Melnick said. If making the movie didn't kill him, the critics certainly would.

Alan Bates? Alan Alda? Gene Hackman? Redford, Ryan O'Neal, and Paul Newman weren't right, Fosse thought, and De Niro too expensive. James Caan? Melnick still dreamed of Beatty. Sam Cohn called Roy Scheider — like Fosse, an ICM client — to find he was interested, even more so after Cohn sent him the script, which Scheider loved. Cohn arranged a meeting at Fosse's office, and when the day came, Scheider arrived fully prepared with a self-deprecating auto-biographical monologue and an overflow of deference and humor. "I told him all of the silly, wild, crazy, dopey, ridiculous parts that I'd ever played in summer stock and a lot of other places that perhaps he never would have dreamed that I would have played that kinda stuff," Scheider recalled, "because I wanted to give him an idea that in my theater background, which was considerable, [I did] fourteen years in a lot of very classical theater but a lot of dumb dopey fun stuff too."

"Look, I'll tell you what," Fosse said. "If you come to my apartment every night this week and read this script with me, I'll consider you for the part."

"It's a deal."

Beginning the following Monday, they met every day that week. It was soon clear that as Joe Gideon, Roy Scheider was wryly, wearily, sexily at ease.

"Okay," Fosse said. "You're the guy."

Scheider had just started filming *Last Embrace,* a thriller, for Jona-than Demme, so *All That Jazz* had to wait, again — until October, three months away. Shutting down, the crew took 50 percent of their salary, and Fosse split himself between shaping up Scheider by day and tightening *Dancin'* at night. Often, Scheider would follow Fosse to the Broadhurst to study him watching the dancers, recording his every behavior and the thoughts he read underneath. They made an amusing pair. A *Dancin'* dancer looking across the stage for a reac-tion would see not one but two Bob Fosses watching her. They spent all day together. Studio, theater, restaurant, cab. Fosse didn't need to say it: Scheider's task was to become him, body and soul. "Roy was so committed," said rehearsal pianist Don Rebic, "if he was there during one of Fosse's coughing fits, he'd follow Bob out into the bathroom. Then Bob would return with a cigarette. Roy too." Fosse worked on

Scheider's cough like it was a monologue, bringing him down to a deeper, gutsier hack—his own. They laughed while they did it, rehearsing dying to perfection.

Dancin', meanwhile, was fraying around the edges. "People were dropping like flies," Christine Colby said. Wayne Cilento pulled his hamstring; Gail Benedict took a spill after a grand jeté and had to literally pull herself off the stage. Colby had consented to swing, learning eight different women's roles before she started going on for men too, but she couldn't cover everyone. From night to night, even number to number, *Dancin'* saw more injuries, and there was more filling in than most swings could keep straight. "[Dancer] Jill Cook would stand in the wings when I came off and she'd say, 'Vicki Frederick!,' and then I'd turn back and do Vicki's part. Then I'd come back off and she'd say, 'Craig!,' then I'd do that, and I'd know which wing to come out of, and I'd come off and she'd say, 'Karen!' It was wild." Being a swing on *Dancin'* was the hardest dance job imaginable—in the running for the hardest dance job in Broadway history—but swings, some said, stood a better chance of survival. Using different parts of their bodies every night, they could, maybe, distribute tension evenly. Maybe. "Any dancer that lasted more than six months was amazing," Allen Herman said. As bodies were gurneyed from the theater and new, not always practiced dancers rushed in, *Dancin'* erupted with emergency scenarios and swings swinging for swings. But enough swinging, and wouldn't swings become principals? There was no time to think it through. Dancers had to be on their toes for any number, until *Dancin'* fell to jigsaw-pieces swings scrambled together in the wings of the Broadhurst. "It was a free-for-all," Wayne Cilento said, "because people would decide they'd be out for three numbers and then be out for the other eight numbers. They were picking and choosing. People were falling apart." On Wednesdays, two-show days, Gail Benedict couldn't walk up the stairs. "I had to drag myself up the railing," she said. Those days, a masseur came for the company. Certain bumps, certain sprains, told the masseur stories of old numbers. Kneading them, he read the Braille of shows past: here, the shellacking of Michael Bennett; there, the raked stage knees of Fosse. These bodies were the corrugated maps of old Forty-Second Street, preserved in hurt's formaldehyde.

All That Jazz rehearsals took over Broadway Arts. Moving from studio to studio, Fosse would check in on Ben Vereen in one room; Gene Foote and Kathryn Doby — taken from *Dancin'* — leading the dancers in another, where he'd offer small notes or ask to see it "once more, kids, do it once more." Then he'd go on to the studio where Ann and Liz Foldi were running "Everything Old Is New Again," the sweetest, most joyful number Fosse had ever created (intended to soften Gideon, as per Melnick's request), after which he'd move on to Roy Scheider, who was working in a studio of his own. Observing him would be Bob Aurthur, touching up scenes as he and Scheider uncovered new ideas for the role.

After weeks of discussion and shared input, Joe Gideon now lived beyond the script. He was now a character independent of Fosse's real life, a creation Fosse and Scheider could step back and interrogate. "What do you think Joe would say to that?" one would ask. "What do you think he'd do?" Scheider had been living with Gideon, and Fosse, long enough to know the answers, and the answers he didn't have, he was expert enough to extrapolate. "Okay," Fosse would say, "but is that truthful?" Meaning, *Do you, Roy Scheider, believe it?* When Scheider stumbled, like he did over Gideon's excesses (Where did all that *all that* come from?), Fosse walked Scheider through Scheider's own memory, drawing comparisons, browsing old songs for the right harmony. "Yes . . ." Fosse would say. "That's good. *That's* the feeling." Fortified, Scheider would do it again the new way, with *his* past for Gideon's, and more often than not, by rehearsal's end, his director would be squinting at him — not a good squint, but not a bad one either. "Are you sure that's right?" Fosse would smile. "You know when it's on film, it's forever." He'd ask for another take, then for one more, and on and on, chipping, chipping, chipping away until the chisel struck a nerve.

And that was just the acting. Scheider had to dance too.

He and Fosse worked at Broadway Arts for two and a half weeks of confidence building and reassurance. But the trouble wasn't the steps, per se; it was the dancing on top of everything else.

"You want me to dance and talk and act at the same time?"

"Yeah," Fosse said. "You'll be ready."

Anticipating Scheider's concerns, assistant director Wolfgang Glattes scheduled a relatively concise pas de deux — Gideon's duet with his daughter — for Scheider's first days of shooting. They shot it on a sound stage at Astoria Studios, replicating the Broadway Arts interior in exact detail, down to the smudgy windows and peeling paint. Fosse gave Foldi a few leaps and ballet poses, nothing substantial, and he choreographed Scheider around her. As promised, it was a simple arrangement; so simple, in fact, the dance seems less like a musical number than a father-daughter dialogue. Of course, it's both, just as *All That Jazz* is a musical and a straight drama, a film that tries to reconcile the two genres as Gideon tries to negotiate work life and real life. The emotional power of this duet comes from that frisson, the convergence of labor and love, a picture of Bob Fosse's perfect peace: rehearsing with his daughter.

"That was the first big hurdle," Scheider said.

For the film's opening number, a giant cattle-call audition shot on location at the Palace Theater, Fosse came to Scheider with an immersion strategy ready-made. "I apologize for having to do this," he said, "but we're going to put this thing in your ear, this little earpiece, so I can direct you from far away." They had only two days at the location, Fosse said; whether that was true or not, the tight schedule was a smooth excuse for Fosse to go almost *literally* inside Scheider's head without insulting the actor or impeding his process. "Bobby would talk to him throughout the entire cattle-call sequence," said sound mixer Christopher Newman, "and Roy, to his credit, never betrayed listening to someone as he was taking his physical direction from Fosse, who was up in a booth, looking down to the stage."

Gideon's cattle call was identical to Fosse's, from "Tea for Two" right up to the regretful, mutually humiliating "Thank you very much for coming." Fosse's earpiece directives to Scheider consisted largely of directives he wanted Gideon to give his dancers — "Tell her *this*"; "Take his arm"; "Smile at them." To capture the best reactions, Fosse had to stay flexible. He dispatched five cameras to scavenge about the Palace stage, as if they were filming a documentary about an open-call audition — the *real* chorus line. The sequence that was supposed to take only a couple of days ended up taking seven. Michael Bennett was on Fosse's mind throughout. To Laurent Giroux, Fosse said, "In this audition, I'm going to do in fifteen minutes what it takes Michael two and a half hours to do every night. And without dialogue."

Sitting in the back of the theater was Robert Alan Aurthur. Having completed his duties as screenwriter, Aurthur, as Fosse's coproducer, shifted his attention to the production — but was basically excluded. "Bob dropped him," Glattes said. "Aurthur had an opinion, and Fosse didn't want to hear it. He was going to be completely in charge." The biting pain in Aurthur's side persisted throughout the Palace shoot and into the examining rooms of New York Hospital, a venue Fosse knew all too well. Aurthur's friends Murray Schisgal and Joseph Heller came by, and Aurthur assured them he would be going home soon. The real problem, he said, was Fosse. "He thought Fosse was killing him," Schisgal said. "He was very disappointed and he was in a lot of pain." His broken ribs — that's what they said it was — continued to hurt through strategy meetings with Melnick, which Aurthur conducted from his hospital bed, and through pro/

con debates over whether to stop shooting while he recovered. They agreed that shutting down (again) would mean losing more money and probably ceding some kind of independence from the studio, and they decided to go on filming. Each afternoon, a secretary shuttled over from Astoria Studios to Aurthur's bedside with news of the day's progress, then returned to the production with his reports, and each afternoon, Aurthur expected Fosse to appear with the secretary. But, his focus on the film, Fosse reasoned that dancers danced with far worse injuries than Aurthur's and never went in to visit him. They spoke by phone. A week in, doctors realized Aurthur's broken ribs were only part of the trouble. A cough had broken his ribs, a cough from fluid in the lungs, lungs full of cancer.

He was dying, fast. "If I die before Fosse," he said in the hospital, "I'll never forgive the SOB."

When he heard Aurthur's prognosis, Fosse finally visited Aurthur in his hospital room. He then returned to Astoria Studios, to a cavernous sound stage where, on November 20, 1978, rehearsing a long white line of Ziegfeldian fan dancers, he got the news that Bob Aurthur had died. Production assistant Jerry Jaffe remembered that "[producer] Kenny Utt came in and told Bob. Bob smoked a cigarette, then went back to rehearsal."

Per Aurthur's will, a memorial party was set for Wally's the following Sunday. To Fosse, who didn't shoot most Sundays, it must have played like a dress rehearsal for his own memorial. Of course Fosse's would be better. It would have to be.

"Who's going to do yours?" asked Jane, Aurthur's wife.

The last time Wolfgang Glattes had AD'd for Fosse, on *Cabaret*, Fosse's set teemed with the excitement of happy collaboration, his Cy Feuer feuds notwithstanding. The current production, beset with tragedy, excess, and an even more demanding and schismatic vision, held Fosse and crew in a loop of frustration and awe. Glattes was the cage protecting both sides, a task generally delegated to the producer. "With each movie he got more frustrated," the AD said. "You had to get to know his problems or know what *would be* a problem. Driving to the set every morning, I would tell him what problems to expect so he could work around them." Scheduling the shoot on production boards — interlocking accordion panels, each lined with colored stripes for every scene, each scene movable in case of delays or changes — Glattes represented the ideal confluence of pragmatism and art, and as Kathryn Doby's husband, he was not suspected of treachery. Glattes carried the rainbow boards with him wherever he went, becoming Fosse's voice of reason on the set, as Alan Heim would be in postproduction. "Fosse had nobody looking out for him," script supervisor Lynn Lovett said. "Kathryn and Wolf were able to be strict with him in a way nobody else could." If Fosse's clothes were covered in ash, Doby had him change; if Glattes caught a crew member working on a crossword puzzle, he calmly asked him to put it away. "Wolf and Kathryn were his caretakers," Lovett said.

Weekends, Glattes and Fosse spent location scouting. They took art director Phil Rosenberg to twenty-five different hospitals, and at each one, Fosse insisted on watching an operation. "His favorite was the hip operation," Glattes said, "because in those days hip operations were the bloodiest of all. It made his day when he could see one first thing in the morning."

"What is it like if you've been through a bypass and then have another heart attack?" Scheider asked his director.

"It's like having an enormous weight, like an anvil, pressing down on your chest."

Built but never opened, Brooklyn's Woodhull Medical Center was the perfect location. With no patients to work around, Fosse could smoke up the halls and generally do as he pleased. By his side at all times, Nancy Bird, head nurse of one of St. Luke's cardiac care units, acted as technical adviser. "I was surprised," she said. "Rather than medicine, he wanted to talk about his feelings, how scared he was when he went into surgery. And as he was talking to me, he of course had a cigarette in his mouth. We joked about that."

"Nancy," he would say, "could you come over here and take a look at Roy's face? Is his coloring right?"

She'd look. "Well, is this how you remember it?"

Authenticity took time. "His stress was incredible," Bird said. "The film was going way over budget. People didn't know whether their scenes were going to be cut. Everyone was just waiting to hear."

All That Jazz was indeed going over, way over, and there was no plan to make up for lost time. On *Sweet Charity* Fosse had storyboarded — which was helpful when it came to pinning down a schedule — but beginning with *Lenny,* he discovered a new freedom in delaying his decisions to the final moment. On *All That Jazz*, his opacity was even more extreme. Few people (other than Glattes) could tell what he was thinking. It wasn't that Fosse was indecisive; he just needed to be there, to see it. "I'd say more than fifty percent of the time on the set was consumed with Fosse trying to figure out how he wanted to shoot it," said Christopher Newman. Unavailable for conversation even during lunch, Fosse could be seen dancing in a corner, a sandwich in one hand and his viewfinder in the other, throwing poses at a mirror he kept for himself. To accommodate Fosse's new ideas, Glattes would break open his production board like a rib cage and rearrange its moving pieces of days, scenes, locations, and actors, minimizing losses wherever possible. Cast and crew buses left Columbus Circle for Astoria at five thirty in the morning, so nearing evening, Glattes and Kenneth Utt had to be careful — overtime was another expense. "At seven o'clock," remembered Lynn Lovett, "Wolf would have to tell Bob, quietly, 'Last shot. That's enough,'" and Fosse would step back from the camera, alive but somewhere else.

After the final shot of the day, Fosse poured himself an ice-cold glass of Pinot Grigio — a signal to all that land was in sight. A round of tired applause followed Fosse and his A-team into a van that took them to dailies, where more wine awaited them — but not to party with. "Dailies are for work, not for popcorn," cinematographer Giuseppe Rottuno said in his rickety English. To protect his focus, Fosse sequestered himself with Heim in the back of the theater, behind Rottuno, a bite-size giant renowned for his work with Visconti and Fellini. Fosse's "Peppino, what would Fellini do here?" was met regularly with Peppino's "Bob, what would *you* do here?" "No one was even allowed to laugh," Lynn Lovett said, "not even at the funny parts. Fosse thought dailies were where you went to learn what you were doing wrong."

While Fosse filmed, Heim and associate editor David Ray synced dailies in their editing suite in the Brill Building, directly across from 1600 Broadway, where Fosse had cut *Lenny* and *Cabaret*. At some point or another, virtually every editor and every director in New York made that square block of midtown his or her home away from home, but only Fosse's team was working with shooting ratios of twenty to one, more than Fosse had ever shot on a single picture, and far more than Woody Allen, Sidney Lumet, Martin Scorsese, or Robert Benton — neighbors and hall mates — ever expected to.

But all that film did not necessarily grant Alan Heim freedom to discover. Unlike *Lenny*, written linearly in large, spacious scenes that allowed Heim to jazz freely from sound to image and unearth his own hidden links, *All That Jazz*'s script, which had been written with Fosse time already built into it, somewhat constricted Heim. "It made it difficult to move things around," Heim said, "to discover, the way we had on *Lenny*." Assistant Wende Phifer sensed his frustration. "At times, Alan felt like he was working as a pair of hands," she said. Why shoot so much film if you're not going to use it? Why get all those angles if the picture's already cut on paper? Having lived with *All That Jazz* in some form for so long — to some degree, his whole life — Fosse found that releasing it from his imagination to the noisy rewind wheels of Heim's Moviola was, as David Ray said, "a process of slowly waking up from the dream where everything's possible." That was a death Fosse had to grieve. "When I was younger, the ideas would just come naturally to me," he told Ray late one night in the Brill Building. "Now I have to struggle. I have to think things through. It's like a deadness."

Fosse's despair bewildered Ray. He thought *All That Jazz* had the best footage of Fosse's career, some of the best film he had ever seen — gorgeous, layered, tough, ecstatic, funny, depressing. But Ray wouldn't show his enthusiasm. "Bob wanted you to be hard on him," he said, "so it was difficult to say you liked it, and I really liked it. I loved it." On guard for yes men, Fosse was near inconsolable. "There's no dress rehearsal for life," he told Phifer. "This is it. Every day, every moment, *this* is the show." Biographical incisions crosscut Fosse into his own life, from the screen to his past. "Everyone left in my family has heart disease," he confessed as they cut the open-heart-surgery footage. Outside their window, the lights came on over midtown, and he sang the blues about his father, a slumped, potato-faced runner-up who used to dress in drag and sing and dance at family gatherings. "That unnerved Bob," Phifer said. "Talking about his dad made him uncomfortable." Cutting the flashback scene of the young Joe Gideon, backstage, ensnared by strippers, he said, "That's exactly what it was like."

They shot the scene in the cramped underground dressing room at the Village Gate, mostly unchanged since the forties. Keith Gordon played the young Joe Gideon (Danny Ruvolo, originally cast in the part, had been killed in a car crash). This was Gordon's biggest and best role yet, and he was incredibly nervous the day of the shoot. On top of the nervousness, he felt unworthy. And he sensed Fosse was doing it — *he* was making him feel bad. He hadn't said anything to Gordon all day, and the kid was beginning to blame himself. Had he done something wrong? Wasn't Fosse supposed to be engaging him, pushing him farther and deeper, the way he had, so famously, pushed Valerie Perrine to her Oscar-nominated performance in *Lenny*? Gordon knew better than to interrupt Fosse, who was whispering to Peppino in a corner of the set, but if he didn't ask for direction, he might fumble the scene and end up alienating his director even more.

The sexual nature of the scene intensified Gordon's anxiety. Of the three naked strippers, one was actually a man, and one — a haggard, drunken actress in middle age — told him, between takes, exactly how she was going to fuck him when the shoot was over. Reporting this to Fosse would only make him look even more like an amateur, so Gordon had to keep it to himself and roll with the punches like a pro. But he wasn't a pro. At seventeen, he hadn't had any real sexual experience — less, in fact, than most boys his age. Really, he knew more about acting than girls.

Gordon looked up. Fosse, stepping through a cloud of smoke, was coming toward him. Finally, he thought, peace of mind. The guidance he was looking for.

"It would be great," Fosse murmured, "if you could really get hard in this scene."

Gordon said nothing.

"It would look more real that way."

Fosse walked away.

He'd failed before he had even begun. Even if he could get an erection, which he surely couldn't under those hot lights and with the entire crew watching him, the fear of humiliation would destroy his concentration. So either way — pleasing Fosse or disappointing him — Gordon would be failing, as an actor and as a man. The scene was ruined. "Looking back," Gordon said, "I realize that was exactly what he was going for — getting that panic on my face."

"That's exactly what it was like," Fosse had said to Phifer. "It was too much for a kid." And yet he never spoke of Gideon as "me," and he recoiled when Heim pointed out the obvious similarities. Pre-empting charges of egomania, Fosse encouraged people to think of his creation as just that — a creation. But his artistic principles undercut the impulse; obsessed with truth, he invited the comparison, even welcomed it, down to the address on Joe Gideon's bottle of Dexedrine — 61 West Fifty-Eighth Street — a made-up address three numbers from 58 West Fifty-Eighth Street, his own.

More footage came in all the time. Struggling to lead his crew through a particularly tricky shot, Fosse called for ten and excused himself from the set to visit the lucky dancing shoes he kept in his dressing room. On his way back he ran into sound mixer Christopher Newman. "What's going on here? Why can't we get this?"

"The crew's tired," Newman explained.

"Why are they so tired?"

"They don't take the same kind of pills you do."

Genuinely surprised, Fosse asked, "How do you know about the pills?"

"I read the script."

"Well, don't let it get around."

Delays persisted to such an extent, Sidney Lumet had to drop out to keep his own film on schedule, and Sam Cohn kept an eye out for replacements. In dailies with Robert Young's *Rich Kids*, Cohn tugged at John Lithgow's sleeve. "Hey, could you do this role for Bobby?" Lithgow didn't hesitate. "Fosse loved the character of Lucas Sergeant," Lithgow said, "because it was a devilish parody of every one of his rivals: Mike Nichols, Hal Prince, Michael Bennett, Gower Champion. He would make wonderful withering jokes at their expense as he was directing the scenes." Rehearsing one of Lithgow's two scheduled scenes, a "seduction" of Sergeant by a traitorous producer, Fosse caught Lithgow lasciviously drumming his fingers as he contemplated the producer's offer. "That was great," Fosse said after the run, "make sure you drum your fingers in the shot." No one in Fosse's shot, Lithgow realized, was exempt from choreography. Even sitting, actors were dancing.

"Hey, John," Fosse said at the end of their second scene. "Do you think you might be able to come up to SUNY Purchase with us?"

"Sure. What for?"

"'Bye Bye Life,'" Fosse said. "The big rock number in the end. I want you to be in the crowd."

He wanted everyone to be in the crowd — everyone important to Joe Gideon and, in most cases, important to Bob Fosse — to watch Gideon, hallucinating in reality, sing goodbye in his mind, absolved by all for all in his last moments of consciousness.

There was no time to skip shooting on New Year's Eve 1979. In between gifts and champagne, the crew filmed every variation on Joe Gideon's bathroom ritual. Fosse staged his daily round of pills, Alka-Seltzer, eye drops, and — hands out in front — "It's showtime, folks" directed at a mirror framed in lights, evoking an actor's dressing room before he hits the stage, and a stage is what Gideon's life is, where his performance of lies, charm, and denial — of his condition, of reality — rivals the razzle-dazzle it's his job to create.

Fosse's clever arrangement of musical numbers describes a feature-length surrender of outer razzle-dazzle to inner. From the opening cattle-call number, "On Broadway," to Gideon's imagined "Bye Bye Life," *All That Jazz* fades from stage-bound numbers set in naturalistic theatrical environments to performances staged in the cluttered proscenium of Gideon's mind, a descent from consciousness to the surreal. As *Cabaret* twisted entertainment to show corruption (and vice versa), and *Lenny* structured Bruce's monologues to better "sing" his life (and vice versa), *All That Jazz* slowly erases the line between onstage and off-, bullshit and truth, finally wedding the creative impulse to death. Death, Fosse's entertainment says, actually gives life; so-called life is just a vaudeville. And vice versa.

"I hate show business," Joe says to Katie.

"But, Joe, you *love* show business."

"That's right." He tips his hat. "I can go either way."

As Gideon comes to his end and his numbers leave the stage, the "Showtime!" affirmations begin to lose their pep, one by one. Slight variations in tempo and imagery convey the physical breakdown Fosse pairs to Gideon's mental breakdown, the stripping away of pretense that leads him to recognize the bullshit in his own work. Gideon's deconstruction of his "Take Off with Us" number — adapted from the airplane orgy ballet Fosse considered mounting for Joffrey — shows his creative and destructive processes to be one and the same, a Möbius strip of relief and despair, death and imagination. Beginning as a light, family-friendly frolic ("Thanks a lot, but it's not exactly over yet"), "Take Off with Us" shatters into "Airotica," a dark burst of sexual fragments ("Now Sinatra will never record it"). Death brings him to the light.

With "Airotica" choreographed and ready to shoot, Fosse announced, in front of the dancers, that he wanted the number to climax with Cheryl Clark taking her top off and writhing on the scaffolding. Clark was stunned; she'd already screen-tested in a sexy black top; she'd already recorded the vocals. No one had said anything about nudity. "This was Friday night," she recalled, "and the number was going to be shot Monday. That was like having a gun to my fucking head." When she resisted, Fosse escorted her to a back office at Astoria Studios where he could attempt to manipulate her in private. She cut him off before he could.

"Bob, there's no nudity clause in my contract."

"There isn't?"

"You know there isn't."

He tried to whimper. "But it will save the number . . ."

"I've seen you exploit girls since I was twenty-one years old and you're not going to exploit me."

She walked off the picture. With no time to lose, Fosse called San-dahl Bergman in LA and convinced her to get on a plane, right away ("I need a favor," he said), to dance the topless lead in "Airotica." It was a bittersweet offer. Bergman had grown up with Cheryl Clark in Kansas — they had had the same dance teachers; their moms were best friends — and she knew filling in for her would be seen as a kind of betrayal. "It was a horrible situation," Bergman said. "I felt bad for Cheryl, I felt bad for me." The next morning, a car picked her up at JFK and drove her to Astoria, where she learned the number in three days.

After they shot it, Fosse took Bergman out to a thank-you dinner. Early in the meal, he put on his little-boy face.

"The dailies, they're really stunning. Everyone thinks you're really good."

She nodded, smiled.

"Sandahl, I'm behind schedule. They're on me."

This was not a lie. He had shut down production for three full weeks to rehearse "Airotica," running up further delays and expenses. It was extreme even for Fosse; he used over twenty-five setups to shoot the number, vowing to an incredulous Albert Wolsky that each would make its way into the final cut (they all would). And now he was paying for all of it. Or, rather, Melnick was.

"I'd like to call up Danny Melnick," Fosse told Bergman, "and I'd like to invite him to dinner with us. I think maybe . . . you and he —"

She knew then he was pimping her. "Bob, if you call Melnick, I'm leaving."

(Fosse didn't call Melnick. He didn't get more money.)

The film's finale — opening night of Gideon's *NY to LA,* which debuts, appropriately, after Gideon's death — was scheduled to film at the grand concert hall at SUNY Purchase toward the end of the shoot. It would follow "Bye Bye Life." The film's sendoff, the opening-night number needed to up the ante on all that had preceded it, and as Gideon's last testament (for which Lucas Sergeant gets the credit), it needed to be a tour de force for maximum irony. Fosse and designer Tony Walton had the whole thing figured: *NY to LA* would begin as a Flentrop tracker organ, one of the largest portable organs in existence, is rolled onstage, completely concealed by a scrim of the New York skyline, with a skyscraper hiding every pipe. A dramatic cross-fade would reveal the organ, transforming it into the city, and then, with a mighty chord, the organ was to slide offstage, revealing LA, this time a palm tree hiding behind every pipe. All hail Lucas Sergeant, genius of Broadway.

Columbia president Frank Price, charged with restoring the struggling studio to financial health, had been tracking Fosse's spending since his first day on the job, in 1978. "Columbia was kind of seat-of-the-pants," Price said. "I inherited a lot of problems." Along with *Altered States* and *Annie* (whose rights the studio had purchased for a preposterous $9.5 million, à la Sam Cohn), *All That Jazz* was one of three productions the board of directors deemed "problem pictures." Price had to fix them. "By the time the [*All That Jazz*] budget reached nine million," he explained, "I had to say, 'Fellas, we're not operating with a blank check.'" Looking to trim, he asked Fosse to budget his big finale. Fosse refused.

Price appealed to Cohn. "We can't have this thing going up any more," he said. "The board is pressing me. I've got to have a budget or this will become a nightmare situation."

Cohn appreciated Price's predicament, but his allegiance was to his client. The big ending — still a work in progress — could not be budgeted.

"Sam, I'm going to have to come to New York, to Astoria —"

"I'll bar the door."

"Sam, I'm going to have to shut you down."

This was seven days before the completion of photography. ("I thought Bobby was going to have another heart attack," Scheider said.)

Assemble the picture, Price advised Melnick, and if they needed those unfilmed sequences — "Bye Bye Life," "NY to LA," and Gideon's dialogues with the Angel of Death — then they could shoot them. Price thought this a reasonable compromise.

Melnick thought it highly impractical. "Are we supposed to stop production, take a few months off to edit, then get everyone back together to shoot it?" he asked.

Apparently, yes.

"Excuse me for a second."

Melnick returned to his office and called Fosse and Cohn. "I want to set up the movie someplace else."

There was silence on the other end of the line.

Changing studios midstream simply didn't happen, especially when there was already so much money in the hole and when the footage — only partially comprehensible without the Angel of Death pieces for temporal segues — smacked of the kind of arty, genre-bending, self-indulgence that marketing departments lived in fear of. But Fosse made a feast of studio pressures, and he said yes, let's do it. Sam Cohn stood with him.

"Fellas," Melnick said, "I just want to make sure, before we go through with this, that you're ready to live with the consequences of the poker game we're about to play"— meaning, if Fosse threatened to leave, he had to be willing to actually leave, to risk his financing, risk finishing the film and not having it distributed, not to mention risking the lawsuits — "Bobby," Melnick said, "do you want this?"

"Go for it."

"I'll call you back."

But that poker game never got to the table. Striking a compromise, Price and Melnick agreed to take on another studio, a partner. It would put up the money for the unfilmed material and share in the profits. All Melnick had to do was sell *All That Jazz* all over again.

"Dan Melnick called," Alan Heim's mother-in-law told Alan. "From California."

Heim called him right back. "Dan, it's Alan."

"Alan, I want you to prepare an hour of the best material we have —"

"What's going on?"

"— and get it out to me by Sunday."

"Today's Friday."

Unsure of what this was all about, Heim took an assistant to the cutting room the next morning and assembled, as directed, an emergency reel of cut and uncut footage, using the cattle-call sequence and certain stand-alone dramatic scenes as set pieces. When time ran out, he called in a messenger and arranged to have the canisters delivered to Melnick's Beverly Hills front door at 6:00 the next morning.

Ten hours later, Dan Melnick's doorbell buzzed him awake. Instead of answering the door, he fumbled for the phone. "Alan?"

"Is it there?"

"Did it have to be six in the morning?"

A salesman in black shades and a designer suit, Melnick dropped the canisters in the trunk of his car and rode from studio to studio. Warner Brothers liked what he showed them, but their key executive was out of town and they couldn't commit without him. So Melnick got back in the car and drove directly to Alan Ladd Jr. Among the most admired and well-liked executives in Hollywood, Laddie, as he was known, had independent taste and a sweeping view of film practice and industry, which, as the son of actor Alan Ladd and stepson of actress/agent Sue Carol, he'd been cultivating since boyhood. He had joined CMA to agent under Freddie Fields before setting out to produce on his own, and eventually he landed on top at Fox, giving easy, clairvoyant yeses to projects as diverse and dicey as *Harry and Tonto, The Rocky Horror Picture Show,* and — when no one else would — *Star Wars.* The Hollywood he imagined had room enough for all. "I just liked it" could have been Laddie's motto; in an industry of panicked arbitrations, Laddie had a laid-back, eloquent instinct, trusting and forthright, and he had earned his stripes, both in the boardroom and at Chasen's.

Laddie invited a few people from the studio to join him and Melnick. He was basically familiar with *All That Jazz,* having turned down *Ending* years earlier. But now that it was *All That Jazz,* a Bob Fosse musical, Laddie's interest shifted back. *My God,* he thought as the lights went down, *if Bob Fosse had been making a musical all along, I never would have passed.* The lights came up forty minutes later and Laddie turned to Melnick: "I'll take it."

Triumphant, Melnick drove back to Columbia, to Frank Price's office. "You're out of the picture," he announced. "I've laid it off for you." For *you:* as if it were a favor to Price.

"Where?"

"Laddie. Fox."

Columbia and Fox elected to co-distribute *All That Jazz,* with foreign rights to one and domestic to the other. Who got which was decided by an official coin toss at the Beverly Hills Hotel. Price had tails, Laddie heads.

It was heads. Laddie took domestic.

Back in the game, *All That Jazz* moved an hour upstate, to a vacant black-box theater at SUNY Purchase, to shoot "Bye Bye Life," which, due to persistent budgetary restrictions, had to work as the final number. There would be no opening night of *NY to LA,* no Flentrop organ. Gideon would simply sing bye-bye to life and drift toward death. Then the zipper would close on his body bag and Merman would belt out "There's No Business Like Show Business" as the credits rolled. *All That Jazz* was a musical.

Translating the *NY to LA* design elements into "Bye Bye Life," Fosse, under deadline, sent Walton and Phil Rosenberg back to the drawing board and closed the door behind them. "It was getting quite frightening," Rosenberg remembered. "We would bring in models and sketches time after time, and he wouldn't know what he wanted and we were only about a week away from having to shoot the scene when he finally said, 'You know, I had a dream last night about cylinders. White cylinders.'" In came yards and yards of silver-coated Mylar — Mirrex Mirror Scrim inherited from the unborn finale, reflective floors, and transparent Plexiglas cylinders with light-bouncing surfaces. Shrouded in black and silver, the intimate five-hundred-seat space did indeed look like a rock concert setting somewhere between life and death.

Crouched behind the bleachers brought in for Gideon's audience, Peppino and Lynn Lovett flipped through a Fellini coffee-table book, one of several Fosse and the cinematographer used to complement their hand gestures. Deferential to his magnificent oeuvre, Fosse gave Peppino very little feedback, which Peppino, taking Fosse's quiet to mean he was disappointed, returned with more silence. Sometimes they wouldn't speak, each wondering what he had done to the other. And they were always together. Harpo trailing Chico, Peppino followed his director wherever he went, at the ready to receive the budding ideas from his brain, but Fosse was mostly too deep in Fosse to notice him there. "Where's Peppino?" he'd ask, and from two paces back would come "I am here, Fosse!," and both would laugh. "Peppino was a gentleman, a man of light to Fosse's dark," David Ray said. "He had a calm personality the process needed." Looking at a still from Fellini's *Casanova,* Peppino and Lovett admired an entombed Venetian opera house dripping with chandeliers. "That's the same shot," Peppino said, his face warming. "But this time I'm going to do it right."

While Fosse built "Bye Bye Life," his actors waited. A few got together in their motel rooms for games, charades, and the kind of truth-telling marathons Fosse might have enjoyed if he weren't confined to the SUNY Purchase black box. The incarcerated dubbed themselves Prisoners of the Performing Arts — POPA for short. "We just sort of occupied ourselves," John Lithgow said. "It was just constant laughter and fun. Even when we went to the bathroom, we would do it together and call it POPA pisses." Actor Anthony Holland brought in his play, and POPA gave a reading of it; Barbara Cook performed somewhere, and POPA organized a field trip.

Meanwhile, delays continued. Fosse built.

The number's two lead dancers — one tall, one short — weren't working well together, a dilemma Fosse was contemplating up until to the very night before the shoot, at dinner with Doby, weighing the pros and cons of their next move. Do they replace one? Both? Proceed as planned? Doby advocated for replacements and additional delays; Fosse had no answer. They ended the evening on a low note and said good night.

Hours later, Doby's phone rang. It was two in the morning on the day of the shoot.

"You're right," he said. "We better change it."

"To who?"

"You and Annie."

Doby and Reinking, just in from New York, were in a rehearsal hall hours later. Albert Wolsky put a rush on their costumes — a pair of full-body leotards with red and blue veins appliquéd onto the fabric, custom-made to represent two halves of a beating heart. That created more delays, and it wasn't until the following Tuesday that Wolsky's order came in, and "Bye Bye Life" was, at last, ready to shoot.

But Fosse wasn't. Once all the pieces had been assembled on set, he had to break down the number into shots. All that had passed was merely preparation for this moment. "Bob started changing things from shot to shot," Doby said, "so we had to keep changing the dance to try to keep up." And when they changed the dance, he changed the shot, which changed the dance, which . . .

All in all, "Bye Bye Life" took them two weeks. "Fifteen days," Glattes said, "for seven minutes of music."

Rehearsing the number, perfecting its climactic baseball slide, Roy Scheider messed up his leg. He said, "It was the hardest physical thing I'd ever had to do." He developed a lump. It made sliding, already a challenge, even harder, and every night, as he lathered himself in Tiger Balm, he refused to think he might not make it through the shoot. He loved this number too much. He loved this man, and he knew what "Bye Bye Life" meant to him. "I think he knew that his death was not going to be as wonderful as this," Scheider concluded, "so that's why he spent so much time thinking about making it wonderful in the movie." Exultant, showy, funky, odd, euphorically mournful, "Bye Bye Life" generated the operatic spirit of a showbiz addict's absolution by death and entertainment — to Bob Fosse, a happy ending. Imagining the real thing, he said, "Maybe somebody will say, 'He was a good showman; he gave us good shows. You could always count on him for an evening's entertainment.'" Maybe for that they would forgive him.

As Fosse was filming the very end of "Bye Bye Life," in which Gideon rushes into his audience of enemies and loved ones for the final goodbye, he called cut and peered out from behind the camera. He wanted to look at them, the people he knew. There were hundreds. Annie, Leland Palmer, *NY to LA*'s "producers," the strippers in the scene with Keith Gordon . . . The way they looked at Gideon seemed a lot like love. Love for him.

He pulled Scheider aside. "You know, that must be kind of exhilarating."

"Yeah, Bobby, it is." Scheider smiled. "Why don't you try it?"

"Naahhhh."

"Come on . . . You'll love it."

Scheider cued the band, the music started, and Fosse dashed from the stage into his people, hugging and kissing, thanking and touching. When it ended, they applauded him — a standing ovation — as he headed back to Scheider, back to the stage, trying to catch his breath.

"Jesus Christ! That's terrific!"

"Yeah, Bobby. It is."

"And you know, Roy," he was said to have whispered, "the best part of it is that they forgive me too."

Scheider saw tears in Fosse's eyes. "Yeah, Bobby. We do."

Rehearsal.
Fred Mann III

RIGHT: Dustin Hoffman as der Führer, goofing on one of Lenny's Hitler bits, on location with Valerie Perrine in Miami.
Valerie Perrine

BELOW: When Hoffman pulled back the covers, he found a giant dildo standing up on Perrine's crotch. He'd been suffering from the flu and she'd planned the stunt to cheer him up.
Valerie Perrine

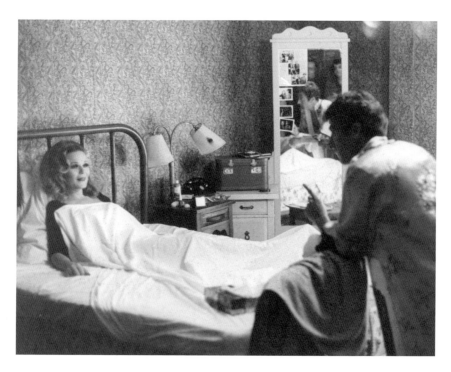

Reinking and Fosse during the filming of *Lenny* in Miami, 1974.
Courtesy of Ann Reinking

Fosse makes a slight adjustment (is it perfect yet?) on Roy Scheider as Joe Gideon in *All That Jazz,* a 100 percent accurate rendering of about 70 percent of Bob Fosse. *Photofest*

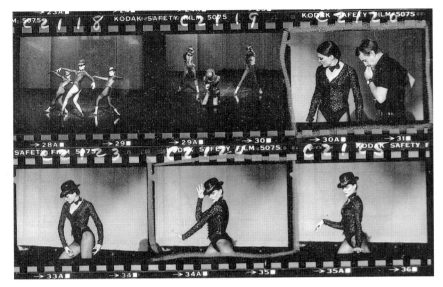

Filming *All That Jazz.*
Fox/Josh Weiner

New Year's Eve, early 1980s. The woman with Fosse is Liz Canney, *Star 80* apprentice editor and girlfriend. *Courtesy of Kenny Laub*

A stolen shot of Fosse, in his office at the DGA building, felled by *Star 80* preproduction blues. The film terrified him — morally, artistically, professionally, personally. "Bob did not seem to be in a mood that indicated he would be receptive to picture taking that day," said Wende Phifer. "Those moods were palpable. So I took it while pretending to take the picture of someone else in the front office, hence the telephoto shot." *Wende Phifer Mate*

Smoking under a NO SMOKING sign, Fosse gives notes to the ladies of *Sweet Charity*. Dorothy Chandler Pavilion, summer 1985. *Christine Colby Jacques*

Father, daughter, mother.
Getty Images/Ron Galella, WireImage

Collaborators, spouses, ex-lovers, friends — Bob Fosse and Gwen Verdon,
East Hampton, 1981. *Eva Rubinstein*

EIGHT YEARS

ASIDE FROM THE PIROUETTES in the audition sequence, which Fosse had Heim cut immediately, the day they were shot at the Palace, the majority of *All That Jazz* was cut after shooting had been completed. "This was highly, highly unusual," said assistant editor Wende Phifer. "Bob didn't even want to think about cutting the movie until he had shot everything. And when he had, we cut in chronological order, taking boxes off the shelf one scene after the next." Editing took more than a year, a colossal amount of time for a feature film. "It was a life," Heim said, "a whole life." Alan's mother died while they cut "Bye Bye Life," and David Ray's marriage collapsed. "It wasn't the movie's fault," Ray explained, "it was probably going to end anyway, but I was there for a good six months working until one in the morning." Alan Heim, on the picture for fourteen months, recalled, "The set dresser [Phil Rosenberg] had a heart attack on the first attempt of the film, and then came back in time for the second one." Of course, Bob Aurthur was dead. Danny Ruvolo was dead. Christopher Newman's wife had a baby.

In need of more space, the team moved from their enclosure in the Brill Building to the Directors Guild of America building on

West Fifty-Seventh, one block from Fosse's apartment, where he kept his production office. Through one window he could see up to Fifty-Fifth Street to where he had lived with Joan McCracken. "All those years and all that work," he told a reporter, "and all I did was move a couple of blocks." Going out to dinner or on his way home from a show, Fosse would drop in on the editors with an idea, sometimes with his girlfriend model-actress Julie Hagerty. "I just want to run through a couple of things," he'd say, and Wende Phifer would cue up a reel. As late as two in the morning, David Ray would leave the DGA building with Fosse and a handful of assistants. Rounding Fifty-Fourth Street, Fosse would light up at the sight of kids crowding into Studio 54. "He would make small talk with these young people," Ray said, "until we realized he wanted us to leave so he could go in and party."

"I still have one artery partially clogged," Fosse admitted in November 1979. "I may get a slight chest pain. Then I just sit down and take a pill."

Heim got most of his work done during the day, not cutting on the beat. "If you stay on the beat," he said, "it becomes too rhythmic. But if you go by the motions of the dancers or the dancers' body parts, it becomes a different experience." Their task was to find and refine visual rhythms and layer them on the eye like phyllo dough. Though confined by the script, Heim cut with New Wave curiosity, dodging time frames and mind frames and circumventing the linearity of the Hollywood musical so skillfully, one couldn't be sure the whole of *All That Jazz* wasn't a flashback confessed to Death in Gideon's final moments or if the Angel of Death was merely another piece of hallucinatory razzle-dazzle he invented to comfort himself.

As they neared a rough cut, Fosse helped Gwen get the first national tour of *Dancin'* on the road. With Gail Benedict, Gwen had been overseeing the Broadway production since Kathryn Doby left for *All*

That Jazz, and not always, Doby thought, with perfect results. "Gwen was trying to make it a little easier on the national company," Doby said, "and we came into a little conflict on that. She was practical. She wanted the shortcut. But I wanted it the way Bob wanted it." Intent on derivations unknown to others, Gwen asserted, often correctly, her expert authority. "That's not how we used to do that step," she said to Benedict on "Percussion III," a number she said came from "Who's Got the Pain?" Who could argue with her? In the absence of Fosse, Verdon was the law. "Gwen was obviously territorial with her knowledge, which was considerable," one dancer said. "That cut both ways." She could share Fosse with other women, but she wasn't prepared to cede his style; it was her bloodline. It was her legacy.

Despite mixed reviews, *Dancin'* was a smash hit on Broadway (and would run through 1982), an achievement Fosse attributed partially to discomania. Thinking franchise, he considered making a documentary about the show, a hybrid half-performance, half-backstage account of the complete *Dancin'* experience. "I'd want to see your quick changes and everything else backstage," he said to Blane Savage, "the show behind the show." And down to the smallest detail. "When I film the section when Charles Ward is doing his solo," he said to Wayne Cilento, "I'm going to film you in the bathroom taking a pee." Fosse entertained the notion of doing *Dancin' Too,* but got only as far as the studio before he concluded, "I'd never do that to a dancer again." Keeping the national and Broadway outfits at their best would be enough. He'd occasionally appear at the Broadhurst unannounced. Shows, like people, were capable of lying, but observing incognito, Fosse could catch them with their guard down. From their place onstage, dancers could see his ropey silhouette passing the exit signs. "That put the fear of God in us," dancer Bill Hastings said.

Fosse watched "I Wanna Be a Dancin' Man," a full-company number inspired by a classic Astaire dance in *The Belle of New York,* fall flat with the audience. Aggrieved to see his life's motto in critical condition, he called a rehearsal for the next day.

Fosse began the rehearsal sharpening the company's coordination, drilling the exact tilt of their heads into the neuronal grooves he'd designed for their safekeeping. But repeating the steps changed little; their "Dancin' Man" was uninhabited. They weren't dancing *from* anywhere, and clearly they had no idea what they were singing. Fosse swore aloud and stormed to the back of the studio. "How do I get you people to *dance?*" he yelled, and then, "Just play the song again. Just *listen.*" With piano:

> *I wanna be a dancin' man*
> *While I can*
> *Gonna leave my footsteps on the sands of time*
> *If I never leave a dime*
> *Never be a millionaire*
> *I don't care*
> *I'll be rich as old King Midas might have been*
> *Least until the tide rolls in.*

"'While I *can*,'" he insisted.

They didn't speak.

"'While I *can*.'"

Still nothing.

"Do you understand? The sand, the *tide*. Then what? *Sand*. It's gone. The tide always comes in, okay?" He looked around the room to see if he was connecting. "This is *your* story, *our* story."

They gathered with him at the piano. "He went through the song line by line," Bill Hastings remembered, "and reminded us of how much we give up to dance. We give up family. We give up wealth. We take a brutal beating daily, physically, emotionally, and in the business. And the world thinks we're crazy for doing it. Our time to do what we love is very short. Bankers do what they do until they're eighty, ninety, a hundred. They get rich. Our legacy is the sand." Beginning with the original company, dancers spoke of the verse containing the lyrics "the sands of time" as the prayer section. "He got introverted when he was showing me those steps," said John Sowinski. "It was a personal, almost private thing he was doing with his body. He was relating to himself."

At the show that night, as the orchestra played the entr'acte, the "Dancin' Man" dancers took their marks behind the curtain. Hastings said, "Normally, we'd be relaxed, some of us talking softly to one another. That night we were perfectly still. Then the curtain went up." This time it was from the inside.

"In the end," Reinking said, "no matter what it does to us, we're lucky to have passion."

A glass of white wine in his hand, Fosse presided over *All That Jazz*'s sound mix. He was in the booth with music editor Michael Tronick, who was seated at the console just above Fosse, awaiting the next take, his gaze fixed to the screen. They were working on a particularly challenging Trumpet passage in "Bye Bye Life." If Tronick missed the cue by a quarter of an inch, Fosse would catch it. His hand would shoot up from below, signaling *too loud* with a friendly wave. "There's a section," Tronick recalled, "when Ben [Vereen] is saying, 'More! Give it to me! More! Give it to me,' with a repeat of the brass. If I was off by one perf—and there are four perfs per frame and twenty-four frames per second, so there are ninety-six perfs a second—so if you're off one-ninety-sixth of a second, Bob would hear it."

Through twelve-hour days, he never flagged. Still dissatisfied with Scheider's cough, which he had revised all through rehearsal and filming, Fosse announced, finally, he was going to record it himself. Ditto the foley work on Keith Gordon's tap dance and the finger snaps in "Airotica." His savage engagement with the subatomic captured their devotion. "Here I am surrounded by all these creative people," he mused aloud, "why can't we figure it out?" It was a genuine question, plainly expressed. *Really, why* can't *it be perfect? Does anybody here know?*

Fosse's early cast and crew screening of *All That Jazz* was an uncomfortable, revelatory experience for many, rife with pity and anger, for him and for themselves. Few saw it for what it was; they analyzed the picture as if it were Fosse. He/it was egomaniacal, narcissistic (an old favorite), courageous, immature, brilliant, fake Fellini — 4¼! It/he was announcing suicide, crying out for attention, apologizing, pleading to be understood, asking to be crowned a genius. It was a Rorschach. "It gave him pleasure to feel that he was being betrayed. He wanted to be the victim," Fred Ebb reasoned. "It was all about Bobby pretending to be honest," Kander said. "He was saying, 'I'm not worth much, but everyone around me is worth even less.'" "When I saw it, I was devastated," said Gordon Harrell, "I thought, *My God, I've been working for a madman.* But at the same time I suddenly understood his moody moments." Harrell was too overcome to face Fosse after the screening. As the lights came up over the closing credits, he left through a side exit and ran into the street.

Fosse leaned in to Ben Vereen. "What do you think?"

Vereen said, "I have to go for a walk."

Fosse anticipated extreme reactions, even backlash. Not just from the critics; from the people he worked with. Fred Ebb, Stephen Schwartz, Hal Prince, countless producers. "He felt guilty about some of the putdowns he put into the movie," Reinking said. "He knew Joe was going to be tough, and he didn't want people to misread him."

He implored Reinking to believe he didn't intend it to hurt anyone. "I really am a nice guy," he insisted. "I really, really am."

She had seen him cry before, but never had she seen him break down. "*I* know you're not that mean. Why didn't you make him more like you?"

"I couldn't make them like Joe Gideon because otherwise they wouldn't get the moral of the story."

Reinking did not need this explained. "*All That Jazz* is about show business can kill you," she would say. "Devoting yourself exclusively to your craft is like an all-protein diet. You may not be hungry, but you're going to starve to death. You need other things. And Bob knew it was killing him, and he knew there was nothing he could do about it. He was hooked. That's why I think *All That Jazz* is very moral, because it says don't do this. You'll lose yourself."

A private screening for Gwen, Nicole, Paddy, Herb, and Sam amounted to a mixed reaction. Fosse was desperate for their feedback, but they were slow to offer it. Nicole hedged longest. She was seventeen now, old enough to have a serious opinion, to hurt and be hurt like an adult. Fosse waited for her reaction in the theater lobby after the screening, but she and Gwen evaded him that night. Overcome with feeling, they walked in silence all the way to Gwen's apartment, unsure of what to think or say. Then Nicole stopped. She looked straight ahead. "You know," she said, "the daughter was the only one who cared whether he lived or died."

Gwen called Bob to tell him that.

The most trying screening of all still lay ahead of him. That summer, Fosse flew to California to watch the film with the executives at Fox. By then Laddie had resigned, leaving a new team in charge. "I can't walk into one of those offices without feeling twelve years old," Fosse said. "Those guys intimidate me, they all have Gucci shoes." Fox's most powerful "guy" turned out to be Sherry Lansing, Melnick's protégée, and they got on instantly. "Bobby had this boyish charm and enthusiasm," she said, "and his pain and vulnerability were right out there for you to see." Sharp, accomplished, humble — a math teacher before she became a model — Lansing was now the president of 20th Century Fox, which made her the first female head of production at a Hollywood studio.

Fosse was late the day of the screening. His wingman Dan Melnick took the floor and smiled at the silence. "Bob's in the bathroom," he announced, "throwing up."

By the end of the picture, Lansing was in tears, "probably the only studio president ever," she would say, "to sob at a screening." She declared *All That Jazz* an absolute masterpiece, said she thought it was one of the best pictures she had ever seen and one of the greatest in the history of film. ("I still do. It still is.")

With nothing to do but wait, Fosse's pre-release terror turned to depression. "I really think Bob Fosse thought he was going to die after *All That Jazz*," Lynn Lovett said. "I think afterward he was sort of like, 'I already died. I wrapped it up.' I'm sure he enjoyed the rest of his life, but I think he was almost embarrassed to still be alive." He disappeared to his apartment, then turned on the TV and disappeared again. "I guess I'm very tired," he told a visiting reporter. "I sit in there like some brainless thing watching game shows. People win prizes and jump on each other and kiss, and it makes me sad that they're so happy. I get all weepy. I don't know what the hell's going on. It suddenly breaks my heart, like there's something I'm missing out on." He wasn't with Annie, he wasn't with Jessica, he wasn't with Julie. "You always think, this will be the one — the one who'll alter your life. With [Julie Hagerty], I tried harder than I used to." He was fifty-two. That was too old. "Julie seemed depressed and hopelessly in love," Lynn Lovett observed. "Fosse would say, 'You need someone younger. Someone who isn't going to die on you.' But she wanted to spend the rest of her life with him."

While Janice Lynde was in town for a TV show, Fosse let her (and her dog) use his office as a temporary apartment. To make her early call in Brooklyn, Janice had to get up at 4:30, hours before anyone at 850 Seventh even thought about coming in. One morning, she heard a scratching at the door.

"Hello?"

"Janice, are you awake?" It was Fosse.

She opened the door to find him leaning against the frame, smoking and crying.

"I've done the worst thing in the world," he said, referring to *All That Jazz*. "They're going to call it Fosse's ego trip. Why did I do this?" The film was opening the following day.

"It may get mixed reviews, but it's brilliant."

"They're gonna kill me, they're gonna kill me, they're gonna kill me . . ."

Janice looked at the clock. "Come on," she said. "You're going to Brooklyn with me."

"No, I don't think so."

"You're not going to sit here and drink all day. Come on."

She packed him in the limousine, and together they drove down to the studio. While Janice filmed, he waited in her dressing room, his cap pulled over his eyes.

As expected, the critical response to *All That Jazz* verged on manic depression. But it made headlines. Listening to his advisers, Fosse toured talk shows with uncommon compliance (*Today, Dick Cavett, Tomorrow with Tom Snyder*) and granted bashful interviews to almost any journalist, fearing the exposure but savoring the attention. (One interviewer, disturbed by young Joe Gideon and the strippers, asked about the effects of burlesque on Fosse's life. "Tragic," he replied. "Absolutely tragic . . . I haven't recovered since.") The publicity worked. The controversy around *All That Jazz* built the film an unexpectedly strong box office and elevated Bob Fosse from famous director to pop-culture personality. The picture couldn't make him a star but it did bring Fosse's life and likeness increased visibility, perhaps even infamy. Joe Gideon and his absorbing mix of vice and self-disclosure would forever be mistaken for the complete Bob Fosse.

No one, not even the film's admirers, expected any Academy Award nominations for *All That Jazz,* let alone the nine it received, including best screenplay, best director, and best picture. Most would go to *Kramer vs. Kramer,* but Fosse's team of Alan Heim, Albert Wolsky, and Ralph Burns, as well as his art directors Phil Rosenberg and Tony Walton (with set decorators Edward Stewart and Gary Brink) all won. If the academy gave Oscars for most defiant musical of the year, *All That Jazz,* enriched by avant-garde techniques and odious subjects uncommon to the form, would have been a sure thing. At a time when revisionist nostalgia and parody set the standard for musical innovation, Fosse imbued his film with the physical and ontological ordeals of contemporary *reality,* naturalizing the most unnatural of entertainment forms: *Meet Me in St. Louis* meets *Citizen Kane.*

Soon thereafter Lansing, Melnick, Scheider, and Fosse took off for the Cannes Film Festival. Before the film premiered, Fosse met network news personality David Sheehan for a drink at the Carlton Hotel.

"Of all the shows you've done," Sheehan asked, "what's the nearest and dearest to your heart?"

"My heart?" He laughed. It was such a reporter's question. "I love them all, but *Pippin's* in a coma."

"A coma?"

"It only exists in the minds of people who saw it. It's on life support."

Dancin' was running strong and *Chicago* was playing London's West End, but *Pippin* had closed, after an incredible five-year run, in 1977.

"Well," Sheehan said, "why don't we put it on tape?"

These were the fledgling years of VHS. "You can't do that," Fosse said.

"I'll talk to pay-TV."

That was new too. "People aren't going to put quarters in slots in their TVs . . ."

Familiar with the technology, Sheehan explained the details, and Fosse's interest was piqued. Resistant to regression but interested in the investment, he could cast and rehearse the show himself, hand it over to Doby, and oversee the project from afar.

The Cannes screening of *All That Jazz* got a standing ovation, but Lansing, Melnick, Scheider, and Fosse returned home before the awards presentation. Fosse knew he wouldn't win and, after the Oscars, didn't want to attend his second consecutive loss. And he caught flak for it too. Sore loser, they called him.

Back in New York, at two thirty in the morning, the phone rang in Sherry Lansing's suite at the Carlyle Hotel.

"Hello?"

Fosse was screaming. "We won! We won! We won!"

"*What?*"

"The Palme d'Or!"

"Oh my God . . ."

"We tied! With Kurosawa, with *Kagemusha*! You've got to get up! We've got to celebrate!"

"Okay, okay, give me a second."

"I'll meet you in the lobby."

They went around the corner to 3 Guys Restaurant. Too happy to keep it to himself, Fosse told the waiter his terrific news. He left Lansing at the table so he could go tell the cashier. He came back and told the loner at the next booth. Lansing thought, *It's like he's never won anything before, like he isn't Bob Fosse.* They celebrated for hours, until the sun came up over Madison Avenue.

"You know, I've got to get ready for my day," she said.

"Just stay with me a little longer please, please, please."

He was irresistible.

They paid the bill and Fosse led her to a building nearby. Inside, he opened a door to a psychiatrist's foyer, where a patient waited to go in.

Dr. Clifford Sager was surprised to see him.

"I won," Fosse said.

Sager beamed. "That's really great. That's really, really great."

Sweet Charity, Cabaret, Pippin, Dancin' — they won for Fosse the director, the entertainer, but *All That Jazz*, directed, choreographed, this time cowritten, and practically starring Bob Fosse represented at last a holistic triumph of authorship, innovation, and personal expression. This time, the success was authentic, undeniably his own.

After he walked Lansing back to the Carlyle, he appeared across town at Ann Reinking's ballet class and strolled right in, unapologetic about the brazen interruption. He found her at the barre. He told her, and she danced all through their rejoicing.

SEVEN YEARS

NICOLE GREW UP. Years of training had given her a ballerina's credentials, but her body showed the biology of a Fosse dancer. The boys caught on. She had burlesquey curves, and a little Know cut behind her smile. Gwen, seeing all, went on red alert. She dug into the mother role and Fosse found himself playing good cop—a honey of a chance if he didn't bungle it. "Gwen was careful with her," he said, "a little more strict than I am. I said, 'I don't have time to watch you. I have to go to work. So I just have to trust you. So if you're anything like your father, you're a pretty good liar, so you could fool me, but I don't want a lot of dope in the house or anything like that.'" She moved in with him for a short span of high school, long enough to see his girlfriends, rapidly approaching her own age, close up. It gave her a new vantage point. They had certain things in common now; namely, her father. Taking their side, Nicole cross-examined him on ancient double standards and refused to let him off the hook. He told her what he told them: He had never claimed to be fair. A woman of the seventies, she cited him for chauvinism and won. She was the joy of his life.

"That's the future," Dr. Sager had said, "and that's where love is."

On weekends, they drove out to Quogue. Nicole running around Manhattan on her own challenged both sides, but by opening the beach house to Nicole and friends for some supervised messing around, Fosse could make her a kind of rehearsal space in which to grow up. One such weekend, he turned them all loose, whipped up a batch of margaritas, and receded into the background. Fosse watched her, drink in hand. If anyone asked how a guy like him had raised a girl like her, he would respond plainly, quietly, he hadn't. Gwen Verdon had. He would say he had been there at the right times and did his best when he could, but the winning moves belonged to her mother. Nicole was only seven when they split up. "Do you want her for the weekend?" Gwen had asked, early in their separation. "I'm not a babysitter" was his reply. In those days, he was a guest in their home. He had to ring the doorbell. Now, sidestepping the girl talk on the back patio, he felt like a guest in his own home, and he was maybe a little drunk too. At least, Nicole thought so. "You shouldn't drink," she said. "You're with minors." She stopped him on his way to the car. "And you're not driving." With her friend to help her, she led Fosse back inside. There they discovered the pitcher of margaritas waiting for them, half full. Nicole's mother heard about it the next day. "These two teenage kids started drinking his margaritas," Gwen said. "They wound up drunk, sick all over the bathroom floor."

He considered, again, doing a full ballet for the Joffrey. There was still *Big Deal*, his musical adaptation of *Big Deal on Madonna Street*, a sentimental favorite for fifteen years. He could do it either for film or on Broadway. Then there was *Atlantic City*, Cy Coleman's idea for a panoramic lowlife musical. That could be for him. And Marty Richards and Alan Carr had *Chicago*'s film rights and interest from Liza Minnelli and Goldie Hawn. But Fosse had made a resolution after *Sweet Charity* never to do onscreen what he'd already done onstage. "Besides," he said, "I can't get it up again for that material. It's like trying to go back to an old girlfriend." But how could the new girlfriend out-gorgeous Jessica Lange? He had already topped *Lenny* with *All That Jazz, Chicago* with *Dancin'*, and truth with self-laceration. What else was there?

There was something, an idea, maybe more of a theme, about the need for the spotlight, within him, within those who *must* act or entertain. It's the primeval hunger. Where does it come from? (Starvation early on?) Do doctors, teachers, and painters have it? Was theirs bottomless, like his? Put to the test, how far could it push someone? How far would it push him? Fosse understood Sally Bowles, Lenny Bruce, and Joe Gideon all ended badly — but why? Beyond *All That Jazz*, he knew, there was a still darker fathom of the performer's consciousness. At their bottom-most floor, a lost harpoon stuck out of the sand. Fosse couldn't know who or what shot it, only that it was in him too, and it hurt. A week after he appeared in Sager's office to announce his win at Cannes, he asked him for psychological intel on the subject of entertainers; research, Fosse said, for a project he had in mind about "the need for attention." Perhaps this would take him past self-laceration into outright despair.

Atlantic City wasn't it, but Fosse met with writer Jack Heifner through the summer, trying to fit into narrative shape the songs Coleman and lyricist Christopher Gore had given them. "Bob and I stared at each other for hours trying to make this work," Heifner said, "but he seemed isolated, like his heart wasn't in it." They worked at Fosse's apartment and sat on his deck at Quogue, tossing story possibilities back and forth. A decaying playpen of failed hopes, *Atlantic City* was turning out to be a loser's *Chicago*, emceed by a couple that crawled up from under the boardwalk. "They were supposed to be like Pied Pipers," Heifner said, "like the Leading Player in *Pippin*." They sing "Toyland," about how the Boardwalk's funhouse became a sex shop; they sing about a dead-end chanteuse, who sang one song, year after year, her whole life; and how the Miss America pageants turn girls into automatons. Heifner said, "I finally put together something Fosse-esque, but more like a musical revue, a *Grand Hotel* in hell." It fizzled soon thereafter, while still in the planning stage.

It was a busy summer. Fosse and Sam Cohn invested in the Laundry, an East Hampton restaurant of the grilled-meat-and-fish variety. To the original brick (the Laundry began as an actual laundry), architect Norman Jaffe added sleek cypress ceilings, skylights, and a bar — said to be the longest in the Hamptons — of strawberry travertine marble. With its wooden chairs and see-through fireplace, the restaurant was informal chic, an Elaine's from the future. It opened on July 12, 1980, with a big, small gathering that included Liza Minnelli, Lauren Bacall, Brooke Shields, Louis Malle, and, of course, Fosse and Cohn.

As he agented deals to clients, Cohn agented his clients to each other, packaging them socially and professionally in town or country. On summer Saturdays, he made a habit of inviting the select to his house on Lily Pond Lane, where he ruled the grill and the tomato and onion salad (inspired by the same at Peter Luger's) while his wife, actor-producer Julia Miles, poured the wine. Fosse was a table regular. So were Roy and Cynthia Scheider and the writers Peter Maas, Steve Tesich, and E. L. Doctorow, all clients Cohn had introduced to one another. "Bob always needed to be around writers," Doctorow said. "I took that as a need to be around people with a formal education." One evening after dinner, Fosse initiated a lightning round of the truth game. When did you lose your virginity? The question circled the group and at Doctorow's response — "I was eighteen" — Fosse's jaw dropped. "He began to get hysterical that it happened so late," Doctorow said. "He took off on that."

The Scheiders were often in Quogue for a weekend with Fosse. Lunches consisted of big bowls of tuna fish (mixed with grapes, raisins, and onions) served with lettuce and Jack cheese on buttery baguettes. They'd talk movies, actors, women, dancers. Dinners ran long and late. "I didn't buy Bobby's dark-guy thing," Cynthia Scheider said. "I really believe he was a sweet, kind, gentle man."

Though the American musical had been sparring with pop since rock 'n' roll, the rise of Michael Jackson made clearer the coming defeat of Broadway. It happened by way of MTV, an up-to-the-minute feed of dance and music far more sophisticated than *American Bandstand* or any concert television that had come before it. Combining the best of Broadway and Hollywood with the newest in pop, MTV held the young spirit of musical theater, and all at home, available most any time, for free. It aged the whole business. By 1980, few Broadway trusts seemed more passé than Gower Champion, former king of the Persian Room. Weaned on the sixties ethic of musical gargantuas, Champion made his reputation as a director-choreographer of sober spectaculars, Busby Berkeley the morning after. From *Bye Bye Birdie* to *Hello, Dolly!,* his old-fashioned extravaganzas were half a great thing, hardly new, simply classic, ideally suited to *42nd Street,* which Champion revived that year under the aegis of legendary producer David Merrick.

Fosse was in the Winter Garden opening night, August 25, 1980, when, after the cast took ten curtain calls, Merrick appeared onstage in the midst of the applause. It had been a fun night and the crowd was pleased to see Merrick enjoying his well-deserved triumph. As the roar escalated, TV crews rushed down the aisle and up to the foot of the stage. Merrick, they had been told, would have an announcement after the show.

Raising a palm to the clamor, he began. "I'm sorry to have to report . . ."

The applause continued.

"No, no, it's very tragic."

You couldn't hear him.

"You don't understand. Gower Champion died this morning." He turned to embrace one of the dancers. It was very effective.

At the party, certain facts emerged. No one but the family, the hospital, and David Merrick knew Champion had been suffering from Waldenström's macroglobulinemia, a rare blood disease. And only they knew he had died that afternoon before the curtain went up on *42nd Street*. Which meant Merrick delayed the announcement all evening and through the show, presumably waiting for his big reveal in front of TV cameras, where the grief-stricken real-time reaction of the cast (he kept it from them too) could be captured, broadcast, and spread through the airwaves that very night — an estimated value of one million dollars in free advertising. Jammed with the likes of Fosse, Neil Simon, Ethel Merman, Joe Papp, and Woody Herman's band, the Waldorf-Astoria's Starlight Roof overheard more talk of Merrick than of Gower Champion. "There were so many rumors that Merrick was just making this announcement as part of his great showman routine," Carolyn Kirsch explained. "Some wondered if it was even true that Gower died that night."

Fosse's reaction was difficult to untangle. "That night my sons told me Bob kind of took them under his wing, trying to shield them from David Merrick," recalled Marge Champion, Gower's former wife. "That son of a bitch," Fosse said to Lee Roy Reams at the party, "I just filmed my own death, and he had to do me one better by doing his live on opening night." A day later, Gower's widow, Karla Champion, asked Fosse if he would speak at Gower's memorial. He replied, "Why would I do that? We were competitors."

Jerome Robbins was a competitor too, but he was also a god. Fosse wrote to him about Nicole: now out of high school, she did not want to be a Broadway dancer like her father or mother (Fosse felt this showed "discrimination" on her part) but a ballerina. "She has two gods," Fosse wrote, "you and Mr. Balanchine." Fosse needed his help:

Training at the School of American Ballet that summer, Nicole was told she wasn't built for ballet and that there might not be room for her in the winter session. She had been offered a full scholarship for an upcoming term with Joffrey and an apprentice position with the Cleveland Ballet, but if there was anything Jerry could do to keep her at SAB, Fosse wrote, anything at all . . . Robbins obliged, but Nicole's ballet career did not progress much further. All torso, no legs, and small, she showed her mother's shape on her father's frame, a body, like Joan McCracken's, more suitable to Broadway. And there it was. Strings Fosse could pull, but he could not protect her from her limitations. It was a short step, he knew, from losing the part to feeling a failure, and a shorter step from failure to believing failure was innate, to living one's life as a reject. The meat grinder of show business: enough turns, and the meat grinds itself.

Reading, at Paddy's suggestion, "Death of a Playmate," Teresa Carpenter's *Village Voice* story about Dorothy Stratten, raped and murdered at twenty, only three years older than Nicole, Fosse observed the meat grinder at its cruelest. In her guilelessness, Stratten reminded him of his younger self, a sweet kid. Vulnerable. Paul Snider, local scum, saw it too. "That girl could make me a lot of money," he said in Carpenter's piece. He took her to her prom and sent her nude photos to *Playboy*. Hefner loved them. He loved her. More than a Playmate, she had Marilyn Monroe potential, the stuff of a genuine crossover, stardom, the big time, and Stratten went higher, and the higher she climbed, the less she saw of Snider, and the angrier he got. When she fell in love with Peter Bogdanovich, Snider went crazy. He shot her and sodomized her and then killed himself. Carpenter concluded, "It was all too big for him. In that Elysium of dreams and deals, he had reached the limits of his class. His sin, his unforgivable sin, was being small time." Fosse was Snider too.

He was Faust and Mephistopheles.

Stratten's tragedy stirred the psychology-of-spotlight ideas Fosse wrote to Dr. Sager about, and pushed his lifelong autobiographical inquiry even farther, into hell. Far grislier than *All That Jazz, Lenny,* or *Cabaret,* "Death of a Playmate" was the most horrific show business tale imaginable — and all true. Coming so soon after the tragedy itself, it smacked of exploitation and immorality. Fosse knew his approach to the story — trying to come at it from Snider's perspective — would be considered a kind of empathy with evil. "I somehow identified with him because he was trying to get in," Fosse said. "It's not that I've been excluded that much, but I know that sense of them all knowing something I don't know. And that makes me very angry."

This script, he would write. No compromises, no collaborators.

He began to research. He studied the autopsy reports, underlining gruesome specifics in red pen. *Postmortem abrasions to forehead, knees, and left shoulder. The brain is pulped. The anus is patulous, shows striations.* Teresa Carpenter led Fosse to public documents. She gave him the taped interviews and transcripts she'd used for her research. Like a detective, he scrutinized property profiles of Bogdanovich's Bel-Air home and the Playboy Mansion; he secured internal *Playboy* correspondence from the time of the murder and conducted interviews of his own with cast and crew from Bogdanovich's *They All Laughed,* Stratten's last movie. This was the Fosse of Broadway Arts, listening to records, watching the mirror. He got Stratten's high-school yearbook and interrogated Snider's private photographs. He made Xerox blowups of Hefner's face. Everything he knew about the case he put into a twenty-two-page history — his road map.

Certain scenes called out as script-worthy. Collecting them, Fosse began to find his story. He began to write.

It came easier than expected. Using real dialogue gave him some grounding, and as expert on the available facts, Fosse had the confidence to charge forth. Some said he didn't know the truth, but who did? He knew Snider; he was uniquely qualified to write that story.

Throughout, he kept Paddy in mind. As coach and guru, Paddy's faith urged Fosse back to the typewriter, back to the script's larger ideas. He began to think of Paul Snider as a modern George Eastman, Montgomery Clift's character in *A Place in the Sun*. Both killed for status; the difference was the sort of business they were in. Though Snider was a psychopath, Fosse could present his mania as a perverted offshoot of the showbiz epidemic, the media-obsessed frenzy of fame, flash, and glossy three-page foldouts. He knew it would take a scholar-dramatist of Chayefsky's caliber to make the analogy into compelling entertainment, and all through the writing of the first draft, he expected to turn the pages over to Paddy for a rewrite. But Chayefsky had other plans for his protégé. "You don't need another writer," he told him. "Finish it yourself."

Paddy was finished with movies. *Altered States* did him in, was *doing* him in. Untoward changes of director (Arthur Penn to Ken Russell), lawsuits, and perversions of Chayefsky's original intent hastened the use of his pseudonym (Sidney Aaron) and increased his smoking. His diet worsened and he stopped going to the gym. Paddy wasn't in the mood. Down in the deli, he told Fosse of the great alienation. His, everyone's. Since getting out of the hospital, he'd become convinced the whole business of living, once marked by possibility and agency, had overrun the population with futility. "What are you going to do about anything?" he shouted. "The problems that face us are beyond any of our conception." Wars, corporations, corrupt politicians. There's nothing we can do, so Americans retreat to our little TVs, our family dinners. "I think perhaps they feel like I do," he said, "they really feel unable to cope. Life is just too much." Paddy used to get to the office at nine; he was coming in now around eleven thirty. He rarely went out to dinner anymore. It exhausted him. Hollywood exhausted him. He told Fosse about the producer who asked him to write a movie based on a Marvin Hamlisch song. A *song*. Was this guy crazy? He couldn't write that. Only Jean Cocteau could write that. "Oh, the hell with the script," the producer said. "Think of the *album*." So was that it? Was he in the music business now?

They laughed. At that.

But it *was* different in the fifties. Television then, Paddy said, was a bohemia.

Before long, Paddy was back in the hospital with pleurisy.

He couldn't join Fosse and Shel Silverstein at Herb's Christmas dinner party, an epic revel that ended with an impromptu round of the truth game. "Do you always sleep with your leading dancer?" Silverstein's date, Pamela Larsson-Toscher, asked Fosse. "Of course," Fosse said. "I have to know we're in perfect sync, and she has to know *exactly* where I'm coming from." Some gave performances. Gardner's wife, Barbara Sproul, read a poem, which Larsson-Toscher translated into sign language. Fosse was so touched by the beauty and precision of her handwork that he insisted she see *Children of a Lesser God*, then running on Broadway. That night he got Larsson-Toscher tickets and arranged for her to meet with the actors backstage.

For all that dissatisfied him, Bob Fosse could never be cynical in the face of true talent. Wherever it showed, the creative bloom was always worth a detour. He attended acquaintances' downtown gigs, listened to their long-in-the-works symphonies, and gave advice (all of it considered, none of it encouraging) to someone's friend's daughter interested in dance. As coach and confidant, he gave them all their next moves. He visited their studios, read their scripts, and went to their previews. If they wrote for his opinion, he'd write them back with itemized lists; I don't have the answers, he would say, but if you want to help yourself, do *this*. Cut your hair, retake your headshot, give up on ballet, pick another dream if you can. He wouldn't sugarcoat the bad news. He knew leaving the business, fleeing a loser's game, was in its way a win. Read *Backstage*, he told them, try out for everything, keep up your education, perform as much as possible, and train, practice, rehearse. How do I become a director? Read. Watch people, *learn* them. Store up memories. The rest was luck, and he couldn't help them with that. Nothing could. Behind every ask hovered a Hail Mary prayer that the great Bob Fosse would see in a life story or girlish cursive on pink stationery or relation to a distant relation some fetal promise or potential and invite the kid to New York, to his office, and make her Gwen Verdon tonight. It hurt him. They were kids — the Nicoles, the Dorothy Strattens.

Paddy Chayefsky turned fifty-eight in January 1981, and Fosse took over a corner of the River Café to throw him a birthday party. Before a sweeping view of the East River and easily the best window on New York City in Brooklyn, Cohn, Gardner, and the rest of the gang celebrated with two cakes, one with the name Paddy Chayefsky and the other with his birth name, credited screenwriter of *Altered States,* Sidney Aaron. The party came right on time. Thin and gray, Paddy needed all the celebration he could get. His movie — psychedelically smothered to death by director Ken Russell, as Paddy had expected it would be — had been a disappointment.

Rather than dwell, Paddy went back to writing plays. In February, he was diagnosed with cancer. He refused surgery, began chemotherapy, and lost his hair. Humiliated, Paddy put on a hat and stopped showing up at the deli. Herb Schlein panicked, and Fosse enlisted Romaine Greene — Stratten's hairstylist on *They All Laughed* — to make him a wig. "It was a very funny situation," Gwen remembered, "and of course, Paddy loved the absurdity of it all." Their laughter was imperative. Not the bullshit kind, the really scared kind. And the bullshit kind too.

Other than doing the odd commercial, Fosse refused a decade's worth of offers to film his shows, even for historical safekeeping. When Lincoln Center's Theater on Film and Tape Archive had asked him to film *Pippin* in 1971, he answered, "So people can come in and rip me off? Absolutely not!" and he did not look back. Ten years later, his vaudeville ethic gave way to the promise of cable TV and videotape, new technologies David Sheehan had explained to Fosse in Cannes. Releasing first on cassette and LaserDisc, then going to cable, and finally to network television, a show—in this case, *Pippin*—could pick up three big paydays, live again in the afterlife, and perhaps even run "forever." Handing the reins to Kathryn Doby, who would direct the show in Toronto before three live audiences, Fosse would have the time he needed to stay in Quogue, working on the Dorothy Stratten script. He could edit the footage remotely, off tapes sent back and forth from Burbank to New York. The terms looked good. According to the *Los Angeles Times*, the *Pippin* deal marked "the first time a work of such scope and commercial success has been attempted specifically for the home video market." The pioneer potential had enormous appeal for Fosse.

But after many nights of wondering what would become of *Pippin*, this time for VHS in perpetuity and without him, Fosse rushed to the phone a day before the shoot in June 1981. He could not simply stand by. At Fosse's insistence, Sheehan sent a jet to Quogue, and Fosse flew to Toronto to run the show to his satisfaction before turning back for home to continue working the Dorothy Stratten movie, which he named—after the vanity plate on Snider's Mercedes—*Star 80*. The weekend Roy and Cynthia Scheider came to Quogue, the conversation about Stratten became a conversation about Paddy. They were so worried about him. Everyone was. Some time before, the Scheiders had referred Paddy to a chiropractor, who sent him to the ICU, where, they were told, he would remain until further notice. The details were unclear. Fosse and the Scheiders stood by the phone, bracing themselves for terrible news, but when the phone finally did ring, it brought news of Paddy's release—a relief.

One night Fosse invited the Scheiders to join him at a bar—he didn't tell them what kind—on the Lower East Side. From their front row seats, the Scheiders were stormed by girls, girls, girls, girls who could blow out candles with their vaginas, vaginas that could smoke cigarettes. It was almost too much for them to take in, but Fosse absorbed the performance with clinical appreciation, explaining to Roy and Cynthia the etymology of each grind and feather. He'd say, "That one's stealing from that one who stole from that one . . ." It could be repulsive, but there was a kind of eloquence in the uncensored circle of sex and money. Here was the oldest truth game on record, the big bang of entertainment. Wasn't ballet born the night some baron asked to see a little thigh?

Fosse and the Scheiders soon discovered they hadn't let Paddy out of the ICU because he was improving. "They took him out," Cynthia Scheider said, "because he wasn't getting any better." Toward the end, when Fosse and Herb visited him in the hospital, Paddy would fake bad death scenes from old B movies. "It's getting dark, fellows! It's getting very dark!" It didn't matter where, it didn't matter why; when they laughed, they burned with mad, fearless hilarity, in the dead center of the bluest part of the flame. Nothing deterred them. Coming and going from Paddy's room, Bob and Herb busted up hearing him holler his old movie clichés out to the hall. Then they didn't hear anything. An emergency tracheotomy took Paddy's voice, so he wrote notes, to Fosse, Herb, and his family. He fell into a coma, and they put tubes in him. "He wasn't conscious," said Chayefsky's son Dan, "but he kept yanking the tubes out." His obstinacy surprised no one; he'd always been terrible with compromise.

Paddy died.

Janice Lynde called Fosse from LA. "Are you okay? Should I fly out?"

"You've got to work."

"I can get time off."

"No, no. The work is the most important."

"Bob," she said, "are you okay?"

"I'm okay."

"Really?"

His voice broke. "How could anyone be okay?"

She stayed in LA.

An estimated five hundred people came to Riverside Chapel — Kazan, Mike Nichols, Comden and Green, David Shaw, Doctorow, Vonnegut, David Mamet, Arthur Miller, David Picker, Lionel Larner, Peter Stone, screenwriter of *Sweet Charity* — so many of them faces from Fosse's life that the gathering must have looked to him a little like his own funeral. And in a way, it was. Paddy Chayefsky's friendship was the happiest love Fosse would ever know. His life with Gwen was too complex to compare. It existed in another part of his heart, much of it shaped by the ruins of their former life, their daughter, and his fear of failing them. But Paddy he could never fail. Eating together, working together, they had cohabited every afternoon for fifteen years, their calendars, like Laurel- and Hardy-shaped Venn diagrams, almost a single circle. And what would Fosse's calendar look like now? Who else could he trust? Under his Howard Beale was the Marty part of Paddy, and that part understood and embraced the Charity Hope Valentine in Fosse. It was they who met at the deli every day.

"I kept looking for Bob before the service," Lionel Larner said. "I couldn't find him." No one likes paying hospital visits to the dying, no one wants to go to funerals, but everyone does. Some are even comforted by the ritual. Fosse was not. As much as he could, he avoided the social customs of grief. He visited Bob Aurthur in New York Hospital only once; Joan McCracken's funeral he observed alone, from across Seventy-Second; and when Mr. Weaver died, Fosse only sent flowers. He made exceptions to bury family in Chicago; in the cases of Carol Haney and Jack Cole — artists he knew personally but never loved — Fosse came to their memorials, sometimes to speak, to give a sincere speech and make a joke, and then he left the theater to be alone. At Paddy's memorial, where his sorrow was doubled by the atmosphere of mourning he dreaded, Fosse had to fight the instinct to disappear to a far corner of the chapel or even to flee. "Then I saw him," Larner said. "He was sitting in the front row."

Herb Gardner gave the opening eulogy.

Arthur Schlesinger Jr. spoke of Chayefsky's big theme, "the corrupt and lunatic energies secreted by our great modern organizations," continuing, "No American in recent times had a more exact and stinging satirical gift, but he never used that gift for purely destructive purposes. He was sardonic, not cynical. He wanted to clear our minds of cant and our souls of hypocrisy. For all his relish in human folly, he never abandoned hope in humanity. His satire, like that of all great satirists, sprang from love — from his instinctive sweet understanding of the inarticulate Martys and Claras of the world, bravely living lives of quiet desperation."

Fosse was the last speaker. "When his turn came," remembered James Lipton, "he mounted the steps slowly, then turned to face us . . ."

He began. "As most of you know, Paddy and I were friends . . ."

Fosse stopped to breathe.

He said he had to audition for the role of Paddy's friend, and it took him eight years to get the part. They laughed.

He explained the deal they had made when Paddy had come to visit him in the hospital six years earlier. At Fosse's bedside, Paddy promised Bob that if Bob died first, he would deliver a tedious eulogy at his funeral. Laughing, Fosse had told Paddy that if he died first, he'd do a little tap dance at Paddy's.

"I hope nobody will be offended."

He performed a soft-shoe. "It was a very quiet dance for about thirty seconds," Doctorow said. "There was nothing funny about it. Bob made it totally appropriate."

Sobbing, Fosse said, "I can't imagine my life without you."

Chayefsky was buried in Kensico Cemetery in Westchester, a forty-minute drive from the chapel. At the graveside, during the first kaddish, Paddy's friend Eddie White looked up from the casket to see Fosse had drifted from the circle to the far edge of the cemetery. He was bent forward, collapsed in grief.

SIX YEARS

DAN MELNICK PASSED on *Star 80*. Dark was one thing, but rape, necrophilia, and murder (without catharsis), he didn't want to see. Who did? Not Alan Ladd Jr., but he had so much faith in Fosse he would have agreed to anything. "Whatever he wanted to do, I would have done it because I thought he was a genius," Ladd said. "I don't know anyone more talented that I've ever worked with, and if you're doing a picture you know doesn't have to bring in vast sums of money, you're happy as a movie studio. I never thought for a minute that *Star 80* was going to be *Star Wars*." Nor was he deterred by the poor commercial prospects of a film of such unrelenting gloom and with such a horrific final scene. That earned Laddie even more respect from Fosse. When the two met for dinner at Village cafés off the showbiz circuit, Fosse left his black armor at home. "On those occasions," Laddie recalled, "when Fosse knew he wouldn't be seen, he would wear color. And he'd only smoke once in a while. That was Bob the guy" — an exotic sighting — "the other was Fosse the showman. He'd come out for Wally's." Laddie saw both Fosses. A Hollywood executive unafraid of his director's power, Ladd too was exotic.

If only *Star 80* were a work of fiction, Fosse might have started casting right away. But the painstaking and (for Stratten's family) painful back-and-forths of rights and releases hobbled his progress through the fall of 1981. With the Stratten tragedy only months in the past and her family beyond devastation, *Star 80* screamed lawsuit. Scalpels in hand, attorneys, executives, and rightfully concerned insurance carriers examined each word of each draft of Fosse's script, hemorrhaging fine print. Prevented from using actual names, Fosse was also required to provide documentation for objectionable dialogue and ordered to refrain from any implication that sodomy preceded the murder. He reluctantly agreed to use close-ups of Snider's face in lieu of more incriminating wide shots, and he consented not to arrange dead bodies in such a way as to suggest consensual sex or rape had taken place. No matter how well intended, each smoothed truth affronted the sincerity of Fosse's effort. But those were the terms.

As promised, David Sheehan kept in close communication with Fosse through the cutting of *Pippin*, dutifully sending him tapes, which Fosse flatly hated. He called Sheehan in the middle of the night, screaming, "You're cutting off the feet! We don't want to see their faces! We want to see their *bodies!*" Sheehan didn't understand. This was TV, he explained, a faces medium. But, Fosse explained, this was *Pippin*, a dance show. You wanted to see the *bodies*. "He would send notes on a Thursday," Sheehan said, "and he would want to see results by the weekend. But we didn't work that fast." Fosse didn't understand why; he could. Railing against Sheehan's dissolves and music-video-like cuts on the beat, Fosse demanded he cut *Pippin* like *Liza with a Z*, keeping its theatricality intact. "I don't think I ever had his trust," Sheehan said, "but he wanted that show immortalized."

It was agony. Late in November, Fosse watched the final cut, expecting to see his notes implemented, as Sheehan had assured him they would be. What he saw appalled him. Not only were his specific instructions ignored, but parts of the show had been outright deleted. After shutting off the television, he wrote to *Pippin*'s cast and crew apologizing for a "foolishly butchered version of the show . . . [that] was mysteriously kept from me." It aired in January 1982 to awful reviews.

Mariel Hemingway, a Cohn client, was desperate to play Dorothy, a role wildly unlike the character she played in her previous film, *Personal Best*. Cohn encouraged Fosse to give her a shot, but Fosse didn't see it. Hemingway had a tomboyish quality that wasn't right for Dorothy. Dorothy was silk, sweet, womanly. He liked Melanie Griffith. But Hemingway persisted. She wrote him letters, begging him to see her. Finally, Cohn got them together on the phone.

"You must read me."

"You're not right for it."

"Let me show you."

"Listen, I like you. You're just not right for this part."

With no other recourse, Hemingway turned up in New York. He had to admit she had the right sort of unused quality, and her relentlessness brought to mind the sort of hunger *Star 80* was about. But breast size was a problem. Hemingway's wasn't a Dorothy Stratten figure — a real concern for a movie about a *Playboy* playmate — but taking Cohn's advice, Fosse let her read, and after the reading, they talked. Instinct told Hemingway this exchange was the real audition. "Fosse had to merge with the actor," she said. "It was really more for him than the other person." The trick was merging on her terms ("But I sleep with all my leading ladies," he pleaded). Trying to facilitate intimacy but unwilling to sleep with him, Hemingway had to walk the tightrope of deep but guarded involvement. "How can I make it feel as though he is having a relationship with me without actually having one?" The question rarely left her mind. "It was a tough line," she said, "because then he'd get mad at me and call me a cocktease, and then I'd be heartbroken." Soon thereafter Hemingway got breast implants, and then she got the part.

For his Snider, Fosse needed an actor with a star's good looks and charm but a character actor's fearlessness—a tall order. Furthermore, he was casting autobiographically, looking for an alter ego, which narrowed the list yet more, and the question "Will anyone do it?" became "Is there anyone who can do it?" The studio answered with Richard Gere, hot off *American Gigolo*. Fosse read him with Hemingway, but Fosse's heart was set on Robert De Niro, whom he couldn't get to read the script. "That fucked him up," Hemingway recalled. "He felt less than, like 'De Niro won't read my script. He doesn't think I'm anybody.'" Fosse asked Hemingway, suspecting De Niro wanted to sleep with her, to finesse the transaction. She refused.

Sam Shepard came to his audition with his friend Cis Rundle, who happened to be Hugh Hefner's social secretary. (The night of Dorothy's murder, Rundle's first on the job, she got the terrible phone call and told Hefner the news. She found him in the game room between a pinball machine and a girl. "It's Dorothy," Rundle said. "She's dead." The girl looked to Hef. "Does that mean we're not going to the Jacuzzi?")

"This is shit," Rundle said, meaning the script, as Fosse emerged from Shepard's audition.

"What's shit?"

"All this about the mansion and Hef. It's wrong." She could see Fosse was listening. "Do you want to make a cartoon or a real movie?"

He made Rundle *Star 80*'s technical adviser and gave her a part in the film. She caught the slips (for example, Hef didn't carry a can of soda, he carried a bottle) and wrote Fosse detailed descriptions of mansion parties and Hef's famous movie nights. She introduced him to Hefner. They got on. Hefner gave Fosse permission to use the *Playboy* logo and allowed him limited access to the mansion for research, once to study the grounds and once to study the parties. They'd film elsewhere, but of course, their copy of the mansion had to be exact. (It was: when Fosse showed Hef a plan of the set, Hef thought he was looking at his own house.) Returning Hefner's kindness, Fosse accepted his feedback on casting. "He asked Bob not to cast Harry Dean Stanton [in the Hefner role]," Rundle said, "and approved of Cliff Robertson."

The search for Snider continued. At his callback, Eric Roberts fielded Fosse's interview questions. Where was he educated? What did he do for fun? (Could they merge? Yes, they could.) For Roberts's second callback, they read through the entire script, and two weeks later, choosing now between Roberts and Gere, Fosse called Roberts back again. "We read the scene he was always rewriting," Roberts said. "The scene where Snider's at the mansion for the first time, a hard scene." It required tremendous control to cover Snider's desperation with charm. But Roberts could do it. He got the part.

What his actors couldn't possibly know about the sex industry, Fosse gave them. While scouting Los Angeles for locations, he personally toured Roberts through the traumatized fringe, its people and pathology. "He educated me on the life of the strip clubs," Roberts said. "He wanted me to know it wasn't about fucking, that every stripper who was a 'lifer' — that's what he called them — has the same issues as children who were molested. Bob believed that. He wanted me to know that this guy [Snider] had expertise, that this guy, if he weren't a psychopath, would have been hugely successful." When they arrived at each club, Fosse would vanish, allowing Roberts to mingle with the strippers on his own.

By contrast, Fosse barred Hemingway from doing her own research. As with Valerie Perrine, he wanted to control everything his leading lady knew about her subject. "He gave me everything," she recalled. "He'd give me tapes to watch, he'd talk about being damaged goods, he taught me how to walk in high heels. He put on my high heels and showed me. Once he said, 'You're so innocent and all-American but you're not. You come from this sick family.'" He wasn't talking about Stratten's family. He was talking about the Hemingways.

His whole life, Fosse had courted despair. He affected it, savored it, feared it, and fled it, but working on *Star 80*, in Los Angeles — Despairsville, USA — reabsorbing the desperate borders of show business ("I'm going to die in one of these places," Fosse said, scouting shitholes with Tony Walton), despair flattened him. Paddy was dead. *All That Jazz* had used up everything he had (he feared), and having surrounded himself with allies, from the laissez-faire Laddie to Wolfgang Glattes and Kenneth Utt, Fosse had no scapegoat to condemn. "On *Star 80* he was just impossible," Glattes said. "It was very frustrating for Bob to not have anyone to blame." Starting fights helped him redirect the anger. So did insisting on the impossible, like getting inside the actual house where Snider lived and killed Dorothy. But Glattes didn't have a permit.

"You have to get in."

"It's trespassing."

"Just do it."

"Bob —"

"*Get in.*"

At dusk, the Santa Monica Freeway clogged over the pale box at 10881 Clarkson Road, and Glattes and his son Michael broke in through the garage.

"Look," Michael said, pointing up.

Cartridges. Still there on the shelf.

Snapping pictures of walls, carpeting, furniture — whatever he could — Glattes moved through the house and into the little bedroom where it happened. Thin coats of new paint didn't cover everything. Glattes found traces of shotgun damage and crusted spurts of blood. "We got the hell out of there," he said.

In Vancouver, Fosse and casting director Lynne Carrow turned a hotel room into a makeshift office and spent days reading and interviewing extras. Though some would appear only in the background of the shot, Fosse auditioned them as if they were potential leads, devoting as much as fifteen minutes to each individual — a long time for a tiny part — to connect to them. "He had this incredible ability to focus so totally on each actor," Carrow recalled. "Bob would sit there a foot away from the actor, pulling a performance out of them, while I read. I never worked with a director who physically sat knee to knee with the actors, coaching them and then turning to me and putting his hand on my shoulder to give me direction, and then turning back to them. It was very intimate. He would touch the women in a way to let them know he was there. But male or female, it didn't matter. He'd be talking to them very gently, very softly, with a cigarette in his mouth. You could see the actor realize they were in the presence of someone who totally understood them. I remember one actress who was having a hard time pulling her performance down and when she got too big he would lean forward and gently touch her knee and say, gently, 'Start that again.' It was sensual."

Fosse scouted Vancouver in a fifteen-passenger van big enough for every department head. He rode up front, smoking far more than his usual too much, his eyes fixed on the window. They couldn't get Dorothy's actual family home so they got one nearby, but they did get the real Dairy Queen, the one where Snider first saw Dorothy, and drove onward to the Penthouse, a strip club perfect for the part of Snider's hangout. There was a lot of downtime in the van, and conversation came easy. Master cinematographer Sven Nykvist took the opportunity to bring up his director's love life. "Bob," he asked, "why all the young girls?" To the window, Fosse replied, "Their stories are shorter."

Currently, Liz Canney headed the pack. (He had met her at a Westhampton Beach bar. She was a waitress.) A pretty, dollhouse brunette,

Canney was young (in her early twenties) and seriously interested in editing. Fosse gave her a job working for Alan Heim, effective as soon as production began. In the meantime, back in New York, they spent New Year's Eve together and went to dinners with Doctorow and his wife, Helen; Sam Cohn; and Steve Tesich. One evening, Fosse's *Star 80* script came up, and Doctorow hedged. He didn't think it worked; the plodding inevitability of Snider's course could make for a tiresome movie. But this close to production, Doctorow felt it would be inappropriate to suggest major revisions. Fosse was already worried enough. Though *Star 80* was his fifth feature film, Fosse approached it like it was his first, with debilitating dread. He told Doctorow he had no idea what he was going to do once he got back to Vancouver. "I'm going to go out there," he lamented, "and they're going to ask me where to put the camera."

FIVE YEARS

BEFORE LEAVING FOR VANCOUVER, Fosse choreographed "The Magic Bird of Fire," a rock-disco reimagin-
ing of Stravinsky's Firebird Suite, for Nicole. It would be
one part of a benefit evening for Ballet Today, Brett Raphael's fledgling dance company, and took the efforts of all the Fosses to mount.
While Bob helped Nicole through the pointe solo he tailored to her
strengths and weakness, Gwen busied herself with Nicole's feathery
unitard and acted as intermediary between father and daughter and
Raphael. The afternoon of May 24, Fosse arrived at FIT's Haft Auditorium for a dress rehearsal, gave only a few notes, and left before the
one-night-only performance. Verdon and Reinking came instead.

The piece gave Fosse an opportunity to try a kind of ballet without suffering the consequences of a highly visible failure. But if "The
Magic Bird of Fire" got a positive response, he might find the courage
to finally accept the Joffrey's offer and put on his first full Fosse ballet. After *Dancin'*, it still seemed to him a kind of finish line. Maybe
even a relief. "It was fierce," Raphael said of the ballet, "with a lot of
jumps. Not a subtle piece." Critic Mindy Aloff wrote, "This piece is
dressed and lit in flame, and features a few singed remnants of danc-

ing: pointe tendu, retiré, and the ever popular pectoral twitch. . . . Nicole Fosse is a pretty teenager; this, however, makes her look as if she's pushing retirement." "The Magic Bird of Fire" was never performed again. Any plans for the Joffrey Fosse sidelined.

With Fosse in Vancouver, Glattes took charge of screen tests in LA. Merely doing the scenes as written rarely gave Fosse as much as he got from getting them laughing or having them tell jokes, so he urged Glattes toward interview-auditions, recommending he interrupt the conversation with a continuous stream of comments and questions. Throwing them off balance could show a glint of real character. To gauge their appearances, Fosse requested close-ups, left and right profile shots, and, of course, full figure (in T-shirt). Glattes knew the drill, but never before had he seen Fosse so blindly adamant about detail. Trivia consumed him.

"We have to use the same carpet, Snider's real carpet."

"Bob, you can't show blood on a brown carpet."

Fosse held his ground and Glattes tested blood for months, a different shade of red every day. As if compensating for being a first-time writer and a longtime success, Fosse indulged his every hypervigilant concern. On *Lenny* he was desperate; on *All That Jazz,* obsessed; on *Star 80,* Fosse was a bottomless wound of insatiability. "It was like none of his successes had ever happened," Doctorow said. In advance of his arrival, Fosse insisted every bookcase on their Playboy Mansion set match every bookcase in the real thing and that every book on those bookcases fit Hefner's personality, whether it was in the shot or not. "It was just a movie," Reinking said, "but it had to be real." Now with a permit to shoot in the actual house where the killing took place, Fosse had the crew dress Snider's former garage with the metalworking equipment he had used to build his sex-torture machine, and he instructed set decorator Mel Cooper to study explicit crime scene photos to assemble the contraption with total and horrendous fidelity. (In the weeds behind the house, Cooper found a Canadian license plate, presumably the one he had ditched to make room for his STAR 80.) The envelopes on the desk that doubled for Hefner's contained letters from Dorothy to her mother — "real" outgoing mail Cooper stayed up nights writing, in Dorothy's hand, in case Fosse decided to open one. "I didn't try to copy her signature," Cooper said, "but it had to be in a woman's writing." Some thought it overkill, but the effect was so lifelike, one could not step on set without feeling a ghostly chill, a premonition. It gradually dawned on cast and crew that Fosse wasn't filming a tragedy — he was re-creating it.

He returned to Los Angeles in June. With his final script revision complete, he rehearsed Hemingway and Roberts for six weeks — unprecedented for a Fosse film — in a vacant studio space at Hollywood United Methodist Church. Each "room" marked off on the floor with tape, they ran through the script, first in chunks, then in full runs, like a play. Only necessary props, blowups of actual locations, and occasional mood music disrupted the totality of their immersion. Midway through the process, Fosse asked second AD Tony Gittelson to put them on the clock. "Start the movie," he would say, and *click* — Gittelson hit the stopwatch. Before long, Hemingway realized that her director was choreographing an entire movie. "It was *all* choreographed," she explained, "every movement. 'You'll pick up this, he'll play the guitar and sing this . . .'" Fosse had never made a movie this way before, but with all he had on the line, staging *Star 80* in full allowed him some kind of insurance, as if by isolating every detail in advance, he could watch a rough cut of the movie before he made it. But the final scene he kept to himself. Fosse hadn't rehearsed that. He did not reveal how he planned to stage the murder-rape-suicide, if he had a plan at all. And so it loomed over the production, a conspicuous and horrific inevitability waiting for everyone.

Filming began in July 1982. "It was so painful to work on," Albert Wolsky said. "Not just in subject matter, but we shot [mostly] in sequence, so the whole shoot was building closer and closer to it. Sometimes on movies you do the worst thing first, to get it out of the way. Not this one."

In Los Angeles, removed from his connection, Fosse had difficulty getting amphetamines. "Cis," he said to Rundle, who was fast becoming a friend, "if you are the actress you think you are, who can you convince you need Dexies?" At night, away from the movie, they laughed, took trips to the Improv, and hung out at the bus stop, people watching. But the dark was always there. Some nights, Rundle just held him. He asked her to and she wanted to help. "Make these last," she warned when she handed Fosse the pills.

A mix of tantrums, charm, and withdrawn silence, Fosse's moods fluctuated throughout the shoot. "It was like sounds were too loud," Hemingway said. What set him off? Was it personal? Not knowing kept the crew on edge. One day he angrily cleared the set, only to look up hours later and ask, "Why isn't anyone here?" Casting director Lynne Carrow thought his moods a function of broken concentration ("I'd say, 'Hey, Bob,' and he'd look at me blankly"). Others had different theories, mostly guesses. They said he was trying to quit smoking; he was taking too many pills; he was quitting pills. Eric Roberts saw a man under impossible pressure. "Everyone was all over him about, 'You can't badmouth Hollywood, you can't badmouth Dorothy, you can't badmouth Bogdanovich, you can't badmouth Hef or we'll lose the *Playboy* logo.' Dorothy's family, people in Hollywood, his lawyers — they were on him about accuracy and morality and the 'real' story." Dorothy's sister Louise sent Fosse a letter, handwritten in her tenth-grade cursive, telling him he didn't know the truth, that he was hurting her and her family. After reading the letter, Fosse professed to be overcome with guilt. He did not want to hurt her. He did not want to hurt anyone.

He called Ann Reinking. "I'm living in a world where nobody wants to live," he told her. "I'm living in this world, and now we got to get to this spot. We've got to get to murder. And I really like these people. I don't want to see them die." He regularly placed a rose bouquet on the craft-service table with a note that said *To Dorothy*.

"He's going to do it," Fosse said to Cliff Robertson, his Hefner. "He's going to kill her, and I don't know how to stop him."

The actor didn't know what to say. He couldn't be sure if this was some kind of Method trick, or the pills.

"We have to do something," Fosse said. "Watch him. Help her."

Roberts had virtually transformed himself into Snider, furthering the illusion and taking the whole production down with him. "He lied about everything," one actor said. He screamed. He locked himself in his trailer. He appeared in the production office in his underwear. "Eric was so volatile," another said, "Fosse had to handle him carefully. He'd have these infuriating moments of *I want to fire him, he drives me fucking crazy*." He would deny it, but Fosse enabled Roberts, reaching raw steaks through his cage, feeding him with friendship and understanding. Without warning, Fosse would show up at Roberts's house, banging loudly on the door in the middle of the night as if to say, *Watch and repeat; this is you.* Before he shot Roberts's sex scene with Hemingway, Fosse asked him to remove the protective dance belt he had used in rehearsal to cover his genitals. Fosse gave Hemingway a feeble explanation for Roberts's sudden nudity, and they proceeded with the shot; her discomfort, which Fosse wanted for Dorothy, showed up on film. On separate occasions, when Roberts went too far, Fosse would take the crew's side against him. "[Roberts] got so into it," Fosse said, "that he began alienating everybody around the set. Costume people and hairdressers would come to me and complain about how horrendously he was behaving. I went to him and was in the middle of reprimanding him when I realized what he was doing. He was trying to feel what it's like to say the wrong things and have people reject you and what that does to you and how it sours you." Fosse nurtured all of it. Playing one side against the other, he introduced Roberts into an atmosphere of exile and estrangement, the kind that drove Snider.

Shooting on a sound stage at Zoetrope Studios, Roberts flubbed a scene.

Fosse's head shot out from behind the camera. "What the fuck is wrong with you?"

"I messed up."

"Get over here."

Fosse got up from the crate he used as a director's chair and took him to the other side of the stage, away from the rest of the crew. "Look at me."

Roberts looked at him.

"*Look* at me."

"I'm looking at you."

"*Look at me!*"

"I'm looking at you!"

"You're playing *me* if I wasn't successful." Fosse got in his face. "Do you understand?"

Do you understand? He asked the question, Roberts remembered, "like, *Can you do this for me? For me.* It was so moving and so gritty and unexpected. By the time we got back to the set, I was copying his every move. I didn't drop one mannerism he had for the rest of the movie. I became Bob Fosse."

Fosse asked Roberts to spend the night in the house on Clarkson Road.

"Can you do it?"

"Yeah, I can do it."

"We're doing it together."

They stayed up, discussed the ending, and Fosse fell asleep on furniture he had brought in to make the house look as it did on August 14, 1980, the day of the killings. Roberts, however, couldn't fall asleep. Freeway traffic kept him up all night. "Playing Snider made me sad," he said. "I was pathetically unhappy during the whole shooting of that movie."

It was the weekend before they were scheduled to shoot the murder. "We were all afraid of it," Alan Heim said. "The actors, Bob. It was inexorable." When Hemingway and Roberts gathered to rehearse the scene, they discovered Fosse had it all prepared, choreographed to the smallest detail, like a dance. To the music of Strauss's *Death and Transfiguration,* he had broken their movements down, from A to B to C. "It was ballet," said Tony Gittelson, "choreographed down to the hands." Fosse talked them through every gesture, whispering direction over their dialogue when necessary. He spoke smoothly, caressingly, interrupting himself with explosive coughing sprees so distressing that factions of the crew actually placed bets on whether he was going to survive the movie.

They wrapped.

Eric Roberts broke into Cis Rundle's house. He trashed the furniture. On more than one occasion, she found him waiting for her on the street, his eyes like empty holes. Once she came home to find him watching TV in her living room. Fosse told Rundle to get a restraining order, but she never did. Somehow she felt sorry for him. Was it her proximity to Hef, and to Dorothy, that drew Roberts to her? Or was it that he didn't know what else to do with what he had left of Snider? He asked Rundle to take him to Dorothy's grave at Westwood Memorial Park Cemetery, hidden famously behind a multiscreen cineplex on Wilshire Boulevard. She did, and watched him from a distance. Across the grass from Marilyn Monroe, he knelt crying at Dorothy's headstone, a simple red plaque near the center of the green. "And then," Rundle said, "I don't know why, Eric ripped up his SAG card and left."

Editing *Star 80* did not demand the same muscle Heim and company had needed to tame *All That Jazz.* Fosse had less footage to bring back to New York — a relief with its own set of problems. For one, Hemingway's weaker points could not unweaken. In an unusual move, Fosse and Heim had her outtakes reprinted, and they gleaned what they could from the scraps, but in the end they found their initial instincts confirmed: they already had the very best of her. Then there was the film's dreaded finale, which Heim had warned Fosse, in dailies, to tone down. He hadn't. Now, in the cutting room, Heim suggested they try to ease off the rape and murder, just a little. He recognized the reality of the story called for horror, but there was such a thing as going too far. "We didn't butt heads," Heim said. "We discussed." For his effort, Fosse dubbed Heim his conscience, but, again, they were stuck with what they had: *Star 80* would end in a sickening display of misery and gore. And yet, despite all that was meant to hurt in his nightmare of showbiz psych, Fosse wanted his film to entertain. "I tried to make it like a musical with one slow scene then a staccato scene," he said. "I put in moments of sheer entertainment just to break up the tension." Only an audience could tell him if he had succeeded.

Outside the cutting room, the musical tide was turning against Fosse. As of the previous June, *Dancin'* had left the Ambassador Theater, making the fall of 1982 the first time since 1977 he had no show on Broadway — and back then, he'd had to wait only a short while to see his name on a marquee once again.

New York wasn't his town anymore.

Breakthroughs in technology, politics, and society begin and end golden ages in the same swoop. One can see the story of Broadway either way, as a sequence of new lives or a series of deaths. Those partial to shows of the 1930s could blame those productions' demise on the radio; in the 1940s, they could say it was the war; in the 1950s, TV; in the 1960s, it was the movies and hippies; and on and on. And yet each modification forced a change to the musical, stimulating an innovation in production, aesthetic ideology, or theme. Only innocence was lost. Each era matured the form, growing it upward from the mulch of shows past. Each generation could have had it both ways. "They don't make 'em like they used to but look how they make 'em now!" One could have said that — then. Not now. "It's just possible that the Broadway musical — like some species of the animal kingdom — may have perfected itself out of existence," Frank Rich opined. The 1979–1980 season featured only three new American musicals. And the musical revival dominated 1981. What happened?

A generation gap, for one thing. The shift of popular music from Broadway to rock drew new talents with it, leaving contemporary musical theater in the hands of old masters. Many seemed out of ideas. Then there were the prohibitively high costs of mounting a big show. Corporations had been investing in Broadway for decades — Coca-Cola put money in *1600 Pennsylvania Avenue*, Columbia Pictures bought into *Dancin'* — but in the early eighties, the Reagan era's fetish for blockbuster spectaculars raised budgets to epic heights, and the corporate investor became an almost essential part of Broadway — which isn't necessarily a bad thing. But when the money tries to protect its investment — at around four million dollars, a considerable one — by getting involved with the creative content of the shows, unhealthy mutations occur. "There is not the same kind of intelligence and cultivation today," Hal Prince told the *New York Times*. "Our times encourage another sort of people — people with new money who are essentially interested in more money, not the arts." The wrong people make the wrong decisions for the wrong reasons. With so many irreducible tastes to fold into one, the likes of Warner Brothers, Paramount, Universal, and other entertainment giants, hoping to draw audiences from New York to Calexico, waved their unmagic wands over Broadway, and musical theater went *pop*, which is to say, mostly bland. And to turn a profit, these expensive shows needed to play longer and to more audiences. But the longer they played, the more new talent they blocked, and there we are again: the generation gap.

That was the first tragedy. Here's the second: big Broadway worked. People paid in record numbers. The summer of 1980 was Broad-

way's biggest ever. And then, self-merchandizing, it got bigger. Strolling midtown in October 1982 — just weeks before Fosse wrapped *Star
80* — many a Broadway rabbi had reason to pause before the Winter
Garden, stroke his long beard, and ponder: "Does *Cats* sell the T-
shirts, or do the T-shirts sell *Cats*?" To see *Cats* at the Winter Garden
— where it ran for almost nineteen years, starting in 1982 — was to
ride giggling into a Disneyland happening as weird and sweet and
thin as a Halloween-themed Miss America Pageant (with cats). High
on aria and low on dance, Andrew Lloyd Webber set the pace for pop
opera, showcasing big songs, big sets, and big voices. "I see shows
having more special effects," Fosse said, "more like Spielberg movies.
Everybody's into short-term concentration, like MTV, with hyped-up
sound and lights." The success of the Broadway spectacular showed
that Robbins, de Mille, Michael Kidd, and Jack Cole were definitely
dead in spirit, even if some of them weren't actually dead. Fosse and
Michael Bennett were all that remained of director-choreographers.
From opposite sides of the same street, each watched the other guy,
regarding him strangely, like the other survivor on his desert island.
They had more in common than they once thought.

Virtuoso in every detail, Michael Bennett's *Dreamgirls* did what
few could have imagined — it outclassed *A Chorus Line*. From the
first note — a single beat — a flood of music continuously transformed
Dreamgirls' fluid network of cultures, personalities, and pop trends,
evolving a panoramic picture of the show-business life, of show business across many lives, many eras. Long, tall light towers moved the
air like tai chi masters, imperiously reinventing the stage space, trans-
porting the drama through time at the speed of a chord change or a
cut. *Sweet Charity* was cinematic; *Dreamgirls* was practically a movie
onstage. "I think he felt like that victory should have been his," Tony
Stevens said. "Fosse was a film genius but Michael Bennett wasn't. But
on *Dreamgirls*, Michael was saying, 'Look, I can do movies too, and I
can do it onstage.'" The hardest part was that Fosse couldn't tell Paddy

about *Dreamgirls;* he couldn't follow him to a corner booth and figure out a way to laugh about it over a drink. Some nights, after leaving the cutting room, instead of heading home, Fosse would walk south to West Fifty-Fifth Street to visit Paddy's old friend Eddie White. An ex-prizefighter, he had Paddy's build, and when the lights were low his silhouette could pass for Chayefsky's. White may even have loved Paddy as much as Fosse did. In the old days, after dinner, Fosse would say good night to Paddy and move on to the female part of his evening, and Paddy, who didn't want to go home to his wife and didn't want to troll the streets for company, would galumph his way to White's, to the big black recliner his pal kept waiting for him, and pass a few hours talking about the fights, about Rocky Graziano, about show business (which was a fight too), until he got tired enough to go home. Now, on those nights that Fosse left the cutting room and didn't go home, he would go to White's and settle into Paddy's big black recliner, sometimes staying until morning. White stayed up with him. Though he was tired, he let Fosse talk on about girls and the movie. "Eddie," he would say, "tell me about Paddy."

He saw Ann Reinking for lunch. Fueled perhaps by the implications of her relationship with Herb Allen, president of Allen and Company and Columbia Pictures (among other subsidiaries), Fosse asked Reinking to marry him. They were in his apartment. "If we'd had a child," he said to her, "he'd be eleven by now." Confused by her emotion, moved by her confusion, she entertained a home movie of what it would look like and skipped to the last scene. "I felt he really wanted to marry me," she said, "but I also felt he knew that he really couldn't. There was no saving him. He knew he was dying, not literally, but that there was something dying in him. You know that something's so wrong and you know that it is killing you but you don't know what it is and you don't know how to stop it. That was Bob. I just loved him so much that if it didn't work out, it would break my heart beyond repair. I don't think I could have survived it."

FOUR YEARS

FOSSE CUT *STAR 80* through spring of 1983 and set his sights on relief. A little vacation first, and then, if he could machete his way through the corporate tangle of Broadway, a *fun* musical; nothing cynical, just a sturdy piece of entertainment, a few laughs and good numbers. The thought of an old-time musical comedy, maybe the kind Abbott used to make — a notion Fosse had spent most of his career resisting — took him back twenty years to *Big Deal on Madonna Street.* "It was about fumblers trying to do something bigger than they were capable of doing and never giving up," he said. "That thread appealed to me — that desire to keep trying all the time." The details were vague — maybe Peter Allen would do the songs and he'd do the book. At this early, early stage, *Big Deal* was a placeholder, Fosse's preemptive retaliation to the post-postproduction blues he saw coming.

The afternoon Michael Jackson invited him to lunch, Fosse called Janice Lynde. "Come with me and tell me what you think."

In June, the *Flashdance* soundtrack bumped *Thriller* off the Billboard Top 200, ending its sensational six-month reign. But Jackson wanted back on the charts. He stayed up nights calling his advisers, nudging them on, toward the next thing. "Billie Jean" and "Beat It," the album's two big singles, had done well as music videos, and they decided to try "Thriller," the title track, as their third.

At lunch, Jackson told Fosse that he was one of his idols, on par with Fred Astaire. "You've changed the face of dance," he insisted. "You've been an inspiration to me." Coming from anyone else, this might have seemed like a sales pitch. But the King of Pop did not need to sell anyone, least of all Fosse, who returned Jackson's admiration with more admiration. Jackson, Fosse said, was one of the greatest dancers he had ever seen, maybe since Astaire, "because he's so fast," Cynthia Scheider explained, "and because when he extends his arm or his leg or whatever it goes completely out and then right back. Not half out, not one quarter, not nine-tenths. It goes completely out and then back — fast. But it's complete. Every action is complete." And Jackson did not have to tell Fosse he had amassed a complete collection of Fosse's work on film and television, which he watched obsessively, for Fosse to realize he'd been a major influence on Jackson. His moves themselves revealed Fosse's influence. Under the pulled-down fedora, Jackson's *Pippin*-like handwork, shoulder isolations, groinology, and upper-versus-lower body contrast — his cooling of hot and heating of cool — danced a page out of "Snake in the Grass" with Astaire-like precision in hip-hop triple time.

After the social part of the meal, Jackson asked to speak with Fosse alone, and Lynde politely withdrew.

"I'll see you at the apartment," she said.

"No, no. Wait at the bar. Would you do that?"

She understood why only after they left the restaurant.

"Do you think he's weird?" Fosse asked on their way up the block.

"Why?"

"He wants me to do 'Thriller' as a music video. But he's just too weird. Don't you think?"

"*You're* saying somebody's weird?"

"What's so funny about that?"

Fosse would turn "Thriller" down, but Jackson kept his door open and they stayed in sporadic communication.

Meanwhile, early test screenings showed *Star 80* did more than merely depress audiences; it actually seemed to traumatize them. Even the hippest crowds in New York fled the theater in abject speechlessness. A Lincoln Center screening ended, Heim said, as "the whole front row walked out. They averted their eyes and held each other as they left." But Fosse didn't make any significant changes. He maintained *Star 80* was his best film; trauma should be traumatic. And though he knew they had a problem, Alan Heim basically agreed with Fosse's assessment. Laddie took a respectful distance. "I was not thinking, *This is a hit*," he said. "I was thinking, *This is nervous time*."

Herb Gardner dragged his feet through the cutting of *The Goodbye People*, refusing to part with or even trim his fulsome monologues or the long silences sandwiched in between. The comedy, which disappointed twice on Broadway, ballooned to over two and a half hours of film, and Cynthia Scheider, sick of Herb's craziness, finally quit the picture, leaving David Picker and United Artists with no editor and a director who preferred to cut alone, in a corner of the Brill Building, doodling hieroglyphics on choice takes he surrendered to no one. "If Herb let me cut twenty seconds in a week," said Rick Shaine, the new editor, "that was major." In came Picker, threatening to kidnap the footage from Gardner if he didn't shape up, and behind Picker came Fosse, to mediate as he had many times before. Taking the reins, he told Gardner to face the wall — literally — to turn away from the flatbed and count how long those too-long silent moments he refused to cut actually lasted. When Herb got up to twenty seconds, he gave in, and *The Goodbye People* passed to Fosse.

Fosse spent his first day as captain getting to know his editor. Did

Shaine have a musical background? What instrument? (Saxophone.) Could he recut the parade scene to a temporary music track? "I don't care what shots you use," Fosse said, "but start here, with close-ups of Judd Hirsch and Pamela Reed, and end up on this master shot . . ." Then he left for lunch. Fosse's strategy surprised Shaine. Rather than asking him to cut the sequence to story, Fosse had asked him to cut by shot size — close-up, medium, and so forth. When Fosse returned, Shaine screened the new parade scene, his eyes watching Fosse's. It worked; the scene crescendoed from small shots to big, building a visual rhythm that actually clarified the story. "I had seen other directors work this way with actors," Shaine said. "He wanted to probe what I could do." Over the next month, Fosse brought in additional temp scores (once "Mr. Bojangles"), and *The Goodbye People* began to slim.

Mostly, Gardner stayed away. "It was painful for Herb," Shaine said.

The morning Shaine came late to work, he caught Fosse skulking in the hall outside the editing room. "You better get in there," he mumbled, and Shaine, unsure of what was happening, did as he said. On his way in, he ran into David Picker. "Do you have any aspirin?" he asked. Shaine looked past him. There was Herb, watching his movie on the Steenbeck. Watching with him was the notoriously, brilliantly, and painstakingly slow director Elaine May, whose oft-delayed *Mikey and Nicky* reportedly reached well over a million feet of film and had taken years to edit (into a wonderful movie). She and Herb were in the middle of a heated exchange. Before her was a document of twenty single-spaced pages — her notes, most of them nanoscale. "If they want tits," May blurted out, "you gotta *give 'em* tits!" Picker intervened, and that was it for Elaine May.

Otherwise, Gardner and Fosse stayed in sync. Over lunch at the Carnegie, they traded *Goodbye People* updates and howled against the gales of Hollywood like the blustery old men of Gardner's new play *I'm Not Rappaport.* As always, Herb Schlein greeted them with the white linen napkins he saved for their table, but only two. "They missed Paddy," Shaine said. "There was a lot of sentiment around Paddy and very little joking."

For Paddy. Lingering at the end of the credits, they were the final words of *Star 80.*

"If you've turned to writing," E. L. Doctorow said to Fosse, "I'm going to turn to dancing."

Fosse lit up.

"We're going to have a dance class called Dancing for Writers."

"Terrific. Who else should we have?"

"Well, Peter Maas."

"Norman Mailer might be interested."

Doctorow considered this. "I can approach Isaac Bashevis Singer."

"How about Herman Melville?"

"I'll call Flaubert."

They settled on three rules, all highly negotiable. One, you had to be published (a couple sentences would do). Two, you had to smoke. Three, you had to be over fifty (no one could show up Fosse that way). Pete Hamill said, "All I wanted to master was that dance all the great dancers did on sand that we saw the beginning of in *The Little Prince.* Or the thing with the hats from *Pajama Game.* To learn either of those would have been enough for one life on this earth and Fosse promised he would do that. All of us — the writers — were nervous of course because once we learned all the moves he was going to get us to perform somewhere, open out of town, wait for the notices, who knew what might happen? Fosse told us the great moment of panic would be when we left the mirror. But he would do it, he said, he would get us through it, he promised that." A short time later Doctorow found a package at his front door: a pair of Capezios with taps, gloves, a scarf, an enameled walking stick, and a sweatshirt that said *Broadway*.

Dancing for Writers never happened, but it didn't have to. Just by their enthusiasm, the writers' ratified Fosse's long-held faith — perhaps his only faith — in what Doctorow called the fraternity of performance. Real writers, Fosse told Peter Maas, were performers in a way too, laying themselves open, putting it all on the line. "Living his entire life in show business, he made performing a metaphor for existence," Doctorow wrote. "Irremediable life was the curtain opening, and the lights coming up, and the world waiting for you to do something." They recognized him.

Fosse gave *Star 80*'s benefit premiere as a gift to Gwen and her most favored cause. Proceeds from the November 9 screening and the Tavern on the Green after-party went to the Postgraduate Center for Mental Health, the oldest low-cost psychiatric clinic in New York City. Verdon had been affiliated with the center for decades, and now, with the opening of a new division specifically for patients in the performing arts, a *Star 80* fundraiser seemed appropriate. Why, Dr. Harry Sands was asked, have a counseling program specifically for performers? "Constant rejection can be devastating," he replied.

Not even Fosse, a lifelong romancer of the worst-case scenario, could have predicted the widespread critical rejection of *Star 80*. With few exceptions (Schickel, Siskel), former allies and detractors came together across all media to catapult a giant tomato at the screen. In certain cases, their disgust rose into a rage so profound it could not possibly be directed at the film alone. They weren't just talking about bad taste; they were talking about a perverted mind. "Fosse has served up a smorgasbord of supercilious mannerisms in one of the most glumly misogynous movies ever produced on this continent," wrote Andrew Sarris, ordinarily the soberest of critics.

"The gruesome ending, particularly, is the biggest treat for women-haters this side of the underground snuff circuit . . . One must concede that Fosse has polished the shrug, stoop, and stutter-step of Jerome Robbins to an all-purpose statement . . . His movies have all been metaphorical antimovies in which very little happens but everything is supposed to Mean Something even when the filmmaker is too proud (or, perhaps, too lazy) to come right out and say what that Something is."

Famously opposed, Sarris and Pauline Kael could have buried the hatchet in *Star 80* and walked into the cinema sunset like Bogart and Claude Rains. "Fosse must believe that he can make art out of anything," she wrote, "that he doesn't need a writer to create characters, that he can just take the idea of a pimp murdering a pinup and give it such razzle-dazzle that it will shake people to the marrow. He uses his whole pack of tricks — flashbacks, interviews, shock cuts, the works — to keep the audience in a state of dread." The moral and aesthetic case they built against *Star 80* was the one-two punch that knocked Fosse out.

"He took to the woods," Heim said, "and said he wasn't going to be leaving Long Island." Why fight? "He really thought he was going to win the Oscar for *Star 80*," Glattes said. There was no hope of reparations and little need; if they hated his best work, then they had at last rejected Fosse, just as he always knew they would. ("I didn't work for years after that," Hemingway said. "Sam Cohn never got me a job after that.") Fosse sent out messages in bottles, calling people he knew, even those he knew only vaguely, to air his depression and field their support. He called Teresa Carpenter. "I found it very strange," she said. "We only met once at Sam's office . . . after we got off the phone, I thought, Why should he care [about the critics]? The man's an artist. You would think, perhaps from his work, he might have been more ego driven." As always, Ann Reinking was empathetic.

She knew his feeling for the dark foundation of showbiz pathology and his attempt to comprehend it were heartfelt. "You really understood this," she said. "Yes, I did," he shot back.

The anger subsided, and Fosse acquiesced to loss. This time he did not fight it. He did not assign blame and hurry toward the next project, as he had after *Sweet Charity* bombed. Instead, he sat in sadness and closed the door behind him. He was getting older.

THREE YEARS

GENUINE DISAPPOINTMENT COOLED his ambition, and Fosse changed, perhaps for the last time. His white Bauhaus castle, site of countless parties and weekend getaways, he exchanged for a plain brown home farther inland, on Quogue's Stone Lane. The former he had rented; this one he bought. He paneled the garage with mirrors and installed a barre, and he stopped making regular trips into Manhattan. It was his new studio, and though it waited only a few steps from his front door, some days Fosse had to fight himself to get himself inside. "It's painful for me to go into my studio," he said in 1984. "You look in the mirrors and your spirit is in the air, but your body is on the ground like a little toad with broken legs."

Now a semipermanent resident of Quogue, he discovered new circles of year-round Long Islanders, like the writer Budd Schulberg and his wife, Betsy. The author of *What Makes Sammy Run?* and *The Disenchanted*, his generation's greatest Hollywood novels, and *On the Waterfront* and *A Face in the Crowd*, two of his generation's greatest screenplays, Schulberg was also showbiz emeritus, the son of Paramount's former chief of production B. P. Schulberg, born inside, and a perfect fit for Fosse. Contentious and expansive, Budd was, like Paddy, a sports-loving tough Jew with a *hamishe* heart and was, of all things, a serious bird watcher, swans in particular. He'd even written a book about it. The simple joy of watching their plumes draw slow circles around the inlet suited the new Fosse, and soon his afternoons filled with all kinds of birds. "For some reason when you get older you start looking at how many cardinals and blue jays are in your feeder and not getting into the studio and sweating it out," he said. He found a mangled stray cat in the brush and took it home. He fattened it up and called it Macho.

Suddenly, he said, I like all the things my dad used to do.

He thought half seriously of unmade movies. E. L. Doctorow's novel *Loon Lake,* a picaresque romance with notes of *An American Tragedy,* stirred the dime-store underdog in him, and its Adirondack setting suited Fosse's elegiac mood. But his mood shifted. He called Doctorow in the middle of the night to talk about his short story "The Hunter," a desolate tale about a lonely schoolteacher. Hardly a movie, it was more of a feeling.

Melnick tried to get Fosse interested in something, but he couldn't bait the hook. The future was a blur to Fosse, and the present had no need for him. "It's generally tough to make serious films nowadays," he said. "I do think that everybody wants to think things are great nowadays, and I think they all want the *Rocky* story in form." Discouraged by the box-office successes of the sort of Spielberg films he admired but could never make, Fosse did not consider his Hollywood exile entirely self-imposed. They simply weren't interested in his kind of movies, not anymore. This was the age of *Porky's.*

"I saw it," the writer Bruce Jay Friedman admitted.

They were at dinner with Pete Hamill.

"You *saw* it?" Fosse asked, hardening.

"Yeah, you know, I'm interested. It's the cultural phenomenon of the moment, like Hula-Hoops."

"How could you?" Fosse lost it. "*You!* You're responsible for *The Heartbreak Kid,* you're good, you're funny!"

"I don't know . . . I wanted to know what it was about . . ."

"How could you sink so low?"

Fosse and Cohn felt the business change. The corporatization of Hollywood disgusted them. Cohn never made his clients sign actual contracts (if they weren't happy, why keep them?), but in recent years, ICM started twisting his arm to get legal and binding commitments from the talent. Cohn openly ignored them. He ignored their requests to curb his "old Hollywood" expenditures on expensive client dinners and shows and he ignored their ingratiating pseudo-complaisance, but he could not ignore what could not be denied: the trend away from pro-director negotiations. Where once he could push through a Fosse or Altman deal, contracts famous for their carte blanche clauses, Cohn now faced stubborn resistance. All they wanted to talk about now was money. The new agents, looking like basketball coaches with their slicked-back hair and matching Hugo Boss uniforms, didn't know the first thing about art. Even worse, they weren't ashamed of it. "Sam would lecture studio executives on honor," Sigourney Weaver recalled. "He couldn't believe these guys didn't care about the theater," said his assistant Susan Anderson. "He hated that they didn't know anything about the law and didn't love the business." For sport, Cohn and Fosse lured them to Cohn's office couch, where Sam bullied them to submission. "It was not Sam's finest hour," Anderson said. To Fosse and Cohn, these assholes were all the same. Todd and Josh, they called them, sometimes to their faces.

In January, Chayefsky was among the Television Hall of Fame's first spate of inductees (a list of seven that Lucille Ball, Norman Lear, Edward R. Murrow, and William Paley), and Fosse broke from his Long Island seclusion to brave Los Angeles and accept the honor on Paddy's behalf. Facing a black-tie audience at the Santa Monica Civic

Auditorium, he told a Chayefsky story. "This is a very fickle business," Paddy had said to Bob one day. "I'll be lucky if they remember I'm the guy who wrote the lines 'What are you doing tonight, Marty?' and 'I'm mad as hell and I'm not going to take it anymore.'" Fosse said, "Paddy, you are wrong. You are remembered. Some of us will never forget you."

In Quogue, he threw the Doctorows a dinner party for their thirtieth anniversary. "Bobby was so taken with the idea that two people could be connected that long in marriage," Doctorow said. When they were certain Fosse had disappeared to the kitchen, Peter Maas, Cohn, and Doctorow hurried into the studio and took their places at the barre. The whole thing had been prearranged. Fosse would come in and find them standing in first position, tutus pulled over their khaki pants, as Nicole, acting as their dance mistress, called out for pliés and arabesques. "It was all very funny," Doctorow explained, "except Bob didn't respond that way." He cried. "I couldn't understand that," Doctorow said. "He sort of smiled through his tears, but he was just so totally wiped out that his three friends would horse around like that." It was as close as they'd get to Dancing for Writers.

Later that evening, good-natured marriage jokes flew around the room and Fosse took offense. "He got pissed," Doctorow said. "We weren't taking the occasion seriously enough. He thought we should be a little more respectful of the achievement. It turned out he had almost religious respect for the institution." Writing and marriage both. "He actually interrogated my parents," actress Deborah Geffner remembered. "Here's the hippest person maybe ever, and he wants to know how my mom and dad managed to stay together so long. It was like anthropological research." The Geffners weren't the only ones he interviewed. Fosse regularly opened up his Quogue parties to his friends' parents, and the longer their marriages the better. Commitment was too exotic a blossom to treat casually.

"He was the ultimate host," Laurent Giroux said, "and a worrywart

too. He threw those parties like they were Bob Fosse shows. He was
going to make sure you were entertained!" He put out cigarettes, and
when the cigarettes were smoked, he passed around cigars; he kept
the fireplace burning and the booze flowing; dashing from kitchen to
deck, he hand-delivered shrimp cocktails and bites of buttered lobster; when it got dark and cooled down, he set up tables for dinner
and passed around sweaters; and if he ran out of propane, he could
call Gwen a few towns over to bring reinforcements. She always did.

And after dinner, he might scrounge up some entertainment.

After the meal one night, he said, "Come on, we're going to do an
old vaudeville number. You do *this*" — a quick step — "then I'll do
— wait, we need a third!" He yanked a body from the couch, gave the
steps, and then he asked to see it. "Good, good, good . . ." He looked
up. "Larry," he said to Giroux, "why are you dancing so slinky and
mushy?"

"You're giving me notes at your own fucking party?"

"Oh, shut up."

Fosse wouldn't go to New York, so he brought New York to
Quogue.

His current girlfriend, Phoebe Ungerer, was by his side throughout. As Verdon well knew, she had to accept her, or seem to. Blocking
his libido would block Gwen from Fosse, so when the crowd looked
for her reaction, Gwen shifted into high doyenne, taking Phoebe
by the arm and introducing her to guests around the grounds like
Fosse's place in Quogue was Gwen's second home. But it was Phoebe's
now.

Bob and Phoebe met at one of Doctorow's garden parties, in East
Hampton, the summer of 1984. Phoebe came with her mother, Mir-
iam, and stepfather, the writer Wilfrid Sheed. They were old friends of
the Doctorows, old friends of everyone's, really, from Kurt Vonnegut
down to Truman Capote. At ease with the big time, Phoebe looked
like a girl Truman would have written about. She had the warmth of

a country morning and a face so pretty it practically pinged. Fosse heard the ping from across the Doctorows' back lawn and turned to look. She was an actress, but she could have been a dancer, or at least Fosse thought so as he cut through the crowd and interrupted her conversation to introduce himself.

"Hi," he said. "I'm Bob Fosse."

She had heard of him. "Phoebe Ungerer."

They shook hands. She was twenty-three; he was fifty-seven.

Looking behind Fosse, Phoebe could see the faces, many she'd known her whole life, turn toward them to watch. They looked concerned, like they knew more about what was happening, or going to happen, than she did. And they did. By then, the major plot points of a Bob Fosse affair were a sad sitcom most Page Six readers had been following for years. They knew it always began like this, with a pretty young girl at the beginning of her career. They knew it always ended. Phoebe was too green to see any of it, but she saw that others could, and it gave her a chill.

One night later, Fosse was serving her lobster and Cristal, his favorite champagne. Quogue brought out the romantic in him. Bustling about the kitchen, lighting tall candles around the table, and dishing out the meal, he was at his best, onstage at home, high on a cozy buzz. Phoebe too.

Six months later, she moved in.

At first, there were few surprises. Off amphetamines (he promised), Fosse watched his days in wide shots and long takes. They took it easy. "I've spent my whole life working on holidays," he explained. Now he had the time to relax.

Quogue lent itself to the comforts of habitual living, to walks with Phoebe, bicycle rides into town to collect ingredients for the evening meal, then the meal. They ate at the Laundry with Sam Cohn and his girlfriend, Dianne Wiest. They watched movies, whatever was on TV. He told her about Kubrick, more of an idol now than

Fellini, and together they swooned over *The Shining*, the Steadicam work in particular. "Bob would teach me about movies and how they were made," Phoebe said. "He thought so much about editing. And where the light comes from. He would always get annoyed when the whole room was lit, or when he saw an establishing shot. He hated that! Who needs that?" When it came time for the Oscars, he let her choose his votes.

He missed his friend. "Losing Paddy," Phoebe said, "was the hardest thing he ever had to do." When Paddy's name came up, Fosse seemed to disappear from his body. "It was like he went to wax," Phoebe said. He got the same look the night they turned on the TV and found that Truffaut had died, of a brain tumor, at fifty-two. Fosse was horrified; he didn't even know Truffaut had been ill. Now there would never be another Truffaut movie. Not eventually, not possibly at some point — *never.*

"Did you know," Phoebe said, "that I grew up at the White House on Eighty-Sixth and Central Park West?"

Fosse turned to face her.

"On the twelfth floor, the same floor as Paddy. I grew up right across the hall from him."

"What?"

"And it was just us and Paddy. There were only two apartments on each floor."

"Yes. That's right."

"I *grew up* there. I don't think I ever spoke with him but I remember I'd see him coming home and leaving. I saw him so many times."

TWO YEARS

FOSSE REVISED HIS WILL for the last time on March 28, 1985. For a man who once carried around a pocket-sized notebook of famous last words, touching up bequests was as much a matter of closing his affairs, of bringing the record of his loves up to date and seeing them provided for, as it was the last shot of the movie. It had to be perfect. Like any memorable ending, it had to be poignant, amusing, revelatory, entertaining, and a touch eloquent. *Poignant* would be easy: he would be dead. For *amusing,* Fosse left his share in the Laundry, by then a flailing, irritating venture, to Sam Cohn, the man who had roped him into it in the first place. For *revelatory,* he left $100,000 to establish a theatrical scholarship in his name "for deserving students in the theatrical arts," and he left $15,000 — here everyone's eyes would widen — to Mary-Ann Niles. *Entertaining:* As original a number as he'd ever choreographed, the big $25,000 dinner party Fosse had been imagining since his bypass surgery in 1974 would be his masterstroke, an evening people would remember until their own deaths. As for the rest of his money, pieces were scattered to the usual suspects (Herb Gardner, Phoebe, his sister Marianne), but the largest amount, an estate that totaled around four million dollars, Fosse left, naturally, to his wife and daughter. Everyone would see that one coming. But the direction he had in mind for his body — to be burned to ash in a *Pippin*-like immolation and the remains divided between earth and sea — had the surprise inevitability of real eloquence.

His year of semiseclusion ended quietly as he paid a house call to Hal Prince's *Grind*, a life-versus-showbiz musical about racial tension at a burlesque theater in Chicago in 1933. Choreographed by Lester Wilson, the show suffered from an overcomplicated story and false start sadly typical of the mid-1980s: too much money. Budgeted at five million and paid for in part by Texas oilmen, *Grind* needed a star to be fiscally secure. One of the Shuberts, Bernie Jacobs, eased Prince into casting Ben Vereen, precipitating an involved series of rewrites to turn an ensemble show into a star vehicle. *Grind* never recovered. "It became for me the most painful working experience of my life," Prince said. Fosse went to Baltimore for a look.

"Bob didn't throw out the choreography," recalled dancer Valarie Pettiford. "He finessed it." Yet his touch was indubitable. In the usual Fosse way, he inflated "New Man," Vereen's solo, with novelty beats, adding percussion wherever he could.

"Mike, do you think we have too many accents?" he asked drummer Mike Berkowitz.

"Nah, there's an eighth note in bar seven we haven't used yet."

His wittiest save was "From the Ankles Down": The curtain rises on act two, and up in an elevated corner of the stage, a knot of naked limbs curl through a lather of golden darkness. What is this? A bit of brass tells us they're strippers — we're in their changing room. But rather than stripping, they're sliding up their stockings, gliding on gloves, dressing with the studied languor of a striptease in reverse. They're getting *dressed*, sexy dressed, but there's a bitter edge to it; even when they're not working, they're working. Frank Rich wrote,

"The interlude gives rueful life — but only brief life — to the show's subsidiary point that grind-show performers are never free of the brutal daily grind that they allow their Depression audiences to escape." *Grind* closed on June 22 after seventy-one performances.

As he worked on *Grind,* Fosse kept thinking about *Big Deal,* considering the rights and wrongs of a Depression-era race musical with an old-fashioned bent. At the height of the civil rights movement, when Fosse first thought of adapting *Big Deal on Madonna Street,* he imagined an all-black show set in Harlem — if it didn't work in Tijuana. Omitting any cultural indicators, Fosse prepared *Big Deal* to go either way, New York or Mexico, film or stage. Now, fifteen years later, preparing to adapt a book from his adapted screenplay *and* musical book of 1969, Fosse decided to make *Big Deal* a predominantly black show. But not in Harlem; in Chicago. And instead of finding new songs, Fosse would build the story on period classics, like a revue. With no composer, songwriter, or co-author, *Big Deal* would be, like *Star 80,* pure Bob Fosse, a single-voiced entertainment unhindered by auxiliary influence. As with *Dancin',* Fosse would answer to no one, not even stars. *Big Deal,* he said to Vereen during *Grind,* would be an ensemble piece. No leading parts, just one exquisite company. Vereen turned it down.

While Fosse wrote, Sam Cohn dealt with Bernie Jacobs. Like an unhappy couple, Cohn and Jacobs were both interdependent and alone; Cohn had the talent, Jacobs had the theaters (seventeen Shuberts, to be exact, more theaters than anyone else on Broadway). Their negotiations were marked by irritation and the sort of squinting that made even the finest-print decisions, like where to eat, a matter of strenuous compromise. (On the issue of lunch, they each refused the other the comfort of his home turf, which disqualified the Russian Tea Room for Sam and Sardi's for Bernie; splitting the difference, they ended up with Joe Allen's.) Cohn hated deliberating. He liked to work fast (he sold the rights to Doctorow's *Ragtime* to Dino De Laurentiis, who hadn't read the book, in three minutes, and over the phone); and described dealing with Jacobs as "the worst migraine you've had in your life." Jacobs accused Cohn of demanding perilously high royalties for his clients, and Cohn asserted that shows like *Annie* made everyone a winner. But they both knew a good thing when they saw it. When Cohn offered him the chance, Jacobs invested in the Laundry.

Big Deal was gestating while Joseph Harris, producer of *Sweet Charity* and *Chicago,* prepared a *Sweet Charity* revival for the Los Angeles Civic Light Opera's summer season. Fosse never liked going back, especially now that his mojo was pushing him forward again, so he shrugged off the revival and sent Gwen instead. "He knew there was never going to be any chance in the world, even if he put his imprimatur on it, [that the revival] ever could be the way it could be, the way it was," said Gordon Harrell. But now that the *Dancin'* tour had ended, Fosse's bank statements had lost a certain something, and in the era of revivalist Broadway, a *Sweet Charity* with Debbie Allen (star of TV's *Fame*) seemed a feasible replacement. In lieu of Fosse, director John Bowab was installed to work the book scenes, while Gwen coached Allen, as she had Shirley MacLaine, and supervised the choreography. Fosse's credit read simply, and obscurely, *production supervisor.* While *Charity* got off the ground, he toiled over the *Big Deal* book.

Reproducing the original dances down to the quickest twitch of the tiniest dancer in the farthest row, Fosse expert Christopher Chadman and Verdon kept 1985 looking like 1966. "Gwen had a photographic memory," Ann Reinking said. "It was unreal. She could tell you all the cues. She knew everything." She was a library. *You'll need to rest here; you'll need to blow smoke up into the garment bag so it ricochets down here; you'll need to breathe here.* Why did they need Fosse? He flew to LA to supervise the transition and then returned to New York.

Though *Sweet Charity* had done right by Fosse in the past, he had a great deal at stake in reviving it. He was thinking now as much about hits as he was about legacy, how — *if*— future generations of theatergoers would receive him. Of course, *The Pajama Game, Damn Yankees,* and even *Little Me* had been revived, and *How to Succeed in Business* would forever be a touchstone of the American musical, but none of those claimed to be Fosse from the ankle up, inside and out, as *Sweet Charity* was. Classic status, if it could be conferred on *Charity,* would show Fosse razzle-dazzle to be, at last, more than razzle-dazzle — more than an extended fad. But no one could say for sure if *Sweet Charity* would work without Verdon in the leading role and twenty years later.

As planned, Fosse returned to LA early in June 1985 to put the finishing touches on the show. The day he arrived at the Dorothy Chandler Pavilion, site of *Cabaret's* Oscar sweep, his dancers bubbled like red-carpet movie fans watching the door of the longest limo as it begins to open. To this current crop of dancers, many of whom had grown up sleeping under *Charity* posters, Fosse was Elvis. And his name was synonymous with the kind of good, hard choreography that the Broadway of late, overrun by spectacle and expensive scenery, had almost abandoned. In 1985, for the first time in its thirty-nine-year history, the Tony nominating committee actually scrapped the award for best choreography (as well as the awards for best actor and best actress in a musical), leaving one to surmise that when Fosse and Bennett took off from Broadway, Broadway took off from dance.

Excitement was very high. Fosse took his seat beside Gwen, and the *Charity* run-through started. But Verdon and Fosse were the real show that afternoon, drawing more attention, and more concern, than anything onstage. Watching them from the wings, dancer Jane Lanier remembered that Gwen seemed to experience the run-through as Charity, practically dancing the part in her seat. "She was going through everything Charity was going through," Lanier said. But Fosse didn't move. In a matter of moments, word of his dissatisfaction filled the theater. Dancer Dana Moore recalled, "Fosse just sort of sat there, his chin down, looking at us over the tops of his eyes, kind of nodding his head, sinking lower in his seat." All the steps were there, the characters were there, but the burn was missing. Director John Bowab had missed the show's innermost core, which gave *Charity* the air of nothing but an expert routine.

Act one ended. Fosse asked the stage manager to call for lunch — a break that went on a little too long to quell the worry. When the company returned to the theater, Fosse made no speeches, offered no explanations or pronouncements; he merely asked to see *Sweet Charity* from the top, and then proceeded to break it down, from scratch, one moment at a time. "After that day," Moore said, "we never saw John Bowab again."

It would take a Fosse, with his encyclopedic archive of erotic buttons, to push his dancers to the burn. "He followed me around as I was rehearsing [the Frug] and he would whisper suggestive or provocative questions in my ear while I was dancing," Moore said. "It was to get me thinking about who I was and where I was and what my life was at that moment, [a reference to] something he learned about me the evening before." As Gwen watched from the house, Fosse slid next to Mimi Quillin, one of the "Big Spender" girls, and whispered, "Pick me, pick me, pick me," in her ear. Then he turned her and made her say it, and mean it, back to his face. "I know that people think it's strange that I thought it was fun to watch Bob flirt with other women," Gwen said, "but he would get so jaunty and he would do such funny things and — I mean, he could be fascinating and you could see the women going for it hook, line, and sinker. I mean, sometimes it was because they wanted a part in a movie, but in spite of that, they would start to be absolutely charmed by him . . ." His kind of sexy had to be got at indirectly; he didn't tell them to seduce but to *expect* the seduction. He would say, "Don't go to them, make them come to you." It's in the eyes, not the groin, and it doesn't ask to be wanted. It knows — it's the Know. ("Bob is more sensual than sexual," Reinking said. "It's one of the biggest mistakes I see when people do Bob's work.")

Rebuilding the ensemble was only half of what Fosse needed to accomplish before he could open the show, two weeks after his arrival, on July 16, 1985. The other half — Debbie Allen's performance — Fosse and Gwen revised in relative isolation. Her "If My Friends Could See Me Now" tested Allen and Fosse both; it had from the beginning and would to the very end. When he first saw the number on Allen, Fosse snapped. "It's awful!" he said. "I didn't choreograph *that!*" Verdon responded defensively, and, Quillin remembered, "It was like a fight was going to break out." But Fosse was reacting more to his work than hers. It had been twenty years since he'd taken the tweezers to *Charity*. Gwen might have predicted this sort of reaction, for large selections of his 1960s trunk occupied that transitional halfway between apprenticeship and maturity, before the watershed years of 1971 and 1972, when Fosse's influences shone brightest. Showing both seed and bloom, "There's Gotta Be Something Better Than This" (borrowed partially from *West Side Story*'s "America"), sections of "The Rich Man's Frug" (thick with 1960s dance vogues), and the particularly frustrating "Rhythm of Life" (classic ensemble choreography by the yard), which had never satisfied him, described both how far he had come and how he'd gotten there. But "If My Friends Could See Me Now" was especially vexing. The number's dense marriage of speed and emotional nuance — a sure thing for Verdon in her heyday — would be hard work for almost everyone else.

Fosse asked Allen to run it again. She began. Then he stopped her.

"What are you doing?"

"I'm dancing."

"That's not dancing."

"It's not?"

"What are you saying with this dance?"

"What do you mean?"

"I mean story." He got up. "Let me show you."

One dancer recalled, "He did the whole dance, every movement, and as he was doing it, he said, aloud, every piece of the story. *I can't believe my luck . . . I'm going to see the girls . . . I'm going to tell them everything.*"

Fatigue alternately softened and exasperated him. "God, I can't do this anymore," he said aloud one day, seemingly with feeling. Speaking with Christopher Chadman before the show's LA opening, he conceded, "Well, I'm probably not going to be around that much longer anyway." The Fosse of the 1970s would have delivered similar remarks with a bitter flash. In the 1980s, he dropped them like feathers. Once hell-bent on souring *Sweet Charity*, Fosse now lightened the ending, one of the show's cruelest moments. "It used to get a little ugly," said Michael Rupert, the new Oscar, "and people would be turned off, start to hate Oscar. Bobby didn't want that." Far slighter than Verdon or MacLaine, the easygoing Debbie Allen brought 1985's *Sweet Charity* closer to the sort of musical-comedy cheer Fosse's 1960s self had tried to avoid. "Everyone seems a little younger and nicer than in previous *Sweet Charity* casts," noted the *Los Angeles Times*, "adding a certain freshness to the cynicism without which no Bob Fosse musical would be complete."

While on *Sweet Charity*, dancer Tanis Michaels, who had fallen ill years earlier, on the road tour of *Dancin'*, was diagnosed with AIDS. Most of the *Charity* company knew about AIDS from reading the headlines and hearing rumors from friends, but at that time, so early in the epidemic, few had had any personal contact with it, and even fewer understood the facts. Crucial details were unavailable — save for one: it meant death. "We didn't know what was happening,"

Donna McKechnie said. "It was like a black wave poured over us." Keeping victims from emergency care, abandoning them in dishonor and neglect, President Reagan refused to publicly acknowledge the AIDS crisis, perpetuating the lie of a gay cancer, leaving open the door to ignorance and allowing death to spread. "By the time I was thirty-nine years old," dancer James Horvath said, "I had buried a hundred and eight people. And these were my friends. There were weeks when we were losing five or six people." Afraid for their own safety and feeling guilty for being afraid, the *Sweet Charity* company held on to Michaels in confusion and love. Could they wash their clothes with his? Was it okay if they danced with him? Could he dance? "Cast members would drink out of Budweiser bottles, and so Tanis had his own Budweiser bottle," recalled Bebe Neuwirth. "He had his own prop, which must have been really, really devastating for him." Michaels, on his day off, would go for radiation treatment. "He would come back the next day," Lanier said, "and his tongue was severely burned and swollen. It was horrible, but he never complained and would dance full out." Days after *Sweet Charity* opened, on July 25, 1985, Rock Hudson issued a press release from Paris — he had AIDS. Reagan's first mention of the disease was still months away, but Hudson's revelation had an immediate impact, generating worldwide attention and transforming the perception of AIDS from an exotic, shameful condition to an immediate threat, dangerous to all. Michaels was given three months to live, but Fosse refused to take him out of the show. "Because Bob said yes to Tanis, I think more of us did too," said dancer Fred Mann III. "He made it okay, for all of us, and somehow for Tanis too. He let him work."

Where once he fought for cynicism, the Fosse of *Big Deal* defended his innocence. Six months before he began casting, he met with Gordon Harrell as he had on *Dancin'* to talk songs. Their long list of Depression-era standards included "Life Is Just a Bowl of Cherries,"

"Pick Yourself Up," "Ain't We Got Fun?," and "Happy Days Are Here Again," which Fosse intended to update with an electronic score. Andrew Lloyd Webber had been composing electronically for well over a decade, but building a whole show on synthesizers was something else entirely — and not entirely welcome. "We used six synthesizers in the pit," Phil Ramone explained. "The musicians union called me up on charges of taking away work from the musicians. But these were sound effects. They weren't replacing what a band or orchestra would do. It was like what they used to do on old radio shows: squeaky doors, slides, foot patters, rain." Electronic capability allowed Fosse to mix audio on Broadway the way he had in films. "Even though the unions were against it, he was afraid not to break tradition," Ramone said. "He wanted to use sound like *Big Deal* were a live-action movie." He put speakers in the back of the house, creating cinematic surround sound live in the theater.

With as many as forty-three separate scenes, the book demanded a cinematic treatment far in excess of the norm. If it could be accomplished, devising — through lighting, staging, and scenery — a means of "cutting" from one scene to the next would be a technical triumph, but Fosse imagined *Big Deal* to be more than merely film-like; he saw the show in his own film style, edited as if by Alan Heim. He spoke to designers Jules Fisher and Tony Walton in terms of crosscuts, close-ups, and fades. "I want the dissolves and softness you get in films," he said, "instead of the usual musical comedy blackouts you get every time the curtain comes in." To create the effect of a zoom, he would throw everything onstage into complete darkness save for a tiny follow spot on a little finger. With such a narrow margin for error, hitting those marks every time demanded total precision on all fronts. But even if Fisher and his team managed to execute Fosse's hair-thin cues, they could not change the physical distance between the audience and the actor, as Fosse and Heim could on film. A spotlight might narrow the periphery like a zoom, but unlike a zoom, it did not appear to bring the subject closer to the audience. To compensate, Fosse rid his stage of as much scenery as possible. The darkness of near vacuity could be modeled like wet clay; with little to move, Fosse and Fisher could move quickly, modifying space and time as if they were making a film.

Thus did *Big Deal* herald the supreme Fosse opus, a total fusion of his cinematic, theatrical, and literary selves, an all-in roulette of Wagnerian scope and Icarusian hubris — in other words, he was asking for trouble. "*Big Deal* turned people against him," Tony Stevens remembered. "I visited him when he was starting to audition, and he knew what people [were] saying: that he couldn't do it, that he shouldn't do it. I asked him why he was doing it and before he could answer he was overtaken by all this horrible coughing and then he lit another cigarette and said, 'That's why.' He was running out of time." Scared and indignant, Fosse went back and forth, letting his antagonists in, blocking them out, throwing in the towel, then pushing up his sleeves. "At a certain point I feel, 'I really don't like what's around, so I'll go out and show 'em.' Then I think, 'They'll chop off my head, so why should I?' And I think, 'I know who and what I am. Why do I have to go out there and have them say either the terrible things or the good things? Why?'"

Auditions and callbacks lasted through November. The recent close of *Dreamgirls* — an undeniable hit after four years on Broadway — freed up stars Cleavant Derricks and Loretta Devine for major roles, and as many as eight hundred others sang and danced for Fosse and casting director Howard Feuer over four long days. "If you know a dancer that's a little off their game today," he whispered to dance captain Valarie Pettiford, "tell me, and I'll try to keep them as long as possible."

For six weeks, Fosse rehearsed his cast at the Minskoff Rehearsal Studios, a fourteen-thousand-square-foot space of eight interconnecting studios three floors above midtown Broadway. Rising costs

in the Times Square area — once a bargain basement of porno theaters and boarded-up lofts — had priced most rehearsal spaces out of
the neighborhood.

It was a telling metaphor. The only comparable rehearsal venue
still in use was Michael Bennett's storied 890 Broadway, a luxuri-
ous downtown complex of bright air-conditioned dance and office
spaces, referred to simply as Michael's. But that too was losing time.
After years of workshops, Bennett mysteriously pulled the plug on
Scandal, the musical he had intended to be his next. Soon thereafter,
a heart ailment reportedly forced Bennett to withdraw from *Chess,*
which he was preparing for London's West End. Concerns about the
fate of Bennett — and his building — followed close behind.

Beset with sciatica, Fosse rehearsed *Big Deal* with a tight back
brace under a baggy shirt. "I can hardly move," he said. "I can't even
tie my own shoes." When he got up to make adjustments, his troupe's
muscles clenched in sympathetic pain. But no one spoke of it. Air-
ing his agony could panic the dancers, the Shuberts, and the press,
and likely slow the rehearsal process, which, bulging with the weight
of two dozen performers, many of them principals, already asked
of Fosse more time than he could afford to give. "He had such a big
principal cast on *Big Deal,*" Diana Laurenson said, "he'd put us ensemble kids in a room with his two assistants for three days and tell
us to figure out something for 'Beat Me Daddy (Eight to the Bar)'
and he'd give us a few ideas — smoky, thirties, late at night dance club,
we're dancehall patrons already clubbing, showing off — and three
days later he'd come back and say, 'Show me what you got,' and each
one of us, as individuals, put choreography into the number. Bob
would say, 'I like that, change that, add this, do that . . .'"

He took dance notes in nine-by-seven-inch composition books
tabbed with song titles, one for each act. Stick-figuring had been a
part of Fosse's practice for decades, but never before had he titled a
notebook "Steps???" On *Big Deal,* his uncertainty was contagious.

Dancer Stephanie Pope said, "The ensemble didn't know what was going on, if there were meetings or what." Full afternoons were spent in waiting. Some sensed Fosse had finally scraped the barrel bottom of his own style; that *Chicago*, a full decade in the past, had taken his minimalism to its farthest point, and *Dancin'* had accomplished the opposite. Creating, from scratch, a wholly new dance vocabulary required more of Fosse than he had to give, especially now that there was no Fred Ebb to revise the book. It was all on Fosse. Once or twice, his back went out and he was carried from the studio on a stretcher.

Christopher Chadman called Candy Brown; after years of working at Fosse's side, Chadman was quick to recognize the decline. "Candy," he said. "We got the best of Bob."

In February, they transferred to Boston. "It's an absolute nightmare of a technical show," Fosse admitted. Maneuvering over sixty microphones, a low-light scheme verging on darkness, and *Big Deal*'s centerpiece — a movable platform of hydraulic bridges continually reshaping stage space and time as in a motion picture — Fosse met his match. The book, meanwhile, needed serious attention. Fosse's characterizations ran thin, and his jokes crossed the lowbrow line. The intrusion of not one but two narrators, rather than smoothing the story, slowed it; four fantasy sequences expunged the urgency from the climax; and at two dozen numbers, *Big Deal* outstayed its welcome. Herb Gardner kindly encouraged Fosse to drop some of the peeing, nose-picking, and blowjob jokes, and Neil Simon came to Boston to write new scenes. But Fosse only half listened — to them and to the critics. "If it's a screw-up," he said, "it's all my screw-up." The Boston opening, Fosse claimed, marked only his third time seeing the show in full — it sputtered together that slowly — an indication that, although time was running out, it was still too early to cut. So he cut fractions, seconds, individual lines. "I've made a tremendous amount of changes," he told a Boston reporter, and then in the next breath, "I've taken about ten minutes off." It had little effect. The show — all five million dollars of it — wasn't selling.

At some point before the show arrived in New York, Gerald Schoenfeld and Bernie Jacobs put their panic and frustration into a three-page low boil of *whiles, howevers, we believes*. It made Fosse sick. His Edward Hopper–like effects were stunning, they wrote; however, they were too dark to see. He had a gift for underscore, but they didn't believe there was enough. No one put buttons on numbers better than Bob Fosse; but any more would diminish the show's energy. And: "Could you possibly choreograph an acrobatic dance number which could be a sure show-stopper?" Hidden in their Shubertese were more than a few good points, but Fosse was too outraged to parse them. For advice, he went to everyone else.

"I don't think they like it," he confessed to Diana Laurenson. "Do you think they like it? Do you think this is going well? I don't think this is going well."

To pianist Don Rebic: "People are telling me it's too dark. Do you think it's too dark? I don't think it's too dark."

Wayne Cilento, warming up before the show, heard a knock at his door. In came Fosse. "Keep going," Fosse said.

Head down, Fosse shuffled to Cilento's dressing table and took a seat. "What do you think we should do about the second act? Is the robbery too long? It's too long, isn't it?" Cilento agreed; something was off about it. Despite all the activity, despite the guys sliding down cables into the pit and through the basement, yes, the robbery was anticlimactic. The audience waits and waits and waits for it, then it comes, and it's *long*. Cilento said they might try it like a music video, with constant dancing. Fosse said nothing. Then: "Do you think that would work?"

He had been unwell for months. Reporting from *Big Deal* rehearsals, journalist Kevin Kelly described his reaction to the angina, the sequence of pain and its neglect: "Fosse makes a sudden gesture, his face creases in pain. He shakes his head, sucks his breath, shifts his weight on the chair. He mentions the heart attack that he presented in living color in *All That Jazz*. He cups his hand as though trapping motes of energy in his palm. He winces." He would not discuss it.

Back in New York, the West Coast production of *Sweet Charity* had come to the Minskoff Theater, the largest stage in New York. Previews were set to begin April 1. *Big Deal* opened on April 10.

"He was in a hyperactive frenzy," *Big Deal* musician Dan Wilensky said, "literally running from our show to [*Sweet Charity*]. It was insane." Sometimes Fosse left his assistants to carry on the show until he came back; other times, they just had to wait — everyone did. Like a teacher called from the classroom, he'd fire off a round of directives as he zipped away, returning hours later to find the company had completed their assignment only shortly after he left. The *Big Deal* orchestra, waiting in the pit of the Broadway Theater, kept watch on the smoke cloud in the back of the house. Seeing it disperse, they knew they were alone. When it got big enough to distress the wind section, they knew he'd returned, but only briefly, and he was probably less patient than before. Perhaps accidentally, *Big Deal*'s God mic had a way of picking up insults. "He would go for the jugular," Wilensky said, "really quickly, brutal and brief. Each instruction was very clear, and let's just say powerfully worded with a fair amount of cussing and yelling, and then he'd go into a coughing fit, and his assistant would pick up from where he left off. Then, boom, we'd look up to see the cloud of smoke vanish, and he was gone, back to *Sweet Charity*."

The other woman, *Sweet Charity*, didn't need his attention, but he ran to her anyway; some thought he was looking to escape.

"What if it isn't any good?"

"Are you talking about the show downtown?" Chet Walker asked.

"No, I'm talking about this."

They were at the Minskoff; it was *Sweet Charity*. "They really loved this show," Fosse said.

"They did."

"But what if they don't anymore?"

ONE YEAR

WHEN THE CURTAIN came down on *Big Deal*'s opening night, Fosse knew where he stood. "The party after was not a pleasant experience," Alan Heim remembered.

Frank Rich's review, a near-pan, read like a double eulogy, for Fosse's show and the musical comedy. "If for only 10 minutes or so just before the end of Act I, Mr. Fosse makes an audience remember what is (and has been) missing from virtually every other musical in town." Those delicious ten minutes, Fosse's big, bashing "Beat Me Daddy (Eight to the Bar)," Kathryn Doby called "ultimate Fosse, a minestrone of everything he knew, like *Dancin'* condensed into a single number." But like too many other numbers, "Beat Me Daddy" chose showcase over story. One couldn't help but extrapolate as Rich had. No longer the hope, the lone exception to the rule, Fosse seemed representative, part of a slope, proof of the decline.

Fosse's defense never assumed a righteous or contrarian edge. "I heard about a couple of reviews," he said, "and I thought, 'Gee, maybe I have deluded myself. Maybe I have really kidded myself and haven't seen it clearly.' So after the opening, I didn't see it for like two weeks.

Then I went to see it again with this fear that I was going to see something that was bad which I had thought was good. And you know what? I liked it *a lot*. I was really proud of it." It was *Star 80* all over again. "He *loved* that show," Ann Reinking said.

"*Big Deal* was ahead of its time," Kathryn Doby said. "It was cut like a movie with a multilayered setup in the right and up in the left. He'd do a big number on the main part of the stage and then have something going on up in one of the corners. You couldn't focus fast enough to get to all of those different places. On a movie, you could do that. But onstage, he hadn't figured out how." E. L. Doctorow saw the makings of a new form. He explained, "What he did was compose a folk opera in operatic time using the found materials of American standards." Not quite sung through, *Big Deal* is not quite danced through either, which is to say it's almost a folk opera, almost a jazz ballet, and, saturated in cinematic visual and audio techniques, almost a movie — an epic multifront assault on the Broadway musical, like *Dreamgirls*. But where Bennett founded his vision on flesh-and-blood characters, Fosse's people are soft pretexts for song and dance. To hold up all the music and moving around — far more than any other Fosse musical — he needed a stronger book.

Ticket sales stayed low, but there was solace in history: A Bob Fosse show had never flopped on Broadway. *The Conquering Hero* was de-Fosse'd before it opened, and *Pleasures and Palaces* closed out of town, which was another thing entirely — that's what going out of town was for. Every other Fosse show had gone on to be a hit, save for *Little Me*, which went on to be a classic. Showing their faith, Schoenfeld and Jacobs went the *Pippin* route, buying up commercial airtime on TV. But the *Big Deal* spots, directed and edited by Fosse, produced tepid results. Some hoped the strong opening of *Sweet Charity* at the Minskoff could reroute attention to *Big Deal* at the Broadway Theater; failing that, its surprise five Tony nominations might help, or perhaps even *Sweet Charity*'s five.

Oddly, the combined total of ten nominations encouraged an alternate reading of 1986, heralding Fosse as a kind of king, if only by default (who else was there?). And Fosse won best choreography for *Big Deal*, and *Charity* took best revival, leading people to wonder where, exactly, his career was heading. Were things slightly better than they seemed? Or were these Tonys, like certain lifetime achievement honors, a good way to say goodbye? Two days later, the answer came. Happy from the win, clumps of *Big Deal* dancers arrived at the Broadway Theater to find the notice had been posted. Some said the Shuberts had hastened the closing to make way for the highly anticipated show to follow — *Les Misérables*.

On closing night, June 8, 1986, Gwen came with Nicole and handfuls of veteran Fosse dancers. The audience met "Beat Me Daddy (Eight to the Bar)" with a standing ovation nearly three minutes long, and onstage, the dancers broke their final poses to embrace one another. Some in the back yelled out, "One more time!," and soon the whole theater was chanting, "One more time! One more time!" At the end of the evening, when the curtain finally came down, a young man appeared at the front of the house, a rose in hand. He placed it on the lip of the stage, turned to face the applause, and left the Broadway Theater. At barely seventy performances, *Big Deal* — a Bob Fosse show — had flopped on Broadway.

He threw a thank-you/goodbye party at Quogue, hiring a boat, putting up a volleyball net, and laying out his traditional fabulous spread. The dance studio Fosse turned into a kind of museum, hanging pictures from the show. All generations of Fosse dancers and collaborators were invited, for they were also there to celebrate stage manager Phil Friedman's retirement after forty years in the theater, thirty of them with Fosse. Despite the valedictories, it was a joyous afternoon, free of sadness and pity. Friedman explained why: "You know how show folks are when you haven't seen each other for a long time. You pick up the friendship as if it were yesterday." By the party's end, the hundred had cleared out, and *Big Deal's* Loretta Devine, Cleavant Derricks, and Valarie Pettiford found themselves at the front of the house, lingering — when Fosse appeared to say a final goodbye. He was crying. "I wanted to make you all stars. I really did. I feel" — his voice caught — "just so bad."

Sam Cohn arranged for the writer Michael Herr to meet Fosse at the Russian Tea Room. Herr had an idea for a movie about Walter Winchell, and Scott Rudin, then head of production at Fox, thought Fosse perfectly suited to direct. He was right. Full of slime and glamour, Winchell's story exposed the corrupt interplay of news and entertainment at the showbiz heart of American journalism. "If people go around today treating themselves like celebrities," Herr wrote, "because not to be a celebrity is just too awful, we may have Walter Winchell to thank." There was a lot for Fosse there. Primed for drama, "his story had such a great shape to it," Herr said, "a tremendous low point rising to incredible power and power and wealth and completely losing it all." And Winchell began as a hoofer in vaudeville.

Herr was waiting for Fosse to arrive when Sam Cohn, Louis XIV of the Russian Tea Room, appeared from across the restaurant and took a seat next to Herr. Invited or not, he was at home at every table, as welcome as a good omen. "Bob's coming," Cohn said, "but you should know, he's in a bad mood. He just [closed] his show *Big Deal*." When Fosse appeared, blue as predicted, Cohn facilitated the introductions — Michael Herr, author of *Dispatches*, co-writer of *Full Metal Jacket* — and bowed out to another part of the Russian Tea Room, presumably for more facilitating.

Without ado, Fosse laid his cards on the table. "You know, I have to tell you I knew Walter Winchell and I really hated the guy. And I can't imagine spending two or three years of my life doing a movie about someone I hated so much."

"There's nothing I can say to that."

Leaving the restaurant, they ended up talking their way through midtown, to the front doors of FAO Schwarz, where, Herr said, he wanted to get gifts for his kids back in London. Fosse decided to join Herr inside. The subject of their meeting long gone from their conversation, Fosse nudged Herr toward the designer stuffed animals, stayed by him through the purchase, and followed him out the door. Herr was having such easy fun, he hardly realized Fosse had walked him to his hotel, the Ritz, a couple blocks away on Central Park South. And then Fosse followed him to his room, a room Fosse didn't like. It was small and dark and in the back of the hotel. The room didn't bother Herr, but Fosse insisted he change. "You should [not] be staying in a room like this," he said, and led Herr back down to the front desk, where he negotiated a room change and then invited Herr for a drink at the bar. They talked for three hours.

"What are you going to do now?" Fosse asked, wrapping up the audition.

"I'm going to go back to London and write this thing."

When he got home, Herr found a message on his answering machine. It was Cohn. He wanted Robert Benton to produce the Winchell movie and suggested they meet again to talk further. Back in New York, in Cohn's office, Herr turned the conversation to directors. Did Sam like the idea of Coppola? "There was silence," Herr recalled. "It was like everybody headed under their desks when I mentioned a non-ICM client." As he had for Kubrick on *Full Metal Jacket*, Herr agreed to write an outline of the Winchell story, which he ultimately sent to Cohn, who forwarded it to Fosse.

It was a powerfully glamorous beginning. Inspired by the long, single-location opening sequence of John Huston's *Moulin Rouge* (a film he didn't know ranked high among Fosse's favorites), Herr began his outline with a giant Stork Club set piece one late afternoon in 1943. Hung prominently in the main room, Winchell's portrait gets a quick dusting, no doubt for the big man's imminent arrival. Deeper in, a member of the kitchen staff stuffs hundred-dollar bills into helium balloons, and a hat-check girl is told, abruptly, to fix her pretty hair. A tablecloth comes down over table 50, Winchell's headquarters, and the opening credits begin. To an eerily calming "Autumn in New York," the booth is set for power: ashtrays, a telephone, a pad and pencils. Then, Herr writes, "one last touch: a glistening orchid is placed on the table, so fresh that it practically shivers." The credits end.

The Stork Club sequence continues to unfold for some twenty pages. We mingle with Ernest Hemingway, Hedy Lamarr, Damon Runyon, and of course Winchell himself. This is the peak of New York society, the highlife young Bob Fosse, new in town after a tour of the Pacific, could only have read about — in Winchell's column. We get the gossip and the music and the terrific uneasy feeling that this fast-talking hotshot has a grip on the skinny throat of American media, which is to say, on everything America thinks, or thinks it thinks. He is the razzle-dazzle demon incarnate. Herr said, "I didn't sentimentalize Winchell. In a lot of ways I made him a hateful character and still kept him a human being." A mix of Paul Snider's barbarity and Hugh Hefner's power, Winchell is the unchecked god of mass manipulation.

"I changed my mind," Fosse told Herr. "I see the movie here. I want to do this."

They continued to meet, socially and professionally. Fosse invited Herr and his daughter over for one of his football-watching parties, the sort he and Paddy used to have. "He was so sweet to my daughter," Herr said. "He wanted to give her a book she might like and found one about dance."

The Winchell movie was an exception: Phoebe could see Fosse extricating himself from all other new projects. Still on the hook for *Big Deal*, he wouldn't plan a new work for Broadway. He could spend afternoons sketching out new dance ideas in Quogue, but at the thought of working those ideas into a story or some kind of bigger picture, he froze. Martin Richards approached him about filming *Chicago* with Michael Jackson and/or Madonna and/or Bette Midler, but Fosse seemed tentative about the idea. Sam had been pushing it for years, never quite convincing Fosse that by going back, he could also go forward. For a brief moment, he considered filming *Dreamgirls* and thought of doing *The Vampire Lestat* on Broadway with David Bowie and Mick Jagger. Phoebe loved the rock-vampire idea, but she couldn't talk him into starting anything from scratch. Cohn sent him the *Good Morning, Vietnam* script, which suited Fosse, but all that scouting, all those months on location, and in Vietnam, turned him right off. "It's a strange paradox," he mused. "I feel I'm getting near the latter part of my career, so I'm getting more picky." Despite his reservations, Fosse resumed the conversation about directing a Michael Jackson music video, and he flew out to Los Angeles for a meeting at Neverland. Again, Jackson freaked him out.

"He has fake plants," Fosse told Phoebe. "They're all over the house."

"Why?"

"Fake plants don't die."

Jackson's "Capone," then in demo, had a rhythm and melody Fosse grooved to, but he wanted more lyrically, and he sent back a request for changes. But the changes didn't come, at least not to his satisfaction. By the time "Capone" became "Smooth Criminal," Fosse had moved on — but judging by the finished product, it would seem Jackson hadn't. His video showcases Astaire and Fosse throughout.

The last time Fosse met with Herr to discuss *Winchell,* he was quite obviously ill. "Phoebe, I could see, was really worried about him," Herr recalled. "I was touched by her." She and Fosse cut short the meal, downplaying his symptoms as they hurried from the restau-

rant. He suffered angina attacks regularly but did not want to pub-
licize his condition for fear of raising his insurance any higher. Too
high, and he would almost definitely never make another movie or
direct another show. If he did — if they let him — backers would glare
at his every move. So Phoebe had to get Fosse out of the restaurant,
quickly. On the street, out of view, she gave him the first of four medications she carried with her at all times — that pill gave immediate
comfort. Then, in a cab, she helped him take the next three. "A couple
of times he was as white as a ghost," she said, "and I didn't know what
was going to happen." He breathed slowly; color returned to his face.
"And he would recover," Phoebe said, "like nothing was wrong."

Award committees must have smelled the blood; they started
honoring him. The Mr. Abbott (as in George) Award came earlier in
the year; the Astaire shortly thereafter. Fosse was said to be drunk at
the ceremony, held at the Plaza Hotel. With Phoebe on his arm, he
rounded the tables, picking fights with critics, causing scenes.

Phoebe, meanwhile, took a steady prescription of acting, voice,
and dance classes in town — and Fosse had her schedule memorized.
At first, his interest touched her. Then she learned he was making
calls to her teachers after class, checking in to see that she was where
she said she would be. In between classes, he questioned her.

"How was it?"

"Good, fine."

"It was?" His silence scared her. "*Really?*"

He called her sister's apartment and demanded to speak with
Phoebe.

"You were late to class."

"There was a traffic jam downtown."

That silence again. "Are you *sure?*"

Their small talk had become an interrogation; dead set on discovering his own betrayal, Fosse badgered her to confess. But for what?

"The problem I find with myself," he would say, "is the closer I get to somebody, the more possessive I get. I'm afraid I start putting restrictions on them."

At one time, Fosse knew he was sexy. Now he was old. His body looked okay, but his legs didn't bend like they used to and he had to take more breaks when he danced. He had to catch his breath. He had to sit down. Having never developed a full vocabulary for his style, Fosse always relied on demonstration to communicate his intention, and in the old days he was forever leaping up from his folding director's chair to bend back an arm or tilt sideways a pretty face. Now that the folding chair directed him, a wealth of intention and imagination stayed locked in his head. And by not showing the best part of himself, he confirmed, more than ever, the worst of his fears. He was done. Old friends tried to cheer him, but Fosse had his proof in the studio mirror. There was the old man's face he hated. Then there was Phoebe's face, at the crest of its beauty, visible every day to the sexy young men of her acting and dance classes. Why was she with him? "He knew people used people in show business as a steppingstone," Phoebe said. "It was because of his post-traumatic show-business-stress disorder, PTSBSD." Less plausible was the possibility that she loved him.

"Roy's been a little down lately," he said to her one night as they were on their way to meet Scheider for dinner. "If you can, please be happy and cheerful with him."

She was her usual fun self at dinner, or at least she thought she was, but when they returned to the apartment, Fosse's scowl told Phoebe she'd made a horrendous mistake.

"You'd really like to fuck a movie star, wouldn't you?"

"You wanted me to be *cheerful!*"

"Oh, I'll have to remember *that*," he sneered. "I'll have to put *that* in a movie."

She ended up sleeping in the studio apartment Fosse kept down-stairs on the eleventh floor. A small office space for his assistant, it doubled as Phoebe's getaway. On bad nights, she could be there awhile. "When he got really angry," she said, "he would completely retreat to Siberia."

Despite his behavior, Fosse still tried to reorder the love-busted part of himself. Years earlier, his whimsy came up with a solution: he imagined his ideal partner as an octopus. "He is neither male nor female," Fosse wrote, "or rather is both. I am likewise. This does not bother our friendship, for when I have need of a male — he is a male — when I desire the female-type companionship — she is a female — when I wish neither or a mixture my friend obliges — I do likewise for my friend — It is effortless transition by both parties." Fosse and Ungerer talked about getting married, but Phoebe couldn't recon-cile the Fosse who followed her home at night, whistling at her and catcalling in the dark just to see if she would turn around with a sexy look in her eye, with the man who sat awestruck at dinner as Richard Attenborough described his four-decade marriage and then questioned him, child to magician, about how he made it work. "Tell me, please," Fosse begged. "Please, Richard, I need to know."

Someone hurt him once, Phoebe thought, and he'd spent his life retaliating. Years of tilting at windmills left him with a conscience he could not abide. He still worried about Mary-Ann Niles. Rumor said she never took off her wedding band, that when asked about her famous genius ex-husband, she talked on about how bad he was to her with a smile on her face. Her friends knew Niles's drinking was killing her, that when they left her apartment for the night, she stayed up laughing alone, hardly moving from the stool she had told them to call Mary's Bar. Fosse sent her money, and more money, year after year, and tried to get her work as a stage manager to keep her in the ring. He couldn't. But Fosse's classic regret, Phoebe thought, was in his memories of Joan McCracken. Phoebe and he were watching an old MGM musical on TV one night, and he brought Joan up. He had that look he had when Truffaut died. "I think the loss of Joan McCracken caused significant damage to Bob's ever loving again," Ungerer said. "I always, always felt like he was haunted by Joan Mc-Cracken." Gwen did too.

Fosse and Cis Rundle spent one afternoon walking and talking around New York, his city. They started in the Village for coffee and by early evening had climbed to the heart of midtown, a few square blocks Noel Behn called Fosse Country. The Deli. The DGA. The Brill Building. The Russian Tea Room. Sam's office at West Fifty-Seventh, which Fosse could see from his place on West Fifty-Eighth. Minus the first twenty years and a couple locations, his whole life had been spent in these buildings. They buffered him from the neon sting of Broadway, ten blocks below, where dreams were torn like tickets and forgotten innocents reached out to him from the dark. "I see a hooker on a corner," he said to Pete Hamill on one such stroll, "and I can only think: there's some kinda story there. I mean, she was once six years old. . . ."

The new Times Square was a lot safer, but it wasn't the real Broadway. Hiltons and Holiday Inns had taken the razor out of Forty-Second Street; the concrete palace fell to towers of black glass and souvenir stands. Now where could he shoot *Winchell*? Not here; not Hollywood either. They made *Porky's* now.

Strolling up Fifth Avenue, he won waves and handshakes from passersby. "The seas parted for him," Rundle said. "They loved him. They ran over to him." Wall Street types stopped midsentence and curled forward, pinching teacup fingers to invisible bowlers. Laughing with them, Fosse answered with a salute or two-second soft-shoe. Being recognized — it was like he had made it.

They came to St. Patrick's Cathedral, and Rundle said she wanted to go inside for Mass. Fosse did too. "I think he would say he was an agnostic," Reinking said. "There is a God and he abandoned Bob." He and Rundle made their way up the grand stairway, and at the large doors he stopped short.

"Wait. I can't go in."

"Why?"

"I'm afraid God might just strike me dead."

He reached into his pocket for a handful of bills. "Here," he said, opening the door for her, "light as many for me as you can."

Award shows or openings had been his only reasons to leave Quogue. Since Paddy died, Fosse had given up 850 Seventh, and his core group, like Cohn, Doctorow, and Schulberg, had homes not too far from his on Long Island. But in the fall of 1986, *Sweet Charity* drew him back to Manhattan, to rehearsal and to his dance captain Gwen Verdon. When Debbie Allen left the show, they returned to Minskoff Studios, where no *Times* critics could touch him, with Ann Reinking their new Charity. Fluent in Reinking for fifteen years, Fosse knew her limits and how to exceed them. Though she had *Pippin*'d, and Roxie'd, and Trumpet Solo'ed, Charity, the most demanding role in Fosse's canon, required sustained and unmatched levels of performance, technique, and endurance. Reinking called it the *Swan Lake* of Broadway. And now was her time. Sliding Reinking's body into Charity's heart, Fosse drew from her a Fosse dancer in full flower.

"Isn't it funny," she said, "that our dreams *almost* come true?"

He smiled. "Quit being so smart."

Was he an artist? The question always embarrassed Fosse. Calling oneself an artist was like calling oneself beautiful; it was for others to decide. But still he wondered. Was he an artist? Did his having to ask the question mean he wasn't? Orson Welles was an artist. He was the Mercury Theater, whose billowing silks Fosse reused in *Pippin* and *All That Jazz*, whose black velour drop he raised up—feet, legs, waist, torso, face, fingers — in *Liza with a Z. Welles* was an artist; Bob Fosse was a craftsman. At his best, he said, a very good craftsman, the number one butcher on the block. Ann Reinking scrunched her nose at this. "Well, okay," he admitted, smiling a little. "Maybe I'm a master craftsman."

Gwen watched Fosse watch Reinking. Fosse watched Reinking watch Gwen. No matter how successfully each had moved on — Fosse to Phoebe, Verdon to Jerry Lanning, Reinking to Herb Allen — they interfaced daily with might-have-beens. Some said Fosse drove Reinking especially hard to make her pay for her happiness, and that Gwen, so often the disciplinarian, eased off to settle the balance, as if keeping Reinking strong against Fosse was her way of looking after him. Gwen always would.

Pianist Don Rebic came early to the Minskoff one morning to find Fosse alone in the studio, looking out the window. Without turning, he asked, "How you doing?"

"I'm getting a divorce."

"How's your professional life?"

"My professional life's great."

Fosse took a long pause. "Well, I think there's a certain balance in that."

By now, cutting his own commercials had become an essential part of Fosse's promotional outreach. Though his approach to the *Pippin* spot had been straightforward and theatrical, a single-number *amuse-bouche,* his concepts for *Dancin'* and *Big Deal* grew progressively unconventional. These were no longer commercials but thirty-second short films, expressly cinematic. On *Dancin',* for instance, he couldn't resist shooting at two hundred frames per second (eight times more than the standard twenty-four) for a slow-motion effect. Rather than appropriate a whole number in full as he had on *Pippin,* he flew and twisted his *Dancin'* dancers before a black drape, as if in limbo. Laying the images on top of one another, Fosse and Heim built a single body of mutant elegance, a new, abstract piece of choreography as startling as the *Pippin* commercial was cheeky, and just for TV.

Heim was busy on another project when the time came to do the spot for Ann Reinking's *Sweet Charity*, so Fosse called Rick Shaine, his editor on *The Goodbye People*. But Shaine was cutting *Dead of Winter* for Arthur Penn. "That's okay," Fosse said. "We'll work at night."

And they did. On the first night, they parsed Fosse's thirty thousand feet of uncut film, basically all of it from "Big Spender" — nearly thirty hours of footage for a thirty-second spot. "Let's make a bet," Fosse purred. "How many cuts do you think we'll end up with?" They made their guesses — Shaine bet on fifty-five, Fosse a few more — and put their twenty-dollar bills down. Four nights later, they reached the finish line, a commercial, but before Shaine could catch his breath, Fosse lit another cigarette and said, "Now let's run through all the outtakes and make sure we didn't miss anything." It was three in the morning. Fading, Shaine climbed onto the daybed they kept nearby, and Fosse settled in at the flatbed for round two. "He watched every single one of those outtakes at high speed," Shaine recalled, "and found a jump of Ann Reinking in slightly better position, her legs were straighter, more parallel to the floor." He woke up Shaine, and they put in the new clip. It threw everything off. A few frames longer than its predecessor, the addition edged the picture off the music; they had to recut the whole thing. Three hours later, at six in the morning, Fosse reminded Shaine they had a bet. Shaine counted fifty-five cuts, right on the nose, and declared himself the winner. Fosse glared and made him recount. Shaine reached the same total, fifty-five. "You know, Rick," Fosse said with a grin as he reached for his billfold, "on *Big Deal*, I think Alan had fifty-seven."

On October 19, 1986, Stanley Lebowsky, Fosse's musical director of many years, suffered a heart attack and died. He was fifty-nine, one year younger than Fosse. When she heard, Verdon came to *Sweet Charity* rehearsal armed with a plan. She passed out copies of Uta Hagen's *Respect for Acting*—a book Fosse had little respect for —explaining, "When Bob comes in, let's all be sitting reading it." It worked. When he saw them all lined up with books to their noses, Fosse laughed. She had been there in *Cabaret,* she had been there in the hospital, and she would be there for him now. "After *Star 80,*" orchestrator Ralph Burns said, "Bob ran back to her womb."

Fosse and Verdon were dressing the same now, coming to rehearsal, Dana Moore recalled, in button-down shirts and slacks — Gwen in navy blue and Fosse, of course, in black. Before he got to rehearsal, she'd come to the studio alone, to pick up the garbage. "Their relationship during *Charity* was very warm and supportive," dancer Lisa Embs recalled. Beyond sharing and thus reading each other's mind, as odd as it sounds, they were said to feel each other's presence. Once, Gwen was working onstage with the company when, "in the middle of it," Mimi Quillin said, "without taking a beat, she leaned into me and in that warbled voice said, 'Bob's here.'" Sure enough, when Quillin looked to the back of the house, he was leaning against the wall, watching.

"You should have seen Gwen in her prime," he said to Dana Moore. "She was one of the most beautiful women."

"But she still is beautiful."

"No, no. Not like she was."

As entertainers, they loved no one more than each other. The Fosse and Verdon legend gave new life to their old act, and they appeared together at public events to give and receive tributes. On May 5, 1987, Verdon took center stage at the Juilliard Theater to present Fosse with the Capezio Dance Award, which he shared that night with Astaire and Nureyev. (Fosse concluded his acceptance speech, "Before I die, I just want the *New York Times* to say one nice thing.")

On June 7, 1987, the night of the Tonys, they presented, together, awards for best choreography and best direction of a musical — to Trevor Nunn and John Caird for *Les Misérables*. On June 22, Fosse and Verdon appeared at the Palace Theater to celebrate George Abbott's one hundredth birthday with a gala evening of song and dance. It was a harrowing night for Fosse; earlier that day, he had gotten terrible news. Fred Astaire had died. Fosse's grief, heightened by the insensitivity of journalists calling him for sound bites, turned to anger. In twenty-four hours, those journalists would be on to their next obituary, and the epochal magnitude of Astaire's death would vanish with them. "His feeling was people just swoop in when people die," Mimi Quillin said. "Then they go."

The next day Fosse turned sixty. He threw himself a party in Quogue, and his life's full company attended: Reinking, Heim, Phoebe, Budd Schulberg, Janice Lynde . . . "He seemed to be taking great care of himself," Lynde recalled, "like he'd found some sort of peace. He was off the booze, off the drugs, and smoking a little bit, but not like he used to." That day they revisited their whole story, from their first meeting at the opening night of *Applause* ("You're so tall"; "You're so short") to the very hard nights. Fosse apologized for calling her middle-class — which he had, hurting her terribly — fifteen years before. "We talked about things," Lynde said. "The ins and outs of our whole friendship. The whole thing."

"You always used to say you didn't want to live past sixty," she teased him. "Why did you pick sixty?"

"Because then I'd be too old to choreograph." He leaned in with a secret. "But sixty is young these days. It's the new fifty."

That evening Fosse's mood fluctuated between euphoria and solemnity. Here he was, older than he had ever intended to be, walled in by six decades of loving friends but closer than ever to the other side of that wall. If he did it right, this scene — the food, the sea air, Gwen, the girls — really could make a good ending to the film. It had

everything: resolution, emotion, full-company power, visual plenitude. It just needed some kind of dramatic incident to catalyze the
movie. Of course, he had an idea; it was one he had used before, but
since when had Fosse claimed to be original? Drawing folks from
their conversations, the director respectfully ordered his guests into
one room and asked them each to stand up, one after the next, and
say something nice about him. They did.

"Didn't the tributes sound like eulogies?" asked one who'd missed
the party.

"Yes. Exactly."

"He was staging his own funeral!"

"I guess he didn't want to miss it."

Now that *Sweet Charity* had closed on Broadway, and the tour, with
Donna McKechnie, loomed, Fosse and cigarettes picked up where
they'd left off. "By the time we were working," McKechnie said, "he
was smoking all the time." After her final performance of *A Chorus
Line*, McKechnie joined Verdon and Mimi Quillin at the Minskoff for
a month of rehearsals, where Fosse, in a neighboring studio, worked
mysteriously and privately. "But I feel I really haven't fulfilled what I
started out to do," he said in 1986. "I think I should have done more
classical dancing. If I had my life to live over again, I would have
gone the route of Jerry [Robbins], would have gone into ballet, choreographed ballets." Was he planning a new show in there? Or was it
nothing, just sketches for his personal amusement? The details were
unclear. But Fosse couldn't keep all of his Minskoff sessions a secret
— McKechnie snuck by, and so did Valarie Pettiford. And Reinking
knew. "He wanted to do a full ballet for the first time in his life," she
said. "He thought he was ready."

Before Fosse was scheduled to appear at McKechnie's Minskoff
studio, he would show up unannounced, waving her on with an "Oh,
don't mind me" or "Pay no attention to this man sitting here." Each

day, he returned, and each day he sat a little closer to his newest Charity, until finally she looked down one afternoon to find him smoking
at her feet. By then, no ice needed rebreaking. The two, who had first
worked together on *How to Succeed,* had been fully and seamlessly
reacquainted, but what McKechnie didn't know (until later) was that
Fosse had been studying her long before those Minskoff sneak-ins.
Slithering by incognito to watch her audition as Cassie and, unknow-
ingly, as Donna, he went to see her in *A Chorus Line* — six times.
That she had been Bennett's muse and offstage partner (his favorite
instrument, he called her) as far back as 1968's *Promises, Promises* did
not keep Fosse from hiring her. By then, his thing with Bennett had
simmered down to a good-humored game, and putting all questions
of trust behind him, he knew McKechnie would be a great Charity — naïve in spirit, but airy where Gwen had guts. The power she
got from Bennett, McKechnie brought to Fosse's style, packing very
big into very small. "Bennett is up and out," she explained, "Fosse is
down and in."

"Can you do that better?" Fosse would ask flatly.

"Yeah."

"Then do it."

He wanted to teach her she was in control of her performance, to
show her she owned her talent and that achievement wasn't a muse
but a muscle. Knowing how high she could go and getting there each
time — that was pro.

Ordinarily Fosse's stage managers and dance captains would lead
the show from town to town, but on this production, he and Gwen
(and Cy Coleman) flew in to personally rehearse the company before
every opening night. Going the *extra* extra mile was well advised.
With Fosse's reputation in decline and *Charity*'s presales disconcertingly low, morale took a hit. "People had given up their homes and
their lives for what was going to be an extended tour," Chet Walker

said, "and things weren't going well. People were worried. I think Fosse felt responsible." The company turned inward with blame and hostility. "It was like the dancers versus the production," one dancer explained. "I heard a lot of negativity in the dressing room." Traveling with *Charity,* Fosse and Verdon could present a united front. "Whatever's going on out there," Fosse announced to the factions, "you have to believe in this little black box." Nothing else concerned them. "He wanted us to know he was on it," Mimi Quillin said, "that he was ahead of what wasn't working, that we were being taken care of."

Verdon and Fosse were there in Toronto on July 2, 1987, before *Charity* opened at the Royal Alexandra Theater. As she readied her dance bag for the first dress rehearsal, Donna McKechnie flipped on the radio and scanned the room for the items on her checklist. Then she heard it: Michael Bennett had died that morning.

AIDS.

The *Times* obituary called him "the most influential theater director and choreographer of his generation."

Later that month, Hugh Wheeler died. Hal Prince hosted his memorial at Sardi's. Both Fosse and Prince shared a long history with Wheeler — book writer of *A Little Night Music* and *Sweeney Todd,* co-screenwriter of *Cabaret* — and judging by the crowd, so did most of Broadway. Between greetings and nervous stares (one at Sondheim), Fosse circled the idea of approaching Prince to inquire about his progress casting *The Phantom of the Opera.* Nicole was still waiting, fingers crossed, to hear if she had made it into the ballet chorus. If she got it, *Phantom* would be her first appearance on Broadway; if she didn't, her chances of ever dancing on Broadway would decrease considerably. Time was against her. Nicole was twenty-four, and her days of being the youngest, strongest dancer in a given company were already years in the past.

Fosse knew *Phantom* had stumbled into delays out of Prince's control, so it was possible certain casting decisions had been unofficially determined, and Prince, as he stood there, had the answer to Nicole's future. All Fosse had to do was ask him. But asking a director, even director to director, to show his hand, even a little, was to apply unfair pressure, and though they went back to *Pajama Game* — debuted with *Pajama Game* — and the air was warm with Wheeler's legacy, talking business felt like an amateur's transgression. But Fosse, to Fosse, was an amateur.

"I've been a performer," he explained to Marty Richards. "You know what it is to wait."

Richards understood Fosse's predicament, but he had no compunction about approaching Prince that very moment and asking the question himself.

"Don't you dare!"

Richards made straight for Prince, and Prince, seeming to comprehend the situation, excused himself from Richards and walked over to Fosse, who, comprehending Prince's comprehension, blushed as he saw him approach. There was an exchange of embarrassments, and Prince immediately assured Fosse *he* was the embarrassed one; the production, he said, should have called Nicole long ago. She had the part, a good part, and Fosse was right to wonder. "This is ridiculous," Prince said to him. "We're both fathers."

Now that *Phantom* had arrived, *Cats* seemed less a one-off than a visitor from the future. And there were more on the way. The yuppie appetite for gargantuan feats of staging — *Phantom*'s chandelier, *Saigon*'s helicopter, *Les Mis*'s turntable barricade — had most certainly brought to visceral life what a *Company* or *Chicago* never could; that was the upside. But with all that stuff onstage, there was almost literally no room to dance and even less reason to. Broadway choreographers could blame the British. "For the New York theater," Frank Rich wrote, "the rise of London as a musical-theater capital is as so-

bering a specter as the awakening of the Japanese automobile industry was for Detroit." The anti-dance rage did not make the world safe
for a Fosse revival.

On September 23, 1987, Fosse and Verdon were on hand at the National Theater to run the last cleanup rehearsal before *Sweet Charity*'s Washington opening, which was scheduled for 7:30 that evening.
The day's work began with a production meeting, held in the theater's
second-floor lobby, where Fosse and Verdon, assisted by Mimi Quillin and Chet Walker, walked the various department heads through
the morning agenda. Fosse hacked through the entire meeting. He
asked Walker about the morale of the company. Walker was tentative.
Worry prevailed, he said. There was concern they were underpre-
pared, that the tour was rushed, that management was guarding the
real truth from the company, and that the show, rather than bumping
along, would close before moving on to Boston and Los Angeles.

Fosse administered general notes around noon and the company
split into groups to rehearse individual pieces of the show. Book
scenes in the lobby, dance scenes onstage. Though he moved between venues, Fosse stayed mostly in the house, first working one-
on-one with McKechnie before he moved to the ensemble. With curtain time only hours away, Fosse and McKechnie rehearsed the bite
Charity gives Charlie's arm in "You Should See Yourself," her first
number. He hurried her delivery of "provolone sandwich and a bottle
of beer" and slowed her rendition of "If My Friends Could See Me
Now," Charity's joy blast, which needed savoring. ("Talk about emotion during the entire number," Fosse wrote to himself. "It's rushed.")
The orchestra needed to clean up "Friends" too, but that would come
later, at the end of the day, with whatever time remained.

"How much time is left?" he asked stage manager Craig Jacobs.
"How much stuff is left to get done?"

At around three o'clock, Fosse led the whole company through

"Rhythm of Life," which he had intended to run the day earlier (he had run out of time) and which had been needling him since he'd first started working with the LA company. "Dance like you're on your way to percussion heaven!" he called out. "Dance like you're in church on your way to heaven!" Walking down the line, he made serious, sustained eye contact with each dancer in "Rhythm," personalizing their relationships to *this moment now*. They were to remember it tonight. "The energy in the room was so incredibly high," dancer Mamie Duncan-Gibbs said. "There was a lot of joy in the room, a sense of accomplishment. I remember even Bob smiling about it."

"He rehearsed us so hard that day," McKechnie said. "Hard even for Bob. He couldn't direct us enough that day."

He called for a break. With his back to the orchestra, Fosse faced the empty seats and watched as they filled one by one with tired dancers. They knew to expect Fosse's opening-night rally speech, his "just do the show, no more, no less," push of customary encouragement. But that particular afternoon they got more. Fosse told them he had done everything he could to save the show. "He said it more like a father than a director," McKechnie recalled. If he could, he said, he would go out there, put on a sandwich board, and sell tickets on the sidewalk. "Your business is to do the best you can," he said. Then his tone changed. Fosse seemed to crumple. He grew philosophical:

"When you get up in the morning, don't compete with anybody.

"Ask yourself, how can I be a better person?

"Save your money.

"I'm *so sorry* this isn't going well."

Usually a man of few words, he spoke for twenty minutes. The curtains, hanging behind Fosse, framed him perfectly, as if he had planned the shot and put himself in it.

"As Bob was talking to us that day, I remember thinking it was like he was reciting his last will and testament," Lisa Embs said. "He was talking about how difficult our lives are in terms of the life of an artist, in terms of trying to take care of daily things like rent and family, and where's our next job, our self-esteem, and that even though it didn't always feel like it, what we're doing is worth something."

He said, "I would do anything to make this show a success."

ONE HOUR AND
FIFTY-THREE MINUTES

AROUND FIVE THIRTY, Fosse ended his speech. With a final apology and a Thank you, *all,* he excused the dancers to their dressing rooms and hotels to eat, change, and ready themselves for six thirty, the half-hour call. Fosse devoted the next hour exclusively to his orchestra. Onstage, Chet Walker stood in for McKechnie, Verdon at his side; on the floor, glued to the podium for maximum control, Fosse and Cy Coleman flanked conductor Wayne Green, watching him closely. Green didn't need the extra pressure, but as they came to "If My Friends Could See Me Now," time did not allow for anyone's needs, least of all his. Fosse's mood was changing. He had been up all day, dutifully caressing them once more unto the breach, but now the clock had gotten the better of him, the better of everyone; the whiplash-inducing collision of slow-down-the-song-and-hurry-up-and-fix-it was twisting the orchestra inside out. "Don't rush this section," he implored Green, and Green tried not to rush, but with less than an hour left to rehearse, rushing seemed the only way out.

It was percussion. It was the cowbell, the *pitch* of the cowbell. *Diggadiggadum:* five burlesquey notes on Charity's little shimmy.

She turns her ass to the audience and wobbles it to *diggadiggadum;* beats that are beat out, in theory, by drummer Allen Herman, Fosse's original drummer on *Dancin'.* But *Charity* had left Herman in a hospital in Philadelphia, being treated for an infected cyst. The show's percussionist, Larry "Spoosh" Spivack, took over cowbell duty. *Diggadiggadum.*

"I don't like that cowbell," Fosse said. But he *did* like that cowbell; it was the cowbell they used in Philadelphia, Toronto, Los Angeles; it *was* the cowbell they used for "If My Friends Could See Me Now," *diggadiggadum;* it was the *Sweet Charity* cowbell. "Fix that cowbell!"

Diggadiggadum.

"Fix it! Fix it!" He was yelling now at Spivack, who was unsure of what else to try. There was no time to get another cowbell that night, so Green suggested getting one the next day. Fosse shook him off. *Tomorrow?* The show went on in under two hours: they had to fix this one, now. But what else could they do? Hit it under, over? Lighter, softer? Quicker —

"Don't rush it!"

Diggadiggadum.

"No!"

They passed the cowbell to the percussionist hired to replace Spoosh to see if he could do something with it. He couldn't. The cowbell then went to the assistant conductor. *Diggadiggadum.* They passed it back to Spoosh.

Spoosh, *Diggadiggadum.* No no no.

"Later I asked [Spoosh] to show me how he was hitting it," Herman said. "He picks up the stick in the proper position and he hit the way any percussionist would hit it — the way he's supposed to. I said, 'Aw, man. Aw, shit.' He said, 'What?' I said, 'You gotta turn the stick around and hit it with the *fat* end!' He said, 'What?' I said, 'That's the way Bob wanted it. He wanted a fatter sound!'"

Spivack couldn't know he was hitting the cowbell with the wrong side of the stick. "Fosse was angry," he recalled, "he was getting angrier, and I was freaking out. The whole theater was waiting for the next twenty minutes of rehearsal, waiting on me, as I tried to fix the cowbell. I must have tried fifteen or twenty times, every combination I could. I was sure I was going to get fired. I was frazzled. All the dancers, all the actors, all the lighting, all the sound people were just waiting for me to get this right. Sixty, seventy people just waiting around. The pressure! The local guys in Washington thought this was very entertaining for them. The trombone player put down his horn, crossed his hands, and said, 'Oh boy, *now* we're getting the show.' I thought my fucking career was over." Fosse was responding to the difference of a quarter-inch of wood.

It was six o'clock. "Ladies and gentlemen," Craig Jacobs announced, "we're out of time."

That was it. There was nothing he could do now.

Fosse picked his hat up off the seat and left the theater to change into his opening-night tux. Gwen was with him.

They went out through the front of the house, passing theater manager Harry Teeter in the business office ("Show's going good," Fosse murmured), and went down a hallway, headed to the street. Mamie Duncan-Gibbs, on her way in to warm up, passed Bob and Gwen ("Have a good show!" Gwen said) as they stepped out onto Pennsylvania Avenue, which was whooshing with rush-hour traffic, the fall air dropping a touch below seventy degrees. Together, they strolled toward the Willard Hotel, where Fosse was staying that night, alone; Phoebe was in New York.

A shady green parkway on their left, Bob and Gwen crossed Fourteenth Street a block from the theater and went up to the great gilded doors of the Willard. Fosse nodded at Steve Blum, the hotel's doorman, as they entered, and a short time later, he and Gwen reappeared, looking their best. "Theater thataway," Fosse said, pointing ahead. Blum tipped his hat.

Inside the Willard's Round Robin Bar, folks had gathered for a quick dinner before the show. A cluster of people at the window stood up.

"Hey!" someone said.

Bartender Jim Hewes turned to face the commotion. The place grew quiet, then suddenly noisy again.

"Hey, someone fell down in the street."

"What?"

"He better get up."

Through the window, Hewes could see the intersection of Pennsylvania and Fourteenth Street. A man had collapsed toward the far side of the crosswalk, a few steps away from the curb. Outside, a crowd gathered, shouting for the paramedics, for an ambulance.

It took twenty minutes for the paramedics to arrive, and by the time they got there, traffic had completely clogged up the intersection. It was chaos, car horns blaring against sirens, but from behind her windshield, Patricia Baughman could see into the swarm. Rush-hour businesspeople grappled with medical personnel, pedestrians hovered for a look, and a shock of orange-red hair flashed by. "She was running around," Baughman said, "pushing people out of the way and screaming."

Thinking Fosse's heart attack was a seizure, Gwen dropped to her knees and held his head in her lap.

He had loved and not loved many women, but the one with him on the pavement, the last one to see him, had been letting go of him the longest.

"I'm very nervous," he had said to her, Lola, at their first rehearsal in 1954.

"So am I."

The ambulance took off for George Washington University hospital, a mile and a half from where Fosse collapsed, and arrived at the emergency room at 6:48. At 7:23, he was pronounced dead.

When I got home, there was a phone message on my machine. It was Bobby. He said he was looking forward to talking to me about this script I sent him about homelessness. He said he didn't think it was for him, but he wanted to help me get it made. By then I knew he was dead, but he was right there on my machine still talking about show business.

— *David Picker*

ACKNOWLEDGMENTS

'VE ALWAYS REVERED the movie musical, its mandate for hard and irrefutable talent, for harmonizing all performing arts into a single expression of pure feeling — every stage at Lincoln Center meshed eloquently into one. But no matter how much Lubitsch and Minnelli thrill me, watching *One Hour with You* and *The Band Wagon*, I can only sometimes escape the sense of having only escaped, of breathing pink helium and no oxygen. Emotions of lasting reverberation are almost irrelevant to those movies; the point seems to be to have a beautiful time, and I do. But a part of me always wished I could inject boiling blood into Astaire's veins. What would happen if Maurice Chevalier lost his cool? What would happen if Cassavetes came back to life and watched nothing but *The Pirate*? That movie would blow my mind.

When Jeanine Basinger, Wesleyan's renowned film professor, brought us, her class, to Cukor's *A Star Is Born*, I could feel, for the first time, real life creeping into the show. When she brought us to *All That Jazz*, I felt something harder and stranger, like depressive exhilaration, which felt real but better, *A Star Is Born* multiplied by all those MGM dream ballets that suddenly made sense. I loved the movie, probably too much. It ate my imagination. I'd had some version of that feeling before, of being consumed by a great work, but it had always registered more like catharsis. It felt good. *All That Jazz* I loved with an intensity that erased me.

That was 2001. Since then I've wanted to do something for Bob Fosse. I did not know what; that seemed to erase me more.

Three years ago, my friend and agent David Halpern suggested a biography. The idea excited me, but I told him I didn't know how to put a whole life into one book — not to mention Fosse's kind of life — that I was sure no one would want it, and even if people did, I'd mess it up. But over one dinner, Halpern delivered the sort of end-of-act-two locker-room sermon that (though I can't remember it) was so heartfelt and fortifying, I'll always think of it as the Agent's Saint Crispin's Day speech. I wrote this book, but David Halpern made it. He invented it, guarded it, cheered it. Then George Hodgman, this book's first editor, acquired it. With a general's conviction, he pointed me toward its future. Scribbling on menus and receipts, underlining big ideas, we debated our Fosse onto the horizon, like Omar Sharif in *Lawrence of Arabia.* Eamon Dolan, this book's second editor, reeled that figure toward us. When I lost sight of him, or it, he held my frustrations. When ideas died, he let me release them with uncommon grace, at my own speed, and he sat shivah with me until I got pregnant again.

Halpern, Hodgman, and Dolan are *Fosse's* Paddy, Herb, and Sam, the studio against the studio. My team.

Every biographer is Dr. Frankenstein and research is the lightning bolt. The single greatest pleasure of writing this book was harvesting that lightning person to person, from Fosse's dancers, friends, family, lovers, collaborators, and enemies. I interviewed over three hundred. The common theme was love: Fosse's for them, theirs for him. Every day since my first interview (Laddie, June 7, 2010), I've been hoping I could take that love they entrusted to me and use it to lightning

Fosse back to life, but without obliterating the anguish, anger, and isolation that so often edged his playful spirit out of view. If I did not succeed, I hope you all know my effort was sincere. For your time and compassion, thank you: Joe Allen, Rae Allen, Carol Alt, Susan Anderson, Eric Angelson, Jane Aurthur, Scott Barnes, Julian Barry, Patricia Baughman, Dwight Baxter, Jeanna Belkin, Gail Benedict, Sandahl Bergman, Mike Berkowitz, Ira Bernstein, Dr. Robert Bilder, Larry Billman, Nancy Bird, Grace Blake, Steve Blum, Shannon Bolin, Michael Bolton, Denice Pence Boockvor, Susan Braudy, Melissa Bretherton, Sandra Brewer, Richard Brick, Candy Brown, Kitty Bruce, Lonnie Burr, Ruth Buzzi, Stephanie Pope Caffey, Kevin Carlisle, Teresa Carpenter, Lynne Carrow, Eileen Casey, George Chakiris, Marge Champion, Emile Charlap, Suzanne Charney, Martin Charnin, Barrie Chase, Sybil Christopher, Wayne Cilento, Cheryl Clark, Madilyn Clark, Jill Clayburgh, Perry Cline, Marya Cohn, Peter Cohn, Christine Colby, Shaun Considine, Mel Cooper, Marilyn D'Honau, Danny Daniels, Joan Darling, Leslee Dart, Loretta Devine, Sara Dillon, Kathryn Doby, E. L. Doctorow, Arlene Donovan, Ervin Drake, Richard Dreyfuss, Diane Duncan, Mamie Duncan-Gibbs, Blake Edwards, Kevin Elders, Lisa Embs, Don Emmons, Harvey Evans, Tracy Everitt, Robin Utt Fajardo, Jules Feiffer, Jules Fisher, Gary Flannery, Ted Flicker, Liz (Erzsebet) Foldi, David Freeman, Bruce Jay Friedman, Victor Garber, Rita Gardner, Dr. Richard Gartner, Gene Gavin, Deborah Geffner, Ken Geist, Gary Gendell, David Warren Gibson, Norman Gimbel, Laurent Giroux, Tony Gittelson, Wolfgang Glattes, Maxine Glorsky, Ellen Graff, Charles Grass, Wayne Green, Robert Greenhut, Joel Grey, Charles Grodin, John Guare, Clyde Haberman, Buzz Halliday, Sonja Haney, Gordon Lowry Harrell, Karen Hassett, Bill Hastings, Bill Hayes, Jack Heifner, Alan Heim, Mariel Hemingway, Jim Henaghan, Allen Herman, Michael Herr, Gregg Heschong, Jim Hewes, Dustin Hoffman, Norman Hollyn, Celeste Holm, James Horvath, Jerry Jaffe, Leilani Jones,

Sherri Kandell, John Kander, Steve Kennedy, Patricia Ferrier Kiley, Peggy King, Carolyn Kirsch, Dorothy Kloss, Alice Korsick, Richard Korthaze, Michael Kubala, Alan Ladd Jr., Nathan Lane, Bonnie Langford, Jane Lanier, Sherry Lansing, Lionel Larner, Pamela Larsson-Toscher, Ken Laub, Diana Laurenson, Carmen LaVia, Dr. Drew Leder, John Lithgow, Jo Loesser, Susan Loesser, Tom Lofaro, Aarne Lofgren, John Henry Loomis, Lynn Lovett, Janice Lynde, Peter MacDonald, Neil Machlis, Norman Henry Mamey, Frankie Man, Fred Mann III, George Marcy, Larry Mark, Mary Ellen Mark, Marsha Mason, Paul Mazursky, Craig McKay, Donna McKechnie, John McMartin, Debra McWaters, John Miller, Dana Moore, Robert Morse, Sharon Murray, Gail Mutrux, Jennifer Nairn-Smith, Lenora Nemetz, Chris Newman, Leslie Newman, Phyllis Newman, Mark Obenhaus, Cynthia Onrubia, Stuart Ostrow, Stan Page, Janis Paige, Valerie Perrine, Valarie Pettiford, Wende Phifer, David Picker, Dean Pitchford, Jonathan Pontell, Linda Posner (Leland Palmer), CCH Pounder, Seymour Red Press, Frank Price, Harold Prince, Mimi Quillin, Tommy Rall, Phil Ramone, Marion Ramsey, Brett Raphael, David Ray, Lee Roy Reams, Donald Rebic, Carl Reiner, Ann Reinking, Frank Rich, Chita Rivera, Eric Roberts, Cliff Robertson, David Rogow, Owen Roizman, David Rose, Bentley Roton, Dr. Charles Rousell, Sandy Rovetta, Cyma Rubin, Eva Rubinstein, John Rubinstein, Cis Rundle, Vidal Sassoon, Blane Savage, Cynthia Scheider, Maurice Schell, Richard Schickel, Murray Schisgal, Betsy Schulberg, Stephen Schwartz, Jay Sears, Jeff Shade, Rick Shaine, Barbara Sharma, David Sheehan, Richard Shepherd, Phyllis Sherwood, Trudy Ship, Dan Siretta, Warren Allen Smith, Lew Soloff, Stephen Sondheim, Pamela Sousa, John Sowinski, Larry "Spoosh" Spivack, Tony Stevens, Leonard Stone, Susan Stroman, Bruce Surtees, Claudette Sutherland, Kristoffer Tabori, Celia Tackaberry, Harry Teeter, Terri Treas, Michael Tronick, Tommy Tune, Paul Turgeon, Larry Turman, Phoebe Ungerer, Ken

Urmston, Beth Kellough Vandenboom, Jack Vartoogian, Ben Vereen, Chet Walker, Marie Wallace, Sigourney Weaver, Raquel Welch, Elmarie Wendel, William Whitener, Dan Wilensky, Kathy Witt, Emanuel L. Wolf, Hilma Wolitzer, Sandy Wolshin, Albert Wolsky, Michael York, Adele Yoshioka, Jimmie Young, and George Zima. I don't believe in ghosts, but now I believe in those who do.

Without librarians and research advisers, I'd be running circles in the storm, swiping at thunder and plunging into mud. Thank you, Walter Zvonchenko, Patricia Baughman, and James Wintle, my Igors at Library of Congress's Performing Arts Reading Room, home of the Bob Fosse and Gwen Verdon Collection, for keeping the box-flow flowing, for putting up with my last-minute queries, and for generally helping me master a holding thousands of items deep. Thank you, Charles Silver and Jenny He at the Museum of Modern Art, for leading me to some precious clippings (with a lovely view of the courtyard) and then letting me alone to Xerox like crazy. Jane Klain at the Paley Center for Media in New York was more than a knowledgeable source d'showbiz; she managed to help me uncover some material I thought had been lost forever. On one great day, she spoke the three little words every researcher dreams of hearing: "I found it." I am grateful to you, Jane.

Aside from being one of the best shows in town, year-round and forever, the New York Public Library's Theatre on Film and Tape Archive is the Père Lachaise of Broadway history. This book's readers know why TOFT has almost zero Fosse, but the archive seems to have just about everything else, and for free, all week (except Sundays and Mondays). Sitting in those little cubicles, I come close to patriotism. Thank you, Patrick Hoffman and the rest of the gang at TOFT. And thank you, Ned Comstock, senior library assistant at USC's Cinematic Arts Library. Everyone in the movie-book business knows and owes Ned. Late in the game, I called him with a long-shot question, and he came through in a way that was so extravagant, I don't want to print it here for fear that no one interested in MGM will ever stop calling him.

The Academy of Motion Picture Arts and Sciences' Margaret Herrick Library made this possible. Aside from being the best in the world, the facility has a beauty and serenity that actually elevates research to a sensual plane. As always, chatting with Sondra Archer down at the periodicals was a welcome relief, and Jenny Romero and Barbara Hall, hidden away like Oz, saved me more than once. Thank you all.

From the Margaret Herrick I go up La Cienega, past the *Point Blank* apartments, to the *Beloved Infidel* house, where a couple of infidels live at point-blank range to some very crisp drinks and a view of the city that should make Mulholland feel bad about itself. Herein dwell Freeman and Gingold, F. Scott and Zelda if they'd lived longer and converted to Judaism. Every evening chez GingFree is blessedly the same, and it has been for years. As the night goes on and the porch gets cooler, we move our drinks inside and start talking about dinner, whether we'll go for Chinese at Genghis Cohen or to Musso's (we pick Genghis), and then David calls ahead for a table and we go. The rest of the evening is spent in a black booth eating, drinking, debating, remembering. The same names come up. Hitchcock, Wilder, Mitchum, the writer Phil Dunne, Mazursky, Tony Richardson. They are our favorite songs. Sometimes we'll be joined by Lynne Littman, Sarah Shepard, or Jack Dolman. The others are less fortunate but no less worthy. They are Jeanine Basinger, Pablo Davanzo, Lisa Dombrowski, Maria Diaz, Bob Dolman, the Goldblatts, Alex Horwitz, Lauren Kirchner, Andrea Martin, Nicky Martin, Jocelyn Medawar, Lynn Povich, Steve Shepard, Mom, Dad, and Sophie. Thank you for asking about Fosse and, in most cases, letting me give a long answer before you even asked. Your interest and encouragement made the small victories bigger, especially in the case of Freeman, this book's

Tom Hagen, and Mom, Dad, and Sophie, this book's Mom, Dad, and Sister. They were flares in the dark.

And also Marie Grass Amenta, Jeffrey Banks, Nikki Donen, Judy James, Nick Kazan, Jacqueline Mention, Mike Ovitz, Rick Pappas, Tracy Roe, Meg Rutenberg, Gil and Joanne Segel, Martin Short, Sally Bedell Smith, and Kenneth Turan. You did mitzvahs. Thank you.

Thank you to Kathy Robbins, whom I must owe a thousand favors. It's hard to tell because, like Zorro or Santa Claus, she works in the shadows and never breaks a sweat. Thank you, Kathy. And thank you to my friends at the Robbins Office, Arielle Asher, Rachelle Bergstein, Katherine DiLeo, Michael Gillespie, Micah Hauser, Ian King, and Louise Quayle. I'm relieved you are behind me and proud that you want to be.

Thank you to Jon Cassir and Matthew Snyder at CAA, who got tough but stayed soft, who reexplained for the billionth time, who had instant faith and never let it wane.

And thank you, thank you, Genevieve, clown-warrior.

SAM WASSON

JUNE 2013

NOTES

I AM FORTUNATE NOT to be Bob Fosse's first biographer. An intrepid guide, Martin Gottfried's trailblazing *All His Jazz: The Life and Death of Bob Fosse* (New York: Bantam, 1990) cut the thicket ahead of me and unearthed bones where I might never have shoveled. Now priceless, his interviews with witnesses long gone helped to recover parts of Fosse that would otherwise be gone for good, and his judicious recounting of events served them well. A complete inventory of the Bob Fosse and Gwen Verdon Collection at the Library of Congress is available online at http://www.loc.gov/rr/perform/special/fosse.html. In this section, the abbreviation *LOC*, followed by a box number, refers to the library's Fosse/Verdon Collection.

Ethan Mordden's magnificent multivolume history of the Broadway musical enlarged my sense of the bigger pictures and brushed up my Shakespeare (and my Abbott and Robbins and Sondheim). Tracing the musical's artistic, cultural, and industrial progress (and regression) from the golden age to the dark age, and in many cases re-creating, magically, the century's high points in drama, music, and dance, Mordden was the dream Emcee/professor and a blast to read.

page **THE END**

1 the Empress: LOC, box 1A, folder 5, *All That Jazz* research, Paddy Chayefsky interview.

miniature black derby: Ben Vereen, interview with the author, January 11, 2011.

2 "Bob always said": Alan Heim, interview with the author, July 22, 2010.

he'd RSVP'd no: Jerome Robbins Papers, box 507, Jerome Robbins Dance Division, the New York Library for the Performing Arts.

3 "If there is an afterlife": Herb Gardner, Bob Fosse Memorial, Palace Theater, October 30, 1987, New York Public Library for the Performing Arts, Theatre on Film and Tape Archive.

more likely to show up: Gwen Verdon interview, *Dance in America,* WNET archives, September 6, 1989.

He would have called Hamill and asked him: Pete Hamill, Bob Fosse Memorial, Palace Theater, October 30, 1987, New York Public Library for the Performing Arts, Theatre on Film and Tape Archive.

"This is incredibly sad": Arlene Donovan, interview with the author, January 10, 2011.

"I'm having the best time": Alan Ladd Jr., interview with the author, June 7, 2010.

4 "It was as if he was orchestrating it": James Barron, "Follow-Up on the News," *New York Times,* December 20, 1987.

"with Fosse's ghost": Martin Gottfried, *All His Jazz* (Cambridge, MA: Da Capo, 1998; first published by Bantam in 1990), 460. Citations refer to the Da Capo edition.

In a quiet room: Phoebe Ungerer, interview with the author, December 13, 2012.

Suddenly Ben Vereen: Ben Vereen, interview with the author, January 11, 2011.

Reinking followed with Nicole: John Rubinstein, interview with the author, September 30, 2010.

Fosse's three women moved closer: Kathryn Doby, interview with the author, November 27, 2010.

SIXTY YEARS

5 He was losing to the blank page: Archer Winsten, "Rages and Outrages," *New York Post,* March 4, 1972.

6 "By the time I was born": "Bob Fosse," *The Dick Cavett Show,* PBS, July 8, 1980.

"It was probably one": Ibid.

When Richard died: Robert Wahls, "Bob Who? Bob Fosse!," *New York Sunday News,* November 26, 1972.

local Norwegian choral group: Charles Grass, interview with the author, September 4, 2012.

"[Cy] would always eat": Ann Reinking, interview with the author, November 15, 2010.

235-pound former spear-carrying: Barry Rehfeld, "Bob Fosse's Follies," *Rolling Stone*, January 19, 1984.

"My mother was": Bernard Drew, "Life as a Long Rehearsal," *American Film*, November 1979.

Sadie had a heart problem: Charles Grass, interview with the author, September 4, 2012.

7 Asthma too: Rehfeld, "Bob Fosse's Follies."

early attacks of pneumonia: Ibid.

Lenny Bruce said: John Cohen, ed., *The Essential Lenny Bruce* (New York: Ballantine Books, 1967), 102.

Sadie Fosse lived in fear: Charles Grass, interview with the author, September 4, 2012.

"If I get pneumonia": Ibid.

They were a bouncy bunch: Ibid.

8 "He used to tell me": Linda Winer, "Shade of Bob Fosse Raised by 'Chicago,'" *Newsday*, November 22, 1996.

"That was one of the reasons": "Bob Fosse," *The Dick Cavett Show.*

"Bob was the favorite": Ann Reinking, interview with the author, November 15, 2010.

"I was a good kid": Rehfeld, "Bob Fosse's Follies."

"I come from a big family": Chris Chase, "Fosse, from Tony to Oscar to Emmy," *New York Times*, April 29, 1973.

He was told to escort: Charles Grass, interview with the author, September 4, 2010.

"I had a crush": "Bob Fosse," *The Dick Cavett Show.*

9 She simply did not: Charles Grass, interview with the author, September 4, 2012.

rumored to have led: Beth Kellough Vandenboom, interview with the author, January 5, 2013.

studied music theory with: Charles Grass, interview with the author, September 4, 2012.

"I, the undersigned": Grass/Weaver Agreement, undated. Collection of Charles Grass.

10 "Mr. Weaver taught us how": Charles Grass, interview with the author, September 4, 2012.

A sign on the wall said: Beth Kellough Vandenboom, interview with the author, January 5, 2013.

"And remember this" *and following*: Charles Grass, interview with the author, September 4, 2012.

11 Behind Weaver's desk: Dorothy Kloss, interview with the author, December 2, 2010.

A real-life Chicago vaudevillian: Ibid.

"She filled me with": Bob Fosse, *Tomorrow with Tom Snyder,* NBC, January 31, 1980.

circus performers: Charles Grass, interview with the author, September 4, 2012.

12 Fosse seemed to disappear: Beth Kellough Vandenboom, interview with the author, January 5, 2013.

"They would accept": Fosse, *Tomorrow with Tom Snyder.*

"He was always told": Charles Grass, interview with the author, September 4, 2012.

Bobby was reprimanded: Ibid.

In Fosse's first: Program, Chicago's Medinah Country Club, June 15, 1936. Collection of Charles Grass.

13 Thus Sadie and Cy: Charles Grass, interview with the author, September 4, 2012.

In November 1937: Martin Gottfried, *All His Jazz* (Cambridge, MA: Da Capo, 1998; first published by Bantam in 1990), 11. Citations refer to the Da Capo edition.

"Mr. Weaver really watched us": Charles Grass, interview with the author, September 4, 2012.

16 "He'd furrow his little eyebrows": Beth Kellough Vandenboom, interview with the author, January 5, 2013.

Astaire and Rogers held the movie slot: Charles Grass, interview with the author, September 4, 2012.

17 Some said it was a fad — they were wrong: For more on the history of vaudeville, see Charles W. Stein's *American Vaudeville as Seen by Its Contemporaries* (New York: Knopf, 1984), a rich and colorful compendium of primary-source documents chronicling vaudeville's fifty-year rise and fall.

"He wanted to dance *with* him": Charles Grass, interview with the author, September 4, 2012.

18 "Weaver didn't care where he put": Dorothy Kloss, interview with the author, December 2, 2010.

"When we started performing": Charles Grass, interview with the author, September 4, 2012.

19 After piling into Weaver's sedan: Ibid.

"I played every two-bit beer joint": William Glover, "A Director Full of Tricks," *Los Angeles Examiner,* December 11, 1968.

"The booker would call you up": *American Musical Theater with Earl Wrightson,* CBS, January 1, 1962.

At ten dollars a night: "Bob Fosse," *The Dick Cavett Show.*

He went to the movies: Drew, "Life as a Long Rehearsal."

The grade-schooler took out: Jan Herman, "Close Up: Bob Fosse," *Daily News,* April 6, 1986.

20 In the house were: Charles Grass, interview with the author, September 4, 2012.

his father drank himself to sleep: Gottfried, *All His Jazz,* 36.

his mother put herself to bed early: Charles Grass, interview with the author, September 4, 2012.

In the summers he shaved: Ann Reinking, interview with the author, November 15, 2010.

"He loved her so much": Ibid.

One Easter morning: Ibid.

Weaver upgraded that same year: Charles Grass, interview with the author, September 4, 2012.

21 "In those days": Ibid.

Fosse also kept quiet his crush: Ibid.

"Dancing at that age": Beth Kellough Vandenboom, interview with the author, January 5, 2013.

"He treated me like family": Ibid.

"All of a sudden, she was gone": Ibid.

"It was another man": Charles Grass, interview with the author, September 4, 2012.

liked the look: Gottfried, *All His Jazz,* 24.

"Ever since I was young": Linda Winer, "Bob Fosse: The Razzle-Dazzle Director Is Planning to Jazz Up Broadway with His New 'Deal,'" *USA Today,* October 30, 1985.

converted to Christian Science: Charles Grass, interview with the author, September 4, 2012.

smoked his while hiding: Ibid.

FORTY-FIVE YEARS

22 "As a teenager in high school": Beth Kellough Vandenboom, interview with the author, January 5, 2013.

Mary Vagos, Mary Farmakis, and Melvene Fitzpatrick: Martin Gottfried, *All His Jazz* (Cambridge, MA: Da Capo, 1998; first published by Bantam in 1990), 34. Citations refer to the Da Capo edition. Also, Kevin Boyd Grubb, *Razzle Dazzle: The Life and Work of Bob Fosse* (New York: St. Martin's Press, 1989).

23 "He had two lives": Charles Grass, interview with the author, September 4, 2012.

Fosse knew right away: "Bob Fosse," *The Dick Cavett Show,* PBS, July 8, 1980.

It didn't get any classier: Ibid.

"I think that [Draper] was probably": *Paul Draper on Tap,* directed by Roger Englander, telecast by Camera Three, WGBH Boston, 1979.

"When the war came along": George Goldberg, "Bob Fosse, Not an Ordinary Man," *Faces International,* Summer 1985.

that burlesque: Actual and authentic burlesque culture, before the modern imagination reclaimed (and misread) basement sleaze as female empowerment, survives in Leslie Zemeckis's documentary *Behind the Burly Q: The Story of Burlesque in America.*

24 "The more we talked about him": Grubb, *Razzle Dazzle,* 8–9.

"There wasn't much dancing": Charles Grass, interview with the author, September 4, 2012.

25 His mother and father didn't really know: Moira Hodgson, "When Bob Fosse's Art Imitates Life, It's Just 'All That Jazz,'" *New York Times,* December 30, 1979.

Mrs. Grass, their stage mother: Charles Grass, interview with the author, September 4, 2012.

"They're not nice girls": Ibid.

26 preyed on him before the show: Paul Gardner, "Bob Fosse Off His Toes," *New York,* December 16, 1974.

When the girls found out: Ibid.

In the tense seconds: Ibid.

27 "They were affectionate": Janice Lynde, interview with the author, May 4, 2011.

"I can romanticize it": Bob Fosse interview, *Datebook,* September 2, 1979.

"It was schizophrenic": Chris Chase, "Fosse's Ego Trip," *Life,* November 1979.

"It just wasn't the same world": Lionel Chetwynd, "Except for Bob Fosse," *Penthouse,* January 1974.

28 at the Cuban Village: Charles Grass, interview with the author, September 4, 2012.

"Bob could charm his way anywhere": Ann Reinking, interview with the author, November 15, 2010.

"She thought you could send": Hodgson, "When Bob Fosse's Art Imitates Life."

"I panicked at the time": Bruce Williamson, "All That Fosse," *Playboy,* March 1980.

bottom-feeding hoods: Lisa Krissoff Boehm details Chicago's myth and image problems in *Popular Culture and the Enduring Myth of Chicago, 1871–1968* (New York: Routledge, 2004).

29 "In 1933 the world will talk": Address of Mayor L. R. Lohr Delivered Over Radio Station WGN, July 10, 1929, second personal scrapbook of Lenox Lohr, box 29, Century of Progress Papers, University of Illinois at Chicago Library.

"The oversized fan poked fun": Rachel Shteir, *Striptease: The Untold History of the Girlie Show* (New York: Oxford University Press, 2004), 147.

"He was fascinated with Sally Rand": Charles Grass, interview with the author, September 4, 2012.

use pitch-black ostrich feathers: Fan dance photograph in LOC, box 60A, folder "Fosse, First Choreography Job."

"was very sophisticated": Beth Kellough Vandenboom, interview with the author, January 5, 2013.

30 "But I like those sequins": Williamson, "All That Fosse."

"Whenever I get close": Hodgson, "When Bob Fosse's Art Imitates Life."

31 "Chairman of senior class": "Nominate Star Seniors at Six N. Side Highs: Tribune Will Query Class Choices," *Chicago Daily Tribune,* December 31, 1944. The students elected him: "Star Seniors Lay Plans, But Put War First: Several Interested in Journalism," *Chicago Daily Tribune,* January 14, 1945. Consisting mostly of sketches and songs: Gottfried, *All His Jazz,* 30.

32 "I think they didn't believe": Charles Grass, interview with the author, September 4, 2012.

took his baby brother: Ibid.

33 "No, no": Ibid.

Fosse's brothers had all served in the war: "Star Seniors Lay Plans."

"wrote to the Great Lakes": Charles Grass, interview with the author, September 4, 2012.

Disguised as an ordinary high-school student: "6 N. Side Highs Will Graduate 1,240 Seniors: Lane Technical Tops List With 313," *Chicago Daily Tribune,* January 21, 1945.

"You want to come with me?": Charles Grass, interview with the author, September 4, 2012.

34 Now that he had gotten a deferral from the war: Gottfried, *All His Jazz,* 36.

"I hate show business": Bernard Drew, "Life as a Long Rehearsal," *American Film,* November 1979.

In the summer of 1945: Charles Grass, interview with the author, September 4, 2012.

"a kind of audition": Ibid.

"That might have saved Bob's life": Ibid.

35 "It was songs and sketches": Buzz Halliday, interview with the author, November 3, 2011.

"very thin, Irish-looking kid": Kenneth Turan, *Free for All: Joe Papp, the Public, and the Greatest Theater Story Ever Told* (New York: Doubleday, 2009), 28.

At twenty-five, Papirofsky, with his streetwise: Ibid.

36 "I saw at once that he was footjoy": John T. McQuiston, "A Veteran at 13," *New York Times,* September 24, 1987.

"I thought plays were effete": Turan, *Free for All,* 27.

37 "that overbite": Kenneth Turan/Bob Fosse unpublished interview, February 19, 1987.

Papp and Bill Quillin: Gottfried, *All His Jazz,* 40.

"I heard about it later": Charles Grass, interview with the author, September 4, 2012.

38 The woman told Mrs. Fosse: Ibid.

"I want you to know": Ibid.

Fosse toured *Tough Situation:* Gottfried, *All His Jazz,* 42.

39 Dancing alone in the forest: Gwen Verdon interview, *Dance in America,* WNET archives, September 6, 1989.

By the time *Tough Situation:* Gottfried, *All His Jazz,* 41.

"That was the first time": Pete Hamill, "Fosse," *Piecework* (Boston: Little, Brown, 1996), 348.

FORTY-ONE YEARS

40 Discharged from service in August 1946: Military service papers, LOC, box 52B.

41 mongrel work in progress: The brief illustration of post–World War II New York as a vaudeville town comes from dozens of primary-source interviews. "In a great musical": Richard Rodgers, *Musical Stages: An Autobiography* (New York: Random House, 1975), 227.

42 "Many a somber problem play": John Martin, "The Dance: De Mille's 'Oklahoma!,'" *New York Times,* May 9, 1943.

"When he talked to you": Lynne Carrow, interview with the author, December 10, 2010.

"I had always wondered why": Robert Greenhut, interview with the author, August 31, 2010.

43 "I think everyone was attracted to him": Christopher Newman, interview with the author, September 10, 2010.

"It was like you were in a tunnel": Trudy Ship, interview with the author, January 21, 2011.

Fosse's bed at the YMCA: George Chauncey, *Gay New York: Gender, Urban Culture, and The Making of the Gay Male World 1890–1940* (New York: Basic Books, 1994), 155–57.

44 "Sing first": Sheila John Daly, "Cross-Country Potpourri of Teen Doings," *Chicago Tribune,* June 21, 1947.

"The Farting Contest": Frankie Man, interview with the author, July 20, 2010.

"He was always there early": Carl Reiner, interview with the author, September 14, 2010.

45 "At the end of that number": Jeanna Belkin, interview with the author, May 8, 2011.

46 "We had a pretty crazy company": Carl Reiner, interview with the author, September 14, 2010.

They called her Spooky: Jeanna Belkin, interview with the author, May 8, 2011.

"Marian was a spitfire": Harvey Evans, interview with the author, January 28, 2011.

"I wanted to walk behind her": Margery Beddow, *In the Company of Friends:*

Dancers Talking to Dancers II, the Women of Fosse, videotaped at the New Dance Group, New York, on October 7, 2007.
"Spooky was a wonderful tap dancer": Jeanna Belkin, interview with the author, May 8, 2011.
"Bobby liked beauty but he loved talent": Deborah Geffner, interview with the author, October 1, 2010.
"No matter where the show took us": Jeanna Belkin, interview with the author, May 8, 2011.

47 "Limehouse Blues": Ronna Elaine Sloan, "Bob Fosse: An Analytic-Critical Study" (University Microfilms International, 1983), 67.
"She was a not too educated girl": Jeanna Belkin, interview with the author, May 8, 2011.
She "had a lot of clarity": Kevin Boyd Grubb, *Razzle Dazzle: The Life and Work of Bob Fosse* (New York: St. Martin's Press, 1989), 19.
The weekend the Ice Capades came: "Bob Fosse," *E! True Hollywood Story,* February 3, 1999.
"Could you imagine": Ibid.

48 Late in the evening: Martin Gottfried, *All His Jazz* (Cambridge, MA: Da Capo, 1998; first published by Bantam in 1990), 44. Citations refer to the Da Capo edition.
"We all knew about Bobby": Jeanna Belkin, interview with the author, May 8, 2011.
Backstage, Fosse pouffed his ascot: Gottfried, *All His Jazz,* 48.
"She was just a very sweet girl": Carl Reiner, interview with the author, September 14, 2010.
"Mr. Weaver was a hundred percent against marriage": Charles Grass, interview with the author, September 4, 2012.

49 "He was very, very nervous": Gottfried, *All His Jazz,* 48.
There was a reception that afternoon: Ibid.
Fosse posted his final review in the scrapbook: Bob Fosse black embossed scrapbook with Dutch boy and girl cover, LOC, box 55A.

50 "Bob likened show business to boxing": Ann Reinking, interview with the author, November 15, 2010.
"He had a drug problem": Charles Grass, interview with the author, September 4, 2012.
The maestro put tens and twenties: Ibid.

51 sensed that Fosse watched them with: Ibid.
"I always thought I'd be dead by twenty-five": Barry Rehfeld, "Bob Fosse's Follies," *Rolling Stone,* January 19, 1984.
"the most promising young dancers": Mark Newton, "The Clubs . . . After Dark," *Montreal Standard,* March 28, 1948.

"When we got off the floor someone said": "The Real Chorus Line," *The David Susskind Show,* WNTA-TV, October 18, 1981.

"They would do their nightclub act somewhere": Eileen Casey, interview with the author, January 31, 2011.

"I get terribly involved in my work": Jan Hodenfield, "Bob Fosse Feet First," *New York Post,* April 21, 1973.

"He thought he was the best and": Ann Reinking, interview with the author, November 15, 2010.

52 they arrived early: Frank Farrell, "Reds Never Rest," *New York World Telegram,* December 8, 1948.

53 "You've heard of Marge and Gower Champion?": Gottfried, *All His Jazz,* 56.

"If they looked good they didn't have": Bill Smith, "Cotillion Room, Hotel Pierre, New York," *Billboard,* December 18, 1948.

"What faith a wife must have": Norman Clark, "Bert Lahr Leads Buoyant Musical On Stage at Ford's," *Baltimore News Post,* February 15, 1949.

54 "There were about fifteen of us": Phyllis Sherwood, interview with the author, December 12, 2010.

"Unless he knew everything perfect": Ibid.

55 "Little bit of comedy in 'showoff' stint": *Variety,* July 13, 1949.

in the audience: Robert Wahls, "Gwen Verdon, the Eternal Gypsy," *New York Sunday News,* June 1, 1975.

THIRTY-SEVEN YEARS

56 with Poe's "Annabel Lee": Lisa Jo Sagolla, *The Girl Who Fell Down* (Lebanon, NH: Northeastern University Press, 2003), 62.

"Her eyes, in particular, often looked": Ibid., 26.

"practically a musical comedy in herself": Sam Zolotow, "Feigay-Smith Show Will Open Tonight," *New York Times,* December 22, 1945.

"There are lots of ballerinas": Sagolla, *The Girl Who Fell Down,* 66.

resembled piano legs: Ibid., 20.

"McCracken was exactly the right kind": Ibid., 71.

57 As one of the original members of the Actors Studio: Ibid., 6.

"I can fall down and make it": *New York Sunday News,* May 7, 1953.

"You could have sopped the audience up": Sagolla, *The Girl Who Fell Down,* 75.

"He would give her a flower": Ibid., 180.

To Mary-Ann, Fosse gave a new: Eileen Casey, interview with the author, January 31, 2011.

But feeling sorry for herself: Ibid.

58 Ol' Spooky (she wanted them to say): Jeanna Belkin, interview with the author, May 8, 2011.

choreographer, Robert Sidney, seemed to give her: Sagolla, *The Girl Who Fell Down*, 181.

styles not necessarily to his taste: George Goldberg, "Bob Fosse, Not an Ordinary Man," *Faces International*, Summer 1985.

59 "Interviewers would say": "Bob Fosse: Steam Heat," *Great Performances: Dance in America*, PBS; first aired February 23, 1990.

"Take care of myself?": Lionel Chetwynd, "Except for Bob Fosse," *Penthouse*, January 1974.

"Since last caught": Bill Smith, "Night Club–Vaude Reviews: Cotillion Room, Hotel Pierre, New York," *Billboard*, January 20, 1951.

The place was so full, chairs had to be: Ibid.

"There wasn't much choreography": George Marcy, interview with the author, February 8, 2011.

60 "We're all here to woo you": Michael Blowen, "Will Gritty 'Star 80' Glitter at the Box Office?," *Boston Globe*, November 6, 1983.

Proser swapped: "Café Theater, N.Y.," *Variety*, April 4, 1951.

Fosse would lead: George Marcy, interview with the author, February 8, 2011.

"I remember going there": Ibid.

"Jesus, she was so in love": Ibid.

61 "She's the one who encouraged me": Chris Chase, "Fosse, from Tony to Oscar to Emmy," *New York Times*, April 29, 1973.

Fosse thought of choreography as: "Is the Director-Choreographer Taking Over?" Roundtable discussion broadcast by radio station WEVD, New York, March 30, 1966.

"Joan was the biggest influence": Bernard Drew, "Life as a Long Rehearsal," *American Film*, November 1979.

62 Joan bloomed with the scent of cypress: Sagolla, *The Girl Who Fell Down*, 164.

she spoke French: Ibid.

she knew about wine: Ibid.

she advised Fosse to enroll in: "Bob Fosse," *The Dick Cavett Show*, PBS, July 8, 1980.

"I was always very bad in class": Richard Philip, "Bob Fosse's 'Chicago': Roxie's Razzle Dazzle and All That Jazz," *Dance Magazine*, November 1975.

Room 3B at the Neighborhood Playhouse: Sanford Meisner and Dennis Longwell, *Sanford Meisner on Acting* (New York: Random House, 1987), 3.

63 Gloria Vanderbilt, Farley Granger: Farley Granger and Robert Calhoun, *Include Me Out* (New York: St. Martin's Press, 2007), 186.

If you do something, you really do it: Meisner and Longwell, *Sanford Meisner on Acting*, 17.

He told them a story about Fanny Brice: Ibid., 176.

"So you're going to be nervous": Ibid.

"I think he had some sort of motto": Bob Fosse, interview with Stephen Harvey, LOC, box 60F.

Meisner saw what few had seen: "Sanford Meisner: The American Theatre's Best Kept Secret," *American Masters*, PBS, August 27, 1990.

64 despite Richard Rodgers's objections to Fosse's: Martin Gottfried, *All His Jazz* (Cambridge, MA: Da Capo, 1998; first published by Bantam in 1990), 62. Citations refer to the Da Capo edition.

Apparently, one of Metro's scouts had seen him: Ibid.

"natural-born hoofer": William Saroyan, *The Time of Your Life* (New York: Samuel French, 1941), 23.

contract for five hundred dollars: Bob Fosse's MGM contract, LOC, box 51A.

She had diabetes: Sagolla, *The Girl Who Fell Down*, 225.

65 "Bobby was great in the show": Phyllis Sherwood, interview with the author, December 12, 2010.

Fosse went up to Sherwood's hotel room: Ibid.

66 "We laughed about it afterward": Ibid.

"He never had a sleaziness about him": Candy Brown, interview with the author, January 7, 2011.

"He always sort of tucked his head": Blane Savage, interview with the author, February 26, 2011.

with chorus girls Norma Andrews: Gottfried, *All His Jazz*, 64.

"When he fell out of love with her": George Marcy, interview with the author, February 8, 2011.

67 some wondered if Niles really understood: Ibid.

"added a lot of talking to his act": Bill Smith, "Empire Room, Waldorf-Astoria, New York," *Billboard*, February 2, 1952.

"Fosse's 'Time of Your Life' bit: "Waldorf-Astoria, N.Y.," *Daily Variety*, January 30, 1952.

he was visibly restless: Gottfried, *All His Jazz*, 64.

Andrews and Jackson suggested: Ibid.

68 filled his stomach with that sour: Chase, "Fosse, from Tony to Oscar to Emmy."

April 28, 1952: "Equity Fines Miss Morrow," *Billboard*, March 29, 1952.

Returning to Hollywood, to MGM, Donen learned: John Anthony Gilvey, *Before the Parade Passes By: Gower Champion and the Glorious American Musical* (New York: St. Martin's Press, 2005), 53.

THIRTY-FIVE YEARS

69 Just outside the high walls: Scott Eyman, *Lion of Hollywood* (New York: Simon and Schuster, 2005), 329.

"You know, Helen": Hugh Fordin, *MGM's Greatest Musicals: The Arthur Freed Unit* (Cambridge, MA: Da Capo Press, 1975), 439.

Mayer hated Smith and Salsbury: Leslie Caron, *Thank Heaven: A Memoir* (New York: Viking, 2009), 60.

Mayer's 167 Culver City acres: Eyman, *Lion of Hollywood*, 1.

"If I start up another studio": Ibid., 436.

70 five-hundred-thousand-dollar budget for a single number: Ibid., 440.

71 Bob Fosse sublet Buddy Hackett's place: Martin Gottfried, *All His Jazz* (Cambridge, MA: Da Capo, 1998; first published by Bantam in 1990), 67. Citations refer to the Da Capo edition.

Fosse endured many screen tests: Kevin Boyd Grubb, *Razzle Dazzle: The Life and Work of Bob Fosse* (New York: St. Martin's Press, 1989), 27.

They gave him a toupee: Ken Geist, e-mail to the author, February 14, 2011.

"That was a trauma for me": Gaby Rodgers, "Bob Fosse: 'Choreography Is Writing with Your Body,'" *Long Island*, October 1, 1978.

the part Kelly was *supposed* to play: John Anthony Gilvey, *Before the Parade Passes By: Gower Champion and the Glorious American Musical* (New York: St. Martin's Press, 2005), 50.

they had a turkey on their hands: Stephen M. Silverman, *Dancing on the Ceiling: Stanley Donen and His Movies* (New York: Knopf, 1996), 181.

The last-minute casting: David L. Goodrich, *The Real Nick and Nora: Frances Goodrich and Albert Hackett, Writers of Stage and Screen Classics* (Carbondale: Southern Illinois University Press, 2004), 194.

Unceasing revisions put a strain: Marge Champion, interview with the author, August 24, 2011.

72 "They were Mr. Show Biz": Gilvey, *Before the Parade Passes By*, 53.

"In my opinion": Stanley Donen, interviewed by Michael Kantor, August 26, 2006, New York Public Library for the Performing Arts, Theatre on Film and Tape Archive.

"Fosse and Donen were wrapped up": Marge Champion, interview with the author, August 24, 2011.

Donen was seen creeping up behind: Ken Geist, e-mail to the author, February 14, 2011.

Fosse was seen creeping up behind: Harvey Evans, interview with the author, January 28, 2011.

73 Out of a distant sound stage sailed: "Bob Fosse: Steam Heat," *Great Performances: Dance in America*, PBS; first aired February 23, 1990.

"Hiya, Foss!": *American Film Institute Salute to Fred Astaire*, CBS, April 18, 1981.

74 "You see it on the screen": Ibid.

they'd never let her dance: Lisa Jo Sagolla, *The Girl Who Fell Down* (Lebanon, NH: Northeastern University Press, 2003), 229.

"After they previewed it": Marge Champion, interview with the author, August 24, 2011.

"Charlie": Charles Grass, interview with the author, September 4, 2012.

75 "That's the teenaged Bob Fosse": Ibid.

"I was living in a one-room apartment": Paul Rosenfield, "Fosse, Verdon and 'Charity': Together Again," *Los Angeles Times,* July 21, 1986.

choreographer Michael Kidd's parties: Interviews with Geraldine Fitzgerald, Gwen Verdon, Marian Seldes, and Elizabeth McCann, *CUNY Spotlight,* CUNY-TV, 1991, New York Public Library for the Performing Arts, Theatre on Film and Tape Archive.

"Dance it like a lady athlete": Glenn Loney, *Unsung Genius: The Passion of Dancer-Choreographer Jack Cole* (New York: Franklin Watts, 1984), 214.

Joan McCracken, Mrs. Bob Fosse, had been one of Verdon's: Gwen Verdon interview, *Dance in America,* WNET archives, September 6, 1989.

76 "Then came *David and Bathsheba*": Hyman Goldberg, "Little Knock-Knees Knocks 'Em Cold," *Sunday Mirror Magazine,* n.d., ca. 1955.

"One more body on the cutting room floor": Jack Stone, "In Hollywood They Call Gwen Verdon the Naughty Girl on the Cutting Room Floor," *American Weekly,* July 31, 1955.

"I never think of myself as sexy": Ibid.

turned into loneliness: Peggy King, interview with the author, February 21, 2011.

77 "My parts were getting smaller": Rosenfield, "Fosse, Verdon and 'Charity.'"

"He was depressed": Peggy King, interview with the author, February 21, 2011.

78 producer Arthur Loew, Kirk Douglas: Jane Allen, *Pier Angeli: A Fragile Life* (Jefferson, NC: McFarland, 2002), 35, 75, 84.

"Anna was moving up": Peggy King, interview with the author, February 21, 2011.

"I think it would have been better if": "AFC's Loew Gives Fosse Salute," *Daily Variety,* September 25, 1987.

Schary's mood worsened several months later: Dore Schary, *Heyday* (Boston: Little, Brown, 1979), 261.

a high-ranking executive: Ibid.

"When I saw the sets for *Kate*": Paul Gardner, "Bob Fosse," *Action,* May/June 1974.

Choreographer Hermes Pan asked: Tommy Rall, interview with the author, April 20, 2011.

79 "I met Bobby for the first time": Ibid.

After the screening, Pan broke: Ibid.

"You just have a way of dancing": "Bob Fosse: Steam Heat," *Great Performances: Dance in America.*

80 to work with Joe Price: Donald Duncan, "They Flip for Joe Price," *Dance Magazine*, August 1964.

81 "I thought choreographers were all": Glenn Loney, "The Many Facets of Bob Fosse," *After Dark*, June 1972.

"Bob knew what was happening": Tommy Rall, interview with the author, April 20, 2011.

the studio granted Fosse: Fosse employment correspondence with MGM, LOC, box 51A.

they bought waterfront land in the Pines area: Sagolla, *The Girl Who Fell Down*, 244.

She wanted a baby: Bill Hayes, interview with the author, December 14, 2012.

Her eye for décor, like her conversation: Sagolla, *The Girl Who Fell Down*, 127.

82 was home to writers, painters, and dancers invited: Ibid., 173.

"She was often very upset": Ibid., 212.

"There were three rehearsal rooms at MGM": "Bob Fosse," *The Dick Cavett Show*, PBS, July 8, 1980.

Can-Can's producers, Cy Feuer and Ernie Martin: Cy Feuer and Ken Gross, *I Got the Show Right Here* (New York: Simon and Schuster, 2003), 121.

a voice she described as sounding like a 78 rpm record: Pierre Bowman, "She's Broadway's Former Dancing Star with a Heart of Gold," *Honolulu Star Bulletin*, October 8, 1985.

83 offered Verdon a fully paid weekend: Verdon interview on *CUNY Spotlight*.

"I was so scared": Chris Chase, "What Gwen Verdon Wants Is to Act," *New York Times*, December 2, 1983.

"It probably sounded like": Ibid.

"Well, Claudine": Ibid.

Gwen went to the Warwick Hotel: Bowman, "She's Broadway's Former Dancing Star."

"How'd it go, honey?": Chase, "What Gwen Verdon Wants."

84 He punched her: Ibid.

director Michael Kidd: Feuer and Gross, *I Got the Show Right Here*, 174.

Jealous of Verdon, Lilo insisted: Ibid., 180.

"I don't really blame Lilo": Rex Reed, "'I Never Wanted to Be Special,'" *New York Times*, February 6, 1966.

phone-booth-size dressing room: Verdon interview on *CUNY Spotlight*.

"I don't know how Michael [Kidd] did it": Cy Feuer, interviewed by Michael Kantor, February 23, 1999, New York Public Library for the Performing Arts, Theatre on Film and Tape Archive.

"Sometimes I'm on stage": Louis Sheaffer, "Sudden Fame Means Busy Schedule to Gwen Verdon," *Brooklyn Eagle*, May 19, 1953.

85 she got on opening night: *American Musical Theater with Earl Wrightson*, CBS, January 1, 1962.

the response to Gwen's Apache dance was so powerful: Cy Feuer, interviewed by Michael Kantor.

Gwen Verdon, meanwhile, was oblivious: Verdon interview on *CUNY Spotlight.*

Michael Kidd figured as much: Ibid.

"You have to go out there": Ibid.

"I could have walked into Tokyo": Ibid.

Gwen had to ride with a policeman: Ibid.

"I remember the first time I saw her": Rosenfield, "Fosse, Verdon and 'Charity.'"

86   Fosse would wait for Joan: Bill Hayes, interview with the author, December 14, 2012.

she led a small acting class: Shirley MacLaine, *My Lucky Stars: A Hollywood Memoir* (New York: Bantam, 1995), 157.

She taught Mary Tarcai: Bill Hayes, interview with the author, December 14, 2012.

Fosse could be seen pacing: MacLaine, *My Lucky Stars,* 157.

"Joan was pregnant": Bill Hayes, interview with the author, December 14, 2012.

she lost the baby: Ibid.

"Joan had hard numbers in that show": Ibid.

Biographer Lisa Jo Sagolla submits: Sagolla, *The Girl Who Fell Down,* 220–21.

The property the Fosses bought: Ibid., 245.

87   "by the time they did *Me and Juliet*": Harold Prince, interview with the author, October 6, 2010.

"Others seemed to be even more shy": George Abbott, *Mister Abbott* (New York: Random House, 1963), 248.

Robbins was aiming higher: Harold Prince, interview with the author, October 6, 2010.

McCracken took Abbott to see *Kiss Me Kate:* Ibid.

"Joanie sounded off about Bob every time": Grubb, *Razzle Dazzle,* 33.

"Have you done much choreography?": George Goldberg, "Bob Fosse, Not an Ordinary Man," *Faces International,* Summer 1985.

88   "Do you think we can talk Robbins into": Harold Prince, interview with the author, October 6, 2010.

Prince called Robbins: Ibid.

Walking up Fifth Avenue after: Abbott, *Mister Abbott,* 248.

Fosse ran into: Carl Reiner, interview with the author, September 14, 2010.

THIRTY-THREE YEARS

90   "[I] let everything that can come out": *American Musical Theater with Earl Wrightson,* CBS, January 1, 1962.

"I go through each number and try to get a combination": Glenn Loney, "The Many Facets of Bob Fosse," *After Dark,* June 1972.

91 "I need to have a sense of insecurity": Kenneth L. Geist, "Fosse Reflects on Fosse," *After Dark,* February 1980.

"I finally [get] to the point": Loney, "The Many Facets of Bob Fosse."

six or seven packs a day: Wolfgang Glattes, interview with the author, November 27, 2010.

thirty thousand dollars short: Allene Talmey, "Biography of a Musical: 'Damn Yankees,'" *Vogue,* March 1956.

92 "Abbott would give you line readings": Rae Allen, interview with the author, September 3, 2010.

If someone started getting arty: Helen Gallagher, interviewed by Liza Gennaro, March 22, 2006, New York Public Library for the Performing Arts, Jerome Robbins Dance Division.

"His legs were so long": Rae Allen, interview with the author, September 3, 2010.

"He was the most disciplined man": Harold Prince, interview with the author, October 6, 2010.

He asked the kids to call him George: Rae Allen, interview with the author, September 3, 2010.

"Bobby was deeply serious": Ibid.

"He was mostly quiet": Janis Paige, interview with the author, July 28, 2010.

Mickey Mouse lunch box and a Donald Duck baseball hat: Rae Allen, interview with the author, September 3, 2010.

93 Fosse was the king of: Shirley MacLaine, *My Lucky Stars: A Hollywood Memoir* (New York: Bantam, 1995), 163.

"Just stage it": Rae Allen, interview with the author, September 3, 2010.

Robbins's coat was off by the time: Janis Paige, interview with the author, July 28, 2010.

"In an hour and a half, [Robbins] had": Gaby Rodgers, "Bob Fosse: 'Choreography Is Writing with Your Body,'" *Long Island,* October 1, 1978.

"You keep the actors moving": Ibid.

94 "In five minutes, Jerry had it solved": Rae Allen, interview with the author, September 3, 2010.

He gave Janis Paige a newspaper: Janis Paige, interview with the author, July 28, 2010.

"That's where Jerry Robbins came in": Sara Dillon, interview with the author, October 8, 2010.

"It was a big egg": Ibid.

"Why don't you do something simple": Richard Adler, interviewed by Michael Kantor, March 29, 1999, New York Public Library for the Performing Arts, Theatre on Film and Tape Archive.

95 "That's it," Fosse said: Ibid.

"He threw about a million steps at us": Kevin Boyd Grubb, *Razzle Dazzle: The Life and Work of Bob Fosse* (New York: St. Martin's Press, 1989), 42.

loved what Fosse did: Bob Fosse, interview with "Haddad," 1982, LOC, box 49A.

"If you want to make a reputation": Ed Blank, "Why Don't They Dance in Films? Ask Fosse," *Pittsburgh Press*, September 8, 1983.

96 "The actual choreography comes out of": Fosse interview with "Haddad."

"The tricks": MacLaine, *My Lucky Stars*, 165.

"Steam Heat" got a standing ovation: Harold Prince, interview with the author, October 6, 2010.

"Bob never forgot how hard Jerry fought": Ann Reinking, interview with the author, November 15, 2010.

"They needed money": Sara Dillon, interview with the author, October 8, 2010.

Before the opening-night curtain went up: Harold Prince, interview with the author, October 6, 2010.

97 That night, May 13, 1954: Alvin Klein, "Hey There! It's Richard Adler," *New York Times*, March 5, 1989.

Richard Adler looked through the clamor: Ibid.

"I don't think any of us touched": Seymour Peck, "Up and Coming Actress," *New York Times*, May 23, 1954.

"What do you think?": Harold Prince, interview with the author, October 6, 2010.

"That night, Carol and Buzz and Peter": Janis Paige, interview with the author, July 28, 2010.

"I think 'Steam Heat' was": "Bob Fosse: Steam Heat," *Great Performances: Dance in America*, PBS; first aired February 23, 1990.

98 Saying nothing, they just looked: Harold Prince, interview with the author, October 6, 2010.

"The last new musical of the season": Brooks Atkinson, "Theater in Review: 'Pajama Game,'" *New York Times*, May 14, 1954.

"The bright, brassy, and jubilantly sassy": Walter Kerr, *Pajama Game* review, *New York Herald Tribune*, May 14, 1954.

"By 9 A.M.": Klein, "Hey There! It's Richard Adler."

Robbins gave Fosse a pair: Ann Reinking, interview with the author, November 15, 2010.

99 After selling their previous lot: Lisa Jo Sagolla, *The Girl Who Fell Down* (Lebanon, NH: Northeastern University Press, 2003), 245.

"I'm confused": Frances Herridge, "Curtain Cues," *New York Post*, May 28, 1954.

ignore the offer from Columbia: Thomas M. Pryor, "'Oklahoma!' Cast Is Named on Coast," *New York Times*, June 19, 1954.

he would go from Joan to Janet: Sagolla, *The Girl Who Fell Down*, 223.

It was immediately obvious to Fosse: Janet Leigh, *There Really Was a Hollywood* (New York: Doubleday, 1984), 177.

100 "I can't wait to see you": Tony Curtis with Peter Golenbock, *American Prince: A Memoir* (New York: Crown, 2008), 167.

"Bob came to the set with a sense": Tommy Rall, interview with the author, April 20, 2011.

"I have always tried to run a dance": Morton Eustis, "Fred Astaire: The Actor-Dancer Attacks His Part," *Theater Arts Monthly,* May 1937.

"How do you know what you're doing?": Blake Edwards, interview with the author, September 10, 2009.

Credited director Richard Quine looked on: Jerome Delamater, *Dance in the Hollywood Musical* (Ann Arbor, MI: UMI Research Press, 1988), 204.

"He was determined to make": Tommy Rall, interview with the author, April 20, 2011.

101 "anything I wanted": Gene Siskel, "Who Killed Dorothy Stratten?," *Chicago Tribune,* November 6, 1983.

On the publicity tour: Delamater, *Dance in the Hollywood Musical,* 204.

complications of diabetes: Sagolla, *The Girl Who Fell Down,* 224.

The problems with Fosse added immeasurably to her distress: Ibid., 226.

tried to make the award show: Arthur Gelb, "Popularizing the 'Tony' Awards," *New York Times,* April 1, 1956.

102 "He was his usual": Rae Allen, e-mail to the author, February 2, 2013.

"Look," he said to Hal Prince: Harold Prince, interview with the author, October 6, 2010.

"I'm very nervous," he said: Interviews with Geraldine Fitzgerald, Gwen Verdon, Marian Seldes, and Elizabeth McCann, *CUNY Spotlight,* CUNY-TV, 1991, New York Public Library for the Performing Arts, Theatre on Film and Tape Archive.

103 "I'm just going to show you": Ibid.

moves she recognized from her early days: Ibid.

104 "It's a vulnerability": "Bob Fosse," *The Dick Cavett Show,* PBS, July 8, 1980.

"Sure, Bob's tough": Robert Alan Aurthur, "Hanging Out," *Esquire,* December 1972.

"The thing that impresses me most": *American Musical Theater with Earl Wrightson.*

"My knees were so badly knocked": Hyman Goldberg, "Little Knock-Knees Knocks 'Em Cold," *Sunday Mirror Magazine,* n.d., ca. 1955.

105 "That child is like wild sunset!": Rex Reed, "'I Never Wanted to Be Special,'" *New York Times,* February 6, 1966.

In the fourth grade, Gwen started signing: "Gwen Verdon and the American Dance Machine," *The Dick Cavett Show,* PBS, December 5 and 6, 1977.

Gwen didn't have technique but: Verdon interview on *CUNY Spotlight.*

"My grandmother was very supportive," Jim Henaghan, interview with the author, January 17, 2013.

"Her dream was to have a home": Ann Reinking, interview with the author, November 15, 2010.

106 Henaghan drank: Verdon interview on *CUNY Spotlight*.

"Jimmy": Jim Henaghan, interview with the author, January 17, 2013.

107 "He would do absolutely true": Ibid.

Cole was mostly silent with Gwen: Ibid.

"Jack was pretty amused": Earl Wilson, "The Girl Who Showed 'Em How," *Silver Screen*, February 1954.

He could see that Gwen had, like him: Tom Prideaux, "A New-Model Verdon," *Life*, February 23, 1959.

"Well, if you say it in English": Robert Rice, "New Star in Town: Gwen Verdon," *New York Post*, June 5, 1957.

"Gwen's answer to Cole": Tommy Tune, interview with the author, January 6, 2011.

"She had an adeptness": Rice, "New Star in Town."

108 "I won't let him beat me": Ibid.

"My mom had to decide": Jim Henaghan, interview with the author, January 17, 2013.

"She understood": Ibid.

"It was quite apparent to everyone": Sagolla, *The Girl Who Fell Down*, 225.

109 "All my women have beauty": Bernard Drew, "Life as a Long Rehearsal," *American Film*, November 1979.

McCracken was the one to urge him: Bob Fosse, interview with Dick Stelzer, *Star Treatment*, LOC, box 47C, folder 1.

Mostly he talked about work: Ibid.

"In my own case these were things like": Ibid.

"I'm a pretty good husband": Chris Chase, "Fosse, from Tony to Oscar to Emmy," *New York Times*, April 29, 1973.

"I think he felt a sense of betrayal": Ann Reinking, interview with the author, November 15, 2010.

110 "I didn't realize until I got into analysis": Jan Hodenfield, "Bob Fosse Feet First," *New York Post*, April 21, 1973.

"If an adult has experienced repetitive trauma": Charles Rousell, interview with the author, July 16, 2011.

111 Beginning March 7, 1955, she zipped: "Making of a Musical," *Life*, May 16, 1955.

Two weeks later, the eighty-three-person company: Ibid.

Prince suggested cutting the big: Harold Prince, interview with the author, October 6, 2010.

113 "Bob and I put the number together": Carol Ilson, *Harold Prince: A Director's Journey* (New York: Limelight, 2000), 22.

"I begged him to see": Harold Prince, interview with the author, October 6, 2010.

"We were tossing out score": Ibid.

"She was very loyal, Gwen": Ibid.

Before the show, McCracken went backstage: Sagolla, *The Girl Who Fell Down*, 226.

"I put it all together later": Ibid.

She had a heart attack, then another: Ibid., 228.

It was in the hospital that he left her: Ibid.

114 Something was wrong with him: Fosse interview with Dick Stelzer.

He saw his psychiatrist as often as: Ibid.

Joan continued to keep her heart attacks: Sagolla, *The Girl Who Fell Down*, 229.

"the most incendiary star on Broadway": Roger S. Hewlett, "The Devil's Disciple," *Time*, June 13, 1955.

A few dancers on their way: Name withheld, interview with the author, September 10, 2010.

115 as she was walking down a busy avenue: Sagolla, *The Girl Who Fell Down*, 244.

At night, he called Joan: Ibid.

THIRTY-TWO YEARS

116 Oakdale Theater: "Irene Manning in 'Pal Joey' at Oakdale Theater," *Hartford Courant*, June 26, 1955.

"In this business": Cynthia Scheider, interview with the author, March 25, 2011.

"Show business is really important": Bob Fosse, *Tomorrow with Tom Snyder*, NBC, January 31, 1980.

117 "I can't do anything but show business": Wayne Warga, "Bob Fosse: Triple Threat Director," *Los Angeles Times*, January 21, 1973.

for ten hours a day, every day for four weeks: Ed Blank, "Why Don't They Dance in Films? Ask Fosse," *Pittsburgh Press*, September 8, 1983.

"At the time the money seemed important": Ibid.

"Bob was always there": Harvey Evans, interview with the author, January 28, 2011.

118 "Robbins would make her nervous": Ronna Elaine Sloan, "Bob Fosse: An Analytic-Critical Study" (University Microfilms International, 1983), 100.

"To Bob, the steps were dialogue": Ann Reinking, interview with the author, November 15, 2010.

"One terrible part of the show": Deborah Jowitt, *Jerome Robbins: His Life, His Theater, His Dance* (New York: Simon and Schuster, 2004), 260.

119 "You develop a certain few tricks": Bob Fosse acceptance speech, *Dance Magazine* awards, New York Athletic Club, April 23, 1963.

the cramped offices they kept: Allene Talmey, "Biography of a Musical: 'Damn Yankees,'" *Vogue*, March 1956.

On Doris Day's recommendation: George Abbott, *Mister Abbott* (New York: Random House, 1963), 253.

"The score": Harold Prince, interview with the author, October 6, 2010.

120 not, he said, to Gwen Verdon: Interviews with Geraldine Fitzgerald, Gwen Verdon, Marian Seldes, and Elizabeth McCann, *CUNY Spotlight*, CUNY-TV, 1991, New York Public Library for the Performing Arts, Theatre on Film and Tape Archive.

"I thought, 'What an extraordinary'": Ibid.

Abbott made Verdon audition: Harvey Evans, interview with the author, January 28, 2011.

Verdon, at Fosse's suggestion: Ibid.

To maximize Verdon's time: Bob Fosse, interview with Stephen Harvey, 1983, LOC, box 60F.

"There's a lot of serious material": Seymour Peck, "'Anna Christie' Sings," *New York Times*, May 12, 1957.

121 "Right away we assumed": Harvey Evans, interview with the author, January 28, 2011.

"They live in their own world": Abbott, *Mister Abbott*, 249.

"Their life": Ibid.

"The school of choreography before": Tony Stevens, interview with the author, February 8, 2011.

"He was so tight with us": Harvey Evans, interview with the author, January 28, 2011.

122 "The Red Light Ballet," the erotic piece: No film of the ballet survives. This re-creation came from interviews with *New Girl in Town* cast members Harvey Evans and Patricia Ferrier Kiley; assorted Gwen Verdon interviews; Harold Prince; Margery Beddow's *Bob Fosse's Broadway* (New York: Heinemann, 1996); and audience members.

"It was the first time that Fosse": Harvey Evans, interview with the author, January 28, 2011.

"And then at the very end of it": Ibid.

123 "Now, I [had] never seen that": Bob Fosse, interview with "Haddad," 1982, LOC, box 49A.

"I think the pornographic ballet": Harold Prince, interview with the author, October 6, 2010.

Abbott argued for narrative consistency: Abbott, *Mister Abbott*, 254.

"They replied that it was high art": Ibid.

Arriving at rehearsal the next morning: Peter Filichia, "Stagestruck," *Theater Week*, May 24, 1992.

Gwen alleged an angry mother had: *Broadway Beat with Richard Ridge*, Manhattan Neighborhood Network, June 22, 1999.

124 demanded Hal Prince deliver George Abbott: Ilson, *Harold Prince*, 30.

To replace her, the production had to: Sidney Fields, "Four Are Needed to Replace Verdon," *New York Mirror,* May 28, 1957.

"Just say the lines!": Harvey Evans, interview with the author, January 28, 2011.

"You cheap son of a bitch!": Ibid.

125 "Gwen and Fosse were now": Harold Prince, interview with the author, October 6, 2010.

"I'd set my hair on fire if he": Robert Wahls, "Gwen Verdon, the Eternal Gypsy," *New York Sunday News,* June 1, 1975.

Gwen's son, Jimmy: Jim Henaghan, interview with the author, January 17, 2013.

"She had had a breakdown": Charles Grass, interview with the author, September 4, 2012.

Fosse wouldn't seek his divorce: Jim Henaghan, interview with the author, January 17, 2013.

126 Fosse got the most appealing offer of his life: Louis Calta, "'Stay Away, Joe' Nearing Stage," *New York Times,* March 14, 1957.

Feuer and Martin, producers of *Can-Can:* E. J. Kahn Jr., "The Hit's the Thing — I," *New Yorker,* January 7, 1956. Also E. J. Kahn Jr., "The Hit's the Thing — II," *New Yorker,* January 15, 1956.

"It's a sounder way of appraising": Ibid.

A month later, MGM called: Sam Zolotow, "'Stay Away, Joe' to Be a Musical," *New York Times,* January 29, 1958.

127 "the reviews it deserved": Harold Prince, interview with the author, October 6, 2010.

"It would be an affecting job": Brooks Atkinson, "The Theater: Singing Anna Christie," *New York Times,* May 15, 1957.

"Little by little": Harvey Evans, interview with the author, January 28, 2011.

Fosse's thirtieth birthday: Margery Beddow, *Bob Fosse's Broadway* (New York: Heinemann, 1996), 12.

"There were long years": George S. Kaufman, "Musical Comedy — or Musical Serious?," *New York Times,* November 3, 1957.

128 "Bob's choreography in the Abbott years": Tony Stevens, interview with the author, February 8, 2011.

"I think of dancing as sheer joy": *American Musical Theater with Earl Wrightson,* CBS, January 1, 1962.

129 Fosse sent those golden cuff links back to Robbins: Ann Reinking, interview with the author, November 15, 2010.

Jerome Robbins talked to God: Barry Rehfeld, "Bob Fosse's Follies," *Rolling Stone,* January 19, 1984.

"Fosse was doing the best he could": Elmarie Wendel, interview with the author, November 2, 2011.

"The dancers started to split": Ibid.

Verdon would join Fosse in Philadelphia: Ibid.

130 "We had never seen that sort of thing": Ibid.

"If something *felt* wrong": Glenn Loney, "The Many Facets of Bob Fosse," *After Dark*, June 1972.

"He would come up with something": Elmarie Wendel, interview with the author, November 2, 2011.

"It was Gwen who kept Bob secure": Fred Mann III, interview with the author, February 22, 2011.

"You could see, from time to time": Linda Posner (Leland Palmer), interview with the author, July 23, 2010.

If the dancers wanted direction: Harvey Evans, interview with the author, January 28, 2011.

131 "Gwen wanted Bobby on the set": Patricia Ferrier Kiley, interview with the author, March 4, 2011.

stationed himself at the camera: Shannon Bolin, interview with the author, February 14, 2011.

"But that's why Bob was there": Ibid.

"At the rushes": Patricia Ferrier Kiley, interview with the author, March 4, 2011.

"It'll look like the black hole": Stephen M. Silverman, *Dancing on the Ceiling: Stanley Donen and His Movies* (New York: Knopf, 1996), 256.

Replacing dancer Eddie Philips: Gwen Verdon interview, *Dance in America*, WNET archives, September 6, 1989.

"The happiest times I ever had with Gwen": Chris Chase, "Fosse, from Tony to Oscar to Emmy," *New York Times*, April 29, 1973.

132 red convertible Fosse called Baby: Patricia Ferrier Kiley, interview with the author, March 4, 2011.

Up late, alone, he'd call Joan: Lisa Jo Sagolla, *The Girl Who Fell Down* (Lebanon, NH: Northeastern University Press, 2003), 244.

At first, she'd hear only silence: Ibid.

"I felt she was almost flattered": Ibid.

"I'm half Irish": Bruce Williamson, "All That Fosse," *Playboy*, March 1980.

he thought of a woman, a sweet: Lionel Chetwynd, "Except for Bob Fosse," *Penthouse*, January 1974.

"I'm fascinated": Chase, "Fosse, from Tony to Oscar to Emmy."

"The problem": Chris Chase, "Fosse's Ego Trip," *Life*, November 1979.

133 "An attraction to death is present": Charles Rousell, interview with the author, July 16, 2011.

In 1937, the American Medical Association: Leslie Iversen, *Speed, Ecstasy, Ritalin: The Science of Amphetamines* (New York: Oxford University Press, 2008), 32–33.

134 Psychiatrists said: Ibid., 79.

by 1959, it was regarded almost as highly: Ibid., 29.

An estimated 3.5 billion doses: Ibid., 39.

And so, neither Fosse nor his psychiatrist: Fosse, interview with Dick Stelzer, *Star Treatment*, LOC, box 47C, folder 1.

135   "Countless nurturing parental acts": Aaron Stern, *Me: The Narcissistic American* (New York: Ballantine Books, 1979), 9.

"It was a constant conflict": Ann Reinking, interview with the author, November 15, 2010.

"[The narcissist's] insatiable hungers are so great": Stern, *Me: The Narcissistic American*, 20.

136   Fosse kept a spiral notebook: "Analyst & Patient Ballet," "Odd Ideas" notebook, LOC, box 53B.

TWENTY-EIGHT YEARS

137   called to tell him about *Redhead:* Details of *Redhead*'s conception from Bill Smith's four-part series "A Show Is Born" for the *Newark Evening News,* June 22–25, 1959.

"Bob," they said: Ibid.

138   Sidney Sheldon, told: Sidney Sheldon, *The Other Side of Me: A Memoir* (New York: Grand Central, 2005), 292–93.

She suggested David Shaw: Gwen Verdon interview, *Dance in America*, WNET archives, September 6, 1989.

Actor Leonard Stone was among the first: Leonard Stone, interview with the author, October 17, 2011.

139   "At the end of every audition": Ibid.

140   "When [Richard Kiley] auditioned": Joyce Haber, "Bob and Emmy and Tony and Oscar," *Los Angeles Times,* February 2, 1975.

"I'd do anything to be up there": Leonard Stone, interview with the author, October 17, 2011.

Variety Arts Studios, 225 West Forty-Sixth Street: Paul Gardner, "Hopeful Actors Blossom in Sun," *New York Times,* May 14, 1962.

"Edith knew absolutely everything": Dan Siretta, interview with the author, February 22, 2012.

Fosse brought on Donald McKayle: Facts of the McKayle/Fosse ordeal obtained via interview notes with Roger Adams (May 25, 1960), Dorothy Fields (June 1, 1960), Albert Hague (June 1, 1960), Kazimir Kokich (June 6, 1960), Robert Linden (May 24, 1960), and David Shaw (May 25, 1960); notes can be found in LOC, box 46B.

141   "He had changed": Harvey Evans, interview with the author, January 28, 2011.

Fosse replaced his boyish sweater vests: Ibid.

"a slick dandy": Leonard Stone, interview with the author, October 17, 2011.

142   "He was getting scary": Margery Beddow, *In the Company of Friends: Dancers*

Talking to Dancers II, the Women of Fosse, videotaped at the New Dance Group, New York, on October 7, 2007.

"He was a slave driver": Leonard Stone, interview with the author, October 17, 2011.

Fosse made them rehearse on Sunday: Ibid.

Scared and angry, one of the dancers: Harvey Evans, interview with the author, January 28, 2011.

"You've got to give the dancers": Ibid.

"He would spend three hours on": James Horvath, interview with the author, January 14, 2011.

Fosse had two cigarettes going: Leonard Stone, interview with the author, October 17, 2011.

"He was so influenced by": Harvey Evans, interview with the author, January 28, 2011.

143 "I saw Bob get really mean": Linda Posner (Leland Palmer), interview with the author, July 23, 2010.

"Yes, he could be cruel": Donna McKechnie, interview with the author, October 14, 2010.

scapegoats were often women and often beautiful: Leonard Stone, interview with the author, October 17, 2011.

"There were rumors he had": Harvey Evans, interview with the author, January 28, 2011.

During these crazy nights: Bill Smith, "Fingers Were Crossed for 'Redhead,'" *Newark Evening News,* June 25, 1959.

upwards of $2,500 a number: Ibid.

144 "She had an entrance in that": Beddow, *In the Company of Friends.*

One night, in the middle of: Harvey Evans, interview with the author, January 28, 2011.

"We don't know how Gwen did it": Ibid.

To keep her weight up, she guzzled: *Broadway Beat with Richard Ridge,* Manhattan Neighborhood Network, June 22, 1999.

"This is the first time in my life": Gilbert Millstein, "New Girl in Town — and How," *New York Times,* February 15, 1959.

One night in Philadelphia, during: Beddow, *In the Company of Friends.*

145 "The amount of physical activity": Kenneth Tynan, "Matters of Fact," *New Yorker,* February 21, 1959.

146 "Perhaps in the future": Brooks Atkinson, "The Theater: 'Redhead,'" *New York Times,* February 6, 1959.

"By the time I got to New York": Carolyn Kirsch, interview with the author, February 11, 2011.

Fosse and Verdon spent weekend time: Jim Henaghan, interview with the author, January 17, 2013.

147 Fosse shied away from large gatherings: Ibid.

He loved the Mets, the losers: Pete Hamill, "Fosse," *Piecework* (Boston: Little, Brown, 1996), 345.

"He admired the difficulty of being": Ann Reinking, interview with the author, November 15, 2010.

Going back and forth from the kitchen: Jim Henaghan, interview with the author, January 17, 2013.

148 "made Bob such a nervous wreck": Cyma Rubin, interview with the author, March 8, 2012.

"You could see they really cared": Leonard Stone, interview with the author, October 17, 2011.

He went for drinks with the cast: Ibid.

"How d'you do it?": Vidal Sassoon, interview with the author, November 22, 2010.

he'd take a room at the Edison Hotel: Kevin Boyd Grubb, *Razzle Dazzle: The Life and Work of Bob Fosse* (New York: St. Martin's Press, 1989), 86.

"All I need": Barbara Rowes, "After Three Coronaries and Critical Surgery Bob Fosse Puts His Heart and Soul into 'All That Jazz,'" *People*, March 3, 1980.

At David Shaw's house in Amagansett: Shaun Considine, *Mad as Hell: The Life and Work of Paddy Chayefsky* (New York: Random House, 1995), 245.

149 He began talks to oversee *Viva!*: Sam Zolotow, "Evans May Star in Play by Shaw," *New York Times*, April 21, 1959.

"Bobby wanted to both direct": Stephen Sondheim, interview with the author, February 15, 2012.

150 Fosse and Browning split: Tommy Rall, interview with the author, April 20, 2011.

"A TV show is put together": John P. Shanley, "Big Stars and One of the Chorus," *New York Times*, October 4, 1959.

151 "He was intrigued by the surrealist painters": Gwen Verdon interview, *Dance in America*, WNET archives, September 6, 1989.

"people all joined together and freaks": Ibid.

Unlike his *Copper and Brass* agreement: Bob Fosse contract, LOC, box 51A.

"Fosse told us he was going to be": Buzz Halliday, interview with the author, November 3, 2011.

Fosse devised a series of fourth-wall-breaking: Ibid.

152 "What a rush!": Ibid.

"Part of the work ethic": Leslie Bennetts, "Bob Fosse — Dancing with Danger," *New York Times*, April 6, 1986.

"I told him, 'I care as much'": Harold Prince, interview with the author, October 6, 2010.

One night in April 1960, Fosse called: Lisa Jo Sagolla, *The Girl Who Fell Down* (Lebanon, NH: Northeastern University Press, 2003), 244.

"We married because we were going to": Robert Wahls, "Gwen Verdon, the Eternal Gypsy," *New York Sunday News,* June 1, 1975.

"I finally decided that I was": Jan Hodenfield, "Bob Fosse Feet First," *New York Post,* April 21, 1973.

153 he had begun psychotherapy: Bob Fosse, interview with Dick Stelzer, *Star Treatment,* LOC, box 47C, folder 1.

"He knew that in order to be": Ann Reinking, interview with the author, November 15, 2010.

154 Whitehead liked the idea of musicalizing: Sam Zolotow, "Lunts May Star in First Musical," *New York Times,* March 4, 1960.

Lunt and Fontanne didn't, though, and: Martin Gottfried, *All His Jazz* (Cambridge, MA: Da Capo, 1998; first published by Bantam in 1990), 120. Citations refer to the Da Capo edition.

155 he had been acting strangely: *All That Jazz,* Gwen Verdon interview transcripts, LOC, box 1A.

Larry Gelbart arrived halfway: Gottfried, *All His Jazz,* 124.

asked about the new lines: Ibid.

Slowly, Fosse turned away from the table: Ibid.

156 "She saw it coming": John McMartin, interview with the author, November 8, 2010.

horseback-riding accident: Trudy Ship, interview with the author, January 21, 2011.

Dilantin, an anticonvulsant: Gottfried, *All His Jazz,* 125.

"It was always controlled by something": Gwen Verdon interview, *Dance in America,* WNET archives, September 6, 1989.

"I got hooked on Seconal and he": Fosse interview with Dick Stelzer.

epilepsy and drug addiction: Gwen Verdon interview, *Dance in America,* WNET archives, September 6, 1989.

disgusted Whitehead: Gottfried, *All His Jazz,* 127.

"That ballet frightened the management": Richard Korthaze, interview with the author, March 24, 2011.

"some of the most innovative work": Beddow, *In the Company of Friends.*

157 "Every time a word [of Truesmith's]": Margery Beddow, *Bob Fosse's Broadway* (New York: Heinemann, 1996), 24.

"the thicket of unreality which stands": Daniel J. Boorstin, *The Image or What Happened to the American Dream?* (New York: Atheneum, 1962), 3.

"I'm not bothered when people refer": Bruce Williamson, "All That Fosse," *Playboy,* March 1980.

158 "Bobby was getting ideas": Gottfried, *All His Jazz,* 126.

"Tom wasn't right for the part": Patricia Ferrier Kiley, interview with the author, March 4, 2011.

"I thought, watching him": John McMartin, interview with the author, November 8, 2010.

"His behavior became so erratic": Beddow, *Bob Fosse's Broadway,* 22.

"If you watch what happens to rats": Robert Bilder, interview with the author, March 27, 2011.

159 "This is a busy bee among musicals": "Musical Opens at Shubert," *Hartford Courant,* November 23, 1960.

Gelbart considered himself available: Larry Gelbart, *Laughing Matters* (New York: Random House, 1998), 204–5.

didn't come for Whitehead either: Gottfried, *All His Jazz,* 128.

Or Poston: Ibid.

"I wonder what the Israelis are": Ibid.

"That's when people started to": John McMartin, interview with the author, November 8, 2010.

I want to do it, Fosse told: Gottfried, *All His Jazz,* 129.

160 "He's doing *Pal Joey*": Ibid.

She laughed through it all: Ibid.

"It was a folie à deux": Ibid.

"I've been fired": Bill Guske, *In the Company of Friends: Dancers Talking to Dancers III, the Men of Fosse,* videotaped at the New Dance Group, New York, December 9, 2007.

TWENTY-SEVEN YEARS

162 Fosse called Jack Perlman: *R. Fosse v. Producers Theatre, Inc.,* legal papers, LOC, box 43B.

163 "I am hopeful": Louis Calta, "Fosse in Dispute over Two Dances," *New York Times,* December 16, 1960.

"unreasonably withheld": *R. Fosse v. Producers Theatre, Inc.*

"An indication of the troubles": Howard Taubman, "The Theatre: 'The Conquering Hero,'" *New York Times,* January 17, 1961.

Standing there, he later said: Bob Fosse, letter to Judy Grossman and Diane Rubin, LOC, box 47C.

"How the fuck can you have": Harold Prince, interview with the author, October 6, 2010.

164 "It made him look like he couldn't choreograph": Ann Reinking, interview with the author, November 15, 2010.

"He sat by her bed a long, long, long time": Ibid.

"After my mother died": Chris Chase, "Fosse, from Tony to Oscar to Emmy," *New York Times,* April 29, 1973.

"Most of what I know about Bob": Charles Grass, interview with the author, September 4, 2012.

seeing another woman: Barry Rehfeld, "Bob Fosse's Follies," *Rolling Stone,* January 19, 1984.

his dad in lipstick: Martin Gottfried, *All His Jazz* (Cambridge, MA: Da Capo, 1998; first published by Bantam in 1990), 158. Citations refer to the Da Capo edition.

165 correspondence with his siblings: Miscellaneous correspondence, LOC, box 47A, folders 7 and 8.

The first time she performed her big: Luke Yankee, *Just Outside the Spotlight* (New York: Back Stage Books, 2006), 101.

"Well," he said: Eileen Heckart interview in Jackson R. Bryer and Richard A. Davison, eds., *The Actor's Art: Conversations with Contemporary American Stage Performers* (Piscataway, NJ: Rutgers, 2001), 116.

"We are going to restage your number": Yankee, *Just Outside the Spotlight,* 101.

"break [the choreographer's] heart if I did that to him": Ibid.

"You know, Heckart": Ibid.

"Yes, it was quite magnificent": Bryer and Davison, *The Actor's Art,* 116.

166 "when we wore the little white gloves": "Dance On: Ann Reinking," *Dance On with Billie Mahoney,* video workshop for Dance and Theater, August 31, 1983.

"Every night": Ibid.

"The high spot": Richard P. Cooke, "The Theater," *Wall Street Journal,* June 2, 1961.

"I saw Bob in *Pal Joey*": Tommy Tune, interview with the author, January 6, 2011.

167 "I remember there was an interview": Stephen Sondheim, interview with the author, February 15, 2012.

she found him ambling around: Buzz Halliday, interview with the author, November 3, 2011.

Getting away from show business: Ann Reinking, interview with the author, November 15, 2010.

Present that season, along with: Arthur Gelb, "Rialto by the Sea," *New York Times,* August 13, 1961.

"This year [East Hampton] seems to": Ibid.

168 "At the first reading": Robert Morse, interview with the author, November 16, 2010.

"He got us into one big clump": Donna McKechnie, interview with the author, October 14, 2010.

held in rooms without air-conditioning: Ibid.

"I'd watch them from the stage": Ibid.

169 "Because Bob had been fired": Gwen Verdon interview, *Dance in America,* WNET archives, September 6, 1989.

"The main problem": Glenn Loney, "The Many Facets of Bob Fosse," *After Dark,* June 1972.

"I took it to its extreme": Ibid.

"On 'Coffee Break,' they": Donna McKechnie, interview with the author, October 14, 2010.

170   all the chorus members: Ibid.

which had been passed around: Susan Loesser, *A Most Remarkable Fella: Frank Loesser and the Guys and Dolls in His Life* (New York: Donald I. Fine, 1993), 203–5.

Unwilling to part with the number, the team met: Cy Feuer and Ken Gross, *I Got the Show Right Here* (New York: Simon and Schuster, 2003), 228–29.

"What did you mean by that?": Gottfried, *All His Jazz*, 141.

"I've got an idea": Feuer and Gross, *I Got the Show Right Here*, 229.

171   "The creative person is an absolute": Moira Hodgson, "When Bob Fosse's Art Imitates Life, It's Just 'All That Jazz,'" *New York Times*, December 30, 1979.

"When you stage a dance": Paul Rosenfield, "Fosse, Verdon and 'Charity': Together Again," *Los Angeles Times*, July 21, 1986.

Fosse called them his care pills: Jennifer Nairn-Smith, interview with the author, January 7, 2011.

"I want to see it full out": Donna McKechnie, interview with the author, October 14, 2010.

"The word *tired* does not exist": James Horvath, interview with the author, January 14, 2011.

"It was his belief in you": Donna McKechnie, interview with the author, October 14, 2010.

"We see the perfection": Ben Vereen, interview with the author, January 11, 2011.

172   Fosse and Verdon, alone except: Feuer and Gross, *I Got the Show Right Here*, 229.

173   "The results were exactly what": Sam Zolotow, "Novel by Sneider Will Be Musical," *New York Times*, September 22, 1961.

There had been a few attempts: "Theatre League Votes Refusal to Recognize Directors' Union," *New York Times*, April 3, 1962.

Fosse bounded into Variety Arts: Barrie Chase, interview with the author, April 21, 2011.

"Crafty, conniving, sneaky": Walter Kerr, review of *How to Succeed in Business Without Really Trying*, *New York Herald Tribune*, October 14, 1961.

"The most inventive and stylized": John McClain, review of *How to Succeed in Business Without Really Trying*, *New York Journal-American*, October 14, 1961.

"It belongs to the blue chips": Howard Taubman, "Musical Comedy Seen at 46th St. Theatre," *New York Times*, October 16, 1961.

"Nobody just walked across": Tommy Tune, interview with the author, January 6, 2011.

174   dancer Barrie Chase: Barrie Chase, interview with the author, April 21, 2011.

175   "Shaking hands with Bob was like": Ervin Drake, interview with the author,
      April 25, 2011.
      "I went along with everything Fosse suggested": Ibid.
      "stayed away": Ibid.
      the production absorbed Fosse completely: Barrie Chase, interview with the
      author, April 21, 2011.
      "He was very involved": Ibid.
      Variety suggested Fosse's audition sequence: "Seasons of Youth" Review, *Variety*,
      November 1, 1961.
      "a total cliché": Barrie Chase, interview with the author, April 21, 2011.
176   "Hiya, Barrie": Ibid.
      Gwen got a call: Lisa Jo Sagolla, *The Girl Who Fell Down* (Lebanon, NH:
      Northeastern University Press, 2003), 257.
      "Gwen," Campbell began: Ibid.
177   "Years from now": Bernard Drew, "Life as a Long Rehearsal," *American Film*,
      November 1979.
      Soon after he got the news, Fosse sat down: "Cleveland, U.S.A.," short story,
      LOC, box 53B.
      De Mille, Robbins, and Richard Rodgers were among: Leo Lerman, *The Grand
      Surprise: The Journals of Leo Lerman,* ed. Stephen Pascal (New York: Knopf,
      2007), 246.
178   Joan's "funeral was dreadful": Ibid.
      Fosse watched from the other side: Sagolla, *The Girl Who Fell Down*, 258.
      got a call from Cy Feuer: Bob Fosse, interview with "Haddad," 1982, LOC, box
      49A.
      "Co-?" Bob asked: Ibid.
179   It was book writer Neil Simon's idea: Feuer and Gross, *I Got the Show Right
      Here*, 234.
      Once, after a performance: Paul Turgeon, interview with the author, March 29,
      2011.
      But only if Feuer and Martin: Sam Zolotow, "Directors' Union Enters
      Broadway," *New York Times*, February 21, 1962.
      now backed by Harold Clurman: "Directors Society Seeks Recognition," *New
      York Times*, December 8, 1961.
      "You know, I never can find": Leo Lerman, "At the Theater," *Dance Magazine*,
      January 1963.
180   every night, Edith: Warren Allen Smith, interview with the author, August 19,
      2012.
      Fernando Vargas, the studio's co-owner, heard: Ibid.
      "Fosse loved the front room": Dan Siretta, interview with the author, February
      22, 2012.

He and Gwen worked: Sally Hammon, "Scene at a 1st Rehearsal: The 'Little Me' Cast Meets," *New York Post,* September 6, 1962.

He had one composition book: Fosse's *Little Me* composition notebook, LOC, box 44C.

181   "I would pass Variety Arts every night": Dan Siretta, interview with the author, February 22, 2012.

Barrie Chase returned to New York: Barrie Chase, interview with the author, April 21, 2011.

"We'd talk for maybe an hour": Ibid.

182   "It looked like we couldn't have one": Jan Hodenfield, "Bob Fosse Feet First," *New York Post,* April 21, 1973.

Neil Simon was rewriting constantly: Neil Simon, *Rewrites: A Memoir* (New York: Simon and Schuster, 1996), 110–12.

"You know at this point": Richard and Betsy Gehman, "The Seven Caesars," *Theater Arts,* November 1962.

"You mean I got to say it exactly this way?": Gilbert Millstein, "This Caesar Has to Take Orders," *New York Times,* November 11, 1962.

"He always seemed like he wanted": Feuer and Gross, *I Got the Show Right Here,* 235.

"Basically, Sid was a brilliant": Linda Posner (Leland Palmer), interview with the author, July 23, 2010.

183   "There was a joke": Richard Lenon, "The Conquest of the Seven Caesars," *Newsweek,* November 26, 1962.

"It was during the Cuban Missile Crisis": Mervyn Rothstein, "The Seven Lives (and 36 Costumes) of Sid Caesar," *New York Times,* November 1, 1998.

Simon took calls: Ibid.

"I don't think there is any": Loney, "The Many Facets of Bob Fosse."

184   "I've never been in this position": Simon, *Rewrites,* 113.

standing in tuxedos at the back: Neil Simon, Bob Fosse Memorial, Palace Theater, October 30, 1987, New York Public Library for the Performing Arts, Theatre on Film and Tape Archive.

"Bob very simply put his arms down": Ibid.

Fifteen minutes later, when Fosse was: Ibid.

"If all the theatrical platitudes of": Walter Kerr, " 'Little Me' — Tour de Farce for Sid Caesar," *Los Angeles Times,* December 2, 1962.

"I have the feeling": Whitney Bolton, "Theater," *New York Morning Telegraph,* November 26, 1962.

185   "If it's a boy, Nicholas": Gottfried, *All His Jazz,* 156.

"I can't explain it": Robert Wahls, "Bob Who? Bob Fosse!," *New York Sunday News,* November 26, 1972.

"I've been dancing since": Bob Fosse acceptance speech, *Dance Magazine* awards, New York Athletic Club, April 23, 1963.

187 "He was so charming and sweet": Kristoffer Tabori, interview with the author, February 23, 2011.

"After his number, he came over": Ibid.

"I adored him": Rita Gardner, interview with the author, February 14, 2011.

"I could see him really helping her": Kristoffer Tabori, interview with the author, February 23, 2011.

Joey seemed softer, with a natural confidence: Ibid.

188 "Fosse had an incredible sense": Ibid.

She could remember flipping between: Robert Wahls, "Gwen Verdon, the Eternal Gypsy," *New York Sunday News*, June 1, 1975.

having lost Jerome Robbins to script: Deborah Jowitt, *Jerome Robbins: His Life, His Theater, His Dance* (New York: Simon and Schuster, 2004), 346.

and, he thought, for Gwen: LOC, box 44A, note to Perlman.

approached Stark and Merrick with the idea: Bob Fosse/Jack Perlman correspondence, LOC, box 44A.

189 the rider stated: Rider to Fosse's *Funny Girl* contract, June 28, 1963, LOC, box 44A.

tabled the rights discussion in good faith: Fosse's handwritten farewell letter to *Funny Girl* company (September 1963), LOC, box 44A.

The lyrics, he said, made no sense: Gottfried, *All His Jazz*, 162.

Fosse heard Stark had placed: Fosse's farewell letter to *Funny Girl* company.

he wrote a six-page letter explaining: Ibid.

fired off a telegram threatening: Ray Stark telegram to Bob Fosse, September 17, 1963, LOC, box 44A.

190 pulled her aside: Linda Posner (Leland Palmer), interview with the author, July 23, 2010.

Palmer's hotel-room phone rang: Ibid.

TWENTY-FOUR YEARS

193 "Nicole kept Bob in life": Ann Reinking, interview with the author, November 15, 2010.

he vowed to put aside, for her: Tony Stevens, interview with the author, February 8, 2011.

"When Nicole came along": Fred Mann III, interview with the author, February 22, 2011.

"He's a fabulous father to Nicole": Suzanne Daley, "Stepping into Her New Shoes," *New York Times*, June 21, 1981.

"There was this point of great happiness": Paul Rosenfield, "Fosse, Verdon and 'Charity': Together Again," *Los Angeles Times*, July 21, 1986.

decided Verdon, at thirty-eight, was too old: Martin Gottfried, *All His Jazz* (Cambridge, MA: Da Capo, 1998; first published by Bantam in 1990), 161. Citations refer to the Da Capo edition.

194 Fosse and Verdon didn't see Nazi Germany: Ibid.
heard at Gus Schirmer's apartment: "Fosse Account of Events" (Jack Perlman's notes on Charnin suit), LOC, box 26C.
told him to see Fellini's film: Ibid.
"Harlequin is a well rounded": "Gwen Verdon as Brokenhearted Harlequin," *Life*, April 14, 1958.
195 midway through, Fosse knew: "Fosse Account of Events" (Jack Perlman's notes on Charnin suit), LOC, box 26C.
Fryer admitted he felt only so-so: Ibid.
privately encouraged Fosse to stay: Ibid.
That night Fosse could not sleep: Ibid.
"Bob would be furious if": Laurent Giroux, interview with the author, December 13, 2010.
In nine pages: Interviews with Geraldine Fitzgerald, Gwen Verdon, Marian Seldes, and Elizabeth McCann, *CUNY Spotlight*, CUNY-TV, 1991, New York Public Library for the Performing Arts, Theatre on Film and Tape Archive.
196 Fosse got a similar response from: Jack Perlman's notes on Charnin suit, LOC, box 26C.
197 the Tango Palace: Bob Fosse's notes for "Dance Hall," LOC, box 26D.
198 This time Fryer, Carr, and Verdon: Jack Perlman's notes on Charnin suit, LOC, box 26C.
Fryer and Carr suggested Martin Charnin: Ibid.
"The first day I met Fosse": Martin Charnin, interview with the author, December 3, 2011.
199 Shopping for a composer, Fosse reached out: Jack Perlman's notes on Charnin suit, LOC, box 26C.
200 "One man did a great big": Susan Loesser, *A Most Remarkable Fella: Frank Loesser and the Guys and Dolls in His Life* (New York: Donald I. Fine, 1993), 242.
"I knew we had trouble": Lionel Chetwynd, "Except for Bob Fosse," *Penthouse*, January 1974.
"Bobby worked morning, noon, and night": Phyllis Newman, interview with the author, February 9, 2011.
"He would always be checking with her": Don Emmons, interview with the author, April 18, 2011.
"In rehearsal, Loesser told me to": Stan Page, interview with the author, July 15, 2011.
suggested they cut their losses: Jo Loesser, interview with the author, May 9, 2011.
201 "Well, so the kid doesn't go": Margery Beddow, *Bob Fosse's Broadway* (New York: Heinemann, 1996), 36.

"The cast was so distraught": Kathryn Doby, interview with the author, November 27, 2010.

202 "Women are very attracted to power": Jan Hodenfield, "Bob Fosse Feet First," *New York Post,* April 21, 1973.

"It takes two to play that game": Christine Colby, interview with the author, March 20, 2011.

"We were almost done with Bob's new": Kathryn Doby, interview with the author, November 27, 2010.

Fosse watched as "Tears of Joy" evolved: Ibid.

"That's how far the cast would go": Ibid.

Fosse took actor John McMartin for a drink: John McMartin, interview with the author, November 8, 2010.

203 Fosse held a backers' audition: Jack Perlman's notes on Charnin suit, LOC, box 26C.

204 "I tried in *Middle of the Night*": Paddy Chayefsky, "Not So Little," *New York Times,* July 15, 1956.

"grasping, vicious, and pandering": Paddy Chayefsky, "In Praise of Reappraised Picture-Makers," *New York Times,* January 8, 1956.

"I swore I'd never again let": Cecil Smith, "Chayefsky: Disciple of Making It Right," *Los Angeles Times,* November 7, 1954.

"I decided to form my own company": Richard W. Nason, "Glimpse of a 'Goddess,'" *New York Times,* August 18, 1957.

"I thought he was a funny fellow": Seymour Peck, "Exit from Realism," *New York Times,* November 5, 1961.

205 "I meant the play to be": "Chayefsky Talks about 'Josef D.,'" *New York Times,* February 15, 1964.

He had taken a part-time teaching position: Clyde Haberman, interview with the author, April 13, 2011.

"From that time on": Shaun Considine, *Mad as Hell: The Life and Work of Paddy Chayefsky* (New York: Random House, 1995), 245.

They got to work in Paddy's office: Jack Perlman's notes on Charnin suit, LOC, box 26C.

"It was like a cave": Karen Hassett, interview with the author, September 5, 2010.

At their second meeting: Jack Perlman's notes on Charnin suit, LOC, box 26C.

206 he called Neil Simon in Rome: Neil Simon, *Rewrites: A Memoir* (New York: Simon and Schuster, 1996), 214–15.

"I love the new lines": Ibid., 217.

"This number," he said through: Ibid., 216.

207 "When you're dancing in one of Bob's": Ann Reinking, interview with the author, November 15, 2010.

"Bob would say that he didn't": Kathy Witt, interview with the author, May 20, 2011.

208 "People have been toying with this": "Is the Director-Choreographer Taking Over?" Roundtable discussion broadcast by radio station WEVD, New York, March 30, 1966.

"We went to a dance hall to observe": Rex Reed, "'I Never Wanted to Be Special,'" *New York Times*, February 6, 1966.

209 "They saw kids doing the Jerk": Diana Laurenson, interview with the author, January 17, 2011.

Arthur, the most exciting new club: Sybil Christopher, interview with the author, January 23, 2012.

"[Arthur] was supposed to be": *Broadway Beat with Richard Ridge*, Manhattan Neighborhood Network, June 22, 1999.

"That's how Bob really developed": Tony Stevens, interview with the author, February 8, 2011.

210 "When he and Gwen were working": Ann Reinking, interview with the author, November 15, 2010.

She saw he was proud of her: Robert Alan Aurthur, "Hanging Out," *Esquire*, December 1972.

They worked after work: Donna McKechnie, interview with the author, October 14, 2010.

"I don't know if this is": Ibid.

211 "It can be as pedestrian as": Betty Spence, "Bob Fosse — He'll Take the Risks," *Los Angeles Times*, May 17, 1981.

"Bob never treated us like a chorus": Kathryn Doby, interview with the author, November 27, 2010.

"He didn't just want to put something": Linda Posner (Leland Palmer), interview with the author, July 23, 2010.

"Ladies," he said: Christine Colby, interview with the author, March 20, 2011.

"She wasn't *the star*": Lee Roy Reams, Theater Production Workshop Dialogue Series Features *Sweet Charity*, Marymount Manhattan College, March 15, 2011.

"Gwen would break the steps": Christine Colby, interview with the author, March 20, 2011

He wanted to direct movies: Margaret Herrick Library, George Cukor Papers, Production files — unproduced, *Bloomer Girl* (20th Century Fox and G-D-C Enterprises); choreography 1965–66.

212 a good hook for Fosse: Ibid.

worried about the offer: Ibid.

Fosse confessed to Fox executive: Ibid.

213 "It was one of the hardest shows": *Broadway Beat with Richard Ridge*.

"Gwen hated singing 'Where Am I Going?'": Reams, Marymount Manhattan College.

"I think the true reason was": Robert Viagas, ed., *The Alchemy of Theatre: The Divine Science* (New York: Playbill Books, 2006), 32.

Privately, Fosse knew his show was hers: Reams, Marymount Manhattan College.

"Gwen was out from time to time": Ruth Buzzi, interview with the author, January 3, 2011.

"I went on a hundred times for her": Helen Gallagher, interviewed by Liza Gennaro, March 22, 2006, New York Public Library for the Performing Arts, Jerome Robbins Dance Division.

214 an ebullient Neil Simon set out: Simon, *Rewrites*, 228.

was a preemptive move, Fosse said: Ibid.

When he awoke Sunday morning: Martin Charnin, interview with the author, December 3, 2011.

"He told me I had to wait and see": Ibid.

215 Fosse asked Stanley Donen to come up: Simon, *Rewrites*, 230.

"The ending," Fosse said: Ibid.

Fosse had decided Irene Sharaff's: Gottfried, *All His Jazz*, 182.

"They fought": Reams, Marymount Manhattan College.

"It should be grittier, darker": Simon, *Rewrites*, 230.

"People in the audience would": John McMartin, interview with the author, November 8, 2010.

Look, Neil Simon said to Fosse: Simon, *Rewrites*, 231.

216 "I still think I'm right," he said: Ibid.

the Palace Theater: Milton Esterow, "Old Palace Theater Prepares for a Musical: Interior Refurbished for 'Sweet Charity' by New Owners," *New York Times*, January 14, 1966.

217 dressing room: Reed, "'I Never Wanted to Be Special.'"

"It opens up the eye": Suzanne Charney, interview with the author, February 20, 2011.

In the first-row balcony, Martin Charnin: Martin Charnin, interview with the author, December 3, 2011.

"There was material on that stage": Ibid.

"The last thing I wanted to do": Ibid.

218 "Talented Bob Fosse": Harold Clurman, "Theater," *Nation*, February 28, 1966.

"The proscenium is all broken up": Ann Reinking, interview with the author, November 15, 2010.

219 "Bob was there from the first day": Dan Siretta, interview with the author, February 22, 2012.

"The only time he spoke directly": Ibid.

"He did come up with the one idea": Gwen Verdon interview, *Dance in America*, WNET archives, September 6, 1989.

"Bob would get so lonely": Dan Siretta, interview with the author, February 22, 2012.

"Fosse would call me at night": Ellen Graff, interview with the author, February 3, 2012.

220 "Bobby was so much a little boy": Dan Siretta, interview with the author, February 22, 2012.

"You are the strangest actor": *Broadway Beat with Richard Ridge.*

"Whose performance do you think": Gottfried, *All His Jazz,* 186.

sense of injustice increased: Ibid.

"During much of their joint professional": Gottfried, *All His Jazz,* 284.

"If Fosse did anything generous": Marie Wallace, interview with the author, February 16, 2012.

221 "She loved being with us": Ibid.

"Those were fabulous parties": Laurent Giroux, interview with the author, December 13, 2010.

"I felt sorry for Gwen": Ruth Buzzi, interview with the author, January 3, 2011.

would visit Gwen in her dressing room whenever they could: Ibid.

"We were in there most nights": Ibid.

Gwen placed a frightened call to Robert Alan Aurthur: Gottfried, *All His Jazz,* 186.

222 Aurthur finally reached Fosse: Ibid.

TWENTY YEARS

223 "Have you finished work yet, Daddy?": Robert Wahls, "Bob Who? Bob Fosse!," *New York Sunday News,* November 26, 1972.

personal resonance: Leslie Bennetts, "Bob Fosse — Dancing with Danger," *New York Times,* April 6, 1986.

224 "This is the manic-depressive floor": Wahls, "Bob Who?"

Fosse's suite was nicely disheveled: Ibid.

850 Seventh was a magical place: Lionel Larner, interview with the author, January 25, 2012.

225 "A man who is not touched by": Herb Gardner, *The Collected Plays* (New York: Applause, 2001), 43.

226 "That was a marriage between": David Picker, interview with the author, October 7, 2010.

he was called the "Corned Beef Confucius": "Max Asnas, Long-Time Owner of the Stage Delicatessen, Dies," *New York Times,* December 12, 1968.

227 "Paddy could tell Bob everything": Ann Reinking, interview with the author, November 15, 2010.

"You'd see them at their table": Karen Hassett, interview with the author, September 5, 2010.

It was just Fosse's *goyishe* sandwich: Alan Heim, interview with the author, July 22, 2010.

228 had his sights set on *Sweet Charity* next: For more on the Hollywood musical

in the late 1960s, see Paul Monaco, *History of the American Cinema, Vol. 8: The Sixties* (Berkeley: University of California Press, 2001); Ethan Mordden, *Medium Cool* (New York: Knopf, 1990); and "*Darling Lili* (1970)" in Sam Wasson, *A Splurch in the Kisser: The Movies of Blake Edwards* (Middletown, CT: Wesleyan University Press, 2009).

Charnin's arbitration: Martin Charnin, interview with the author, December 3, 2011.

"Fryer and Carr had to admit to it": Ibid.

"Okay, kid": Shirley MacLaine, *My Lucky Stars: A Hollywood Memoir* (New York: Bantam, 1995), 175.

"I remember feeling tentative": Charles Champlin, "Finest Hour for Bob Fosse and Feet in General," *Los Angeles Times,* May 11, 1969.

229   "I hate show business and I love it": Bernard Drew, "Life as a Long Rehearsal," *American Film,* November 1979.

Surtees liked to joke that one day: Bob Fosse correspondence with Robert Surtees, LOC, box 47A.

"Bobby was fascinated with": Sonja Haney, interview with the author, February 27, 2011.

"Anyone less charming than Bob": Bruce Surtees, interview with the author, March 28, 2011.

Ross Hunter had soft-focus ideas in store: "Ross Hunter Withdraws from U's 'Charity' after 'Difference' with Fosse," *Daily Variety,* November 6, 1967.

"There was quite a fight": Champlin, "Finest Hour for Bob Fosse."

230   "He wanted to be an artist": Bruce Surtees, interview with the author, March 28, 2011.

Fosse talked to Surtees about McCracken, about ideas she had: Ibid.

"If there were people," McCracken had written: Joan McCracken, "Thoughts While Dancing," *Dance Magazine,* April 1946.

They discussed John Huston's: Bruce Surtees, interview with the author, March 28, 2011.

"*Moulin Rouge* was the first time": Moira Hodgson, "When Bob Fosse's Art Imitates Life, It's Just 'All That Jazz,'" *New York Times,* December 30, 1979.

Fosse began wearing a viewfinder: Bruce Surtees, interview with the author, March 28, 2011.

231   "How do you feel about it?": Chris Chase, "Fosse, from Tony to Oscar to Emmy," *New York Times,* April 29, 1973.

232   "I loved rehearsing with Shirley": Sonja Haney, interview with the author, February 27, 2011.

233   "It had to be one of the worst things": John McMartin, interview with the author, November 8, 2010.

"The fact that she was there at all": Chita Rivera, interview with the author, February 3, 2011.

One would glimpse her whispering: Ibid.

"They literally finished each other's": Suzanne Charney, interview with the author, February 20, 2011.

Gwen turned down the title role in: Lewis Funke, "Will Rogers Recalled," *New York Times*, October 13, 1968.

"If I'd known how he worked": "Won't Sit Down on the Job," *Chicago Daily Defender*, April 4, 1968.

"One of the reasons you wanted to work": Lee Roy Reams, Theater Production Workshop Dialogue Series Features *Sweet Charity*, Marymount Manhattan College, March 15, 2011.

"His anxieties and indecisions": Marilyn Beck, "There's Been Trouble on 'Sweet Charity' Set," *Hartford Courant*, February 27, 1968.

234 "I knew that he felt he was under": Sonja Haney, interview with the author, February 27, 2011.

"He missed nothing": MacLaine, *My Lucky Stars*, 179.

"Everything about films": Bob Boyle, "Bob Fosse Began Early on Successful Career," *Nevada Daily Mail*, February 4, 1969.

sent out for Preparation H: Sonja Haney, interview with the author, February 27, 2011.

"If only all the fuses would blow": John Hallowell, "Rebellion on Broadway as Stars Balk at Lengthy Runs," *Life*, July 21, 1967.

235 "Both Gwen and I were watching": Sonja Haney, interview with the author, February 27, 2011.

"Bob wasn't really into the dancing": Larry Billman, interview with the author, February 21, 2011.

"He was so involved": Sonja Haney, interview with the author, February 27, 2011.

Fosse sat down at the lighting console: Ibid.

"Bob was so focused on technique": Lonnie Burr, interview with the author, February 21, 2011.

"Hey, Bob!" Sammy yelled: Ibid.

"That's when Bob and I really": Sonja Haney, interview with the author, February 27, 2011.

236 "Big Spender" Fosse shot twice: Ibid.

would have kept shooting: Ibid.

"Seeing how upset I was": MacLaine, *My Lucky Stars*, 179.

The dailies were a sensation: Sonja Haney, interview with the author, February 27, 2011.

Meanwhile, Fosse fought Universal over: Martin Gottfried, *All His Jazz* (Cambridge, MA: Da Capo, 1998; first published by Bantam in 1990), 198. Citations refer to the Da Capo edition.

237 "That last minute in": Terry Clifford, "Home Town Boy Bob Fosse Makes Good," *Chicago Tribune*, April 20, 1969.

vacillated up to the very last minute: Sonja Haney, interview with the author, February 27, 2011.

Both endings tested to mixed results: Ibid.

"When I saw the movie": Ibid.

"If a director overuses it": Boyle, "Bob Fosse Began Early."

"If it's a flop": Sonja Haney, interview with the author, February 27, 2011.

"Every moment of creating this dance": Reams, Marymount Manhattan College.

238 "Didn't do anything except feel sorry": Bob Fosse, 1969 daily diary, LOC, box 55G.

"That was my fault": Lionel Chetwynd, "Except for Bob Fosse," *Penthouse*, January 1974.

Screenwriter Peter Stone would indict: Gottfried, *All His Jazz*, 197.

239 midway into Fosse's *Little Me* deal: Extensive legal documents and correspondence pertaining to *MCA Artists v. Robert Fosse*, LOC, box 51A.

240 getting a little foothold on the deal: For more on the background of Creative Management Associates, see David McClintick, *Indecent Exposure* (New York: William Morrow, 1982).

Fosse signed with CMA: Fosse's 1969 CMA contract, LOC, box 51A.

Back in New York, he kept: From "A Concerned Friend," LOC, box 53B.

for her, he vowed to control his death wish: Ibid.

Herb Schlein, permanently concerned: Rosemary Edelman, "The Pastrami Philosopher," *New York*, July 23, 1979.

"He knows every cockamamie show": Ibid.

241 "You would look over": Dan Siretta, interview with the author, February 22, 2012.

"[Paddy's] a very compassionate": Sondra Lowell, "Fosse: Still Explaining His Movie," *Los Angeles Times*, February 3, 1980.

So when Paddy told Fosse: Bob Fosse/Paddy Chayefsky, *Big Deal* correspondence, LOC, box 66A.

242 "marred only by Fosse's depression": Robert Alan Aurthur, "Hanging Out," *Esquire*, August 1973.

for an amazing $800,000: Gottfried, *All His Jazz*, 202.

"It's a strange relationship, friendship": Steve Tesich, Bob Fosse Memorial, Palace Theater, October 30, 1987, New York Public Library for the Performing Arts, Theatre on Film and Tape Archive.

"It's like having a tiny apartment": Ibid.

Prematurely, Fosse sent *Big Deal*: Bob Fosse/David Picker *Big Deal* correspondence, November 11, 1969, LOC, box 66A.

243 Fosse was so desperate to work he even: Bob Fosse/Ray Stark *Big Deal* correspondence, December 29, 1969, LOC, box 66A.

One night, Hal and Judy Prince invited: Gottfried, *All His Jazz*, 203.

244 "There were two musicals onstage": Harold Prince, interview with the author, October 6, 2010.

"The first day of rehearsal": John Kander, interview with the author, November 10, 2010.

Fosse started calling: Cy Feuer with Ken Gross, *I Got the Show Right Here* (New York: Simon and Schuster, 2003), 242–43.

Feuer had pasta: Ibid.

245 He got a call from Sue Mengers: Larry Turman, interview with the author, July 26, 2010.

Fosse took a trip up the California coast: Bob Fosse/Larry Turman, *Burnt Offerings* correspondence, LOC, box 13C.

he expected to meet with Marasco: Ibid.

246 "I knew the best time to get": Emanuel Wolf, interview with the author, March 17, 2012.

247 "The worst tragedy can befall me": Drew, "Life as a Long Rehearsal."

"I was living like a wife and a mother": Suzanne Daley, "Stepping into Her New Shoes," *New York Times*, June 21, 1981.

"They *all* thought I could be controlled": Aurthur, "Hanging Out."

248 Sitting across from: Marty Baum interview, *Cabaret*, special ed. (Warner Home Video, 1998), DVD.

A meeting of the *Cabaret* production team was set for January 20: Bob Fosse, 1970 daily diary, LOC, box 55G.

"I didn't find him the happiest": Patrick McGilligan, ed., *Backstory 3: Interviews with the Screenwriters of the '60s* (Berkeley: University of California Press, 1997), 127.

249 "I lied": Feuer and Gross, *I Got the Show Right Here*, 245.

too loud, the *New York Times* thought: John S. Wilson, "Liza Minnelli Charming Empire Room Audiences," *New York Times*, February 10, 1970.

"It's a long, hard battle": Ibid.

Fosse met Minnelli in the Waldorf: "Liza Minnelli," *The Rosie Show*, OWN-TV, aired March 12, 2012.

250 dove deeper into research: Fosse correspondence, LOC, box 55G.

George Grosz: Kathryn Doby, interview with the author, November 27, 2010.

the Surtees issue had stalled: Feuer and Gross, *I Got the Show Right Here*, 246.

"No," Fosse heard around midnight: Bob Fosse/Ernie Martin correspondence, LOC, box 16B.

he should do whatever he wanted: Gottfried, *All His Jazz*, 209.

251 "If you quit": Shaun Considine, *Mad as Hell: The Life and Work of Paddy Chayefsky* (New York: Random House, 1995), 294.

"You no-good son of a bitch": Feuer and Gross, *I Got the Show Right Here*, 247.
He could see Fosse hadn't slept: Ibid.

SIXTEEN YEARS

252 "You were either a friend or": Cy Feuer, interviewed by Michael Kantor, February 23, 1999, New York Public Library for the Performing Arts, Theatre on Film and Tape Archive.

Fosse barred him from discussions: Peter MacDonald, interview with the author, March 8, 2012.

"For six weeks": Wolfgang Glattes, interview with the author, November 27, 2010.

"Bob was obsessed with blood": Ibid.

253 this time, with Fosse's blessing: Bob Fosse/Mary Dorfman correspondence, December 11, 1971, LOC, box 16B.

Michael York: Michael York, interview with the author, December 22, 2010.

"That two weeks": Ibid.

Trailed by her dog Ocho: Rex Reed, "Liza Minnelli Filming 'Cabaret,'" *Washington Post*, July 25, 1971.

Louise Glaum: Liza Minnelli interview, *Liza with a Z* (Showtime Entertainment, 2006), DVD.

"needed to be special": Liza Minnelli AFI Interview, http://www.youtube.com/watch?v=vkqK6oeGkq.

254 "Well?" she asked, modeling: "Liza Minnelli," *Inside the Actors Studio*, Bravo, February 5, 2006.

"If you feel like crying," he told her: Gwen Verdon interview, *Dance in America*, WNET archives, September 6, 1989.

"What's wrong?" Wolf asked: Emanuel Wolf, interview with the author, March 17, 2012.

He called Wolf: Ibid.

255 "His concentration was so intense": Wolfgang Glattes, interview with the author, November 27, 2010.

256 "When he was ready to go": Ibid.

"It was always very comfortable": Michael York, interview with the author, December 22, 2010.

"I tried to make the dances look like": Glenn Loney, "The Many Facets of Bob Fosse," *After Dark*, June 1972.

opted out of storyboarding: Wolfgang Glattes, interview with the author, November 27, 2010.

"I basically try to get an overall shot": Betty Spence, "Bob Fosse — He'll Take the Risks," *Los Angeles Times*, May 17, 1981.

257 "Every time I do that": Ibid.

"I keep my options open as long as possible": Ibid.

"You see, the wonderful thing about a camera": Bob Fosse, *Tomorrow with Tom Snyder,* NBC, January 31, 1980.

"They have to keep pulling me out": Spence, "Bob Fosse."

"Feuer wanted a kind of Barbra Streisand": Peter MacDonald, interview with the author, March 8, 2012.

258 "All through the shooting": Michael York, interview with the author, December 22, 2010.

"After a run-in with Feuer": Peter MacDonald, interview with the author, March 8, 2012.

"I'm sure it was a miscommunication": Kathryn Doby, interview with the author, November 27, 2010.

259 "I asked for some real thirties clothes": Reed, "Liza Minnelli Filming 'Cabaret.'"

"Gwen came and literally went": Michael York, interview with the author, December 22, 2010.

opposite sides of the screening room: Wolfgang Glattes, interview with the author, November 27, 2010.

Fosse turned around and asked Feuer: Peter MacDonald, interview with the author, March 8, 2012.

260 "Watching dailies": Michael York, interview with the author, December 22, 2010.

Fosse was already referring to: Emanuel Wolf, interview with the author, March 17, 2012.

"By the end of the shooting day": Louise Quick, *In the Company of Friends: Dancers Talking to Dancers II, the Women of Fosse,* videotaped at the New Dance Group, New York, on October 7, 2007.

playing badminton on a patch: C. Robert Jennings, "Divine Decadence Provides the Theme for German 'Cabaret,'" *Los Angeles Times,* June 27, 1971.

reminiscing all the way back to: Joyce Haber, "Joel Grey Talks about the Good Old, Bad Old Days," *Los Angeles Times,* March 4, 1973.

"Friday nights after shooting": Wolfgang Glattes, interview with the author, November 27, 2010.

"It would sometimes go on to five": Ibid.

261 "Ilse was a lovely lady": Peter MacDonald, interview with the author, March 8, 2012.

"It was as if he lived": Cy Feuer and Ken Gross, *I Got the Show Right Here* (New York: Simon and Schuster, 2003), 246.

"Do you think Bobby's gay?": Peter MacDonald, interview with the author, March 8, 2012.

"She was angry, no?" Ilse asked: Martin Gottfried, *All His Jazz* (Cambridge, MA: Da Capo, 1998; first published by Bantam in 1990), 213. Citations refer to the Da Capo edition.

262 Ilse, meanwhile, did Fosse's spying: Peter MacDonald, interview with the author, March 8, 2012.

Feuer appeared: Ibid.

"Bob," Feuer said: Ibid.

Furious, Fosse wrote a letter: Bob Fosse/Ernie Martin correspondence, LOC, box 16B.

263 dark blue velour: Gwen Verdon interview, *Dance in America*, WNET archives, September 6, 1989.

"He's impossible," she complained: Ibid.

"She walked in on him": Janice Lynde, interview with the author, May 4, 2011.

Fosse got her letter in Berlin: Gottfried, *All His Jazz*, 219.

The evening before *Cabaret* wrapped: Peter MacDonald, interview with the author, March 8, 2012.

"Now that I bought you all dinner": Ibid.

Michael York attempted very graciously: Michael York, interview with the author, December 22, 2010.

264 "If you don't know what I fucking think": Peter MacDonald, interview with the author, March 8, 2012.

"It was glorious": Ibid.

could not fill the vacuum: Gottfried, *All His Jazz*, 220.

He called Gwen: Ibid.

The villa turned out to be an estate: Neil Simon, *Rewrites: A Memoir* (New York: Simon and Schuster, 1996), 346–47.

265 She took him back: Gottfried, *All His Jazz*, 222.

"Don't think you're going to get": Peter MacDonald, interview with the author, March 8, 2012.

"I'm in the camera department!": Ibid.

"Liza was in heaven": Ibid.

he was shocked: Betty Spence, "Film Editor as Creator: Artist with Bits, Pieces," *Los Angeles Times*, January 11, 1981.

"Well," Fosse said: Vincent LoBrutto, *Selected Takes: Film Editors on Editing* (Westport: CT: Praeger, 1991), 55.

266 "He paced like a panther": Spence, "Film Editor as Creator."

267 "Every cut you make changes another": LoBrutto, *Selected Takes*, 58.

268 He asked Ilse never to answer: Gottfried, *All His Jazz*, 222.

Nicole, he told Ilse: Ibid.

Janice Lynde soothed him *and following*: Janice Lynde, interview with the author, May 4, 2011.

270 "I remember him saying it was": Ann Reinking, interview with the author, November 15, 2010.

"He took me to these strip clubs" *and following*: Janice Lynde, interview with the author, May 4, 2011.

271 David Begelman told Fosse he was: Gottfried, *All His Jazz*, 224.

272 one hundred identical (numbered): Richard Shepherd, interview with the author, March 13, 2009.

"The shibboleth": Sam Cohn interviewed by William Wolf for NYU's School of Continuing Education Class, the Filmmakers, New York Public Library for the Performing Arts, William Wolf Film and Theater Interview Collection.

At his peak, Sam Cohn saw: Mark Singer, "Dealmaker," *New Yorker*, January 11, 1982.

"Sam," his client Herb Gardner: Ibid.

273 "I have a neurotic response": Sam Cohn interviewed by William Wolf.

274 "Unless it was extremely urgent": Arlene Donovan, interview with the author, January 10, 2011.

"He was supposed to meet me [once]": Ibid.

"He seemed totally oblivious": Teresa Carpenter, interview with the author, July 23, 2010.

"You remember that deal we made?": Alan Ladd Jr., interview with the author, June 7, 2010.

"It's a very small group of people": Sam Cohn, interviewed by William Wolf.

"The different disciplines exist within": Jon Bradshaw, "May I Kiss You on the Forehead, Sam?," *New York*, December 29, 1975.

275 "Sam loved talent so much": Alan Ladd Jr., interview with the author, June 7, 2010.

"His clients": Marya Cohn, interview with the author, December 11, 2012.

"Sam was just overwhelmed by": Arlene Donovan, interview with the author, January 10, 2011.

"Those guys had a true guy-code": Susan Anderson, interview with the author, January 14, 2013.

"But Bobby is an extremely intelligent man": Bernard Drew, "Life as a Long Rehearsal," *American Film*, November 1979.

There were no pictures of his children: Peter Cohn, interview with the author, December 6, 2012.

"Family dinners?" Cohn once asked: Leslee Dart, interview with the author, July 25, 2012.

"At any time of day": Susan Anderson, interview with the author, January 14, 2013.

276 Susan Anderson peeked through the lens: Ibid.

Fosse told Sam about an idea: "Foreward [*sic*]," original concept for *Liza with a Z*, May 1971, LOC, box 45A.

277 Fosse sent Ilse back home: Gottfried, *All His Jazz*, 222.

"Fellas, this is much too long": Emanuel Wolf, interview with the author, March 17, 2012.

"There's a certain amount of self-delusion": "Bob Fosse," *The Dick Cavett Show*, PBS, July 8, 1980.

"Bob would do a movie": Wolfgang Glattes, interview with the author, November 27, 2010.

278 "Now, serious theater must": Otis Guernsey, "Edward Albee Confronts Broadway," *Diplomat*, October 1966.

he momentarily considered *Promises, Promises:* "Merrick Will Do 2 New Musicals: First Will Be a Goldman and Sondheim Show in Fall," *New York Times*, May 31, 1967.

Hair was a landmark musical, Fosse thought: Bob Fosse interview with Pete Hamill, *The Barry Gray Show*, December 1, 1979.

279 "I took somebody to an experimental": Tom Burke, "Steve Has Stopped Collaborating," *New York Times*, May 10, 1970.

"the challenge of maintaining relationships": Stephen Sondheim, *Finishing the Hat* (New York: Knopf, 2010), 165–66.

280 "a metaphoric explosion!": Mel Gussow, "Prince Recalls the Evolution of 'Follies,'" *New York Times*, April 9, 1971.

"I was looking at the past with affection": Ibid.

Fosse liked it and asked Sondheim: Stephen Sondheim, interview with the author, February 15, 2012.

"Out of politeness I said I would": Ibid.

281 "He called me up out of the blue": John Rubinstein, interview with the author, September 30, 2010.

"Fosse told me of his enthusiasm": Stephen Schwartz, interview with the author, January 29, 2011.

282 Fosse and producer Stuart Ostrow met *and following:* Stuart Ostrow, *Present at the Creation, Leaping in the Dark, and Going Against the Grain* (New York: Applause, 2006), 66.

"Stu Ostrow trusted Bob and that made": Wolfgang Glattes, interview with the author, November 27, 2010.

Strolling through the woods around: Ostrow, *Present at the Creation*, 66.

"I don't want to," she said *and following:* Janice Lynde, interview with the author, May 4, 2011.

FIFTEEN YEARS

286 For three consecutive days before: Emanuel Wolf, interview with the author, March 17, 2012.

Emanuel Wolf tried to calm him: Ibid.

he called *Cabaret* the perfect movie: Martin Gottfried, *All His Jazz* (Cambridge, MA: Da Capo, 1998; first published by Bantam in 1990), 228. Citations refer to the Da Capo edition.

"Bob and I were standing in the back": Emanuel Wolf, interview with the author, March 17, 2012.

287 "Until now there has never been": Pauline Kael, "Grinning," *New Yorker,* February 19, 1972.

288 cameras each held a twelve-hundred-foot: Barbara Goldsmith, "Barbara Goldsmith on Film," *Harper's Bazaar,* September 1972.

289 "the real me": Cecil Smith, "Liza Minnelli Hopes 'Real Me' Shows Up in Special," *Los Angeles Times,* September 3, 1972.

"Fosse wanted to bring reality" *and following:* Phil Ramone, interview with the author, October 10, 2010.

290 "When the sponsors would come around": Liesl Schillinger, "Suddenly Liza," *New York,* February 26, 2006.

"He could not be stopped": Owen Roizman, interview with the author, September 2, 2010.

"Now, you've gotta imagine": Liza Minnelli interview, *Liza with a Z* (Showtime Entertainment, 2006), DVD.

291 "I always watched [Fosse's] face": Ibid.

"Liza really, really wanted to learn": Candy Brown, interview with the author, January 7, 2011.

"One night": Owen Roizman, interview with the author, September 2, 2010.

"When you get out there": Ibid.

What Minnelli needed now: Liza Minnelli interview, *Liza with a Z* DVD.

292 "It was a hooker hotel!": Ibid.

"Liza was very nervous": Christopher Newman, interview with the author, September 10, 2010.

293 "I think she's great because": Fred Ebb, interviewed by Michael Kantor, March 29, 2009, New York Public Library for the Performing Arts, Theatre on Film and Tape Archive.

294 Candy Brown took the long way out: Candy Brown, interview with the author, January 7, 2011.

295 It always began the same: Bob Fosse describes his audition process in pages 54 to 57 of his May 13, 1976, deposition for *Grove Entertainment v. Pippin/Ostrow,* LOC, box 24C.

"What do you see in 'Tea for Two'?": Chet Walker, interview with the author, December 22, 2010.

"It has jumps, turns, rhythm": Ibid.

"Sometimes, he'd put in this": Jane Lanier, interview with the author, February 10, 2011.

"A lot of people wouldn't see": Kathryn Doby, interview with the author, November 27, 2010.

296 "He was always there to": Gordon Harrell, interview with the author, February 23, 2011.

"He would tell people in": Candy Brown, interview with the author, January 7, 2011.

"I've seen Bob audition people": Laurent Giroux, interview with the author, December 13, 2010.

"Our eyes met during": John Sowinski, interview with the author, February 1, 2011.

"It was like he was cutting himself": Albert Wolsky, interview with the author, August 11, 2010.

"He would literally walk over": Valarie Pettiford, interview with the author, February 2, 2011.

297 "I think I've turned down": "Bob Fosse," *The Dick Cavett Show*, PBS, July 8, 1980.

On the day Sacco was cut: McCandlish Phillips, "For Stage Tryouts, 4 Seconds of Hope," *New York Times*, February 9, 1972.

298 "I remember once": Ken Urmston, interview with the author, May 12, 2011.

"He would cast dancers": Stephen Schwartz, interview with the author, January 29, 2011.

"You couldn't have gotten a more": Candy Brown, interview with the author, January 7, 2011.

Ann Reinking arrived at *and following*: Ann Reinking, interview with the author, November 15, 2010.

300 "Ann extended Bob's talent": "Bob Fosse: Dancing on the Edge," *Biography*, A&E, August 24, 1999.

That night he called her: Ann Reinking, interview with the author, November 15, 2010.

Reinking was cool: Ibid.

301 "*Separate* is not the right word": "Bob Fosse: Steam Heat," *Great Performances: Dance in America*, PBS; first aired February 23, 1990.

"I want to be a good father": Chris Chase, "Fosse, from Tony to Oscar to Emmy," *New York Times*, April 29, 1973.

"Bob was the most notorious": Cyrus M. Copeland, *Farewell, Godspeed: The Greatest Eulogies of Our Time* (New York: Harmony Books, 2003), 9.

"I always look up to you, Bob": Ibid., 10.

302 Fosse asked John Rubinstein to: John Rubinstein, interview with the author, September 30, 2010.

"When I *really* read the script": Ibid.

"The place had a fun and temporary feel": Sandahl Bergman, interview with the author, April 27, 2012.

"We were sort of looking at each other": John Rubinstein, interview with the author, September 30, 2010.

303 The morning after the fire, a sentimental stranger: Warren Allen Smith, interview with the author, August 19, 2012.

304 "Bob would always be pushing people": Alan Heim, interview with the author, July 22, 2010.

"I arranged a very elaborate system" *and following:* Trudy Ship, interview with the author, January 21, 2011.

306 "the Fosse diet" *and following:* Alan Heim, interview with the author, July 22, 2010.

307 "Don't worry about it": Ben Vereen, interview with the author, January 11, 2011.

308 "On the page": Ibid.

Schwartz and Hirson liked the idea: Stephen Schwartz, interview with the author, January 29, 2011.

"The show was being discovered": Ibid.

"I realized [Fosse] was having me": John Rubinstein, interview with the author, September 30, 2010.

309 "I didn't feel Bob's dominance was": Stephen Schwartz, interview with the author, January 29, 2011.

Angrily annotated scripts: *Pippin* scripts, LOC, boxes 24A and 24B.

"There's a theory": Harvey Evans, interview with the author, January 28, 2011.

"*Pippin* is classic vaudeville with": Ann Reinking, interview with the author, November 15, 2010.

310 It was an interesting idea, Schwartz thought: Stephen Schwartz, interview with the author, January 29, 2011.

"There was a cloud over his head": Candy Brown, interview with the author, January 7, 2011.

311 "I sort of aired some of the dirty": Stephen Schwartz, interview with the author, January 29, 2011.

"I think he's very talented": Laurie Johnston, "Fosse Discusses Creation of 'Pippin,'" *New York Times,* November 7, 1972.

"Bob wanted no chorus in *Pippin*": Pam Sousa, interview with the author, January 11, 2011.

The girls would have poker nights: Ibid.

"We called Kathryn Mother": Cheryl Clark, interview with the author, April 19, 2011.

They would play tricks on: Candy Brown, interview with the author, January 7, 2011.

312 "We were a family on *Pippin*": Ibid.

MGM days: Pam Sousa, interview with the author, January 11, 2011.

"People in plays and in movies": Julian Barry, interview with the author, September 6, 2010.

"He was a star director": Name withheld, interview with the author, September 10, 2010.

"Most of us got those calls": Candy Brown, interview with the author, January 7, 2011.

313 "I get involved in the material and the people": Johnston, "Fosse Discusses Creation of 'Pippin.'"

"It made me nervous": Candy Brown, interview with the author, January 7, 2011.

"I think it's fair to say": Pam Sousa, interview with the author, January 11, 2011.

"I was never attracted to him" *and following:* Jennifer Nairn-Smith, interview with the author, January 7, 2011.

314 "There was always one person": Candy Brown, interview with the author, January 7, 2011.

"She would be in tears, sobbing": John Rubinstein, interview with the author, September 30, 2010.

315 "He was a director": Jennifer Nairn-Smith, interview with the author, January 7, 2011.

he threatened to kill him: Ibid.

"I was working in the theater and": Maxine Glorsky, interview with the author, September 7, 2010.

"Bob protected me from": Jennifer Nairn-Smith, interview with the author, January 7, 2011.

"Jennifer and Ann came in one day": Candy Brown, interview with the author, January 7, 2011.

316 "There were lots of poppers backstage": Name withheld, interview with the author, September 10, 2010.

"Someone dropped a lude": Cheryl Clark, interview with the author, April 19, 2011.

"I talked so much on the phone" *and following:* Ann Reinking, interview with the author, November 15, 2010.

"I know enough about emotions": Chase, "Fosse, from Tony to Oscar to Emmy."

317 "When Bob finally told us": Kathryn Doby, interview with the author, November 27, 2010.

"We didn't realize that": Gene Foote, *In the Company of Friends: Dancers Talking to Dancers III, the Men of Fosse,* videotaped at the New Dance Group, New York, on December 9, 2007.

"Bob would remind us": Candy Brown, interview with the author, January 7, 2011.

"Some people came up": Ken Urmston, interview with the author, May 12, 2011.

318 "The audience is expecting me": John Rubinstein, interview with the author, September 30, 2010.

319 "I used to be more involved in patterns": Johnston, "Fosse Discusses Creation of 'Pippin.'"

"We did not work *with* each other": Foote, *In the Company of Friends.*

"Jolson's, Martha Graham's": Walter Kerr, "It's a Lovely Way to Do a Show," *New York Times,* October 29, 1972.

320 "I don't hesitate to lift from": Johnston, "Fosse Discusses Creation of 'Pippin.'"

"The follow spots for Fosse": Maxine Glorsky, interview with the author, September 7, 2010.

"I kept telling him he was a good person": Ann Reinking, interview with the author, November 15, 2010.

"We now get to New York": John Rubinstein, interview with the author, September 30, 2010.

321 "Candy, Candy, Candy": Candy Brown, interview with the author, January 7, 2011.

John Rubinstein felt the audience recoil: John Rubinstein, interview with the author, September 30, 2010.

"Part of the problem": Stephen Schwartz, interview with the author, January 29, 2011.

322 "The statement of [*Pippin*]": Johnston, "Fosse Discusses Creation of 'Pippin.'"

"He never seems to enjoy achieving": Bernard Drew, "Life as a Long Rehearsal," *American Film,* November 1979.

"There's something deflating in that": Kerr, "It's a Lovely Way to Do a Show."

flew to Vegas to see Liza: Wayne Warga, "Bob Fosse: Triple Threat Director," *Los Angeles Times,* January 21, 1973.

323 "I never use my name to get tickets": Robert Wahls, "Bob Who? Bob Fosse!," *New York Sunday News,* November 26, 1972.

"Don't worry about it, pal": Warga, "Bob Fosse: Triple Threat Director."

Fosse brooded on the offer: Bob Fosse letter to Stanley Donen, March 29, 1972, LOC, box 47A.

"You can even wear a bowler": Gottfried, *All His Jazz,* 267.

"Nicole was crazy about that book": Gwen Verdon interview, *Dance in America,* WNET archives, September 6, 1989.

"One sting": Janice Lynde, interview with the author, May 4, 2011.

Fosse bought his Snake costume: Bob Fosse to Stanley Donen, March 29, 1972, LOC, box 47A.

324 Dazzled, Herb Gardner thought: Herb Gardner, Bob Fosse Memorial, Palace Theater, October 30, 1987, New York Public Library for the Performing Arts, Theatre on Film and Tape Archive.

Meeting him was Ilse: Gottfried, *All His Jazz,* 269.

Strolling the Madeira coastline: Ibid.

325 he felt he owed her: Tony Stevens, interview with the author, February 8, 2011.

Abend had to hire a private detective: Louise Kiernan, "Murder She Wrote," *Chicago Tribune,* July 16, 1997.

now writing Hallmark cards for a living: Andy Seiler, "Pssstttt! 'Chicago' Has a Secret Past," *USA Today,* March 24, 2003.

Columbia concluded that grim material *and following:* Julian Barry, interview with the author, September 6, 2010.

327 "I want to go out and find where we're shooting" *and following:* Patricia Ferrier Kiley, interview with the author, March 4, 2011.

328 "They told us to bring resort wear": Janice Lynde, interview with the author, May 4, 2011.

On the morning of February 13: Bob Fosse, interview with Stephen Harvey, 1983, LOC, box 60F.

329 "We knew what that meant": Emanuel Wolf, interview with the author, March 17, 2012.

"When we left Africa, we came back" *and following*: Janice Lynde, interview with the author, May 4, 2011.

330 "a harmless preoccupied guy": "Wally Cox, TV Mr. Peepers, Dies at 48," *New York Times*, February 16, 1973.

"They were roommates at one time" *and following*: Janice Lynde, interview with the author, May 4, 2011.

331 "When you sat in the room" *and following*: Julian Barry, interview with the author, September 6, 2010.

332 "They were diet pills": David Freeman, interview with the author, April 12, 2013.

333 "He was not the sort of guy": Drew Leder, interview with the author, November 18, 2012.

his secretary, Vicki Stein, did the lion's share *and following*: Julian Barry, interview with the author, September 6, 2010.

334 "He was a master watcher": Christine Colby, interview with the author, March 20, 2011.

"He had a way of— how shall I": Richard Korthaze, interview with the author, March 24, 2011.

"You'd be talking to Bob": Alan Heim, interview with the author, July 22, 2010.

335 "The way you're bounding ahead": Sherri Kandell, interview with the author, July 8, 2012.

"I was just blown away": Ibid.

"Lenny Bruce would push people's buttons": "Bob Fosse: Steam Heat," *Great Performances: Dance in America.*

"He could get so mean about it": Jane Aurthur, interview with the author, September 9, 2010.

"He'd love to set up some kind": Arlene Donovan, interview with the author, January 10, 2011.

"What I really want to do is find": Lionel Chetwynd, "Except for Bob Fosse," *Penthouse*, January 1974.

336 "You know, Julian" *and following*: Julian Barry, interview with the author, September 6, 2010.

337 he knew the more good press he got: Tony Stevens, interview with the author, February 8, 2011.

338 "I confess I thought I had a shot": Tony Awards, videotaped by the ABC Television Network at the Imperial, New York, March 25, 1973.

he flew to the Beverly Hills Hotel: Janice Lynde, interview with the author, May 4, 2011.

339   "He was really, really nervous then": Ibid.

Shoring himself up with booze and tranquilizers: Chase, "Fosse, from Tony to Oscar to Emmy."

In the limo to the ceremony, Fosse repeated: Janice Lynde, interview with the author, May 4, 2011.

341   Janice decided to say nothing: Ibid.

"He was very still": Emanuel Wolf, interview with the author, March 17, 2012.

Janice was not with him: Janice Lynde, interview with the author, May 4, 2011.

342   "My legs were like cooked spaghetti": Jan Hodenfield, "Bob Fosse Feet First," *New York Post*, April 21, 1973.

343   "Hi, Dad": Chase, "Fosse, from Tony to Oscar to Emmy."

They convened in Fosse's suite and opened: Janice Lynde, interview with the author, May 4, 2011.

"I'll walk you one more block," he had said: Herb Gardner, Bob Fosse Memorial, Palace Theater, October 30, 1987, New York Public Library for the Performing Arts, Theatre on Film and Tape Archive.

344   "Would you do *anything* to win one?": Janice Lynde, interview with the author, May 4, 2011.

345   "His pain was extreme": Ibid.

"He was afraid he would not be able": Ibid.

"There's this Looney Tunes cartoon": Ann Reinking, interview with the author, November 15, 2010.

FOURTEEN YEARS

346   He was no longer interested in therapy: Ann Reinking, interview with the author, November 15, 2010.

Since getting off Seconal: Bob Fosse, interview with Dick Stelzer, *Star Treatment*, LOC, box 47C, folder 1.

Someone, Fosse used to say, must have scared: Bernard Drew, "Life as a Long Rehearsal," *American Film*, November 1979.

That boy, Dr. Sager told him, was: *All That Jazz*, Clifford Sager interview transcripts, LOC, box 1A.

Fosse thought both: "Odd Ideas" notebook, LOC, box 53B.

347   He lasted only a few days: Ann Reinking, interview with the author, November 15, 2010.

Fosse hated the lithium: Ibid.

"I knew it was time to check out": Ibid.

was concerned their hero was losing: Bob Fosse/Marvin Worth correspondence, May 8, 1973, LOC, box 20B.

a scene Fosse and Barry had completely invented: Ibid.

Worth said all the chronological: Ibid.

"We'd be talking about the form": John Kander, interview with the author, November 10, 2010.

"I was malleable": John Kander and Fred Ebb as told to Greg Lawrence, *Colored Lights: Forty Years of Words and Music, Show Biz, Collaboration, and All That Jazz* (New York: Faber and Faber, 2003), 126.

348 "He would say, 'Oh, this is'": Ibid.

"He's an arrogant son of a bitch": Ibid., 127.

Experts believed TV audiences were uninterested in: http://www.playbill.com/news/article/153521-Jeffrey-Ash-Broadway-Ad-Man-and-Producer-Dies-at-65-Stuart Ostrow.

"This cameraman was just shooting us": Pam Sousa, interview with the author, January 11, 2011.

349 Therein lay the beauty of United Artists: A witty, concise rendering of the history of United Artists can be found in Steven Bach, *Final Cut: Dreams and Disaster in the Making of* Heaven's Gate (New York: Morrow, 1985).

"to protect the great motion picture public": Ibid., 36.

350 "The thing about UA was we didn't": David Picker, interview with the author, October 7, 2010.

"I'd do anything to make it possible": Ibid.

"I want you to play Lenny": Dustin Hoffman, interview with the author, September 13, 2012.

351 "It was not the right way to": Ibid.

He tried Raquel Welch: Raquel Welch, interview with the author, May 9, 2012.

He considered his sometime girlfriend Joey Heatherton: Robert Greenhut, interview with the author, August 31, 2010.

Her mother had been a showgirl: Judy Klemesrud, "Valerie Perrine, or, The Return of the Hollywood Sex Kitten," *New York Times*, December 1, 1974.

"That was": Valerie Perrine, interview with the author, February 26, 2011.

"We read two hundred and fifty actresses": David Picker, interview with the author, October 7, 2010.

352 "I'm Leonard Albert Schneider" *and following*: Valerie Perrine, interview with the author, February 26, 2011.

353 Fosse respectfully rented his own: Martin Gottfried, *All His Jazz* (Cambridge, MA: Da Capo, 1998; first published by Bantam in 1990), 300. Citations refer to the Da Capo edition.

"I remember how Gwen suffered": John Rubinstein, interview with the author, September 30, 2010.

"He suddenly allowed a lot of": Gottfried, *All His Jazz*, 284.

a short distance from the sand was a white cypress: Jay Sears, interview with the author, February 16, 2012.

354 lobster especially, and Chinese spare ribs: Ann Reinking, interview with the author, November 15, 2010.

"I would have made a terrific waiter": Linda Winer, "Shade of Bob Fosse Raised by 'Chicago,'" *Newsday*, November 22, 1996.

Brahms, Chopin, or: Richard Natale, "Dining with Bob Fosse," *Viva*, 1973.

Too much scotch could take Fosse down: Ann Reinking, interview with the author, November 15, 2010.

"I love big parties": Natale, "Dining with Bob Fosse."

"Most nondancers don't understand": Fred Mann III, interview with the author, February 22, 2011.

began after Ann's last matinee *and following*: Ann Reinking, interview with the author, November 15, 2010.

356 "We were just reading scenes" *and following*: Julian Barry, interview with the author, September 6, 2010.

357 the more he came to believe that Lenny's layers *and following*: Dustin Hoffman, interview with the author, September 13, 2012.

360 "Bob insisted that no extra could": David Picker, interview with the author, October 7, 2010.

as Fosse had promised Hoffman they would: Dustin Hoffman, interview with the author, September 13, 2012.

361 "We got a problem" *and following*: David Picker, interview with the author, October 7, 2010.

"what's your shlong doing on that ashtray?": Dustin Hoffman, interview with the author, September 13, 2012.

362 "You're ugly! What are you doing here?": Ibid.

"It was vicious": Ibid.

"Bob, it's not working": Ibid.

"Dustin felt I was restricting him": Kenneth L. Geist, "Fosse Reflects on Fosse," *After Dark*, February 1980.

363 "Nobody talks like this, Bob": Dustin Hoffman, interview with the author, September 13, 2012.

he liked what the speed and exhaustion: Bruce Surtees, interview with the author, March 28, 2011.

"All Dustin wants to do is talk!": Ibid.

"Someone tell Fosse I'm not a machine!": Dustin Hoffman, interview with the author, September 13, 2012.

"[Fosse] wanted to be Lenny": Ibid.

"There are not a lot of movie directors": David Picker, interview with the author, October 7, 2010.

"We can know what this means": Robert Greenhut, interview with the author, August 31, 2010.

"It was ballsy": Bruce Surtees, interview with the author, March 28, 2011.

364 "I want this to be like": Ibid.

"We would just run the whole magazine": Robert Greenhut, interview with the author, August 31, 2010.

They shot the final monologue twice: David Picker, interview with the author, October 7, 2010.

"You're worse than your father" *and following*: Robert Greenhut, interview with the author, August 31, 2010.

365 "Why are you doing this?": Neil Machlis, interview with the author, September 1, 2010.

"Who would ever dream of": Ibid.

Greenhut's phone rang. "Hello?": Robert Greenhut, interview with the author, August 31, 2010.

366 "I had complete trust in Bobby": Valerie Perrine, interview with the author, February 26, 2011.

An acting robot: Ibid.

"He spent more time rehearsing": Larry Mark, interview with the author, September 17, 2010.

"Hi, Bobby" *and following*: Valerie Perrine, interview with the author, February 26, 2011.

367 "It wasn't sexual": Dustin Hoffman, interview with the author, September 13, 2012.

"Bobby, I can't do it": Valerie Perrine, interview with the author, February 26, 2011.

"That's why he got to know you": Ibid.

368 "I'm embarrassed by that story": Bob Fosse interview, *Midday*, CBC-TV Canada, July 7, 1987.

told Perrine to think of her Great Dane: Valerie Perrine, interview with the author, February 26, 2011.

"In the beginning, we were going": Neil Machlis, interview with the author, September 1, 2010.

"We were burning film": Robert Greenhut, interview with the author, August 31, 2010.

"The guy is overrated and he knows it": Tim Cahill, "Dirty Lenny on the Silver Screen," *Rolling Stone*, December 5, 1974.

"There came a point late in the shoot": Bruce Surtees, interview with the author, March 28, 2011.

The cinematographer gave Larry Mark a coconut: Larry Mark, interview with the author, September 17, 2010.

"It was like [Fosse] was trying to get even": Dustin Hoffman, interview with the author, September 13, 2012.

369 "Fosse showed no remorse": Bruce Surtees, interview with the author, March 28, 2011.

"Because there was no money": Albert Wolsky, interview with the author, August 11, 2010.

Dustin Hoffman behind a baby grand: Tom Lofaro, interview with the author, February 10, 2011.

It was an atmosphere *and following*: Kitty Bruce, interview with the author, February 15, 2013.

370   "His cough would wake me up": Dustin Hoffman, interview with the author, September 13, 2012.

"He just wanted to be there": David Picker, interview with the author, October 7, 2010.

Swiss cheese sandwich with mustard on white *and following*: Larry Mark, interview with the author, September 17, 2010.

"Can you make it smaller?" he would ask: Bruce Surtees, interview with the author, March 28, 2011.

"What are you doing?": Julian Barry, interview with the author, September 6, 2010.

371   would lean into Trudy Ship: Trudy Ship, interview with the author, January 21, 2011.

Hoffman wanted to join, but Fosse: Alan Heim, interview with the author, July 22, 2010.

"He was never totally specific": Albert Wolsky, interview with the author, August 11, 2010.

"I'm so depressed": Ibid.

he'd seen a big, bearded man: Ibid.

372   "He fought everything so hard": Dustin Hoffman, interview with the author, September 13, 2012.

about 360,000 feet of printed film to: Cahill, "Dirty Lenny on the Silver Screen."

"He taught me how to be hard on material": Alan Heim, interview with the author, July 22, 2010.

Sometimes lunch would be personally delivered: Ibid.

"There were times in the cutting room": Jonathan Pontell, interview with the author, February 7, 2011.

He made no effort to hide the attaché: Alan Heim, interview with the author, July 22, 2010.

"I'm positive that Bob did this intentionally": Ibid.

373   "Bob would talk to me about": Trudy Ship, interview with the author, January 21, 2011.

He would laugh at himself for dating: Ibid.

"Who was it last night?": Ibid.

One night Fosse invited Kim and Ann: Gottfried, *All His Jazz*, 301.

At home, Fosse found Kim had: Ibid.

"If you can't go by the rules": Ibid., 305.

The performance, Fosse decreed: Alan Heim, interview with the author, July 22, 2010.

374 "It was the racial monologue": Ibid.

"[Fosse] was frequently demeaning him": Trudy Ship, interview with the author, January 21, 2011.

"Throw it out," Fosse said: Ibid.

"We discovered that by fragmenting": Alan Heim, interview with the author, July 22, 2010.

Ralph Burns called "Fosse time": Ibid.

375 "Film is just like music": Michael Blowen, "Will Gritty 'Star 80' Glitter at the Box Office?," *Boston Globe*, November 6, 1983.

Fosse wrote him asking for co-credit: Bob Fosse/Julian Barry correspondence, June 6, 1974, LOC, box 47B.

"I wrote back and told him no": Julian Barry, interview with the author, September 6, 2010.

Fosse said he'd never bring it up: Ibid.

"He was coughing and coughing": Trudy Ship, interview with the author, January 21, 2011.

"The nerve-racking thing": Robert Greenhut, interview with the author, August 31, 2010.

376 singeing one side of his mouth: Wolfgang Glattes, interview with the author, November 27, 2010.

"Although we had worked on each other's" *and following:* Herb Gardner, Bob Fosse Memorial, Palace Theater, October 30, 1987, New York Public Library for the Performing Arts, Theatre on Film and Tape Archive.

377 "We used to turn on the radio": Paddy Chayefsky on *Dinah!*, CBS, March 2, 1977. Around ten every morning, John Kander: John Kander, interview with the author, November 10, 2010.

378 "We were pregnant a lot in those days": "Dialogue with Liza Minnelli, Fred Ebb, and John Kander," January 14, 1974, New York Public Library for the Performing Arts, Theatre on Film and Tape Archive.

"I would never write a completed lyric": John Kander and Fred Ebb's *Chicago*, Martin Gottfried on Bob Fosse, "Theater Talk," videotaped at Top Line Studios, September 27, 1996.

"Put in two finger snaps": John Kander, interview with the author, November 10, 2010.

379 "Our copy was so messy": Ibid.

Verdon's *Chicago* contract was a valentine: Gwen Verdon's *Chicago* contract, September 27, 1974, LOC, box 18C.

380 "Gwen knew a child needed both parents": Ann Reinking, interview with the author, November 15, 2010.

"And she continued to love him": Ibid.

"If you want to make something good": Paul Gardner, "Bob Fosse Off His Toes," *New York,* December 16, 1974.

"I'd wake up in the morning": Barry Rehfeld, "Bob Fosse's Follies," *Rolling Stone,* January 19, 1984.

381 "In American writing now": Anatole Broyard, "Love on the Critical List: Books of the Times to Control the Uncontrollable Greatest of All Obstacles," *New York Times,* July 30, 1974.

"Above all, *Ending* made me feel": Ibid.

likening it to a string-quartet: Stuart Ostrow, *Present at the Creation, Leaping in the Dark, and Going Against the Grain* (New York: Applause, 2006), 81.

"My characters were as far from": Hilma Wolitzer, interview with the author, July 5, 2010.

they should turn the script away: Robert Alan Aurthur's sixteen-page step outline, December 23, 1974, LOC, box 13D.

382 Fosse talked Aurthur into inventing: Ann Guarino, "The Fall of a Curtain, the Rise of an Idea," *New York Daily News,* March 17, 1976.

"What'll happen is I'll probably die": Barry Rehfeld, "Bob Fosse's Follies."

"Don't let me do anything I've done before": Tony Stevens, interview with the author, February 8, 2011.

Stevens soon realized exactly what: Ibid.

Ann Reinking called it "the Know": Ann Reinking, interview with the author, November 15, 2010.

"You have to have the magnificent stare": Ibid.

had fascinated Fosse since he saw Tony Richardson's: Marilyn Stasio, "A Tough 'Chicago' Is Where Bob Fosse Lives," *Cue,* July 7, 1975.

"The performer portrays incidents": Bertolt Brecht and John Willett (ed. and trans.), "Alienation Effects in Chinese Acting," *Brecht on Theater: The Development of an Aesthetic* (New York: Hill and Wang, 1992), 93.

383 "'Gest' is not supposed to mean gesticulation": Ibid., 104.

"The reason I haven't called you" *and following:* Julian Barry, interview with the author, September 6, 2010.

"People would walk into the editing room": Alan Heim, interview with the author, July 22, 2010.

384 "You were a better cutter before": Ibid.

"I just don't feel good": Ann Reinking, interview with the author, November 15, 2010.

The first week of dance: "Fosse Fatigue Causes Delay in Start of 'Chicago' Rehearsals," *Variety,* November 6, 1974.

"The number started with me": Chita Rivera, interview with the author, February 3, 2011.

385 Fosse showed the company images of: Graciela Daniele, interviewed by

Michael Kantor, March 30, 1999, New York Public Library for the Performing Arts, Theatre on Film and Tape Archive.

"Go over there": Ibid.

"In 'All That Jazz'": Gene Foote, *In the Company of Friends: Dancers Talking to Dancers III, the Men of Fosse,* videotaped at the New Dance Group, New York, on December 9, 2007.

"It was the crown": Tony Stevens, interview with the author, February 8, 2011.

386   "It got so that he wouldn't put on": Ibid.

Heim said Fosse didn't look so good: Alan Heim, interview with the author, July 22, 2010.

Reinking was worried about the purplish color: Ann Reinking, interview with the author, November 15, 2010.

"Are you okay?": Alan Heim, interview with the author, July 22, 2010.

387   placed a big bouquet of red roses: Gary Gendell, interview with the author, June 12, 2012.

Tony Walton showed off a model: Gottfried, *All His Jazz,* 316.

"I was shocked": Moira Hodgson, "When Bob Fosse's Art Imitates Life, It's Just 'All That Jazz,'" *New York Times,* December 30, 1979.

He asked stage manager: Gottfried, *All His Jazz,* 316.

Like a truck was driving: *All That Jazz,* Phil Friedman interview transcripts, LOC, box 1A.

Friedman called Leder, as directed: Gottfried, *All His Jazz,* 316.

Joe Harris and Ira Bernstein ran into Neil Simon: Ira Bernstein, interview with the author, May 17, 2011.

388   Fosse — trying to keep calm — told Harris: Gottfried, *All His Jazz,* 317.

"The show is over": Ibid.

"What do you mean?": Gardner, "Bob Fosse Off His Toes."

1 to 2 percent on the value: Kenneth Turan, "Insuring the Stars: You Think Your Policy's High-Risk?," *Washington Post,* September 19, 1977.

389   At 3:30, Fosse's doctors called Broadway Arts: *All That Jazz,* Phil Friedman interview transcripts, LOC, box 1A.

"[Gwen] really went through this": Gottfried, *All His Jazz,* 318.

She believed this was, in a way: *All That Jazz,* Gwen Verdon interview transcripts, LOC, box 1A.

"Please don't let them keep me": Suzanne Daley, "Stepping into Her New Shoes," *New York Times,* June 21, 1981.

"Alan," Verdon said to Heim: Alan Heim, interview with the author, July 22, 2010.

At 5:30 that evening, producers Fryer and Harris: *All That Jazz,* Phil Friedman interview transcripts, LOC, box 1A.

"It's exhaustion," they said: "Fosse Exhausted, 'Chicago' Tryout Opening Delayed," *Daily Variety,* October 31, 1974.

Dr. Ettinger moved Fosse: Ann Reinking, interview with the author, November 15, 2010.

390   He asked if he could have a smoke: Gottfried, *All His Jazz,* 320.

They would take a vein: Ibid.

The following day, the *Chicago* company: Candy Brown, interview with the author, January 7, 2011.

Pam Sousa booked a couple commercials: Pam Sousa, interview with the author, January 11, 2011.

She threw parties: Jan Hodenfield, "Gwen Verdon & Chita Rivera: 2 from the Chorus," *New York Post,* May 31, 1975.

he called the theater to check up: Laurent Giroux, interview with the author, December 13, 2010.

Heim came to the hospital with a report: Alan Heim, interview with the author, July 22, 2010.

Cinema One's best opening day: *Variety,* full-page advertisement, November 14, 1974.

"Fosse has learned": Pauline Kael, "When the Saints Come Marching In," *New Yorker,* November 18, 1974.

391   Drugged out, he called Annie: Ann Reinking, interview with the author, November 15, 2010.

"I'm going to a real opening": Ibid.

Fosse made a pass at almost every nurse: Gardner, "Bob Fosse Off His Toes."

Outside his door, the ICU nurses held: Ann Reinking, interview with the author, November 15, 2010.

"Bob, are you smoking?": Janice Lynde, interview with the author, May 4, 2011.

394   "We sure picked the right subject": Gottfried, *All His Jazz,* 324.

THIRTEEN YEARS

395   America had become a showbiz nation: Ambitious scholars take note: bridging 1970s disenchantment culture with the rise of our current (perhaps ancient) showbiz reality is a subject that deserves its own book. In the meantime, I took them piecemeal. For a fine survey of the 1970s, see Bruce J. Schulman, *The Seventies: The Great Shift in American Culture, Society, and Politics* (New York: Free Press, 2001). For fine surveys of showbiz culture, see Neil Postman, *Amusing Ourselves to Death: Public Discourse in the Age of Show Business* (New York: Penguin, 1985), and Neil Gabler, *Life: The Movie: How Entertainment Conquered Reality* (New York: Knopf, 1998). Or just watch Scorsese's *The King of Comedy* (1983) and Weir's *The Truman Show* (1998). Their prescience is delightful and terrifying.

"We all have to put on": Bob Fosse, May 18, 1986, interview with Kevin Boyd Grubb, LOC, audiocassette.

396 "The 70s was the decade in which": Norman Mailer, "Mailer on the '70s — Decade of 'Image, Skin Flicks, and Porn,'" *U.S. News and World Report*, December 10, 1979.

397 "Bob took me to Patsy's for dinner": Deborah Geffner, interview with the author, October 1, 2010.

"Young choreographers": Alan Heim, interview with the author, July 22, 2010.

"It was spy versus spy": Tony Stevens, interview with the author, February 8, 2011.

"I remember when I walked into": Donna McKechnie, interview with the author, October 14, 2010.

398 They had him on an ice mattress *and following*: Ann Reinking, interview with the author, November 15, 2010.

"There is this profound period": Nancy Bird, interview with the author, February 16, 2011.

399 "It is a little difficult to, you know": Bob Fosse, *Tomorrow with Tom Snyder*, NBC, January 31, 1980.

He got sentimental one night: Paul Gardner, "Bob Fosse Off His Toes," *New York*, December 16, 1974.

Chayefsky promised Bob that if Bob died first: Roderick Mann, "Bob Fosse — Writing 'Star 80' Was Easy, Filming It Wasn't," *Los Angeles Times*, November 13, 1983.

Actor John McMartin called in the middle: John McMartin, interview with the author, November 8, 2010.

The *Pippin* cast took up a collection: Laurent Giroux, interview with the author, December 13, 2010.

400 Garson Kanin sent a book: Book referenced in miscellaneous correspondence, LOC, box 47B.

Valerie Perrine sent a life-size: Valerie Perrine, interview with the author, February 26, 2011.

Dustin sent zinnias: Gardner, "Bob Fosse Off His Toes."

"How long has it been since you've": Joyce Haber, "A Possible Dream for Rod McKuen," *Los Angeles Times*, December 3, 1974.

"Tony": *All That Jazz*, Tony Walton interview transcripts, LOC, box 1A.

Wolfgang Glattes saw someone: Wolfgang Glattes, interview with the author, November 27, 2010.

Nurses unplugged it: Gardner, "Bob Fosse Off His Toes."

Student nurse Kathy Zappola *and following*: *All That Jazz*, Kathy Zappola interview transcripts, LOC, box 1A.

There were fights: Martin Gottfried, *All His Jazz* (Cambridge, MA: Da Capo, 1998; first published by Bantam in 1990), 327. Citations refer to the Da Capo edition.

"The hospital staff didn't know who": Ibid., 329.

401 Gwen had to disguise Nicole: *All That Jazz,* Gwen Verdon interview transcripts, LOC, box 1A.

he looked to her more like a machine: *All That Jazz,* Nicole Fosse interview transcripts, LOC, box 1A.

bust pads: Ibid.

As Gwen looked on, Nicole put his heart: *All That Jazz,* Phil Friedman interview transcripts, LOC, box 1A.

Long after she left, his mind was still: Ann Reinking, interview with the author, November 15, 2010.

Being in the hospital was starting to do weird things: Ibid.

402 regrets lined up: Scott Hornstein, "The Making of Lenny: An Interview with Bob Fosse," *Filmmakers Newsletter,* February 1975.

making quiet, shaky love to Ann Reinking *and following:* Ann Reinking, interview with the author, November 15, 2010.

403 nuns danced: "Bob Fosse," *The Dick Cavett Show,* PBS, July 8, 1980.

404 "I had a strange dream": Shirley MacLaine, *My Lucky Stars: A Hollywood Memoir* (New York: Bantam, 1995), 186.

He was discharged on December 10, 1974: Tom Buckley, "Ann Reinking Plays Herself in 'All That Jazz,'" *New York Times,* January 4, 1980.

she in her back brace and he: Ibid.

Fosse quit smoking: Ann Reinking, interview with the author, November 15, 2010.

Gwen threw a Christmas party: Jan Hodenfield, "Gwen Verdon and Chita Rivera: 2 from the Chorus," *New York Post,* May 31, 1975.

at Herb Gardner's party, he got drunk: Bob Fosse and Robert Alan Aurthur, interview with Dr. Joe Wilder, August 26, 1975, LOC, box 14B.

"Can you get me some Dexies?": Janice Lynde, interview with the author, May 4, 2011.

405 He took off for Palm Desert, and then: Army Archerd, "Just for Variety," *Daily Variety,* January 14, 1975.

"Bob looked terrible" *and following:* Emanuel Wolf, interview with the author, March 17, 2012.

He explained to Welch that: Raquel Welch, interview with the author, May 9, 2012.

406 At three o'clock that morning, Emanuel *and following:* Emanuel Wolf, interview with the author, March 17, 2012.

TWELVE YEARS

407 "After the heart attack, he was getting": Ann Reinking, interview with the author, November 15, 2010.

"Hal offered in the spirit of": Ira Bernstein, interview with the author, May 17, 2011.

he wondered if they wondered if he: Tony Stevens, interview with the author, February 8, 2011.

"He got winded": Pam Sousa, interview with the author, January 11, 2011.

"That will hold," he would say: Candy Brown, interview with the author, January 7, 2011.

408 "It got creepy": Tony Stevens, interview with the author, February 8, 2011.

"You want me to tell Bob Fosse": Ibid.

"I'm not sure he even wanted to be there": Cheryl Clark, interview with the author, April 19, 2011.

"treat this section like an E. E. Cummings poem": Ibid.

"Bobby doesn't know how he wants" *and following*: Richard Korthaze, interview with the author, March 24, 2011.

"Their love was reinitiated in the": Tony Stevens, interview with the author, February 8, 2011.

409 "They were having a difficult time": John Kander, interview with the author, November 10, 2010.

If everyone runs out on Roxie, Verdon argued: Tony Stevens, interview with the author, February 8, 2011.

"She asked Fosse for it": Ibid.

"She knew": Ibid.

"I thought Bob was like the Emcee": Ibid.

There were two ways to get results, Fosse told: Ann Reinking, interview with the author, November 15, 2010.

"If you ever want anything from anybody": Laurent Giroux, interview with the author, December 13, 2010.

410 "He made Gwen unattractive": Tony Stevens, interview with the author, February 8, 2011.

"That's the great Gwen Verdon": Chita Rivera, interview with the author, February 3, 2011.

"*Chicago* was always cynical but": John Kander, interview with the author, November 10, 2010.

"There was a feeling of tension": Ibid.

411 "I'm walking off the stage": Chita Rivera, interview with the author, February 3, 2011.

"I felt pretty bad about it": "Bob Fosse," *The Dick Cavett Show.*

"Going out of town was": Pam Sousa, interview with the author, January 11, 2011.

were discovered in the alleyway: Tony Stevens, interview with the author, February 8, 2011.

he agonized through every rewrite: John Kander, interview with the author, November 10, 2010.

"Their angsts were not well matched": Tony Stevens, interview with the author, February 8, 2011.

Fosse snapped at him publicly: John Kander, interview with the author, November 10, 2010.

Candy Brown found Ebb in the bathroom: Candy Brown, interview with the author, January 7, 2011.

"Why don't we get on a train": John Kander, interview with the author, November 10, 2010.

"We made a pact": Chita Rivera, interview with the author, February 3, 2011.

412 Fosse was drinking more than usual *and following*: Tony Stevens, interview with the author, February 8, 2011.

413 "I'm afraid this show is my image": Marilyn Stasio, "A Tough 'Chicago' Is Where Bob Fosse Lives," *Cue*, July 7, 1975.

"I'm a target now": Ibid.

"*Chicago* was theater and politics": "Bob Fosse: Steam Heat," *Great Performances: Dance in America*, PBS; first aired February 23, 1990.

"Neil hated it": Greg Lawrence, *Colored Lights: Forty Years of Words and Music, Show Biz, Collaboration, and All That Jazz* (New York: Faber and Faber, 2003), 125.

414 "We were in Philadelphia for": John Kander, interview with the author, November 10, 2010.

After each of the many previews: Tony Stevens, interview with the author, February 8, 2011.

"They were the tiniest things": Chita Rivera, interview with the author, February 3, 2011.

"Come in, honey": Ibid.

415 The phone rang in Cheryl Clark's room *and following*: Cheryl Clark, interview with the author, April 19, 2011.

417 "She was screaming and crying": Tony Stevens, interview with the author, February 8, 2011.

"We had to toe a line": Ibid.

"Bobby was almost embarrassed" *and following*: John Kander, interview with the author, November 10, 2010.

418 "She was standing at the end" *and following*: Chita Rivera, interview with the author, February 3, 2011.

419 "I was sitting at the piano": John Kander, interview with the author, November 10, 2010.

"Bobby, I know what you're doing": Fred Mann III, interview with the author, February 22, 2011.

"Sharing the wealth is a difficult" *and following:* Ann Reinking, interview with the author, November 15, 2010.

420 "choreography and direction burn up": Clive Barnes, "'A Chorus Line,'" *New York Times,* May 22, 1975.

"*A Chorus Line* is a great *concept*": Robert Berkvist, "'This Show Is about the Sheer Joy of Dancing,'" *New York Times,* March 26, 1978.

"They can only buy one hit": Fred Ebb, interviewed by Michael Kantor, March 29, 1999, New York Public Library for the Performing Arts, Theatre on Film and Tape Archive.

"Well, we fooled 'em again": Joe Allen, interview with the author, January 27, 2011.

Gwen arrived in a sequined spaghetti-strap: Chicago opening night party photographs, LOC, box 59A.

Now twelve, she needed a chaperone for: Scott Barnes, interview with the author, January 14, 2012.

421 "I would say it's not a good life": Gaby Rodgers, "Bob Fosse: 'Choreography Is Writing with Your Body,'" *Long Island,* October 1, 1978.

"I'd rather you swallowed": "Bob Fosse: Steam Heat," *Great Performances: Dance in America.*

"one of those shows": Clive Barnes, "Stage: 'Chicago,' Musical Vaudeville," *New York Times,* June 4, 1975.

"It was a steal": Harold Prince, interview with the author, October 6, 2010.

422 Frank Rich saw it: Walter Kerr, "'Chicago' Comes On Like Doomsday," *New York Times,* June 8, 1975; Barnes, "Stage: 'Chicago,' Musical Vaudeville"; Frank Rich, interview with the author, February 6, 2011.

"What happened is [Fosse] saw": Stephen Sondheim, interview with the author, February 15, 2012.

423 "At first Fosse seems to be saying": Stephen Farber, "Bob Fosse's Acid Valentine," *New York Times,* August 3, 1975.

Then Gwen sucked down some of *and following:* Tony Stevens, interview with the author, February 8, 2011.

425 "The cast seems altogether tighter": Clive Barnes, "Liza Minnelli Lends Talents to 'Chicago,'" *New York Times,* August 15, 1975.

producer Martin Richards, who had given: Joyce Haber, "Liza's Last Night: Hamming It Up," *Los Angeles Times,* September 17, 1975.

"Never before": Ibid.

"Good," Fosse said: Tony Stevens, interview with the author, February 8, 2011.

Fosse deliberately led his daughter to all sorts of: Nicole Fosse interview, *Dance in America,* WNET archives, September 6, 1989.

she was named, he liked to say, for: Emory Lewis, "Fosse Can't Get Used to Success," *Sunday Record,* July 8, 1973.

It was the basis for all movement, she told *and following:* Nicole Fosse interview, *Dance in America,* WNET archives, September 6, 1989.

426 Fosse wrote urgently to Lennie Strauss: Bob Fosse/Lennie Strauss correspondence, October 22, 1975, LOC, box 47B.

427 "The black attaché case Fosse carried": Julian Barry, interview with the author, September 6, 2010.

As a boy, Fosse had personally defended: Bob Fosse/Lennie Strauss correspondence.

"Bob was not a multimillionaire": Ken Laub, interview with the author, February 13, 2012.

"We had this jokingly competitive": Charles Grodin, interview with the author, March 7, 2012.

428 A slow and stubborn collaborator: Cynthia Scheider, interview with the author, March 25, 2011.

"Herb said once he'd rather not": Charles Grodin, interview with the author, March 7, 2012.

Sam called Chayefsky, Fosse, and: Craig McKay, interview with the author, February 26, 2011.

"We were Sam's children": Cynthia Scheider, interview with the author, March 25, 2011.

"What do they want from me?" *and following:* Craig McKay, interview with the author, February 26, 2011.

430 Fosse considered borrowing what Ostrow: Stuart Ostrow, *Present at the Creation, Leaping in the Dark, and Going Against the Grain* (New York: Applause, 2006), 82.

Ending was relentless, Hamill explained: Pete Hamill/Bob Fosse correspondence, April 25, 1976, LOC, box 14B.

ELEVEN YEARS

432 "We were pretty sure they were going": Ann Reinking, interview with the author, November 15, 2010.

"It was hell": Tony Stevens, interview with the author, February 8, 2011.

"It was like you start disappearing": Ann Reinking, interview with the author, November 15, 2010.

"Every time they cut back to Bob": Alan Heim, interview with the author, July 22, 2010.

433 "You know she can't act": Scott Barnes, interview with the author, January 14, 2012.

"Being depressed is not a bad thing": Fosse quoted in "Bob Fosse," October 24, 1983, interviewed for William Wolf for NYU's School of Continuing Education

Class, the Filmmakers, New York Public Library for the Performing Arts, William Wolf Film and Theater Interview Collection, 1972–1998.

"He put himself down": Ann Reinking, interview with the author, November 15, 2010.

"What do you think?": Dustin Hoffman, interview with the author, September 13, 2012.

434   Fred Ebb got a call: Greg Lawrence, *Colored Lights: Forty Years of Words and Music, Show Biz, Collaboration, and All That Jazz* (New York: Faber and Faber, 2003), 121–22.

Herb Gardner said when Fosse openly: *All That Jazz*, Herb Gardner interview transcripts, LOC, box 1A.

435   Nicole confessed she knew all about: *All That Jazz*, Nicole Fosse interview transcripts, LOC, box 1A.

Verdon, interviewed by Aurthur, remembered: *All That Jazz*, Gwen Verdon interview transcripts, LOC, box 1A.

Ann admitted that he'd changed: *All That Jazz*, Ann Reinking interview transcripts, LOC, box 1A.

Chayefsky said he was punishing Ann: *All That Jazz*, Paddy Chayefsky interview transcripts, LOC, box 1A.

It's the same story with every girl: Ibid.

He loses them, Paddy said: Ibid.

But, Dr. Sager explained, he let: *All That Jazz*, Clifford Sager interview transcripts, LOC, box 1A.

He wrote to Robert Joffrey in June 1976: Bob Fosse/Robert Joffrey correspondence June 24, 1976, LOC, box 47C.

436   almost a hundred, Fosse claimed: Bernard Drew, "Life as a Long Rehearsal," *American Film*, November 1979.

Using actual names: Draft of *All That Jazz* screenplay, August 3, 1976, LOC, box 1A.

Aurthur wrote a first draft quickly: Betty Spence, "Bob Fosse — He'll Take the Risks," *Los Angeles Times*, May 17, 1981.

437   "Bob Aurthur said that I was crazy": Ibid.

"I've only got one more film": Craig McKay, interview with the author, February 26, 2011.

"He knew he was going": Ibid.

to meet with Melnick: For an in-depth consideration of the producer at home and at work, see David Thomson, "Footloose and Fancy Free," *Film Comment*, May/June 1984.

438   The studio encouraged Melnick to: AMPAS cast and crew reunion screening of *All That Jazz*, the Academy of Motion Picture Arts and Sciences' Samuel Goldwyn Theater, videotaped September 21, 2001.

But Beatty (after his customary): *Los Angeles Herald Examiner,* November 22, 1976.

Nicholson, who took Fosse to: Kathy Witt, interview with the author, May 20, 2011.

read the script and found it surprisingly: Dustin Hoffman, interview with the author, September 13, 2012.

"I think you're wonderful": "Jessica Lange," *Inside the Actors Studio,* Bravo, June 12, 1996.

"He befriended me in a very": Ibid.

"This is a man who did not want": Ann Reinking, interview with the author, November 15, 2010.

"When you think something's about to": Bruce Williamson, "All That Fosse," *Playboy,* March 1980.

439 Angelique, Fosse said, was the one: Roy Scheider commentary, *All That Jazz* (Twentieth Century Fox, 2003), DVD.

"He used to tell people": "Jessica Lange," *Inside the Actors Studio.*

"He assumed she was my girlfriend": Charles Grodin, interview with the author, March 7, 2012.

"Is it good?": Ann Reinking, interview with the author, November 15, 2010.

440 "He was hooked on his stress": Ibid.

"You know what?": Laurent Giroux, interview with the author, December 13, 2010.

"If Bob had a free evening" *and following:* Ken Laub, interview with the author, February 13, 2012.

441 "I think he wanted to prove": Ann Reinking, interview with the author, November 15, 2010.

442 "I don't know what I want" *and following:* Gordon Harrell, interview with the author, February 23, 2011.

444 "He was moving closer": Ann Reinking, interview with the author, November 15, 2010.

he unlocked the studio door *and following:* Nicole Fosse interview, *Dance in America,* WNET archives, September 6, 1989.

445 "Don't dance": Gary Flannery, interview with the author, January 26, 2011.

"I don't want a caricature": Ibid.

"The character of Bojangles never": Gordon Harrell, interview with the author, February 23, 2011.

"It wasn't that we drifted apart": Ann Reinking, interview with the author, November 15, 2010.

Their old arguments, once fought *and following:* Ibid.

446 Chayefsky had been working on *and following:* Shaun Considine, *Mad as Hell: The Life and Work of Paddy Chayefsky* (New York: Random House, 1995), 351.

447 "Our family has never taken death": Chayefsky Funeral Arrangements, New

York Public Library for the Performing Arts, Paddy Chayefsky Papers, box 166, folder 9.

"In 'And All That Jazz'": Susan Stroman, interview with the author, January 14, 2011.

448 After a tech run at Boston's: Carolyn Kirsch, interview with the author, February 11, 2011.

"I wanna smell you girls": Susan Stroman, interview with the author, January 14, 2011.

"You could see his joy": Maxine Glorsky, interview with the author, September 7, 2010.

"It was like applause": Ibid.

"Is he dead?": Carolyn Kirsch, interview with the author, February 11, 2011.

"It scared him": Ibid.

"As soon as we got together": Drew, "Life as a Long Rehearsal."

449 "Sign this or I'll kill you": AMPAS cast and crew reunion screening of *All That Jazz.*

"So what do you think": Gail Benedict, interview with the author, January 6, 2011.

line around the theater for two hours: Christine Colby, interview with the author, March 20, 2011.

for as many as six hours: Ibid.

"He didn't want to see your technique": Ibid.

"We were afraid the show was not": Gail Benedict, interview with the author, January 6, 2011.

450 Jill Cook brought a snake: Blane Savage, interview with the author, February 26, 2011.

"That show's a huge hit": Sandahl Bergman, interview with the author, April 27, 2012.

"Gail": Ibid.

"Everyone was fighting for": Wayne Cilento, interview with the author, January 27, 2011.

451 "He really liked Sandahl": Blane Savage, interview with the author, February 26, 2011.

Savage reasoned that Fosse thought his open: Ibid.

But Bergman didn't take Fosse: Sandahl Bergman, interview with the author, April 27, 2012.

"You know," Fosse said: Ibid.

"looking like a raptor": Blane Savage, interview with the author, February 26, 2011.

"I've really tried to vary my choices": Robert Berkvist, "'This Show Is about the Sheer Joy of Dancing,'" *New York Times,* March 26, 1978.

"One valve is still partially clogged": Ibid.

452 the producers asked the dancers to: Sandahl Bergman, interview with the author, April 27, 2012.

"We were always together on that show": Ibid.

"Everyone was talking about it": Blane Savage, interview with the author, February 26, 2011.

"It was obvious yuk-yuk humor": Christine Colby, interview with the author, March 20, 2011.

453 "It was like he was killing Charles": Don Rebic, interview with the author, February 28, 2011.

Drummer Allen Herman recalled they kept: Allen Herman, interview with the author, March 3, 2011.

"I remember looking at the Trumpet": Christine Colby, interview with the author, March 20, 2011.

rerouted Fosse's dancers: Ibid.

The production hired horse-drawn carriages: Eric Angelson, interview with the author, June 27, 2012.

Stagehands met dancers at the station: Christine Colby, interview with the author, March 20, 2011.

down into the basement, where a strip: Ibid.

454 brought on two more in Boston: Ibid.

"It was absurdly hard": Gail Benedict, interview with the author, January 6, 2011.

for a few *Dancin'* dancers, the only: Name withheld, interview with the author, September 10, 2010.

"We were so tired": Ibid.

"I haven't been asleep for three days": Blane Savage, interview with the author, February 26, 2011.

455 "Don't spend your life at the mall": Diane Duncan, interview with the author, April 9, 2011.

"You look tired": Ibid.

Reinking's relationship with Ward: Ann Reinking, interview with the author, November 15, 2010.

"All she wanted to do was please him" *and following:* Allen Herman, interview with the author, March 3, 2011.

who appeared one day in Boston, dressed: Christine Colby, interview with the author, March 20, 2011.

Months earlier, he had had the idea to: Kevin Kelly, "Fosse, at 58, Finds No Security in Success," *Boston Globe,* February 9, 1986.

"He really knew the way": Jessica Lange, *Inside the Actors Studio.*

456 Suspecting another man in her life, Fosse: Kelly, "Fosse, at 58."

"All of our eyes popped out": Christine Colby, interview with the author, March 20, 2011.

The following day she came late: Blane Savage, interview with the author, February 26, 2011.

"It's not just *your* rehearsal, Annie": Gail Benedict, interview with the author, January 6, 2011.

"René," he said into the hush: Ibid.

"They've forgotten there's a thing": Berkvist, "'This Show Is about the Sheer Joy of Dancing.'"

"Precision and style mark the evening": Richard Eder, "'Dancin', Fosse's Musical, Opens at the Broadhurst," *New York Times,* March 28, 1978.

"Fosse knows his limitations": Arlene Croce, "Broadway Downbeat," *New Yorker,* April 24, 1978.

457 Fosse called Ann Reinking from Payne Whitney *and following*: Ann Reinking, interview with the author, November 15, 2010.

"You can't kill love": Ibid.

Removing sex only nurtured the friendship: Ibid.

"You can't live without trust": Ibid.

NINE YEARS

458 "I want you to do the Gwen" *and following*: Linda Posner (Leland Palmer), interview with the author, July 23, 2010.

459 Reinking he made audition for: Roy Scheider, *All That Jazz* DVD commentary. Fosse ran hundreds of girls: Jennifer Dunning, "Serene Young Hoofer of 'All That Jazz,'" *New York Times,* January 11, 1980.

"You're not going to read a hundred": Larry Mark, interview with the author, September 17, 2010.

Erzsebet Foldi, a twelve-year-old student: Erzsebet Foldi, interview with the author, January 26, 2011.

"Will you light my cigarette?": Ann Reinking, interview with the author, November 15, 2010.

"You got the job": Ibid.

460 He suspected Dreyfuss was talking to: Name withheld, interview with the author, September 10, 2010.

"In my test, they were fighting": Sandahl Bergman, interview with the author, April 27, 2012.

"I can't get up there with": AMPAS cast and crew reunion screening of *All That Jazz.*

461 "I don't think I want to do": Roy Scheider, *All That Jazz* DVD commentary. Then Aurthur told Fosse *and following*: Martin Gottfried, *All His Jazz* (Cambridge, MA: Da Capo, 1998; first published by Bantam in 1990), 374. Citations refer to the Da Capo edition.

Alan Bates?: *All That Jazz* casting correspondence, LOC, box 48A.

462 "I told him all of the silly, wild" *and following:* Roy Scheider, *All That Jazz* DVD commentary.

Shutting down, the crew took: Wolfgang Glattes, interview with the author, November 27, 2010.

Often, Scheider would follow Fosse: Ibid.

"Roy was so committed": Don Rebic, interview with the author, February 28, 2011.

Fosse worked on Scheider's cough: Roy Scheider, *All That Jazz* DVD commentary.

463 "People were dropping like flies": Christine Colby, interview with the author, March 20, 2011.

Wayne Cilento pulled his hamstring: Wayne Cilento, interview with the author, January 27, 2011.

Gail Benedict took a spill: Gail Benedict, interview with the author, January 6, 2011.

Colby had consented to swing: Christine Colby, interview with the author, March 20, 2011.

"[Dancer] Jill Cook would stand": Ibid.

"Any dancer that lasted more": Allen Herman, interview with the author, March 3, 2011.

"It was a free-for-all": Wayne Cilento, interview with the author, January 27, 2011.

464 "I had to drag myself up the railing": Gail Benedict, interview with the author, January 6, 2011.

Those days, a masseur came: Laurent Giroux, interview with the author, December 13, 2010.

"once more, kids, do it once more": Eileen Casey, interview with the author, January 31, 2011.

intended to soften Gideon, as per: AMPAS cast and crew reunion screening of *All That Jazz.*

"What do you think Joe would say" *and following:* Roy Scheider, *All That Jazz* DVD commentary.

466 "Bobby would talk to him throughout": Christopher Newman, interview with the author, September 10, 2010.

He dispatched five cameras to scavenge: Betty Spence, "Bob Fosse — He'll Take the Risks," *Los Angeles Times,* May 17, 1981.

ended up taking seven: Ibid.

"I'm going to do in fifteen minutes": Laurent Giroux, interview with the author, December 13, 2010.

but was basically excluded: Ibid.

"Bob dropped him": Wolfgang Glattes, interview with the author, November 27, 2010.

The biting pain in Aurthur's side persisted: Gottfried, *All His Jazz*, 381.

"He thought Fosse was killing him": Murray Schisgal, interview with the author, September 24, 2012.

strategy meetings with Melnick *and following*: Gottfried, *All His Jazz*, 381.

467　"If I die before Fosse": Paul Rosenfield, "Long, Winding Road of 'Jazz,'" *Los Angeles Times*, January 6, 1980.

Fosse finally visited Aurthur: Gottfried, *All His Jazz*, 381.

he got the news: Ibid.

"[producer] Kenny Utt came in": Jerry Jaffe, interview with the author, February 16, 2011.

Per Aurthur's will, a memorial party: Gottfried, *All His Jazz*, 382.

"Who's going to do yours?": Ibid.

468　"With each movie he got": Wolfgang Glattes, interview with the author, November 27, 2010.

"Fosse had nobody looking out for him": Lynn Lovett, interview with the author, February 17, 2011.

"Wolf and Kathryn were his caretakers": Ibid.

"His favorite was the hip operation": Wolfgang Glattes, interview with the author, November 27, 2010.

"What is it like if you've been through": Roy Scheider, *All That Jazz* DVD commentary.

"I was surprised" *and following*: Nancy Bird, interview with the author, February 16, 2011.

469　"I'd say more than fifty percent of": Christopher Newman, interview with the author, September 10, 2010.

Cast and crew buses left Columbus Circle: Jerry Jaffe, interview with the author, February 16, 2011.

"At seven o'clock": Lynn Lovett, interview with the author, February 17, 2011.

470　"Dailies are for work, not for popcorn": Ibid.

"Peppino, what would Fellini do here?": Bob Fosse/Federico Fellini correspondence, May 15, 1981, LOC, box 49A.

"No one was even allowed to laugh": Lynn Lovett, interview with the author, February 17, 2011.

shooting ratios of twenty to one: Alan Heim, interview with the author, July 22, 2010.

"It made it difficult to move": Ibid.

"At times, Alan felt like he was": Wende Phifer, interview with the author, February 15, 2011.

471　"a process of slowly waking up" *and following*: David Ray, interview with the author, March 25, 2011.

"There's no dress rehearsal for life" *and following*: Wende Phifer, interview with the author, February 15, 2011.

mostly unchanged since the forties: "Billion Dollar Backlot," *All That Jazz* press release, Twentieth Century Fox.

Danny Ruvolo, originally cast in the part: "Danny Ruvolo, 22, in Car Crash; Danced in 'Chorus Line,' 'Rex,'" *New York Times*, November 22, 1978.

he was incredibly nervous the day of the shoot *and following*: Keith Gordon interview, http://sensesofcinema.com/2004/feature-articles/keith_gordon/.

472 "That's exactly what it was like": Wende Phifer, interview with the author, February 15, 2011.

473 "What's going on here?": Christopher Newman, interview with the author, September 10, 2010.

"Hey, could you do this role" *and following*: John Lithgow, interview with the author, August 9, 2010.

474 There was no time to skip shooting: Lynn Lovett, interview with the author, February 17, 2011.

475 "This was Friday night" *and following*: Cheryl Clark, interview with the author, April 19, 2011.

476 Fosse called Sandahl Bergman *and following*: Sandahl Bergman, interview with the author, April 27, 2012.

vowing to an incredulous Albert Wolsky that each would: Albert Wolsky, interview with the author, August 11, 2010.

"I'd like to call up Danny Melnick" *and following*: Sandahl Bergman, interview with the author, April 27, 2012.

477 "Columbia was kind of": Frank Price, interview with the author, February 26, 2013.

"By the time the [*All That Jazz*] budget reached": Rosenfield, "Long, Winding Road of 'Jazz.'"

"We can't have this thing going up": Frank Price, interview with the author, February 26, 2013.

478 This was seven days: Rosenfield, "Long, Winding Road of 'Jazz.'"

"I thought Bobby was going to": Roy Scheider, *All That Jazz* DVD commentary.

Assemble the picture: Bernard Drew, "Life as a Long Rehearsal," *American Film*, November 1979.

"Are we supposed to stop production": Ibid.

"Excuse me for a second" *and following*: AMPAS cast and crew reunion screening of *All That Jazz*.

479 "Dan Melnick called" *and following*: Alan Heim, interview with the author, July 22, 2010.

drove directly to Alan Ladd Jr. *and following*: Alan Ladd Jr., interview with the author, June 7, 2010.

480 "You're out of the picture": AMPAS cast and crew reunion screening of *All That Jazz*.

Who got which was decided by: Alan Ladd Jr., interview with the author, June 7, 2010.

had to work as the final number: Vincent LoBrutto, *By Design: Interviews with Production Designers* (New York: Praeger, 1992), 126–27.

481 sent Walton and Phil Rosenberg back to: Ibid.

"It was getting quite frightening": AMPAS cast and crew reunion screening of *All That Jazz.*

In came yards and yards of: LoBrutto, *By Design,* 126.

Crouched behind the bleachers: Lynn Lovett, interview with the author, February 17, 2011.

Peppino, taking Fosse's quiet to mean: Ibid.

"Where's Peppino?": Ibid.

"Peppino was a gentleman": David Ray, interview with the author, March 25, 2011.

482 Peppino and Lovett admired an entombed: Lynn Lovett, interview with the author, February 17, 2011.

"That's the same shot": Ibid.

The incarcerated dubbed themselves Prisoners *and following:* John Lithgow, interview with the author, August 9, 2010.

Doby advocated for replacements *and following:* Kathryn Doby, interview with the author, November 27, 2010.

Albert Wolsky put a rush on their costumes: Albert Wolsky, interview with the author, August 11, 2010.

483 "Bob started changing things": Kathryn Doby, interview with the author, November 27, 2010.

"Fifteen days": Wolfgang Glattes, interview with the author, November 27, 2010.

"It was the hardest physical thing" *and following:* Roy Scheider, *All That Jazz* DVD commentary.

"Maybe somebody will say": Leslie Bennetts, "Bob Fosse — Dancing with Danger," *New York Times,* April 6, 1986.

484 "You know, that must be kind of exhilarating" *and following:* Roy Scheider, Bob Fosse Memorial, Palace Theater, October 30, 1987, New York Public Library for the Performing Arts, Theatre on Film and Tape Archive.

EIGHT YEARS

485 Aside from the pirouettes *and following:* Wende Phifer, interview with the author, February 15, 2011.

"It was a life": Alan Heim, interview with the author, July 22, 2010.

"It wasn't the movie's fault": David Ray, interview with the author, March 25, 2011.

"The set dresser [Phil Rosenberg] had": Alan Heim, interview with the author, July 22, 2010.

486 "All those years and all that work": Bernard Drew, "Life as a Long Rehearsal," *American Film,* November 1979.

"I just want to run through": Wende Phifer, interview with the author, February 15, 2011.

"He would make small talk": David Ray, interview with the author, March 25, 2011.

"I still have one artery partially clogged": Martin Burden, "Fosse Lights Up," *New York Post,* November 14, 1979.

"If you stay on the beat": Alan Heim, interview with the author, July 22, 2010.

487 "Gwen was trying to make it": Kathryn Doby, interview with the author, November 27, 2010.

"That's not how we used to do": Gail Benedict, interview with the author, January 6, 2011.

"Gwen was obviously territorial": Name withheld, interview with the author, September 10, 2010.

Fosse attributed partially to discomania: Laurent Giroux, interview with the author, December 13, 2010.

"I'd want to see your quick changes": Blane Savage, interview with the author, February 6, 2011.

"When I film the section when Charles": Wayne Cilento, interview with the author, January 27, 2011.

"I'd never do that to a dancer again": Laurent Giroux, interview with the author, December 13, 2010.

"That put the fear of God in us" *and following:* Bill Hastings, interview with the author, January 8, 2011.

489 "He got introverted when he was": John Sowinski, interview with the author, February 1, 2011.

"Normally, we'd be relaxed": Bill Hastings, interview with the author, January 8, 2011.

"There's a section" *and following:* Michael Tronick, interview with the author, March 22, 2011.

490 "He wanted to be the victim": Greg Lawrence, *Colored Lights: Forty Years of Words and Music, Show Biz, Collaboration, and All That Jazz* (New York: Faber and Faber, 2003), 122.

"It was all about Bobby pretending": Ibid., 120.

"When I saw it, I was devastated": Gordon Harrell, interview with the author, February 23, 2011.

"What do you think?": Ben Vereen, interview with the author, January 11, 2011.

"He felt guilty about some of" *and following:* Ann Reinking, interview with the author, November 15, 2010.

491 A private screening for Gwen, Nicole *and following:* Chris Chase, "Fosse's Ego Trip," *Life,* November 1979.

"I can't walk into one of those": Ibid.

"Bobby had this boyish charm and enthusiasm": Sherry Lansing, interview with the author, July 22, 2010.

492 a math teacher before she became: Aljean Harmetz, "Sherry Lansing, Former Model, Named Head of Fox Productions," *New York Times,* January 2, 1980.

"Bob's in the bathroom" *and following:* Sherry Lansing, interview with the author, July 22, 2010.

"I really think Bob Fosse thought": Lynn Lovett, interview with the author, February 17, 2011.

turned on the TV and disappeared again *and following:* Chase, "Fosse's Ego Trip."

"Julie seemed depressed": Lynn Lovett, interview with the author, February 17, 2011.

While Janice Lynde was in town *and following:* Janice Lynde, interview with the author, May 4, 2011.

493 "Tragic," he replied: NewsCenter 4, NBC, February 28, 1980.

494 "Of all the shows you've done": David Sheehan, interview with the author, July 23, 2012.

495 got a standing ovation *and following:* Sherry Lansing, interview with the author, July 22, 2010.

SEVEN YEARS

497 "Gwen was careful with her" *and following:* Chris Chase, "Fosse's Ego Trip," *Life,* November 1979.

"That's the future": *All That Jazz,* Clifford Sager interview transcripts, LOC, box 1A.

498 On weekends, they drove out to Quogue *and following:* Nicole Fosse interview, *Dance in America,* WNET archives, September 6, 1989.

He considered, again, doing a full ballet: Army Archerd, "Just for Variety," *Daily Variety,* December 21, 1979.

Atlantic City, Cy Coleman's idea: Carol Lawson, "Broadway," *New York Times,* January 11, 1980.

interest from Liza Minnelli and Goldie Hawn: Martin Gottfried, *All His Jazz* (Cambridge, MA: Da Capo, 1998; first published by Bantam in 1990), 351.

"Besides": Kenneth L. Geist, "Fosse Reflects on Fosse," *After Dark,* February 1980.

499 "the need for attention": Bob Fosse/Clifford Sager correspondence June 2, 1980, LOC, box 48B.

Fosse met with writer Jack Heifner *and following:* Jack Heifner, interview with the author, June 25, 2012.

500 Fosse and Sam Cohn invested in the Laundry *and following*: Susan Anderson, interview with the author, January 14, 2013.
"Bob always needed to be around writers" *and following*: E. L. Doctorow, interview with the author, May 5, 2012.
Lunches consisted of big bowls: Cynthia Scheider, interview with the author, March 25, 2011.
501 "I didn't buy Bobby's dark-guy thing": Ibid.
Fosse was in the Winter Garden opening night: Carolyn Kirsch, interview with the author, February 11, 2011.
Merrick, they had been told, would have: Marie Brenner, "Like No Business I Know," *New York,* September 8, 1980.
"I'm sorry to have to report": Cliff Jahr, "'42nd Street' Log — the Making of a Hit," *New York Times*, September 7, 1980.
502 No one but the family: John Anthony Gilvey, *Before the Parade Passes By: Gower Champion and the Glorious American Musical* (New York: St. Martin's Press, 2005), 297.
Jammed that night with the likes of Fosse: Brenner, "Like No Business I Know."
"There were so many rumors that": Carolyn Kirsch, interview with the author, February 11, 2011.
"That night my sons told me": Marge Champion, interview with the author, August 24, 2011.
"That son of a bitch": Lee Roy Reams, Theater Production Workshop Dialogue Series Features *Sweet Charity,* Marymount Manhattan College, March 15, 2011.
"Why would I do that?": Gail Benedict, interview with the author, January 6, 2011.
That summer, Fosse wrote to him *and following*: Bob Fosse/Jerome Robbins correspondence, July 25, 1980, Jerome Robbins Papers, box 507, Jerome Robbins Dance Division, the New York Library for the Performing Arts.
503 Reading, at Paddy's suggestion: Roderick Mann, "Bob Fosse — Writing 'Star 80' Was Easy, Filming It Wasn't," *Los Angeles Times,* November 13, 1983.
Stratten reminded him of his younger self: Ann Reinking, interview with the author, November 15, 2010.
"That girl could make me a lot of money": Teresa Carpenter, "Death of a Playmate," *Village Voice,* November 5, 1980.
"It was all too big for him": Ibid.
504 "I somehow identified with him": Barry Rehfeld, "Bob Fosse's Follies," *Rolling Stone,* January 19, 1984.
underlining gruesome specifics in red pen: Dorothy Ruth Hoogstraten autopsy report, case number 658824, filed August 25, 1980, Los Angeles Superior Court.
Teresa Carpenter led Fosse to public documents: Teresa Carpenter/Bob Fosse correspondence, LOC, box 31C.
It came easier than expected: Mann, "Bob Fosse — Writing 'Star 80' Was Easy."

505 "You don't need another writer": Ibid.

"What are you going to do about anything?" *and following:* Ronald Davis Oral History October 17, 1979, Academy of Motion Picture Arts and Sciences' Margaret Herrick Library.

506 Paddy was back in the hospital with pleurisy: Shaun Considine, *Mad as Hell: The Life and Work of Paddy Chayefsky* (New York: Random House, 1995), 392.

Herb's Christmas dinner party, an epic *and following:* Pamela Larsson-Toscher, interview with the author, February 14, 2011.

I don't have the answers, he would say: Miscellaneous correspondence, LOC, box 47A.

507 Fosse took over a corner of the River Café *and following:* Considine, *Mad as Hell,* 393.

"It was a very funny situation": Ibid.

"So people can come in and": Laurent Giroux, interview with the author, December 13, 2010.

508 "the first time a work of such scope": Lee Margulies, "'Pippin' to Bypass Normal Channels, Due on Pay TV," *Los Angeles Times,* June 6, 1981.

Fosse rushed to the phone a day before: David Sheehan, interview with the author, July 23, 2012.

Sheehan sent a jet to Quogue: Ibid.

The weekend Roy and Cynthia Scheider came *and following:* Cynthia Scheider, interview with the author, March 25, 2011.

509 Paddy would fake bad death scenes *and following:* Considine, *Mad as Hell,* 395.

"He wasn't conscious": Ibid., 396.

"Are you okay?": Janice Lynde, interview with the author, May 4, 2011.

510 An estimated five hundred people came: Herbert Mitgang, "Chayefsky Praised for Passion in Exposing Life's Injustices," *New York Times,* August 5, 1981.

"I kept looking for Bob before": Lionel Larner, interview with the author, January 25, 2012.

when Mr. Weaver died: Charles Grass, interview with the author, September 4, 2012.

511 "Then I saw him": Lionel Larner, interview with the author, January 25, 2012.

"the corrupt and lunatic energies": Mitgang, "Chayefsky Praised for Passion."

"When his turn came": James Lipton, *Inside Inside* (New York: Dutton, 2007), 150.

"As most of you know, Paddy and I": Ibid., 150–51. See also "Soft-Shoe Tribute at a Playwright's Funeral: Chayefsky Mourned with Laughter and Dance," *Los Angeles Times,* August 5, 1981.

"It was a very quiet dance for about": E. L. Doctorow, interview with the author, May 5, 2012.

512 Fosse had drifted from the circle to: Gottfried, *All His Jazz,* 406.

SIX YEARS

513 he didn't want to see: Martin Gottfried, *All His Jazz* (Cambridge, MA: Da Capo, 1998; first published by Bantam in 1990), 409. Citations refer to the Da Capo edition.

"Whatever he wanted to do": Alan Ladd Jr., interview with the author, June 7, 2010.

"On those occasions": Ibid.

514 back-and-forths of rights and releases hobbled: Rosenfeld, Meyer and Susman/Jay Kanter correspondence, August 31, 1981, LOC, box 31B.

Fosse was also required to provide documentation: Ibid.

He reluctantly agreed to use close-ups: Bob Fosse/Jay Kanter correspondence, October 27, 1981, LOC, box 31B.

sending him tapes, which Fosse flatly hated: Kathryn Doby, interview with the author, November 27, 2010.

"You're cutting off the feet!" *and following:* David Sheehan, interview with the author, July 23, 2012.

515 "foolishly butchered version of the show": Bob Fosse/*Pippin* cast correspondence, November 23, 1981, collection of Kathryn Doby.

Mariel Hemingway, a Cohn client, was desperate to: Mariel Hemingway, interview with the author, May 30, 2011.

Cohn encouraged Fosse to give her a shot: Phoebe Ungerer, interview with the author, December 13, 2012.

He liked Melanie Griffith: Ibid.

"You must read me": Mariel Hemingway, interview with the author, May 30, 2011.

Hemingway turned up in New York: Ibid.

But breast size was a problem: Susan Anderson, interview with the author, January 14, 2013.

Instinct told Hemingway this exchange was *and following:* Mariel Hemingway, interview with the author, May 30, 2011.

516 The studio answered with Richard Gere: Eric Roberts, interview with the author, May 7, 2012.

"That fucked him up": Mariel Hemingway, interview with the author, May 30, 2011.

Sam Shepard came to his audition *and following:* Cis Rundle, interview with the author, July 21, 2011.

517 Eric Roberts fielded Fosse's interview questions *and following:* Eric Roberts, interview with the author, May 7, 2012.

"He gave me everything": Mariel Hemingway, interview with the author, May 30, 2011.

518 "I'm going to die in one of these places": Gottfried, *All His Jazz,* 412.

"On *Star 80* he was just impossible" *and following:* Wolfgang Glattes, interview with the author, November 27, 2010.

519 "He had this incredible ability": Lynne Carrow, interview with the author, December 10, 2010.

Fosse scouted Vancouver in a fifteen-passenger: David Rose, interview with the author, December 10, 2010.

"Bob," he asked: Ibid.

He had met her at a Westhampton Beach bar: Gottfried, *All His Jazz,* 414.

520 Fosse gave her a job working for Alan Heim: Alan Heim, interview with the author, July 22, 2010.

In the meantime, back in New York, they: Ken Laub, interview with the author, February 13, 2012.

"I'm going to go out there": E. L. Doctorow, interview with the author, May 5, 2012.

FIVE YEARS

521 gave only a few notes, and left before *and following:* Brett Raphael, interview with the author, July 23, 2012.

"This piece is dressed and lit": Mindy Aloff, untitled copy, September 27, 1982.

522 Glattes took charge of screen tests in LA: Bob Fosse/Wolfgang Glattes correspondence, April 2, 1982, LOC, box 35A.

"We have to use the same carpet": Wolfgang Glattes, interview with the author, November 27, 2010.

"It was like none of his successes": E. L. Doctorow, interview with the author, May 5, 2012.

Fosse insisted every bookcase on their: Mel Cooper, interview with the author, February 4, 2011.

"It was just a movie": Ann Reinking, interview with the author, November 15, 2010.

Fosse had the crew dress Snider's former *and following:* Mel Cooper, interview with the author, February 4, 2011.

523 Each "room" marked off on the floor: Eric Roberts, interview with the author, May 7, 2012.

"Start the movie": Tony Gittelson, interview with the author, November 19, 2010.

"It was *all* choreographed": Mariel Hemingway, interview with the author, May 30, 2011.

"It was so painful to work on": Albert Wolsky, interview with the author, August 11, 2010.

524 "Cis," he said *and following:* Cis Rundle, interview with the author, July 21, 2011.

"It was like sounds were too loud": Mariel Hemingway, interview with the author, May 30, 2011.

One day he angrily cleared the set, only: Mel Cooper, interview with the author, February 4, 2011.

"I'd say, 'Hey, Bob'": Lynne Carrow, interview with the author, December 10, 2010.

"Everyone was all over him about": Eric Roberts, interview with the author, May 7, 2012.

Dorothy's sister Louise sent Fosse: Louise Hoogstraten/Bob Fosse correspondence, LOC, box 35A.

Fosse professed to be overcome with guilt: Bob Fosse/Louise Hoogstraten correspondence, LOC, box 35A.

"I'm living in a world where nobody": Ann Reinking, interview with the author, November 15, 2010.

525　He regularly placed a rose bouquet: Cis Rundle, interview with the author, July 21, 2011.

"He's going to do it": Cliff Robertson, interview with the author, September 28, 2010.

"He lied about everything": Name withheld, interview with the author, September 10, 2010.

He appeared in the production office in: Grace Blake, interview with the author, May 10, 2011.

"Eric was so volatile": Name withheld, interview with the author, September 10, 2010.

Without warning, Fosse would show up: Eric Roberts, interview with the author, May 7, 2012.

Fosse asked him to remove the protective: Mariel Hemingway, interview with the author, May 30, 2011.

"[Roberts] got so into it": Tom Hinckley and Kevin Gault, "Bob Fosse," *Cable Guide*, November 1984.

526　"What the fuck is wrong with you?" *and following*: Eric Roberts, interview with the author, May 7, 2012.

527　"We were all afraid of it": Alan Heim, interview with the author, July 22, 2010.

To the music of Strauss's *Death and Transfiguration*: Michael Blowen, "Will Gritty 'Star 80' Glitter at the Box Office?," *Boston Globe*, November 6, 1983.

"It was ballet": Tony Gittelson, interview with the author, November 19, 2010.

Fosse talked them through every movement: Alan Ladd Jr., interview with the author, June 7, 2010.

factions of the crew actually placed bets: Mel Cooper, interview with the author, February 4, 2011.

Roberts broke into Cis Rundle's house *and following*: Cis Rundle, interview with the author, July 21, 2011.

528　"We didn't butt heads": Alan Heim, interview with the author, July 22, 2010.

"I tried to make it like a musical": Barry Rehfeld, "Bob Fosse's Follies," *Rolling Stone,* January 19, 1984.

529 "It's just possible that the Broadway musical": Frank Rich, "Where Are the New Musicals?," *New York Times,* July 12, 1981.

"There is not the same kind of intelligence": Margaret Croyden, "The Box-Office Boom," *New York Times,* May 10, 1981.

The summer of 1980 was Broadway's biggest ever: Ibid.

530 "I see shows having more special effects": Linda Winer, "Shade of Bob Fosse Raised by 'Chicago,'" *Newsday,* November 22, 1996.

"I think he felt like that victory": Tony Stevens, interview with the author, February 8, 2011.

531 Some nights, after leaving *and following*: Martin Gottfried, *All His Jazz* (Cambridge, MA: Da Capo, 1998; first published by Bantam in 1990), 421. Citations refer to the Da Capo edition.

"tell me about Paddy": Ibid.

Fosse asked Reinking to marry him *and following*: Ann Reinking, interview with the author, November 15, 2010.

FOUR YEARS

532 "It was about fumblers trying": Leslie Bennetts, "Bob Fosse — Dancing with Danger," *New York Times,* April 6, 1986.

maybe Peter Allen would do the songs and: Miscellaneous correspondence, LOC, box 8B.

The afternoon Michael Jackson *and following*: Janice Lynde, interview with the author, May 4, 2011.

He stayed up nights calling his advisers: Nancy Griffin, "The 'Thriller Diaries,'" *Vanity Fair,* July 2010.

533 they decided to try "Thriller": Ibid.

"You've changed the face of dance": Janice Lynde, interview with the author, May 4, 2011.

"because he's so fast": Cynthia Scheider, interview with the author, March 25, 2011.

he had amassed a complete collection: Phoebe Ungerer, interview with the author, December 13, 2012.

Jackson asked to speak with Fosse alone: Janice Lynde, interview with the author, May 4, 2011.

"I'll see you at the apartment": Ibid.

534 "the whole front row walked out": Alan Heim, interview with the author, July 22, 2010.

But Fosse didn't make any significant changes: Ibid.

"I was not thinking": Alan Ladd Jr., interview with the author, June 7, 2010.

refusing to part with or even trim *and following:* Rick Shaine, interview with the author, July 11, 2012.

536 "If you've turned to writing": E. L. Doctorow, interview with the author, May 5, 2012.

They settled on three rules: Ibid.

"All I wanted to master was that dance": Pete Hamill, Bob Fosse Memorial, Palace Theater, October 30, 1987, New York Public Library for the Performing Arts, Theatre on Film and Tape Archive.

537 Doctorow found a package at his front door: E. L. Doctorow, interview with the author, May 5, 2012.

Real writers, Fosse told Peter Maas: Peter Maas, Bob Fosse Memorial, Palace Theater, October 30, 1987, New York Public Library for the Performing Arts, Theatre on Film and Tape Archive.

"Living his entire life in show business": E. L. Doctorow, interview with the author, May 5, 2012.

Fosse gave *Star 80*'s benefit premiere as: Fred Ferretti, "The Evening Hours," *New York Times*, March 1, 1985.

"Constant rejection can be devastating": Ibid.

Schickel, Siskel: Richard Schickel, "A Centerfold Tragedy of Manners," *Time*, November 14, 1983; "The Best of 1983," *At the Movies with Gene Siskel and Roger Ebert*, Tribune Entertainment, 1983.

"Fosse has served up a smorgasbord": Andrew Sarris, "The Pimp and the Simp," *Village Voice*, November 15, 1983.

538 "Fosse must believe that he can make": Pauline Kael, "The Perfectionist," *New Yorker*, November 28, 1983.

"He took to the woods": Alan Heim, interview with the author, July 22, 2010.

"He really thought he was going to win": Wolfgang Glattes, interview with the author, November 27, 2010.

"I didn't work for years after that": Mariel Hemingway, interview with the author, May 30, 2011.

"I found it very strange": Teresa Carpenter, interview with the author, July 23, 2010.

539 "You really understood this": Ann Reinking, interview with the author, November 15, 2010.

THREE YEARS

540 he exchanged for a plain brown home: Jay Sears, interview with the author, February 16, 2012.

He paneled the garage with mirrors: Phoebe Ungerer, interview with the author, December 13, 2012.

"It's painful for me to go": R. E. Krieger, "People in the News," *Hartford Courant,* January 4, 1984.

541 Contentious and expansive, Budd was: Phoebe Ungerer, interview with the author, December 13, 2012.

"For some reason when you get older": Tom Hinckley and Kevin Gault, "Bob Fosse," *Cable Guide,* November 1984.

He found a mangled stray cat: Pete Hamill, "Fosse," *Piecework* (Boston: Little, Brown, 1996).

He called Doctorow in the middle of the night: E. L. Doctorow, interview with the author, May 5, 2012.

"It's generally tough": Hinckley and Gault, "Bob Fosse."

"I saw it": Bruce Jay Friedman, interview with the author, August 20, 2012.

542 Cohn never made his clients sign *and following:* Susan Anderson, interview with the author, January 14, 2013.

"Sam would lecture": Sigourney Weaver, interview with the author, August 19, 2012.

"He couldn't believe": Susan Anderson, interview with the author, January 14, 2013.

Chayefsky was among: Tom Bierbaum, "ATAS Inducts Seven into Hall of Fame," *Daily Variety,* January 23, 1984.

543 "This is a very fickle business": Shaun Considine, *Mad as Hell: The Life and Work of Paddy Chayefsky* (New York: Random House, 1995), 399.

he threw the Doctorows a dinner party *and following:* E. L. Doctorow, interview with the author, May 5, 2012.

"He actually interrogated my parents": Deborah Geffner, interview with the author, October 1, 2010.

"He was the ultimate host": Laurent Giroux, interview with the author, December 13, 2010.

544 He put out cigarettes, and when: Ibid.

"Come on, we're going to do": Ibid.

Bob and Phoebe met at one of Doctorow's garden parties *and following:* Phoebe Ungerer, interview with the author, December 13, 2012.

TWO YEARS

547 establish a theatrical scholarship: "Fosse Leaves Money for Scholarship, Friends Dinner," Associated Press, October 3, 1987.

548 Budgeted at five million and paid for: Carol Ilson, *Harold Prince: A Director's Journey* (New York: Limelight, 2000), 328.

One of the Shuberts, Bernie Jacobs, eased Prince: Ibid., 332.

"It became for me the most painful": Ibid.

"Bob didn't throw out the choreography": Valarie Pettiford, interview with the author, February 2, 2011.

"Mike, do you think we have": Mike Berkowitz, interview with the author, March 1, 2011.

549 "The interlude gives rueful life": Frank Rich, "Stage: 'Grind,' from Harold Prince," *New York Times,* April 17, 1985.

Big Deal, he said to Vereen: Ben Vereen, interview with the author, January 11, 2011.

550 in three minutes, and over the phone: E. L. Doctorow, interview with the author, May 5, 2012.

"the worst migraine you've had" *and following:* Samuel G. Freedman, "How an Uneasy Alliance Helps Shape Broadway," *New York Times,* April 1, 1984.

"He knew there was never going": Gordon Harrell, interview with the author, February 23, 2011.

Fosse's bank statements had lost a certain something: Ibid.

"Gwen had a photographic memory": Ann Reinking, interview with the author, November 15, 2010.

551 Fosse took his seat beside Gwen and: Dana Moore, interview with the author, February 11, 2011.

552 "She was going through everything Charity was": Jane Lanier, interview with the author, February 10, 2011.

"Fosse just sort of sat there" *and following:* Dana Moore, interview with the author, February 11, 2011.

Fosse slid next to Mimi Quillin: Mimi Quillin, interview with the author, February 2, 2011.

"I know that people think it's strange": Gwen Verdon interview, *Dance in America,* WNET archives, September 6, 1989.

553 "Don't go to them, make them": Dana Moore, interview with the author, February 11, 2011.

it had from the beginning: Carol Alt, interview with the author, April 1, 2011.

"It's awful!": Mimi Quillin, interview with the author, February 2, 2011.

"It was like a fight was going to": Ibid.

Fosse asked Allen to run it again *and following:* Carol Alt, interview with the author, April 1, 2011.

554 "God, I can't do this": Mimi Quillin, interview with the author, February 2, 2011.

"Well, I'm probably not going to": Ibid.

"It used to get a little ugly": Janice Arkatov, "Rupert Is at Home in 'Charity,'" *Los Angeles Times,* July 27, 1985.

"Everyone seems a little younger": Dan Sullivan, "Stage Review: Allen Puts Sweetness Back in 'Charity,'" *Los Angeles Times,* July 22, 1985.

While on *Sweet Charity*, dancer Tanis Michaels: Fred Mann III, interview with the author, February 22, 2011.

"We didn't know what was happening": Donna McKechnie, interview with the author, October 14, 2010.

555 "By the time I was thirty-nine years old": James Horvath, interview with the author, January 14, 2011.

Afraid for their own safety and feeling guilty: Name withheld, interview with the author, September 10, 2010.

"Cast members would drink out of Budweiser": Dann Dulin, "Bebe Neuwirth Moves Through Life Helping Others," *A&U*, December 2011.

"He would come back the next day": Jane Lanier, interview with the author, February 10, 2011.

Michaels was given three months to live, but: Ibid.

"Because Bob said yes to Tanis": Fred Mann III, interview with the author, February 22, 2011.

Six months before he began casting: Gordon Harrell, interview with the author, February 23, 2011.

556 "We used six synthesizers in the pit": Phil Ramone, interview with the author, October 10, 2010.

"Even though the unions were against it": Ibid.

He put speakers in the back: Ibid.

"I want the dissolves and softness": Kevin Kelly, "Fosse, at 58, Finds No Security in Success," *Boston Sunday Globe*, February 9, 1986.

557 "*Big Deal* turned people against him": Tony Stevens, interview with the author, February 8, 2011.

"At a certain point I feel": Kevin Kelly, "Bob Fosse's New 'Big Deal,'" *New York*, April 7, 1986.

as many as eight hundred others sang and danced: Ibid.

"If you know a dancer that's a little off": Valarie Pettiford, interview with the author, February 2, 2011.

558 The only comparable rehearsal venue still in use was: "The Minskoff Studio Closing Over Rent," *New York Times*, June 15, 1989.

a heart ailment reportedly forced Bennett: Jeremy Gerard, "Michael Bennett, Theater Innovator, Dies at 44," *New York Times*, July 3, 1987.

Beset with sciatica, Fosse rehearsed: Kelly, "Bob Fosse's New 'Big Deal.'"

"I can hardly move": Kelly, "Fosse, at 58, Finds No Security in Success."

"He had such a big principal cast": Diana Laurenson, interview with the author, January 17, 2011.

but never before had he titled a notebook: LOC, box 11B.

559 "The ensemble didn't know what": Stephanie Pope Caffey, interview with the author, March 1, 2011.

his back went out and he was carried: Ibid.

"Candy," he said: Candy Brown, interview with the author, January 7, 2011.

"It's an absolute nightmare": Bob Fosse, May 18, 1986, interview with Kevin Boyd Grubb, LOC, audiocassette.

Maneuvering over sixty microphones: Ibid.

Herb Gardner kindly encouraged Fosse to: Herb Gardner/Bob Fosse correspondence, LOC, box 8B.

Neil Simon came to Boston to write: Gordon Harrell, interview with the author, February 23, 2011.

"If it's a screw-up": Kelly, "Fosse, at 58, Finds No Security in Success."

"I've made a tremendous amount of changes": Larry Katz, "Fosse's Big Gamble," *Boston Herald,* February 28, 1986.

560 "Could you possibly choreograph": Gerald Schoenfeld/Bob Fosse correspondence, March 19, 1986, LOC, box 8B.

Fosse was too outraged to parse them: Phoebe Ungerer, interview with the author, December 13, 2012.

"I don't think they like it": Diana Laurenson, interview with the author, January 17, 2011.

"People are telling me it's too dark": Don Rebic, interview with the author, February 28, 2012.

"What do you think we should do": Wayne Cilento, interview with the author, January 27, 2011.

Fosse had been unwell for months: Phoebe Ungerer, interview with the author, December 13, 2012.

561 "Fosse makes a sudden gesture": Kelly, "Fosse, at 58, Finds No Security in Success."

"He was in a hyperactive frenzy" *and following:* Dan Wilensky, interview with the author, October 2, 2010.

"What if it isn't any good?": Chet Walker, interview with the author, December 22, 2010.

ONE YEAR

563 "The party after was not a pleasant experience": Alan Heim, interview with the author, July 22, 2010.

"If for only 10 minutes or so": Frank Rich, "Theater: 'Big Deal,' from Bob Fosse," *New York Times,* April 11, 1986.

"ultimate Fosse, a minestrone of everything": Kathryn Doby, interview with the author, November 27, 2010.

"I heard about a couple of reviews": Kevin Grubb, "Fosse and His Followers," *Dance Magazine,* August 1986.

564 "He *loved* that show": Ann Reinking, interview with the author, November 15, 2010.

"*Big Deal* was ahead of its time": Kathryn Doby, interview with the author, November 27, 2010.

"What he did was compose a folk opera": E. L. Doctorow, Bob Fosse Memorial, Palace Theater, October 30, 1987, New York Public Library for the Performing Arts, Theatre on Film and Tape Archive.

565 to find the notice had been posted: Wayne Cilento, interview with the author, January 27, 2011.

Gwen came with Nicole and handfuls *and following*: Grubb, "Fosse and His Followers."

"You know how show folks are": Kevin Boyd Grubb, *Razzle Dazzle: The Life and Work of Bob Fosse* (New York: St. Martin's Press, 1989), 263.

566 found themselves at the front of the house, lingering: Valarie Pettiford, interview with the author, February 2, 2011.

"I wanted to make you all stars": Loretta Devine, interview with the author, November 19, 2010.

Sam Cohn arranged for the writer Michael Herr *and following*: Michael Herr, interview with the author, April 13, 2011.

567 Herr began his outline with *and following*: Michael Herr, *Winchell* (New York: Knopf, 1989).

568 "I changed my mind" *and following*: Michael Herr, interview with the author, April 13, 2011.

Phoebe could see Fosse extricating: Phoebe Ungerer, interview with the author, December 13, 2012.

He could spend afternoons sketching: Ibid.

569 Martin Richards approached him: Martin Gottfried, *All His Jazz* (Cambridge, MA: Da Capo, 1998; first published by Bantam in 1990), 447. Citations refer to the Da Capo edition.

Sam had been pushing it: Phoebe Ungerer, interview with the author, December 13, 2012.

he considered filming *Dreamgirls:* Ann Reinking, interview with the author, November 15, 2010.

and thought of doing *The Vampire Lestat and following*: Phoebe Ungerer, interview with the author, December 13, 2012.

"It's a strange paradox": Tom Hinckley and Kevin Gault, "Bob Fosse," *Cable Guide,* November 1984.

Despite his reservations *and following*: Phoebe Ungerer, interview with the author, December 13, 2012.

The last time Fosse met with Herr *and following*: Michael Herr, interview with the author, April 13, 2011.

570 she gave him the first of four medications *and following*: Phoebe Ungerer, interview with the author, December 13, 2012.

Fosse was said to be drunk at the ceremony *and following:* Gottfried, *All His Jazz*, 440.

Phoebe, meanwhile, took *and following:* Phoebe Ungerer, interview with the author, December 13, 2012.

571 "The problem I find": Sondra Lowell, "Fosse: Still Explaining His Movie," *Los Angeles Times*, February 3, 1980.

"It was because of his" *and following:* Phoebe Ungerer, interview with the author, December 13, 2012.

572 an octopus: LOC, "Odd" notebook, box 53B.

Fosse and Ungerer talked about getting married *and following:* Phoebe Ungerer, interview with the author, December 13, 2012.

Rumor said she never: Gottfried, *All His Jazz*, 452.

Fosse sent her money *and following:* Phoebe Ungerer, interview with the author, December 13, 2012.

573 Gwen did too: Bernard Drew, "Life as a Long Rehearsal," *American Film*, November 1979.

Fosse and Cis Rundle spent one afternoon: Cis Rundle, interview with the author, July 21, 2011.

blocks Noel Behn called Fosse Country: Gottfried, *All His Jazz*, 370.

"I see a hooker on a corner": Pete Hamill, "Fosse," *Piecework* (Boston: Little, Brown, 1996), 344.

Strolling up Fifth Avenue, he won: Cis Rundle, interview with the author, July 21, 2011.

"The seas parted for him": Ibid.

"I think he would say he was": Ann Reinking, interview with the author, November 15, 2010.

574 "Wait. I can't go in": Cis Rundle, interview with the author, July 21, 2011.

Fosse had given up 850 Seventh: Phoebe Ungerer, interview with the author, December 13, 2012.

Reinking called it the *Swan Lake* of Broadway *and following:* Ann Reinking, interview with the author, November 15, 2010.

575 "How you doing?": Don Rebic, interview with the author, February 28, 2011.

he couldn't resist shooting at two hundred: Richard Brick, interview with the author, May 3, 2012.

576 Heim was busy on another project when *and following:* Rick Shaine, interview with the author, July 11, 2012.

577 "When Bob comes in": Mimi Quillin, interview with the author, February 2, 2011.

"After *Star 80*": Gottfried, *All His Jazz*, 444.

Fosse and Verdon were dressing the same now: Dana Moore, interview with the author, February 11, 2011.

pick up the garbage: Cynthia Onrubia, interview with the author, October 10, 2012.

"Their relationship during *Charity*": Lisa Embs, interview with the author, April 26, 2011.

"in the middle of it": Mimi Quillin, interview with the author, February 2, 2011.

"You should have seen Gwen": Dana Moore, interview with the author, February 11, 2011.

"Before I die, I just want": Robert Greskovic, "Gala Touch to Capezio Awards," *Los Angeles Times,* May 6, 1987.

578 the night of the Tonys: Jeremy Gerard, "Quiet Transitions Mark Tonys' Brisk Evolution," *New York Times,* June 1, 1987.

"His feeling was people just swoop in": Mimi Quillin, interview with the author, February 2, 2011.

"He seemed to be taking great": Janice Lynde, interview with the author, May 4, 2011.

579 "I guess he didn't want to miss it": James Lipton, *Inside Inside* (New York: Dutton, 2007), 151.

"By the time we were working": Donna McKechnie, interview with the author, October 14, 2010.

"But I feel I really haven't fulfilled": Kevin Kelly, "Fosse, at 58, Finds No Security in Success," *Boston Sunday Globe,* February 9, 1986.

"He wanted to do a full ballet": Ann Reinking, interview with the author, November 15, 2010.

"Oh, don't mind me" *and following:* Donna McKechnie, interview with the author, October 14, 2010.

580 *Charity*'s presales disconcertingly low: Mimi Quillin, interview with the author, February 2, 2011.

"People had given up their homes": Chet Walker, interview with the author, December 22, 2010.

581 "It was like the dancers versus": Name withheld, interview with the author, September 10, 2010.

"Whatever's going on out there": Mimi Quillin, interview with the author, February 2, 2011.

"He wanted us to know he was on it": Ibid.

Donna McKechnie flipped on the radio *and following:* Donna McKechnie, interview with the author, October 14, 2010.

"the most influential theater director": Jeremy Gerard, "Michael Bennett, Theater Innovator, Dies at 44," *New York Times,* July 3, 1987.

Hal Prince hosted his memorial at Sardi's *and following:* Gottfried, *All His Jazz,* 446.

582 "For the New York theater": Frank Rich, "Broadway: The Empire Strikes Back," *New York Times,* March 29, 1987.

583 Fosse hacked through the entire meeting: Mimi Quillin, interview with the author, February 2, 2011.

He asked Walker about the morale: Chet Walker, interview with the author, December 22, 2010.

There was concern they were: Ibid.

Fosse administered general notes around noon: Mimi Quillin, interview with the author, February 2, 2011.

Fosse and McKechnie rehearsed the bite Charity gives Charlie's arm: Ibid.

"Talk about emotion during the entire number": Fosse rehearsal notes for September 23, 1987, courtesy of Mimi Quillin.

"How much time is left?": Gottfried, *All His Jazz*, 4.

At around three o'clock, Fosse led: Mimi Quillin, interview with the author, February 2, 2011.

584   which he had intended to run the day earlier: Ibid.

"Dance like you're on your way": Mamie Duncan-Gibbs, interview with the author, February 18, 2011.

he made serious, sustained eye contact: Ibid.

"The energy in the room was so": Ibid.

"He rehearsed us so hard that day": Donna McKechnie, interview with the author, October 14, 2010.

"just do the show, no more, no less": Chet Walker, interview with the author, December 22, 2010.

told them he had done everything: Stephanie Pope Caffey, interview with the author, March 1, 2011.

"He said it more like a father": Donna McKechnie, interview with the author, October 14, 2010.

If he could, he said, he would: Stephanie Pope Caffey, interview with the author, March 1, 2011.

"Your business is to do the best": Donna McKechnie, interview with the author, October 14, 2010.

Fosse seemed to crumple: Ibid.

"When you get up in the morning": Ibid.

"Save your money": Chet Walker, interview with the author, December 22, 2010.

"I'm *so sorry* this isn't going well": Wayne Green, interview with the author, April 25, 2011.

he spoke for twenty minutes: Lisa Embs, interview with the author, April 25, 2011.

"As Bob was talking to us that day": Ibid.

585   "I would do anything to make": Wayne Green, interview with the author, April 25, 2011.

ONE HOUR AND FIFTY-THREE MINUTES

586   Around five thirty, Fosse ended his speech: Fred Mann III, interview with the author, February 22, 2011.

Fosse devoted the next hour exclusively to: Mimi Quillin, interview with the author, February 2, 2011.

Onstage, Chet Walker stood in for: Chet Walker, interview with the author, December 22, 2010.

on the floor, glued to the podium: Wayne Green, interview with the author, April 25, 2011.

"Don't rush this section": Ibid.

587 *Charity* had left Herman in a hospital: Allen Herman, interview with the author, March 3, 2011.

Larry "Spoosh" Spivack, took over: Larry Spivack, interview with the author, March 4, 2011.

"I don't like that cowbell": Wayne Green, interview with the author, April 25, 2011.

it was the cowbell they used in Philadelphia: Allen Herman, interview with the author, March 3, 2011.

"Fix it! Fix it!": Larry Spivack, interview with the author, March 4, 2011.

"Later I asked [Spoosh] to show me": Allen Herman, interview with the author, March 3, 2011.

588 "Fosse was angry": Larry Spivack, interview with the author, March 4, 2011.

"Ladies and gentlemen": Ibid.

Fosse picked his hat up off: Mimi Quillin, interview with the author, February 2, 2011.

They went out through the front: Harry Teeter, interview with the author, June 23, 2011.

"Show's going good": Ibid.

"Have a good show!": Mamie Duncan-Gibbs, interview with the author, February 18, 2011.

they strolled toward the Willard Hotel, where: Phoebe Ungerer, December 13, 2012.

"Theater thataway": Steve Blum, interview with the author, June 23, 2011.

589 A cluster of people at the window stood up: Jim Hewes, interview with the author, June 23, 2011.

"Hey!" someone said: Ibid.

It took twenty minutes for the paramedics: Ibid.

"She was running around": Patricia Baughman, interview with the author, June 23, 2011.

Thinking Fosse's heart attack was a seizure: Martin Gottfried, *All His Jazz* (Cambridge, MA: Da Capo, 1998; first published by Bantam in 1990), 5. Citations refer to the Da Capo edition.

arrived at the emergency room at 6:48: Charles W. Hall and Douglas Stevenson, "Bob Fosse Dies After Collapsing on D.C. Street: Choreographer and Director Bob Fosse Dies Here," *Washington Post*, September 24, 1987.

591 "When I got home": David Picker, interview with the author, October 7, 2010.

INDEX

Specific dance numbers are listed by title of work.
Specific productions are listed under the headings *movies; music videos; stage productions; television.*